WINN L. ROSCH'S PRINTER BIBLE

Winn L. Rosch

A Subsidiary of
Henry Holt and Co., Inc.

a subsidiary of Henry Holt and Company, Inc.
115 West 18th Street
New York, New York 10011

First Edition–1996

Printed in the United States of America.

Library of Congress Cataloging-in-Publication Data

Rosch, Winn L.
[Printer bible]
Winn L. Rosh's printer bible / by Winn L. Rosch.
p. cm.
ISBN 1-55828-436-2
1. Printers (Data processing systems) I. Title.
TK7887.7.R67 1995
004.7'7—dc20 95-40388
CIP

10 9 8 7 6 5 4 3 2 1

MIS:Press books are available at special discounts for bulk purchases for sales promotions, premiums, fund-raising, or educational use. Special editions or book excerpts can also be created to specification.

For details contact: Special Sales Director
MIS:Press
a subsidiary of Henry Holt and Company, Inc.
115 West 18th Street
New York, New York 10011

Associate Publisher: *Paul Farrell*
Managing Editor: *Cary Sullivan*
Acquisitions Editor: *Jono Hardjowirogo*
Development Editor: *Michael Sprague*
Copy Edit Manager: *Shari Chappell*
Production Editor: *Anne Incao*
Copy Editor: *Suzanne Ingrao*

CONTENTS

CHAPTER ONE
Introduction

1

CHAPTER TWO
Background
17

CHAPTER THREE
Buying a Printer

65

CHAPTER SEVEN
Consumables

CHAPTER NINE
Printer Sharing
373

CHAPTER TEN
Fonts
419

CHAPTER ELEVEN
Languages
475

CHAPTER TWELVE
Maintenance and Troubleshooting
567

APPENDIX A
Plotters

INDEX

CHAPTER ONE

Introduction

Your printer is the most important peripheral to your PC. It alone makes your computer's fleeting electronic thoughts tangible, portable, and sharable with the world at large. It links the age of electronic communications with the classical realm of the printed word. Your printer makes your first impression when you send out résumés and makes lasting impressions that can survive the ages.

What's there to know about printers? You just plug it into you parallel port, load it with paper, and watch the pages pour out. Ideally you should have no problems for years. You could just keep on computing, and you'd have absolutely no need for this book.

Of course, all those pages zipping out of your printer might each be bedecked with but a single character or be lined wall-to-wall with text about as understandable as Klingon. Worse, most problems you suffer through with your printer are so subtle you might not even notice them for years. You might miss many of the convenience features of your particular machine, you may pay more per page than you need to, and you might never get all the quality from the machine that it's designed to deliver.

The real problems with an uninformed approach to printers and printing are subtle, pernicious, and usually, expensive. They begin at the beginning, when you wander into the computer or appliance store with wide eyes and open pocketbook or page through the magazine ads with visions of sugar plums and perfectly typeset newsletters of your own dancing through your head. You could spend hundreds or thousands of dollars more that you need to on a new printer yet still not get all the features that you want. Or, by making the wrong hardware choice, you might never be able to print high-resolution graphics or load the new font you want to use.

Potential problems with printers don't end when you and your money are parted. With an inappropriate printer (or simply a bad pick from the available multitude) you might waste a page for every job you print, enough to total up a small forest of pulp over the life of your investment. Even with the wisest possible printer choice, one made after months of careful deliberation, you can still waste hours of your life in frustration just trying to figure out the simplest of its functions. In fact, some folks suffer through months of inadvertently double-spaced pages before they find out the solution is a simple as sliding a DIP switch.

Know what you're doing, however, and printer problems vanish fast as a sandlot baseball game at the sound of breaking glass. All that mastering the hard copy capabilities of your PC takes is a bit of knowledge about printers. Once you understand the fundamentals, you can get better quality from your printer without increasing your investment. In the long run, you'll get more out of your printer while putting less in—more pages for fewer pennies.

Understanding printers and printing is a worthy goal, one you can certainly achieve if you read on through these pages.

Although the many pages of this tome tell of a long journey, it won't be difficult. Moreover, you can set your own pace. We've organized everything to help ease you into understanding what you need to know. In fact, you can use this book both as an introduction to get you started and as a reference if you already know your way around. Along the way we'll try to keep a light tone and not weigh things down with more technicality than you need, but still give you enough detail that you can impress your friends or put that pernicious salesperson in his or her place. Sure, that's a big promise, but so is our topic and this book.

Your Next Printer

Why now? Why yet another book about printers? Because great changes are sweeping through printing technology and the printer industry. The requirements for a modern PC printer are changing dramatically, and the industry offerings are changing to match. More importantly, what you expect from a printer is changing, too. After more than a decade of promises, the graphical operating system has become *de rigueur* for PCs. Not only does this new look require better graphics from printers, but also it has put new emphasis on color. Creative printer makers have adapted new technologies to meet these demands.

Printers have come a long way since the first models were introduced for connecting to PCs. They are faster, sharper, more colorful, and less expensive in real terms than ever before. They are more versatile, able to print text, graphics, even photographs, often with bright colors. They have become so much a part of our lives and business that the next generation of workers are apt to give only an uncomprehending glance should you utter the archaic word "typewriter."

According to a survey polled by the Gallup organization at the behest of computer-and-printer-maker Epson and released in May 1995, for the first time more laser and inkjet printers are being sold than impact dot-matrix printers, with 30% of all printers of the former versus 29% for the latter. Among other trends, this shift marks a move to word quality. Even the best impact printers produce text and drawings that have fuzzy edges because of their fuzzy ribbons. Today's inkjets and lasers are, for the most part, noticeably sharper. In addition, these newer technologies produce text and graphics that are typically darker and more uniform.

Better still, the price of quality has plummeted. The hard numbers of the list prices suggested by manufacturers have never been lower. Adjust those figures for inflation, and today's printer is a true bargain. You can buy a printer with double the resolution of a two-year-old laser printer for about $200 on the street–and get color capabilities almost for free. Moreover, the low prices of these new machines don't demand any compromise in quality. In fact, even the most affordable printers are pushing the standards of resolution ever higher. Print quality today only starts at the 300 dpi that was top of the heap only a few years ago. Even if you have a tight budget, your next printer will likely double that quality level.

Several new trends have started over the past few years. The fastest growing printer technology is the color-capable inkjet–at one time little more than a footnote to the industry. Some laser printers now cost less than impact dot-matrix machines. An entirely new class of printers, portable machines, is slowly gaining form and strength. Without a doubt, other trends are developing, too, some that we might not notice until we have the benefit of hindsight.

Along with these changes in the market, applications, and hardware has come a change in selection strategy. Nearly all general purpose printers today are based on one of three basic technologies: impact, inkjet, and laser. Unlike days gone by, however, choosing one of these print technologies no longer dooms you to any particular level of quality. Any one of these three can produce output suitable for correspondence or great graphics. Today your choice of printer technology and a specific printer must be guided by subsidiary considerations. Some technologies endow printers with specific abilities–for example, better transparency output–while others make working with a particular machine more pleasant. These characteristics arise from how each technology forms images on paper. If you based a purchase decision on a preconceived idea about what printer technology you want based on past advice or experience, you're likely to miss making the best choice.

With the entire world going on line, however, you might have your doubts about the need for a new printer. After all, the future of hard copy might be a short one. Hardly. Wipe the dust off your crystal ball, and you'll see that the role of the PC printer is assured for decades to come. The dream of the paperless office predicted in the long-ago 1980s promised to put an end to concerns about printers. You would read everything directly from the screen, carry a DynaBook instead of a newspaper on the trolley, and watch forests once again overtake the landscape as pulp mills reverted to their old purpose of churning out bad fiction. Instead the modern office drowns in more paper than ever before.

There's one consolation. The advances in printer technology have made each page better looking, likely even more colorful. And new printers push out those pages faster than ever before and cost less. New, better printers won't solve the world's problems but at least we won't ruin our eyesight so quickly as we muddle through.

What You Need to Know

Printers are different from most else that you would want to connect to your PC, mechanical in nature and purpose while most everything else is more logical and electronic. Where other peripherals aim for data, the printer is more materialistic, designed to give you something you can hold in your hand.

As a consequence, the things you need to know about printers run a slightly different range than with most PC products. In this book, we'll be concerned with four particular aspects of printers and printing. These include buying a printer, installing it, using it effectively and economically, and taking command to make your machine do exactly what you want it to.

Buying a Printer

Before you can share the great joys and heart-stopping tribulations of using your PC printer, you've got to own one. That might just be the scariest aspect of the modern printer, confronting the myriad models and finding the one machine that's right for you and your applications.

If your goal is to find the perfect printer, you have about as much hope as in locating an honest politician, a task far harder than Diogenes's quest for an honest man. At least he had hope, a lamp, and apparel suitable to a toga party to take the edge off the failure at the end of an unsuccessful week. Your quest is indeed hopeless, principally for lack of subject matter. No single printer can hope to be perfect for every person or PC because every print job, every PC application, every office, every profession, and just plain everyone has their own particular needs and desires when it comes to the means, methods, and look of on-paper output.

If you could find an honest politician, finding the perfect printer would be easier. Every choice of printer has to be a compromise, something at which the politician excels–be it compromising to find a middle course suitable to disparate parties and viewpoints or compromising ethics to find the most profitable course for himself or herself. In choosing a printer you have to compromise among goals of quality, speed, and price to find the one machine that brings together the right technologies and capabilities to suit your personal requirements. The good news is that you can likely find a printer to suit your needs, be they fast drafts or typeset-quality offset masters. More likely, you'll find several, all better than you might have dreamed about only a few years ago.

Indeed, in those scant years printers and the printer market have changed dramatically. No more are particular print methods marked by eye-straining output. With one arm's length look, you might be hard pressed to tell whether a particular sheet emerged from an impact, laser, or inkjet printer. Nor will studying the price list alone settle the matter. For what was once the going price for an ordinary impact printer, today you can buy a personal laser printer.

As a result, the old strategy of beginning your search for a printer by picking a broad class of printers–like laser or inkjet–just doesn't work any more. Instead, you should start by looking at what you have and what you want.

Installing Your Printer

Once you have a printer, you'll want to put it to work. You've got to connect it to your PC and to your software. The process involves two separate issues, the hardware and the software. The choices involved are more varied than you might think.

First, you must consider how and where to plug in your printer. Sure, there's a printer port on the back of your PC most of the time, but that's not necessarily the best choice for getting the most from your printer. For example, getting the most value from a printer in a business setting often calls for sharing it. Depending on your finances and philosophy, you have your choice of a number of means of sharing your printer. Some of those will dictate using a connection other than your PC's printer port.

Then you must link your printer to your software. Again, that seems simple on the surface, and it can be if you're willing to settle for a generic solution. For example, adding a printer to Microsoft Windows requires merely making the right choice from a list provided with the operating system. But specific printer models are often newer than the current version of Windows, and even older printers are sometimes blessed with driver software newer than the latest Windows release. Avoiding bugs and getting control of all your printer's features requires installing the latest printer driver.

Moreover, the standard Windows installation may not be the best one for you. Individual manufacturers have optimized particular parts of the Windows system for their products. For example, some models of Epson printers are blessed with a proprietary version of Print Manager written specifically for them.

You also have a choice of add-on hardware and software accessories. You can put your printer on a stand or desktop, roll it around, and hide it in a closet (where it might fry from lack of air circulation). Some software publishers offer special utilities and drivers for printers that can speed performance. For example, you might replace the print spooler part of Windows Print Manager to move spooling upstream and regain full control of your applications faster. You'll find a variety of subtle but effective enhancements to your printer installation.

Using Your Printer

Certainly using a printer is child's play. Press a couple of keys from within your favorite application, and your printer whirs into action. And with every sheet that rolls out you could be wasting money, too. Printers get designed with many goals in mind, like optimizing speed or quality or looking good on magazine tests. Few seem optimized for output economy. After all, printer makers want you to part with your money, not save it. When they sell you all your supplies, you can bet that your potential profits (and losses) come in second as a concern compared to their own.

Operating your printer most economically calls for careful consideration of all the materials it consumes when it does its job. Certainly you can shop around and find the cheapest possible paper for your laser printer, but your savings will evaporate when sheets stick together and roll through two at a time or when the machine jams every ten minutes. You can recycle your toner cartridges, but often you'll lose the output sharpness for which you paid extra.

To buy these supplies wisely, you need to know the differences between kinds of paper and the specific needs of your printer. You need to know about the changes made in laser toner over the years and how budget refills sometimes don't fit the bill. Cartridges for your inkjet printer and even ribbons are all plagued by similar concerns. Operating your printer effectively and economically requires a basic understanding of all these *consumables* that you must deal with as part of your daily life dealing with your printer.

Controlling Your Printer

Sometimes you've got to take command. You may want to write your own utilities to switch your printer between modes, alter margin settings, or change typefaces. You may even want to design your own fonts. You need intimate control of your printer.

You can do it. All you need is a knowledge of the control codes and language that your printer uses. Once you and your machine speak the same tongue, it will follow orders like any good trooper (or take direction like a good trooper).

Don't be scared by endless listings of C++ code. You don't have to be a programmer to put printer controls to work. As long as you can type into an editor, you can create your own simple DOS programs to issue instructions to your printer. Some word processors give you the opportunity to embed special codes in your documents (or even add them to their setup repertory). Know the code and you can take command.

This Book

The goal of this book is to give you the most useful mix of the technical and practical, everything that you need to know. You'll get enough background to understand how printers work so that you can find the best one for your particular application. You'll also see why they do what they do and how to control them. With this background you'll be able to go beyond simply pressing the "print" button and extend the capabilities of your printer. Along the way, you'll see how to make your work look better, even artistic.

Besides aesthetics, this practical approach will help you find the best buy in a new printer. Beyond purchase price, however, you'll see how to identify the printer that will be least expensive in the long run, not just when you buy it but as you use it for its entire life. You'll also see how to keep the costs of printing low, as affordable as possible given the need to generate a constant flow of paper.

One ramification of this historical approach is that we'll start in ancient times, those dreary dark years when printers had only one color of ink and offices still had an unfortunate underclass called secretaries, a great fraction of whose duties involved the production of hard copy.

I. Introduction

This is the chapter that you're reading. It tells you what a wonderful purchase you've made in this book and outlines what you're going to learn from reading it. It even has a self-referential section describing this self-same introduction. Fortunately this section is short and ends right here.

II. Background

Before we can begin a discussion about anything, we need to at least speak the same language. The world of printers has its own cant rife with specialized terms and subtle variations. This chapter sets the foundation for our enlightened discussion of printers by providing the background you need to understand the terminology and put essential issues in perspective.

We'll start our approach to understanding printer technology from a historical perspective. Not only does history provide a logical structure, it gives us the perspective so hard to find in the fast changing world of personal computing. The structure is the only objective one. Moreover, it shows the progress of the years, the emergence and development of technologies. In particular, we'll see how the control afforded by computer-based circuits has taken over from the cleverness and refinement in mechanical design.

When we reach the current printer era, we'll cover all the current technologies and look at basic terminology. We'll lay in a cursory understanding of concepts like character formation, impact versus non impact printing, memory, and paper handling so we can discuss them more fully later on.

III. Printer Selection

You can learn anything about your printer by trial and error, at least given enough time and paper. Unfortunately "enough" often means an unlimited supply because you will inevitably make not one but many mistakes and consign them to the trash can (or shredder or recycling bin, depending on which operating system's metaphor you abide). One place where the mistakes of trial and error are particularly costly is buying a printer. If you don't want to throw out your mistakes, you have to eat them—and a diet of inappropriate printers can be bad for the digestion, to say the least.

Avoiding such costly mistakes is probably one reason for buying a book that purports to be the bible about printers. The good word is that this chapter is devoted to helping you select the right machine to buy. The only reason it's not first is because you need to know what the printer salespeople are talking about (or think they are talking about) before you even tread into the showroom or crack the cover of a catalog or shopping magazine.

The main thrust of the guidance given in this chapter is that your purpose should dictate your choice. That is, selecting the right printer depends on what you want to do with it. And once you know what you will do with your printer, the hard part of the purchasing decision will automatically fall into place.

In this chapter we'll run down the various applications to which you may submit a computer printer and see what are the most important concerns for each one. We'll look both at general applications like correspondence (including envelopes and labels) as well as more specialized areas like workgroup printing, desktop publishing, prepress proofing, presentation preparation, and portable printing.

IV. Technologies

If you want to understand how different kinds of printers work, this chapter will explain it to you, probably telling you more about printer technologies than anyone short of a designer thinks he wants to know. But as your parents probably told you, it's good for you no matter what it tastes like.

Understanding the technology that makes your printer work has practical benefits. For example, knowing how a printer works can be an invaluable aid in understanding, even repairing, commonly occurring problems. If you know what the printer is supposed to be doing, it's a lot easier to figure out what it isn't doing or what it's doing wrong. Errors that otherwise would seem strange make sense when you know how the printer makes its images.

Moreover, even the most jaded of us still have a bit of curiosity lurking within. You might just want to know how your printer does its job simply for the sake of knowing. In this increasingly complex and technical world, understanding even a small part of it can give you a feeling of mastery and superiority.

You'll learn about how all the major printer technologies manage to mark up and mangle the paper that you run through them. Among others, we'll discuss impact dot-matrix, non impact inkjet printers, laser printers and their friends LCD shutter and LED printers, thermal wax transfer printers, and dye sublimation printers.

V. Graphic Printing

Printers are not just for text anymore. The modern world is one of images, and you expect (or should) that your printer can deal with them as easily as you. Even text has become a graphic as far as most printers are concerned, thanks to Windows and TrueType, and the Macintosh and PostScript.

The world of graphics has several aspects. Line drawing has long been the fodder for printers. Even the earliest dot-matrix machines could draw lines and duplicate the black-and-white graphics you could display on your monitor screen as easily as pushing the print-screen button. More troubling for printers are capturing the finer points, such as the realism of photographs (which, speaking technically, requires continuous-tone reproduction). In addition, modern printers have extended their range to include colors other than white and black.

In this chapter, you'll learn about how an ordinary printer tackles the challenge of reproducing continuous-tone images using *electronic halftone techniques*. You'll also see how the same technology gets extended to nearly the full range of color that you can see using a technology called *dithering*.

VI. Operation

Once you know *how* your printer works, you'll want to make it do its job. This chapter discusses issues that need to be considered in the every day operation of a computer printer. We'll start by looking at basic printer controls and what they do—after all, there's more to the life than just pressing the "on-line" button. We look at stuff that's far from the mundane, like shades of cloak and dagger. With some printers, for example, you can make a duplicate printout long after the original has been safely and secretly spirited away.

From the Control Panel, we'll leap to the control systems, venturing on to commanding your printer through your applications and operating system. In particular, we'll look at Print Manager, the Windows program that organizes your printing sessions and lets you print while your work. First, we'll consider what Print Manager is and what it does—as well as its limitations and shortcomings (and alternatives). Then we'll put Print Manager to work. We'll take a look at how to reorganize your printing assignments to get that important job done first, the best way to make multiple copies, how to kill the a job gone awry, and how to route different jobs to specific printers.

In addition, we'll look at several popular printer utilities, programs that let you do strange and amazing things with your printer. A utility can multiply the value of your printer or just make your use of the machine easier.

VII. Consumables

Much to the dismay of environmentalists and cost accountants, you can't print without something to print on and something to print with. Both of those somethings–paper and ink (or their equivalents)–are the raw materials that your printer must consume to do its jobs. For obvious reasons, printer people call them collectively *consumable.*

This chapter will examine that oft-neglected side of printing, both technical details and the expenses involved. We'll take a look at paper in its various sizes, contents, weight, and finishes. The emphasis will be on what you need to know about the raw material of printing to make the best looking, most affordable, and smoothest running print jobs possible,

We'll also get a taste for ink and toner, considering related issues such as recycling and reinking. And we won't ignore the oft-neglected consumables like optical-photoconductor drums, print heads, and electricity. In the end, we'll come up with a way to judge the overall cost of printing and how to keep the cost of hardcopy low.

VIII. Interfaces

To get your printer working on anything but a self-test, you've got to plug it into your PC. For the most part, that's as easy as plugging in a vacuum cleaner–just jab the plug into the socket. Take the teensiest step beyond the ordinary (if such a thing exists) and you'll feel the quicksand slowly slipping into your nostrils. Even seemingly commonplace printers are apt to have peculiar requirements for their interfaces and cables.

This chapter will help guide you in connecting your printer to your PC. In most cases, connecting a printer is straightforward–plug it into the printer port. But the printer port is no longer so straightforward. Moreover, other options are becoming important. Issues to be discussed include:

- **Parallel ports.** Once upon a time, a parallel port *was* a printer port. No longer. There's not even a single thing that can be called a parallel port. This basic printer connection is plagued by four variations, each of which behaves differently. We'll look at all four variations (including the "official" standard that you won't need to deal with, at least with your printer. You'll find a lot of practical help, including a general reference with pin-outs of cables needed to get specific printers and ports working.
- **Serial ports.** Although serial printers are becoming rare, they are among the most troublesome to connect. After we verse ourselves in serial fundamentals, we'll examine what's required to make serial connections work. Again, you'll find a practical guide that includes wiring diagrams for making specific printers work with a serial connection.
- **Video and SCSI interfaces.** A few special applications require more speed than an ordinary serial or parallel port will support. One technique adopted by some older laser printers was to give direct access to the laser beam itself, letting you send your own raster directly to the printer as a kind of video signal. Another strategy adopted by a small but growing number of printers is to exploit the high speed of a SCSI connection. We'll take a look at both technologies, learning along the way how to sort through the exigencies of the SCSI port.

IX. Printer Sharing

Getting the most from a printer means giving it a full load of work. In that it's unlikely a single person can use up all the power of a printer (particularly high-speed lasers) you can usually make your office printing more cost effective by sharing one printer among a workgroup.

In this chapter, we'll evaluate all the different ways of sharing, from the simple to the complex. The cheap way means using an A-B switch that lets you connect two PCs to one printer (or two printers to a single PC port, if you wish). The easy way is with a true printer sharing device–a box that lets you plug multiple PCs into one printer and automatically controls access.

If you already have a network, you know you can use it to share a printer, too. But you have several ways of linking a printer to a network. We'll figure out which is best for your particular application, network, and printer. And if you don't have a network, we'll evaluate whether you can benefit by adding one to share a printer.

X. Fonts

Even ordinary typing has its aesthetics. In fact, every character you print was probably created by a gifted artist called a typeface designer or *typographer*. Using the typographers work, you build your own masterpieces by choosing and arranging characters.

To help you get a handle on what you're doing, in this chapter we'll discuss typography and fonts–everything from what a typeface is to the standards among today's PCs. You'll learn the terminology of typography, the difference between typefaces, modern PC and print font technology, and how to put it all to work. We'll even look at how you can design your own characters and fonts.

XI. Languages and Standards

If you want to take full command of your printer, you need to know how to issue instructions that it will follow. To do that, you need to know the printer's language. This chapter will lend you an ear so that you can learn how to talk the language of your printer.

This is mostly a reference chapter about the major printer languages such as those used by Epson-compatible dot-matrix printers, PCL-compatible laser printers, and PostScript printers of all kinds. We'll begin by discussing issues in printer control and describing the relationships among the languages. We'll then take a deep enough look at each so that you can take command yourself using your favorite programming language or your applications and utility. We'll include a command reference for each of the major languages.

XII. Troubleshooting

This chapter looks at problems you're likely to encounter with a PC printer, including everything from trouble getting started to strange errors that pop up out of nowhere. We'll take a look at basic troubleshooting and cover some of the more common problems that you might encounter when using today's applications. Although we won't be able to solve all the problems (all possible problems haven't yet occurred, let alone been anticipated), we take a logical approach that will help you solve many difficulties.

We'll start with the printer that refuses to work from the moment you free it from its box and the printer that makes an effort to work but doesn't succeed–the machines that double-space every line, skip every other page, or print characters that resemble hieroglyphics more than English. Finally, we'll consider printers that suddenly go off-color or stop working entirely. Although what you learn won't put the local service center out of business, you'll come to know what you can–and can't–fix easily.

Appendix A. Plotters

Printers aren't the only devices for turning your PCs evanescent thoughts into hard copy; plotters tackle the chore, too. In this appendix, we'll examine the fundamentals of plotters, distinguish their applications from those of the printer, and see which does what best (as well as how to find the best plotter for your PC).

The CD

You expect it, you got it. Every computer book these days requires a CD as a "free bonus" to help you think you're getting more than some inky paper one step away from the remainder bin. If that's what you want to think, that's fine. But no free bonus CD is really free. You pay for it as part of the purchase price of the book. The publisher simply factors it in as an additional cost that helps determine the price. So much for our beneficence.

But we have tried to make this CD useful if not valuable to you. It holds a collection of spiffy things that you can spend hours playing with–and years exploiting usefully. We've included easy-access reference material, printer drivers, fonts you can experiment with, and utilities to try out to see if they help your daily work.

To be honest, most of this stuff is available elsewhere. This CD brings it together in one place for your convenience and with no on-line charges. That should be enough of a treat in itself.

Hypertext

A printed book is a wonderful companion. You can carry it anywhere, read it with one or fewer hands under conditions that would make the most rugged PC sizzle or choke. But a printed book is also confining, limiting your view of the world to the linear arrangement of words upon the page. Certainly you can flip ahead or back through the leaves, but you will lose context.

Switching to an electronic version will allow you to pore through a tome in context, leaping from reference to reference without losing your chain of ideas or train of thought. Hypertext links text by context, making your journey more direct and letting you rather than the author (me) choose the detours.

To give you the best of both worlds, we've included the full text of this book in Windows Help hypertext format on the enclosed CD. It is entirely self-contained, and after a simple installation will let you find what you need with digital speed. You can even install it on your hard disk as a valued companion (until you discover that you value disk space even more!)

Reference

In addition, you'll find an electronic reference as part of the hypertext. You'll find in it all the charts from the book so you can look up details as you need them. You'll be able to look up command codes without smudging your thumb or interface wiring with a couple of keystrokes.

Fonts

One of the joys of modern printers is freedom from the chains of Courier. Once upon a time, all that you could expect from your printer was icky monospaced Courier characters that looked like refugees from an old Remington typewriter. Today you can download nearly any font that you want into your printer and use it instead. All you need is the font to download.

With that in mind, we've included a number of fonts in various formats for your experiments and enjoyment. These fonts come from a number of sources. Some of them free, come-ons from the typographers to get you to try their other offerings. Others ask you buy a license to use them if, after you try them, you decide to use them. In any case, they'll get you started in the wide world of fonts. You'll probably find playing with fonts is addictive, which is exactly why typographers are willing to offer them to you free. (Do we feel bad about helping you get hooked? Hey, you're an adult. You can handle it.)

Utilities

This is our try-before-you-buy section. We've included a number of printer utilities that will help you get more from your printer, make your life easier, or just let you have fun. These are actually published as shareware. That is, the authors of the programs distribute copies through various sources (of which this CD is but one) so that you can try out their work. If you like it and decide you want to use the program, you're expected to pay a licensing fee back to the author. Although this software isn't really free, the trial is. This approach means you don't have to spend anything for software that's not useful to you. Not only do you get something that makes your printer more useful but you won't have to waste any money to find out that it's not.

See? This book is all about saving money. And saving frustration. More than that. This book is all about printers.

CHAPTER TWO

Background

The world of print spans the ages, from the first clay tablets and reed styli to today's fastest laser printers. In every case no matter where or when, however, the aim is the same–to produce records legible to the world. The technologies of print have been as diverse as the span of development, formulated to match the needs and abilities of each generation. This chapter traces the history of printing from quills to color lasers. Along the way you'll meet the terms and technologies that underlie today's hard copy output.

The written language not only has accompanied humanity through history but also has defined history. The words we print have recorded our finances, deeds, and thoughts, usually in that order of importance, through the ages. From poking clay to painting papyrus to Spencerian script took thousands of years but brought no real change. Each word was hand-crafted with care or carelessness, every document unique.

Somewhere along this perilous journey the printing press appeared. Johannes Gutenberg worked on the invention of movable type in Mainz, Germany, ran out of money, and was finally repossessed by his investors. His dream finally came to fruition in 1454 when his famous Bible was squeezed out by his successors, Fust and Schoeffer. Along with the good word, the printing press brought the world of writing the precision of the machine. Instead of unique, hand-wrought characters came the precise replicas molded in a foundry, every "i" dotted and "t" crossed forever in molten lead. Whether the work of the machine rivaled the aesthetics of the scriptorium remains in the eye of the beholder. Once typefaces became familiar, however, there was no mistaking one character for another and no need to guess exactly what was written. For the published word, the printing press brought easy, accurate reading, legibility that would not be rivaled by one-off writing for hundreds of years. That's the job of today's computer printer, putting the same quality and legibility on paper that once was the province only of the commercial printshop with its mass-produced output.

History

Today's PC printer traces its roots back to the very first of all individual printing machines, the typewriter. This first mechanical printer served as a means to add legibility to writing, to eliminate the vagaries of cursive script and remove its ambiguities and misunderstandings, to make the transcribed word as formal as the work of the printing press.

As initially conceived, the typewriter was hardly the breakneck-paced device we came to know in the generation before PCs. It was hardly able to keep up with the fleeting fingers of the scribe. The mechanism was slow and clumsy, prone to jamming, requiring force and memory to make work. At most, two fingers first did the work. It took more than 20 years to develop the modern concept of touch-typing with all ten. The men who had to labor over the machines—and they were men, the hard-to-kill stereotype of the female secretary grew only generations later—pecked the typewriter into the expected standard for business papers and correspondence.

Despite its initial disadvantages, the typewriter paved the way for the computer printer. It set a high standard, indeed, for the quality of its output. Typed characters could be trusted, whereas hand-lettering could not, although banishing errors entirely was an arduous chore, as anyone suffering through an academic dissertation in the days before the PC can attest.

The same technology underlying the humble typewriter has survived through to today and served as the foundation of the first computer printers. In fact, some primitive PC printers back in the days when hackers were hobbyists rather than criminals were electric typewriters modified to hammer on electronic command. Some of today's least expensive printers still rely on facets of typewriter technology and rank as the direct descendants of Sholes's original office machine.

Although an old-fashioned typewriter is a mechanical complexity (as anyone knows who has tried putting one back together after taking it apart), its operating principle is quite simple. Strip away all the cams, levers, and keys, and you see that the essence of the typewriter is its hammers.

Each hammer strikes against an inked ribbon, which is then pressed against a sheet of paper. The impact of the hammer against the ribbon shakes and squeezes ink onto the paper. Absorbed into the paper fibers, the ink leaves a visible mark or image in the shape of the part of the hammer that struck at the ribbon, typically a letter of the alphabet.

One way or another, all impact printers rely on this basic typewriter principle. Like Christopher Sholes's first platen-pecker, all impact printers smash a hammer of some kind against a ribbon to squeeze ink from the ribbon onto paper, making their mark by force fact. If any difference exists between an impact printer and a typewriter at all, it is that the typewriter directly links your fingers to the mechanism that does the printing. A printer, on the other hand, inserts your personal computer between your mind and the printed word.

In the earliest days of personal computers—before typewriter makers were sure that PCs would catch on and create a personal printer market—a number of companies attempted to adapt electric typewriters to computer output chores. The happily forgotten Bytewriter of 1980 was typical of the result—a slow, plodding page-pounder with full typewriter keyboard. It could do double duty, controlled by your PC or by you, as fast as your fingers could fly, but, it was no match for the computer's output.

Another device, short-lived on the marketplace, claimed to turn your typewriter into a printer simply by squatting atop the keyboard. The box was filled with dozens of solenoids and enough other miscellaneous mechanical parts to make a pinball machine look simple. The solenoids worked as electronically controlled "fingers," pressing down each key on the appropriate command from the connected PC, player piano technology adopted to the computer. As interesting as this mechanism sounds (and it probably made some *very* interesting sounds), it treaded the thin line between the absurd and surreal. More than a little doubt exists as to whether these machines, widely advertised in 1981, were ever actually sold.

Today, the most popular low-cost printers are impact dot-matrix machines, most often clipped to simply the name "dot matrix." Although they use a different character-forming method than the classic typewriter, they rely on the same hammer-and-ribbon impact printing principle.

Epson claims to have invented the personal computer printer, having introduced its first model, the *MX-80*, in 1978, three years before IBM ushered out its first PC. In fact, IBM's first printer offering, the Graphics Printer, was manufactured by Epson and was little more than that company's MX-80 mechanism with a change in ROM to reflect IBM's choice in character set. The dot-matrix printer flourished for the first decade of the PC age and now has gone into slow but accelerating decline. Currently between one-quarter and one-third of the printers sold still rely on impact dot-matrix technology.

At the time, however, printing technology was already well established in the office automation market. The machines of choice were essentially fast typewriters lacking keyboards. These offered something the dot-matrix machines could not, the same character clarity as pounded out by the best typewriters. These daisy-wheel printers are now best regarded as dinosaurs, both in size and survivability. Their role was overtaken by a new development.

This challenge, the first real revolution in personal printing in 100 years, came in 1984 with the introduction of the first laser printer, the Hewlett-Packard LaserJet. Even this new technology grew from old roots. The basis of the laser printer process was exactly the same as used by the Xerox photocopier, although the print engine in the LaserJet was made by Xerox competitor Canon. At heart, this and all ensuing laser use a kind of heat-set, light-inspired offset printing. The laser now claims the high end of computer output, except where color counts, as its own territory, about 30% of the PC printer market.

The big hole between the impact dot-matrix printer and laser printer—more than a third of the market—is dominated by a newcomer, an improved dot-matrix printer called the inkjet. Silent, fast, and good looking, particularly on paper, the inkjet is rapidly becoming the most popular PC printer technology. It offers nearly the same quality as the laser at a fraction of the price, and it readily adapts to printing color graphics. Like the laser printer, the first inkjet was introduced in 1984, also by the Hewlett-Packard Company.

INTELLIGENCE

A modern printer must be more than a brute-force paper-pounder. It needs brains to control the placement of every dot on paper or whatever you plan to print. Even the cheapest impact dot-matrix printer has to be smart enough to know the one exact instant it must trigger each of its printwires to ram each of its ribbon-fuzzy dots at exactly the right spot. Laser printers have to match each character in their font cartridges with the proper on-paper position or arrange each of the hair-width dots of a graphic image on a sheet, possibly flicking their light beams 7 million or more times for each printed page they roll through. Most of the brain work is invisible. Behind the scenes, every printer must sort through a raft of commands, often embedded in the stream of characters to print, to find instructions for carrying out advanced operations such as switching to bold characters or changing fonts.

Printers vary substantially in their native intelligence. While many printers operate as little more than slaves, taking simple orders from your PC and carrying them out to the letter, many printers have much greater abilities. Many can go so far as to format the data as they print it. In fact, today's higher-power printers often have data processing abilities on par or beyond the typical PC.

Character Printers

The basic printer from which all output technology springs, was the *character printer*, typified by the classic all-mechanical teletype, was so dumb that it did not even know when it came to the edge of the paper. It would gladly perforate its platen with the text of an entire novel if the data it was sent was not broken into short lines with the appropriate carriage return and line-feed characters mixed in with the text. Many of today's printers have brains almost equally as primitive and rely on the computer and its software to tell them exactly what to do. Some computer programs, like word processors designed to be used with specific printers, may include special printer drivers software that adds in all sorts of extra ASCII code symbols to the data stream. Every fractional-inch movement of the print-head between proportionally spaced characters, every character to be pecked, every roll of the platen, is specifically indicated by the computer program and sent to the printer.

On the other hand, smart printers can take over these same text-processing functions on their own. They can accept an almost completely unformatted string of text, break it into proportionally spaced lines, and leave the proper margins at the top and bottom of the page. To handle these and other chores, even inexpensive printers nowadays have their own built-in microprocessors. The internal microbrain helps the printer position the proper petal of the daisy-wheel in front of the print hammer or calculate when to fire the wire of a dot-matrix printhead.

Line Printers

As the name implies, the *line printer* sees the world in terms of the single printed line. The line printer absorbs the individual characters sent to it by your PC but does nothing until it gets a carriage return, its end-of-a-line command. The carriage return tells the line printer to dash out all the characters it has received since the last carriage return, which it obediently does. The basic line printer doesn't think beyond the confines of a single line. This effect becomes particularly apparent when printing graphics. Every image must be sent as a line of graphics commands. For a dot-matrix printer–the pre-eminent line printer–a line of graphics comprises a series of instruction for printing short columns of dots, one dot wide and the height of the printhead. The printer has no conception what the printed page will look like and doesn't care. Your PC must instead track the progress down the page, breaking the image into individual lines to send to the line printer.

Page Printers

The wisest of modern printers visualize their work as an entire printed page. The machines, called *page printers*, acquire a page full of text or data before they begin printing, typically waiting for a form feed command as the cue that a page of data is complete. The page printer then arranges a full page of dots before running a sheet of paper through its mechanism.

Although the page printer may receive data as individual text characters, it deals with printing only as dots. Consequently, it must work out the dot pattern of each character it prints and place each dot at its precise location on the page before printing begins. Similarly, if the line printer is to draw a line or copy a bit-mapped image, it must calculate every point on the line and dot in the bit-mapped image and determine where each point or dot appears on the page. The conversion of characters and drawings to dot patterns is called *rasterization.* In a printer, the rasterization process produces a bit-image of an entire page. The printer mechanism then reads one row of dots at a time from memory and scans it across its imaging system exactly as a television camera deconstructs an image into individual scan lines.

The part of the printer that does the actual work of creating the bit image is called the *raster image processor* or RIP. Although any logic design could be used for the RIP of a printer, today microprocessors are the rule. RIPs require exactly the same functions as video processors and use similar designs. The printer RIP differs only in that it works at higher resolutions (one square inch of paper often holds as much data as a full monitor screen) but need not finish its job in real time. Raster image processing usually takes much longer than the time required for the printer engine to scroll a sheet of paper through. To keep things rolling as fast as possible, today's printer RIPs are most often based on *Reduced Instruction Set Computer* or RISC microprocessors. These chips are distinguished by design and performance. Engineers created RISC processors to carry out a few instructions (the reduced instruction set) at high speed by making the instructions more uniform and optimizing programs by preprocessing them during compiling.

Because rasterization typically requires carrying out a few basic operations repeatedly, the RISC design is suited perfectly to rasterization.

Character Printing Techniques

Developing character is not taken lightly, either in Boy Scouts or PC printers. In either case, two chief techniques have emerged, the trial by fire and the accumulation of wisdom. In the former case, a single cathartic experience etches a lifelong personality. In the latter case, the personality develops slowly with experience, gradually building to maturity. In printers, these development paths take the guise of fully formed character printer and the bit-image printer.

Fully Formed Character Printers

The image-forming technology of the typewriter was adopted by the first generation of word-processing printers used in conjunction with PCs. These machines made each character they printed in one quick action, a kind of catharsis-comes-to-paper printing Each character was fully formed from the outset, leading to the name of the technology, fully formed character printing. One characteristic of this printing technique is comparatively high quality. The only other print technology available in these early days of the PC printed characters as rough matrices of dots that were considered ugly and hard to read.

Fully formed character printers were essentially an analog technology, one that recorded the smooth curves of characters with essentially infinite detail. As with other analog technologies, the quality limit of a fully formed character printer was noise, something extraneous to the character formation process itself. In fact, the limit was the fuzziness imposed by the fabric of the inked ribbon, when you used a smooth mylar ribbon, by the texture of the paper. The quality limits of this technology were in its implementation.

On the downside, the quality of printing came at the cost of speed. Printing a full page of text often would take three minutes or more. In addition, these machines had limited versatility. They were designed solely for typing characters and had rudimentary (at best) graphics printing abilities. Although text-only printing was adequate in the early days of computing when word work constituted most of what a PC did, as graphics rose in importance, these fully formed character printers become less desirable. Few remain on the market, although their influence survives, as we shall see.

Bit-Image Printers

The alternate way of printing to smashing down characters all at once is to build them up from individual dots, much as a television set builds up its image from individual pixels on scan lines. Get far enough away or make the lines or dots fine enough, and your eye ignores them and goes for the overall image.

Essentially a digital technique, the quality of bit-image printing depends on pragmatic design choices. The more information devoted to individual characters, the higher their quality.

Although this technology can correctly be called dot-matrix printing, because most people think only of impact dot-matrix machines when they hear the term, bit-image is the term of choice for the technology.

Graphics Printing Techniques

Bit-image printers compatible with the IBM character set give you two methods for printing graphics, block graphics and all-points-addressable graphics. The principle differences between the two are quality and compatibility. Block graphics are ugly, but any software that can generate them operates any printer that can print them. Bit-image graphics are sharper, but require that your software know exactly how to control your printer.

Block Graphics

Think of block graphics as an extra set of characters built into a printer that permits you to draw pictures out of building blocks of simple shapes—like squares, rectangles, triangles, horizontal and vertical lines, and so on. Each of these shapes is electronically coded and recognized by the printer as if it were a letter of the alphabet, and the printer merely lays down line after line of these block characters to make a picture, like filling in each square on a piece of graph paper with different shapes. The pictures look a little chunky because the building blocks are big, just a little under 1/8 of an inch across in most printer's default text modes.

All-Points-Addressable Graphics

The native mode of most bit-image printers allows you to decide where to place individual dots on the printed sheet using a technique called all-points-addressable graphics or APA graphics. With a knowledge of the appropriate printer instructions you or your software can draw graphs in great detail or even make pictures resembling the halftone photographs printed in newspapers. The software built into the printer allows every printable dot position to be controlled–specified as printed (black) or not (white). An entire image can be built up like a television picture, scanning lines several dots wide (as wide as the number of wires in the printhead) down the paper.

This graphics printing technique takes other names, too. Because each individual printed dot can be assigned a particular location or "address" on the paper, this feature is often called dot-addressable graphics. Sometimes, that title is simplified into dot graphics. Occasionally, it appears as bit-image graphics because each dot is effectively the image of one bit of data.

The problem with all-points-addressable graphics is that your software must know the codes for telling your printer where to put each dot. Although a number of standards have arisen in the printer industry, some manufacturers have elected to go in their own directions and use their own codes. Most, however, follow the codes set by the industry leaders. For example, most nine-pin and 24-pin impact dot-matrix printers use the same codes as Epson or IBM printers. Most laser printers use the same codes as Hewlett-Packard LaserJet printers.

Banded Graphics

Banding is a technique that Microsoft developed to allow printers that only understand bit-mapped graphics to take full advantage of the Windows graphics device interface (GDI). The languages used by most printers do not understand drawing commands such as polygons or lines that Windows uses to create some forms of image. Such machines are designed before the emergence of Windows or in ignorance of it and can only print bit maps and text.

To allow such printers to handle its GDI output, Windows takes care of the rasterization process, converting drawing commands into bit maps inside your PC. It sends the bit maps to your printer. In pure form, this technique has a drawback in that it requires the printer to have sufficient memory to store an entire page (so that it can acquire the page image before printing it).

Banding helps sidestep the need for a printer to have a large amount of memory by subdividing the image bit map into a number of rectangles, which Microsoft calls *bands*, each of which is small enough to be held inside the confines of the printer's memory. Windows rasterizes each band separately and then sends it to the printer. It then instructs the printer to print the band without advancing to the next sheet, allowing the limited memory of the printer to accept the next band. After all the bands of the page have been printed, Windows and the printer advance to the next sheet.

Output Quality

Consistent quality and legibility underlie the development of printer technology, and it remains one of your leading concerns in selecting a modern PC printer. Most people believe the philosophy that the better their documents look, the better they look, especially when it comes to letters of introduction, *curricula vita*, and resumes. Top quality shows you've mastered the technology, that you care about detail, and that you hope a good first impression will give you the superficiality you need to make you stand out among all the other comers. When printer quality gets high enough, you can substitute it for the work of a professional typesetter for mastering newsletters, instruction manuals, and even full-fledged books.

Output quality is always a tradeoff with cost and speed. Printers that produce better looking hard copy inevitably cost more. And with many printers, particularly dot-matrix machines, producing the best quality means sacrificing throughput. Notching up one level of quality may cut print speed to one-half or one-quarter its fastest rate.

Printer makers use a number of nebulous terms to describe or mislead you about the quality produced by their printers. All talk about resolution but many really mean addressability. More often than not, the quality of the specification sheet is, like speed, a theoretic value–calculated rather than measured, scientifically defensible but rarely produceable in the real world.

Resolution

The most prominent measure of output quality of printers and other devices is *resolution*, a term that's also used to describe general graphic image quality. When applied to PC printers, the most common measure of resolution in printers is *dots per inch* which indicates the number of individual dots that could be distinguished in one linear inch of printing. (Some manufacturers express resolution in dots per square inch; you must take the square root of such measurements to reach a dots-per-inch value.) Strictly speaking, resolution should reflect your ability to distinguish individual dots. Most manufacturers of impact dot-matrix printers often use the term resolution to describe what really is addressability. This error raises the dots-per-inch figure and exaggerates image quality.

Resolution is also a measure of halftone image quality including the digital halftones produced by PC printers. In the case of halftones, however, resolution is measured in *lines per inch* reflecting the means by which halftones were traditionally made–by imposing a screen between the image and the camera making the halftone.

Addressability

When many manufacturers talk resolution, they really mean *addressability*, the degree of accuracy at which print controls and commands are understood and executed. That is, when a printer has an addressability of 360 dpi, your PC can instruct the printer to place a dot anywhere on a sheet of paper with an accuracy of 1/360 of an inch. More likely, the manufacturer means that the printer has a command in its repertory that lets you specify head movement in increments of 1/360 of an inch.

Addressability is a software issue. Its high degree of precision often falls apart when the software commands get translated into physical movement and ink. Although you may be able to instruct your printer's printhead to move 1/360 of an inch, whether the mechanism can actually move that precisely is another issue.

Even when a printer has adequate precision to mechanically reproduce its full addressability, you're unlikely to see all that quality on paper. For example, the image-forming printhead wires are often substantially larger than the smallest addressable increments of the printer. Although the printer may be able to place individual dots precisely, the dots remain large and obvious, obscuring detail and your best intentions. Impact printers also suffer from the resolution-robbing fuzziness added by interposing a ribbon between printhead and paper.

Laser printers typically do not suffer the same quality-robbing mechanical problems as dot-matrix printers. In general, the resolution of a laser printer is the same as its addressability, but not always. Toner particles can produce the same effect as impact ribbons and printhead wires. The individual toner particles can be larger than the addressability units of the printer, making resolution less than the claimed addressability. Most lasers with true resolutions in excess of 300 dpi require the use of *microfine toner*, which has reduced-size pigment particles, to deliver full quality. Manufacturers use a variety of names for fine-particle toner. For example, Epson calls it *MicroArt* toner. In addition to making sharper images, microfine toners also help produce darker blacks, minimize toner blurring, and reduce the *edge effect* that makes the edges of solid shapes to appear darker than the center part of the object to appear darker.

Resolution Enhancement Technology

When Hewlett-Packard Company introduced its LaserJet III line of printers, it was able to improve apparent output quality without increasing resolution or addressability. The company called the method by which it achieved this contradictory result *resolution enhancement technology* or RET. The process works by smoothing the edges of text and graphics by adjusting the size and placement of certain dots–mostly those on the edges of curves–that make up characters and lines. For example, by placing small dots in the white corners of jagged diagonal lines, RET reduces the harsh contrast of the stairstep shape, making the line appear to be smoother and sharper. Although RET does not increase the objective quality of a printer, it makes hard copy look subjectively better.

Epson calls its equivalent to RET a similar name, *resolution improvement technology*, abbreviated as RITech. It was first implemented in the company's ActionLaser 1500 to similar effect, smoothing the rough edges of text characters and straightening the jaggies in diagonal lines.

Text and Characters

The makers of dot-matrix printers often designate several quality levels for the text output of their machines. The descriptions are entirely subjective and essentially at the whim of the manufacturer. In that the same terms are commonly used by all manufacturers, you need to know what they mean–or are supposed to mean.

- **Draft quality** is generally a euphemism for the worst on-paper quality produced by a dot-matrix printer with the offsetting benefit that it is generated at the highest speed at which the printer is capable. Draft quality uses the minimum possible number of dots to indicate each character and, on many printers, gives the impression that the font designer was inspired by the St. Valentine's Day massacre. Each dot appears with stark individuality, and the sparse placement of those dots in the matrix gives text a grey appearance even when you don't try to squeeze ten times the recommended life from a ribbon. Draft quality earns its name because it's supposedly good enough for drafts, output that you will proofread but would be unwilling to share with the rest of the world.

- **Near letter quality** means that a dot-matrix printer attempts to duplicate what you'd get from an old-fashioned typewriter. Instead of distinct individual dots, near letter quality shoves the dots one upon another, even overlapping them, so that characters have a continuous rather than fragmented appearance. Dot-matrix printers achieve near letter quality by slowing down their print heads while maintaining the same firing rate for the printhead wires so the printer puts more dots in every inch. Many printers will go over each line twice to further increase the dot density. Both the slowing printhead and repeating lines takes a toll on speed, so near letter-quality printing is inherently slower than draft quality.

  Some manufacturers give near letter quality a more specific definition. Epson, for example, uses the term to describe the highest quality output of the company's nine-pin printers, in deference to the "letter quality" produced by 24-pin machines.

- **Letter quality** means different things to different manufacturers. Most use it to describe the best quality output that a given printer will produce, however good or bad, that may be on an objective scale. To achieve this level of quality, the printer uses exactly the same techniques as near letter quality, in some cases slowing further and switching to unidirectional printing for more accurate dot placement. Epson reserves the letter quality term for the best output of its 24-pin dot-matrix printers. Other manufacturers do not distinguish letter and near letter qualities. The term originates in the belief that letter quality is good enough for you to use for correspondence and other documents that you would be willing to share with the world without embarrassment.

- **Typeset quality** is what the best printers aim for. Today's top lasers claim the ability to deliver true 1200 dpi resolution, making the output of ordinary lasers look coarse in comparison. But even these machine still fall short of the ideal that is produced by typesetting machines. The standard among typesetters, which are used to create the text for master plates for offset printing, is about 2500 dpi.

In truth, the only time you'll see true typeset quality is on the masters for offset printing. The printing process itself smears and smudges the tack-sharp quality of the original master to yield somewhat lesser resolution. In fact, the visual quality of the *originals* produced by a top laser printer is probably equal to the printed *copies* of masters originating on typesetters.

Fonts

Traditionally printers have specialized in putting text on paper. Graphics only became a concern later, after PCs learned how to do graphics themselves. Printing text seems like a simple process, and it is the least complicated form of printing your machinery faces. But the increasing versatility of the PC has transformed text printing as it has transformed everything else (including the world). No longer is your chief concern merely with moving ASCII characters from your PC to printer. You now have all sorts of aesthetic concerns: typefaces, type sizes, and orientations. You have to tell your printer not just to print the letter "C," but also which letter "C" down to its shape, size, and boldness. You face more choices than a child in a candy store armed with a blank check and sweet tooth. The once simple chore of printing has become an art form, transformed from mere copying to the same aesthetic challenge faced by the designers of forms, magazines, and books. Running a printer is no longer a job for the mere typist; it's now in the realm of the artist, graphic designer, and you.

Probably the most important concern is the way the text looks, and how you make it look that way. In printer terminology, you are dealing with *fonts*. Think of a font as an entire alphabet, set of numerals, and punctuation marks of a single size and typeface design.

Fonts are not a singular technology for PC printers. They come in wide variety, not just the typefaces but the underlying technology that determines how you can use them. Some fonts are built into printers. Others only take up temporary residence in the printer. Still others never even see the printer and are manipulated only inside your PC, sent as graphics to the printer.

From the standpoint of how fonts are stored and used, fonts come in two varieties, bit mapped and outline. Some printers (and other display devices) can use only bit-mapped fonts. All of today's quality publishing applications and even most word processors now prefer to use outline fonts because they offer greater versatility.

Bit-Mapped Fonts

The bit-map is the basic way to store any graphic image, and clearly the letters of the alphabet are graphic images like any other that your can draw, paint, or print on paper. When fonts are stored as bit maps, each character pattern gets recorded as an individual pattern of dots. The pattern of the bit map is a matrix of dots, and the larger the matrix and the greater the number of dots the more detail in the character. In general, one dot represents the smallest individually addressable unit in the display system, be it the monitor screen or printer mechanism. Consequently, dots are fixed in size and the number of dots in a character matrix determines the size of the character. Larger characters, made from a greater number of dots, have more detail.

Bit-mapped fonts have two primary advantages. They are fast and simple to use because they never change. Each dot is fixed forever in its position in each character. Text processing a bit-mapped font requires only moving the bit pattern itself; so no other time-consuming data processing such as adjust the size or shape of the character is ever needed. A printer stores the bit maps of each character in a table, and it only needs to look up the appropriate entry to retrieve and print each character.

On the other hand, you usually need a separate bit-mapped font for each size, typeface, and style that you want to print. Bit-mapped fonts are not readily adjusted in size. Consequently a print job with multiple type sizes will require a multitude of bit-mapped fonts. If you have an aesthetic license (or are aesthetically impaired) and plaster every page with a dozen or more different fonts, your storage needs can become prodigious if you use naught but bit-mapped fonts. Your poor printer won't likely have room to accommodate them in its limited RAM.

Nevertheless, the resident fonts in most inexpensive printers are bit mapped. For example, inexpensive dot-matrix printers store their coarse, monospace fonts in their ROM. Even early Hewlett-Packard laser printers came with bit-mapped fonts in ROM.

Bit-mapped fonts are not used solely in budget-oriented applications, however. Bit-mapped fonts can produce the highest quality available at a given resolution. Because each character pattern is separately defined and stored, each one can be optimized. This feature is particularly welcome in small fonts for which the placement of each dot is critical to legibility. Instead of an unthinking algorithm deciding each dot position, a human typeface designer chooses the look of each character and can weigh aesthetics, which remain out of the reach of modern computers.

In today's world of graphic operating systems, any bit-mapped fonts built into a printer are essentially irrelevant to your purchase decision. You'll want at least one so you can print from DOS (if you ever print from DOS), but for serious printing you'll rely on your graphic operating system and an entirely different font technology.

Outline Fonts

Instead of a map of individual dots, you can use equations to describe and store the characters of each font. The formulae are mathematical equations that serve as drawing instructions that tell your PC or printer how to construct a character. The formulae are essentially quadratic equations for Bézier lines, and each one is described in terms of a variable scaling factor. Altering the scaling factor changes every dimension of the character uniformly, making the character print any size that you want. Because you can adjust the size of these fonts so easily, they are often called *scalable* fonts. The more common name is *outline* fonts because the drawing commands describe the shape of each character as an outline, later filled in during the display or printing process.

- **Proportional spacing** describes the characters in some typefaces that are different widths to suit their individual shapes. In other words, some characters are wider than others. For example, a lowercase "i" would be printed substantially narrower than an uppercase "W." Most commercial printing uses proportional spacing because it is more natural and easier to read than the alternative, fixed spacing or monospacing. On the other hand, proportional spacing is more demanding of computing resources, particularly when paragraphs are justified. The varying widths of individual characters must be considered when calculating the lengths of lines. Because characters have different shapes in different fonts, you cannot rely on the character widths being consistent between two different proportionally spaced fonts.
- **Monospacing** is a font design technique that assigns an equal width to every character. This equal spacing was necessary in early typewriters, which advanced their carriages by a fixed amount for every keypress. It simplifies printer design, particularly in inexpensive dot-matrix printers where it is still commonly used. Monospacing also aids in the legibility of certain kinds of information such as tables or program listings because it makes every character and space distinct. Designing a monospaced font takes some ingenuity to produce aesthetic results, extended serifs on narrow characters to make them appear wider and squeezing wide characters to make them appear narrower.
- **Pitch** is the traditional method for measuring the width of the monospaced characters produced by typewriters and printers. Pitch is measured in characters per inch, the number of any alphanumeric characters that

fit within one linear inch of a line of type. (Because pitch applies only to monospaced typefaces, all characters have the same width.) The higher the pitch, the smaller the characters.

Resident Fonts

The fonts that come built into printers are called resident fonts. To be able to print simple, old-fashioned text sent to the printer as a string of ASCII codes, a printer needs at least one resident font. Your printer stores its resident fonts in its ROM.

Resident fonts can be either bit mapped or outline. Some printers have some of each. Most dot-matrix printers have several bit-mapped fonts. Better laser printers have several outline fonts resident. Because they are stored inside the printer, these fonts are sometimes called *internal* fonts.

Downloadable Fonts

Most better printers allow you to enlarge your printing possibilities by adding more fonts to the printer's repertory by downloading them from your PC. These *downloadable* fonts work exactly like resident fonts but are stored in the printer's RAM rather than ROM. In general, you must download these fonts once each session before you can print with them. When you switch off your printer, the downloadable fonts disappear, and you have to load them anew the next time you run your printer. Each font you download steals part of the printer's RAM so that it cannot be used for another purpose, such as buffering. Because downloadable fonts are not part of your printer's hardware or firmware, they are sometimes called soft fonts.

Downloadable fonts do no good if a printer cannot use them in its work. For the most part, however, the task is easy for a printer. It only needs to know how route the code stream containing the font into its memory and how to reroute character searches from the ROM font to the new font in RAM. Nearly all modern printers from inexpensive dot-matrix engines to top-of-the-line lasers accept downloadable fonts. With banded and bit-image printing of text pages through modern operating systems, you have little need for downloadable fonts, at least as long as you don't stray back to DOS.

Note that all downloadable fonts are not the same. Their memory image must match the format that the printer knows how to handle. Consequently, downloadable fonts are to some degree printer specific. Leading printer standards such as Esc/P and PostScript stringently define font standards, so downloadable fonts matching those formats have wide application among compatible printers. You can even define your own fonts to download.

Cartridge Fonts

Before the wide acceptance of outline font technology, many printers depended on bit-mapped fonts. Manufacturers found it improvident to build a substantial number of them into ROM simply because it was expensive, if just for the cost of chips. Moreover, desktop publishing was then new, so few people demands a wide variety of fonts. (When the whole world is Courier, it's hard to see the usefulness of Caslon Old Style.) For those few who wanted or needed a wider variety of fonts, printer makers allowed you to add them in the form of expansion ROM—not loose chips but in packaged in plug in cartridges. For obviously reasons, these quickly became known as *cartridge* fonts.

Cartridge fonts have the unique strength that they don't take away anything from your printer the way that downloadable fonts steal RAM. they only add to it. Most people found downloadable fonts more convenient (if just because they are easier to steal). Because of the ready access to downloadable fonts and the versatility of outline fonts, cartridge fonts have fallen into disfavor. Although still present in new printers, they are of doubtful utility, especially if you plan to use a graphic operating system like Windows 95.

In order to use cartridge fonts, a printer requires a cartridge slot. Most printers that have cartridge slots pattern them after the design developed by Hewlett-Packard for its LaserJet series of machines. A few manufacturers use proprietary slots, which limits your choice of fonts to those available from the printer manufacturer.

Screen Fonts

The goal of the modern desktop publishing or graphics program is true What You See Is What You Get—the infamous WYSIWYG—printouts where what comes out on paper exactly matches what you've worked with on the screen. True WYSIWYG remains but a dream because of the ingrained differences between video and hard-copy technology. If nothing else, the resolution of monitors is far below that of printers. Making a match between screen and paper requires finding a low resolution font that has the same look as a high-resolution twin designed for your printer. These approximately matching low-resolution fonts that are meant for showing on your video screen are called *screen* fonts.

In general, screen fonts are most often used when you print with bit-mapped fonts. In such instances, you need fonts of the same typeface, size, and weight for both printer and screen. When you don't have an exact match, your software may try font mapping, that is, substituting an available font for one to which it does not have access.

When you use outline fonts, a *font manager* program may be able to translate the printer outlines to those suitable for the screen. For example, Adobe Type Manager converts fonts meant for PostScript printers to match your screen. Windows versions since 3.1 use TrueType, which has built-in font management and mapping abilities. In general, TrueType will attempt to put the best looking face it can on your screen.

Color Printing

A growing number of applications demand color output, and the printer industry has responded with a number of different technologies to suit individual color applications, from low cost to photo-like quality

A number of impact dot-matrix printers allow you to add color to both the alphabets and graphics they put on paper. A few have two color ribbons (like old-fashioned typewriters) and special software instructions to control shifting between them.

Most color printers now use ribbons soaked with three or four colors of ink, and can achieve seven colors on paper by combining color pairs. For example, laying a layer of blue over a layer of yellow results in an approximation of green. To switch colors that they print, they merely shift the ribbon up or down. The extra mechanism required is simple and inexpensive, costing as little as $50 extra. (Of course, the color ribbon costs more and does not last as long as its monochrome equivalent.) A few machines use multiple ribbons, each one a different color, to achieve the same effect.

Non impact matrix printers excel at color. Inkjets are well suited to the task because their liquid inks can actually blend together on the paper before they dry. Color inkjet printers are, however, substantially more complex and expensive than their monochrome equivalents because each primary color requires its own separate ink reservoir and nozzle. Most thermal-wax matrix printers are designed particularly for color output. They achieve on-paper color mixing by using transparent inks that allow one color to show through another. The two hues blend together optically.

The only problem with color printers is that they need special software to bring their rainbows to life. Without the right software, you have to understand computer programming to take advantage of multicolor capabilities. Today, most impact color printers follow the standard set by the Epson JX-80, which adds one escape code to its normal command set for changing ribbon color. Thermal-wax and phase-change printers normally use PostScript, and PostScript 2 gives them a common color language.

Page description languages can actually slow down graphic printing–particularly color printing–when you deal extensively with bit images. To print a bit image with a page description language, your PC must first translate the bit image into commands used by the page description language. Then the printer must convert the commands into the image raster before it can print out the image. This double conversion wastes time. Printers that sidestep the page description language by using their own specialized drivers typically send only the bits of the image through the printer interface. The printer can then quickly rasterize the image bits. The down side of the special driver technique is that each application (or operating environment) requires its own driver software, which usually means that such printer work only with Windows and a handful of the most popular applications.

Memory

All but the most basic printers require memory of some kind. A line printer needs at least enough memory to store the characters in a printer; a true page printer requires at least full page of memory (although engineers have found ways of cheating on paper printing memory needs).

Printer memory is no different from other memory used in PCs. In general, printer memory uses ordinary *dynamic random access memory* or (DRAM) technology. Because print jobs usually are not a critical application–few are matters of life or death–printer memory usually does not require error-detection techniques like parity-checking.

Raster Memory

Raster or image memory stores the bit image that will be printed onto a page. One bit of raster memory corresponds to each dot that appears on paper. The higher the resolution, the more dots in each square inch and page, and the more raster memory a printer needs. With true page printers that require the full pages to be rasterized before printing, memory needs can be prodigious, as shown in Table 2.1.

Table 2.1 Memory Requirements for an 8-by-10 Inch Image (8.5-by-11 inch page) at Various Resolutions

Resolution (dots per inch)	Page Size (total dots)	Memory (kilobytes)
75 by 75	450,000	55
150 by 150	1,800,000	220
300 by 300	7,200,000	879
600 by 600	28,800,000	3,516
1200 by 1200	115,200,000	14,063

Clever programmers have devised methods of printing full-page bit images with less than the number of bytes indicated by this table. These schemes shift the rasterization process from printer to PC, potentially and probably slowing down the PC and the print job (see the discussion of banded graphics, which follows). When the printer handles rasterization (as it will in a pure PostScript system), these raster memory requirements usually apply, although some newer printers can sneak past these limits using designs like memory enhancement technology (see the next section).

Processor Memory

Processor memory or working memory is used by the raster image processor for running its program to calculate dots and their positions. As with any other microprocessor, the RIP requires RAM for holding program code during execution and for temporary storage of data. Among other things, processor memory stores the soft fonts you download into your printer.

The more complex the print job, the more memory will be required by the processor for its operation. In most printers, raster and processor memory are drawn from the same pool so that the overall memory in the printer gets allocated as it is needed. In some circumstances, however, the processor may demand so much memory that the machine has insufficient reserves for holding the completed bit image of a full page. To avoid such problems, printers use page protection. This design forces the printer to set aside enough memory to create a full-page raster before memory is allocated to the processor. This assures that the printer will not run out of raster memory in the middle of receiving a page of data from your PC.

Some printers set aside part of their RAM supply to serve as a processor cache. As with cache memory inside a PC, the printer processor cache helps improve performance by storing common or previously used instructions for later recall. Because the instructions don't need to be reloaded into memory, the cache can improve the performance of the printer's processor and the overall performance of the printer.

Buffer Memory

Buffer memory is additional storage space that a printer can allocate to temporarily hold data before it is printed or even rasterized. Not a mere dumping ground for data, the buffer helps hold incoming text when the data arrives at a faster rate than the printer's engine can handle.

The chief advantage of buffering is that your PC need not get entirely tied up when you have to print something out. As mechanical devices, typical printers splatter out characters and graphics much more slowly than the electronic mind of your PC can crank them out. Without the aid of a buffer, your PC would sit around waiting for your printer to catch up, wasting its processing power spinning its logical wheels. A printer buffer accepts characters and commands from your PC as fast as they can be generated, so your PC works at maximum efficiency and wastes the minimum time on the print job. When it's done sending data to the print buffer, it gives control back to you so you can continue with your everyday work.

Beside simply quickening the speed at which control of your PC returns to you, buffer memory enables a number of additional speed-up and convenience technologies, such as the following:

- **Job overlap** allows a printer to start processing a subsequent print job before it finishes printing the previous one. Although job overlap does not actually speed up printing–print speed in most modern printers is mostly determined by the print engine–it does make printing apparently faster to your PCs. You and your PC wait less time for access to the printer. With modern operating systems that incorporate print spoolers that release control back to your programs quite quickly, job overlap becomes less of a concern.

- **Simultaneously active ports** describes a feature of advanced printers that allows multiple computer systems to share the printer using different ports. The computers can send data at the same time to the printer, and the printer keeps each print job straight, outputting them one after another. Some systems permit their parallel and serial input ports to be simultaneously active. Others have multiple parallel ports. Some allow a network interface to be active along with the ports. If you have two PCs and a printer with simultaneously active parallel and serial ports, you can use this feature as a primitive form of printer sharing, as long as you can tolerate the low speed suffered by the serial connection with the printer.

Print buffer memory need not be physically inside your printer. You can also buy standalone print buffers and printer sharing devices with built-in buffer memory. In addition, *print spooler* software lets you use the memory inside your PC to buffer print jobs. All advanced operating systems come equipped with print spoolers. All network operating systems include print spooler software as well. Except when you need other special features, these software buffers minimize the need for buffers inside your printer.

The size of buffer memory inside a given printer varies. Some allow you to expand their buffers. Some printers allow you to allocate the amount of their RAM that will be devoted to print buffering. Finding the optimum size is a trade-off between the speed up of buffering and accelerated processing of having larger processor memory.

Physical Memory

Printers use exactly the same kind of physical memory as PCs in general. When memory needs are small, as they are in the case of a line printer with a small internal buffer, printers get along with a few dozen kilobytes of RAM in discrete memory chips soldered down to their circuit boards. Sometimes the memory in these machines is expandable to accommodate additional downloadable fonts or increase the size of the internal buffer. Most such expandable printers use plug-in proprietary memory boards to hold their extra kilobytes.

Because laser printers make such heavy memory demands, on par (and sometimes exceeding) the requirements of PCs, they use the same memory technology as today's PCs, typically single in-line memory modules (SIMMs), which pack several discrete memory chips on a small circuit board. Depending on the whim of the printer's designer, a specific printer may use generic SIMMs or proprietary expansion memory. Obviously the use of industry standard SIMMs should be preferred in a printer should you ever want to add memory. Standard SIMMs are less expensive than proprietary memory and, although individual modules may be more difficult to install than proprietary expansion boards, most people can handle SIMM installation.

In general, the more memory in your printer the better. With older application software, larger memory endowments permit you to download more fonts and use higher resolutions. Windows 3.1 and Windows 95 use TrueType to take advantage of many memory-saving techniques (such as banded graphics, see above) that allow your printer to get by even with less RAM than would be required to store a full-page bit image. On the downside, however, TrueType moves most of the image processing chore to your PC, which may slow the rasterization process (your PC probably doesn't rasterize as fast as the RISC processor in your printer) and even slows overall system performance (because your PC has to process the page image instead of just downloading a page description to the printer).

Memory Enhancement Technology

Operating system designers discovered long ago that the most convenient way to store data often is not the most efficient. The result was the creation of disk compression programs that were able to effectively double the capacity of hard disk drives. It's not much of a leap of faith to try to use the same techniques to squeeze more capacity from the confines of printer memory, too.

This line of reasoning led engineers at Hewlett-Packard to develop *Memory Enhancement technology* (abbreviated as MEt) for its line of LaserJet printers. Using adaptive data compression technology, MEt lets a LaserJet with as little as 1 megabyte of physical memory to store raster data for complex documents and accept multiple downloaded fonts.

Print Speed

On the surface, speed seems the most straightforward and objective measure of a printer. Like everything else about printers, speed is not a single or simple thing. It can be measured in various ways with various units, and it varies with what you do and the quality of the results you expect. Specification sheets most commonly describe print speed in one of two units, characters per second and pages per minute.

- Characters per second or cps units are typically used to measure the speed of dot-matrix or line printers. In pure form, cps expresses how quickly a printer can put individual characters on paper. In reality, printer manufacturers don't measure cps by how long a document takes to print. Instead they deduce the cps rate from the speed at which the printhead travels across the paper. For example, if a printhead can speed across a full 80-character line of text in two-thirds of a second, the manufacturer rates the printer at 120 cps, even though it may not print a character in each position.

  Because the speed at which the printhead moves and the width of a full line in most printers are fixed, the cps rate will vary with the number of character positions in a line. Because a twelve-pitch line holds 20% more characters than a ten-pitch line, most dot-matrix printers produce twelve-pitch output 20% faster than ten-pitch. Although most manufacturers will quote a cps rate for ten-pitch printing, some more optimistic manufacturers may opt for a rate based on narrower characters (perhaps even fifteen-pitch).
- **Pages per minute** or ppm units are most often used to measure the speed of laser printer or other page printers. It represents the number of full pages of text that the printer can work through in any given minute.

You can measure the speed of a laser printer in pages per minute in two ways. *Engine speed* is the rate at which paper rolls through the imaging mechanism of the printer. With most laser printers, this is the rate you can expect output when printing text using the printer's internal fonts. *Throughput* is the rate at which a printer produces hard copy from raw data. Although engine speed and throughput can be equal (as in the above instance of using internal fonts for text), modern printing techniques make the RIP of the printer labor mightily indeed. Rasterizing a page can take a few minutes to over an hour. The actual rate, hence the throughput, varies with what and how you print. Faster processors and larger memories tend to increase throughput.

Assuming you want single-spaced output, the rough conversion formula for characters per second into pages per minute is as follows:

```
Pages per minute = characters per second / 80
```

This basis for this formula is that a single-spaced page comprises about 60 lines, each of which has 80 character positions.

If you assume the standard format of 80 characters per line and 60 lines per page, you can work out similar conversion factors for other speed designations. Table 2.2 lists the conversion factors that will let you approximate printer speed ratings given in different measurement units.

Table 2.2 Printer Speed Conversion Factors

	Characters Per Second	Lines Per Minute	Pages Per Minute
Characters Per Second	1.0	0.75	0.0125
Lines Per Minute	1.33	1.0	0.0167
Pages Per Minute	80	60	1

To make a conversion, select the units from the left hand column, then find the conversion factor under the appropriate units column to the right. Multiply the original units to find the new units. These conversion factors assume 80 column pages 60 lines long.

Note that all such speed conversions are approximate. Line printers and page printers use entirely different technologies that have a dramatic impact on speed as soon as you vary from the standard 80-column, 60-line page. For example, as soon as you shift to double-spaced printing, the comparison changes. Although a page printer produces single- and double-spaced pages at exactly the same number of pages per minute, a double-spaced page takes a line printer about half as long to print–although the cps remains unchanged, the ppm rate for the line printer effectively gets cut in half when you double-space. Moreover, if a page has a lot of white space, the line printer will skip over it to increase its effective throughput while the page printer typically will be locked to its engine speed.

Paper Handling

The computer printer is stuck with the same dilemma faced by the modern office worker. Although it has an official job–moving ink to turn the ephemeral thoughts of your PC into hard copy–most of its time gets occupied with paperwork. Every printer is stuck with the chore of shuffling through reams of paper. Although some move sheets a line at a time and others work with pages, all have to somehow scoot it through their mechanisms. Engineers have concocted various schemes for moving paper through PC printers. Their choices depend on the needs of the printer itself, the kind of medium meant for the printer to handle, and how much trouble you're willing to endure.

The needs of line and page printers differ. Line printers are concerned solely with a single line at a time. They require the paper to move in distinct one-line increments, stop, wait for the line to be completed, then move on to the next line. Page printers, contrary to what you might expect, demand more precise motion. They work a dot's width at a time rather than the width of a full multiple-dot line. Instead of stopping for each dot, however, page printers are machines on the move, smoothly sweeping the paper (or other printing medium) past their wide print heads for the length of a page. Where the line printer operates in start–stop mode, the page printer is a smooth operator.

Paper makes a bigger difference. Designers target specific kinds of paper for their mechanisms. The major division is between two styles of paper. *Cut sheets* are the familiar individual pages that you're used to handling. *Continuous-form paper* puts hundreds of cut sheets end to end to make one long strip. It may take the form of a roll much like paper towels or *fan-fold paper*, the strip folded back upon itself to resemble a stack of cut sheets, each linked to the next by perforated edges. Continuous-form paper may or may not have *sprocket holes* at its long edges to aid the operation of some paper-feeding mechanisms.

If there is any trend in printer paper and its handling, it's toward cut sheets, led by the wide popularity of laser and inkjet printer, which use it. Certainly, continuous-form is the less convenient form of paper in that you have to tear apart the individual sheets before you can pass them off as your work. On the other hand, you can buy continuous-form carbon (or carbonless) copy sets that allow you to print multiple copies of documents such as forms in a single pass through the printer.

Friction Feed

The earliest and the most recent printers share the same paper-moving technology, friction feed. Both printers derived from the old-fashioned typewriter and modern laser machines rely on a tight grip on paper to usher it through their tortuous mechanisms. They grab each sheet between the rubber rollers and use the force of friction to keep it from slipping.

In the prototype form of friction feeding as used in typewriter-derived mechanisms, one large rubber roller serves as both platen and drive wheel. Smaller rollers hold the paper or other medium tightly against the platen roller and force the paper to move as the platen spins. In many printers, a movable frame with additional rollers called the *bail arm* adds additional grip to the platen and also holds the paper flat against the platen so the hammering of the printhead doesn't move the paper backward. This design ensures a sharper on-paper image.

Although strictly speaking the elaborate paper-moving mechanisms inside laser printers are friction feed, in general use the term is reserved for describing the typewriter-like printers with these large platen rollers. The term *friction feed* implies that loading paper in a printer so designated must be a manual operation. Each sheet is a ritual in itself–you pull out the bail arm, slide each individual sheet in behind the platen, run it partway through the printer, line up its edges to be certain the top edge is parallel to the platen (so that the printhead does not skate diagonally across the paper), lock the paper in, and finally push down the bail arm.

No one wants to repeat this ritual the dozens or hundreds of times required by each printout. Understandably then, most printers that offer friction feed combine it with some other paper-handling method. While you'll want to use an automated paper-feeding system for most printouts, you can opt for friction feed when you need additional versatility. Most friction-feed mechanisms will handle any kind of paper you can fit between their rollers, from your own engraved 100% rag stationery to newsprint. It adroitly handles envelopes and other oddly shaped media. When you need to print a single sheet or special job, say a preprinted form, friction feed can save the day. When you need to print out an instruction manual, friction feed may take up your entire day.

Cut-Sheet Feed

Should you want to automate the friction-feed system, you can add in some inventiveness and subtract out inspiration to create a set of mechanical hands that would carefully slide in individual sheets for printing, then pull out and stack the output. Most printer manufacturers have at one time or another concocted such abominations for their friction-feed printers, typically with more cams, gears, and levers than a cuckoo clock factory. They give a variety of names to their creations. Foremost is *cut-sheet feeder* or automatic sheet feeder because they feed individual cut sheets through the printer. Alternately, they are termed *bin-feed systems* because they draw the sheets they use from their own supply bin.

Some printer makers offer cut-sheet feeders with two bins so that you can select between two different paper supplies without reloading the printer. For example, you might load one bin with printed stationery and the second with plain bond paper for the later sheets of multipage letters. Printer makers typically call this kind of mechanism a *dual-bin cut-sheet feeder.*

No matter the name, these devices rank among the most mechanically complex accessories you can add to your computer system. They appear to be afterthoughts. One design team dreamed up the basic printer, and after it was done a committee of aesthetically impaired tinkers grafted on the cut-sheet mechanism. In most cases, they are accessories that snap or latch onto the basic friction-feed printer.

They can be fascinating to watch, the PC equivalent of a juggler with a dish twirling on a stick balanced on his nose. As with any mechanical device, reliability goes down as the number of moving parts goes up, so you can imagine the typical cut-sheet feeder as an innovation designed to keep repair centers busy.

Thankfully, such add-on cut-sheet feeders have gone the way of all things, including the basic friction-feed printer. Today's tray-fed printers have cut-sheet mechanisms conceived and designed integral with the rest of the printer that are able to whisk individual sheets through simple paper paths without reliability worries.

Roll Feed

Another obvious way to trim the number of times you're forced to slide sheets of paper into a friction-feed printer mechanism is to use longer sheets that hold more printing. Take that concept to the extreme–a single, almost endless sheet–and you have the basis of the *roll-fed printer*. This design relies on the same expedient as toilet paper. You start with a roll and pull off only as much as you need. Although the roll of paper sometimes may be perforated at regular intervals approximating a standard paper size, most roll-feed systems include a *tear-off bar* so you can just rip when the printing ends. You waste little paper, but you can get some odd-length sheets.

Most roll-fed printers rigidly hold the paper roll square to the rear of the mechanism, assuring the system maintains the proper alignment. The paper from the roll always goes in perpendicular to the platen, and the sturdy mounting prevents it from drifting askew. You only need to load paper at the end of each roll. Although rolls often are hundreds of feet long, they are carefully measured at the factory to end right in the middle of important documents. The shortcoming of the roll-fed system is, of course, that you end up with one long sheet with torn edges at top and bottom.

The classic roll-fed printer was the news teletype that coughed up a continuous play-by-play of happenings that crossed the newswire. Reporters could tear off as much of the printout as they needed. Broadcasters often read the news copy straight from the wire (no rewrites), earning them the name rip-and-read journalists. Printing calculators and many dedicated-purpose printers such as those that rattle out your credit card chits still use roll-feed.

Pin Feed

The primary reason that roll-fed paper usually is not perforated at sheet-size intervals is slippage. Even the slight drag of a full roll of paper is enough to make paper, even when tightly gripped between rubber rollers, slip a fraction of an inch over the length of an 11-inch page. Although you might not notice a page that's compressed by 1/16th of an inch, such slippage errors are cumulative. Over the course of a printout, the errors pile up until the perforations and the page breaks in the text no longer line up. The image in the mind of your PC gets out of sync with what's printed on paper.

Mechanics know that gears eliminate slippage. Although actually gearing paper isn't practical, adding sprocket holes to paper takes advantage of the same concept. The holes engage positively with sprocketed wheels on the printer platen and prevent the paper slipping as it is pulled through the mechanism. This design results in the *pin-feed* system. The pins of the name are the individual teeth of the sprockets that engage the paper.

True pin-fed printers permanently affix their sprocket wheels to the edges of the platen rollers, absolutely assuring that the sprockets, platen, and paper all move in sync. On the downside, this arrangement prevents any adjustability. The design fixes the distance between the sprockets once and for all.

The width of paper to take advantage of the pin feed system must match the sprocket spacing for the system to work. Nearly all pin-fed printers use sprockets spaced for paper 9.5 inches wide. Once you strip the edges with the sprocket holes from this paper, you get standard 8.5-inch-wide sheets.

Because pin feed is basically the friction feed system with added sprockets at the edges, you can also use a pin-fed printer as a friction-fed machine with any paper that fits between the sprockets. In other words, pin feed gives you the benefit of positive paper positioning without sacrificing the versatility of friction feed.

Pin-feed printer designs are not popular today. The single-width paper requirement, although a small practical limitation (how often do you print on paper that differs from the standard 8.5-inch width?), seems too restrictive. Moreover, pin feed is based on the typewriter mechanism with a large, spinning rubber platen roller. Modern impact dot-matrix printers eschew this design in favor of a fixed platen.

Tractor Feed

Overcoming the limitations of the pin-feed system takes separating the sprocket mechanism from the platen. The *tractor feed* system does exactly that, giving over the paper moving function to a separate drive mechanism called the *tractor*. Instead of wheels, the first tractor-fed printers used short, flexible bands with projecting sprockets to drive the paper through the printer, rolling around like the treads of tractors. The term *tractor* actually means anyone or anything that can pull something around; hence these drive elements are termed, quite correctly, tractors.

Because the tractors are not affixed to the platen but are separate elements of the mechanism, they can be adjusted without regard to the width of the platen. The tractor-feed system can thus accommodate any width of paper up to the maximum permitted by the design of the printer. Although most tractor systems also have a minimum paper width because of mechanical constraints, they allow you to set any paper width between their limits.

Over the years, several variations on the tractor design have evolved. They are designated by the location of the mechanism and how they move the paper through the printer.

- **Bidirectional tractors** hold paper precisely so that the printer can shift it forward or backward while maintaining absolute alignment. Most bidirectional tractor systems comprise two sets of drive sprockets, one in the paper path before the platen and one afterward. You adjust the pairs of tractors so that they put the paper under tension and wrap it tightly across the platen so that there's no chance it will bunch up or bulge away from the platen no matter which direction it travels.

  The distance between the tractors and platen can be substantial in some printer designs. It may span as many as three sheets. In any case, with a bidirectional tractor you have to keep two or three sheets constantly threaded up. If you want to tear off a complete print job, you have to advance at least one additional sheet through the printer to keep the paper threaded. In effect, you lose one sheet for every print job you tear off.

Outside of a tendency to stretch sprocket holes when you apply too much tension between the tractors, the only other substantial shortcoming of the bi-directional tractor system is complexity. The complex mechanism is relatively expensive to build. Moreover, you have to deal with two complete tractor systems and the tension between them every time you want to thread the printer.

- **Unidirectional tractors** drive paper through the printer in only one direction, ever onward. Although they may be able to reverse for a fraction of a line, they cannot maintain precise paper positioning during backward motion. In general, this arrangement is okay because most documents get printed with only forward paper movement.

  A unidirectional tractor system requires only one set of tractors. Depending on the position of the tractors in the printer, they are classified as push or pull tractors.
- **Push tractors** are located before the platen. They push the paper up to the platen. In most push tractor systems, the tractor is used mostly for alignment. A conventional rolling rubber platen acts as the actual drive mechanism.
- **Pull tractors** are located after the platen. They pull the paper across the platen around out of the printer. Many pull tractor systems have fixed platens, so the tractor is the only paper moving mechanism in the printer.

Printers with pull tractors are usually mechanically simpler and hence less expensive to build (and probably more reliable). But the pull tractor design suffers one of the same shortcomings as the bidirectional tractor. Keeping paper threaded through the tractor mechanism requires running an extra sheet through the printer every time you want to tear off a print job. Because pull tractor printers are often designed for high-speed output and generating huge stacks of printout, people who print in great volumes don't see the occasional waste of a single sheet as a problem.

Push tractors don't suffer the wasted-paper shortcoming. In fact, many push tractors have a special tear-off function that automatically advances the paper to a tear-off at the completion of a print job. When you to start the next job, the printer retracts the paper back to the top of the form.

Tray Feed

The integral cut-sheet mechanisms used by nearly every laser printer and most inkjets store paper inside trays and are sometimes called *tray feed*. The actual mechanism uses a friction-feed system with numerous rollers and guides to conduct each sheet along the proper path around the drum or past the printhead. Most paper-feed trays are removable, whereas output trays usually are not. The feed trays themselves are a convenience feature, one that allows you to switch paper supplies in seconds with relatively little hassle. The removable trays also allow you to load paper in a place or position more comfortable than would otherwise be demanded by the mechanism–you can slide in a stack of paper and align it on a table top instead of trying to squeeze your hands into the guts of the printer.

The *feed trays* used by different printers to hold blank stock are not the same. Beside the design differences relevant only to the engineer who has to draw a blueprint of the printer and have all the pieces fit together, one variable in feed-tray design is of particular practical importance to you: capacity. Some trays hold more paper than others. The printers that are aimed primarily at personal use–most inkjets and slower lasers–have trays with modest capacity, typically capable of storing about 50 sheets. With a high throughput print job, for example, a simple text draft, you'll be reloading the machine every 10 to 15 minutes. Printers designed for work group operating such as high-speed lasers demand greater tray capacities, and more is usually better. You'll want a printer with capacity suited to your operating style.

Output trays also vary in capacity. In normal operation, however, another difference has an even greater effect on convenience–the orientation of the output. When tray-fed printers disgorge their output, the individual sheets can fall into the output tray in one of two orientations, face up or face down. If you want to get the immediate gratification of seeing the abominations you've committed to paper immediately, even in process, you'll want to see pages curl out face up. But if you want to get your work done with a minimum of hassles, face down rates higher because you won't have to sort through the stack and reorganize all the pages. Although most early laser printers piled out paper face up because of their engine designs, face down has become the more popular configuration for obvious reasons of convenience. For your peace of mind, you may still want to check the output sheet orientation before you buy a new printer.

Duplex Printing

The ultimate in paper handling as far as convenience and economy are concerned is *duplexing*, the ability of a printer to print on both sides of each sheet of paper with one pass through the mechanism. Using both sides of a sheet of paper obviously saves the cost of paper and helps you take one small step in lowering the environmental costs of doing business. Duplexing not only makes two-sided printing easier, it even makes the process possible.

Certainly, you can run a stack of paper through your laser printer, flip it over, then print on the other side. But this technique is problematic for several reasons. If your print job is long, you have the logistical problem of interleaving sheets. You need to first print the odd-numbered sheets, then make the flip and do the even-numbered sheets (perhaps in reverse order, depending on how your printer stacks its output). Of course you must spend your time flipping and reloading the paper, and woe unto you if you get a jam in the middle of the run! Worse, with laser printers you stand a chance of melting off the toner from the previously printed side of the sheet when the machine tried to fuse the second side, potentially contaminating the mechanism. A printer designed for duplexing eliminates all of these concerns. If you print a lot of reports, the cost savings in cutting your paper consumption in half may more than pay for a more expensive duplex printer.

Paper Paths

The route that each sheet takes as it courses through your printer is called the *paper path*. The journey can be a tortuous one, around multiple bends and sharp curves, or it can be a straight line. As you might expect, the more direct route is usually preferred because jams are less likely. One of the major innovations in more recent laser printers has been the straightening of the paper paths.

Many printers allow for *multiple paper paths*, letting you choose (to some extent) exactly how each sheet gets where it's going. The available options may let you choose how each printed sheet is delivered to you or where you must locate the blank paper to feed into the printer.

Cut-sheet printers like lasers may give you the choice of output trays, for example, at the top or back of the printer. One tray–typically the one with the more tortuous passage–dumps paper face down; the other face up.

Continuous-form printers allow you to select various locations for the paper supply. Put a machine on a true printer stand, and *bottom feed* will probably be best. You can put a box of stock under the printer and thread it up through a slit in the stand and past the printhead. The primary alternative is feeding paper from the rear, which allows you to puts the printer and its stack of feed stock on the same desk.

Paper Size

Although the 8.5-by-11-inch letter-size sheet has become the nearly universal standard in American business, it is not the only size you might want to print. Some legal communities cling to longer sheets for the motions, brief, and other papers. Newsletters naturally lean toward larger dimensions so that a single fold will produce four pages of standard-size sheet. You may even prefer to nonstandard size as your statement of independence—both aesthetic and economic.

Most printers, however, stodgily stick to the letter-size standard. If you want to vary from the norm, you'll have to look carefully at the claims of printer makers to determine whether a particular machine will meet your needs and paper specifications.

Tray Size

The trays used by laser and other printers designed to handle cut sheets are the most visible and immediate limit on the size of paper you can use. After all, if the paper won't fit in the tray, you can't easily load it into the printer. You can usually adjust the guides in trays to hold smaller sheets down to some minimum limit, but larger stock is prohibited.

The trays actually only enforce a limit created in the design of the printer. The engine width of a laser determines the widest possible printed area, and a slightly larger width that allows for margins is set by the paper handling mechanism. The engine width cannot be violated because the printer can put ink or toner where it cannot reach. Length is another matter. In theory, you could design a laser to print continuously on a never-ending roll. Cut sheets, however, are constrained by practical tray designs, which in turn reflect the popular available paper sizes.

Put simply, most laser printers can handle sheets 8.5 inches wide with a printable area of about eight inches. Most will accommodate both letter- and legal-sheet sizes, although some may require special trays for the latter, which may be an extra cost option. Most of these machines will also accommodate smaller standard sizes and even custom sizes within the limits of the adjustability of their trays. Lasers for larger sheets are available but expensive because demand for them is small and the larger print mechanisms are necessarily more costly. For example, newspapers often use 11-by-17-inch lasers for proofing. You can even find continuous-form laser printers, although they are also expensive because of their small volume of sales.

Carriage Width

Printers for continuous-form paper abide by similar limitations as do cut-sheet machines. They can print sheets of almost any length. You only need to roll a long sheet into the printer and instruct your software about its length to print as long as you want. But these printers are limited in the width of the media they can handle by their physical designs of the guide for their printheads and other physical constraints. Just as with the engine-width of a laser, the distance a printhead can move horizontally limits the width you can print on paper. The maximum sheet width a continuous-form printer can use is called its *carriage width*, a term carried over from the days of mechanical typewriters when you rolled each sheet around the rubber platen that ratcheted past the hammers on a subassembly called the *carriage*.

Among PC printers, two carriage widths are nearly universal standards to the extent of having their own, well-understood names. A *narrow-carriage* printer can print a line of ten-pitch (pica) characters 80 positions long, yielding a printable width of eighty characters at ten pitch (that is, eight inches). A *wide-carriage* printer extends the length of the longest line it can print to 136-pica-width characters, a distance of 13.6 inches. The actual paper-handling mechanisms of these machines accommodate sheets somewhat wider then their maximum printed widths to allow for both blank margins and for the perforated edges of continuous-form paper. Most narrow-carriage printers accommodate paper measuring 9.5 inches wide; most wide-carriage printers, sheets up to 15 inches wide. These widths correspond to 8.5 and 14 inches, respectively, once you strip the perforated edges off.

Paper Control

Printers differ to a great degree in how precisely they can move paper through their mechanisms. Some are designed to allow exacting tolerances and move each sheet in increments of the tiniest fractions of an inch (as small as 1/216th of an inch). A few still cling to their typewriter heritage and restrict you to shifting paper to one line (or half-line) at a time.

The trend has been to more precise control because it allows more format versatility in printing text–for instance, you can change line spacing from six lines per inch for manuscripts to eight per inch for business letters or add a few extra inch-fractions to each line to stretch ten pages into 12 pages when you have a tough essay assignment–and more accuracy in printing graphics.

Printers also vary in the control they afford in the other direction, the horizontal movement of the printhead across the paper. A few primitive machines still stick with the mechanical cog of the typewriter. Most modern machines, however, let you vary the character pitch in text mode and the spacing of dots and speed of printing in graphics modes. This versatility is necessary for the rendering of proportionally space d text and for printing multiple graphic densities.

Bidirectional Printing

The old-fashioned typewriter printed characters exactly the way you thought of them and they were to be read, from right to left. Printers, however, hold an advantage: they can memorize an entire line before printing it. Better still, they can retrieve the individual characters from a line in reverse order, a trick you would be hard-pressed to duplicate. But using that trick, the printer can print from left to right or right to left.

A technology called *bidirectional printing* takes advantage of this ability. Bidirectional printing means that the printer first pecks out one line in the traditional manner from left to right, then prints the next line from the other direction, right to left. More than a good trick, bidirectional printing allows the machine to print subsequent lines without the typewriter's carriage return. This simple omission can cut printing time by up to 50%.

The biggest drawback of bidirectional printing is that alignments are more difficult to maintain when the print head is moving from different points of reference, starting at either the left or right end of the line. Consequently, to achieve highest quality, most bidirectional dot-matrix printers revert to unidirectional printing in their letter-quality modes and when generating their best quality graphics.

Horizontal and Vertical Tabbing

One place the intelligence of a printer can be put to use is in optimizing printhead motion, making every movement of the printhead the most efficient possible. The internal microprocessor in a printer can look ahead in the memory, see what is coming up next and optimize the positioning of the printhead or print wheel by finding the shortest difference between consecutive lines. The goal is to move between printhead positions as quickly as possible. Often called logic-seeking printers, these machines use a number of techniques to optimize printhead movement. Using horizontal tabbing, they can breeze over oceans of blank space in each line without dwelling on each individual space and deciding what not to print. With vertical tabbing, they can be equally adept at skipping blank lines on the page. Both techniques, combined with bidirectional printing, allow a printer so blessed to type normal documents faster than machines with the same characters-per-second speed rating that lack these features.

Advanced Paper Handling

Over the years, as the processor in printers has become more sophisticated, designers have added a number of convenience features to the paper handling abilities of their machines. Collectively called *advanced paper handling* (and known under the proprietary name *Smart Park*), it comprises several functions.

Among the most common features included in advanced paper handling is *paper parking*, which helps you save time loading and unloading continuous-form paper from your printer to print single sheets or envelopes. Paper parking moves the continuous-form paper out of the way without unthreading so you can manually load envelopes or individual cut sheets. When you're finished with manual paper handling, you can instantly resume the use of continuous-form paper without further ado.

Short tear-off saves paper when you use continuous forms. At the end of a print job, a printer with the short tear-off feature advances the continuous paper to the tear-off bar so you pull off the print job. When you start the next print job, the printer automatically retracts the paper down to the top of the form and starts printing there. In net effect, you don't waste a sheet with every printjob as you normally would.

Microadjustment allows you to move paper electronically by pressing front panel buttons to align the top of the form (or any other position on the paper) with a high degree of precision. Some Epson printers, for example, allow you to manually control paper positioning in increments of 1/180th of an inch.

Command

Somehow you've got to control your printer. After all, you don't want it running amuck and crashing down buildings in Tokyo. More importantly, you need to be able to tell it what to do, where to place each character, how to arrange every dot, and when to move the paper and head on to the next page. In other words, your PC needs a language with which to communicate with your printer.

For mundane operations, you don't need all the complexities of a real language. In fact, the electronic equivalent of switches would work, letting you toggle between print modes such as boldfacing and underlining. Simple codes work for these function and others like them, for example, to tab, advance to the next line, or backspace. These simple commands take two forms. The most basic are special, nonprinting characters called *control codes* that have near-universal meaning. Related are *escape sequences*, which use multiple characters to command more complex and advanced functions.

Printer Control Languages

By using a combination of control codes and escape sequences, your PC can command any function of a printer. The combination of these codes constitutes the printer's language. Because it directly commands the functions of the printer, the combination of codes is called a *printer control language* or a command language.

Although many printer makers have developed their own command languages, the systems developed by two manufacturers dominate the industry. Most dot-matrix printers, both nine- and 24-wire, emulate the corresponding Epson series of machines. This Epson emulation is sometimes called Esc/P because of the form of the most often duplicated commands. The update of this language to work with 24-pin printers is called Esc/P-2. Laser printers usually follow the language developed by Hewlett-Packard for its line of LaserJets. These machines use the Hewlett-Packard Printer Control Language (usually called HPPCL or simply PCL). The latest version is Enhanced PCL 5, which accommodates machines operating at addressability levels up to 600 dpi.

Printer control languages command the printer mechanism itself. They instruct the printer on how to move its printhead, which font to make active, or when to eject a sheet of paper. The actual content of the image that appears on paper has little relevance to the language. Moreover, printer control languages are, for the most part, device-specific. A given set of printing commands works only at one resolution level and, perhaps, with only one model of printer. After all, sending an instruction to print 300 dots in a row will have dramatically different results on printers that lay down 72 and 600 dpi.

Page Description Languages

The alternate approach to controlling a printer is to concentrate on the output and let the printer do its own thing in generating the output. Instead of directly instructing the printer what to do, you tell the printer the way you want the final pages printed. The language (and what generates the code) is only concerned with results and doesn't care *how* the printer goes about generating the actual page. Languages aimed at results rather than method are called *Page Description Languages* (PDLs). The most common PDL is Adobe PostScript, the most recent version being Level 2.

PDLs are chiefly used in laser printers because the nature of the control system demands a page printer. After all, the entire page must be defined before it can be printed out. In contrast, the commands of old printers that only use escape sequences and the like are termed a command language. When using a command language, the printer works more like a line printer, beginning to print as soon it has interpreted the first commands.

A PDL code stream is device-independent. That is, a given document will look the same (at least in its general structure) no matter what printer generates the output from the commands. Of course, you cannot expect exactly the same output from all printers that use a given PDL because a page printed on the 72-dpi printer won't look as clear as one from a 1200-dpi machine. This device independence means that when you use a PDL, it doesn't matter what you plug into your PC. As long as your software generates a PDL language stream, any printer (or typesetter or whatever) that uses the same PDL should accept the code and work perfectly. Moreover, you can copy the PDL code to a disk file, ship it halfway around the world to a low-cost service bureau in Bangladesh, and have it completely understood by the equipment there (that uses the same PDL, of course).

The downside of the PDL is that it requires a printer with a powerful processor. With a PDL, the printer must interpret every command and rasterize the resulting image before printing it out. In general, using a PDL is more time consuming than sending simple commands to a printer. A command language requires little in the way of processing power in the printer–your PC does all the thinking for it.

Emulations

The range of functions that can be commanded by command languages is rich, varied, arbitrary. Printer designers can pick any code for any function. Moreover, they can add new functions and escape sequences to elicit them whenever they see fit. Such design freedom is an invitation to chaos. Somehow your PC and its software would need to know what each sequence means for your specific printer. And with thousands of printer models on the market, the potential for confusion is undeniable.

Fortunately for us all, printer designers are not so blind. They don't choose escape sequences at random. In fact, a few sets of them have become standard. Not because of the restraint of printer designers, however, but thanks to the laziness of programmers who couldn't be bothered to write code for every possible printer. Instead they chose to support a top-selling few and ignored the rest. The designers of the also-ran printers quickly capitulated and followed the leaders. They made their printers understand the escape sequences used by the more popular printers so that their printers were able to act like or *emulate* the leaders. The list of the printers that a given machine can emulate is called its *emulations*. In effect, a printer's emulations describes its software compatibility, the range of programs that can properly control the printer.

Often a manufacturer will describe a printer not by the command language it uses but by the machines that it emulates. That's actually a convenience because when you install your software, you only need to specify the emulated printer rather than worrying about languages and codes.

Automatic Language Switching

Many printers can understand more than one language or emulate multiple printer models. Most allow you to select which standard to follow when you set up the printer. Some machines still use DIP switches to set emulations. Others have elaborate front-panel menuing systems controlled by an array of pushbuttons only slightly more modest than the dashboard of the Space Shuttle. You simply pick the emulation you want, then configure your software to match.

Some printers are more flexible. They can recognize the commands used by a specific language and automatically switch themselves into a mode that uses that language. Manufacturers call this feature *automatic language switching*. In its most common application, printers equipped with automatic language switching recognize two languages, a command language and a page description language.

The most common choices are HPPCL and PostScript. When these machines detect a change in the language being sent to them, they can switch on the fly to the new language. This allows these machines to operate in mixed computing environments where a single printer is shared among a network of machines running different software using different languages.

Connectivity and Interfacing

No printer is an island. It serves you best as a peninsula, connected at one point or another to the mainland of your PC. To be at all useful, every printer must somehow connect to your PC. To use computer lingo, every printer needs an *interface*, the place where its circuitry and commands meet with those of your PC or PC network.

Once upon a time, PC engineers designated exactly one port to be used by printers, the parallel port, which even DOS calls LPT ports, for Line PrinTer. Over the years, however, a diverse profusion of ports have polluted this original connection simplicity. Each, of course, boasts its own virtues and each has its own collection of drawbacks, which range from daunting complexity to pernicious pricing.

- **Parallel ports** remain the most common connection for printers, and most new machines will offer this connection. For character-based printouts in text mode and most PostScript documents, the parallel connection works fine. When you shift to printing with bit graphics, however, the simple parallel lags behind. Designers have advanced several improvements to the standard parallel design. When buying a printer that will need to print in bit-image mode (which means just about anything under Windows) you'll want a machine that uses one of these more advanced designs. The most common designation for these are EPP for Enhanced Parallel Port (which also goes under the Hewlett-Packard proprietary name of the *Bi-Tronics interface*) and the ECP or Extended Capabilities Port.
- **Serial ports** allow you to connect a printer directly to a modem or move it further from your PC than the ten feet recommended for a parallel connection. But all serial technologies are inherently slower than parallel connections, and in bit-mapped printing a serial connection may be too slow to be tolerated.
- **Connectivity** is often used as a generalized term for any form of linking computers together, be it through a local area network, modem connec-

tion, or simple data transfer cable. When use in regard to a printer, connectivity describes the ability of the printer to link with host computer systems and networks. The connectivity of a printer determines its compatibility with hardware interfaces and software protocols used in networking. Connectivity considerations include the port used to provide the hardware connection between printer and computer, the language used by the printer to control its functions, the topology of the network to which the printer is linked, and the network protocol and operating system. Many printers link to networks only through a host computer. Others (typically high-performance laser printers) feature direct network connections and link as dedicated network nodes.

Some printers are able to understand the signaling systems used by more than one network. *Automatic protocol switching* allows such a printer to recognize the protocols used in different network systems and switch to the proper protocol on the fly. This feature can be helpful when you have to run several network protocols over the same physical network and still share one printer among all network users. Even if you use a single network and protocol, this feature simplifies the set-up procedure–the printer will automatically select the protocol to match what you're using.

You can connect a printer to a network in several ways. Most simple networks allow all (or selected) network users to share the printer connected to a single PC. More advanced networks allow a printer to be a node unto itself, either through a special external network adapter or through a network adapter built into or installable into your printer. For example, Hewlett-Packard printers offer *modular input/output slots* (or MIO slots) to accommodate its JetDirect interface card as well as a number of third-party interfaces that allow you to plug your printer directly into your printer. The specification for these slots has gone through several revisions. The current standard is called *MIO*.

- **Control-panel lockout** is a feature of many printers designed for shared use in conjunction with local area networks. It allows the network manager or administrator to disable the set up and configuration facilities that would normally be accessible through the Control Panel of the printer. In typical use, the network administrator would set up the printer for normal operation, then lock out the Control Panel so unauthorized users cannot alter the settings. This prevents both accidental and intentional changes to the printer's settings.

- **Software drivers** are the second half of connection between your PC and your printer. Your hardware passes the signals between the devices; the software driver determines what those signals will be. The driver serves both as a command translator and communication manager, linking your applications to your printer. The driver is a layer of program code interposed between your application program and the hardware of the printer port. Your application generates generic output instructions. The driver then translates those instructions into the printer's language, for example, telling the printer the resolution to use, which characters use specific fonts, the printable area of the document, and even managing the flow of paper through the printer.

Software drivers take any of several forms. They may be built into your applications, added on to applications, built into operating systems, or constructed as modules that you must install into your operating system. Printer drivers that link with operating systems allow all the programs that are written to the specifications of the operating system to share the same driver and link to your printer. For example, once you've installed the correct driver for your printer into any versions of Windows, all of your Windows applications should link properly to your printer.

To work properly, the driver must match both ends of the connection: it has to understand the codes sent out by your application and must know the language understood by your printer. At one time you needed a specific driver for every program you ran to match your particular model of printer. Multiply the number of available programs by the number of different printer models, and you'll see the kind of chaos the need for printer drivers can create. Fortunately the standardization of printer languages and the wide use of Windows (and to a lesser extent, OS/2) have simplified the driver situation. For example, the universal printer driver included with Windows will handle the vast majority of printers available today.

Your primary concern when buying a new printer is the availability of software drivers that suit the particular application software that you plan to run. If your printer doesn't have a driver for your application or operating system–or the printer doesn't emulate a machine that your application or operating system has its own driver for–you won't be able to take advantage of all the features of your printer (if you can get it to work at all). Fortunately nearly all printers will work with Windows and Windows applications. Drivers supplied with your printer may, however, enable special features that are not accessible using the universal Windows drivers. Moreover, newer drivers prepared and related by your printer manufacturer typically eliminate bugs and can add further features to your printer.

Printing Costs

Price is only part of the story. Certainly it's what you pay for a printer when you buy it, but it tells you almost nothing about what printing actually costs. After all, you're not really shopping for a printer. You're buying the output, what the printer does. The printer and its price are only one factor in the total cost of printed output. If you think that's all you'll have to pay, you'll be in for a big surprise when you start totaling up your expenses.

The real price with which you should be concerned when selecting a printer is its *cost per page*, how much you'll end up spending for each sheet you print. Cost per page is the most popular way of quantifying the true cost of ownership of a printer. The exact formula for determining cost per page varies with different manufacturers. In general, the cost per page should include both the cost of used-up items like paper, ink, and toner, and the capital cost of the printer itself amortized over its expected life.

Consumables

All of the supplies that get used up with each sheet your printer uses are called *consumables*. Exactly what constitutes the consumables varies with printer technology. All printers use a medium of some sort. Usually it is paper, but in preparing presentations you may make acetates for overhead transparencies. In addition, consumables include the ink or toner used by the printer in whatever form: cartridges, ink sheets, toner bottles, or whatever. In addition, some printer parts naturally wear out as part of the printing process, and these must be considered consumables as well. In some laser printers, you must periodically replace the *optical photo conductor* (OPC) drum, a fuser, and sometimes a toner overflow cartridge. Impact and inkjet printers often require periodic replacement of their print heads.

Some printer makers help you trim the cost of toner when you don't need the highest quality output. They endow their machines with a draft mode (called *EconoMode* by Hewlett-Packard) that alters the amount of toner spread on each character rather than printing speed. Although these draft modes help retain both the definition and legibility of normal printing, they lack the true dark blacks. According to Hewlett-Packard, using their EconoMode can cut the cost of toner by up to 50%.

Estimating the cost of consumables can itself be complex. With a laser printer, for example, you must add the price of a sheet of paper to the fraction of the toner and other replaceable items used in producing a single page. In computing the cost of toner, you must also make allowance for *coverage*–how much of the paper gets covered with toner. Printing text usually requires only 3% to 5% coverage, while graphics may involve substantially more. To expedite cost per page, you can simply divide the cost of a toner cartridge (and drum, if the printer uses a separately replaceable toner and drum design) and divide that by the manufacturer's rated print capacity (expressed as a number of pages).

Electricity is a consumable product not often considered in making a printer purchase. Although some printer technologies use so little power as to be considered negligible, lasers can be another matter entirely. The fusers in laser printers demand high peak powers, sometimes in excess of 1000 watts, while the complex electronics inside the machine may continuously draw 200 watts or more.

Most recent printers shift into a power-saving idle mode when they are not used for a while. Such an economy mode can trim power demand to a few dozen watts. The Department of Energy has developed Energy*Star standards for printers. A printer that is certified to conform to the Energy*Star standard minimizes its electrical needs. An Energy*Star-compliant monochrome laser printer has a sleep mode that uses less than 30 watts. It will automatically switch into this mode when it is idle between print jobs. A color laser will reduce its consumption to less than 45 watts. In fact, some of the latest laser printers, such as the Canon LBP-430 and HP LaserJet 4L, are so power-economical that the manufacturers have omitted on/off switches from them.

Workload

If you do a lot of printing, you may try to squeeze every possible page you can from your printer during your workday. Not all printers are up to such a workload. Many machines are designed as personal printers, built to withstand only the rigors that may be wreaked by a single individual with an occasional print job. Plugged into a network, such machines may choke and sputter to a premature demise.

Printer manufacturers use the term duty cycle to describe how hard a given machine is designed to work. It essentially tells you how much printing you can expect to get from the printer. Duty cycle reflects the workload that a given printer is designed to handle without suffering damage. Most manufacturers rate their printers in the number of pages they expect the machine to make in a typical month, although you may encounter all sorts of different quantifications such as pages per hour or time percentages (a printer with an 80% duty cycle is expected to be actively printing 80% of the time it is turned on). In general, you can assume that the greater the duty cycle the sturdier the printer and the better it is suited to running for long periods of printing. If a given printer doesn't have a sufficient duty cycle to cover the needs of your office, you may need multiple machines–or a more expensive printer rated to handle your work.

CHAPTER THREE

Buying a Printer

Buying a printer can be easy or a source of anguish, depending on how you approach the task Any printer you purchase will give you output of some kind, probably legible, perhaps even acceptable. But getting the optimum match of quality, speed, and price takes more careful consideration, not only of the available hardware but also about how you plan to use it.

The stage magician knows what you will pick even before he says, "Pick a card, any card." Only through misdirection does he make you think you have a choice. Every card he offers may be the same–he subtly switches what he holds with the varied selection he proffered face up to assure you a random selection. In the end, you're amazed when he pulls out the card that perfectly matches your random selection, but the right choice was never in doubt. After all, that's the magician's job.

Choosing a printer can be exactly the same. Getting the perfect choice can seem like magic, but if you know what you're doing there's never any doubt. Your choice is entirely decided beforehand–not by stacking the deck with aces but by knowing the applications that you plan to do. You need to know what you expect to accomplish to know the best way of doing it. It's better to fit your printer to your purpose than to spend too much for something you don't need or too little for something that can't do what you want.

The one right printer isn't necessary a particular brand or model. No one company is privy to the secrets of a particular application area or style of printing. The basic technologies of printing–impact dot-matrix, inkjet, laser, thermal-wax, and dye-diffusion methods–are widely used. Although each individual manufacturer may add its own refinements, these are rarely enough to open a new application area to a given technology. Although one dot-matrix printer may prove better than another, it will still be most suited to those jobs at which dot-matrix printers excel.

General Printing

Perhaps the most common plea when searching out a printer is for something that will handle all of your printing needs. You don't have a specific application in mind because you do so many different things. You send out business letters, pore through spreadsheets, track inventory with a database, and print the clues in your favorite mystery game. Sometimes you want to print graphics to make a hard copy of your new kitchen plan you've just laid out on your PC. Or you might craft an oenofile newsletter specializing in bottles for under a buck for a rather discriminating audience and want to include photographs and charts. Sometimes an idea hits you that only color can convey, and you want to make it into a transparency for your next motivational talk. You want your printer to do it all.

Surprisingly, in today's marketplace you *can* find a printer that will do it all. Certainly there are some compromises, primarily speed and quality versus cost, but you could satisfy your every general-purpose printing need with a single printer.

But it's not quite that easy. Not just one but dozens of different printers are aimed at exactly you, the generalist. Your choice is wide, matched only by the confusion. Choosing requires setting some targets. The primary one is determined by your budget. Price is your first guide.

One application is paramount even in a general-purpose printer: correspondence. Inevitably you need to send letters to someone, even if just to complain about your new printer purchase.

Beyond these general-purpose applications are a number of specialized applications that require specific printer features. They are discussed in the next section.

Division by Cost

Buying a printer is as much a matter of finding the right strategy as finding the right hardware. You need to organize your priorities. If your PC is for mere pleasure–playing games, surfing the Internet, or trying to unknot the puzzle of computers in general–your budget may be tight and the overriding concern in any purchase. Matters of money are issues only for PC people in penury. Few of us have truly unlimited budgets. Moreover, those who do have unlimited budgets probably got that way by watching their expenditures and insuring they always got the most for their investments. Even when your involvement with your PC is more purposeful, you will need to keep an eye on price.

If you are forced to examine your prospective printer purchase strictly on a cost basis, you'll find the technologies and capabilities divided into three primary levels: the minimum price you can pay, midrange inkjets, and office-duty laser printers. A fourth class, the special application printer, doesn't fit into this nice price hierarchy because the needs of your application override the basic cost considerations. Of course, as with the rest of the PC universe you'll find the lines between these ranges to be shadowy and blurred. There is wide overlap of pricing across these distinctions.

Budget Range

When cost is everything and you have nothing, at least in the form of cash reserves, you'll end up looking for the least expensive printer offerings. Unless you're aiming to take advantage of the bankruptcy laws, you will want to tip-toe as gently past your nonexistent budget as the marketplace allows.

Of course, penury isn't the only reason to look at the low end. If you don't do much printing, you might want to lay out as little cash as necessary for something that's hardly a necessity. If all you print is an occasional program list, a handful of invoices at month's end, or the labels for your annual greeting cards, you're not going to stress even the flimsiest machine. You probably won't even worry about quality as long as it's legible. So a minimal printer makes sense.

You can take this strategy to the extreme, too. No printer at all can make sense in some situations. If you have access to a printer somewhere else–at your office, at the neighbors, or at the local copy center–you might not even need a printer. Even if you have to pay a nickel a page for a printout, you'll have to go through a couple of thousand pages before you approach the price of a new printer, and that's ignoring the cost of consumables, cables, and the other idiocies that go along with buying something you don't really need. Moreover, the high-resolution laser printout from the copy center will likely look a lot better than the dotty work of a bargain printer. Even if you do buy a minimal printer, you'll be sorely tempted to visit the copy center when you have to set out another ream of resumes.

Should you decide that you do need the least of all possible printers, you'll find yourself in the realm of the impact dot-matrix printer. Prices of bare-bones models begin at about $100 and run up to several times that–into an entirely different class.

Budget-oriented printers are designed with one chief goal in mind: to give you something that you can hold in your hand. They shine at neither speed nor quality, although these days you get a remarkable dose of each. After all, nothing says "cheap dot-matrix printer" quite like the output of a cheap dot-matrix printer. If you want to impress a prospective employer, you won't want to typeset your resume with one of these dot-matrix marauders, although one will be perfectly adequate for making drafts you can check over before taking your file to the copy center for a quality printout.

The lowest of the low bear a remarkable resemblance to the very first PC printers. They are typically nine-pin impact dot-matrix printers that can generate from 80 to 120 characters per second, given an adequate tailwind and a head start. They differ dramatically in price, some with retail tags one-fifth that of their predecessors, even if you don't consider the effects of more than ten years' inflation. Obviously, corners must have been cut somewhere, and you'll usually find that it is everywhere. These minimal printers lack the robustness and solid feel of older, more expensive machines. You'll find them mostly molded from plastic—thin at that—with simple metal stampings serving as the chassis and lightweight metal parts for the platen, bail wires, and printhead guide tube.

From a software standpoint, you'll find today's budget machines to be direct substitutions for their forebears. They will work with the same applications and deliver essentially the same results. Technology here has been harnessed not for pushing limits but for limiting costs.

If you clear your mind of preconceptions, you'll find two alternatives to the minimal printer: the close-out and the used printer.

Close-out machines let you buy last year's technology at a deflationary price, typically between 50% and 70% of the street price of the hardware when it was new. For the better deal, you give up the refinements the printer maker has added to its latest models. When your needs are minimal, however, you might never wander into the exotic realm where new features make a difference.

You will lose in two areas, however. The supplies accompanying an older printer will themselves be old. In particular, the ribbon packed with last year's impact dot-matrix machine may be dry and incapable of making strong blacks. In addition, the manufacturer's support for an older printer will disappear more quickly than for a current model. Although most printer makers will continue to give support to their products for years, you lose one of those years when you buy a model that's a year past its prime. If the close-out model you choose was not particularly successful (leading to its close-out status), you may find few new drivers forthcoming to match new applications and operating systems.

Sometimes you'll find current models at close-out prices. A close look at the ad may reveal that the printer is "remanufactured." Although that term can cover a multitude of sins, the most likely one is that the printer was once sold and proved dead on arrival. The manufacturer took the ailing machine back and replaced it with a new one. Instead of getting tossed out, the DOA machine popped back to the service shop where its problem was found and corrected. Because it was once sold, the repaired machine no longer qualifies for sale as "new." As a result, it wears the remanufactured label and a remanufactured price. Such a printer is equal to a new machine and can be a good deal.

Used printers are another matter. To be offered for sale, the used printer must have an owner who wanted to be rid of it. The reason may be benign (a glorious new printer makes the old one a superfluous paperweight) or malignant (the printer has a subtle problem that will only become obvious after you buy and have used the machine for a few days). In any case, a used printer has some of its life rattle squirted or blasted out of it. Most will require new consumables soon after your purchase. After all, no one will likely put a new ribbon or a new drum in a machine slated for quick sale.

Midrange Machines

The *midrange* means that you have to trade something off–speed, output quality, or life expectancy. What you give up is reflected in the price, which is why these machines fall in the midrange. You'll find a wondrous mix at this level, from good-quality inkjets to low-end lasers. As long as you can work within the imposed primary limit, you'll get excellent results and return on your printer investment.

What kind of printer to buy depends on what you want to give up. Opting for the midrange automatically means that you won't get the best of anything–not the highest resolution or the fastest output or a machine that will survive Armageddon. Many midrange machines will rival those that fall in the high end on at least some of these qualifications. Some deliver blazing speed, others deliver beautiful image quality. Each is a specialist in its own way, and it will succeed and suffer depending on how your work matches their specialty.

Which you get–speed, quality, or longevity–depends on both your specific printer choice and the underlying technology of the machine. Your technological choices in the midrange in the modern printer market are three: better impact dot-matrix printers, mainstream inkjets, and budget lasers. Each has strengths and weaknesses.

Impact dot-matrix machines inevitably suffer the problems inherent in their technology: they are noisy and yield fuzzy output. At best, they will generate on-paper quality on a par with a vintage typewriter. But to gain higher quality they must slow down, often substantially. Printer programs and drivers that eke out the last bit of quality from impact dot-matrix machines often double- or quadruple-print each line and cut printhead speed to squeeze in as many dots as possible for a higher apparent resolution. No matter how precise their dot placement, however, these printers can never overcome the fuzziness inherent in hammering through a ribbon. Moreover, the hammering itself is a curse, generating drill-like whines that appeal only to dentists with sadistic streaks.

On the positive side, impact dot-matrix printing is where PC output originated. The technology is old, proven, and essentially trouble-free. You don't have to worry about clogged printheads, contamination, and ink-wasting cleaning cycles. In fact, the cost of ink rates as the lowest of any printer technology that uses a separate source (that means excluding printers like thermal engines that use expensive treated paper instead of ink). You can use the same ribbon nearly forever—and some folks seem bent on stretching a single ribbon well beyond forever, as their pale grey printouts will testify. If individual ribbons are not cheap enough for you, you can always re-ink them.

Impact dot-matrix printers also bring the benefit of automatic copies using carbon or carbonless forms. If your application demands an exact duplicate, you may need impact technology.

A midrange impact printer will undoubtedly have a 24-wire printhead. It will come with pretenses of letter-quality output and graphic resolution of 360 dpi, both of which are more promise rather than reality.

In strong competition, you'll find the low end of the inkjets that aspire even higher, claiming laser quality. They actually come close to the high standard set by the last generation of laser printers and can produce output that's demonstrably superior to most impact printers. On the other hand, they lack the impact printer's ability to make carbon copies.

High-End Machines

The high end of the printer spectrum isn't the place just for the best. It's more the place of the perfect fit, where you find the machine that best suits a particular application. When you're willing to pay more, you can look in the specialized niches for a machine with extraordinary speed, resolution, or color. (Modern technology still can't deliver all three in a single package.)

Once your budget exceeds $1000 to $1500, you're out of the range of general-purpose printers. Individual features go in their own directions, to higher speed, precision-matched color quality, full-tone color reproduction, and machines with automatic duplexing. At this point, you should consider whether you want to invest in a single printer or more than one, each targeted at a specific need. One of them may be a lower-cost general-purpose printer.

Correspondence Issues

When you plan to use a printer primarily in a business setting, the needs of correspondence dominate. Much of what a business does is paper work, and much of that ends up in the mailbox.

Envelopes

Most modern printers are designed to primarily handle flat sheets of paper; after all, few people prefer to print on thicker things like grapefruit or granola. Envelopes may give some printers problems; envelopes are thicker than ordinary paper and they are sized differently. They simply don't fit into the flow of normal paper.

Envelopes are naturally thicker than ordinary paper because they have to be at least two sheets thick (otherwise they'd have no inside, and they wouldn't be very useful as envelopes). Worse than the thickness is their variety. Most envelopes have areas where their flaps are overlapped and glued together. In printing on an ordinary envelope, your printer will encounter areas with three different thicknesses: a single sheet where the flap is not yet folded down, two sheets over most of the envelope area; and three sheets where the glued-down flaps overlap. Impact printers in particular sometimes have problems with these changing media thicknesses.

Envelopes are also shaped differently from the ordinary rectangular sheet of paper. They must naturally be somewhat wider than the paper you use for your correspondence so you can fold your sheets and have a reasonable expectation of the paper fitting in the envelope. Envelopes have to be somewhat wider than the standard 8.5 inches expected by narrow-carriage printers. For example, the widely used commercial number 10 envelope measures 9.5 inches wide.

Printer manufacturers make a number of concessions to people who want to print envelopes. Some help adapt their printers to cope with the exigencies of envelope printing. Others point you toward dedicated hardware to handle the chore. Among your options in expediting envelope printing are:

- **Dedicated envelope trays.** Loading envelopes into a normal feed tray will bring to mind memories of pounding pegs into holes into elementary school, only you're stuck with square pegs, round holes, and a hammer inadequate to the task. A dedicated envelope tray not only makes things fit but also makes the changeover easier. You only need to pull out the paper tray and slide in the envelope tray to get the job done.
- **Envelope feed slots.** Most folks don't need to print a million envelopes at a time, a circumstance that delights most letter carriers. It also makes a dedicated envelope tray a luxury you may not want. After all, you might buy a separate inexpensive printer just to do envelopes for the price of an extra dedicated tray. You'll find envelope slots on both lasers and some impact dot-matrix machines. Operation is easy and obvious–these printer weren't designed for Ph.D.s but for regular office staff, which might include temps with little familiarity of equipment or office procedures. If you plan to print many envelopes a few at a time, an envelope feed slot will save both time and the paper that gets wasted in rethreading a printer.
- **Paper parking.** A number of printers designed for continuous-form paper allow for paper parking. They can move the continuous-form paper out of the way and allow you to hand-feed individual envelopes as you need to print them out. This frees you from the chore of unloading the continuous-form paper, sliding your envelope in, then reloading the paper and hoping it's properly aligned at the right top-of-form position. Run through this ritual a couple of times a day, and you'll see it's well worth advancing to an upgrade-model printer to get paper parking.

Labels

The easiest way to deal with envelopes is to keep them away from your printer entirely. If you don't print envelopes, you don't have to worry about envelope issues. You can simply buy the best printer for your flat sheet needs. When you need to do an envelope, you can put a dedicated machine to work, one that makes labels. Instead of typing directly on the envelope, you print a pressure-sensitive label and stick it in place.

The one great strength of the dedicated label printer is convenience. Not only do you save the ardor of switching your principal printer between sheets and envelopes, but you gain other amenities. The label printer itself can perform many jobs besides making stickers for envelopes. You can add clarity to file folder labels, identify cassette tapes, or even make labels for the jars in your sand collection or your home-brewed beers. Moreover, most dedicated label printers come with special software that lets you capture addresses from your monitor screen, so you can press a couple of buttons and watch a label curl out of the printer. Although you can route anything on the screen to the label printer, this software is amazingly accurate in finding addresses in most word processors' displays of business letters. This software can also add Postnet bar codes to your labels to expedite the Postal Service's handling of your mail.

One drawback of using a dedicated label printer to handle your envelope addressing is aesthetic. Labels on envelopes look like, well, labels. They reek of junk mail and mass merchandising, not personal attention to correspondence. Of course, this perception will change as the technology becomes entrenched. Moreover, you can minimize the aesthetic impact by using clear instead of white labels. With a clear label, your recipient won't be jarred by the contrast in label and envelope color when you opt for colored stationery.

Adding a dedicated label printer also increases your correspondence costs. You must not only pay for the printer but also for every label you use. And labels can be surprisingly expensive, often costing as much as the envelopes you stick them on. Little wonder that the manufacturers of blank labels offer their own printers.

One surprising circumstance in today's printer market is that the dedicated label printer is not the lowest-cost means of adding dedicated label making to your PC. You can buy an inexpensive impact-dot matrix printer for less than most thermal label printers. Moreover, sprocket-feed plain paper labels are often less expensive than the thermal label stock used by the dedicated label printers. Although the commercial thermal machines come equipped with their own address capture and label management software, you can find good shareware equivalents without much effort on most bulletin boards. And of course an inexpensive dot-matrix printer can serve as an emergency backup for your regular machine. Or you can save the price of labels entirely by feeding envelopes into your inexpensive dedicated printer.

Spot Color

When you want to add emphasis to your text or make a small graphic image stand out from the sea of grey, nothing beats mixing in a bit of color. The use of color for accent is termed *spot color* by printer makers, and it marks the one obvious advantage of the computer over old-fashioned typing. It adds a new dimension to your work.

The requirements for spot color differ from other color applications. Most of what artists, publishers, and presenters want to do with color involves full-page images. The highest-quality color printing processes are specifically aimed at painting graphics that cover a full sheet. Indeed, the thermal-transfer and dye-diffusion print processes work more economically printing full-page graphics. Spot color, on the other hand, requires adding only a bit of color, and the full-page printing processes make it uneconomical. You must waste enough ink to cover a full sheet of medium simply to highlight one word.

Inkjet printing in all of its guises–thermal, piezoelectric, and phase-change–excel at spot color because they meter their ink so you use color ink only when you print with a specific color. Better still, color adds minimally to the cost of most inkjet printers. Many, in fact, allow you to buy in basic black and upgrade to living color later.

Several impact dot-matrix printers also have spot color abilities, either as special color models or as upgrades to monochrome printers. Because of the limitations of the impact printing process, however, the quality they achieve falls short of inkjet printers. Individual hues typically lack saturation or intensity, and colors do not blend well. Primary colors print with relative purity, but the secondary spectrum of primary color mixtures (for example, green from yellow and blue, or purple from red and blue) are less satisfying because the actual inks never mix but are instead simply overprinted.

Color lasers work well for spot color, too, using toner only for colors that print. However, color adds substantially to the cost of a laser printer. No current laser printers allow upgrades from black-and-white to color.

Special Applications

Several of the jobs you give a printer require a specialist's work. They call upon particular talents that most general-purpose printers handle reluctantly, if at all. These machines may speak a particular language, have fine-tuned color capabilities, or handle extraordinary media. If your application demands more than a general purpose printer can deliver, you'll have to shop for a machine that matches your particular needs.

Among the many specialized applications that you might have are desktop publishing, workgroup printing, large-sheet printing, portable printing, prepress proofing, and presentation preparation. We'll discuss these applications, their particular needs, and the printers or technologies that best serve them separately.

Desktop Publishing

Desktop publishing and your printer concerns have two sides, depending on what you plan to produce. If you're working on a tight budget to make a personal newsletter–the classic labor of love of the true amateur–what you produce with your printer may be the master you'll use for distribution. A quick trip to the strip-mall printshop will photocopy every page you need. You may even print out each newsletter copy on your own printer to save time or trouble.

To get higher quality on the printed page, you'll want to have printing masters made by a typesetter or service bureau. What comes out of your printer is not the final copy but merely a reference, something to pass around for comment and criticism. In this application, your printer is actually making a prepress proof, although this term is usually reserved for color output (see below).

Technologies

The primary printer technology used for desktop publishing is the laser printer because lasers most closely approximate the work of the modern printing press. Lasers are the best way of getting high-resolution black-and-white images. They are also fast, and their consumables are inexpensive enough to make printing a small run of newsletters feasible.

Should you seriously consider using a laser printer as your personal printing press, you'll want to investigate duplex models that print on both sides of a sheet. The chief advantage is, of course, saving in printing and mailing costs (after all, half as many pages means lower rates if you're sending your newsletter first class). You can also make single-fold half-size (5.5 by 8.5 inches) jobs more easily.

If you're on a particularly tight budget, you may be able to get away with using a quality inkjet printer. Most offer resolutions as high as midrange lasers. The downside is speed. If you need to print 100 copies of your newsletter, you'll be tending your print job for a long time.

Color

A moderately priced inkjet will allow you to include color illustrations in the pages you print individually. Getting that color will cost you. You'll either have to print each copy of your newsletter individually on your inkjet (which will cost you in time, considering the slow speed at which color rolls out) or you can have the local office center make color photocopies (which will just cost you).

Workgroup Printing

Because it is unlikely if impossible for one person and PC to tie up a printer continuously–after all, you need to spend some time getting information into a PC before you can print it out–sharing a printer has always made economic sense.

Obviously, a shared printer will print at higher volumes, and the higher workload raises important issues. You need adequate tray capacity so someone doesn't have to play jack-in-the-box and spring up every five minutes to reload the feed tray. (Then again, you could institute a policy that whoever takes output from the printer must put in a fresh supply of paper. Guess how long that will last.)

Speed is always a concern, particularly when you share a printer. A shared printer need not be faster than an individual printer. After all, the entire reason for sharing is to put the printer's idle moments to use. However, you'll find that printers specifically designed for sharing tend to be substantially faster than those designed for more personal use. Whether you need speed is a judgment call based on the number of users and the print load each adds.

A shared printer must be more rugged than a personal printer. After all, it will be doing more work, running nearer capacity more often. Moreover, a shared printer is more likely to suffer abuse. Blame is harder to assign when something is shared, and those doing the sharing and abusing know this. Printers designed specifically for sharing typically take these considerations into account and feature more robust print engines and overall designs.

Buffering

When two or more people attempt to print at the same time, someone will have to wait unless you allow some means to store the print job until earlier jobs are finished. In other words, each worker needs some kind of print buffer. In a shared printer environment, this buffering can take a variety of forms.

For example, each PC can have its own buffer that can store the job until the printer is free while quickly returning control to the individual user. The Windows Print Manager takes care of this kind of buffering. But individual printer buffers suffer from several shortcomings. The PC buffer may complain when access to the printer is too long denied–and if it doesn't, you stand the risk of delaying too long (say forever) when real printer trouble shows up. The integral PC buffer inevitably steals both performance and memory from the PC in which it is running. Moreover, buffer memory, like the printer itself, is more efficiently shared because not everyone needs to use it simultaneously.

A shared buffer can take two forms: integral to the printer or external to it. From the standpoint of workstation printing efficiency, there's little difference between the two. Integral buffering has the advantage of versatility. The printer can allocate the same memory for whatever it more urgently needs, be it raster processing, simple buffering, or smart buffering with protocol switching. An external buffer may hold a price advantage. The external buffer will likely use inexpensive generic memory modules while a printer may require proprietary memory expansion. Amortized over the life of the printing system, however, the memory price difference will likely be insignificant.

Interfacing

To be shared, a printer needs to be connected to the 1 it serves. Again, you have several alternatives: switch boxes, dedicated print spoolers, or a network. The *switch* is cheapest and least convenient. The *print spooler* is convenient and less of a hassle to connect than an entire network, particularly if all you want to do is share a printer. The *network*, of course, gives you all the wonders and migraines of networking.

Networking gives you two connection options: tying your printer to an individual workstation or linking your printer directly to the network. The former works with any printer; the latter requires a machine with innate network compatibility. Usually the needed network resources take the form of an input/output slot in the printer into which you can slide a network adapter. Other manufacturers choose to build the network circuitry into the printer proper and give you a simple network connector on the back of the machine. In either case, you need to be sure the printer you choose supports the network you run, in terms of both hardware and protocol. (You'll find an in-depth discussion of this in Chapter 8.)

Tying a printer to a network workstation has several advantages. If your network doesn't support the direct connection of printers, it may be the only avenue available to you. Moreover, you have a wider variety of machines from which to choose. You don't have to restrict your choices to network-capable printers; any machine becomes a potential choice. In addition, the network interface will be less expensive. The workstation will need its own network adapter anyway, so you pay nothing extra to link the printer. In addition, you can add inexpensive memory to the print server for buffering network print jobs.

The downside to connecting through a workstation is that the workstation suffers. It will occupy a substantial portion of its processing power and memory to serving printing needs. Whoever gets stuck with the print server won't be happy, because of both impaired PC performance and the cacophony of sitting next to (or near) a constantly chugging printer. On the other hand, no one needs to sequester himself with the print server. The processing demands aren't so high that they can't be served by a minimal PC, even a 286 or 386SX machine, so you can put that computer you were about to toss out to work with your printer.

Big Sheets

Some jobs call for larger-than-normal sheets of paper. For example, when you have a spreadsheet with 10,000 columns, a printer that's limited to 8.5-by-11-inch paper can fit them all onto a single page only with type the size of gnats' teeth. Having access to a printer that takes bigger paper—for example, B-size or 11 by 17 inches—will help you get an overview of such big printouts. Big sheets are also handy when proofing big things such as pages of a newspaper or making masters for newsletters meant to fold down to standard 8.5-by-11-inch size.

If you just need the big sheets for drafts and personal review, you have a good case for a wide-carriage line printer. Even an old-fashioned impact dot-matrix printer will fit the bill and do it without an inordinately large invoice drifting down upon your desk. A growing number of large-format laser printers are also becoming available. These, however, cost several times as much as a normal-size laser or a wide-carriage line printer.

To make the investment in a large-format laser worthwhile, you'll probably want to share the machine with the entire office. You will want some form of connectivity built in to the machine, either a network interface or simply integral sharing abilities.

Portable Printing

When you're constantly on the move—always one step ahead of the competition, creditors, or process servers—you need to travel light and fast. Too often, however, you also need access to hard copy so, for example, you can always have a fresh contract at hand. Toting along a conventional printer is sort of like joining a chain gang where all the rest of your partners are rocks. You can hardly make a quick escape when tethered to a nearly immovable object.

An entire class of printers has emerged to meet the needs of the worker on the go (or on the lam). You have a choice of technologies, prices, and handicaps, all designed to accompany you in your travels.

First a negative word (or two): Why bother? Anywhere you go in the civilized world you're likely to encounter a PC-compatible printer. It's not like there aren't a few million machines out there. Most use the ubiquitous parallel connection, so you can just plug in your notebook PC and print away, often with laser quality and speed.

On the other hand, when you're most in need of a printer, you're likely to be stranded in the middle of a Macintosh shop with nary a parallel port in sight, nothing but a LaserJet driver installed with only PostScript printers awaiting your words. Or you may lounging on a train like the *20th Century Limited* when you run into Carol Lombard and need a contract to tie her to a starring role on Broadway. A portable printer (and a good screenplay) can save the day.

Portable printers are not distinguished from the common mien by spectacular technologies. They use the same sorts of mechanisms as their deskbound kin. Two characteristics make the portable printer stand out: portability (of course) and power.

Portability

To be portable, a printer needs to be manageable without reliance on a hand truck. How small and how light depends on your own strength, endurance, and masochism. For most people, the less the printer weighs, the more portable it is. Three to five pounds falls well into hand. Moreover the machine should be small enough to fit into a briefcase with your briefs or an attaché case with your, uh, notebook computer. Size must necessarily be a compromise, however, because the printer must be large enough to cover an entire sheet–about ten inches wide.

Power

Although electricity is widely available in the United States, you can still find yourself without a ready supply: on the red-eye from the far coast, sitting in the parlor on an Amish farm, at home with a stack of overdue utility bills threatening to collapse and suffocate you. At such times a printer that accepts battery power can help you muddle through.

Be wary about power sources when considering portable printers, however. Many ads happily quote the weight of the portable printer sans batteries, and toting a full charge can double your burden. Worse, most portable printers require external transformers when you use them with utility-supplied electricity. That's another couple pounds to carry along, although you can deport the burden to your checked luggage (if you have unfathomable faith in the airline baggage handling system).

Applications

Every manufacturer's portable printers seem to use a different technology. Among those you'll find are thermal, inkjet, and ink-transfer printers. Although all claim suitability to portable use, some are better at specific applications than others. Thermal-transfer printers, best represented by the Citizen PN60 Pocket Printer, produce remarkable quality, with deep blacks as sharp as many lasers. Eminently suited for correspondence and contracts, these machines make graphic printing a slow, expensive chore because of their ribbon needs. inkjets, such as the Hewlett-Packard 310 and 320, bring good text quality (not quite up to laser level) along with good graphics and optional color. These machines are particularly suited to taking presentations on the road; you can generate new transparencies with excellent quality in hotel rooms or a taxicab. Thermal printers, like the Kodak Diconix line, are great when you need to keep down weight, though you'll have to balance mass against quality and the need for special paper.

Prepress Proofing

Color matching

The most important aspect of prepress proofing is that what rolls out of your printer exactly matches what gets stacked at the far end of the printing press. The matching job is more difficult than you might expect. Certainly red is red and blue is blue, but the pigments used by printers and printing presses vary widely. Where your color printer likely uses inks based on dyes and waxes, printing press inks are usually pigments ground into vegetable oils. The color effects in the two media can be entirely different, particularly when you deal with subtle hues.

Technologies

If you're only dealing with black-and-white, any printer capable of handling bit-image graphics will help you preview your publications. Higher resolutions will help you better approximate what you will get back from the printer. In that the vast majority of PostScript printers use laser technology, however, that's your likely choice for the best preview.

The leading color technology for prepress work is thermal-wax transfer printing. Although the color range of thermal-wax is substantially more limited than dye-diffusion printing (say 16 colors versus 16 million), the dithered color output of the thermal-wax machines better approximates the halftone process.

Inkjet technology can also be a candidate for prepress work. The best color comes from the solid inkjets. Their wax-based inks rival (some say surpass) the work of thermal-wax printers. Even if you consider the relative quality of the two technologies equal, the solid ink takes the lead when your use of color or full-page graphics is minimal. Because solid inkjets use their expensive inks only for the image that actually appears on the page, they are more economical in their use of consumables.

Thanks to ever-improving quality—higher resolutions and brighter colors—ordinary liquid-ink inkjets are also in contention for prepress work. They take the lead when initial cost is your primary concern. To get the best prepress quality, however, you'll have to use more expensive paper. When ink gets absorbed into your printing medium, it gets diluted with the white of the medium and becomes fuzzy around the images. Coated stock prevents both problems. Even with the more expensive medium, liquid ink doesn't quite reach the brilliance and intensity of solid wax ink if only because it's thinner on the paper and lacks depth.

Presentations

When you have to convince others of the merits of your ideas, you want to take advantage of every tool and technique available to help make your point. If you don't make a good impression, you will lose your battle before you begin.

Visual aids are almost *de rigueur* when making business presentations today, if just to keep your audience from nodding off. A bright image on the screen can chase the slumber from their eyes. More importantly, you can use graphics to make obscure points clear or to emphasize what should be obvious. A chart pointing skyward says success more poignantly than all the figures you recite. Bulleted lists on the screen will get compulsive note-takers to diligently copy down the finer points of your arguments. And if you want your persuasion to last longer than the few minutes you're allowed on the grandstand or podium, you'll want to leave your audience with something tangible, a handout that summarizes and reiterates your arguments.

For both visual aids and handouts, one of your best choices (though not always the very best choice) is a PC printer. You can make colorful projection acetates in a few minutes and generate handouts by the dozen.

Even the best color printers do not give you the utmost in quality for presentations. Photographic processes still have an edge when you need the last iota of detail or rich color saturation. Moreover, if you want to make a slide presentation, including the kind with half a dozen projectors, a supersonic sound system, and a technician with fingers gnawed down to stubs, you'll need 35mm slides made by a service bureau or film recorder. On the other hand, most projection foils produced photographically tend to be small, at least when compared to full-page acetates.

If you have a huge audience you want to regale or blackmail with handouts or you make the same presentation again and again, commercial offset printing costs far less than feeding paper into your personal printer. Offset printing usually yields higher quality, particularly in the reproduction of halftones, than does PC printing.

One word of warning: For many people, presentations inevitably bump against deadlines so that you're still preparing down to the very last minute. If your presentation involves many colorful slides or transparencies, you'd better leave yourself a wide time buffer. Few printers that excel at making presentation transparencies are fast. Some will labor an hour or more on a single full-page graphic image; the fastest may take 15 minutes for a fairly complex image. If you have to revise three transparencies and your presentation is scheduled to begin ten minutes from now, you're better off writing your visual aids out of the show. By the way, none of the leading color technologies is severely hampered by engine speed. Processing time for full-page graphics is what takes its toll. You get more speed from faster processors inside the printer or special streamlined driver software that sidesteps the printer's processor entirely.

Projection Transparencies

If you want to enhance a speech with visual aids, the first requirement for your printer is that it be able to print on a projection medium. Not all printers can. Thermal printers cannot, many impact dot-matrix printers cannot, some laser won't. In addition, you'll want a printer with color capabilities to give the best impression.

Three technologies have the right media and color capabilities to make them viable choices for projection transparencies: solid and liquid inkjets, and thermal-wax dye-diffusion printers. Each technology has strengths and weaknesses. Liquid inkjets are the least expensive, yet they can deliver surprisingly good projection quality.

Three primary factors influence the on-screen image quality of projection transparencies: resolution, color, and transparency.

You'll want resolution high enough that you won't see jaggedness on diagonal lines. Resolution is even more important in color printing because it influences the dither pattern use to simulate a wider color spectrum. Coarse resolution can result in some particularly obnoxious screen patterns projected in front of your audience.

Color has many aspects. The biggest difference you'll find among presentation printers are in purity, saturation, and dither quality. Saturation and the purity of color are both influenced by the inks or dyes chosen by the printer maker. Some inks yield brighter, truer colors that create greater impact. Others look flaccid and even pastel when printed. (Be wary. The quality and look of printouts on acetates when not projected don't even hint at what colors will look like when they are glowing on the screen.) Beyond the choice of inks, how the ink is laid down also influences color quality. Ink that's too thinly spread on the acetate looks washed out; too thickly spread, and colors become dark and murky. Although the printer mechanism influences how heavily the ink gets laid down, the software driver of a printer may also have a substantial effect.

When the ink gets too thick, your transparencies lose their transparency. Not only does color grey out, so does the readability of what you project. If the room's too bright or the projector too dim, your acetates may blend into a dark morass on the screen. A few inkjet printers have problems with image transparency.

Overall, liquid inkjet printers are the lowest cost choice for making projection transparencies. They can come surprisingly close to the color produced by other technologies costing several times more, measured both per page and per printer. Software drivers exert a particularly strong influence on the quality of liquid inkjet output. You'll find more experienced manufacturers have better drivers that produce better projected image quality.

If liquid inkjet printers have any consistent image defect, it is *banding*. With many machines you can distinguish each pass of the printhead individually, by a slightly light line where two passes were too far apart, a dark line where two passes overlapped, or a gradient banding across the width of a single pass of the printhead. Thermal-wax printers avoid this banding because they have a single printhead as wide as a sheet. As a result, most thermal-wax printers give the most uniform color available with any technology.

Solid inkjet printers use bright, transparent ink but tend to make their colors too dense. As a result, projection transparencies look excellent when you hold them in your hand but inadequate when projected on a screen.

Hand-Outs

The materials you leave behind are, for the most part, ordinary printouts. The same considerations apply as when preparing a newsletter through a desktop publishing system. After all, a handout is published; only the distribution system is changed. The only difference is that the volume of copies you need will be low enough that you may consider making them all with your printer or making one copy as a master and letting the photocopier do the rest of the work.

When you only want black-and-white, your prime quality concern will be resolution. You'll want laser-level quality, at least 300 dpi. You don't want to leave the coarse peckings of an impact dot-matrix printer behind. A good-quality inkjet may suffice, particularly if you feed what it makes into the photocopier. Otherwise, you might have to wait too long to satisfy the needs of a large audience.

Cost makes color for handouts mostly a matter of who is in your audience. Although you're not likely to think $5 per page too scandalous when you need ten copies for the board of directors overseeing a $1 billion deal, the same price for 200 pages for the monthly PTA meeting may be a bit much. The lower cost of dot-matrix printouts shifts the equation but doesn't change the underlying issue. Color handouts are costly and hard to justify unless you're a color printer manufacturer trying to make an impression.

Buying Checklist

Printers in any category have never been more affordable or such great values. In fact, you could blindfold yourself, poke a finger down into the ads, send in a check, and end up with a decent printer at a good price. The best buy, however, comes from making an informed choice–finding the one printer that best suits your particular requirements without wasting money on features you don't need.

Start methodically by considering your needs and comparing the capabilities of the printers available to you. This shopping list will help you get organized and find the right questions to ask to locate the right printer and the right printer vendor.

Plan the Purpose for Your Printer

The place to begin any purchase decision is by determining exactly what you want to accomplish with your printer. In other words, set yourself a goal. If you're buying your first or only printer that you plan to use with your PC, you'll probably be looking for a general purpose machine, one that can handle any job you give it, from flinging out quick drafts to making the most detailed bit-image graphics.

If your printer must take on a multitude of chores, list them in order of importance. Your list might include anything from writing letters to creating your own greeting cards to proofing photographs. Decide which task you'll need most. In particular, try to identify a specialized kind of output you need. If you're planning to write a newsletter of your own someday, you might best buy a PostScript printer now to get access to Adobe Type One fonts. If you need a lot of output, concentrate on printer speed. If you need to share a printer among several people, look for one with built-in connectivity. If you want color, narrow down your needs. Do you want spot color for accents or do you need full-page color graphics for proofing and presentations?

Knowing your needs will help narrow down the printer technology you want and will help make many of your decisions for you.

Two Printers Can be Better than One

If your applications are divergent, you may find your needs satisfied more affordably or conveniently by opting for two printers, each aimed at its particular strengths. For example, if you want PostScript laser quality for desktop publishing and you occasionally need to make color transparencies for presentations, you could buy a color laser printer and spend more than $5000. Or you could get an inexpensive laser printer (say $500) and a top-quality color inkjet (say $300). Better still, with two printers you don't have to worry about getting stuck in an emergency. Even if one fails, you can still roll out letters or transparencies (although maybe in monochrome) when the need arises.

Convenience can rally for two printers as well. For example, you may want a laser printer with a special envelope feed slot so you can print all your correspondence on one machine. A specialized label printer will take care of the same needs, without the need to stand next to your laser printer and manually feed envelopes through.

Set a Budget

Knowing how much you have available to spend will help guide your search and should help you avoid overspending when tempted by too much technology or salesmanship.

Some people set out to buy the cheapest possible printer and are disappointed when they find that they've actually bought what they went looking for–the cheapest possible printer. The better strategy is to start by setting a budget, then starting your search.

Your budget will help narrow down your choice of technology. Small budgets and big printers don't match. You can't expect to get a workgroup laser printer when you can't afford the ribbon for a dot-matrix machine.

The tighter your budget, the more compromises you'll need to make. Fortunately, modern technology makes for few compromises. The primary one is speed. You can get laser quality for $200, but laser speed will cost a laser price (now down to less than $500). The more you pay, the faster you will get, at least within a given technology.

If you have no budget–if money is no object–first buy another copy of this book and give it to a friend, or give each of a dozen friends a dozen copies. That may not help you choose between printers, but it will reinforce the old saw about the fool and his money. Setting a budget even when you have unlimited funds will help focus your decision.

Determine Printers Compatible with Your Applications

The most useful printer you can find is the one that works best with the software applications that you use most. After all, if your printer won't work with your software, it won't work at all.

Start your printer search by checking your software manuals for supported printers or printer control languages. Draw up a list of compatible printers, and look for machines on the list or those promising compatibility with listed printers.

Unusual or vertical market applications constrain your printer choices most. DOS applications require built-in support or individual drivers to bring to life all the features of many printers. Without program support, your new printer will likely work no better than a vintage daisy-wheel, if at all.

If you plan to limit yourself solely to Windows or OS/2 applications, you'll want a printer listed in the printer driver Set-up screen (or one that comes with its own drivers for your chosen operating system). Although the lists of printers supported by these operating systems is wide, and printer emulations make it even wider, you can still find machines that won't work or won't work well. Almost any modern dot-matrix printer will understand Epson's **Esc /P** commands, but if you only use that emulation you may limit yourself to 120-dpi quality even if your printer is capable of 600 dpi.

In other words, don't trust to faith (at least when it comes to printers). Limit your search to models with specific application support.

Make Sure Paper Handling is Compatible with You

Your printer needs to work with the kind of paper you want to use: you'll tractor feed for continuous forms, bin feed for cut sheets. Don't forget to check the capacity of cut-sheet feed trays. If your printing demands are heavy, you'll probably want the largest capacity available so you don't have to chain yourself to the printer all day.

As important as the type of paper handling is the sheet size. If you need to print larger spreadsheets or proofs of big pages for a newspaper, you'll want a wide carriage printer or a large-format laser or thermal-wax transfer machine.

Consider the Full Cost of Printing

In other words, don't forget supplies, service, and consumables. You should regard whatever price you pay to buy a printer as a down payment. You'll face additional payments over the life of the printer to buy the supplies you need. You need to buy paper, ribbons or toner, maybe a printhead or drum, and electricity for as long as you own (and use) the printer. Any printer that requires a specific kind of paper will almost surely cost more per page that you print. Even within a given technology (such as thermal-wax transfer printers) the paper sold by one manufacturer for its printers may be priced dramatically differently from that offered by another manufacturer.

You may be surprised that in the long run you'll probably pay more for these consumables than you did for the printer itself, particularly if you invest in a technology that requires the periodic replacement of high-priced consumables. For example, the cost of toner and replacement drums can overshadow the purchase price of a low-cost laser printer. Moreover, the consumables for different printer models vary widely in cost and life. In some cases, a printer with lower consumable costs can be less expensive in the long run than one with a lower purchase price.

Even the best printer will sometimes malfunction, particularly when put to heavy use in an office situation. Most machines come with a warranty that will take care of the cost of these problems, at least initially. But after the warranty runs out, you'll be stuck with the cost of repairs. Most businesses like to hedge their bets with a service contract or extended warranty, which essentially amortizes the cost of repairs. You'll want to figure in such costs over the life of your printer when comparing purchase price.

Even if you don't buy the extended warranty or service contract, these numbers will give you guidance as to what you can expect to pay for maintenance of your printer throughout its useful life. You can take your chance without this kind of insurance or maintain the printer yourself (which has its own hidden costs). But you can't ignore this aspect of the cost of printing.

Bottom line: Be sure to factor in all of these long-run incidental costs when comparison shopping. A bargain printer may not be a bargain once you total up all of its costs.

Even the purchase price itself may not tell you the whole story of what you'll initially pay. Take a close look at what comes with your printer. You want to be sure that what you buy comes with everything you need to get started. Some manufacturers include what others sell as extra-price accessories. Worse, some vendors (particularly the rock-bottom prices mail-order sort) give themselves an edge in pricing by stripping the toner cartridge from a new laser printer package and charging you extra for what should be standard. Be wary and check that what you pay includes everything you need to set up and use your new printer.

Check the Interface and Cable

Until the development of electronic clairvoyance, you will always have to somehow connect your printer to your PC. While some printers give you your choice of connections–parallel or serial port, sometimes a network interface–most of the time linking a printer means using a parallel port. For personal printing, the parallel port is fine, but you're likely to get better throughput through a network. Make certain your network will connect directly to your printer and that the printer hardware is compatible with your network architecture.

Don't forget to get a cable for your printer. PC makers never include serial or parallel cables with their machines. Printer makers rarely include the required cable either. So you're stuck with the need to buy one if you want to plug in your printer.

Fortunately, the parallel cables used by most modern printers are generic, which translates to cheap and widely available. You can probably find what you need at any computer store or Radio Shack for less than $10.

Some machines require special cables, however; this situation applies most specifically to printers with serial interfaces. Some parallel printers won't work with the generic cable because of their own subtle variations from the prevalent port standard. In such instances, you'll need a cable particularly tailored to match your printer. A matching cable is particularly important if your system requires something other than a standard IBM printer cable (36-pin Centronics to 25-pin D-shell).

Even if your printer uses a standard parallel connection, you'll probably want to order a new cable with the machine. There's nothing more frustrating than having a new printer and no way of plugging it into your PC. Even when you're upgrading to a new printer and plan to plug the new one in place of the old, you'll still want a new cable. Eventually you're going to want to attach that old printer to something (maybe LPT2 on your PC so you can use it as a label printer), and you'll naturally need a cable for it. Getting it now saves later frustration and additional shipping and handling fees from direct vendors or the cost of a second trip to your computer dealer (not only travel expenses but also the time involved and the embarrassment of admitting you forgot such a necessity).

Check Technical Support

If you don't regard yourself as being a computer expert, you need to know that there is a hand to hold when you reach for it. This book does its best to extend its mitt, but sometimes even it can't answer all your questions; even the most imaginative author can't anticipate every situation and problem.

If you venture far from the ordinary, you'll probably want to know that some additional help is available somewhere. For example, you may have a job that calls for inverted boldfaced italicized superscript characters printed vertically in a Cyrillic font. A quick answer from someone intimate with the printer's commands can save you hours of poring through a manual or even the charts in this book.

Your dealer is your first line of support. Of course, you should expect your dealer to help you with any product he offers. And, of course, you'll often be disappointed—not necessarily because of incompetence of the dealer but because his experience will be limited to his customers, which may be but a small sampling of all the users of a given product. The dealer simply may never have encountered the problems troubling you and might have the same difficulty as you finding the right solutions.

Printer makers have more experience with the problems with their product, and most can provide answers when you need them. Getting those answers is another matter. Different printer makers provide various means of support. Most common is simple telephone support, but it comes in several variations. As with any telephone support, toll-free is best whether from vendor or manufacturer. A dial-in bulletin board system is useful for support but won't give you the instant answer that the telephone will. Then again, it won't keep you on hold for half your lifetime either.

Some manufacturers now have *fax-back support*. You call a number and use your telephone's touchpad to wend your way through a menu. (What? You only have a rotary-dial telephone? Maybe you should stick with your typewriter, too.) The printer company then faxes the data sheets you want to your fax machine. (What? You don't have a fax machine? Do I detect a pattern here?)

Although not provided directly by the manufacturer, another form of support may help point you toward a particular printer maker. Many PC Users' Groups have special sections, some of which may deal with printers and printing issues (such as desktop publishing). If you check with the group for the machine with which they are experienced and for which they can provide support, you may narrow your printer search.

Don't Forget Delivery

If you elect to take advantage of the low-ball prices you find listed in magazines, don't forget that the hardware has to make its way from the vendor's warehouse to your loading dock or backdoor. You can bet that those rock-bottom prices you see advertised don't include delivery charges for something that takes a team of elephants to deliver.

Some printers are lightweights, like the portable machines that you're expected to stow in your briefcase. But many laser printers, particularly the large-format models, would give Hercules a hernia. The shipping costs for such behemoths is far from trivial and can add substantially to the cost of a machine bought from a distant vendor.

Before you buy, check the transportation arrangements made by your vendor. If the vendor pays the shipping, you can save UPS or other delivery charges of $20 or more. Beware of any product that must be delivered by motor freight or truck. Most trucking services believe that their responsibility ends when they get the box to your address. You're responsible for wrestling whatever you order from the truck through your door and to its final resting place. Many trucking companies charge extra for residential delivery (in which case you should expect them to lend a hand in getting the box into your house). A few transportation services will actually put your printer in place or even set it up.

On the other hand, you may actually want to pay *more* for delivery, especially if you want your printer *now*. Many direct-purchase vendors offer special rates for next-day or second-day air deliveries. Remember, though, impatience has its price, one that you'll end up paying.

Research the Service Policy

No printer, no matter how well designed and ruggedly built, can be expected to run forever without problem or failure. Being works of man rather than works of

God, all printers are inevitably flawed. If something happens to your printer, you're going to need help to get it going again. Although you may pray for divine assistance, you'll probably have to rely on your dealer or the printer maker's service center to bring the printer back to life.

When your printer does fail, you won't lose your work as you might with a hard disk crash. Nevertheless, you'll lose valuable time waiting for repairs. Getting your machine going again should be as high a priority for your dealer or the printer maker as it is for you. Before you buy any machine from anyone, check where and how you can get your printer serviced, both in and out of warranty.

Many computer dealers are ill-equipped to handle mechanical printer repairs. They will have to send your machine out for service exactly as you would, probably to the same place that you would–the manufacturer's service center. In that case, the dealer provides only an extra layer of waiting.

You'll find that some manufacturers have local service depots akin to the typewriter repair shops of days gone by. These local service centers usually will take care of mechanical problems without imposing the vagaries of shipping the printer back to points unknown.

With more expensive printers, you'll want the same kind of service policy you've got on your PC–on-site service is best. Many manufacturers now offer service contracts for their products; these may include on-site service. Such service contracts provide you with the equivalent of an insurance policy. You pay a little bit over a long period to avoid having to shell out a lot for a major disaster. They spread the risk–while giving the manufacturer another source of profits.

Watch the Warranty

Warranties help take the risk out of a new printer purchase. Moreover, a longer warranty takes the risk out of using your printer and can lower its total cost per page (because you have to figure the inevitable cost of services into each page you print).

Depending on their confidence in their products and their ability to avoid your claims, printer manufacturers offer warranties of many lengths. The minimum warranty appears to be 90 days. Some stretch for one or more years. Longer is, of course, measurably better. You can figure its value from the price of a service contract covering the warranty period.

Some printers are not covered by manufacturers' warranties. For example, grey market printers that you buy from a direct vendor may not be eligible for warranty service by the manufacturer or official importer. However, every printer (or product you buy) is warranted by its vendor *unless such warranty is specifically disclaimed.* By law, your dealer must extend specific warranty protection to the products it sells. The specifics are, however, complex. If you get to the point of arguing about them, you'll probably want to consult with a lawyer. Reputable dealers won't let things go that far. Ideally you'll want the dual protection of both the vendor's warranty (with return privileges) and the manufacturer's.

Note that if your dealer says that a printer will fit a particular application, he has made a warranty. If the printer later does not serve what the dealer says, the dealer will have to somehow make good on his claim (for example, by taking the printer back).

Modern printers are so reliable that you're unlikely to need to make a warranty claim. But it's always good to know you have a warranty to depend on, just in case something does go wrong.

CHAPTER FOUR

Technologies

How you get an image on paper is a matter of technology. Today's PC printers use a variety of methods for making their marks, pounding ink to paper, spraying it on, relying on attraction and the magic of mirrors, even melting wax. Each of these printer technologies has its strengths; weaknesses; finding the best one for you requires matching these technologies with your output applications.

Just as you can take any one of a variety of routes to get to a given destination—the shortcut that takes you there quickest, the scenic route, the one with the least confusion and fewest turns, which make the directions understandable, one that goes past the doughnut shop—printers give you different paths to your printout. The differences are twofold, philosophical, and practical.

At the philosophical level, you can ponder such concepts as what makes a character a character, or is a printed character a single whole, a gestalt that cannot be understood except in its complete form or is the character like matter itself, made from individual atoms stacked and arrayed into physical form? If the latter, at what point does the character appear from the sea of atoms? How many atoms does it take to form a distinguishable character, to form an aesthetically appealing character?

These questions underlie a fundamental difference between printer technologies, character formation. The former concept, the character gestalt, results in the fully formed character printer. The atomistic view yields the bit-image (or dot-matrix) printer. Each has its own merits, and you can argue about them until a bug causes the e-mail system to collapse. The printer industry has, however, answered the question for you and pushed the fully formed character printer far into the background, forgotten perhaps, but not dead.

The practical side of PC printer technology involves how you get marks on paper. The range of technologies is as wide as your imagination, as wide as the collective imagination of mankind. Printers mash and spray, singe and melt, some let color seep into the paper, others dust it on. As long as you get your expected results, you might think your means of getting there doesn't matter. But each different print technology comes with its own repercussions in cost, convenience, quality, and longevity. Some printers are cheaper than others or make pages at less expense. Some make you wrestle with ribbons that leave your skin more decorous than the tattooed lady, others are surgically clean. Many machines claim typeset quality, others will send you shopping for a guide dog. And some make pages permanent as the national debt, others fade faster in the light of day than a politician's promise.

Finding the right printer is a matter of informed choice–you choose what you want, but you must have information about all your options. Much of the information you need involves the technology of printing, how the various varieties of printers work. In this chapter, you will learn how your words and images take form on paper, acetate, or vellum. We'll start with the underlying philosophies of character formation and then quickly move on to the actual mechanics of printing.

Character Formation

The history of print technology has been one of ever finer control. The first mechanical prints were essentially full-page images. Although the print machinery allowed you to make as many copies as you needed, you could re-use the image only as itself in its entirety. Terms "impact" and "non impact" describe the kind of deviltry involved in getting any marks at all to appear on paper. But the method of making those marks is independent of what they are and how they are shaped. While differing printing technologies have some effect on the image quality and what the printer is used for, other considerations are just as important in regard to image quality. The most important among them is the character-forming method used by the printer.

Fully Formed Character Printers

The original typewriter and all such machines made through the 1970s were based on the same character-forming principal as the original creation of Johannes Gutenberg. After laboriously carving individual letters out of wood, daubing them with sticky black ink, and smashing paper against the gooey mess, Gutenberg brought printing to the West by inventing the concept of movable type. Every letter he printed was printed fully formed from a complete, although reversed, image of itself. The character was fully formed in advance of printing. Every part of it, from the boldest stroke to the tiniest serif, was printed in one swipe of the press. Old-fashioned typewriters adapted Gutenberg's individual-character type to an impact mechanism.

In the early days of personal computing, a number of machines used this typewriter technology and were grouped together under the term fully formed character printers. Other names for this basic technology were letter-quality printers, daisy-wheel printers, and a variation called the thimble printer.

Fully formed character technology produces good-quality output, in line with better typewriters. The chief limitation, in fact, is not the printing technology but the ribbon that is used. Some daisy-wheel printers equipped with a mylar film ribbon can give results that almost equal the quality of phototypesetter.

While daisy-wheel printers still are available, they are passé, from the PC perspective. Gutenberg-era technology finally is showing its age. The movable-type design limits them solely to text printing and crude graphics. Fully formed character printers also limit you to a few typefaces. You can only print the type faces–and font sizes–available on the image-forming daisy-wheels or thimbles. These machines also are slow–budget-priced machines hammer out text at a lazy 12 to 20 characters per second, and even the most expensive machines struggle to reach 90 characters per second. Other technologies (in particular, laser printers) now equal or exceed the quality of fully formed character printers, run far ahead in speed, and impose little or no price penalty.

Bit-Image Printers

The way to break free from the binding of Gutenberg is to go him one further. Gutenberg broke the page into tiny, separate elements–individual letters. The next step would be to follow suit with the letters themselves– break them into dots. The result is the bit-image printer.

Where fully formed character printers remember the shape of each letter mechanically, the bit-image printer stores each shape electronically (or relies on your printer to store the image information). It forms each character on-the-fly, based on the bit arrangements stored in memory.

The raw material for characters on paper is much the same as it is on the video screen–dots. A number of dots can be arranged to resemble any character that you want to print. To make things easier for the printer (and its designer), printers that form their characters from dots usually array those dots in a rectilinear matrix like a crossword puzzle grid. Because most bit-image printers form their characters from dots placed within a matrix, they are usually termed dot-matrix printers. Most people, however, restrict the use of the dot-matrix term to impact dot-matrix machines.

Bit-Image Technologies

All popular, non impact printers and the surviving impact technology use bit-image technology; the reason is versatility. A bit-image printer can generate both text and graphics at virtually any level of quality. The dot patterns that make up individual characters are computer controlled and can be changed and varied by your computer (or the computer-like control electronics built into the printer) without your needing to make any mechanical adjustments to the machine. A daisy-wheel, fully formed character printer may allow you to shift from roman to italic typeface or from pica to elite type size simply by swapping printing elements (the daisy-wheels themselves), but matrix printers make the switcheroo even easier and the repertory wider. Just send a computerized instruction to the printer, and you can change the typeface in midline, double the height of each character, squeeze type to half its width, or shift to proportionally spaced script. The same dots can be formed into a chart, graph, drawing, or simulation of a halftone photograph. Using bit-image techniques, one printer can put virtually any image on paper.

The quality and speed of the output of bit-image printers vary with the technology used. At the low end, dot-matrix printing can look simply awful. At the high end, better laser printers can generate book-quality output. Speeds vary from less than a page a minute to dozens of pages in the same period. The following outline describes how each of the most important bit-image printer technologies works.

Bit-Image Quality

The quality of the characters printed by the bit-image printer is determined by three chief factors–the number of dots in the matrix, the addressability of the printer, and the size of the dots. The denser the matrix (the more dots in a given area), the better the characters look. Higher addressability allows the printer to place dots on paper with greater precision. Smaller dots allow finer details to be rendered.

The minimal matrix of any printer measures 5x7 (horizontal by vertical) dots and is just sufficient to render all the upper and lowercase letters of the alphabet unambiguously–and not aesthetically. The dots are big, and they look disjointed.

Worse, the minimal matrix is too small to let descending characters (g, j, p, q, and y) droop below the general line of type and makes them look cramped and scrunched up. Rarely do you encounter this minimal level of quality today except in the cheapest, close-out printers.

The minimum matrix used by most commercial dot-matrix printers measures 9x9 dots, a readable arrangement but still somewhat inelegant in a world accustomed to printed text. Newer 18- and 24-pin impact dot-matrix printers can form characters with 12x24 to 24x24 matrices.

Other bit-image technologies go even further. Laser printers pack tiny dots very densely, 300 per inch. At a 10-per-inch character pitch, a single letter is formed from a 30x50 matrix. The latest generation of ink-jet and impact dot-matrix printers also approaches that quality level. Newer lasers can double or quadruple that matrix quality. For comparison, commercial typesetting equipment achieves character matrices of about 240x400 for 12-point (that is, 10-pitch) type.

As with computer displays, the resolution and addressability of dot-matrix printers often are confused. When resolution is mentioned, most of the time addressability is intended, particularly on dot-matrix printer specification sheets. A printer may be able to address any position on the paper with an accuracy of, say, 1/120th inch. If a printwire is larger than 1/120th inch in diameter, however, the machine never is able to render detail as small as 1/120th inch.

The big dots made by the wide printwires blur out the detail. Better quality impact dot-matrix printers have more printwires, and they are smaller. Also, the ribbon that is inserted between the wires and paper blurs each dot hammered out by an impact dot-matrix printer. Mechanical limits also constrain the on-paper resolution of impact machines.

Printer Electronics

Character Mode

On the surface, printing in character mode couldn't seem simpler: Send an ASCII code to the printer, and it responds by putting the corresponding character on paper. Behinds the scenes–and inside the printer's case–there's a lot more going on. The ASCII code sent to the printer looks nothing like the character you want to see. After all, it's nothing more than a bunch of bits, at best electronic pulses most of the time totaling about eight.

Fully Formed Character Printers

In fully formed character printers, the translation is the matter of timing noted before. In its most elementary form, a fully formed character printer interprets the bit pattern of a character as a delay period. The printer constantly keeps its full alphabet (and then some) moving past its print head. At a generally uniform rate, printhead steps to each position where a character might be printed. It waits for the delay specified by the character code, then prints whichever character is ready in the printhead. The designer of the printer arranges the characters streaming past the printhead to ensure that the desired character is in the proper place when its delay ends. Think of it as the printer mechanism adjusting its timing to hit the right character as being like playing miniature golf. You've got to have your timing down pat, hitting the ball at exactly the right instant to sneak it past the slowly spinning blades of a windmill straddling the fairway.

This rudimentary form of fully formed character printer moves its printhead from character position to character position at a constant rate, halting at each place just long enough to squeeze out one character and then move on. Smarter printers gain extra speed by predicting the future. They anticipate where the next character will be needed and move their printhead to it the most efficient way possible, skipping over seas of unprinted paper as necessary. Rather than rely on clairvoyance, they see into the future by delaying it. They accumulate characters in an internal buffer, and read through them before making a move. That way they know what they will have to do before they start doing it.

To determine character positions, the printer doesn't have the luxury of looking at the paper. Most of the time, it guesses. It drives its printhead and platen roller with stepper motors, specials motors that notch around in discrete intervals, a fraction of a turn at a time. The printer counts the number of steps it makes to each character position. Because it knows how wide each step is and the number of steps it has made, it knows about where it is all it needs is a point of reference.

Most printers set up their reference point every time they move their printhead over to the left edge of the mechanism. From this point, they can count up to any horizontal location on the paper. To determine the correct vertical location, they rely on the top-of-the-form setting you've made to indicate the beginning of a page.

Bit-Image Line Printers

When they print text, bit-image printers work electronically in a manner that's similar to fully formed character printers. Their electronic systems generate signals to sweep the printhead smoothly across each line, driven by a stepper motor so that the printer knows the exact location of its printhead. But the bit-image printer has no preformed characters to draw upon.

In order to figure out the shape of each character it prints, the bit-image printer must look up the definition of the character in memory. (In fact, you can think of the preformed symbols used by the fully formed character printer as mechanical memory.) The printer uses the ASCII codes it receives to tell it where to look in memory for the bit patterns of the character to print. It reads its memory one vertical line of bits of a single character at a time. The printer uses each bit of the vertical line as a separate signal to control the firing of an individual printwire. It fires an entire vertical line of printwires at once, and then lets the printhead shift to the next position. It then gulps down another vertical line of bits, and fires its printwires again.

Although the bit-image line printer normally looks in its ROM chips to find the character definitions it needs to fire its printwires, the location of the character memory need not be forever fixed. In most such printers, the character definitions are arranged as a table, and the printer uses a pointer to reference the base location of the table. By changing the pointer, you can make the printer look somewhere else to find the character shapes to use.

Most bit-image line printers use this trick to allow you to download your own character sets. All you need to do is load a table of character definitions in the printer's RAM, then change the pointer to indicate the address of the new table in RAM. Viola! You're printing with the definitions you downloaded.

Bit-image line printers can use exactly the same future-prediction technology as fully formed character printers to optimize the movement of their printheads, peeking in their buffers to find the future positions of the printhead and the best way of getting there. Better still, they can read backward through their buffer to find characters in reverse order and read the individual lines of their character definitions backward, too. The printer can then print an entire line backward and print an entire document bidirectionally.

Bit-Image Page Printers

Oddly enough, printers that generate a page at a time read their character memories in smaller doses, a single bit at a time. Yet because of the great speed of the page printer image-forming mechanism, most page printers don't get keep up with line printers but beat them soundly.

In character mode, serial page printers such as lasers work as if each was a line printer that has a printhead exactly one wire high. The image-forming mechanism traces across each character–actually, each line of characters–multiple times; the multiple equals the height of a line in bits. In effect, the page printer scans the page the same way a television camera scans a full picture.

Non scanning page printers like thermal-wax and dye-sublimation printers work a bit differently. They route the bit-high line of data directly to their pagewide printheads, much like line printers tilted 90°.

In character mode, the page printer uses ASCII codes just as does the bit-image line printer, as keys to access the table of character definition. Where the line printer reads the bits of each character shape vertically, the page printer reads them horizontally. The data bits it reads can be used to directly control the image mechanism, for example, triggering the laser on and off in a laser printer. More usually, however, the bit-stream gets routed through a buffer that's many lines long. The buffer helps ensure that the data will be ready so that the mechanism can smoothly scan down the page without interruption or pause. Of course, the electronics of scanning page printers must develop the signals that control the sweep mechanism and keep it synchronized with the bit-stream.

Printer Mechanics

Just as you can hold a pencil in any of a multitude of positions to make a mark on paper, you can design printers to use different technologies to accomplish the same task. Of course, some ways of holding a pencil result in more successful and legible writing than others. Similarly, some printer technologies are more successful than others.

Printer technologies divide in many ways. You can make the split by how they handle lines and pages, whether they impact the paper or gently caress it, the number of colors they use, or how much the mechanism weights. The classic division divides the race of printers between impact and non impact machines, that is, those that hammer ink to paper and those that use more subtle forms of persuasion. The dividing line is drawn across the surface of the paper and marks whether anything mechanical actually hammers against the paper to render letters and graphics. To put it simply, an impact printer beats your paper into submitting to its will. Non impact technologies are kinder and gentler and rely on scorching, electrocuting, and spray painting to make their marks.

This division also marks the split between old technologies and new. When the concepts underlying mechanical printing developed, the only means available required impact. Non impact designs require precise control that is afforded only by computer technology. Moreover, non impact designs require technologies based on chemistry and other physical changes that weren't even dreamed about when impact printing debuted.

As with any dated technology, impact printing has for the most part been pushed aside. It survives only at the bottom of the market, where long years of experience and design economies keep prices low, or in particular niches where engineers can exploit the unique properties of impact technology.

Certainly there are other, equally valid ways of dividing printer technologies for discussion: line printers versus page printers, monochrome versus color, low versus high price, performance, or quality. None of these is as distinct as the impact/non impact demarcation. Moreover, the impact/non impact distinction marks fundamental differences in the underlying technologies that are used.

Impact Printers

If you want to impress someone, few things work as dramatically as the simple hammer. Central to all impact printers is a hammer or something with a more elegant, descriptive, or misleading name, which accomplishes the same purpose– It pounds what you want to print on paper.

Hammers have been used to craft lettering since some stone mason first chiseled an inscription on a rock. As long lasting as stone engraving may be, neither the process nor the product is suitable for the purposes filled by the written word. But the hammer became an intrinsic part of the technology that led to today's first PC printers.

The idea was to interpose ink between the hammer and paper. The sharp impact of the hammer could shake, batter, or squeeze the ink to paper, driving it into the paper fibers where it would lodge and dry to make a permanent mark.

Background

Although an old-fashioned typewriter is a mechanical complexity (as anyone knows who has tried putting one back together after taking it apart), its operating principle is quite simple. Strip away all the cams, levers, and keys, and you quickly see that the essence of the typewriter is its hammers.

Each hammer strikes against an inked ribbon, driving it against a sheet of paper on which you want to print. The harsh and hard impact of the hammer against the ribbon and paper shakes, squeezes, and presses ink from the cloth or mylar carrier onto the paper. Absorbed into the paper fibers, the ink leaves a visible mark or image in the shape of the part of the hammer that struck at the ribbon. In the first printer, the typewriter, the impression left by the hammer was typically one of the letters of the alphabet.

One way or another, all impact printers rely on this basic typewriter principle. Like Christopher Sholes's first platen-pecker, all impact printers smash a hammer of some kind against a ribbon to squeeze ink from the ribbon onto paper, making their mark by force. In fact, if any difference exists between an impact printer and a typewriter, it is that the typewriter directly lines your fingers to the mechanism that does the printing. A printer, on the other hand, inserts your personal computer between your mind and the printed word.

In the earliest days of personal computers—before typewriter makers were sure that PCs would catch on and create a personal printer market—a number of companies adapted typewriters to computer output chores. The Bytewriter was typical of the result—a slow, plodding computer printer with full typewriter keyboard. It could do double duty as fast as your fingers could fly, but, it was no match for the computer's output.

One device, short-lived on the marketplace, even claimed that you could turn your typewriter into a printer simply by setting a box on the keyboard. The box was filled with dozens of solenoids and enough other mechanical parts to make the Space Shuttle look simple. The solenoids worked as electronically controlled "fingers," pressing down each key on command from the host computer. Interesting as it sounds, they tread the thin line between the absurd and surreal. More than a little doubt exists as to whether these machines, widely advertised in 1981, were ever actually sold.

Today, the most popular low-cost printers are impact dot-matrix printers, most often clipped to simply the name dot-matrix. Although they use a different character-forming method than the classic typewriter, they rely on the same hammer-and-ribbon impact printing principle.

Impact Advantages

As with typewriters, all impact printers have a number of desirable qualities, at least from the perspective of the printer maker. Thanks to a design and technology that has been developed and refined for more than a century, engineers have mastered most of what goes on inside the impact printer. At least they know how to make things go bang and get ink on paper along the way.

Most impact printers can spread their output across any medium that ink has an affinity for, including any paper you might have lying around your home, from onion skin to thin cardstock. While both impact and non impact technologies have been developed to the point that either can produce high-quality or high-speed output, impact technology takes the lead when you share one of the most common business needs, making multipart forms. Impact printers can hammer an impression not just through a ribbon, but through several sheets of paper as well. Slide a carbon between the sheets or, better yet, treat the paper for non carbon duplicates, and you get multiple, guaranteed-identical copies with a single pass through the mechanism. For a number of business applications–for example, the generation of charge receipts–exact carbon copies are a necessity and impact printing is an absolute requirement.

Impact Noise

Impact printers reveal their typewriter heritage in another way. The hammer bashing against the ribbon and paper makes noise, a sharp staccato rattle that is high in amplitude and rich in high-frequency components, penetrating and bothersome as a dental drive or angry horde of giant, hungry mosquitoes. Typically, the impact printer rattles and prattles louder than most normal conversational tones, and it is more obnoxious than an argument. The higher speed the impact printer, the higher the pitch of the noise and the more penetrating it becomes.

Some printer makers have toned down their boisterous scribes admirably–some printers as fast as 780 characters per second are as quiet as 55 dB, about the level of a quiet PC fan. But you still want to leave the room when an inexpensive impact printer (the best-selling of all printers) grinds through its assignment.

Daisy-Wheel Printers

Nearly all of the fully formed character printers that are likely to be connected to a personal computer use the impact principle to get their ink on paper. Rather than having a separate hammer for each letter, however, the characters are arranged on a single, separate element that is inserted between a single hammer and the ribbon. The hammer, powered by a solenoid that is controlled by the electronics of the printer and your computer, impacts against the element. The element then squeezes the ink off the ribbon and onto the paper. To allow the full range of alphanumeric characters to be printed using this single-hammer technique, the printing element swerves, shakes, or rotates each individual character that is to be formed in front of the hammer as it is needed.

Most often, the characters are arranged near the tips of the spokes of a wheel. These machines are called "daisy-wheel" because the hubs resemble flower petals. Hold the daisy horizontally and bend those petals upward, and the printing element becomes the thimble (or what you might call a "tulip-wheel").

Band Printers

The speed demon among fully formed character printers is the *band printer* The band in question is not a musical group but rather a continuous loop embossed with characters. Think of an alphabetically decorated rubber band running across a print hammer and you'll have the general idea.

The operating principle of the band printer is exactly the same as any other fully formed character printer. With one swifting whack from the printhead hammer, the band printer pounds ink from a ribbon to paper in the shape of the character embossed on the band. Choosing the correct character remains a matter of timing–the hammer must fire when the character you want is directly in front of it.

The chief advantage of using a band instead of a ball is that you can put many bands side-by-side, running parallel to each other like an array of conveyor belts. The more bands, the more characters the printer can put down in a given time. Consequently, the band printer has the greatest speed potential of any fully formed character printer.

On the other hand, the quality from the band printer will inspire you to try to rub your spectacles clean and make an appointment with the optometrist. In general, band-printed text appears uneven and fuzzy.

Impact Dot-Matrix Printers

The prototypical, bit-image printer is that impact dot-matrix machine. Those normally used by PCs are line printers. Each one uses a printhead that shuttles back and forth across the width of the paper to create one line of characters or graphics at a time. As impact printers, these machines pound out characters by driving ink from ribbon to paper. Instead of a single hammer, however, they use several, usually arranged in a vertical line down the printhead for the entire height of a character. The hammers take the form of long and thin wires, which are often called *pins* (as in a "nine-pin" printer). Fired all at once, these small printwires would pound out an upright line on the paper. As the printhead scans across the paper, the hammers can dot the paper across its width, potentially creating a series of lines, which blends into a one-line-wide horizontal band.

The vertical position of the wires in the printhead and the horizontal position of the head across the paper maps out a band of hammering positions, corresponding to the cells in the matrix. The impact dot-matrix printer can selectively use its hammers to put a dot in any one or all of these cell positions. The trick to impact dot-matrix printing is this selective pounding of the printwires.

To print a line of characters, the printhead moves horizontally across the paper, and each wire fires as necessary to form the individual characters, its impact precisely timed so that it falls on exactly the right position in the matrix. The wires fire on the fly–the printhead never pauses until it reaches the other side of the paper.

In most dot-matrix printers, a seemingly complex but efficient mechanism makes this magic and controls when each of the printwires pounds the paper. The printwire normally is held away from the ribbon and paper, and against the force of a spring, by a strong permanent magnet. The magnet is wrapped with a coil of wire that forms an electromagnet, wound so that its polarity is the opposite of that of the permanent magnet. To fire the printwire against the ribbon and paper, this electromagnet is energized (under computer control, of course), and its field neutralizes that of the permanent magnet. Without the force of the permanent magnetic holding back the printwire, the spring forcefully jabs the printwire out against ribbon, squeezing ink onto the paper. After the printwire makes its dot, the electromagnet is de-energized and the permanent magnet pulls the printwire back to its idle position, ready to fire again. The whole process takes a fraction of a second, just long enough for the printhead to move to the next position in the matrix of dots.

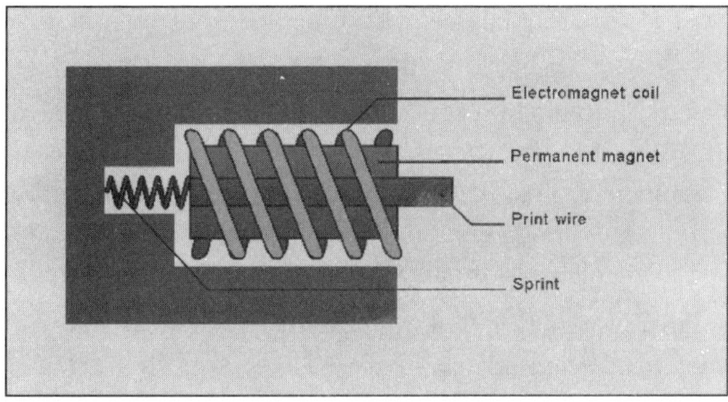

Figure 4.1 The printing mechanism for an impact dot-matrix printer.

The two-magnets-and-spring approach is designed with one primary purpose—to hold the printwire away from the paper (and out of harm's way) when no power is supplied to the printer and the printhead. The complexity is justified by the protection it affords the delicate printwires.

A major factor in determining the printing speed of dot-matrix machine is the time required between successive strikes of each printwire. Physical laws of motion limit the acceleration each printwire can achieve in ramming toward the paper and back. Thus, the time needed to retract and reactivate each printwire puts a physical limit on how rapidly the printhead can travel across the paper. It cannot sweep past the next dot position before each of the printwires inside it is ready to fire. If the printhead travels too fast, dot positioning (and character shapes) would become rather haphazard.

Note, however, that the next firing position may not necessarily be the adjacent cell in the matrix. In the most popular impact dot-matrix design, that used by Epson, the printhead moves faster than the firing mechanism operates. When the printhead moves from the adjacent cell to one that was just printed, the printwire is not yet ready for a second firing. Consequently, these machines can put a dot only in every other cell across the width of a line using a single pass of the printhead. As a result, the highest ink density that these machines can achieve in a single pass is about 50%. Printouts made this way consequently cannot achieve full black. That's one of the reasons why drafts printed at the highest speed on impact dot-matrix printers look pale grey.

To make truly black characters, these impact dot-matrix printers must make two or more passes of the printhead. On the second pass, they fill in the gaps left by the first pass, again printing every other cell position but offset one cell from the first pass. Additional passes, with offsets of half a cell, can produce even darker characters.

Impact dot-matrix printers differ in the number of wires they array in their printheads. Most of the earliest machines had nine wires for forming characters because this is the minimal number for creating legible text with lowercase characters with true descenders. The nine-wire design continues to dominate the lowest end of the printer market. Moreover, many high-performance printers retain the nine-wire design.

Machines aiming for better looking text—so-called near letter quality—often use more complex printheads with 24 wires. These are often arranged in parallel rows with the printwires vertically staggered by the width of one printwire arranged so that they can fill adjacent matrix cells in a single pass. This allows darker characters of higher apparent quality. Unfortunately, on some early machines this stagger led to a wavy appearance of individual characters when the printers were operated in their draft modes. During normal operation, these pack more dots in each vertical column. The wires are finer than those in nine-pin printers, allowing 24-pin machines to achieve higher true resolutions and make sharper characters and graphics.

There's nothing inherently magical about 24 wires, not even the mundane practicality of the nine-wire design. Some printer makers have tried other numbers and arrangements of printwires, for example, 18-wire models that simply expand on the nine-wire design. The 24-wire arrangement dominates because most printer makers now use the same command system, one based on the 24-wire design used by Epson.

The highest speed impact dot-matrix printers use multiple printheads. Rather than divide the work vertically and assign different lines to each printhead, these machines usually array their multiple printheads so that they work on the same line at the same time, offset horizontally. For example, one head might print on the left half of a page and the other on the right half. The arrangement minimizes the travel of both printheads.

Non Impact Printers

Non impact printers can use any of a diverse array of technologies, from laser beams to miniature toaster heating elements that fry pigment to paper, to bubbles of ink blown into place. The sole characteristic that can be assumed for any non impact printer is that nothing forcibly smashes into the paper during the image-making process.

The obvious opposite to impact technology is non impact printing. A number of other ways of putting images on paper without the typewriter-like hammer impact have been developed through the application of new technologies and a good deal of imagination. The three leading, non impact technologies are the ink-jet, thermal, laser, wax-transfer, and dye-diffusion.

Ink-Jets

Superficially, you can consider an ink-jet printer as just another dot-matrix printer with the hammers left back at Zeus's forge and rocket technology substituted. The "jet" in the name should elicit the essence of the technology–a miniaturized fire hose spray of turgid ink at some unsuspecting target, technology akin to a squid under computer control. Key to ink-jet technology are the miniaturization and the tight tolerances. The jets spurted at your paper measure hardly larger than strands of hair, splattering droplets of ink as fine as the dust called toner by laser printer makers. The control afforded by modern computer circuits allows the ink-jet printer to place each of its dots with a precision that puts a Rolex and the Swiss watchmaking industry to shame.

As with conventional impact dot-matrix printers, ink-jets are line printers. They are designed around printheads one line wide, which course across paper or acetate laying down dots along the way. Instead of printwires, the ink-jet has nozzles from which the spray of ink emerges. The geometry of the mechanism and the printing are the same as those with impact dot-matrix printers.

Hallmarks of the ink-jet process are quality, quiet, and color. Precision dot placement allows the best ink-jet printers to equal mainstream laser printers in the sharpness of the text and graphics they render. Without hammers pounding ink paper like a myopic carpenter chasing an elusive nail, ink-jet printers sound almost serene in their everyday work. The tiny droplets of ink rustle so little air that they make not a whisper. All you hear is the regular course of the printhead cruising across the paper. Best of all, however, are the color capabilities added economically because of the simple, even elegant design of the ink-jet print mechanism. The single term ink-jet belies important differences in the design and operation of printer hardware. Currently three different technologies wear the ink-jet name.

Most of the machines rely on the combination of a small orifice and the surface tension of liquid ink to prevent a constant dibble from the jets. That is, the ink puckers around the hole in the ink-jet the same way that droplets of water bead up on a waxy surface. The attraction of the molecules in the ink (or water) is stronger than the force of gravity, so they scrunch together rather than spreading out or flowing out the nozzle. The ink-jet printer must apply some force to break the surface tension and force out the ink.

Thermal Ink-Jets

The most common ink-jet technology is called *thermal* because it uses heat inside its printhead to boil a tiny quantity of water-based ink. This thermal process produces a tiny bubble of steam that balloons out from the orifice of the ink-jet. The printhead carefully controls the formation of this bubble. When the bubble reaches the critical point at which it can no longer hold itself together, its burst and the force of the blast sprays the ink from the nozzle to the paper.

A research specialist at Canon discovered the thermal ink-jet process in 1977, although practical printers came many years later. Canon derives its proprietary name *BubbleJet* from this technology, although the design is also used in printers manufactured by DEC, Hewlett-Packard, Lexmark, and Texas Instruments.

Heat that makes the bubbles is the primary disadvantage of the thermal ink-jet system. It slowly wears out the printhead, requiring that it be periodically replaced to keep the printer working at its best. Some manufacturers minimize this problem by combining their printers' nozzles with their ink cartridges so that when you add more ink you automatically replace the nozzles. With this design, you never have to replace the nozzles, at least independently, because you do it every time you add more ink. Because nozzles ordinarily last much longer than the supply in any reasonable ink-jet reservoir, other manufacturers make the nozzles a replaceable part. The principle difference between these two systems amounts to nothing more than how you do the maintenance. Although the combined nozzles-and-ink approach would seem more expensive, the difference in the ultimate cost of using either system is negligible.

Piezo Ink-Jets

The alternative, used primarily by Epson in its Stylus line of ink-jet printers (except for the Stylus 300), sprays ink electomechanically instead of thermally. The ink-jet nozzles in these printers are made from a *piezoelectric crystal*, a material that bends when you apply electricity to it. When the printer zaps the piezoelectric nozzle with a voltage jolt, the entire nozzle flexes inward, squeezing the ink inside and driving it out to the paper.

According to Epson, this design results in a longer-lived printhead. The company also claims it yields cleaner dots on paper, free from the halos of ink splatter that sometimes appear with bubble-based ink-jet printers.

Solid Ink-Jets

Taking the thermal ink-jet idea to the extreme, solid ink-jet printers melt sticks or chunks of wax-based ink into a liquid, which they then spray onto paper. Although this inky spray makes such machines ink-jets, they differ fundamentally from other designs. Where classic ink-jets spray volatile inks at paper that are fixed by the evaporation (or absorption) of a solvent, the solid ink-jet melts the ink, flings it at paper, and lets it harden there. Because going from solid to liquid (and back) marks a phase transition, this technology is sometimes called *phase-change* printing.

The first printer to use this design was the Howtek Pixelmaster. The technology received a major push with the introduction of the Tektronix Phaser III PXi in 1991. Where the Pixelmaster used plastic-based inks that left little lumps on paper and sometimes clogged the printhead, Tektronix opted for wax-based inks. It also added a final processing step, a *cold fuser* which is simply a steel roller that then squashes the ink dots flat, or nearly so, as the printing medium rolls out of the printer. According to Tektronix, its inks and fuser smooth out the image and allow for brighter, transparent colors that work well for paper and transparency media. Moreover, heat alone will remove clogs from the Tektronix printhead.

One secret to the success of the ink-jet is that it has no ribbon to blur the image. On-paper quality can equal that of more expensive laser printers (see below). The laser-less technology of the ink-jet machines equates to lower costs–and lower prices–budget ink-jets rival low-end dot-matrix printers in affordable price.

But ink-jets are slower at producing high quality than laser printers because they rely on a printhead that mechanically scans across each sheet instead of lightning-fast optics. Ink-jets also require periodic maintenance because they use liquid ink. If not properly cared for, the ink can dry in the nozzles and clog everything up.

To avoid such problems, better ink-jets have built-in routines that clean the nozzles with each use. Most nozzles now are self-sealing, so that when they are not used, air cannot get to the ink. Some manufacturers even combine the ink-jet and ink supply into one easily changeable module. If, however, you pack an ink-jet away without properly cleaning it first, it is not likely to work when you resurrect it months later.

Because ink-jets are non impact printers, they are much quieter than ordinary dot-matrix engines. About the only sound you hear from them is the carriage coursing back and forth. On the other hand, ink-jets require special paper with controlled absorbency for best results–that means you are likely to pay more per page. If you try to get by using excessively porous, cheap paper, the inks wick away into a blur. If the paper is too glossy, the wet ink can smudge.

The liquid ink of ink-jet printers can be a virtue when it comes to color. The inks remain fluid enough even after they have been sprayed on paper to blend together. This gives color ink-jet printers the ability to actually mix their primary colors together to create intermediary tones. The range of color quality from ink-jet printers is wide. The best yield some of the brightest, most saturated colors available from any technology. The vast majority, however, cannot quite produce a true-color palette.

Most thermal and piezo ink-jets have difficulty achieving the rich, deep blacks produced by laser printers when you print in color. A critical look reveals that black text printed with the Canon BubbleJets making cool grey-blacks, the Epson Stylus rendering a dark charcoal grey, and HP Deskjets producing a warmer, dark sepia black. One reason is that many ink-jet printers cannot print a true black when in their color mode. Instead they use a *composite black*, made by blending their three inks together. In theory, the three primary colors of ink should yield black, but the ink hues used by the different manufacturer vary a bit from perfect, resulting in the imperfect black. To avoid this problem, many ink-jet printers use four ink colors, adding a true black to their three color primaries.

As important as the underlying print mechanism, is the choice of ink. After all, a color printer cannot make colors that are not in its inks. Ink-jet ink tends to blur (which reduces both sharpness and color contrast) because it dries at least partly by absorption into paper. Most ink-jet printers work with almost any paper stock, but produce the best results—sharpest, most colorful—with specially coated papers that have controlled ink absorption. On nonabsorbent media (for example, projection acetates), the ink must dry solely by evaporation, and the output is subject to smudging until the drying process completes.

Direct Thermal

A technology common among low-cost printers but no longer in the mainstream uses heat to make its mark—sort of a branding iron for digital data. Because they use thermal energy to effect their purposes, these machines are termed thermal printers.

Certainly heat alone is sufficient to deface paper, as an ordinary match will ably demonstrate. Taken to its enthusiastic extreme, thermal technology could end your paperwork problems forever. The trick to making thermal energy work is control—and specially prepared paper.

A printer that works on the same principle as a wood-burning set might seem better for a Boy Scout than an on-the-go executive, but today's easiest-to-tote printers do exactly that—the equivalent of charring an image onto paper. Thermal printers use the same electrical heating of the word-burner, a resistance that heats up with the flow of current. In the case of the thermal printer, however, the resistance element is tiny and heats and cools quickly, in a fraction of a second. As with ink-jets, the thermal printhead is the equivalent of that of a dot-matrix printer, except that it heats rather than hits.

Thermal printers do not, however, actually char the paper on which they print. Getting paper that hot would be dangerous, precariously close to combustion (although it might let the printer do double-duty as a cigarette lighter). Instead, thermal printers use special, thermally sensitive paper that turns from white to near-black at a moderate temperature.

Thermal technology is ideal for portable printers because few moving parts are involved–only the printhead moves, nothing inside it. No springs and wires means no jamming. The tiny, resistive elements require little power to heat, actually less than is needed to fire a wire in an impact printer. Thermal printers can be lightweight, quiet, and reliable. They can even run on batteries.

The special paper they require is one drawback. Not only is it costly (because it is, after all, special paper) but it feels funny and is prone to discolor if it is inadvertently heated to an extremely high temperature. For example the paper may discolor if left in your car in the hot sun.

Gradually, thermal printers are becoming special application machines. Ink-jets have many of the same virtues and more reasonable paper, therefore low-cost ink-jets are invading the territory of the thermal machines.

Thermal Transfer

Thermal transfer is the leading technology for printing pure, saturated colors. As with other thermal processes, thermal transfer uses heat to help along the printing process. As the name implies, the heat is used to transfer ink to the output medium. Thermal transfer systems use inks coated on a thin plastic substrate called a *carrier.* A special *binder* makes the ink adhere to the substrate. The heat of a thermal printhead melts the binder and releases the ink from the substrate. Pressed against paper, the ink adheres, forming an image on the paper. Because the binder is often a wax, this kind of printing is sometimes called *thermal wax.*

Compared to plain thermal printing, thermal transfer is more independent of the output medium, which works well for both paper and acetate media. For best results, however, it requires extremely smooth coated paper to ensure uniform adhesion of the ink.

Thermal transfer printing sees application in two areas that use very different implementations of the technology. A few portable printers use a thermal transfer design in what otherwise looks like a conventional line printer mechanism with a printhead that moves back and forth. The primary application of the technology is in high-quality color page printers.

In portable printing, thermal transfer technology has several advantages. The printhead itself has no moving parts, making it very rugged and reliable. The printhead makes no noise and can be designed for resolutions of 300 dots per inch and higher. Moreover, the small thermal printhead requires little energy so the technology lends itself to battery operation.

The few implementations of the thermal transfer design to portable printers have suffered from their miniaturization, however. The primary defect is limited carrier capacity. In these machines, the ink sheet takes the form of a conventional typewriter ribbon. Thermal transfer technology forces the use of a single-strike design: Each character space on the ribbon can be used only once. Printing a single character totally removes the ink from an area that may be as large as the character, preventing the reuse of that spot on the ribbon. Unfortunately, the compact design of portable printers precludes the use of long ribbons. The net result is that current implementations of thermal transfer technology in portable printers can output very few sheets per ribbon cartridge. As a result, you may have to tote a large number of cartridges with you. Worse, you have to pay for them. And with one cartridge producing as few as two or three sheets, the cost of consumables can be much larger than the printer itself.

Color thermal transfer page printers produce the richest, purest, most even and saturated hues of nearly any color printing technology. Designers can make their resolutions arbitrarily high because the thermal printhead elements, which have no moving parts, can be made almost arbitrarily small. Most modern thermal transfer printers claim resolutions of at least 300 dots per inch. Many extend their resolution to 600 dots per inch, although not by improving the printhead. Instead they alter the speed of paper travel to squeeze more dots down the length of the paper while maintaining the same resolution across the sheet. In other words, these machines achieve a resolution of 300 dots per inch horizontally and 600 dots per inch vertically.

Compared to other technologies, however, today's commercial thermal-transfer printers are slow and wasteful. They are slow because the thermal printing elements must have a chance to cool off before advancing the 1/300th of an inch to the next line on the paper. Also, they are wasteful because they use wide ink transfer sheets, pure colors supported in a wax-based medium clinging to a plastic film base–sort of like a mylar typewriter ribbon with a gland condition. Each of the primary colors to be printed on each page requires a swath of inked transfer sheet as large as the sheet of paper to be printed–that is, nearly four feet of transfer sheet for one page. Consequently, printing a full-color page can be expensive, typically measured in dollars rather than cents per page.

Because thermal-wax printers are not a mass market item and each manufacturer uses its own designs for both mechanism and supplies, you usually are restricted to one source for ink sheets–the printer manufacturer. While that helps ensure quality (printer makers pride themselves on the color and saturation of their inks), it also keeps prices higher than they might be in a more directly competitive environment.

For color work, some thermal-wax printers give you the choice of three- or four-pass transfer sheets and printing. A three-pass transfer sheet holds the three primary colors of ink–red, yellow, and blue–while a four-color sheet adds black. Although black can be made by overlaying the three primary colors, a separate black ink gives richer, deeper tones. It also imposes a higher cost and extends printing time by one-third.

From these three primary colors, thermal-wax printers claim to be able to make anywhere from seven to nearly 17 million colors. That prestidigitation requires a mixture of transparent inks, dithering, and ingenuity. Because the inks used by thermal wax printers are transparent, they can be laid one atop another to create simple secondary colors; they do not, however, actually mix.

Expanding the thermal-wax palette further requires pointillistic mixing, that is laying different color dots next to each other and relying on them to visually blend together in a distant blur. Instead of each dot of ink constituting a picture element, a group of several dots effectively forms a *super-pixel* of an intermediate color. A super-pixel is a group of dots on paper that functions as a single image pixel.

The penalty for this wider palette is a loss of resolution. For example, a super-pixel measuring 5x5 dots would trim the resolution of a thermal-wax printer to 60 dots per inch. Image quality looks like a color halftone–a magazine reproduction–rather than a real photograph. Although the quality is not perfect, it is good enough for proofs of what is going to a film recorder or the service bureau to be made into color separations.

A variation of the thermal wax design combines the sharpness available from the technology with a versatility and cost more in-line with ordinary dot-matrix printers. Instead of using a page-wide printhead and equally wide transfer sheets, some thermal wax machines use a line-high printhead and a thin transfer sheet that resembles a mylar typewriter ribbon. These machines print one sharp line of text or graphics at a time, usually in one color–black. They are quiet as ink-jets but produce sharper, darker images.

Dye-Diffusion

For true photo quality output from a printer, today's stellar technology is the thermal dye-diffusion process, sometimes called thermal *dye sublimation*. Using a mechanism similar to that of the thermal-wax process, dye-diffusion printers are designed to use penetrating dyes rather than inks. Instead of a dot merely being present or absent, as in the case of a thermal-wax printer, diffusion allows the depth of the color of each dot to vary. The diffusion of the dyes can be carefully controlled by the printhead. Because each of the three primary colors can have a huge number of intensities (most makers claim 256), the palette of the dye-diffusion printer is essentially unlimited.

What is limited is the size of the printed area in some printers. The output of most dye diffusion printers looks like photographs in size, as well as color. Another limit is cost. The more exotic technology pushes the cost of dye-diffusion pages into the pricing stratosphere. Running a single page through some dye-diffusion printers can cost $5.

The price per page as well as the initial cost of dye-diffusion printers has been sliding closer and closer to the affordable range. The least expensive machine—the Fargo Primera with its continuous-tone upgrade—can be purchased for under $1000. (The low price results from foregoing the PostScript language used by most more expensive machines, a less robust design, and sometimes marginal output quality.)

Laser Printers

The one revolution that has changed the faces of both offices and forests around the world was the photocopier. Trees plummet by the millions to provide fodder for the duplicate, triplicate, megaplicate. Today's non impact, bit-image laser printer owes its life to this technology.

For a laser printer, a print job begins when the printer receives data from your PC. The raster image processor in the printer then interprets the command it receives, composes the pages to be printed, and puts the bit-image data into its memory, from which it can be read during the actual printing operation.

To transfer the image to paper, the printer projects a modulated laser beam onto a rolling drum or belt that's part of what is normally called the drum of the printer. When light strikes the photosensitive material on the drum—called an *optical photo conductor* or OPC—the light creates an electrostatic charge on the drum. As the beam scans across the drum and the drum turns, the system creates an electrostatic replica of the page to be printed.

The printer then dusts the drum with particles of toner, the black ink powder used by the printer. The light-struck areas with an electrostatic charge attract and hold the toner against the drum; the unexposed parts of the drum do not.

The printer presses the paper against the drum. An electrostatic charge attracts the toner to the paper. The paper is next squeezed through a fuser, which heats the toner and presses it permanently to the paper. The completed page rolls out the printer. Meanwhile, as the drum turns, it is wiped clean of excess toner. It is then ready to accept a new image.

At heart, the principle of the laser printer is simple. The optical photo conductors react to light in strange ways. Selenium and some complex organic compounds modify their electrical conductivity. Copiers and laser printers capitalize on this by focusing an optical image on a photo conductive drum that has been given a static electrical charge. The charge drains away from the conductive areas that have been struck by light but persist in the dark areas. A pigment called toner is then spread across the drum, and it sticks to the charged areas. A roller squeezes paper against the drum to transfer the pigment, which is fixed in place by heating or "fusing" it.

The trick to the laser printer is that the laser beam is made, as if by magic, to scan across the drum (magic because most printers use rotating mirrors to make the scan). By turning the drum, it automatically advances to the next line as the scanning is done. The laser beam is modulated, rapidly switched on for light areas, off for dark areas, one minuscule dot at a time to form a bit image. Similar optical printers use LCD-shutter technology, which puts an electronic shutter (or an array of them) between a constant light source (which need not be a laser) and the drum to modulate the beam. LED printers modulate ordinary light-emitting diodes as their optical source.

As exotic as these different technologies sound, these imaging parts of the laser printer are of little concern in buying such a machine. Nearly all laser and laser like printers produce similar results–you need an eye loupe to tell the difference–with today's incarnation of the technology producing resolution of 300 dots per inch. You find that the biggest differences between lasers and related LCD shutter printers are found in their paper-handling and data-handling.

Impact dot-matrix printers use a variety of tricks to improve their often marginal print quality. Often, even bidirectional printers slow down to single-direction operation when quality counts. To increase dot density, they retrace each line two or more times, shifting the paper half the width of a dot vertically, between passes, filling in the space between dots. Unidirectional operation helps ensure accurate placement of each dot in each pass.

With non impact bit-image printers, resolution and addressability usually are the same, although some use techniques to improve apparent resolution without altering the number of dots they put in a given area.

Laser Resolution Issues

The best resolution available in moderate-cost PC printers comes from laser machines. The minimum resolution offered by these machines is 300 dots per inch, and newer machines are pushing the expected standard to 600 dots per inch (some go to 1200 dpi). Several factors control the resolution that slides out of a laser printer.

In most lasers, the resolution level is fixed primarily by the electronics inside the printer. The most important part of the control circuitry is the Raster Image Processor, also known as the RIP. The job of the RIP is to translate the string of characters or other printing commands into the bit-image that the printer transfers to paper. In effect, the RIP works like a videoboard, interpreting drawing commands (a single letter in a print stream is actually a drawing command to print that letter), computing the position of each dot on the page, and pushing the appropriate value into the printer's memory. The memory of the printer is arranged in a raster just like the raster of a videoscreen, and one memory cell–a single bit in the typical black-and-white laser printer–corresponds to each dot position on paper.

Most dot-matrix printers accept dot-addressable graphics on the fly. That is, the printer obediently rattles data bytes to paper as soon as the bytes are received or, at most, after a full line has been accepted. They operate one line at a time, as line printers.

Lasers cannot work so quickly. They work a page at a time (earning them the epithet page printers), digesting an entire sheet of graphics before committing a dot to paper. The laser mechanism is tuned to run at exactly one speed, and it must receive data at the proper rate to properly form its image. In addition, many lasers recognize higher level graphics commands to draw lines and figures across the entire on-paper image area. To properly form these images, the laser needs to get the big picture of its work.

For these and other reasons, lasers require prodigious amounts of memory to buffer full-page, bit-mapped images in their highest resolution modes. The size of the memory in the laser printer, consequently, limits the resolution of graphics that can be printed. Enough memory must be present to store a whole page at the resolution level to be printed. If not enough memory is available, only a portion of a page can be imaged or the full page must be imaged at a lower resolution. An 8x10.5-inch image (about a full page on an 8.5x11-inch sheet) at 300 dpi requires 945,000 bytes–essentially one megabyte of printer memory. The 512K that is packed in some printers as standard equipment allows only 150 dpi across a full 8.5x11-inch sheet. Even more memory is needed if you want to use the printer's memory for functions other than storing a raster—for instance, holding downloadable fonts.

NOTE

Most lasers operate in a character-mapped mode when rendering alphanumerics, so memory usage is not as great. The printer can store a full-page image in ASCII or a similar code, one byte per letter, and can generate the dots of each character as the page is scanned through the printer.

The RIP itself may by design limit a laser printer to a given resolution. In many lasers, however, the RIP can be replaced by an add-in processor using the video input of the printer. The video input earns its name because its signal is applied directly to the light source in the laser in raster scanned form (like a television image), bypassing most of the printer's electronics. The add-in processor can modulate the laser at higher rates to create higher resolutions.

Hewlett-Packard's LaserJet III series of printers introduced another way to improve sharpness that the company called Resolution Enhancement Technology. This technique works by altering the size of toner dots at the edges of characters and diagonal lines to reduce the jagged steps inherent in any matrix bit-image printing technique. With Resolution Enhancement, the actual on-paper resolution remains at 300 dots per inch, but the optimized dot size makes the printing appear sharper.

Moving from 300 dots per inch to 600 dots per inch and 1200 dots per inch means more than changing the RIP and adding memory, however. The higher resolutions also demand improved toner formulations because, at high resolutions, the size of toner particles limits sharpness much as the size of printwires limits impact dot-matrix resolution. With higher resolution laser printers, it becomes increasingly important to get the right toner, particularly if you have toner cartridges refilled. The wrong toner limits resolution just as a fuzzy ribbon limits the quality of impact printer output.

Laser Color Issues

In the mainstream printer market, lasers still give you the same choice of color that Henry Ford offered with his Model T—any color you want as long as it is black. Most laser printers have a single-imaging system able to handle only a single color of toner, so they can print only a single hue on your paper. Although you can print different colors by loading toners of strange and wonderful hues, you still get one color per pass.

Exactly what constitutes a pass varies among manufacturers. Most color laser printers use three or four distinct passes of each sheet of paper. The paper rolls around the drum and makes four complete turns. Each color gets images separately on the drum, and then separately transfers them to the sheet. The printer wipes the drum clean between passes. Hewlett-Packard modifies this printing method into something it calls "one-pass" printing. In the HP color laser process, each color again gets separately scanned on the drum, and toner is dusted on the drum separately for each color. Figure 4.1 shows the layout of this design. Note, however, that the four colors are built up on the drum in sequence without transfer to the paper. After the last color–black–is coated on the drum, the printer runs the paper through and transfers the toner to it. The paper thus makes a single pass through the printer.

With scanners and the like, single-pass technology has the advantage of speed. With the HP one-pass color process, no real speed advantage occurs. The photo conductor drum spins around the same number of times, but during three out of four of the spins it doesn't dance with the paper. The speed at which the drum turns and the number of turns it makes determines engine speed, so the one-pass process doesn't make a significant performance increase.

On the other hand, HP's one-pass technology does help registration. With conventional color laser systems, the alignment of the paper must be critically maintained during all four passes for all the colors to properly line up. Paper alignment is not a problem with the HP one-pass system. Only the drum needs to maintain its alignment, which is easy to do because it is part of the mechanism rather than an interloper from the outside world.

Color-capable lasers are slowly but steadily invading the marketplace. As with any new technology, these initial entries are at the high end. For example, the first three major models were the HP Color LaserJet, QMS magicolor, and Xerox 4900 Color Laser Printer, priced at $7,295, $9,999, and $8,495 respectively. Only the HP deigns to advance beyond the 300-dpi resolution of the first generation of monochome lasers. QMS goes to 600 dpi with a $1,299 memory upgrade, and with a $949 RAM upgrade the Xerox machine will print at 1200x300 dpi.

Switching to color puts new demands on the laser printers. All existing models run each sheet through individual passes for each color. Consequently, color printing speed is a fraction of monochrome speed, typically one-quarter or less. For example, the Xerox 4900 is rated at 12 ppm in monochrome but only 3 ppm in color.

As the memory upgrades required for high-resolution color indicate, RAM needs increase with color content. After all, you need to store image data for each color you print. Without using memory conservation technology, you need up to four times the memory for color as you need for monochrome printing.

Color lasers are faster than other color page printers, such as those using thermal-wax transfer technology. They are also often quieter. Because they use toner only for the actual printed image instead of a full page for each sheet, they are more economical than transfer printers when coverage is low. At 5% coverage, about what you'd use for normal text or line graphics, you can expect a page to cost a quarter or less (only about a dime with the HP).

Photo Typesetters

The highest quality available in the printed word comes from the classic phototypesetter. They generate their output on special paper, at heart the same stuff that photographs get printed on. Because there's no toner, no ribbons, and no ink to spread, the photographic paper can form an image as sharp as the best black-and-white photographs. Its grain is virtually invisible.

The first phototypesetters operated much like non impact band printers. They used a long strip of photographic negative bearing all the characters in a given typeface. By moving the appropriate character between a light source and the photographic paper, then briefly flashing the light, the typesetter would expose the paper. After a long sequence of these exposures–one for each character on the page–the machine would automatically develop the paper and slide it out, ready to be cut and pasted into a master for a printing plate. Using the miracle of optics, the phototypesetter could generate a range of type sizes from a single strip of negative by varying the magnification–or actually, reduction. The optical phototypesetter started out with large character images on the negatives and reduced them to the appropriate size. This reduction shrinks flaws in the negative and helps the typesetter achieve extremely high quality, at least when everything went right.

Digital technology has overtaken the typesetter. Instead of photographic negatives, today the typesetter works more like a laser printer, the best dot-matrix printers that technology can conceive. Although these machines still rely on photographic technology to eliminate the graininess of toners and inks, they often write directly to printing plates instead of making intermediate masters on paper. The resolution of a modern typesetter starts at 2500 dots per inch.

Portable Printers

No fundamental technological difference separates portable printers from desktop models. Portable printers use many of the same methods of making characters and graphics as their more stationary kin. The fundamental difference between portables and desktops is construction.

More than anything else, shape plays the prime roll in determining whether a given printer is portable. Modern printers are surprisingly lightweight, light enough that you might consider many models portable were you able to pack them readily. Most, however, are pumped up with air to become bulky rather than massive. Part of the reason for this printer inflation is image–a bigger printer looks like more for your money. Moreover, having more room to work makes the designer's chores easier. Increased air volume also makes the mechanism easier to cool.

Truly portable printers are more–and less–than desktop machines with the air pumped out. Once the manufacturer goes to the effort of reducing size, it has made a commitment to portability. And new concerns arise; in particular, power. Reducing power demand removes several technologies from contention. Lasers at idle draw more than most notebook PCs and when fusing could drain a battery in seconds. (Most laser engines themselves are too large and bulky for portable consideration.) Even dot-matrix draws more power than most portable printer makers would like.

The dominant technologies in portable printers are ink-jet, direct thermal, and thermal transfer. The leading contenders product quality comparable to last generation's 300-dpi laser printers.

Currently the lightest-weight portable printer is the Pentax PocketJet, which weighs about 1.1 pounds and was priced at $499 at its introduction. It uses direct thermal technology, which requires special paper. Although not outrageously expensive (about eight cents per sheet), it does have the greasy sheen of most thermal papers. Suited for drafts and printing out prepared speeches for delivery, you probably wouldn't want to use the output for general correspondence. Quality is good enough, at 300 dpi, that you could photocopy it for public consumption.

The next-lightest portable printer (at 1.5 lb with battery) is the Citizen PN60, a thermal transfer machine capable of color output. You select color or monochrome operation by loading the appropriate transfer ribbon into the machine. With 360-dpi resolution, output quality is good. But the cost per page can be high and ribbon life short for full-page graphics making the machine, initially priced at $399, expensive to use in image-intensive applications.

CHAPTER FIVE

Graphics Technologies

We live in the space-time of images. Words are no longer enough to make a point or an impression. Your printer must be as adept at making graphics as he is at making text, a consummate challenge for output technologies. Today's PC printers combine several images technologies to put pictures on paper.

Our four-dimensional universe no longer is content with mere one-dimensional media. Everything seems to have developed a visual, even graphic, component. Even ordinary music has given way to the music video.

Your documents can survive in the sea of competing interests if they're stuck with row upon row of black-and-white numbers (and we hope never red on the balance sheet) or long grey paragraphs of text. With a couple of keystrokes or a quick tickle of your mouse, you can import a chart, a chunk of clip art, or a photograph of Noah's ark into your most blasé document. You add the interest and the impact. And you could give your printer a case of indigestion akin to your swallowing a swordfish whole. It might explode from data overload–too many bytes and no knowledge of what to do with them.

Once upon a time, images were a source of amazement in the computer room. One or another operator with too much idle time coerced the laboring line printer to print out a graphic using text characters to represent dots in the picture: big dense capital "M"s for dark spots, tiny periods of the lightest of greys. With enough distance and imagination, you could see Einstein's face staring out of the textual wilderness.

Printers have come a long way since then, out of the computer room and closet, into your office, onto your desk, or even the kitchen counter. Along with them have come a number of new technologies for rendering images with precision approaching the photographic. Today's PC printer only starts with line drawings of charts and graphs. Most modern machines can print photos with higher quality than most newspapers. The best not only rival the drugstore photo lab but even send serious shivers into the Great Yellow Father of chemical photography, so that even Eastman Kodak Company got dragged into the computer age of electronic imaging.

The image-making abilities of modern printers run a wide gamut, from zero to full-color photo realism. The basic technologies involved are few, however. The heart of printer image-making is halftone technology, developed a century ago for rendering photos in newspapers. Printing color adds more hues to the halftone, enough to get the printer into a real dither. Along the way, your PC may have to calculate the colors to render, translating from color space to color space to match what you get on paper to what you see on your monitor screen.

Monochrome Graphics

Ever since the advent of mechanical printing, producing realistic images has been problematic. The principal difficulty is that ink is a single color or tone–generally black–while the rest of the world covers the full range of color. Even when reduced to monochrome, the world has a limitless supply of shades of grey while the printer's ink remains unremorseful black.

Try to print a real-world image with continuous tones with a printer that's locked in the Manichean world where everything is black or white, and the results are far from realistic. All shades of grey disappear, and what are left are sharp contrasts.

Continuous-tone photographs directly rendered into mere black-and-white become blotchy, vast areas one or the other color. Sometimes the effect can resemble the original, but more often the result is incomprehensible.

For hundreds of years, the only alternative were line drawings with cross-hatching to represent shading. Although there's nothing reprehensible about this technique–Albrecht Durer and Rembrandt (among a multitude of others) raised engraving and etching to art form status–the result is stylized rather than realistic. Worse, making the conversion required the skilled handiwork of an artist. Each line had to be engraved or etched separately. Getting the best-looking image was a matter of line style and placement, matters that were completely up to the artist.

Artistry is wonderful and–like artists themselves–an anathema to business people. The quality of the renderings varies with the artist employed and the effort devoted to the process. Moreover, the vagaries of employing human beings for a task adds even more unpredictability to the business of printing. Consequently, business people and inventors spent no small effort in mechanizing the process of translating continuous-tone images into printable form. Eventually, they developed a continuous-tone technology that we'll discuss next.

One issue in the conversion of continuous-tone to black-and-white is the grey level at which the transition occurs, which is called the *threshold*. Set it low, and even the darkest greys turn white and the image is little more than a few dots or scratches. Set it high, and the image becomes a mass of black with little relief.

The image-processing abilities of the PC have given us other ways of converting a continuous-tone image into black-and-white. In one refinement, image-processing software can locate edge transitions—contours at which grey levels change—and convert them into lines. This process is called *edge-detection*, and it results in an outline of the basic image shapes. By selectively enhancing the transitions in certain directions, the processing program can give the black-and-white image a two-dimensional, embossed effect. Some software attempts to mechanically create the equivalent of the artist's engraving or even woodcuts with varying degrees of success (which depends mostly on the original image).

Whatever means you use to transform a continuous-tone image into black-and-white for printing, the process inevitably changes the quality, tone, and subjective look of the image. For example, Figure 5.1 compares an original image with two of the basic conversions. The threshold conversion gives a dark, dramatic effect. Edge detection yields a lighter, more refined look.

Figure 5.1 Greyscale to black-and-white conversions.

Even these mechanistic conversions require judgment, even artistry, to get the best possible image quality. You have your choice of a vast range of thresholds by varying the brightness of the rendering of the original continuous-tone image. Similarly, adjusting the brightness and contrast will alter exactly where the edge transitions fall, and hence the look of the edge-detected conversion. You can even combine these and other conversions to create more artistic effects, all in black-and-white, all readily handled by the simple black-and-white printing process.

GREYSCALE GRAPHICS

The breakthrough in printing continuous-tone images came with the discovery that images could be broken into fine dots with different patterns, shapes, or sizes of dots rendering various grey tones. The result of the process was called a *halftone* as it contained various shades of grey, halftone being an artistic term for the shade between the tones of black and white.

The halftone process works because at a distance, your eye can no longer resolve the individual dots, which blend into grey tones. Various grey levels are possible by filling blank areas with different densities of dots.

In the classic photographic halftone process, an image gets broken into dots by photographing, applying a process called *screening*. This optical screening process illuminates an image with light that has been broken into dots by projecting it through a *screen*. The screen optically produces a pattern of light and dark areas that resembles what you see when looking through an ordinary window screen. Instead of being a fine mesh (like that window screen) the halftone screen is a pattern of dots arranged in a matrix.

The screened light serves to break areas of continuous tone into dots. By adjusting the optics of the system, when the screened image is photographed, the size of the dots corresponds to the brightness of the image. Actually, through the magic of the photographic negative, the relationship is inverse–darker areas make larger dots.

Although you might normally consider dots to be round, nothing about the halftone process dictates a perfectly circular shape for the individual dots. The holes in the screen and thus the dots in the halftone can take any form and render an image made of minuscule squares, stars, diamonds, or even dragons. The shape of the individual dots is called the *grid pattern* of the halftone. Although most optical halftones do, in fact, use circular dots, other halftone techniques favor different shapes for technical or aesthetic reasons. For example, diamond-shaped grid patterns are becoming popular with digital halftones because the digital process naturally produces square pixels that look better when rotated 90° into a diamond shape.

During the printing process, the various sizes of halftone dots provide space for the ink of the printing process to spread and cover a greater percentage of the paper surface to make an area of the image appear darker. The deepness of the grey tone rendered by the dot depends on the area within the screen cell that actually gets covered with ink. The classic halftone process controls this coverage with the various sizes of dots. Larger dots cover more area with ink and consequently look darker. Tiny dots cover less paper, letting more white shine through and making the image look lighter. An exact midtone requires 50% coverage, so a midtone dot would fill half a screen cell with ink.

As should be obvious, the photographic halftone making is an analog process. In theory, a dot could cover any fraction of a screen cell, so it renders any shade of grey within an infinite range. In practice, however, a typical photographic halftone has five to ten grey tones.

The fineness of the screen, the spacing between the holes in the grid, determine the quality of the image, roughly corresponding to resolution. The halftone quality is measured in lines per inch, which measures the distance between the lines of the screen and, hence, the centers of the dots in the resulting halftone image. The number of lines per inch is also called the *frequency* of the halftone. The frequencies of photographic halftones typically fall into the range from 50 to 200 lines per inch.

This range is constrained at the high end by the reproduction process and materials. Vagaries of the printing process such as the tendency of ink to flow across the boundaries between dots (a defect called blocking up the printing plate because halftones screened too finely print as solid blocks of ink instead of discrete dots), ink bleed in absorbent paper, even the coarseness of the paper limits the ultimate resolution. At lower frequencies, the screen becomes so coarse that the individual dots no longer hang together, the halftone effect disappears, and the image may be unintelligible at reasonable viewing distances.

Over the years, the screening process has become an art form. Early on, halftone makers discovered that they could improve the look of the final image by rotating the screen so that the grid did not run perfectly horizontally and vertically with the image borders. The most common screen angle used now in photographic halftone making is 45°. This rotation doesn't affect the individual dots–after all, they are usually circles which look the same no matter how you rotate them–but changes their overall pattern. Figure 5.2 shows the effect of a 45° screen rotation. Look at almost any published halftone, and you'll see the dots in rows running in this diagonal pattern.

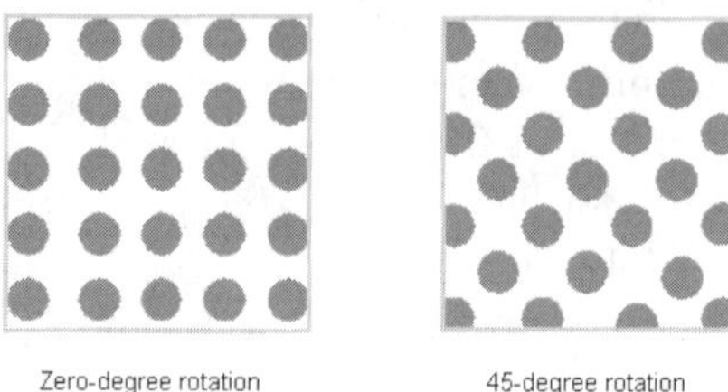

Figure 5.2 Comparison of 0 and 45 degree screen rotations.

To display images on a television or computer monitor, the halftone process is unnecessary. These display processes are much like photography. Although printers have only one color of ink available, monitors and televisions have a wide range of grey (and color) tones. Although the video processes do fragment the image much as does a halftone, each fragment fills its respective cell with a uniform tone. One of the challenges faced by your printer is the translation of this variety of tones into a form that your printer can render.

To give a semblance of continuous tones to the printed image, the printer driver makes a digital halftone. The resulting halftones are quite similar to the optical variety–the image is broken into dots–but the technique of their production is quite different. The optical halftone process breaks the image into cells, evaluates the brightness of each cell, and scales a dot to the brightness in one step (see Figure 5.3). The digital process works with images that are already broken into cells. The next step is to evaluate the tone of the cell and finally generate a printable pattern that will maintain the brightness relationship between the tone and all the other tones in the image.

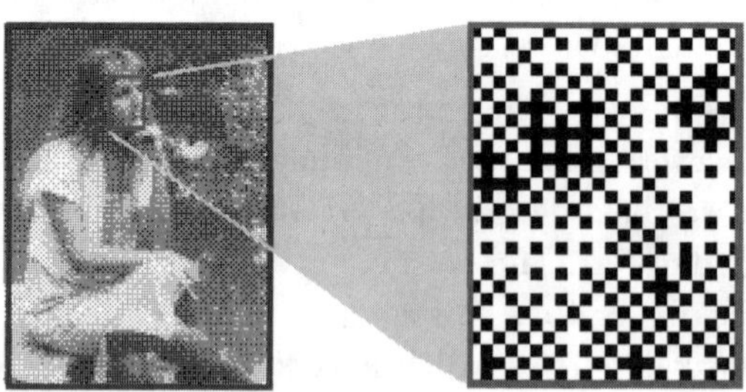

Figure 5.3 Digital halftones break an image into a pattern of square dots.

The digital halftone process differs in another way. PC printers suffer the same limitation as these other mechanical reproduction processes. The ink is one color and cannot adequately convey intermediate tones. Worse, unlike the halftone screening process that produces dots of different sizes and shapes, a computer printer generally produces a single dot size (with the exception of those using technologies akin to Hewlett Packard's Resolution Enhancement Technology and similar processes). Fortunately, printer designers discovered that they could simulate the halftone effect using patterns of identical individual dots. Thus, where the optical halftone varies the tonality of the image with dots of various sizes, the digital halftone usually relies on *patterns* of dots to convey tonality.

Each image cell of a digital halftone—which may contain any number of individual printed dots—corresponds to one pixel of the original rasterized image. It also corresponds to a dot of a photographic halftone. Consequently, the cell size and not the printer's dot-per-inch capability determines the visual resolution of the image. In other words, a printer gives up some of its resolution (in reality, a lot of its resolution) for the ability to produce a halftone effect.

Image Cells

The digital halftoning process works by subdividing the raster generated by the printer into *image* cellseach of which being a matrix of dots. Unlike optical halftones, however, in digital halftones the dots are actually squares. Figure 5.4 shows the difference between a digital halftone image dot and image cell with a 3x3 dot matrix.

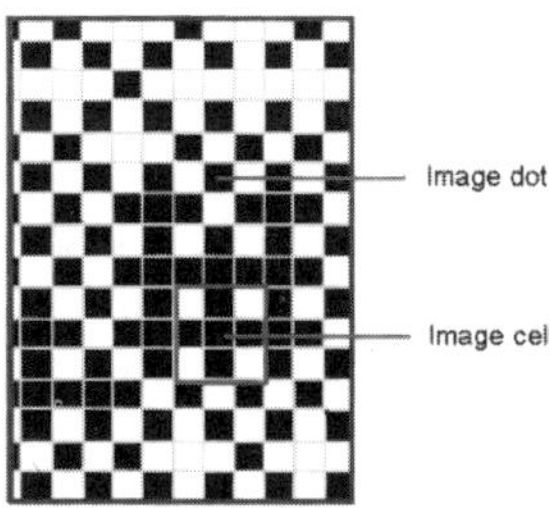

Figure 5.4 Image dots and cells for a 3x3 digital halftone matrix.

To add a greyscale to images, the printer can control the density of paper coverage—and hence the apparent shade of grey of the cell when viewed from a distance—with the number of dots it places into each cell. The more dots in the cell area, the greater the ink coverage, and the darker the grey tone.

The choice of cell size—that is, the number of dots that make up each cell—determines the number of different greys that can be produced, at least theoretically. The more dots, the greater the number of greys. Because each dot in the cell adds to the density, the potential number of greys is directly proportional to the number of dots—plus one for the special case of zero dots (white paper).

Most digital halftoning systems use square cells as well as square dots within them. Consequently, the number of possible greys is the square of the linear dimension of the cell plus one. For example, a 5x5 cell is sufficient to reproduce 26 different grey tones including full white and black (because (5 * 5) +1 = 26). Table 5.1 shows the relationship between the number of greys and the effective resolution of the printing system expressed as screen frequency for several combinations of printer resolution and cell size.

The non integral cell sizes in Table 5.1 result when the halftone screen is rotated, as is customary in the graphic arts industry.

NOTE

Most photographic screens are rotated 45°. Digital systems may alter the amount of rotation to minimize image artifacts.

Because the screen is rotated, the measuring axis does not align with a single row of dots but cuts across several rows.

Table 5.1 Greyscale Range Versus Cell Size at Common Printer Resolution Levels Using Uniform Dot Size

Printer Resolution	Number of Grays	Screen Frequency	Cell Size
300	26	60	5x5
300	33	53	5.7x5.7
300	50	43	7x7
600	26	120	5x5
600	33	106	5.7x5.7

600	50	85	7x7
600	101	60	10x10
600	129	53	11.3x11.3
600	197	43	14x14
1200	50	170	7x7
1200	101	120	10x10
1200	129	106	11.3x11.3
1200	197	86	14x14
1200	226	80	15x15
1200	401	60	20 x 20
2400	226	160	15x15
2400	401	120	20x20
2400	798	85	28.2x28.2

In theory, the larger the cell, the greater the range of tones that can be reproduced. With a large enough cell size, continuous-tone images should be easy to simulate. Unfortunately, every increase in cell size results in a decrease in apparent resolution. For example, with our 5x5 cell, linear resolution is one-fifth of what it would be for black-and-white images. That's a substantial loss. A 300-dpi laser printer would actually produce an image with 60-dpi resolution on paper. Because this more limited on-paper resolution corresponds to the coarseness of a conventional halftone screen, it is usually called *screen frequency*

The one best compromise is a trade-off between grey scale and resolution. Whether you want more grey or higher resolution depends on your applications–the image itself, your printer hardware, the kind of paper you choose, and simply what looks best to you.

Note that our math determines the number of grey tones available from a given size cell; it says nothing about the arrangement of dots within the cell. Certain patterns look better than others. For example, some cell arrangements produce distinct and distracting patterns when arranged together–white globs, black splotches, and herringbone lines. Creating the optimum arrangement is more a matter of art than science. Printer and driver makers (and particularly printer driver makers) choose the best-looking patterns from the available range.

Not all driver writers use the same pattern assortments, so the work of one printer may look better than that of another even if the resolutions or the engines of the two machines are identical.

Hewlett-Packard's latest LaserJets subvert this rule of resolution versus grey scale. According to HP, the LaserJet 4 operating at a resolution level of 600 dots per inch can produce 120 levels of grey at an apparent resolution of 106 lines per inch using a printer driver with Resolution Enhancement technology capabilities. The trick is the same as that which is used to increase the apparent sharpness of individual characters. Resolution enhancement technology varies the size of the individual dots in the halftone patterns. As a result, the halftone cell effectively appears to be twice its real size. Because this enlargement applies in two directions, the modification of dot size quadruples the number of potential pattern combinations, allowing for the increase in apparent resolution.

The increase is apparent rather than real. The actual digital screening of the image is still carried out at the actual resolution level (53 lpi). Consequently, the resolution enhancement approach doesn't add new information to the image. It can also introduce some subtle defects into images, particularly technical illustrations that have precise mathematical patterns rather than the random patterns of naturalistic images. The HP approach can yield a noticeable trellis or horizontal/vertical grid appearance to some patterns instead of the more conventional 45° screen angle. Sometimes an apparent white line separates adjacent rectangles with different fill patterns for contrasting grey levels.

Contrast

In printing, *contrast* describes the difference between the lightest and darkest values, the dynamic range of a display medium. Contrast is usually measured as the ratio of light to dark so that a contrast ratio of 10:1 means that the lightest tones appear ten times brighter than the darkest.

Different display media impose their own limits on contrast ratio. Quite simply, some media can handle a wider dynamic range than others. Moreover, the available contrast of most media depends greatly on viewing conditions. Bright ambient light tends to wash out self-illuminated media such as video monitors while it enhances reflective media such as printing or photographs. Table 5.2 lists the contrast ratios of some common display media under different viewing conditions.

Table 5.2 Contrast Ratios of Common Display Media

Medium	Viewing Conditions	Ratio
Human vision	Bright environment	100:1
Projected motion picture	Darkened theater	80:1
Photographic print	Brightly lit room	80:1
Television or monitor	Darkened room	30:1
Offset printing	Brightly lit room	10:1
LCD display, backlit	Normal office	5:1
Television or monitor	Bright office	5:1

When printing a greyscale image, exactly duplicating the digital original held in memory often leads to disappointing results: The printed image takes on plain grey tones with little contrast. In many cases the range of tones in the original image extends far beyond the limited abilities of a PC printer to reproduce. The brightest whites and the dimmest blacks get clipped, leaving a stark high-contrast image with little tonal separation or detail. Alternatively, when the range of tones is within the replication range of the printer, the on-paper results may turn into a sea of grey, with nearly all the shade reproducing as a uniform murk.

The issue is *tonal mapping*, that is converting the greyscale of the original to take best advantage of the printer's capabilities. In the ideal case, the whitest white in the image will be mapped to match the paper itself with no ink or toner intruding. The blackest black will be represented by an unrelieved expanse of ink at its highest density. The range of grey tones will then be expanded or compressed to fit within the range the printer can reliably produce. With a sufficient range of greys, you won't be able to see individual steps between them: Tones will blend smoothly from light to dark exactly as they do in a good quality photograph. Unfortunately, most printers lack the ability to produce enough greyscale steps to make smooth tonal transitions.

This linear mapping with compression or expansion is usually sufficient to make an adequate image, although the result usually appears to be lacking contrast.

The shortcoming is emphasis: In most images, the importance of one set of tones dominates, containing most of the image information. Other tones have less importance. This linear mapping assigns essentially the same importance to all values.

Required Grey Range

Certainly it is tempting to want as many levels of grey as possible to best reflect the real world in which brightness can take any of an infinity of ranges. Fortunately for the designers of printers and other display media, the limitations of the human eye lessen the need for an infinity of greys. The typical human eye can detect differences in greys when the contrast between them is about 1° under optimal viewing conditions to which the eye has adapted. That is, if you lay two greys next to one another and one differs by less than 1%, then the two will appear to be the same shade. There would be no point to coding or printing these two greys as different values. In fact under optimum conditions, the human eye can handle that 100:1 contrast ratio, which works out to be 463 different shades of grey.

Because actual display media have contrast ratios lower than the range of human vision, the number of greys they need to be able to handle decreases. The range is unimportant in judging between greys; contrast, rather than absolute brightness, is the issue.

For the convenience of programmers and storage systems, grey levels are typically encoded as one byte. This coding allows for a contrast range of about 12.5:1 with smooth grey shading. Although this range is clearly insufficient to record the entire wealth of human visual experience, it is more than broad enough to accommodate the most widely used display system (the television set and computer monitor) in a well-lit environment as well as offset printing and the output of most PC printers.

Note that this kind of coding is both optimal and nonlinear. When you use a linear code for grey levels, accommodating a 100:1 contrast range would require 10,000 grey levels for smooth shading.

The linearity (or lack of it) of the contrast coding of a display media is often termed *gamma*, although the word has separate and distinct technical definitions in different fields. For example, in photography, gamma refers to the ratio between negative density and the logarithm of film exposure. In television, it represents the power relation between video voltage and display intensity.

Halftone printing appears to be a medium with linear contrast. You deal with percentage of ink coverage and you control the number of dots in a given area. Offset printing is not truly linear, however. Because ink tends to smear and papers absorb some inks, thereby spreading them around, halftone dots grow larger when printed on a traditional press. This phenomenon results in a non-linear relationship between what you would expect and the actual visual look of a printed halftone. Akin to gamma, the correct technical term is *dot gain.* It refers to how much light a dot printed in the final image absorbs compared to the dot coverage in the original halftone.

At 50% coverage, normal offset printing results in a dot gain of about 24%. That is, what you expect to be halfway between white and black veers dramatically toward black, producing an actual coverage of 74%. Actual dot gain varies with the ink and paper used in printing, even the speed of the printing press. Glossy or coated paper, for example, produces a lower dot gain because it absorbs less ink.

With PC printers, dot gain varies as well. A high-resolution laser printer may produce little dot gain while ink-jets may have substantial dot gain. This difference in dot gain explains part of the readily apparent difference when printing the same bit-mapped halftone on printers using different technologies (or again, different papers).

If you have a critical application, dot gain can be important. Most people tend to ignore it for most purposes. After all, both video display systems and the human eye are nonlinear. Many printer makers compensate for it in the firmware inside their printers or in their printer drivers, although this compensation is ineffective when your PC sends an image to your printer as a bit map. When printed images seem skewed toward being too dark or too light, adjusting their gamma (which can help compensate for dot gain) rather than brightness of the image before making a digital halftone will often have a more pleasing and realistic effect.

Image Key

To make a more pleasing image, the tone range in one range–the one of primary interest–can be expanded at the sacrifice of less important ranges. The more important range is called the *key* of the image.

An image that has its most important elements in the midtones is called a *normal key* image. When bright shades dominate, for example, a bride in her boudoir or polar bear in a snowstorm, the image is termed *high key.* When dark shades dominate–a moonlit rendezvous or the Welsh coal miner at work–the image is called *low key*. Optimal reproduction of a high key image expands the range of bright tones, while letting the darker shades fall off to black. With a low key image, the tonal range of shades and details in the shadows are extended while letting the bright tones disappear into whiteness.

Note that neither your printer nor your printer driver has any idea about the key of the image. Without a knowledge of the subject matter and a good dose of aesthetic appreciation, the printer cannot hope to optimize image reproduction. Consequently, when you want the best image quality on paper, you are stuck manually tuning the image; adjusting contrast is key to the emphasis you want to create. Part of the process can be automatic–matching the tone range of the original image to the range of the printer by expanding or compressing tonal reproduction. But you must determine the image you want–whether bright or dark, joyful or foreboding–and adjust the reproduction of the image appropriately.

Typically you'll want to make your adjustments using an image editor such as Adobe PhotoShop, Corel PhotoPaint, or Micrograf Picture Publisher, and store your enhancements as part of the image.

Dithering

The process using multiple pixels with a limited range of tones to represent a wider tonal range is called *dithering* It is an essential part of the digital halftone technique. The process can be entirely automatic, guided by algorithms, and can take many forms (and produce different results) depending upon the algorithm you choose.

The most popular dithering algorithms fall into four general classes. Listed in order of complexity (and visual quality), these are random, pattern, ordered, and error diffusion dithers. Rather than different technologies, each is built upon the foundation of the simpler schemes.

Random Dither

To make a random dither, you first generate a random number within the range of values represented by the image data. For example, if you have a 24-bit color system, each color is represented by an eight-bit value, so the range of values would be from 0 to 255. Next, compare the random number you have generated to the value of an individual pixel. If the image value is less than the random number, plot the pixel as white. If the image value is equal to or greater than the random number, plot it in color. Repeat this entire process for each pixel, generating a separate random number for each.

Random dither results in images that are plagued by noise, like the snow in a TV picture. If your random numbers are truly random, however, you will see no image artifacts such as moiré patterns.

Pattern Dither

Choosing the patterns to use for a pattern dither system is itself an art. The patterns that produce the worst artifacts are easy to eliminate from consideration. For example, using a predominance of patterns with dots arranged essentially horizontally will result in the appearance of horizontal lines through the image; vertical dot patterns would create vertical lines.

Some studies have shown that patterns for adjacent tones should be made to look similar to eliminate the appearance of edges where you would like a smooth transition. The effect, essentially an optical illusion, is called *contouring*.

In general, the individual dots can be grouped together to produce a cluster. This has the effect of an optical halftone with dots of different sizes. Alternately, the individual dots can be scattered or dispersed through the positions in the cell. Although this scattering of dots does not increase the resolution of the dithered image, it can make the image appear less grainy. It can also be more difficult to reproduce, particularly with fine dots and offset printing. When dots blur together, you lose not only the fine-grain effect but also accuracy in greyscale rendering.

Ordered Dither

The most common digital halftoning technique is the ordered dither. It combines random and patterned dithering. Instead of making a pixel-by-pixel comparison with random numbers, however, the ordered dither makes the comparison to a master cell pattern.

To make an ordered dither, first divide the image into cells. For example, if you plan to use a 5x5 dither, divide your image into groups of pixels measuring 5x5. Then create a master pattern for your image by assigning each bit position in a 5x5 matrix a numeric value corresponding to the number of available grey tones. A 5x5 matrix can produce 26 grey tones (0 through 25), so number the bit positions in the master pattern 0 through 25. Next overlay the master pattern on each cell into which you've divided the image. Compare each bit of the image to the corresponding bit of the master pattern. If the image bit value is less than the pattern value, make the corresponding bit in the dither white; otherwise, make it black.

As with the pattern dither, the appearance of an ordered dither depends on aesthetic judgment. Some master patterns will result in distinct image artifacts—not just horizontal or vertical lines but cross-hatch or x-like patterns within individual cells. Because ordered dithering superimposes a pattern on the image, it can produce obvious moiré patterns when used on screened or already dithered images that already have an intrinsic bit pattern.

Beyer dithering uses the ordered dithered method and patterns shown mathematically to produce the highest frequency visual noise (and thus finest "grain"). Unfortunately, it also tends to produce cross-hatch-like artifacts in the image. Figure 5.5 shows the number of matrix cells for the two smaller Beyer master dither patterns.

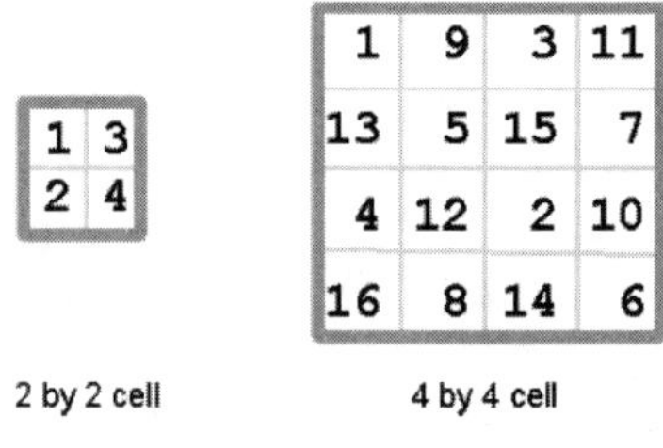

Figure 5.5 Beyer dither master pattern cell values.

The Beyer method of dithering is used by the Windows GDI in creating dither patterns, although it uses a larger 8x8 cell. Beyer dithering is also used by proprietary driver software such as the Advanced pattern mode of some Hewlett-Packard printers.

Error Diffusion Dither

The chief shortcoming of the random dither scheme is that it ignores the error between the random number and bit value. This error information is lost and results in the noise in the resulting images. Error diffusion dither retains as much of that error as possible by spreading it among adjacent picture elements. When viewing the error diffusion dither from a distance, your eye optically blends the error that's recorded in the adjacent image elements back in, making the image appear more natural. The result is a high-quality image with the fine grain of random dither but with much less noise.

Making an error diffusion dither pattern starts out as with random dither. You generate a random number within the range of bit values and compare the image bit to the random number to determine whether the dither bit is white or black. Instead of discarding the result of the comparison, you add a fraction of it to one or more of the nearby image bits, changing their value as you go along.

This error value is spread out in a pattern, and the choice of pattern determines the visual look and quality of the dithered image. In the language of dithering, the patterns for distributing error values among adjacent pixels are called *filters*. For example, the Floyd-Steinberg filter diffuses the dithering error over four adjacent pixels using the values shown in Figure 5.6. In the figure, the red dot is the sample pixel.

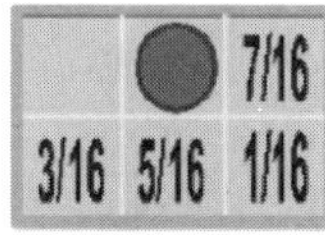

Floyd-Steinberg filter

Figure 5.6 A sample error-diffusion filter.

The Floyd-Steinberg filter is used by the Advanced Scatter dithering mode used by some Hewlett-Packard printer drivers (among others).

As with all dithering patterns, picking the best error diffusion filter is as much art as science. Because every error number you generate results in more math later on, filters that use fewer error values are faster. On the other hand, filters that spread errors over more pixels tend to produce better quality. For example, the Burke filter shown in Figure 5.7 diffuses the error over seven adjacent pixels instead of the four in the Floyd-Steinberg filter. Note, too, that the Burke filter uses relatively simple math, requiring only that you calculate 1/16, 1/8, and 1/4 of the total error for diffusion.

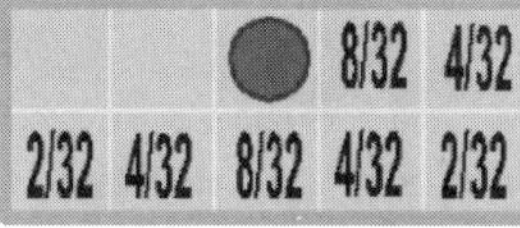

Burke filter

Figure 5.7 The Burke filter distributes the total error over seven pixels.

The Stucki filter extends the Burke filter to an additional row, spreading the error still further while preserving the simplified math. The Stucki filter weightings are shown in Figure 5.8.

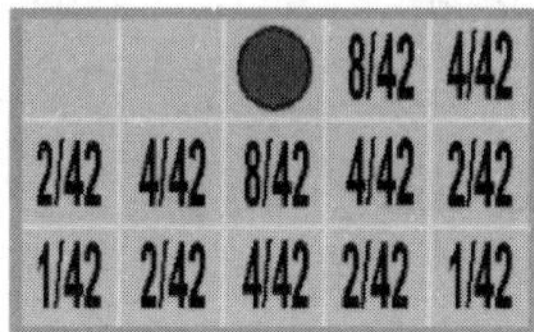

Figure 5.8 The Stucki filter distributes errors over 12 pixels.

One common problem is that large errors swamp adjacent pixels, pushing up their values dramatically, even beyond the range of the system. This unrestrained growth of pixel values can lead to streaks appearing in the final dithered image. Consequently, most error diffusion systems clip pixel values. Although this clipping helps eliminate the streaks, it also adds noise to the image. Another technique to minimize streaking is to spread smaller error values among a wider range of pixels. Of course, these techniques increase the number of necessary calculations and increase the time required for creating the dither.

Note, too, that error diffusion dithering is directional. Because later pixel values are dependent on the previously evaluated pixels, the order in which they are analyzed is important. In general, the rows of pixels are scanned a line at a time, most commonly from left to right, top to bottom. You can often obtain better results (meaning fewer artifacts) by scanning bidirectionally–the first line left-to-right, the next right-to-left.

Dithering is a one-way process that forever changes your image. Practical dithering systems force you to give up resolution to increase the range of colors that you can produce. In other words, once you dither you cannot undither. When editing images and preparing them for printing, dithering should always be the *last* step in the process.

Random-Dot Halftones

These digital halftone techniques attempt to duplicate the effects achieved optically using a conventional screen. Optical screening is only an expedient way of defining halftones; it is hardly the optimum method. The regular size and spacing of dots in the halftone is the easy way of making a halftone, one that's particularly amenable to mechanical screening. When you have adequate microprocessor power, as you do with today's latest chips like the Pentium, you can step beyond traditional fixed halftone cell sizes. Instead, you can mix cells of various sizes, even overlap cells. With some printers, you could even vary the size of individual dots to optimize halftone rendering.

The result of this process is called a *stochastic* or random halftone. Look at one of these closely, and instead of the ordered and repetitive pattern of a conventional halftone, you'll see a random-looking pattern akin to the splatter of paint dots. Because the repetitive pattern is gone, artifacts disappear and the halftone appears more realistic–even more regular because of its randomness.

In addition, stochastic technology holds the potential to increase the number of available grey levels without decreasing resolution. For example, whereas a 7x7 dot cell can produce 50 grey levels using conventional techniques, 5040 patterns can actually be created from the 49 dots. A stochastic halftone system exploits these patterns to achieve its greater greyscale range. The penalty, of course, is the need for processing power to determine the optimum dot arrangement. Although the stochastic process currently is not exploited by any of the drivers from major printer vendors, the technology may see wider application in the future.

Supercell Screening

Several new digital halftoning processes, including Accurate Screens (developed by Adobe Systems), Balanced Screens (developed by Linotype-Hell), and HQS Screens (developed by Agfa-Compugraphic) use a technique that approaches the random-dot principle. Rather than evaluating the image at each pixel, these processes sample groups of 300 to 3000 halftone cells called the *supercell.* The placement of each dot can then be optimized across cell boundaries to yield a smoother halftone that's free from visual artifacts such as moiré patterns.

Accurate Screens is hardware based and designed to be device independent so that it can be used in a variety of platforms, accessed through the PostScript language. All high-resolution PostScript Level 2 devices–which means typesetting equipment but not most PC printers–include Accurate Screens technology. Both HQS and Balanced Screens are software-based products that are designed to work with a small number of typesetters. Currently, no PC printers use them.

Rendering Greys

Most bit-image printers have no grey rendering abilities of their own. Instead they rely on your PC and its printer driver software to render greys as bit images by dithering. These the driver then sends these bit maps to your printer dot-by-dot. The printer places each dot in its proper position in the image raster, and prints them out.

There are two important exceptions to the rule that greyscale rendering is always done in your PC. PCL printers can generate a limited number of greys that they can use to fill shapes. PostScript printers handle the actually grey rendering inside the printer.

PCL

The first version of Hewlett-Packard's Printer Control Language to give printers grey-rendering abilities was PCL4, which was introduced with the LaserJet II printer. Under PCL4, printers can render seven grey values (for a total of nine brightness levels when you add in pure white and black), which they can use to fill arbitrary shapes such as rectangles. The printer renders these greys using a 53-lpi screen frequency regardless of whether the printer is operating at 300 or 600 dpi. Although PCL4 allows you to encode any brightness level as a grey percentage, the printer will substitute one of the seven brightness values that it can produce. Table 5.3 summarizes the translation.

Table 5.3 Translation of Grey Percentages to Discrete Grey Values in PCL

Grey Percentage	Grey Level
0	White
1–2	Lightest grey
3–10	Light grey
11–20	Medium-light grey
21–35	Medium grey
36–55	Medium-dark grey
56–80	Dark grey
81–99	Darkest grey
100	Black

Printers that use PCL5 also have access to the HP Graphics Language/2 plotter language. These commands extend the grey rendering abilities of printers to polygons and wedges, although still limited to only seven grey levels. The incorporated HPGL/2 command also allows filling polygons with cross-hatchings. Starting with the LaserJet IIIP printer, Hewlett-Packard extended PCL5 to allow user-defined fill patterns.

NOTE

Except for these limited applications, PCL printers depend on your PC to handle the rendering of grey tones, rasterizing the greys in your printer driver.

PostScript

PostScripts printers render halftone shades internally instead of accepting dot patterns from the printer driver. All PostScript language interpreters include a command to fill an arbitrary shape such as a bar on a chart, a polygon in a drawing, or a large text character with grey. The printer driver sends a **fill** command specifying the grey level, and the PostScript interpreter then generates the appropriate pattern of dots and places them within the confines of the shape. This design allows PostScript drivers to send out exactly the same instructions regardless of your printer's resolution.

Most PostScript printers that operate at a resolution level of 300 dpi generate their greyscales using a screen frequency of 53 lines per inch. This screen can simulate 33 levels of grey. Should your PostScript driver send out instructions specifying more than 33 grey shades, the interpreter in the printer renders a shade as close as possible to the desired one using its limited repertory.

At higher printer resolutions, the screen frequency for producing grey values varies with manufacturer and printer model. For example, the 600-dpi Hewlett-Packard LaserJet 4M uses a screen frequency of 85 lpi, which can render 50 distinct grey levels. Lexmark keeps the 53-lpi screen frequency in its-600 dpi printers, enabling its machines to produce 129 grey values.

The PostScript language includes commands for altering screen frequencies and screen angles so that you can force a printer to use other values that are within its capabilities. Some drivers give you direct control over these values. Taking such intimate control forces the PostScript driver to produce instructions for a specific resolution level to match your printer. If you want to maintain the hardware independence of the driver output, you must not tamper with these values and instead rely on the driver and printer defaults.

The PostScript approach to greyscale rendering has two practical implications. It conserves the processing power of your PC by moving the rasterization of greys to the printer and its microprocessor. Its resolution and hardware independence helps ensure that every application gets the best possible quality, including the most faithful greyscale rendering.

Color Printing

Adding color is never easy, as any botched paint job will readily attest. With electronic technologies, however, the problems are different from those of the workaday world of painters. One issue is standards. The standards of the painting profession are such that you consider yourself lucky if the pigment doesn't peel from your house before your check clears and that the petunias are only a trifle flattened during the process. In the world of electronics, standards are further reaching and much more persnickety. They require that diverse group of engineers, each with his or her own agenda, to agree on a common language even though the people themselves might not speak in the same tongue.

Moreover, with printing, you expect a greater degree of precision than house painting. When it comes to painting your house blue, you try to match a chip to your dreams and communicate your color choice in a language rife with terms as imprecise as Navy, cobalt, powder, cerulean, robin's egg, and true. Satisfaction often means that the result isn't too ghastly. With computer printing, however, you want an exact match–the color that ends up on paper must be the same as what you saw on the screen–and cornflower blue doesn't cut it as a description.

The issue is more than names. Getting the right colors–or even good-looking colors–with a PC printer requires more than familiarity with the labels on your crayons. You need to know the correct ways of describing and creating colors. You need to know how your printer simulates colors that it truly cannot print by optical prestidigitation with the colors it can. In other words, to master color printing, you need to understand color from the first quivering of a photon to the evaporation of the last molecule of solvent from your printer's ink.

The place to begin any discussion of color printing is with color itself. Color, at least color as it is dealt with by your printer, isn't the same stuff they taught (or tried to teach) you in elementary school art class. In other words, you have to know a bit about physics to master aesthetics–and have a bit of psychology thrown in.

Background

The perception of color is a personal, even phenomenological, experience. Because it is impossible for anyone to truly see through another's eyes and see exactly what and how someone else sees, we can never be sure that the way you see red is exactly the same as the way anyone else sees it. Although such arguments give philosophers and psychologists something to argue about at their conventions and may explain why some people see beauty in dressing themselves in several assorted varieties of plaid, they have little relevance to color theory.

Color is how we perceive light–or rather the individual *photons* that make up light. A photon is the basic unit of light, akin to the atoms that lumped together make matter and all material things. Each photon has a specific energy, which correlates to its *wavelength*, which, in turn, corresponds to its frequency. You might not want to be concerned with such esoteric things as the energies of photons, but, oddly enough, your eye is finely tuned at distinguishing photon energies. You perceive each photon as a color that's determined by its energy (and thus frequency and wavelength). The human eye is precise enough to distinguish millions of different colors–quite a sensory feat considering your tongue is sensitive to only four tastes. The wavelengths of visible light stretch between about 7000 angstroms and 4000 angstroms [an angstrom being one-tenth a nanometer or one ten-millionth of a millimeter]. Wavelengths longer than 7000 angstroms are invisible and called infrared. Those less than 4000 angstroms are invisible and called ultraviolet. Figure 5.9 shows the relationship between color and wavelength of visible light. That range corresponds to frequencies from about 428 to 750 terahertz.

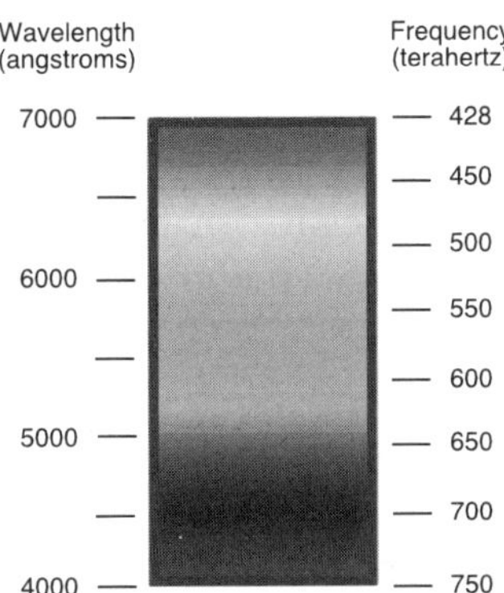

Figure 5.9 Wavelengths and frequencies of the color spectrum.

Color vision depends on the cone cells in the retina in your eye. Most eyes have three types of cones, each of which has a peak sensitivity to a particular wavelength of light. Your vision system measures the relative intensity of each of the three different cone sensors to determine a specific wavelength and color. (The human eye also has another kind of light receptor, the rod cells, which are insensitive to color but acutely sensitive to photons. They provide night vision, the ability to see in dim light, albeit without color.)

This trio of color light sensors is important to specifying, duplicating, and recording colors. Because the three visual sensors measure separate and distinct phenomena, representing a color requires three values. These may correspond directly to what is sensed by each type of cone cell. For storage, transmission, or editing these values can be transformed into more convenient values (which ultimately can be transformed back into the original).

No matter how we each see individual colors, certain aspects of color theory are universal. Basic to such concepts is the idea that any color can be mixed from a very limited set of *primary colors*. The explanation of this principal arises from the theory of color vision which states that the perception of individual hues stems from the differing levels of excitation of three types of cone cells in the retina of your eyes.

You probably learned about primary colors in elementary school. You were told that from the three primary colors–blue, red, and yellow–you could make any color. You diligently drew a color wheel to illustrate this essential fact. And when you were given three crayons of the appropriate colors, you could never duplicate the alleged color effects no matter how hard you tried or whatever the teacher said. You had to take the explanation of color primaries on faith. Sorry, you still do, but now we can complicate matters be adding a new layer of confusion. Rather than a single set of color primaries, there are two. The three you were taught in elementary school are known as the *subtractive primary colors*. You probably remember them as the familiar trio of blue, red, and yellow. These are also known as the primary colors of pigments. They are called *subtractive primaries* because pigment colors arise from the reflection of light.

A pigment reflects only the colors you see from it. The other hues are absorbed by the pigment, subtracted from those that you see. Mix two pigments together, and both subtract from the colors that are reflected. Because they subtract, every color of pigment you add to a mixture takes you closer to black, which ideally reflects no light. Figure 5.10 shows how the subtractive primaries blend.

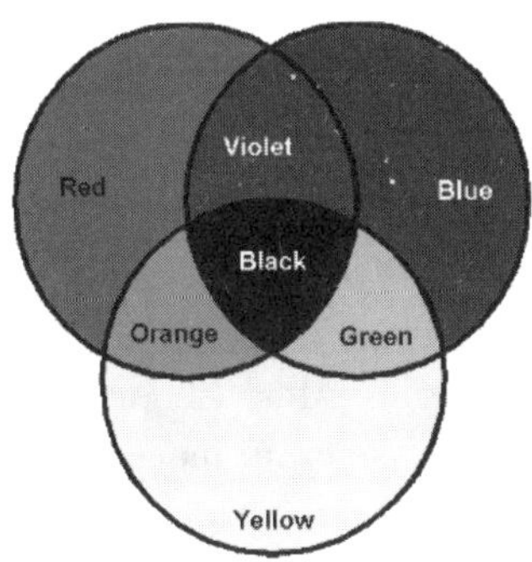

Figure 5.10 The subtractive primary colors and secondaries.

As with much of what you were taught in school, these subtractive primaries are wrong, at least as far as printing is concerned. They work well enough when you're mixing tubs of non toxic paint to smear across paper, easel, and classroom with your fingers, but they don't make the right blends to work with printers for critical color reproduction. Most printers substitute the trio of cyan (a pale greenish blue), magenta (a pale bluish red), and yellow for the familiar colors. This combination of primaries allows for the greatest range of color mixtures.

The other variety of primary colors that you probably weren't taught in school are the *additive primary colors* Also called the primary color of light–specifically the blue, red, and green you may be familiar with from working with color monitors–they work by each adding spans of wavelengths together. Add together all the wavelengths of visible light, and you get the sensory equivalent of white light. Figure 5.11 shows these additive primaries and how they blend together.

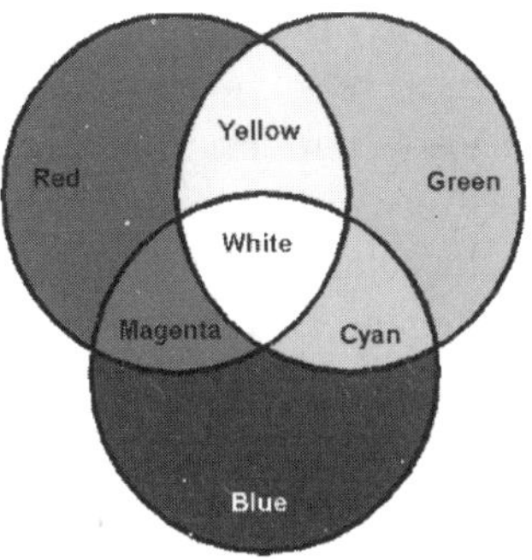

Figure 5.11 The additive primary colors and secondary colors.

More than merely an issue to help you win at Trivial Pursuit or amaze your friends at parties, the distinction between additive and subtractive primaries is one of practical import. The color system used by printers is based on subtractive primaries. That of monitors and video systems is based on additive primaries.

Although the two sets of color primaries appear in texts as if they have been divinely determined, there is nothing sacred about them. You could develop other sets of colors to serve as primaries. Most PC printers and the mechanical print process used in color publishing use cyan, magenta, and yellow as their color primaries and print the familiar subtractive primaries (red, yellow, and blue) as their secondary colors.

If that's not enough confusion, take note that neither of the three-primary systems can adequately describe the colors that you see. These simple three-primary color systems describe only one dimension of color, more technically termed *hue* or more technically, *chromaticity*. Perceived colors have other aspects, which are sometimes called intensity and saturation. Our usage of these words here is loose. All of these descriptive terms have tight, formal definitions used in defining standards—formal definitions that are often ignored even in technical discussions.

In general (rather than technical) discussions, intensity or brightness describes how a color fits in the range from black to white. Pink, for example, is red diluted with white, whereas maroon instead adds black to red. The three-primary color wheel that your third-grade teacher rolled into your classroom is clearly inadequate to describe all the potential hues and tones. You need more dimensions than are available with the color wheel. Color specialists prefer to use a three-dimensional arrangement and description of colors called a *color space*. Unlike the two-dimensional color wheel, which has a seemingly obvious layout (if you allow for the variations of two sets of primary colors), the three dimensions of color space lend themselves to any of many ways of organization, just as an interior decorator has many options in arranging the three-dimensional space of a room. Most of the choices inevitably lead to chaos (often despite the best intentions of the interior decorator or color specialist). No one arrangement can be objectively perfect, but you and the decorator—or all the color specialists in the world—can come into agreement about a workable, even elegant, arrangement.

To give a common language to discussions of color, a group of specialists did get together in 1931 to form an international organization called the *Commission Internationale de L'Eclairage* (which translates to the International Commission on Illumination but is more familiarly called by its abbreviation from the French, CIE). Among its other accomplishments, the CIE developed the world standard for measuring color (a process called *colorimetry* based on a theoretical *Standard*

Observer an idealized human being whose perception of color was based on surveys and scientific studies. In 1967, the CIE released a chart of the color space that today is used worldwide to describe colors. The CIE standards allow any color to be precisely described independently of how it is created or viewed.

A color space has three dimensions (if it didn't, it wouldn't be a space), so three numbers are necessary and sufficient to describe any location within it. These numbers correspond to locations on the X, Y, and Z axes of the color space. The CIE assigns each axis to an aspect of color. In the CIE system, the Y axis corresponds to luminance, a term of art that roughly matches the perceived brightness of a color. The two additional components, X and Z, represent different bands of light using spectral weighting curves the CIE derived from experiments conducted on human vision. The spectral composition of each signal corresponds to the color-matching characteristic of human vision, although the magnitudes of the signals correspond to physical (rather than perceived) radiant energy.

The standard CIE space includes all visible colors. Being three-dimensional, however, the color space is difficult to print in books or charts. Consequently, the widely reproduced CIE chromaticity chart is a two-dimensional reduction of the color space. It is shown in Figure 5.12. The missing dimension is the luminance value, Y. Consequently, the CIE chart shows all visible combinations of what are commonly hue and saturation.

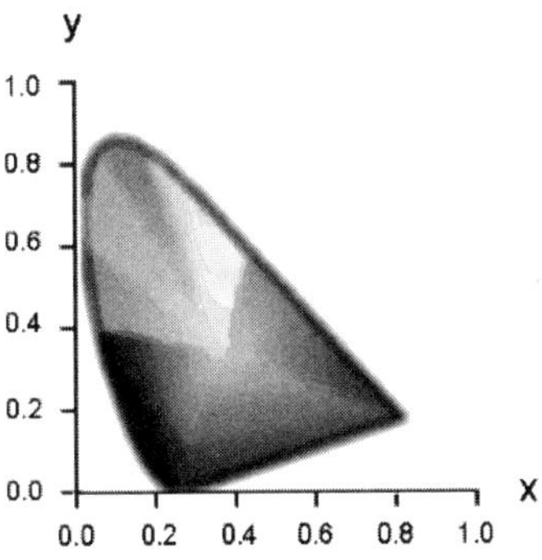

Figure 5.12 The CIE color space.

To develop the values for the x and y axes of the chromaticity chart, the CIE uses mathematical transformations on the X, Y, and Z values, consequently X does not equal x and Y does not equal y. To compute the x and y values for the coordinates on the chromaticity chart, the CIE uses these two formulas:

```
x=X/(X+Y+Z)
y=Y/(X+Y+Z)
```

The flat bottom on the chromaticity chart results from the difficulty in producing the sensation of the color purpose. No single wavelength can make you see purple; you need a mixture of long and short wavelengths to make a true purpose. The flat line on the bottom of the chromaticity chart shows this combination.

As noted before, the CIE representation of color is completely arbitrary. There are any number of ways that you can find three values to completely describe any color. Moreover, you can transform any such value into the CIE system mathematically, although the math quickly becomes complex. The chief importance of CIE chromaticity is that it gives the world a convenient standard on which to reference color descriptions.

Describing Color

Terms defined by the CIE also give us common ground on which to describe color and color systems. Once you venture into the world of color, terms get technical indeed. Words that you banter about in normal conversation become precisely defined terms of art.

A color space has three dimensions and thus three axes, and any color can be precisely located and completely defined by assigning it a position on each axis. Each axis represents a perceptual aspect of color. The most common way of describing these color attributes are as hue, saturation, and brightness.

Hue

To the CIE, the term hue means the part of your visual sensation that makes an area appear similar to one of the perceived colors (red, yellow, green, and blue) or a combination of two of them. It generally corresponds to the quality you see that's associated with a given frequency or wavelength of light. The range of hue represents the familiar color spectrum from red through violet free from the effects of shading. Figure 5.13 shows this range of hues.

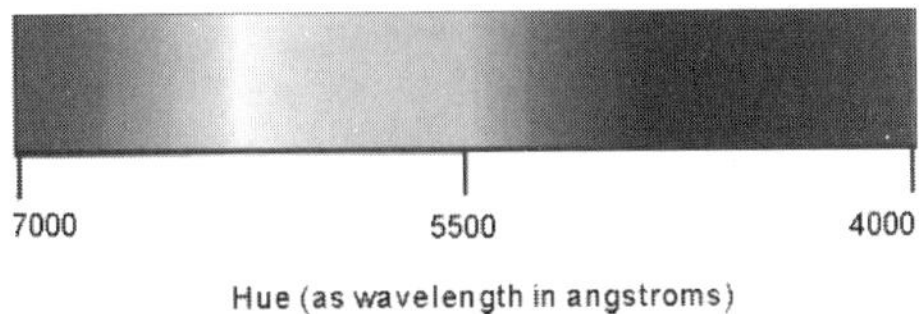

Figure 5.13 Hue (in relationship to wavelength).

Saturation

The strict definition of *saturation* is the relationship between the colorfulness of an area to its brightness. In other words, saturation separates color from grey. A color without saturation would be grey. Add saturation and it becomes a dirty pastel. Push saturation to the extreme and you end up back in the 60s with Peter Max, flower children, and flashbacks. Saturation provides contrast between colors, and you can desaturate colors by mixing in the broad spectrum of white light (which lowers the contrasts) while holding the brightness constant. Figure 5.14 illustrates saturation.

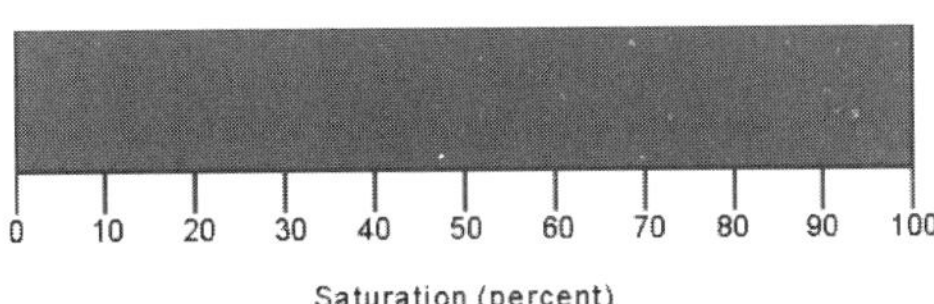

Figure 5.14 The range of color saturation (using red as an example).

Brightness

Generally speaking, brightness is how intense light appears to your eye. An object without any brightness would be black as night at the bottom of the sea. An object with extreme brightness would be the sun. Figure 5.15 shows a representation of brightness.

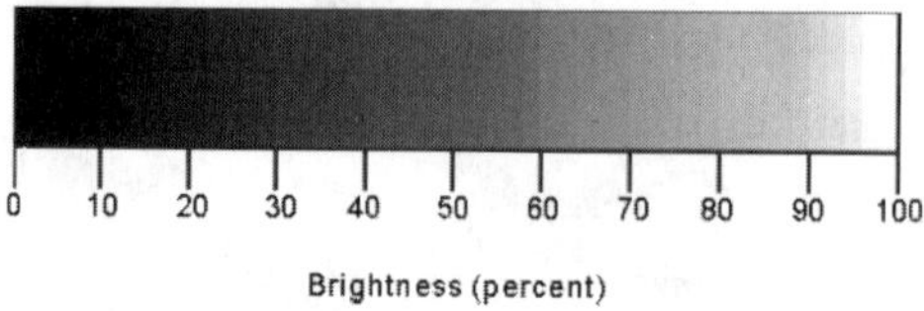

Figure 5.15 A representation of the range of brightness.

But the concept of brightness is much more complex than it first appears. What one person calls brightness may be something altogether different than what another thinks it is. In fact, in addition to brightness the CIE uses three distinct terms to describe what you might think of as the same thing: *luminance*, *intensity*, and *lightness*.

Under the strict CIE definition, brightness is the attribute that makes an object you see seem to emit more or less light. In other words, for the CIE, brightness is an entirely subjective quality. To make it more useful, however, the CIE studies what most people think of as brightness and defined it mathematically using terms derived from a number of physical quantities involved in its perception. The CIE created its more specific definitions of these factors so that these terms could be discussed more scientifically.

Luminance

According to the CIE, *luminance* s the radiant power of the light source described in a way that conforms to how you would perceive the intensity of that power. To make luminance correspond better to human visual perception, the definition of luminance applies a *weighting factor* to the raw power value that adjusts the measurement to reflect human spectral sensitivity. In other words, luminance is a power value measured across a limited range of frequencies with the frequencies to which the human eye is most sensitive more emphasized. For example, because the human eye is most sensitive to green, the power in the green region of the spectrum is the most important factor in a luminance measurement.

Intensity

Remove the weighting factor from the luminance value and what you have left is the measure of the raw power of a light source. The CIE calls this raw power measurement *intensity*. It is measured over a limited range of frequencies (which may correspond to the entire range of visible light, which is itself but a small chunk of the electromagnetic spectrum). Intensity is essentially a linear measurement that is expressed as units of power divided by the area over which it spreads. Common measurement units would be watts per square meter.

Lightness

To most closely approximate the way that people perceive color, the CIE developed the concept of *lightness.* Not only does the human eye perceive certain colors more strongly than others, but its response is also nonlinear. That is, a color that has twice the physical intensity of another will not appear to be twice as bright. An object that perceptually appears half as bright as another actually emits (or reflects) only 18% as much light. Lightness adds a nonlinear factor to the luminance value.

According to the CIE, lightness varies as the modified cube root of luminance. The precise formula of lightness as defined by the CIE is as follows:

$$\text{Lightness} = -16 + (116 * (Y/Yn)^{1/3})$$

In the previous formula, Yn refers to the luminance of the white reference. In most cases this value will be one, reducing the fractional value to Y. (Strictly speaking, this formula is only part of the CIE definition. Near black, the CIE adds a short linear region that can be ignored for practical purposes. This region allows CIE measurements to suppress the noise that appears near black in video systems.) More important than the formula is this underlying concept: The human response to brightness is nonlinear, varying roughly logarithmically in accordance with luminance (which is itself a weighted value).

Although this discussion appears esoteric, it explains one of the great mysteries of printing: why 50% black doesn't appear half as dark as 100% black, the midpoint between black and white. The nonlinear response of the human eye forces the use of a nonlinear greyscale in printing to preserve tonal relationship. To the human eye, the halfway point between black and white is 18% of true black.

Measuring Light and Color

To measure the different aspects of color, engineers use several different instruments. These include the light meter, densiometer, colorimeter, and spectrophotometer.

A *densitometer* measures density, which can be either transmitted or reflected. A transmission densitometer detects how much a semitransparent medium obstructs the passage of light. A reflection densitometer evaluates the amount of light reflecting from a surface. The densitometer is not a color-oriented device, it ignores hue rather than evaluating it. The transmission densitometer is often used in photographic processes to evaluate the exposure of developed negatives. A reflection densitometer is typically used in printing to evaluate the density of ink on a sample.

A photographic *light meter* measures the intensity of light independent of color. Typical light meters apply no weighting to their evaluations except that imposed by the sensitivity of their sensing elements (in modern meters, silicon photocells). The overriding concern is the exposure of film or an electronic imaging device.

The *colorimeter* is the CIE's contribution to color measurement. It is designed to evaluate color in the same way that the human eye sees it. In other words, it quantifies color in the way most people subjectively see it, at least as agreed by the CIE in 1976.

A *spectrophotometer* is the most sophisticated and accurate instrument for evaluating color. It evaluates each wavelength of light that is emitted or reflected from an object. It assigns a value to the power in each wavelength. From this data, a color can be precisely and objectively described. Because it works in the realm of physics rather than perception, it requires skilled operators and is generally reserved for critical applications, such as evaluating ink samples for an exact match to a color standard.

Viewing Conditions

Although the CIE color space gives us a standard means for describing color no matter what its source is or how it is presented, it does not guarantee that a given color will look the same to you wherever it appears. Even a color that is precisely defined as to its absolute frequency can look different to you in different situations. This variation arises not because of any property of colors themselves (the frequencies do not change) but because of how your eye sees color.

Color Temperature

One issue is color temperature. You might consider white light to be a mixture of many colors (some people say *all* colors, but strictly speaking that's not true). All of the various colors present in white light are not equally represented. In fact, the amount of each color is skewed so that less higher frequency (shorter wavelength or bluer) colors are included. The exact mix depends on the source of the color. Physicists base all their descriptions on an ideal they call the *black body*–an object that radiates a continuous spectrum of colors. The mixture of colors radiated by the black body depends on its temperature. The hotter it is, the more higher frequency, shorter wavelength colors it emits. One consequence of this effect are the colors of the iron heated in a blacksmith's forge. As it gets hot, an iron bar in the furnace first begins glowing a dull red. As it gets hotter, the color changes to orange and then yellow and then white. Note that the bar does not radiate a single color but a mxiture of all colors. At first the red frequencies dominate, then orange, and so on. By the time it gets to white, enough red is still mixed in so that you see white instead of a shift through the spectrum green to blue.

Scientists describe the mixture of colors emitted by an ideal radiator as the *color temperature*, which directly corresponds to the temperature of a black body radiating the color mix, approximately equal to the colors you see in the farrier's forge. Color temperature is measured in *Kelvin* and abbreviated K, which is equivalent to the number of Celsius degrees above zero of a black body radiating the particular mix of colors. Sunlight and all incandescent lights–in fact, all light sources based on hot objects emitting radiation–have characteristic color temperatures and, thus, mixtures of colors. A typical incandescent light bulb emits light at a color temperature of 3400 K. Direct sunlight at midday is about 5600 K. Because the incandescent bulb is cooler than the sun (thank goodness), its light appears orange in comparison to sunlight. Early and late in the day, the color temperature of sunlight goes down (the sun doesn't change, but the shorter wavelengths of light are more absorbed by the atmosphere because the sunlight must travel through it at an angle and consequently farther). That's why sunrises and sunsets glow in glorious oranges and reds.

When an image is projected in a darkened room, as in a movie theater or the screen of your monitor in a cave-like office, your eye creates its own white reference based upon that of the projected beam. Consequently, whites appear white and colors assume their familiar relationship. If, however, another light source dominates over the project image, for example, your monitor in a brightly lit office, your eye may adapt to the ambient light, making the screen appear bluish or yellowish.

Human vision has a limited range of adaptation to color temperature, although this aspect of vision rarely gets discussed. Most people are able to compensate for color temperatures within the range from 5000 K to 5500 K. Consequently, many computer color monitors (most of which use phosphors that produce a color temperature of 9300 K) appear bluish and incandescent tungsten lighting (with a color temperature of about 3200 K) appears yellowish.

Self-Illuminant Versus Reflected Colors

Here's a problem when viewing printed colors. Your eye wants to see red as red and green as green. Over the millions of years that human sight has developed, our eyes have learned to compensate for the changes in color temperature of sunlight as the sun courses through the heavens from sunrise to noon to sunset. Your eye automatically shifts the balance of light it expects to compensate for color temperature changes. And it works, approximately. Unfortunately, while your eye compensates to adapt to a wide range of color temperatures so that you see overall illumination as white, pigments behave differently under different color temperatures. The pigment looks different, subjectively, even though none of its characteristics such as reflectance and absorption have actually changed.

Contrast

Ambient lighting has another effect on the way you perceive colors. The ambient illumination can alter the apparent contrast of an image. For example, if you create an image in a dark office and later view it on a monitor in bright surroundings, it will appear to have increased contrast. Similarly, if you create an image in a bright office, its contrast will be too low when viewed on a monitor in a dark room. On the other hand, lower ambient brightness tends to subdue contrast from printed images.

Other factors also influence the color that you subjectively perceive. Adjacent colors, background hues, contrasts, even the level of illumination all affect the way you perceive a given color. Consequently, for precise comparisons and matching of colors, you must tightly control viewing conditions.

Color Printing

Adding color to the traditional printing process is easy. You simply send the pages through the printing press a second time after loading the press with a different color ink. With PC printers, you can do the same thing, even to the extent of putting a mauve ribbon in the old dot-matrix machine for a second go around. In either case, the process is messy and ugly. It's messy for the printer who has to clean up tubs full of ink; messy for you because you have to reel back half a ream of paper before letting it run through a second time. And it's messy because nothing in the world is perfect, and printing often falls farther from the mark than most things.

Registration

Even at this primitive level of color, problems quickly become apparent. The odds highly favor you wanting to have some kind of fixed relationship in the physical arrangement of the two different colors. For example, you might want to highlight a word in mauve in the middle of the sentence. If the highlighted word appears two lines lower in the document, in a different sentence and probably printing over something else, the emphasis would be lost–along with much of the meaning and aesthetics of the page.

The process of aligning the different ink colors with one another is called *registration*. Correctly aligned colors–those that print with the proper physical relationship–are said to be "in register."

Achieving correct registration of colors has been a challenge for printers and printing presses since the days back to when printers loaded individual sheets by hand through their hand-mangling machines. The critical factor is getting the paper to line up in exactly the same place with each journey through the printing press (or, with modern color rotary presses, throughout is circuitous travels through the press).

With most PC printers, the problem of paper positioning is readily solved, at least with line printers. Instead of separate passes through the printer for each color, the impact dot-matrix printer shifts the ribbon to change colors without altering the alignment between the mechanism and the paper. Ink-jet printers simply squirt out their various ink colors at the same time, without registration worries. Page printers have greater difficulty because most use multiple-pass processes, moving the paper through the mechanism several times. They prevent registration problems by grabbing hold of the sheet at the beginning of the print process and not loosening their grasp until all colors are laid down.

Matching Colors

When you use your PC to prepare color materials for printing out, you will encounter another problem: color systems. Your PC works with additive color to display on your monitor screen, whereas your printer uses subtractive colors when it prints with ink or toner. Simply sending the levels of primary colors from your PC to the printer won't ensure a color match.

Getting a perfect match faces one fundamental obstacle: The range of colors that can be reproduced with video systems is different from the range that can be printed. If you want to match reality, the situation is even worse. The color ranges of both video and printing are much smaller than the entire range of colors that most people can distinguish, and the colors spectrum available through the print process is dramatically smaller than what you can see on your screen. The range of each system varies depending upon who's talking. Figures commonly quoted list the color range of computer monitors as about 250,000 colors and the perceptibly different color range of four-color process printing as about 5000 colors. Figure 5.16

illustrates this problem, contrasting the total visible color space with the range of typical video displays and printing systems.

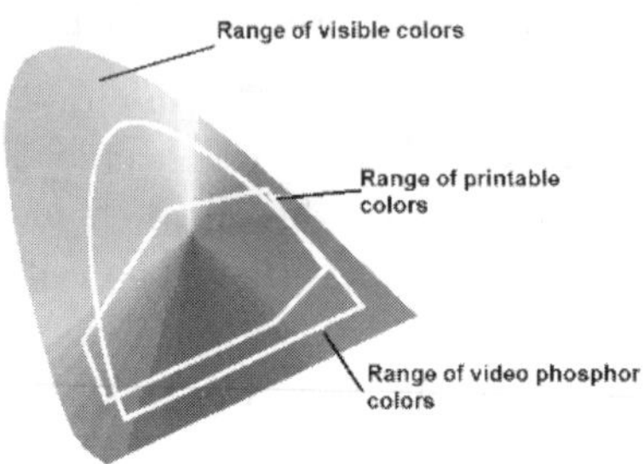

Figure 5.16 Comparison of the color ranges of vision, video, and printing.

Despite the huge color ranges quoted for some color printers (most claim a range of a full 16.7 million colors), the actual number of perceptibly different colors falls closer to that available from process printing than from monitor displays. The four-color process printing and PC printers share essentially the same technology of visually mixed reflective inks, whereas video is self-illuminating. Some software attempts to avoid the problem of the different ranges of video and print media by letting you choose a display mode that constrains the colors that they show on your screen to the printable range.

Even when you confine the colors that you use to the common area within the roughly hexagonal shape in Figure 5.16, you still face problems in matching the colors on your monitor to those that you can print. The two systems use entirely different color systems; they don't even describe colors in the same way.

In fact, several systems are commonly used for describing colors. Most are identified by initials describing the color primaries they use. The most common are RGB, CMYK, HSB (or HSI or HSL). The first is the most familiar, at least if you work with PCs. The initials stand for red, green, and blue, the additive primaries, and the names given to the three color channels used by the system. CMYK stand for the inks used in four-color process printing, which essentially means all full color commercial printing. The colors are cyan, magenta, yellow, and black (the use of the K distinguishes black from blue). The odd colors are actually the correct ones for subtractive processes. HSB stands for hue, saturation, and brightness. The variations include hue, saturation, and intensity, but the intensity value often refers to something closer to luminance rather than true intensity as defined by the CIE;

and HSL, where the "L" stands for luminance, which again does not correspond to the strict CIE definition.

Color Management

Matching printed output to screen colors is not as easy as you might think. In general, you must calibrate the monitor to your output and adjust the mixture of each color to find the best match. When you add other devices that use color graphics to your PC such as scanners or want to work with images from outside sources such as PhotoCDs, the complications multiply. *Color management* software helps ensure you that you can maintain consistent colors regardless of the origin or output of an image.

Color management works by assigning a color space definition to each device or image source you want to use. It calibrates each to its own virtual *Reference Color Space* (RCS). It can then use the RCS as a common standard, like helping a tourist who only speaks English speak to a shopkeeper who speaks only French by way of a Swahili translator who also speaks both English and French. The color management system translates the source colors into its RCS, then translates those color references to match those of the output device.

Color management adds a layer of software between your application and the various output devices–monitor, printer, and so forth. Using a *color profile* hat tells the software the nature and range of colors that the device can produce and even the color system (RGB, CMYK and so forth) used by the device. The color management software adjusts the signals going to the device so that its output will match that of other devices connected to the management system.

Neither DOS nor Windows 3.1 (not the Macintosh) have built in color management. Windows 95 does. Microsoft licensed CMS (Color Management System) technology from Kodak to develop the *Image Color Matching* (ICM) system for Windows 95. The goal of ICM was to provide better color consistency between what you see on your monitor screen and the paper that curls out of your color printer. It extends the concept of WYSIWYG graphics to color. What you see on the screen is the same as what you get on paper. Windows 95 includes ICM support for monitors, color printers, and color scanners.

Taking advantage of ICM technology requires that programs be specially written to use its functions. Consequently, older applications can't guarantee the same color consistency that new Windows 95 applications will.

ICM is tied to the CIE colorimetry standards. To match specific hardware devices, ICM uses *color profiles* hat store the color properties of scanners, monitors, and printers. These profiles use a standard format created by an industry consortium called *InterColor 3.0* a group of computer and imaging industry companies including Apple Computer, Kodak, Microsoft, Silicon Graphics, and Sun Microsystems. Using the InterColor 3.0 standard assures that you can match colors not only within your own PC and hardware but across a wide variety of hardware platforms.

The color management abilities built into individual graphics applications may differ in the details of their implementations, but all follow the same basic principles. For example, Figure 5.17 shows the color management screen used by Corel PhotoPaint.

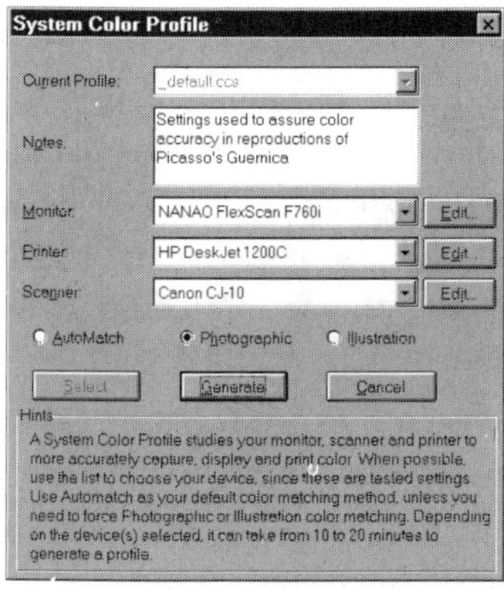

Figure 5.17 The Corel PhotoPaint color management window.

Working with this kind of color management is easy. You simply select the devices you want to use, and the software automatically makes its own adjustments to keep the colors as constant as possible. However, this scheme is not an ideal solution because it gives you no objective reference to color. It helps make what you print match what you see on your screen, but the adjustments won't work if you give a file to someone else (such as a service bureau) to print out, unless the service bureau uses exactly the same software.

You have two choices for an objective standard: (1) use a recognized standard that has profiles to match your equipment or (2) meter both your monitor and printer and adjust your system to produce the colors you want. These *color calibration system*-sensure the best possible color matching in critical applications.

Color Halftoning

The traditional means of reproducing color images relies on an elaboration of the black-and-white halftone technique. As with monochrome halftones, the color technique relies on breaking the image into a series of dots of different sizes to give each single color of ink a range of tones. Instead of the single ink color used in black-and-white printing, color printing relies on the mixing of inks of the primary colors to produce a full spectrum.

Most color printing uses four rather than three primary colors. Although it seems that every color chart in existence purports that the three subtractive primaries yield black when combined together, the actual hue of the blend doesn't have the same depth and richness as a true black ink. Such a mixed black is rarely perfect. Usually it appears to be a murky brown or purple. To print a true black, the standard color process adds a true black ink to the blend. Consequently, most commercial full-color printing is called *four-color-process* printing.

Using black ink instead of a combination of three colors can also have other benefits. Black ink is, in general, much cheaper than colored inks, which are usually made with expensive organic dyes or rare metals. Printing black rather than an overlaying of three colors also makes for thinner, quicker drying ink, which allows for greater throughput because sheets can run through printing presses more quickly and stick without smearing. And printing black instead of the three primaries also makes visual sense because it eliminates registration problems. Where a dot made from three colors usually will have color fringes, a dot printed only in black will have sharp edges. For all of these reasons, text is printed solely with black ink even on four-color printing presses. Full-color images are printed using all four colors, black overprinting the three primary colors.

In the four-color process, each ink color gets printed separately using a separate printing plate. The color image must consequently be converted into four separate images, one for each color plate. These single-color images are called *color separations.*

When quality is paramount, four-color-process printing often is not enough. As noted earlier, all visible colors cannot be blended from the four primaries used in the process. Actually, the limitations of four-color printing are even more severe. Mixtures of the standard four colors used in process printing typically can match only about half the colors that can be made with custom blended pigments. That is, you can blend together different mixtures of color in ink and print them as solid colors that can't be matched by the four-color process. The colors green, orange, and violet are particularly hard to make and match using the standard four-color process primaries of cyan, magenta, yellow, and black.

For high-quality color work, seven or more colors may be used in process printing. Typically the four-color primaries are augmented by the hard-to-mix trio of green, orange, and violet. Pantone has developed a six-color process it calls *Hexachrome* that they claim yields results comparable to seven- and eight-color process printing.

In any case, to use any of these color processes, you require color separations to make individual plates for each color you plan to print. Before the advent of computerized graphics, making color separations was an optical process much like making a halftone. To make the color separations, a color image was photographed using a screen four times—once without a filter to produce the black plate, then one time each with a cyan, magenta, and yellow filter to produce each of the separations. The film itself was black-and-white and the grey tones of the color separation corresponded to the intensity of the color of each separation.

Overlaying geometric patterns often results in moiré patterns, new and different patterns that mysteriously emerge from the combinations. The most familiar moiré patterns arise when patterns of lines and curves are combined, but dot patterns can also result in moiré. The simple color screening process outlined previously inevitably produces moiré patterns from the dots.

Eliminating moiré requires careful balancing of the angle of the screen used in making the halftones, the screen frequency, and even the shape of the individual halftone dots. Experience has shown the optimal arrangement of dots forms a *rosette*, a flower-like pattern of the four-color dots, which is visible only under microscopic examination.

In theory, the optimum relationship among the color screen angles to produce the most pleasing rosette is 30°. Unfortunately, because a 90° rotation of a screen appears identical to a 0° rotation (or 180°, 270° or 360° rotation), the math doesn't work out for four screens. The conventional compromise is to maintain the black screen at the same 45° angle as is used in black-and-white halftoning. The cyan and magenta screens get shifted the optimum 30° from black, one in each direction. The yellow screen is rotated a further 15°. Yellow was chosen for the reduced rotation because it has the least optical prominence and it positioning yields the least visible effect on the optimal rosette. Table 5.3 summarizes the screen angles most commonly used in making color separations optically.

Table 5.3 Traditional Halftone Screen Angles (optical screening)

Color	Screen Angle
Yellow	0°
Cyan	15°
Black	45°
Magenta	75°

Because computers can take intimate control over every pixel, they aren't limited by the conventions of the optical halftone process. In fact, a new technique called *Flamenco screening* that uses identical screen angles for all four-color screens is used by some printer drivers. Flamenco screening allows the appearance of higher resolution but requires precise control of registration to completely carry off its illusion.

Print Order

Most PC colors lay down the four inks used in the four-color process in a fixed sequence. Yellow is almost invariably the first color printed, and it is followed by magenta, cyan, and black in that order. You can remember it as its mnemonic, YMCK, one that sounds like a youth organization that's gone amuck.

The rationale behind this ordering of inks is that yellow is the least powerful of the primary colors; it is easily overwhelmed by the others. Not only do yellow inks usually have less tinting strength, the color yellow appears weaker to the human eye. Overprinting yellow on another color usually is unsuccessful, having little affect on the tone or hue of the underlying color–printing yellow over black yields black. On the other hand, magenta and cyan easily overprint yellow, and black can overpower any color.

In commercial four-color-process printing, the most common print-run color sequences are black, cyan, magenta, then yellow; and cyan, magenta, yellow, then black. The common PC printer order (YMCK) is probably the third most popular. The color renditions produced by each of these print orders is perceptibly different–and probably out of your control. If you want to ensure consistent color results across multiple print runs, you should insist that the same color order be used for each run.

Color Dithering

Digital storage and display systems don't need to worry about the halftone process. They used essentially continuous tone storage and display. Each image pixel can have one of many color values. In modern PCs, the smallest range of colors is usually 256, that is, eight-bit color. In quality image editing systems, 16- and 24-bit colors are typically used, and some systems (notably a little-used Macintosh mode) support 48-bit color.

A problem arises when you want to display or print one of these multicolored images on a system with a limited range of colors. For example, most ink-jet, wax-transfer, and color laser printers can print no more than 16 pure colors, whereas True Color images use eight bits to encode color data in each of three color channels, producing 24-bit color and the ability to define 16.7 million distinct hues. This range presents a challenge to the typical color printer that has only four colors of ink or toner at its disposal.

Most color printers (except for continuous-tone machines such as those using dye-sublimation technology) claim the ability to directly produce a spectrum of eight colors—magenta, cyan, yellow, and sometimes black directly from inks of those colors: red by combining magenta and yellow; blue by combining magenta and cyan; green by combining cyan and yellow; black by combining all three ink colors; and white by not using any ink at all. Some manufacturers tune their colors so magenta appears close to red and combines with yellow to yield a more orange shade as well as a darker cyan that looks nearly blue and combines with red to yield violet. Regardless of the tuning, however, these printers can produce no more than eight distinct colors.

Note that these colors can combine physically, mechanically, or optically. That is, the inks may actually mix by being sprayed wet into wet on the paper. The inks may be transparent and overlaid so that they act as glazes or filters. Or the inks may dry separately but adjacently so that they blur together only at a distance, their hues fusing together optically by the failure of your eye to resolve patches of individual colors.

These 16 colors are the maximum that most color printers can directly print, no matter how wide a spectrum they claim. The only exceptions are the few continuous tone technologies, the dye-sublimation process being the most common. Increasing the color range of a printer requires augmenting this basic color printing ability with some other technology.

The most common method for extending color range is an adaptation of the halftone dithering technique. Your software divides the image into sets of dot patterns. Instead of simply altering the density of dots to produce grey levels, however, the software separately adjusts the density of the dots of each color. More red dots in a given area yields a redder, more intense hue. Fewer dots lowers the intensity of color and reduces red to rose or pink. The process of making these halftone-like color images is called *color dithering* As with the halftone process, dithering is an illusion of color caused by your eye blending together the adjacent color pixels. At a distance, the size of individual printed dots becomes smaller than your eye can individually resolve, so they and their colors naturally blur together.

As with monochrome digital halftones, the basic dithering system groups an array of printed dots together as an image cell. The printer can create a much wider spectrum by filling the cells with various numbers of dots of the eight or 16 different colors that it directly generates.

As with halftones, quality is a trade-off with resolution. Rather than grey tones, however, the issue is hues. For example, if you limit yourself to patterns of two dots, you have the potential for 64 different combinations (one of eight colors for the first dot, and another choice from the eight for the second dot). The more dots, the more potential patterns of color. But the relationship isn't quite so simple. Even with a simple two-dot arrangement, however, some of the choices are redundant. Red next to blue gives exactly the same visual effect (from an appropriate distance) as blue next to red. With a two-dot pattern, about half the potential pairs are redundant–the actual effective yield is 36 (eight choices for the first dot, seven for the second, and so on, that is $8+7+6+5+4+3+2+1$).

Calculating the potential number of hues and shades from the cell size requires more complex math as the number of primary colors increases, but there are always substantially fewer hues than dot combinations. Producing a full True Color spectrum consequently requires a large number of dots.

For example, the DeskJet 1200C and PaintJet XL300 Windows PCL driver ink-jet printer assembles its True Color spectrum from a 16x16 array of dots. Such a large array allows for 18,446,744,073,709,500,000 combinations (that's 256^8), not all of which are optically unique. Hewlett-Packard maps the 16,777,216 color possibilities (that's 2^{24}) allowed by 24-bit color coding into the possibilities of the 16x16 dither by choosing unique patterns for each color that meet mathematical criteria for yielding optimum color.

Graphics Storage

The quality of graphic image that your printer can produce of course depends on the quality of the digital original. As good as modern printers are, they cannot work miracles and give you a better image then what you give them.

Image quality depends on where the image comes from or how you make it. These are issues of access and taste beyond scientific scrutiny. However, the format of the image and the way it is stored also influences its output quality, and this aspect of the image follows rules independent of your aesthetic judgment.

Image Formats

Monochrome (Two Color)

Storing monochrome images is almost trivial–you need only a one-bit code, one that indicates the presence or absence of color. However, most graphics programs give you a choice of image conversions to produce a monochrome file, and each choice can have a dramatic effect on the appearance of the image. For example, you may be given a choice of line art, black-and-white, dithered, and halftone. Line art and black-and-white refer to essentially the same thing, a reduction of the image to two colors. As noted in the Monochrome Graphics section you can make any of a wide variety of conversions to line art images. Halftone renderings are essentially the same thing as dither in the two-color world. You have your choice of dithering methods and little else.

On the positive side, monochrome storage is the most efficient way of saving shapes in a bit map, at the sacrifice of all shading and color information. It requires only one data bit for every pixel of storage. For drawings and reproductions of some graphic arts media (etchings, engravings, single-color seritypes), it makes sense.

Greyscale

The number of shades of grey in an image determines how many bits you need to store a greyscale image. Common formats use 16, 64, and 256 shades of grey. These formats correspond to four, six, and eight bits of data per image pixel to record greyscale data. As noted above, eight bits are close to sufficient to code an image meant for typical PC display devices and environments with imperceptible transitions between different greys. Consequently, for most greyscale printing, you'll work with an eight-bit format for greyscale images, which require one byte of storage for every image pixel.

Color

Color storage is an issue of how many and what kind. How many refers to the number of colors in the actual image. The range allowed by different applications and file types is large, indeed. The color ranges common among personal computers stretch from simple four-color images to those having 281,474,976,710,655 hues and shades. The former is the basic digital RGBI color system used since IBM introduced its color graphics adapter in 1982. The latter is a little-used Macintosh format.

As you can see, the number of available colors rapidly gets unmanageable, or at least, hard to remember. Consequently, the range of colors in computer files and display systems is most often described as the number of bits required to encode a color range. You can find the number of codable colors by raising two to the power of the number of bits; that is, eight-bit color can encode 2^8 hues and shades.

This relationship breaks down in some higher resolution modes. In video systems, for example, a 32-bit mode is often configured as three color channels, one byte for each of the primaries, and a one-byte alpha channel that encodes control information such as that used for keying or overlaying images. The alpha channel doesn't add new color capabilities; instead it aids in image management. In publishing, however, 32-bit color mode usually devotes one byte to the four-color-process primaries (cyan, magenta, yellow, and black). Similarly, 48-bit color is usually arrayed as four 12-bit channels (three color, one alpha) or as three 16-bit primary color channels.

Table 5.4 lists the common bit ranges and the number of colors that each can encode.

Table 5.4 Bits-to-Color Translation

Bits	Colors	Common Use
1	2	Monochrome
2	4	CGA, color halftones
4	16	Basic VGA
8	256	Ubiquitous
16	65,536	Ubiquitous
18	262,144	VGA CLU
24	16,777,216	TrueColor (Ubiquitous)

Table 5.4 continued

Bits	Colors	Common Use
32	16,777,216	Video production
32	4,294,967,296	DTP
48	4,294,967,296	With alpha channel
48	281,474,976,710,655	Two bytes per color

The most common of these use 8, 16, or 24 bits because it conforms with full bytes of storage while keeping storage requirements reasonable. The more colors you use, the more realistic you can make images appear. After all, reality offers a near infinite range of colors. Although the human eye is limited in the number of colors it can distinguish, estimates run from 1 million to more than 20 million. (One reason for this wide range: A trained eye can distinguish more colors than an untrained eye.) On the other hand, the more bits used for color, the more cumbersome it is to use and store. More bits means more memory to store, whether in RAM (for example, a video board frame buffer or printer buffer) or in disk files. More bits also mean more processing time when working with an image, running it through a driver to print, or rasterizing it inside your printer. Consequently, the number of colors used in image creation and storage is a compromise.

Newer image capture hardware such as color scanners produce higher color resolution (greater color bit depth). For example, 12 bits per primary has become popular in better scanners. These greater resolutions allow you a wider range for image manipulation but images captured in them usually are reduced to a more common format (most often 24-bit color) for storage. For example, this higher color resolution may allow more detail in the brighter parts of an image. If you then want to alter the gamma of the image to compress the higher key colors, you can do so without clipping them (which would cause bright areas to assume a uniform tone). Even though you don't use the greater number of bits for storing the image, these higher color depths can allow you to adjust an image to look better when you print it out.

Direct Color

When you assign one digital value to each color that you want to store or display, you are said to be using *direct* color. It's direct because there is a direct relationship between the individual colors and the digital code that are used to store each one. Each color requires its own digital code, so the more colors you want to store, the larger and more cumbersome the bit code must be, as demonstrated in the previous table. Although direct color technology is the most straightforward, it is not the most efficient way of coding an image.

Mapped Color

One saving grace of the real world is that you rarely see all of the millions of colors that you can perceive in a single view. Most images use a relatively small number of colors drawn from the full array available. The designers of color imaging systems have taken advantage of this aspect of color to make a more efficient storage system, *mapped* color.

A mapped color system reduces the storage by recording only the colors that appear in the image or, more often, only the colors that appear most often in the image (or colors approximating the most common ones in the image). To eliminate the need to use the full number of bits to name and store each color, a mapped system adds a new code for each color in the image, one with fewer bits than would be required by direct color. The system then uses a *color map* to store the relationship between the new code value and the direct color codes. This color map is called the color *palette* of the system because the system draws the colors it can use from this map like an artist selects his colors from his palette. In operation and effect, the color map consists of a number of pointers, each of which indicates a direct color value. Some systems (such as the VGA display system) call the color map a *color look-up table* or *CLU*.

Another term for mapped color is *indexed color* Instead of viewing the table of color codes as a map, the people who developed this term saw it as an index much like the index in a book that allows you to quickly look up references.

When storing a color-mapped image, you must include both the mapped values for each image pixel as well as the color map. After all, without the color map, you wouldn't know which color each code referred to. Use the wrong color map with an image, and it will take on a strange look indeed.

Practical systems use a fixed number of codes for storing image data, typically eight bits. They reduce the image data to a mere 256 different colors so that the eight-bit code will suffice. Mapped images with 256 colors give a good (or at least tolerable) approximation of the original image, particularly when the original tends to be rich in one particular hue.

In a practical color-mapping system, image processing starts by first counting the distinct colors in the original image. If the range is more than 256, the system reduces the number to fit. Image-processing software can use any of several strategies to make this reduction. It can start with a fixed palette of color and find the closest match to those required by the image. For example, when image-processing software matches an image to the Windows palette, it uses this technique. You can achieve higher quality by optimizing the palette, choosing its color to match those in the image instead of some arbitrary standard.

Converting Color to Geryscale

PCs today have become primarily color machines, and the work you do on them is filled with more and brighter colors than even the most ambitious rainbow. Despite the rise in popularity of color ink-jet printers (which owe much of this popularity to the bright hues you work with on your PC), more than half the printers sold still provide one color at a time, usually black. Moreover if you aim to produce something to be printed commercially, you'll get stuck in the same monochromatic rut.

You've probably learned to see the world in shades of grey and to convert all issues into terms of black and white–especially if you're a politician–but PCs and printers aren't as facile at changes of context and color value. They can, however, derive a single monochrome signal from the three used for color.

Green to Grey

The easiest conversion method to derive monochrome from color is to ignore all but one of the color channels. Universally, such systems use the green signal as the gauge of brightness. Surprisingly, the results can be convincing.

The effectiveness in green conveying brightness is a matter of human nature. Having evolved from creatures that frolicked mostly in the jungle or savanna (depending on your anthropological allegiance), our ancestors lived in a world awash in green. Their eyes developed a supreme keenness for green; they are still more sensitive to it than to any other hue. The effect of green light dominates in our eyes, weighing most heavily in our interpretation of brightness.

If you plug a monochrome VGA monitor into a standard VGA jack when your PC is running in color mode, you will get a green-for-brightness monochrome mapping. Some image editing programs allow you to make a similar conversion.

While the green-for-brightness approach works well for images of the real world in which few colors are pure and some green sneaks into most hues, it fails in the realm of the PC and its pure, artificial colors. For example, a pure red signal that lights your monitor almost to full brightness carries zero green information. Similarly, an equally bright blue would produce a negligible green signal. As a result, charts that you paint with vivid color contrasts may reproduce as uniform black when you derive monochrome brightness solely from the green signal.

Weighted Translation

To avoid such problems, most conversions from color to monochrome involve blending the three primary color signals together. As with any blend, however, you can use any ratio of the various constituents. Because of the sensitivity of the human eye, achieving a semblance of apparent brightness from a three-color signal requires more green than red and more red than blue in the mix.

When you edit images on your PC, its video system automatically takes care of the color balancing act. Your PC handles colors as if they were all equally important. For example, you may be able to assign many of 256 intensity values to each color in a 24-bit color system. Your PC assumes that a signal with an equal mix of each of these signals will produce a tone without hue–white, a pure grey, or black. Your video board adjusts the values of these full-range signals to produce the proper mix that will appear on your monitor with the proper color balance.

Neither your PC's printing system nor your imaging editor program participates in the video system's color mixing and adjustment process. Consequently, your imaging editor must add its own compensation when converting a color image to greyscale. A simple sum of the primary color signals will not yield a proper greyscale rendering of the color image. The program must apply the proper weighting to each signal.

PostScript Monochrome-Color Mapping

In monochrome PostScript printers, the conversion from color in the input image to a black-and-white printout is handled automatically. When the data calls for an object to be rendered in color, the PostScript interpreter in h printer converts the color into the appropriate greyscale value. This allows the same PostScript code to work with monochrome and color printers, as well as other output devices.

Some applications take over the greyscale conversions of images before sending them to the PostScript driver. These programs send the bit-image data to the PostScript printer in black and white. Obviously, the resulting code is specific to monochrome devices and won't produce color on color printers. Moreover, this technique subverts any hardware-specific features of a printer that are designed to enhance greyscale rendering. The result may look worse than if a color image had been sent to the printer.

On the other hand, PostScript code with color instructions may cause errors on old PostScript machines (those predating the addition of color in 1988). Of course, if your printer is that old, you can't expect to get the same quality as with today's latest printers.

CHAPTER SIX

Operation

Putting your printer to work can be a easy as plugging it in. Getting a printer to do what you want is another matter–you have to deal with simple printer mechanics (loading paper) and control systems, both the buttons on the printer and the commands available to you through your operating system and application software. Although every printer is different, the common ground among printers is wide.

A printer is one of the least exciting peripherals you can add to your PC, second only to a back-up system in tedium value. You don't enjoy a printer as you would a new game or modernistic warped keyboard. At best, you use it for its anointed purpose. At worst, it makes a dead albatross look like a desirable lavilier. A printer can be a plague on your house or office, particularly when the essence of its operation is far from obvious and you're stuck with reading the manual to discover the secrets to its mysteries; if you have a manual, that is, and if it is readable.

Even though every printer model is, to some extent, unique in design as well as execution, enough common thread unites their operation that if you master one machine, you can probably get any one working.

The common mien for printers extends beyond a few front panel pushbuttons or even elaborate command languages. From any number of angles, getting to know one printer is getting to know them all. Most printers share the same mechanical considerations, like placement and paper loading. They all have the same rudimentary controls. Even complex machines with their own internal programs rely on the same concepts for their menuing systems. Nearly all printers require some kind of installation procedure that requires hardware and software. They need drivers to deliver all their features.

The printing process doesn't suffer a single means of control. In the typical PC system, you command the print process at five different levels: at the application, at the driver, with your print spooler, at the interface, and on the printer itself. Figure 6.1 shows the five levels of printer control.

Figure 6.1 The five places the printing process can be controlled.

Initially, you prepare what you want to print using your application software. You key in text and lay out graphics in the arrangement that best conveys your ideas. With your PC you make an image on the screen, and you depend on your printer to translate that image into reality. How you go about making the initial image for the printer depends on your application. Your printer neither knows nor cares about what your application does during the creation process; only the results count. Because this is a book about printers and not applications, we'll leave the image-making part of the printing process to your own imagination and software.

Once you have an image, your software and printer both depend on the printer driver to translate the image or text of your application into printer commands. Your choice of driver determines not only how accurate that translation is but also whether your printer will recognize the commands at all. Because the driver acts as a translator, it must understand two languages, that of your application and that of your printer. Matching the driver is probably the most critical part of getting your printer to work properly–and giving you full control over the printing process.

Most modern operating systems impose an extra layer of software on the printing process, the print manager or print spooler. Most people use the two terms interchangeably. Strictly speaking, however, a *print spooler* is a only a temporary repository for printer commands that holds them until the printer can use them, and the *print manager* guides the one or more sets of related commands and data (each set comprising a print job) through the spooler. The print manager lets you schedule print jobs, putting the most important one first. It also lets you pause, restart, and cancel print jobs when you change your mind or have a problem.

The interface controls how the print job reaches the printer. It can be a simple hardware port or a more elaborate network connection. In effect the interface is the conduit that channels the commands and data of the print job to your printer. Interfaces are so complex that they get their own chapter in this book, Chapter 8, "Interfaces." Networks and related printer sharing systems are covered in Chapter 9, "Printer Sharing."

Finally, you get a last chance at controlling your printouts on the printer itself. The Control Panel on most printers lets you command paper movement and sometimes other details, such as print speed, font, or number of copies. Many printers give you mechanical control, too, so that you can directly alter the physical placement of the image on paper by moving the paper in the printer mechanism.

This chapter covers the basic issues of using and controlling a printer, from the initial installation during which you select the proper driver for the printer through operating the printer manager to the Control Panel on the printer itself. Because every make and model of printer has its own peculiarities, our discussion will have to be somewhat general (although highlighted with specific examples). It will help you understand everything you need to know to install a printer–darned near any printer–set it up and use it with your applications.

We'll work our way back up the chain of control. We'll start with the printer itself–after all, that's what this book is supposed to be about. From there, we'll examine the control afforded through the spooler and print manager (skipping the nitty-gritty of the interface until Chapter 8), getting an overview of how this kind of control actually works. Then we'll look at the both print management functions and drivers from the perspective of the operating system, the level at which most of today's print managers and drivers operate. We'll consider both installation and everyday operation. Finally, we'll take a look at common problems that occur in the normal operation of a printer and how to correct them.

Mechanical Matters

Many of the concerns in operating a printer are purely mechanical. After all, that's the printer's primary job, changing ephemeral electronic signals into visible, mechanical reality. The printer needs to deal with some very physical things: paper, ink, and contaminants. Moreover, you need to deal with the printer.

We'll only look at a few of the mechanical aspects of the media–in particular, how to handle and load it. Chapter 7, "Consumables," will discuss issues involving the selection of paper and ink.

Location

Any real estate agent will tell you the three most important factors in pricing a house are location, location, and location (although privately they may confide the real answer is commission, commission, and commission). The same trio should be your first considerations in setting up a new printer.

Printers need space. They need space for their own mechanism. They need space to accommodate the supplies they use to make a print job (such as their supplies of paper). And you need space to access the printer and take care of its maintenance. Nearly every printer's manual will advise of its location and space needs, and the reasons for these requirements will soon become obvious—particularly if you don't follow the guidelines.

The obvious need is the space for the printer itself, but the footprint of a printer almost always extends beyond the space on the desktop the printer's case occupies. You could just clear a corner of your desk that matches the dimensions of the bottom of your printer, but most machines have trays that extend well beyond their perimeters. Even those that kindly tuck their trays inside require an empty area for pulling the tray out. If you don't plan ahead, you'll knock half the stuff off your desktop every time you pull out the paper tray. (Certainly the best location of a printer with a front-loading tray is at the front edge of a desk or stand, but then that leaves you with the question of what to put behind the printer.)

With printers that use continuous-form paper, you'll need access to the back of the printer, either to load stock or unload printed sheets. Although you may think you can pull paper up from the back of the printer, the fates weigh the odds heavily against you. They will ensure that the paper will snarl itself up so you can't pull it out but, of course, only on time-critical print jobs. Either provide access to the rear of the printer or put the printer on a movable stand so that you can pull it out for access.

NOTE

Many laser printers have hinged tops that allow you to delve inside to pull out shredded sheets or load toner and drums. Wherever you locate such a printer, make sure you have adequate room for the top to swing.

Printer Stands

Back in the days when a printer required a moving crew to put it in its place, every machine got its own printer stand, a sturdy contrivance capable of propping up the leaning tower of Pisa should the dire need arise. The printer itself was deported to the wasteland where its clatter and heat would be unnoticed–generally that means a computer room filled with operators so used to the noise and air conditioning that they could sleep through any printer's commotion. Today the PC printer has little need for the isolation and support of its ancestors, but a printer stand can still help out.

The foremost reason for plopping your printer on its own stand is that the stand is an additional piece of furniture. Not only do you save the desktop space you'd otherwise give up to the printer, but also you get an additional option is for arranging the furniture in your office as well as storage for supplies. With printers that use continuous-form paper, you get another, more valuable benefit–proper paper feeding.

Continuous-form paper can be troublesome. Instead of neat little stacks, you get boxes, typically designed to be just large enough to be inconvenient to carry. Worse, many inexpensive PC printers don't afford you the luxury of putting the paper just anywhere. Their anemic tractor systems can barely tug a single sheet of paper. Fold the continuous-form stream around the corner of your desk and you may add enough friction to keep the feed mechanism stalled in the middle of a single sheet. Even when your printer has the strength to deal with the twists of fate, you still have to figure out how to arrange the paper. When the paper streams both in and out of your printer from the rear (a not too unusual arrangement), the inbound and outbound paper fold together into a confused mass. If you're particularly unfortunate, your printer will eventually reel in the outgoing paper along with the inbound supply, resulting in a rather interesting (and bothersome) paper jam.

Put the printer on a stand, and you can feed paper from the bottom and collect it in the rear. The isolated streams prevent jams, and the straight-through path allows even weakling printers to run unmolested.

A printer stand also helps enforce a demilitarized zone around your printer. With the freedom of placement afforded by a printer stand, you can put the machine someplace more out of the way than the top of your desk. That allows you to provide adequate clearance around the machine to aid in cooling and provide space for access when you have to load paper, toner, or other consumables. A printer stand consequently helps out even with desktop-style machines such as laser and thermal-wax machines.

Roll-around printer stands are great when you have to shuttle one printer between several systems. For example, if you have a spare printer, you can roll it into service complete with paper loaded and ready with but a few seconds of notice. But when you leave shuttling to the astronauts and just get a stand with wheels because that's the way it comes, you may be paving the way for disaster. Roll the printer away for whatever reason, even if just to sweep the carpet, and forget to unplug it from your PC, and you may be set for a demonstration of the law of gravity as your PC plummets, probably onto your foot.

My preference is for the least expensive printer stand you can find. Most printers are so unappealing that trying to match your decor is futile. Moreover, you don't have to worry about giving the stand a beating, smearing it with ink or toner, or scratching the finish by dropping a tray. All you need is something sturdy enough to hold up your hardware. About the only thing that doesn't qualify is that metal roll-around typewriter stand left over from the days when there actually were typewriters.

Stands for bottom-fed continuous-form printers work nicely for lasers. They are about the right size and, moreover, the space on the bottom for feed stock works well for holding your inventory of laser paper. The paper is always there when you need to reload, and its weight also helps lower the center of gravity of the printer-and-stand tower and stabilize it.

Tractors

The least-fun aspect of continuous-form paper is loading paper tractors. Until you get a knack for this arcane process, you'll rue not opting for a neat, new ink-jet printer with a cut sheet feeder. After you master the tractor, however, you're understanding will become complete, and you'll know why continuous-form paper is now for specialized applications only.

If you've had a tractor-feed printer for years, you've probably tried the lazy man's approach. Ignore any tractor adjustments or releases and just slide paper up to the closed tractors. Then roll the platen until the tractor pins grab the sprocket holes of the paper. Old pin-feed printers require this approach. With any luck, your paper will be threaded and you'll just have to set the top of the form. More likely, the tractor will grab the sheet halfway between two holes and start to make a path of its own.

At that point it's time to get serious and actually do it right. Tractors have two adjustments to worry about. They have snaps that release their covers to allow you to lay paper upon their pins to get proper alignment. And they have friction releases that allow you to slide the tractors horizontally across the platen so that you can adjust the placement of your paper.

Pull Tractors

With a pull tractor, the best way to load paper is to release both the snaps and the slides. Pull the paper through your printer until you have enough to lay onto the tractor so that the perforation between the first and second sheet of the continuous web fall on or near the tractors. Slide the tractors to the correct distance apart to match the width of the paper between sprocket holes.

- Lay the paper on the tractor so that the tractor pins pop through the holes. You can use the perforation to check to be sure you've threaded the paper squarely. Make sure the relationship between the pins and the perforation is the same on both tractors and you can be certain the paper is square.
- Snap the tractors closed, leaving the tractors loose on their platen slide.
- Align the top of a sheet where you think the top of the form should be, then print a test sheet.
- If you're quick, you can slide the paper along with the tractors horizontally so you can put the left margin of the paper exactly where you want it.
- The test sheet also lets you be sure you have the top of the form set correctly.
- Finally make sure there's a slight amount of tension across the paper between the tractors so that the paper doesn't pucker out, but be sure the tension is not so great that the tractor pints damage the sprocket holes in the paper.
- Once you're satisfied that your alignments are correct, lock the tractors in place and print away.

With pull-tractor printers, you should release the friction feed mechanism when you use the tractors. Otherwise, slight differences in the feeding of the paper between the platen and the tractors may strip the perforations from pages or cause the paper to buckle between the platen and tractor. Fixed-platen printers usually make this point moot, having no friction feed option. They rely on the weight of the paper and friction of its travel through the mechanism to hold the medium against the flat platen.

Push Tractors

Printers that use push tractors require a slightly different strategy. You have to push the paper around the platen (pull tractor printers invariably have round rubber platens), so you must release the pressure on the platen, typically by pulling the bail arm out.

- Again, open the tractors and release the catches on the tractors so that they can slide horizontally across the platen.
- Slide the paper past the tractors and around the platen until the perforation between the first and second sheets is near the tractors.
- Align the paper in the tractors using the perforation as a guide to be sure that the paper is square.
- Close the tractor covers.
- Now adjust the tractors both for horizontal placement and the correct tension across the paper. (It is inadvisable to do this when printing because you'll be working against the grip of the platen.
- Put the paper under the bail arm, and push back the bail arm to its operating position.
- Print a test sheet and check for proper paper alignment.

Bidirectional Tractors

Printers that use bidirectional tractors give you one further adjustment: You can alter the distance between the tractors to pull the paper taut against the platen.

- The first step is to be sure that you've released friction-feed pressure on the platen. Bidirectional tractors do not require platen pressure and in fact will not operate properly if you engage the friction feed mechanism of the printer.
- Release the vertical tractor lock and slide the tractors down so that they are as close as possible to the platen.
- Open both sets of tractors and release them so that they slide horizontally.
- Slide the paper around the platen and align its end with the midpoint of the second tractor, the one that pulls the paper from inside the printer.
- Make sure the paper is square using the top of the sheet as a reference.
- Snap the pull tractors closed.
- Pull back on the paper from behind the push tractors, applying slight tension to the paper around the platen. This will help assure that the paper is squarely threaded.

- Push the paper down on the push tractor, align the holes to the closest pin that does not force your to add tension to the paper. The paper should be wound loosely around the platen.
- Now snap the push tractor closed.
- Add tension to the paper by sliding the tractors away from the platen. At this point apply only light tension.
- Make a test print, sliding the tractors horizontally to properly align the left margin of each page.
- After your test sheet is done, increase the paper tension around the platen roller to its normal operating value and lock the platens down. Correct tension holds the paper tightly against the platen without the tractor pins distorting the sprocket holes in the paper.

With some microperforated paper, the stress of loading tractors is sufficient to pull off the perforations. If you encounter this problem, fold over the first sheet of paper, and thread the printer with a double-thickness of paper.

Envelopes

Not all tractor-fed printers are designed to print across the uneven thickness of envelopes. If you are careful, you can usually print on them. For best results (and to lessen the likelihood that you might damage your printer), you should take a few precautions.

Start by choosing the most appropriate envelopes for your printer. Printers without envelope capability are typically oriented to single-sheet thicknesses, so you'll want the thinnest envelopes possible. You'll also encounter fewer paper-advance problems if you use tractor-feed envelopes with strippable sprocket holes at the edges.

Set the paper thickness adjustment to match the prevailing thickness of the envelope. Nominally that means two sheets thick. Most envelopes vary from a single sheet to three overlapped sheets, and the two-sheet setting is the best middle ground.

Adjust your software to use the proper paper size. You don't want your PC to tell your printer to keep printing beyond the confines of the envelope. Running past the edge of the medium can cause damage to the printheads, ribbon masks, motors, and even printed circuits of some printers. Just to be sure, run a test print on a full-sized sheet of paper using your envelope print-area settings.

When loading envelopes, leave the flap open. This will make the envelope thinner for smoother feeding. You may also have to push the envelop down against the platen as you roll it in to ensure it travels smoothly through the mechanism.

Trays

Some sources may recommend riffling through cut-sheet stacks before loading them into your tray to help ensure that they don't stick together during printing. Your stacks will be smoother if you don't. Moreover, sticking sheets more usually results from improper physical conditions such as high humidity in your office or in the paper itself than it does from the stacking of sheets.

NOTE

With any sheet-fed printer, be it ink-jet or laser or whatever, you need to learn about paper orientation. Each sheet the machine sucks in has a particular orientation.

Special Stock

When you use a printer that requires special paper such as the coated sheets of thermal-wax systems and many ink-jets, you must be careful to have the coated side of the stock in the proper orientation for the system or you will lose print quality. Depending on the printer, the coated side of the paper must be up or down. Either check your manual for proper orientation or print one sheet each way and determine for yourself which way looks best.

Plain Paper

With plain paper printers like lasers, the orientation of individual sheets might seem insignificant. But even plain paper isn't so plain–most sheets have differing textures on each side (see Chapter 7, "Consumables") that can affect print quality. Moreover, when you want to print on paper that isn't so plain, such as stationery or gilt-edge paper for certificates and awards, you need to align the input sheets so that the output looks right. You don't want your address to appear upside-down on the backside of each sheet. Determining the right orientation just takes a single test run. Just run one sheet through and compensate for the error however necessary. Then, make a note–say on a label you stick to the printer or paper tray–indicating the proper orientation for the next time you load stationery. It is a peculiar quality of human nature that causes you to forget the correct alignment between bouts of printing on stationery.

FRONT PANEL CONTROLS

Nearly ever printer gives you an array of controls to operate the most important functions of the machine. These typically include paper handling and speed or font selection. In a given class of printer, the available controls have become somewhat standardized, so you can expect the same functions from whatever machine you buy.

The typical dot-matrix printer you should expect four buttons: On-line, Line feed, Form feed, and Draft/LQ with innumerable variations such as Fonts, Paper feed, and Eject. Neither the names nor the functions of any printer control have been standardized, so each manufacturer follows his own star.

On-Line

Nearly every printer offers you an on-line/off-line button. The "line" that it refers to is the control link between your PC and the printer. On-line therefore means your printer is connected through to your PC and obeys the command it gives. The distinction between on- and off-line is more fundamental. On-line means that the printer monitors the data and control lines from your PC. The data lines are the more important because your computer can send elaborate commands in the data stream. Just about anything you can do with your printer can be actuated through a data stream command.

When your printer is off-line, it doesn't listen to the data stream commands. It doesn't listen to anything. In fact, it signals back to your PC that it is not ready to print so that your PC will not send any data or commands to it.

Many printers make the operation of the control buttons dependent on the setting of the on-line switch. These machines monitor their control panels only when they are off-line. When they are on-line, they ignore the buttons your press and listen only to commands sent from your PC.

Line Feed

When you want to advance a sheet of paper just a bit at a time, you press the *Line feed* button. As the name should imply, each press advances the paper one line. It's a control only relevant to (and available on) line printers. Straightforward as the control sounds, what constitutes a line varies with the printer set-up and the designer's whim.

For example, when you set a printer to 10-pitch or pica characters, you'd expect it to advance one-sixth of an inch with each press of the line feed button because that's the height of 10-pitch characters. When set for 12 pitch you'd expect the printer to advance each sheet by one-eighth of an inch each with every line feed press. In fact, most modern line printers advance each sheet by the same increment no matter what pitch you set them to. The actual height of a printed line is set by the physical height of the printhead–for example, nine or twenty-four print wires high–and cannot be varied. So the printer invariably advances each sheet by that increment. In general, that's one-sixth of an inch and 66 presses equal one full page.

Some printers offer a *microline feed*. Instead of advancing the paper by the height of a full character, a press of the line feed button of a printer using this design moves the paper up by the minimum addressable vertical unit of the printer, often a fraction as small as 1/216th of an inch. The purpose of this fine degree of control is to allow you to exactly align the paper in your printer so that what you think is the top of a sheet corresponds precisely to what the printer believes is the top of the sheet.

When you're impatient, moving the paper in such fine increments can be frustrating. Most printers that use microfine line feeds automatically shift to normal line feeding when you hold down the line feed button for more than one second.

Form Feed

When you want to feed a full sheet through your printer, press the *Form Feed* button. This control signals the printer to advance to the top of the next sheet of paper or form. Continuous-form line printers will roll through to the next sheet. Page printers will eject one sheet of paper.

A form feed differs from making a succession of line feed in that the form feed is indexed. That is, your printer knows where to find the top of a sheet of paper and only advances as far as it needs to get to the top of that sheet. Consequently, some printers label the form feed button *Top of Form* or *TOF*.

To be able to advance to the top of the form, your printer needs to know exactly where it is. For printers like lasers that use cut sheets, finding the top of a page is unambiguous and automatic. Printers using continuous-form paper face a challenge because most have no way of detecting the perforations that separate individual sheets. They rely on you to set the top of the form properly. Thereafter, they merely advance the distance they equate with the length of a page (which you may also need to set).

The procedure for setting the top of the form so that a printer has the proper index varies with the make and model of the machine. Typical implementations rely on you physically putting the paper in the proper position, then telling the printer to use that position as its index value. Some machines rely on you pressing a combination of keys to set the top of the form. Inexpensive printers use another expedient: They assume that the position that the paper is in when they are powered on represents the proper top of the form. To set the top of the form with these machines, you spin the paper to the proper position, then switch the machine off, wait a few seconds (so that it can forget its old setting), then switch it back on.

WARNING

With these machines, be careful not to inadvertently manually roll partly down a sheet when the power is off–the new (and wrong) paper position will automatically be set as the top of the form.

Printers commonly use one or more of three means for setting the page length they use for the form feed command, which they call the *form length*: a physical adjustment of DIP switches, selecting a menu command from their Control Panel, and software commands sent from your PC. Because most printers default to a form length of 11 inches, which is exactly what most people in the United States use, you normally don't have to deal with this setting. If you opt to use legal-size paper, however, you'll need to make an adjustment. The DIP switch settings should be documented in your printer's manual; the menu setting is supposed to be obvious (and a graphic interface is supposed to be intuitive–yeah, sure); and software commands are covered in Chapter 9, "Printer Commands and Languages."

Most continuous-form printers assume by default that an 11-inch sheet is 60 lines long rather than 66. The extra six lines constitute a *perforation skip*. That is, the printer is designed not to print over the perforated edge separating individual sheets of continuous-form paper. To allow you a bit of freedom in aligning sheets and generally making things more aesthetic, most perforation-skip settings allow a margin of one-half of an inch (or three lines) at the top and bottom of each sheet. Actually, the printer just skips six lines on every page, and you must position the page so that the skip appears in the center of the skip or wherever might appeal to you more. You can typically defeat the perforation skipping feature using a DIP switch or menu setting.

Some printers lack a separate form feed button but instead use a combined line-and-form feed button. Pressing the button momentarily advances one line at a time; holding the button down for about a second forces the printer to advance to the top of the next form.

Menu Systems

Once the realm of only printers with elaborate LCD displays and dozens of pushbuttons, even some of the least expensive printers now allow you to set them up using a system of menus. Printer designers figured out that instead of adding the cost of an LCD display to the printer, they could shift the cost to you and let you use the paper stock of your printer as a display.

The first printers to have menu control included a large array of pushbuttons, occasionally understandably labeled, that allowed you a relatively straightforward control system. Of course, every pushbutton adds a few cents to the cost of a printer, so clever manufacturers found ways of conserving on pushbuttons by nesting menus and letting a few buttons serve many functions.

Most menu systems are built around a skip/select design. Typically two buttons let you skid and one or two let you select. To make a menu selection, you press the skip buttons to step through the various offerings of the menu. When you see the selection you want, you press the select button. In most systems, this will slide you into the next level down the menu system in which you press the skip buttons again to cycle through the options. Once you find what you want, press the select button again to make your choice.

One complication is that sometimes you have to step through several menu items to find the option you want to change. Some printer makers seem to take particular glee in hiding common options in obscure places in the menu Fortunately, most of the changes that you need to make with the menu system will be for the initial set-up of your printer. After that, your printer will remember the settings using EEPROM memory (or similar nonvolatile technology that keeps its settings even when you switch off the power).

Software Overview

Everything you do on your PC involves software. Without a program, your PC doesn't even rise to vegetable status. It doesn't think, it doesn't grow. It only consumes and sits there. Brain dead perhaps, more like an unwelcome brother-in-law. Software brings the system to life, gives it purpose, gives it brains, gives it a job.

Because your printer is part of your PC, it needs software, too. To link your printer to modern applications and operating systems, you need driver software. In addition, you can take command of your printer using two types of utility software, programs that control what you print and others that manage how and when each job gets printed.

Control utilities include those that let you change the typeface, pitch, or other aspect of character-based printing, those that change a print mode (for example, from draft to letter quality), and those that copy graphic images from files to your printer. Software that manages print jobs allows you to send several individual jobs to your printer at a rate faster than your printer can pound them out, arrange the jobs in order of priority, make additional copies without printing a second time from your application software, and canceling print jobs when something goes awry.

Utilities

Most printer control utilities have a simple design. They send control codes to your printer using whatever language the machine understands. You only need to choose a function, and the utility translates your desires into the proper commands and sends them to your printer port.

This simple design belies the amazing diversity of printer utilities. Some are so simple as to send a single one character command to your printer, for example, to advance to the next sheet using the **Form Feed** command. You can write such a program to run at the DOS command prompt that takes little more than a dozen bytes. You can use the same basic program structure to send whatever commands you want to your printer. The Appendix tells you how to create simple command files for your printer.

On the other hand, printer utilities can be elaborate menu-control structures that allow you to adjust every aspect of your printer's operation. These may let you select font, speeds, margins, even rotate pages to print sideways. Under the skin, however, these utilities are similar. Most of their code is used by the user interface, the part of the program that make it understandable to human beings rather than those who teethed on microprocessors and machine language.

Because these programs take direct control of your printer, they must know the commands and language your printer understands. Many such utilities are machine specific. They work with only one make and model printer (and those that emulate their favored machine). Others include installation routines that allow you to set them up to match your printer. In either case, you must match the software to your printer if you expect the commands to work properly.

Another class of utilities acts as translators, converting data in one format to another. Typically you'll use one of these programs to print out a graphic file. Most common file formats bear little resemblance to the commands a printer needs to render the image in the file on paper (the exception being PostScript files). The utility converts the bit-image data of the file into your printer's language.

Printer utilities are conveniences that let you get the most from your printer. They free you from needing to master the front panel commands and menu systems of your hardware.

Queuing

In printer management, the most important concept to understand is *queuing*. As in real life, a queue to a print job is a line awaiting service. A print queue is simply a number of print jobs lined up, waiting to be sent to your printer.

Print queuing software, usually called a *print spooler* or simply a spooler, wedges itself in your PC's memory between your application software and your printer. Most spoolers accept the output of your printer driver software and send their output to the port driver (or directly to your printer port). The design concept behind the print spooler is let your application software print as fast as it can. Most applications fully occupy themselves when making a printout, so you can do nothing with these applications while they are printing. The sooner they finish printing, the sooner you can get back to doing something useful with your PC.

The spooler works by capturing the commands and data bound for the printer with electronic speed and routing it to a temporary holding ground called a *buffer*. Most print spoolers save printer-bound data to your hard disk (or a hard disk on your network server). Because your application software does not have to wait for your printer to struggle through the mechanical challenge of printing, it can get back to work sooner. The spooler simply reels out the data it has saved to disk at a rate that your printer accepts it. It works in the background, almost invisible–not truly invisible, because the operation of your PC (particularly if it's an older, slower model) will lag because of the processing time devoted to the spooler.

Most spoolers accept more than one print job at a time. All the jobs waiting to be printed form the print queue.

In a perfect world, that would be enough in itself. But the world is far from perfect, and printers can become a significant blemish on it. One screw up in one of the jobs in the queue, and all will suffer. An errant control code could shift your printer into **graphics** mode, and all later text could turn into alien scribbles. Or a call from the boss could demand a duplicate of last month's report *immediately* while your printer is laboring away with your latest fractal composition. Print management helps take command of such problems. You can assign your monthly report top priority so that it sneaks ahead in the queue. You can stop the queue to fix printer problems. You have total control, at least to the degree that the author of the spooler thought to give you.

DOS

By itself, DOS does amazingly little with printers. Perhaps the most important DOS function is simply to give your printer a name—not Frank or Ethel or anything human or friendly, but a name by which your software can get its attention. Beyond that, DOS lets you send data directly to your printer (without the least investigation into what the data might be and whether it could cause your printer to choke and die. DOS also includes rudimentary abilities in managing print sessions and the ability to copy an image from your monitor screen to your printer. To say that DOS manages printers is a lot like contending that a clock controls the hours of the day.

But DOS does work with printers to some extent, and DOS programs have to abide by some of DOS's conventions in using your printer. Even in this day of advanced operating systems—a term which in itself means "anything other than DOS"—you still should know the rudiments of DOS printer functions. If nothing else, they can be useful in setting up and testing your printer.

Printer Naming

To DOS, every printer is a line printer. DOS was designed to work with simple line printers (as was the first PC) because at the time that's all there was. As a consequence, the name that DOS gives to a printer is LPT, short for Line PrinTer.

The LPT nomenclature may be familiar as a way of describing parallel ports. The jacks on the back of your PC may even be labeled LPT1 and LPT2. In general, the parallel port and printer names correspond exactly—or at least once did—because a printer was the only thing you were likely to connect to be parallel port and because a parallel connection was the only one that a sane person was likely to use (absent extenuating circumstances like pure necessity). However, the correspondence between ports and printers does not hold in every case. Connect a serial printer to your PC and you're apt to need to give it an LPT name to bring it to life or even use it with DOS applications.

LPT names are, in fact, automatically assigned to the parallel ports in your PC by its BIOS. When your system boots up, the BIOS looks at particular I/O address ranges to see if you have parallel port hardware attached. As the BIOS finds a set of port hardware, it assigns it an LPT name in serial order. The first port it finds become LPT1; the second, LPT2; and the third, LPT3. These are all the names that the BIOS can use.

The BIOS has a fixed search order for parallel ports. It starts with I/O address 3B0-3BF, then looks at 378-37F, and finally 278-27F. The first address was used by IBM's first video adapter, which also included a parallel port. This address is rarely used by parallel ports today. Consequently most PCs today assign LPT1 to 378-37F and LPT2, if it is present, to 278-27F.

After the BIOS assigns names to parallel ports, DOS and your programs can later access the ports using the LPT name without worrying about hardware addresses and the like. The BIOS of your PC automatically passes the data or commands your programs send to an LPT name to the proper hardware connections.

If you have a serial printer, you must assign an LPT name to it for DOS and many of your DOS-based programs to access it as a printer. You assign an LPT name to a printer using the **DOS MODE** command (which has several other functions as well). After you make the assignment, your serial printer will look like an ordinary line printer to DOS.

DOS uses one more name to describe printers, PRN. In general, DOS refers to your primary printer, the one connected to LPT1, as PRN. The name PRN can be used interchangeably with LPT1 by DOS and many applications.

Note that these DOS device names are reserved. That means you cannot use them as file names, even if you have a passion for three- or four-letter names. Instead of acting on a file, DOS acts on the device you name (which can have surprising results in itself). Rather than a drawback, these device names can be a useful feature of DOS, as you shall see.

The MODE Command

For DOS, the **MODE** command is a catch-all for handling housekeeping functions. It not only allows you to assign names but also sets serial port communications parameters and changes the operation of your PC's video system.

If you have a serial printer, you'll need to call on two of the functions of **MODE**. First you must set serial communications parameters so that your PC and printer can understand one another. Then you must assign your serial printer an LPT name so that your programs know where to send data to it.

Setting DOS's communications parameters to match your printer first requires that you know what parameters your printer uses. You set these values when you perform your printer's hardware configuration process, typically by altering entries in your printer's menu system or (with older and cheaper printers) by adjusting DIP switches inside the machine. At this point, how you make the adjustment is immaterial. All that matters is what you switch the settings to. (We'll cover the details of this aspect of printer configuration in Chapter 8, "Interfaces.")

The serial parameters you need to know to set up the **MODE** command include the serial port speed, the word length, parity, and number of spot bits. Table 6.1 summarizes the parameters you need to know, typical values you can set them to, and the typical value used in most printer set-ups. You also need to know the DOS name of the serial port to which you've connected your printer. This name must be in the range COM1 to COM4.

Table 6.1 Serial Port Parameters

Parameter	Units	Typical Range	Typical Default
Speed	Bits per second	300-115,200	9600
Parity	None	Even, Odd, Mark, Space, None	None
Word length	Bits	7 or 8	8
Stop bits	Bits	0, 1, 1.5, 2	1

These parameters are important because you enter them as command line options to the **MODE** command. Because **MODE** is an old, and therefore rather primitive, program, the order and form of the options you give to it are critical. You must first tell the **MODE** command which port you want to set up, then specify the parameters in the order speed, parity, word length, and stop bits. You must insert an equals sign between the port name and the parameters. The parameter values must be separated by commas. In addition, when configuring a printer, you should append a "P" to the end of the parameter string (also separated by a comma, which tells DOS that you've connected a printer and to ignore time-out problems, which are normal for printers but unusual for serial ports used for communications. You can use upper- or lowercase characters for the "P," parity value, or even COM port name; **MODE** is not case sensitive. Although you don't have to give the **MODE** command a value for every setting, **MODE** examines the parameter list and tracks the identity of each parameter using the commas. If you omit a parameter, you still need to put in the comma that would have gone with it.

A typical mode command would look like this:

```
MODE COM1=9600,n,8,1,p
```

This command takes control of your first serial port (COM1) and sets its speed to 9600 bits per second with no parity (n), eight-bit words (8), one stop bit (1), and warns your system that you have a printer connected to this port.

MODE recognizes a restricted range of parameters. Accepted speeds include the following values: 110, 150, 300, 600, 1200, 2400, 4800, 9600, 19,200, 38,400, 57,600, and 115,200 bits per second. It understands two word lengths: 7 or 8; three parity settings: odd, even, and none; and three stop-bit settings: 1, 1.5, and 2.

Assigning an LPT name to a serial printer using **MODE** is much simpler because there are no parameters. You just specify **MODE** to the COM port and LPT port names you wish to use, separating them by an equals sign, a syntax that pretty much describes the function of the command. A typing **MODE** command to names of printers would look like this:

```
MODE COM1=LPT1
```

After issuing this command, DOS will send whatever data you specify for your first printer to the serial printer connected to COM1.

COPY

The **COPY** command is DOS's all-purpose duplicating engine, probably the one command you tangle with most (if you bother to tangle with DOS at all). Hardly surprisingly **COPY** can be useful with printers as well as files. After all, **COPY** is a simple function that moves bytes from one place to another. It can just as easily move them from file to printer as from file to file. All you need to do is substitute the DOS name for your printer for the destination name in the **COPY** command. (In that most printers are one-way machines, using a printer name as a source file will likely bring your system to a halt–it could wait forever for your printer to say something or simply end the **COPY** command.)

For example, the command

```
COPY ANY_FILE.TXT LPT1
```

tells DOS to move the contents of the file ANY_FILE.TXT to your printer character by character. If your printer is in a receptive move, it will diligently type out each character. Most of the time you'll want to use plain text files because nontext characters will be interpreted by your printer as commands, which may lead to some surprising results.

Ordinarily you won't use the **COPY** command for printing. Most programs have their own print routines and drivers that send not only text but the proper formatting commands to your printer to make everything look perfect. Knowing how to use **COPY** can often be useful however.

Many programs give you the option of printing to a file. This function routes the output normally sent to your printer to a disk file, text complete with formatting commands. Once you have a file on disk, you can send it to your printer using the **COPY** command. Because the file encapsulates all the formatting commands, it will print exactly as it would had you made an ordinary printout. Saving and later printing files in this manner can be useful when your printer is tied up or broken. Or you can take a disk image of a document somewhere else to be printed out without having to install the application that generated the printout.

One disadvantage of this technique is that error handling is nonexistent. One error can screw up an entire print job. And if your printer develops a problem on page 99 of a 100-page job, you'll have to print out all the pages over again just to get to the last one. (And you'll probably encounter another error in exactly the same place.)

The **COPY** command is also useful in testing your printer. You can verify that your printer is installed properly to work with DOS by simply copying a text file to the printer. This is usually an all-or-nothing test. If the text prints, all is well. If it doesn't print, something is wrong. It's your problem to figure out what.

If you don't have a text file handy, you can always type directly to your printer using the **COPY** command. The command

```
COPY CON LPT1
```

will send the characters that you type at the keyboard directly to the printer, printing them out one at a time like an old-fashioned typewriter. To end this direct typing command, you must send an end-of-file character to DOS, which tells it to end the **COPY** command. This character is called "Control-Z" and has the value of 01A(Hex). You can type it by holding down the **Ctrl** key while pressing the **Z** key.

In truth, characters will generally not appear as you type them. Line printers, such as most ink-jets and impact dot-matrix machines, must receive an entire line before they start printing. In other words, you must press a line feed (which gets sent to the printer along with a carriage return when you press the **Enter** key), and then the printer will type out the entire line. Lasers and other page printers require even more coaxing. They need to receive a complete page before they print. Some will wait until they receive a sufficient number of lines to equal a page (for example, 60 line feeds/presses of the **Enter** key) or they get a form-feed character, ASCII value 0B(Hex), typed with the **Ctrl-L** key combination. Again, typing in this mode is useful in determining whether your printer is working.

You can also take advantage of the ability to use **COPY** to print a file by storing special set-up commands in disk files. To carry out a command such as to change fonts, just copy the appropriate file to your printer. If that's too hard to do, make a batch file with an appropriate name. For example, SCRIPT.BAT might contain the single command **COPY SCRIPT.DAT LPT1**. In SCRIPT.DAT you would store the command to switch to a script typeface.

PRINT

Using the **COPY** command for print jobs is a big waste of time. Not that the command is ineffective. It does exactly what it's supposed to do. But it also ties up your PC for the duration of the print job. Almost as bad, it requires your constant attention when you want to print multiple separate files. You have to copy each file to your printer individually after the previous print job completes.

The DOS command **PRINT** helps you sidestep these wastes of time. **PRINT** works like **COPY** and transfers files to your printer, but it also includes two welcome features–background operation and print job management.

Background operation means that you can start a file spooling out to your printer, then go on to another job *before* your job has finished printing. **PRINT** lets your PC print and do other work at the same time, a primitive form of multitasking. Command-line options to the **PRINT** command allow you to adjust how much of your PC's thinking time gets devoted to background printing and how much is left for carrying out your other applications.

Print job management means that **PRINT** will let you queue up several files to print with a single command. It will then print each one in sequence without further intervention. Beyond that, **PRINT** lets you change your mind and prevent pending jobs from getting printed.

The basic form of the **PRINT** command is just the command name followed by the file you want to print. If the file is not in the current directory, you must help DOS find the file by including the drive and path to the file. For example, the command

```
PRINT BALLOF.WAX
```

would send the characters from the file BALLOF.WAX to your printer. By default, the characters will go to the PRN or LPT1 device and take advantage of background operation.

PRINT also lets you list multiple files on a single command line. You list the files one after another, separating the names with spaces. For example, the following command:

```
PRINT FIRST.FIL SECOND.FIL THIRD.FIL FOURTH.FIL
```

will print out the files FIRST.FIL, SECOND.FIL, THIRD.FIL, and FOURTH.FIL without any further attention from you (other than to monitor the printer and ensure that paper flows smoothly through it). By default you can list 11 files—one printing and ten queued up—unless all the names won't fit on a single command line, in which case what you can type on a single line will limit the number of files in the queue.

PRINT allows for a number of options that control the operation of the program and the printer that you use. Most of these operations appear on the command line before the list of files you want to print, although three of the options may be mixed in with the filenames.

The options that must appear before the filenames include the following:

- **Buffer size.** You specify the size of the internal buffer to be used by **PRINT** to store data before it is sent to the printer with the **/b:** option, which you follow with the numerical buffer size in bytes.

NOTE

You can specify any size buffer in the range 512 to 16384 bytes. Each byte comes from the pool allocated to DOS programs, so you lose working memory with larger buffers. On the other hand, larger buffers can speed printing in some circumstances. The default setting for the **/b:** option is 512 bytes.

- **Printer name.** You can route the files you want to print to any printer connected to your PC. You specify the printer that you want to use with the

/d: (for "device") option. The **PRINT** command recognizes valid DOS device names for ports including LPT1, LPT2, LPT3, COM1, COM2, COM3, and COM4. You can also specify PRN, which is the default. **PRINT** is not case sensitive, so you can type the device names in upper- or lower-case (or a mixture of both). **PRINT** does not check whether you actually have a printer connected to the specified port. When it is unable to print successfully, however, it will give an error message.

- **Time to ready.** **PRINT** doesn't instantly send out an error message when a printer doesn't respond. Instead it waits a predetermined period, which you can change with the **/u:** option. If your printer is laggardly about coming on line, you can extend this delay.

  PRINT measures this delay in timer ticks, each one 1/18th of a second long. Normally, **PRINT** waits one tick for the printer to signal it is ready. The printer normally is ready and on-line before you issue the **PRINT** command, anyway. You can set the waiting period to be from one to 255 ticks (that's about 14 seconds).

- **Character wait.** **PRINT** always waits a predetermined time for a character to print before issuing an error message. **PRINT** waits a reasonable time, and if the character does not get printed, **PRINT** forces DOS to put an error message on your screen. Normally **PRINT** waits two clock ticks, roughly 1/10th of a second, before posting the error. The **/m:** option allows you to specify any waiting period for a character to print between 1 and 255 clock ticks.

- **Background operation**. When **PRINT** runs in the background, your PC's microprocessor must split its time between the foreground task and **PRINT**. By default, **PRINT** takes about 1/32 of your PCs power. Using the **/s:** command line option, you can change the time allocation between foreground and background tasks. Following the /s:, you indicate the number of system clock ticks to allocate to **PRINT>**. By default, **PRINT** gets 8. The maximum is 255, which essentially gives over all of your PC's time to printing (which means, of course, that **PRINT** takes over your PC rather than truly running in the background. The minimum number of ticks you can assign to background operation is one. With fewer than that, **PRINT** would get no time at all, and running **PRINT** would be pointless.

- **Queue size**. You can alter the number of files you can load into **PRINT**'s queue using the **/q:** command line option. The number you append to the option sets the number of files allowed in the print queue. The minimum is 4; the maximum, 32; the default, 10. Unlike ordinary DOS, **PRINT** allows only 64 characters to identify each file, a total that includes the filename as well as the path and drive letter.

- **File management.** Three command-line options to **PRINT** allow you to add and subtract files from the print queue. The **/p** switch adds files to the print queue. The **/p** option adds the file preceding the option on the command line and all files following the option. The option **/c** allows you to cancel one or more files from printing. The **/c** option acts first on the file preceding the option on the command line and applies to all files following the option until an add option appears on the command line. The **/t** option cancels the printing of all files, including all listed before and after the option on the command line.

Keystroke Print Functions

Even before the PC was invented, small computers followed a custom carried over from the days of printing terminals–you could make your printer echo (or copy) every character that appeared on your monitor screen. With printing terminals, this process was entirely automatic. In fact, teletypes were output-only terminals that had no monitor screens but only typing functions.

The first PCs also incorporated this ability to echo screen characters to their printers. It was incorporated as a separate operating mode, which had its own simple control system. To turn echo printing on, you pressed the **Ctrl-P** key combination on terminals or **Ctrl-PrtScrn** on the PC. A second press of the appropriate key toggled your PC out of its echo-print mode.

This function was a natural to the first PC display systems that incorporated the printer interface on the display adapter board, the IBM Monochrome Display Adapter (MDA) board. Later video systems divorced the video and print functions and rendered this mode obsolete. If you're a careless typist, the omission is a blessing. Leave your printer turned off (or worse, don't connect one at all) then type the revered **Ctrl-P** combination, and your PC would apparently die, awaiting your nonworking or nonexistent printer's acceptance of the characters appearing on your screen. Even when the printer is on, its slow speed could make every action on your PC an agony.

Ctrl-P has long been superseded by IBM's creating of the **Printer Screen** function for which the **PrtScrn** key was actually named. Instead of streaming monitor characters to the printer immediately as they appear, the **Print Screen** function gathers up everything that's visible on the screen and sends it out in one shot to your printer. Pressing the **Shift-PrtScrn** combination sends a copy of what's on your screen for character-by-character duplication on your printer.

DOS being as it is–essentially slow and stubborn–you have to wait while your screen images gets duplicated to your printer before you can do anything useful with your PC once again. With inexpensive dot-matrix printers, you could be waiting quite a while. Modern printers with large buffers make the process much quicker, almost instant.

NOTE

The **Print Screen** command sends the text of the screen image and nothing more to your printer. The image is not completed by a form feed command. With line printers, that means that the image will print out, and your printer will stop in the middle of a page because it will print only 25 lines on a 60-line sheet. With lasers and other page printers, nothing will happen until you send more lines or a form feed command to the printer.

GRAPHICS

Ordinarily the **Print Screen** command works only with text when your system is operating in **text** mode. If the screen display uses block graphics, such as boxes to highlight text or menus, these will be sent to your printer in the form of the IBM extended character set high-bit characters. If your printer is not set up to use the IBM extended character set, on-screen and on-paper graphics won't match. What appears are lines on the screen that will likely be rendered as a string of ordinary text characters. If you encounter this problem, you need only reconfigure your printer to use the IBM extended character set. With dot-matrix printers (the ones most likely to demonstrate the problem), you'll need to reset a DIP switch.

Graphics rendered in **graphics** mode are another matter. Because DOS ordinarily has no idea what kind of printer you have attached to your PC or even how to translate screen **graphics** to print language, running Print Screen in a graphics mode doesn't produce acceptable results.

DOS allows for printing a **graphics** screen using a limited range of printers. The terminate-and-stay-resident utility GRAPHICS acts as a translator for print screen. It takes the bit-image date from the screen and translates it into the codes understood by a limited range of printers. In other words, running GRAPHICS once installs a special printer driver for the **Print Screen** function.

To learn the language of an individual printer, GRAPHICS looks up the printer's profile in a file called GRAPHICS.PRO, which is ordinarily located in the same directory as the utility GRAPHICS.EXE, usually your DOS directory. GRAPHICS uses a keyword you add as a command line option when you run the program to search out your printer's profile in GRAPHICS.PRO. Table 6.2 lists the printer profiles contained in the GRAPHICS.PRO file along with the option you must add when running the GRAPHICS program. For **Print Screen** to work properly, your printer must be on this list or emulate a printer that is on the list.

Table 6.2 GRAPHICS Utility Printer Type Options

Manufacturer	Model	Option
Generic	Any PCL printer	hpdefault
Hewlett-Packard	Deskjet	deskjet
Hewlett-Packard	LaserJet	laserjet
Hewlett-Packard	LaserJet II	laserjetii
Hewlett-Packard	PaintJet	paintjet
Hewlett-Packard	QuietJet	quietjet
Hewlett-Packard	Quietjet Plus	quietjetplus
Hewlett-Packard	Ruggedwriter	ruggedwriter
Hewlett-Packard	Ruggedwriterwide	ruggedwriterwide
Hewlett-Packard	Thinkjet	thinkjet
IBM	Graphics, narrow carriage	graphics
IBM	Graphics, wide carriage	graphicswide
IBM	PC Color with black ribbon	color[1]
IBM	PC Color with CMY ribbon	color[8]
IBM	PC Color with RGB ribbon	color[4]
IBM	PC Thermal	thermal
IBM	Proprinter	graphics
IBM	Quietwriter	graphics

DOS Applications

Under DOS, printing from a specific DOS application is left completely under the control of the application. DOS never interferes but it does not help either. The program itself must take control of your printer, and send it all the commands it needs to print text or graphics.

Many applications have built in support for a wide variety of printers. In truth, they support only a few command sets and languages, but judiciously choose those to allow the widest possible use. They use the common command systems such as the Epson Esc/P sequence for graphics and simple formatting commands for text. (You'd be surprised how well ancient word processors were able to control page formatting using nothing but tabs, spaces, and the backspace commands.)

Many DOS applications use their own driver system to match with specific models of printers. Such a design allows the software publisher to write a few common drivers to match the popular command systems (that pesky Esc /P system again). Printers out of the mainstream (or simply out of the program publisher's ken) are left driverless. The printer manufacturer is expected to supply the driver to match the program so that you can put its printer to work. Of course this strategy works only for the most popular programs (under DOS, those are typically AutoCAD, Lotus 1-2-3, Microsoft Word, and WordPerfect.) Other programs may get no support. Some software publishers skirt the issue by designing their programs to use the same drivers as more popular software. Graphic environment and graphic development systems once promised to make driver-matching easier, but with one exception these never won wide support. The exception is Microsoft Windows, the subject of the next section. Most programmers have given up this flimsy strategy and moved to Windows, which does not require printer drivers for individual applications.

Some general rules to follow in matching impact dot-matrix printers:

- Follow your printer manufacturer's recommendation. After all, whoever made your printer should have the best idea of the command system he or she put into it. Your printer may be designed to exactly emulate a more popular model. Then again, remember that the manufacturer may be guessing at the command system used by a particular printer model and that even this recommendation is apt to be inexact.

- Match the number of print wires used by your printer. Although most 24-wire printers can emulate nine-wire models, the results are often unsatisfying. Moreover, nine-wire printers usually cannot emulate 24-wire models. A mismatch of the number of wires often results in odd output—strange-looking graphics with skewed aspect ratios, odd sizes, or a pale grey appearance.
- Match the carriage width of your printer. Some software automatically tries to take advantage of the full width of your printer's carriage, spreading text and graphics across a full 15-inch width if that's what it thinks you have. Install the wrong driver, and the last seven inches of your printout will get scrunched into the right margin or rollover to the next line. On the other hand, specify too narrow a margin, and you may never be able to put an image on the right half of a page.
- Match the color capabilities of your printer. If your printer can print color, ensure that the emulation you specify also supports color, otherwise you'll waste the money you paid for the added hues. Although monochrome printers generally ignore color commands, they may waste time printing the same line several times, each time in basic black.
- When in doubt, use drivers for older models. Newer printers have newer features. If new features were added *after* the maker of your printer burned the ROM chips in your printer, your machine can't possibly match. Compatibility always lags the original product because the compatible makers must learn from the original in order to incorporate its features. Staying with an older driver helps ensure that your software won't generate codes too new for your printer to handle. The downside of this strategy is, of course, that some updates involve bug fixes. A newer driver may incorporate bug fixes that an older driver does not.

Matching printer models is always an approximation. You can never be sure that one printer will act exactly like another. Nevertheless, if you're trying to work with DOS applications, printer drivers will remain important to you.

Canon

Canon developed its own language for its printers, called CaPSL (for Canon Printer Scripting Language). CaPSL is an amalgam of other standards. The current version is CaPSL III. CaPSL is not widely supported by other printer manufacturers (although some of the standards it incorporates are) and Canon itself uses other control systems (such as PostScript) in many of its products.

Epson and Esc /P printers

The one level of support built into nearly all software packages is that of Epson's Esc /P control system.

Epson embellished its own standard and created a new language, Esc /P2, that incorporates features such as scalable fonts.

If you don't have an Epson and can't find support for the particular make and model of printer that you want to use, the next step is to come as close as possible. In general, that means selecting the driver for the Epson model that most closely matches your printer. You'll face some degree of trial and error, but you won't damage anything. The worst possible outcomes of using the wrong driver are locking up your system (a reboot will cure that) and racing through a ream of paper, printing one character per page (quickly stopped with the expedient of switching off your printer–and perhaps your PC). Universal support falls apart with ink-jet and laser printers, however.

Hewlett-Packard and PCL Printers

Most programs identify PCL drivers not by level but by the corresponding Hewlett-Packard printer that uses that PCL level. In addition, several models of LaserJet offer particular features that your software may want to use. Use the corresponding HP driver only if your printer supports that feature. For example, if your printer cannot handle duplexing (printing on both sides of a sheet), don't use a LaserJet IIIsi or LaserJet 4si driver. Table 6.3 lists the PCL versions and features of many HP laser printers.

Table 6.3 PCL Version and Feature Support of HP LaserJet Models

HP Model Name	PCL Version	Special Features
LaserJet	PCL 3	512K RAM
LaserJet 500+	PCL 3	

LaserJet 2000	PCL 3	
LaserJet Plus	PCL 3	
LaserJet II	PCL 3	
LaserJet IID	PCL 3	
LaserJet IIP	PCL 3	
LaserJet IIP Plus	PCL 3	
LaserJet III	PCL 4	
LaserJet IIID	PCL 4	
LaserJet IIIP	PCL 4	No RET
LaserJet IIIsi	PCL 4	Duplexing
LaserJet 4	PCL 5	
LaserJet 4L	PCL 5	
LaserJet 4M	PCL 5	
LaserJet 4ML	PCL 5	
LaserJet 4P	PCL 5	
LaserJet 4MP	PCL 5	Postscript resident
LaserJet 4M Plus	PCL 5	
LaserJet 4MV	PCL 5	
LaserJet 4si	PCL 5	Duplexing
LaserJet 4V	PCL 5	
LaserJet 5	Enhanced PCL 5	
LaserJet 5P	Enhanced PCL 5	

IBM/Lexmark

IBM and Lexmark are twisted together in history and fact. IBM spun off its printer, keyboard, and typewriter business in March 1991, to create Lexmark. As part of the transition, Lexmark licensed the use of the IBM name on its products for five years so that Lexmark printers were entitled to wear the IBM nameplate while the new company established its own identity. Many products developed by

IBM continued in production by Lexmark and wore either or both corporate names. Although the two companies are separate entities today (IBM owns a 10% interest in Lexmark), the control systems used by their printers are much the same and will be discussed together here.

Although the printer that IBM sold as its Graphics Printer in 1981 was actually manufactured by Epson, it used its own ROM with several important differences: its own character set that reflected the extended attribute characters used on PC screens, a few commands lacking in the matching Epson model, and the omission of several other Epson commands. In general, the IBM and Epson dot-matrix control systems are the same, but in some cases the differences will become apparent. In general, you can get away with substituting the driver for one company's products for a printer of the other but the match will not be perfect. Always match IBM to IBM and Epson to Epson when possible. The Graphics Printer was superseded by the IBM Proprinter in 1982, which continued in production until 1992. In that period, 3,000,000 Proprinters were sold.

The initial IBM/Lexmark laser printers used their own command system in addition to sporting PCL compatibility. Although Lexmark has been downplaying its own controls, they still remain viable and supported by a number of products. Consequently you'll often find Lexmark drivers for software products. Of course, you should match your printer's set-up with the driver you choose–switch to PCL mode to use a PCL driver and Lexmark mode to use Lexmark drivers.

Lexmark uses two conventions for naming the drivers used by the company's various printers. Although early drivers did not follow the current scheme, which was introduced on May 1, 1993, as the company releases new versions of drivers, they will move to the new naming convention.

The first two characters describe the printer type, the next two indicate the software for which the driver is meant to work using an abbreviation of its name, the next two distinguish the version or release number of this software, the next (seventh) character indicates the data stream or printer type, and the final character indicates the country for which the driver is designated. For example, the driver named 39FL401E.EXE is designed to work with the Model 4039 printer (code 39) and the Freelance software program (FL) version 4.0 (characters 40) and to provide PostScript Level 1 support (1) in the English language (E).

In general, the printer code in the first two characters is drawn from the IBM or Lexmark model designation of the printer. Table 6.4 summarizes most of the codes used by the Lexmark driver system for this purpose.

Table 6.4 Lexmark Driver Designations; Printer Codes (first two characters)

Code	Printer
02	IBM 6902 Correcting Wheelwriter, 6783 Wheelwriter 10 Series II
03	IBM 6903 Correcting Quietwriter
05	IBM 2205 PS/1
19	IBM 4019 LaserPrinter
12	IBM 4212 Proprinter 24P
26	IBM 4226 Model 302 Printer
29	IBM 4029 LaserPrinter
37	IBM LP 4037 5E Printer
38	IBM 38XX Pageprinter
39	IBM 4039 LaserPrinter
3A	IBM 4039 Plus LaserPrinter
3L	Lexmark 4039 10 Plus
42	IBM 42XX Proprinter family
47	ValueWriter 600 by Lexmark, 4047 5E
49	Lexmark Optra family
50	IBM 6750 Quietwriter 7/8 and IBM 674X Wheelwriter 3/5/6
52	IBM 52XX Quietwriter family
70	IBM 4070 IJ
72	IBM 4072 ExecJet Printer
76	IBM 4076 ExecJet II Printer
7C	ExecJet IIc 4076 by Lexmark
79	IBM 4079 Color JetPrinter PS
83	IBM 5183 Portable Printer
8P	IBM 238X Plus Personal Printer Series II
8X	IBM 238X Personal Printer Series II
9P	IBM 239X Plus Personal Printer Series II
9X	IBM 239X Personal Printer Series II
MP	Multiple printers

The various codes used to indicate the application for which the driver is to be used vary. In general, these two characters will be initials or a simple abbreviation. The version code usually follows the convention of the publisher of the application.

The data stream code indicates the language that the driver sends out to the printer. These include various versions of both Hewlett-Packard's PCL and PostScript as well as several more esoteric command formats. Table 6.5 summarizes the definition of the data stream code character.

Table 6.5 Lexmark Driver Designations; Seventh Character

Code	Definition
1	PostScript language Level 1
2	PostScript language Level 2
3	PCL 3
4	PCL 4
5	PCL 5
A	PostScript language Level 1 & 2
D	Diskimage File
E	Epson
F	Fonts
N	Network Utilities
P	PPDS
U	Printer Utilities

The final character, the national or language designation, follows a simple scheme. In general, the letter value is the first character in the name of the language in English. For example, German is "G" rather than "D" (for *Deutsch*). When the first character would be duplicative, Lexmark substitutes the second character in the language name. Table 6.6 summarizes these national language abbreviations.

Table 6.6 Lexmark Driver Designations; National Language Abbreviations (eighth character)

Code	Language
D	Danish
E	English
F	French
G	German
I	Italian
N	Norwegian
S	Spanish
U	Dutch
W	Swedish

PostScript Printers

Unlike other printer control systems, PostScript was developed by a software company, Adobe Systems, rather than a printer manufacturer. PostScript was first released in 1985. Over the years, it went through minor revisions including the addition of color commands in 1988. In 1990, it was superseded by PostScript Level 2.

The structure and core of commands of the two levels are the same. Level 2 can be considered a superset of Level 1. Level 2 printers are generally backwardly compatible with Level 1 drivers, although there are some peculiarities. Most of the time a PostScript Level 2 printer will work flawlessly with Level 1 code, but all of their features will not be available.

Adobe currently uses a three-step system for indicating versions of its drivers. The first number indicates the PostScript level. Currently, only 1 and 2 are used. Following a period, the next number is the major revision number. After a second period comes a minor revision number. The current level of PostScript drivers when this book was written was version 2.1.2, which replaced version 2.1.1. The difference between the two versions involves a bug fix for printing TrueType characters from Adobe Acrobat files.

Despite PostScript's recognition as an industry standard, it is not invariable. PostScript drivers from printer manufacturers often include printer-specific features. Adobe drivers are generic and will control any PostScript printer of the appropriate level. Printer-specific drivers give access to additional features not supported by the general PostScript language. You should always use the manufacturer-supplied PostScript driver instead of the general Adobe driver when you have the choice–and the printer that matches the driver.

Windows 3.x

The great joy of graphic operating environments when they were first introduced was freedom from the need for special drivers for each application you wanted to run. The environment's drivers for both display systems and printers covered all applications that ran within the environment. The original incarnation of Windows (introduced in 1985) was only one of many graphical environments. All aimed to give programmers a common application interface that would allow them to take advantage of this unified driver approach. Freed from the need to craft drivers for every available printer (or at least the major models), the programmers could concentrate on making the core code better.

The near-universal acceptance of Windows 3.x among PC users has helped promote this philosophy and has helped make Windows a success.

Normally, you need to tangle with only two issues when using a printer with Windows 3.x. First, you must deal with the installation process to be sure that you have installed the proper driver for your printer. After that one-time-only chore, your dealings with printer involve little more than selecting the right menu entry from your application software and using Print Manager to control your print jobs.

As with the rest of the code used by Windows 3.x, Print Manager is a 16-bit application. It runs in the background using co-operative multitasking. Its spooling operations can only be used by Windows applications because only Windows applications use the program calls needed to access it. DOS applications that run under Windows connect directly to your printer using their own driver software.

Driver Installation

You need to install a driver for every printer you want to use with Windows. When you have two printers that are exactly the same but connected to different ports, each requires its own, separately installed driver (even if the drivers are identical). If you have two printers that share a single port–for example, using a switch box–you should install a driver to match each one unless the two printers are identical and used identically.

Under Windows 3.x, installing a printer driver is called adding a printer. You start the process from **Control Panel**, which is installed by default in the Main program group in Program Manager. Double-click on the Control Panel icon, and you'll have a wide variety of options available to you. One of these is the Printer icon. Double-clicking on this icon initiates the driver installation process.

The first thing you'll see when you install drivers is an opening screen that looks like Figure 6.2. The display lists the printer your Windows system will use as a default when you simply run a **Print** command as well as any other printers you've installed in your system. The Windows definition of printer includes any device that accepts text output from your applications, so you may see devices (which may be nothing more than software) in addition to physical printers listed. The example shows three different fax products besides a single printer.

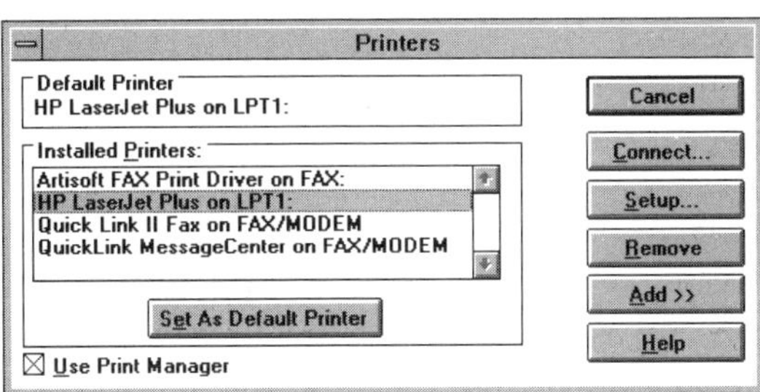

Figure 6.2 The Windows 3.1 printer installation opening screen.

The printer installation system gives you several options for action, represented by the buttons on the right side of the screen. These allow you to cancel out of the procedure if you decide you goofed and don't want to alter your current settings, help if the screen has left you perplexed, and four choices to aid in adding or removing a printer.

The order of the buttons follows no particular logic. The first button to click on to install a new printer is **Add**, near the bottom of the list. Once you click on **Add**, the printer installation window will lengthen to give you a choice of printers to install, as shown in Figure 6.3.

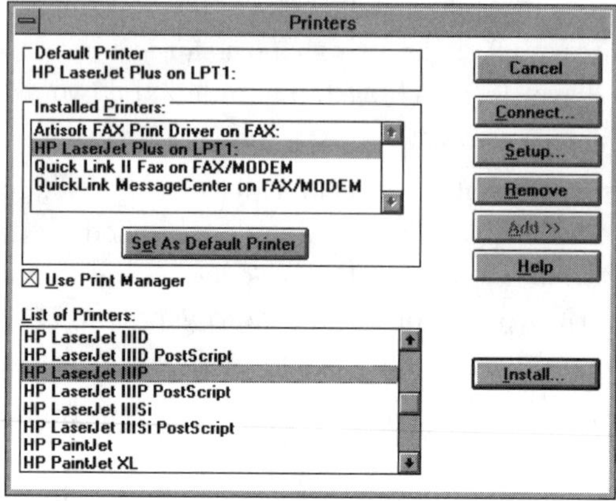

Figure 6.3 Selecting a printer make and model to install.

To select the printer you want to install, you only need to highlight its name. Just scroll through the list until the name of your printer is highlighted by the color bar. If your printer is not listed, select the option at the top of the list for printers not supported by Microsoft's own driver. If your printer is listed but also comes with its own driver disk, you should also choose this option as if your printer were not listed.

Once you have your printer (or its lack) highlighted, then click on the **Install** button. Windows will then begin the installation process.

Part of the process is copying the driver software into your \Windows\System subdirectory. If you've previously installed a similar printer, Windows may find the driver already installed, and will query you whether you want to use your old driver or add a new one. If, as is most common, Windows finds no suitable driver already in the \Windows\System directory, it will prompt you to load the driver software into drive A:. You'll see a screen like that shown in Figure 6.4.

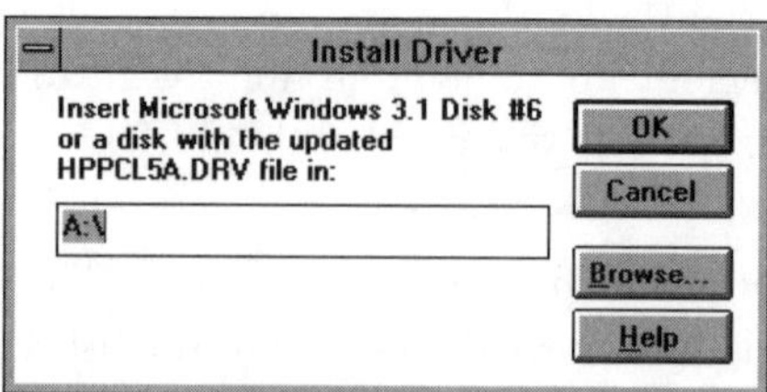

Figure 6.4 Windows prompting for a driver disk.

You can substitute any drive or directory for the **A:** including network drives and directories. Windows looks for a series of files–the driver itself as well as files providing installation information–and if any are missing, it will give you the same prompt all over again, asking you to please put in a valid driver disk. If Windows obstinately keeps posting this same prompt, check to be sure you're listing the right drive and directory. And make sure the right disk is in your floppy disk drive.

Once you've installed the driver software, you will need to indicate how you have connected it to your PC. You tell Windows about the connection by clicking on the **Connect** button at the Printers window. You will then see a new window that looks like that in Figure 6.5.

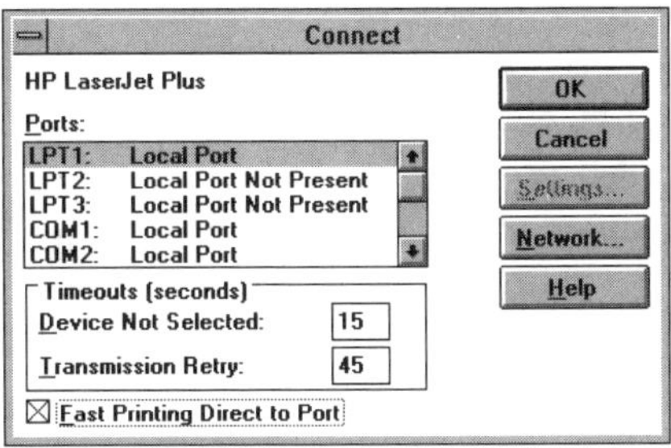

Figure 6.5 Selecting a port during printer installation.

The Connect window lists your various port options, including all the potential hardware ports supported by the PC standard. Selecting a parallel port gives you no further options. When you select a serial port, however, the Setting button will become active. You can then click on it to adjust the serial port parameters to match those used by your printer. Note that the parameters used by Windows need not be the same as those you may have loaded previously with the **MODE** command under DOS. The settings you make under Windows only apply when Windows is operating. Figure 6.6 shows the serial port options that Windows provides.

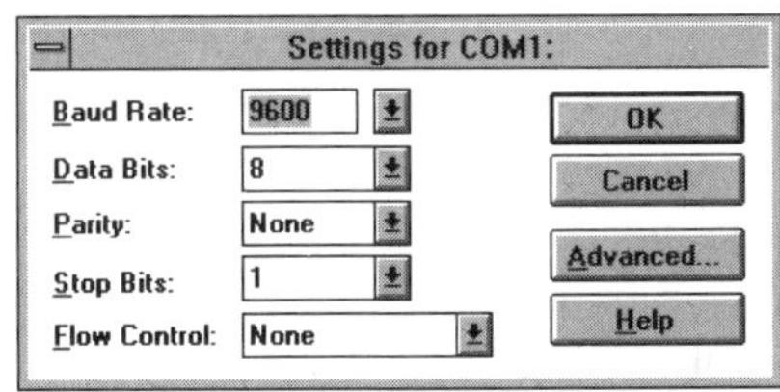

Figure 6.6 Setting up serial port communications parameters.

You only need to select the speed, word length, parity, stop bits, and handshaking used by your printer. The Advanced button is of interest only if you've elected to use COM3 or COM4 as your printer port. It allows you to specify the I/O port and interrupt used by the serial port for the printer. Set these values to those you give to your COM port when you install the hardware.

Once you've completed the installation of your printer, you can configure it for normal operation. You can set your configuration from the Print menu within your applications (in general, you select **File**, then **Printer Setup**) or you can set the defaults back at the Printers windows. Just click on the **Setup** button. You'll then see a screen like that shown in Figure 6.7. The exact look of the screen will vary of course with the printer make and model that you've installed.

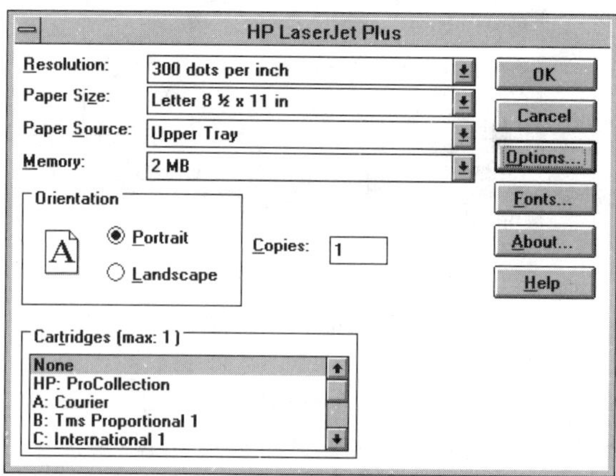

Figure 6.7 Set-up options during printer installation.

For example, the figure shows the set-up option for the HP LaserJet Plus. These include the resolution, paper size, the paper try to use, page orientation, installed font cartridges, the memory installed in the printer, and the number of copies to make in each print session. Ordinarily, the defaults suffice for most printing, but the set-up options allow you to customize printer operations to suit your work and life style.

Note that the set-up options allow you two further choices, accessed through the Options and Fonts buttons. Again, whether these choice are available depends on the printer that you've installed. With the HP LaserJet, clicking on the **Options** button opens a window like that shown in Figure 6.8.

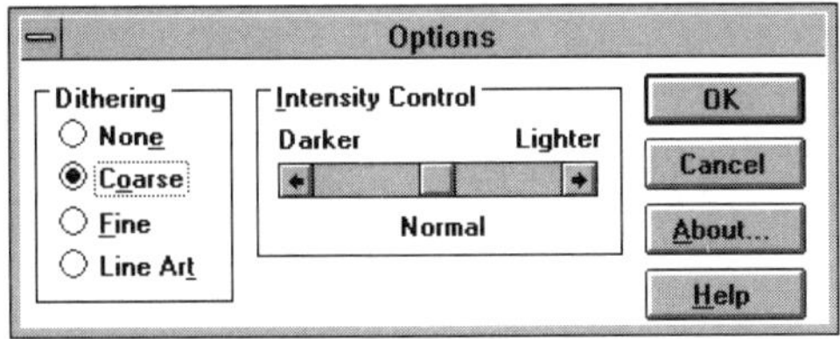

Figure 6.8 Printer dithering and intensity options.

With the LaserJet, you get to alter two options from this window: the type of dithering to use and the print density. Your dithering choices (None, Coarse, Fine, and Line Art) follow a progression in the number of available greys—coarse allows more greys at the price of larger image cells. The density adjustment allows you to compensate for applications that print too light or heavy.

The other advanced choice at the Options window is Fonts. Clicking on that button when you have an HP printer (or one that uses the HP driver) installed brings up the HP Font Installer program, a utility written by Hewlett-Packard but distributed by Microsoft with Windows. Its principle window is shown in Figure 6.9.

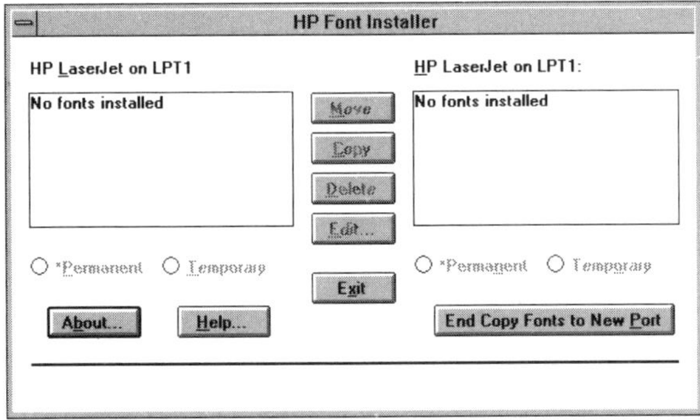

Figure 6.9 The Hewlett-Packard Font Installer.

The HP Font Installer copies fonts from floppy to hard disk and manages them, making them available to all your Windows applications. It also ensures that individual fonts get installed into your printer when you need them.

Other printers may allow you different set-up options. All have the same effect and goal, letting you customize your normal printing process.

PRINT MANAGER

Windows lets you control your print queue through its Print Manager. Click on the **Print Manager** icon, and you'll see a screen like that shown in Figure 6.10.

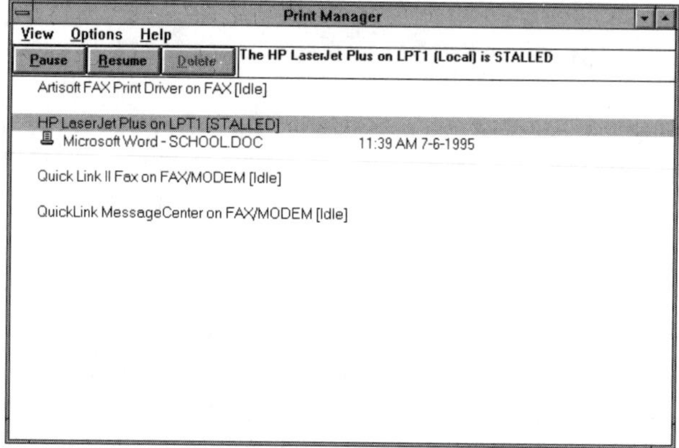

Figure 6.10 The Print Manager control system.

Print Manager lists all available print devices and all pending print jobs in its initial screens. It lists the print jobs by the device you told Windows to print them to. Under each print device, you'll see all its queued up jobs listed by originating program and file name as well as the time the job got sent to the spooler.

Many printers include their own Windows control programs. These typically are specially written to control special features of the printer. In general, they offer superior support than the drivers that come standard with Windows offer, if just because they are more recent. In other words, if your printer comes equipped with its own driver software for Windows 3.x, you should install that driver.

Printer makers and utility publishers sometimes include their own enhancements to other Windows functions. These promise improved versatility or greater performance. For example, Epson includes its Spool Manager with many of its newer printer models and PC-Kwik includes its own Windows printer driver. Both of these products substitute for Print Manager and, while not exactly accelerating printing, they do make the print process quicker.

OTHER UTILITIES

Windows 3.x allows you to have more than one print management program. For example, the Epson Spool Manager happily coexists with Print Manager, and you can select which control system to use either by port or by designating which you wish to use with the Control Panel.

The Epson Spool Manager is contained in the program EPSPLMGR.EXE, which normally installs itself in your /Windows/System directory. You must run it to use it, by clicking on its icon or by adding it to the list of applications to Load in your SYSTEM.INI file. After you use Epson Spool Manager for a print job, the program remains in memory, ready for its next assignment. If you want to recover the memory it uses, you must manually close it. The next time you want to print, it will start up automatically. If you use Epson Spool Manager on a printer server in your network, you should leave it constantly running so that it will print the files that it spools from workstations as they come in. (Epson calls these spooled-but-unprinted files "journal" files.)

If Epson Spool Manager accepts a print job from an application but does not print it out, first ensure that your printer is switched on, ready, and connected to the correct port. The spool program also has a **Hold** function, so you should verify that you have not inadvertently put printing on hold. (**Hold** is located in the spool manager's Document menu.)

When print jobs stop partway through, it can indicate that your spooler has run out of free disk space or it may have encountered a badly fragmented disk. These problems are not readily solved during a printout, so you should always be sure you have adequate free disk space and that you regularly defragment your hard disk. Epson, for example, recommends you have at least 20MB of free disk space to take advantage of its Spool Manager, and notes that 100MB is even better. Remember, color graphics printing involves three or four times as much data as monochrome.

Some spooling errors are caused by interaction between your video and printer drivers. You can determine whether you have such a conflict in your system by temporarily reverting back to the basic VGA driver and then trying to duplicate the spooling problem. If the spooling problem does not occur, a driver interaction is the root of your problem. One solution is to forego either your high-resolution video driver (your poor eyes) or the enhanced spooler (your poor patience). Better still is to obtain the latest versions of both drivers.

Video drivers can also cause your PC to slight on colors in printouts. In addition, some programs (notably Windows' own Paintbrush) are limited to printing the color range of the current video display. If you use 16-color mode, Paintbrush will print only in 16 colors even from 24-bit True Color files.

Windows 95

Windows 95 adds a wide variety improvements (and simple changes) to printer control, compared to earlier Windows versions.

The biggest difference–and the first you're likely to notice–is the absence of Print Manager from the scene. Instead Windows 95 uses a Printers folder that normally resides in the Settings menu available from the Start bar. Click on the Printers icon (under settings) to open the Printers folder and you'll find both the printer installation wizard and the Windows 95 control system for any of the printers you've already installed.

Although the control afforded through the Printers folder is much the same as that which is available with Print Manager, you'll find some important differences. First, because each printer has its own control system, you can customize the properties of each printer individually. For example, you can assign each printer its own job separator rather than making such assignments globally.

As with other Windows 95 configuration information, you store and control printer configuration information using a property sheet much like that used by your applications. That way you only need to learn one interface to control the set-up of every aspect of your PC. Each printer gets it own property sheet (and its own icon). To access the property sheet to alter the printer configuration, you only need to click on the icon of your printer in the Printers folder or select **Properties** from the Printers menu selection after you open your specific printer. The property sheet will let you change nearly every set-up parameter of your printer and its connection with your PC, including the printer port or network path used by the connection, the paper options used by the printer, your choice of printer fonts, and other options specific to the specific printer model.

This design brings other benefits. For example, because each printer has its own control system, you can customize the properties of each printer individually. If you wanted to, you could assign each printer its own job separator rather than making such assignments globally.

The differences behind the scenes are even more dramatic. Microsoft rewrote the entire print system for Windows 95. The new design restructures printer drivers and radically alters the operation of the print spooler. Where the Windows 3.1 print system used code scatter among several Windows components, Windows 95 integrates them all as a series of 32-bit virtual device drivers. Moreover, the Windows 95 print system was rewritten using 32-bit code (much of it drawn from the Windows NT print subsystem) instead of the 16-bit instructions used by Windows 3.x, giving it an automatic performance edge. It fully supports the pre-emptive multitasking design of the overall Windows 95 architecture.

Printer drivers under Windows 95 follow the operating system's new minidriver model. This design splits drivers into two parts, a generic half that supports the features common to a given type of device and a product-specific half that adapts the features of a particular model of printer to the system. This two-part design makes writing drivers easier. A printer manufacturer needs to be concerned only with the product-specific part of the driver. Microsoft itself has exploited this technology to give Windows 95 extensive built-in printer support. From the box, using all the manufacturer's defaults Windows 95 can take control of over 800 different printer models.

In the Windows 95 printer system, spooling has moved from after to before the page rendering and rasterization for most printers. Instead of creating the data for the printer before spooling it, the Windows 95 system creates an *enhanced metafile*, which the printer driver interprets as it runs as a separate thread while your applications execute. As a result, old applications that shift control to the print process regain control significantly faster.

Under Windows 3.1, your Windows applications sent raw data to the printer driver, which translated the Graphic Device Interface commands into printer commands to build an output image before sending the image to the spooler (and then to the printer). In effect, this design was equivalent to attaching a hardware spooler between your PC's parallel port and your printer. You had to wait while the application and printer driver generated a print image. The only time you saved was the excess required by the printer for its mechanical operation.

Under Windows 95, the printer driver forms the page image in the background. For example, if you wanted to draw a big, blue circle using Print Manager, you'd have to wait while the printer driver drew the circle and painted each bit blue before you could enter further data into your application. With Windows 95, your application needs only to send out GDI function calls to build what Microsoft calls an *enhanced metafile* or *EMF*. The EMF contains a list of Windows graphic commands that can later get interpreted into printer commands by a background program. As a result, the hard (and thus time-consuming) work of interpreting them into raw printer data no longer keeps you from interacting with the application. While you type away, the printer driver draws the circle and paints it. Then, without further intervention, it sends the image to the spooler, which reels it out to your printer.

With multithreaded Windows 95 applications, the change is not an issue because the applications themselves can assign printing to a separate, concurrent thread. Nor does this improvement affect PostScript printing. PostScript code is accepted by the Windows 95 queue and passed along to your printer without change. In addition, Windows 95 expands its spooling function to embrace DOS applications as well as Windows programs. When you run a DOS application under Windows 95 and issue a **Print** command, Windows 95 reroutes the output of your DOS print stream through its own printer subsystem. Although your DOS application still uses its own DOS printer driver and doesn't make use of the EMF system, the output of the driver feeds into the Windows 95 print queue. You can then manage your DOS print job as if it were a Windows print job, changing its priority or even canceling it as you would with regular Windows printing. Compared to running under DOS alone or Windows 3.x, you get back control of your application sooner because the spooler accepts the printer driver output faster than can a printer or even the printer port itself.

Unlike the spooling function of earlier Windows versions, the spooler in Windows 95 allows for *deferred printing*. The Windows 95 print subsystem will carry out every step of the print operation from application to driver to metafile to spooler without sending the actual **Print** command through the port. The print subsystem saves the output that would go to the printer in a disk file and can accommodate multiple print jobs, limited only by your free disk space. You can later print out these files.

Deferred printing can be useful if your printer dies in the line of duty or if you are working on your notebook PC and don't have a printer readily available. You can run the **Print** function and hold the output until you return to home base and can plug back into your printer.

The actual spooler is made from several 32-bit protected mode device drivers. Microsoft designed it to operate more smoothly when running in the background. For example, while Print Manager in Windows 3.1 handed down a block of data to the printer whether or not the printer was ready to receive it, forcing the system to wait until the printer was ready, the Windows 95 spooler only sends out data when the printer signals that it is ready.

Installation and Set-Up

Despite the unified Windows 95 configuration process, Microsoft made printers a special case and gave their installation a special entry point separate from the rest of the hardware you might want to install. (This honor was also bestowed on a few other devices, such as modems.) As a consequence, the printer installation process has its own installation wizard (Microsoft's clever term for "utility program") called, as you might expect, the *Add Printer Wizard*. Although the wizard is supposed to make printer installation a "no-brainer," if you have never confronted its sort of enforced-choice prompting, you might feel out of your element. Old hands at using PCs know that any so-called intuitive interface requires more than a bit of explanation the first time through. So let's take a look at the Add Printer Wizard and see how its magic works.

Plug and Play for Printers

For anyone who has ever gotten a migraine from trying to install a peripheral to his PC—a class that generally includes anyone who's tried to add anything to a PC—one of Windows 95's greatest blessing is its support of the Plug-and-Play standard. In fact, Windows 95 is the first operating system to fully implement Plug-and-Play.

Using a combination of Plug-and-Play technology and support of bidirectional parallel ports through which your PC can communicate with your printer (and carry on a full two-way conversation), Windows 95 can automatically detect what kind of printer you have when you install it, when you install the operating system for the first time, or even when you simply boot up your PC. You can also explicitly command Windows 95 to look for your printer and configure itself (which sort of defeats the purpose of Plug-and-Play, but the Windows 95 developers planned for many strange contingencies). Using the information supplied by your printer, Windows 95 can select the proper printer driver to use or ask you to install a new driver if it cannot find one that will work. The only unfortunate aspect to this process is that your printer must be capable of carrying on the required Plug-and-Play conversation, and only newer printers have the needed Plug-and-Play support. For example, the entire Hewlett-Packard LaserJet 4 line (including the LaserJet 4L, 4 Plus, 4ML, 4MP, 4M

Plus, 4P, and 4si), the Lexmark 4039 and 4039+, and the ValueWriter 600 all currently support the Plug-and-Play standard.

The Plug-and-Play process for printers is a step-by-step process that depends on both hardware and software support. When you first install Windows 95 on your PC and whenever you boot it up after that, the operating system loads the Plug-and-Play configuration program. This software routine sends commands out through your PC's parallel port (which must comply with the IEEE 1298 standard, see Chapter 8, "Interfaces") and awaits responses from your printer. If the printer complies with the Plug-and-Play standard, it will identify itself to the operating system. Windows 95 then runs through its list of printers to determine whether it has configuration information to tell it how to use the printer it has detected.

If Windows 95 discovers that it has not been set up to work with the printer you've connected to your PC, it will post a message on your monitor asking you whether you would like to install the machine. If you answer in the affirmative, and Windows 95 has a matching printer driver in its repertory, it will automatically install the driver and configure it to match your printer. If Windows 95 can't find a driver that will work with your printer, it will ask you to insert the one of the Windows setup disks to search for a driver. If Windows 95 still cannot find a driver that will work with your printer, it will then ask you to slide in whatever disk that came with the printer that contains the manufacturer's own printer driver.

Add Printer Wizard

The first step in installing a printer is calling up the Add Printer Wizard. To do that, you need to know which rock to look under. The place to start is the Start bar. Put your mouse pointer on Start, then click to bring up the main menu. Run your mouse up to **Settings**, and click or simply hold it there for a second.

You'll then see a submenu offering you the choice of the Printers folder, among others. Click on the **Printers** folder to open it, and you'll see a screen like that shown in Figure 6.11.

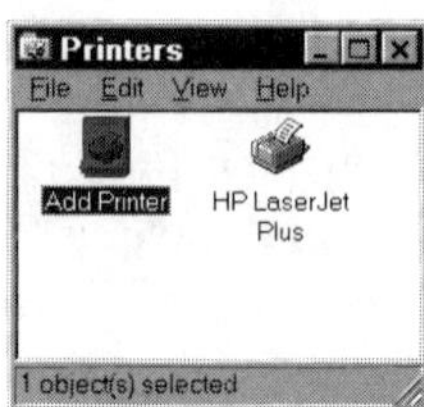

Figure 6.11 The Printers folder once opened.

Once you've opened the Printers folder, you'll see the Add Printer Wizard. If you haven't installed any printers before (including during your initial Windows 95 set-up operation), it will be the only icon you can see in the open window. If you've already installed one or more printers, you'll see the Wizard accompanied by the printers you've previously installed.

To activate the Wizard, click on it. After a slight flurry of disk activity as Windows 95 loads the appropriate code, the Wizard will swing into operation, and you'll see a screen like that shown in Figure 6.12.

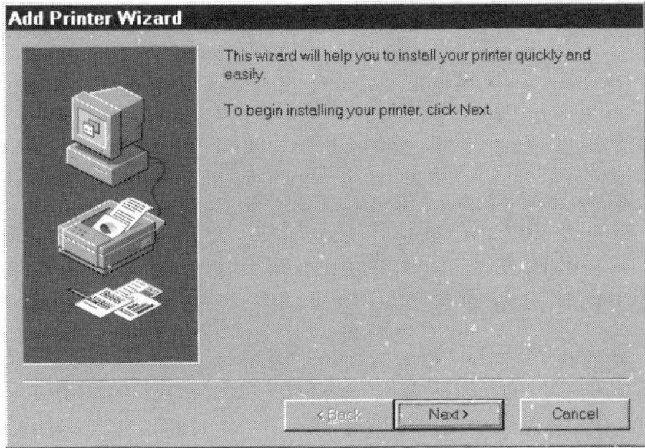

Figure 6.12 The Add Printer Wizard opening screen.

At this point, the printer installation process appears straightforward, and your choices are only two: continue with the process (which requires merely pressing **Enter** or clicking on the **Next** button; or canceling the process (press **Tab** then **Enter** or click on **Cancel**) because you really don't want to install a new printer. For example, you may have clicked on the **Add Printer** icon out of curiosity or mistakenly thought you'd need to use it to change the defaults on your printer (you don't).

If you choose the **Next** button, you'll quickly get into the meat of the printer installation process. If your printer supports the Plug-and-Play process, you'll need to do nothing more in the installation process. Windows 95 will automatically figure out what kind of printer you have (by asking the printer, naturally) and find the appropriate driver, if it has it available. If not, you'll be prompted for it.

If your printer does not support Plug-and-Play, the Add Printer Wizard needs to know what kind of printer you do have. It will ask you with a new window, which should look like the one shown in Figure 6.13.

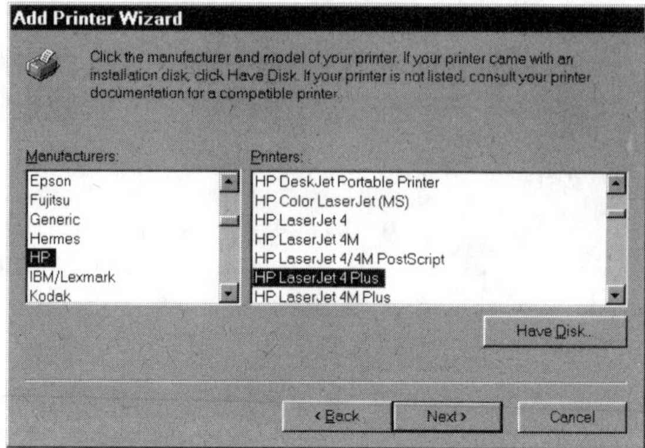

Figure 6.13 Selecting a printer manufacturer and model with the Add Printer Wizard.

Selecting a make and model of printer using the Add Printer Wizard is simple. First, find the name of the manufacturer of your printer in the left column, scrolling down as necessary. As you highlight manufacturers, the right list changes to reflect a lengthy selection of printers offered by that manufacturer. Highlight your particular model by scrolling to it and clicking on it. If you can make an exact match *and* you do not have an updated printer driver, click on **Next** to continue the installation process.

The Add Printer Wizard prompts you that if your printer came with a disk, you should click on the **Have Disk** button. This tells the wizard that you want to substitute a different driver from the one that Microsoft includes with the Windows 95 package. You can also click on **Have Disk** if your make or model of printer is not listed but comes with a Windows 95 driver on disk.

As the wizard notes, if your printer is not listed you can still install it by specifying a compatible printer from the list. Choose the make and model that's closest to your own. If your printer's manual lists models with which your printer is compatible, select one of those.

Clicking on the **Have Disk** button opens another window that prompts you to slide a disk into your floppy disk drive, like that shown in Figure 6.14.

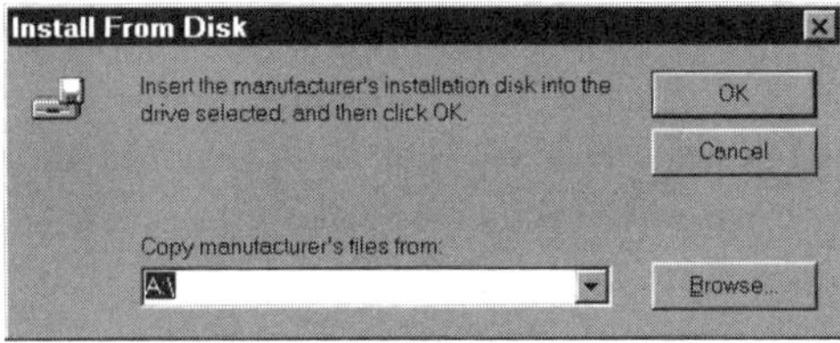

Figure 6.14 Substituting or adding driver files from another disk.

You can specify another disk drive or directory by typing in response to the prompt, "Copy manufacturers files from:" or, if you are not sure where the installation files are located, you can click the **Browse** button to search them out, shifting between disks and directories as necessary.

Once the Add Printer Wizard has found the drivers associated with your printer and is ready to copy them to your \Windows\System directory as necessary, it needs a bit more configuration information. Specifically, you must tell it how you plan to connect your printer to your PC. That is, you must specify an interface.

The Add Printer Wizard automatically pops up a window querying you for the proper port connection that looks like Figure 6.15.

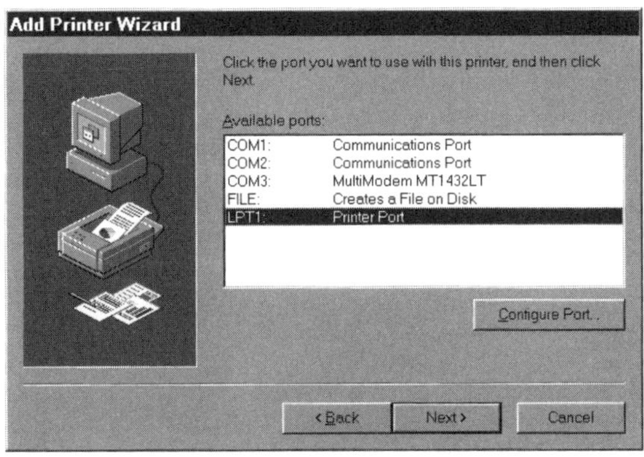

Figure 6.15 Selecting a port with the Add Printer Wizard.

The Add Printer Wizard lists all available ports, network connections, and the option of writing files to disk. You only need to choose the interface from those listed.

Ports require their own configuration, however, and the Add Printer Wizard integrates that function with the regular installation process. After you've selected a port, click on **Configure Port** to set it up. The response of the Add Printer Wizard varies with the kind of port you've chosen.

If you select an LPT (parallel or printer) port, the wizard displays a simple screen like that shown in Figure 6.16:

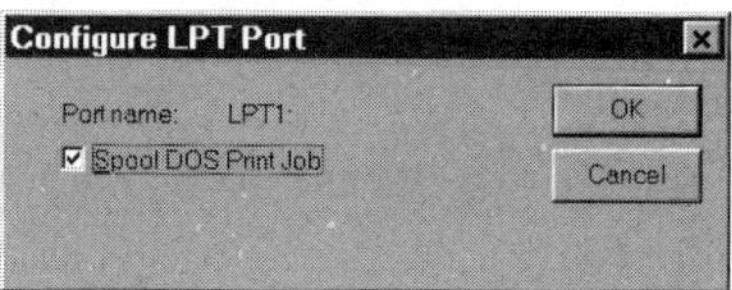

Figure 6.16 Options for parallel port configuration.

As you should note from this window, your only option is whether to spool DOS print jobs. As the default, Windows 95 will capture the data your DOS applications send to a printer port and will add them to the queue in its spooler. By clicking on the checked box in front of the Spool DOS Print Jobs prompt, you can deselect this feature. The only time you will want to deselect spooling DOS print jobs is when one of your applications refuses to work with the spooler.

If you have connected your printer with a COM (serial or asynchronous) port, the Add Printer opens a more complex window, the properties sheet shown in Figure 6.17.

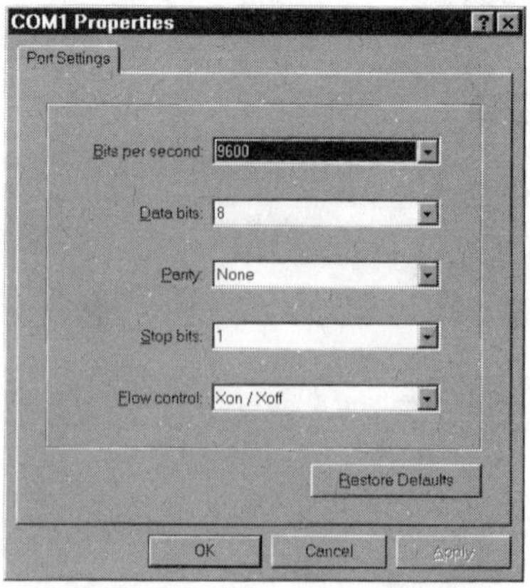

Figure 6.17 Serial port setup options.

This properties sheet allows you to change the communications port parameters that Windows 95 will use to communicate with your printer. You should select setting that match the ones you've chosen for your printer. Note that Windows 95 defaults to software flow control (XON/XOFF), which can cause problems when printing graphics. Instead, you should choose the alternate setting, hardware flow control. Of course, to make hardware flow control operate properly, you'll need to use the proper serial cable, one that supports hardware handshaking. Chapter 8, "Interfaces," describes the proper cables and will help you ensure you can make hardware handshaking work. (Note that the Add Printer Wizard does not give you the option of spooling or not spooling DOS print jobs with serial printers.)

After you've chosen and set up your printer port using the Add Printer Wizard, click the next button for the next step of the installation process. The wizard will respond with a window like that shown in Figure 6.18 to give a name to your printer.

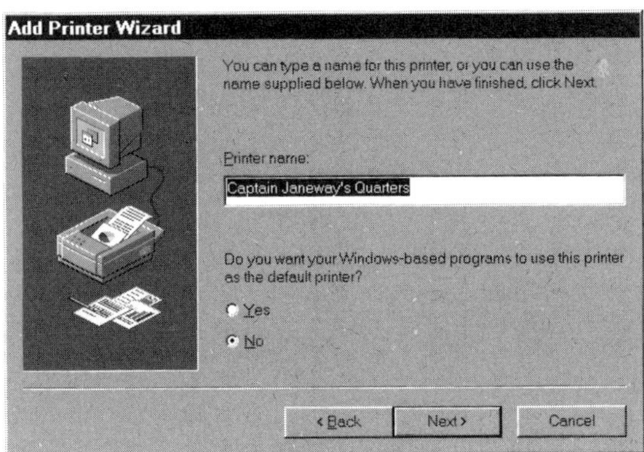

Figure 6.18 Giving your printer a name.

You can give just about any name you want to your printer. Ordinarily the Add Printer Wizard names your printer after the manufacturer and model number, but you may prefer something more user oriented. These printer names are most useful when you use a networked printer. You can identify the location of the printer or one of its characteristics (for example, "Color Proofing printer") so you can quickly and unambiguously identify it when managing your print jobs.

The Add Printer Wizard also gives you the option of making the printer you're installing your default printer–that is, the printer that Windows 95 will use when you select **Print** from the File menu within your applications. Windows 95 requires that you specify one of your printers as the default, but it doesn't care which one.

The Add Printer Wizard asks one more question before it completes the installation process. With the windows shown in Figure 6.19, it asks whether you want to print a test page so that you can verify that the installation process was successful.

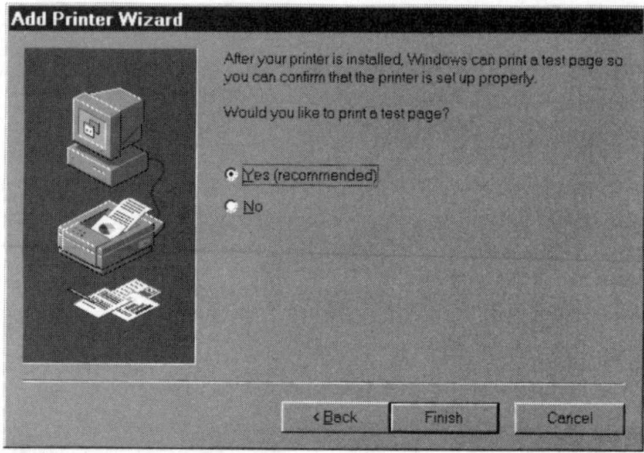

Figure 6.19 The option to print a test page.

Make your choice and click on **Finish**, and you've finished the first stage of the installation process, the preparation. Only one step remains, for the Add Printer Wizard to copy your driver files and make the proper entries in the Windows 95 Registry, where the operating system keeps all of its hardware and software set-up information. If the Add Printer Wizard requires files to which it does not have access, it will prompt you to slide a disk into your A:\ drive or indicate other disk location. You'll see a window like that shown in Figure 6.20 as the wizard completes the printer installation process.

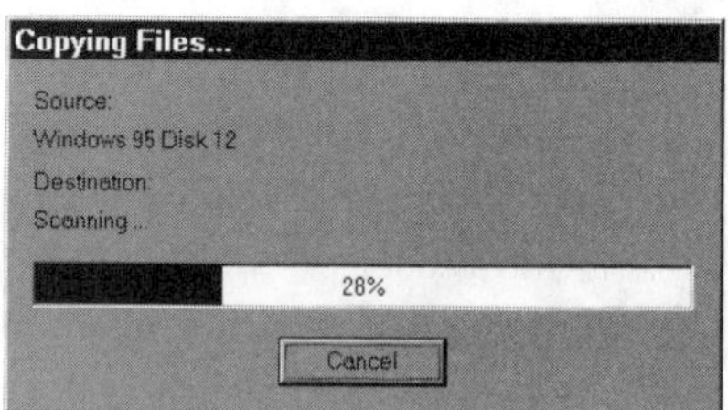

Figure 6.20 Windows 95 automatically finishing printer installation.

Even at this point you have one last chance to abandon the process. Clicking on **Cancel** will halt everything you've done and dump the Add Printer Wizard. Of course, you may not realize a mistake until it's too late and the printer installation process has completed. Or you may want to get rid of a print you've already installed for other reasons. For example, you may buy and connect a new printer and have little need to keep seeing the icon for the old machine in your Printer folder.

To remove an installed printer, you only need to complete a simple, three-step process. First, highlight the printer you want to eliminate by clicking on it. Then select the **Files** option from the Printer folder menu. Finally, click on **Delete**, as shown in Figure 6.21.

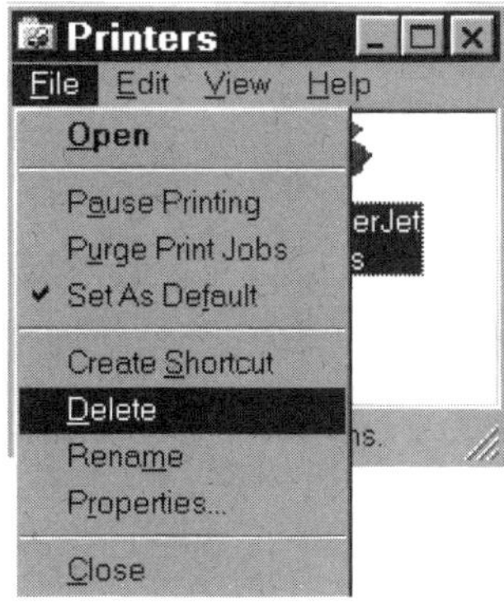

Figure 6.21 Removing an installed printer in Windows 95.

Windows 95 will query you to be sure you want to kill off your installed printer. It will also ask if you want to delete the drivers associated with the printer from your disk. Respond in the affirmative, and Windows 95 will eradicate the last vestiges of your old printer.

Network Connections

Windows 95 includes its own **Network** functions that allow you to link several PCs together in a peer-to-peer configuration. That is, as a simple network that allows you to share the disk drives in the various PCs with other PCs instead of requiring a separate server. Part of the resource sharing you gain by linking your PCs together is the ability to share one or more printers. You can make the printer connected to one PC accessible to other PCs in the network as if it were a local printer. In fact, setting up and controlling a shared printer through Windows 95 works almost exactly like connecting and using a printer with a single PC.

Networked Printer Installation

If you rely on a printer connected to a network directly supported by Windows 95 for making your printouts, the operating system makes installation easy. You don't have to worry about any of the many variables in printer set-up. Instead, Windows 95 examined how the printer has been setup on the network server, and copies that configuration to your PC. If your network administrator has made the printer drivers you need available on the network, Windows 95 will copy those, too, and will make the entire installation procedure automatic.

Network Job Management

Before the advent of Windows 95, managing a job sent to a network server for printing meant finding the network administrator (in the case of a large network) or leaving your workstation and going to the server to take control. Once you send a job from Windows, it is out of your control.

The integrated Windows network environment puts you in continuous control of the jobs you dispatch for printing. You can use the same control system as you would for a local print job, initiated by clicking on the icon of the network printer. In fact, if you've set up your network to give you administration privileges, you can completely control a printer on a remote node from any system linked to the network. For example, you can hold any print job or completely cancel it, reassign priorities, or restart printing after a pause.

OS/2

As with Windows, OS/2 links your applications to your printer using an overall software driver instead of individual drivers for each application. Versions of OS/2 before Warp used a variety of drivers for different printers. OS/2 has combined most of these to make its OMNI driver. Most printers use the OMNI driver.

NOTE

IBM wrote the OMNI driver itself. It uses 32-bit technology. As with any "one-size-fits-all" product, its match for particular printers may not be optimum. For example, it does not support the internal fonts of most printers. You must use the OS/2 ATM fonts with it.

Some Hewlett-Packard DeskJet owners have expressed dissatisfaction with it. They prefer to use the old HPDJPM.DRV, which accompanied versions 2.x of OS/2. It also comes with Warp but is not installed as the default driver. HPDJPM.DRV works with all HP portable DeskJet printers and the 500-series of DeskJets except the 540.

NOTE

HPDJPM.DRV is a 16-bit driver, and it lacks a number of features such as support for internal fonts and soft fonts and higher resolutions. You can still use this driver with Warp by copying it from its distribution disk (it's found on Printer Driver Diskette #1 or the equivalent place on the Warp CD). If you drag it to your desktop, OS/2 create a new printer icon for you automatically.

Printer installation under OS/2 Warp is handled the same as adding any device driver. You use the OS/2 System configuration menu, available by clicking on **Control Panel**, to select the printer or other device you want to install. Figure 6.22 shows the OS/2 System Configuration menu.

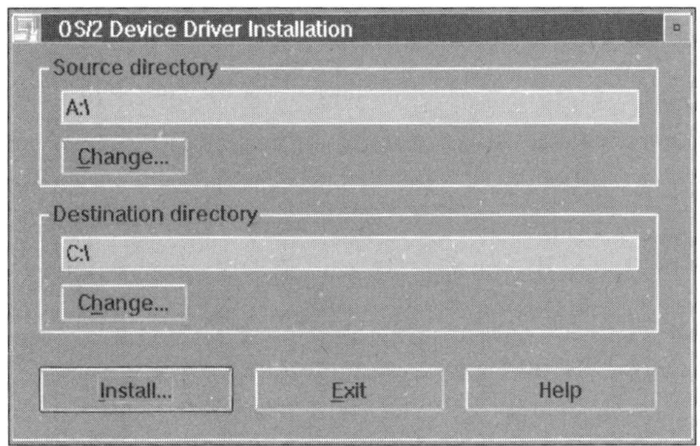

Figure 6.22 The OS/2 System Configuration menu.

If OS/2 comes with an appropriate driver, it will automatically install it to match the printer you specify. If you have an unsupported printer or if you want to use an updated driver for a supported device, you have the option of installing the software form disk. OS/2 will prompt you for the appropriate drive using a pop-up Device Driver Installation window like that shown in Figure 6.23.

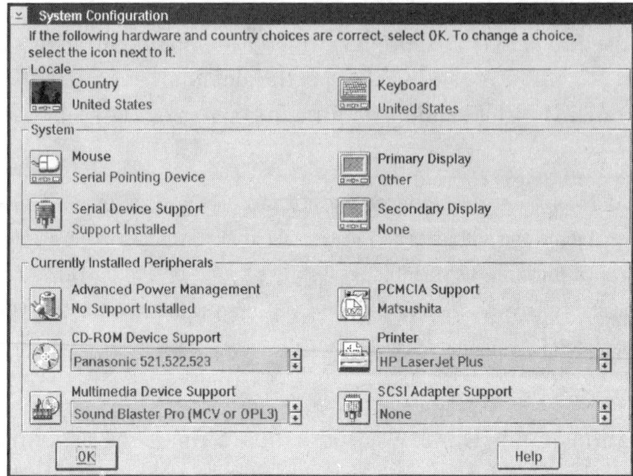

Figure 6.23 The OS/2 Device Driver Installation window.

Once you indicate the proper source for your driver files, click on **Install**, and OS/2 will manage the rest of the installation process.

Although this installation will allow you to use your printer with OS/2 applications, DOS programs will still use their internal print facilities, so you must install the appropriate printer drivers to work with any DOS applications that you plan to run under OS/2. Similarly, if you want to print from Windows applications that you run under OS/2, you'll want to install the Windows driver for your printer under Windows 3.1, as described earlier in the Windows 3.x section.

Because OS/2 has its own print management function, you'll want to *disable* Print Manager using the Control Panel. Having two layers of printer management adds nothing in terms of control but does stack on the overhead, slowing things down. In particular, you'll have to wait while your Windows printer driver generates printer code before you'll regain control of your Windows application.

You should also disable the **Direct Print to Port** option if it has been activated. Rather than sending data to the physical port, you want Windows to send it to the OS/2 printer driver or else the data will never make it to the OS/2 print management system. Using the physical port will cause OS/2 to make you wait while your Windows application finishes printing before you gain access to your Windows application again. You'll find the OS/2 port driver listed as LPTx.OS2 when you configure your printer under Windows.

Note that the OS/2 spooler will only work when you have an OS/2 printer driver installed, even though you won't use the driver when printing from a Windows application. Normally OS/2 will set up the driver for you when you install the operating system. If you don't plan to print anything through OS/2, you can even install the IBMNULL driver that comes with OS/2 and assign it to the port you want to print from. That will be sufficient to make the OS/2 spooler work.

CHAPTER SEVEN

Consumables

***Consumables** are those things that you printer uses up, wears out, or burns through as it does its work. Paper is the primary consumable, and the need for it is obvious with any printer. Without paper (or similar print medium) your printer couldn't give you any output. Other consumables are less obvious, sometimes even devious in the way they can eat into your budget. This chapter details consumables and the role they play in your printouts and finances.*

Many people think they know everything they need to know about their printers' consumables as soon as they master the paper trays. The paper goes in the tray in front and pops out on top or at the rear. Every so often you drop in another toner cartridge, fiddling with a handful of levers and latches. The printer complains when it runs low on paper or toner. Both cost more than anyone wants to pay, so they buy the cheapest they can find.

Once upon a time, about when Rip van Winkle fell asleep, you could get away with knowing little more than that. A couple of months after the old dot-matrix ribbon starts printing too faintly to read, you finally get around to ordering a new $5 ribbon to hold you through for the rest of the decade. But if you buy one of today's top- quality printers–laser, thermal-wax, and dye-diffusion–you may be in for a surprise. When the toner or transfer sheet runs out, the replacement may cost as much as did your old dot-matrix printer.

The effects of your choice of consumables can be subtler–and more pernicious. Choose the wrong paper for your laser printer, and the toner may flake off or your machine might suck two, three, or four sheets at once (alas, printing only on one of them).

Cost is the primary concern with consumables, of course. Although you only write one check to buy a printer, you pay as you go for its consumables. Printer supplies are a constant drain on your purse. And modern technologies have opened the sluices. Where once that $5 ribbon would last you until your vision blurred, you need a $50 to $100 toner cartridge as often as every few weeks.

The reason that laser printer consumables cost so much is that a bit of the machine is used up with every page that rolls out. The organic photo conductor drum on which images are made gradually wears out. (A new drum material, silicon, is supposed to last for the life of the printer, but few printer models currently use silicon drums.) Toner is spread across each page. The charging corona or other parts may also need to be periodically replaced. While thermal-wax printers do not waste their mechanisms, they do slurp up ink—up to four pages full of ink for every page of paper that spools through.

These consumables costs can add up. With laser printers, consumables, not including paper, cost between two and five cents a page. With thermal-wax printers, costs can range as high as $5 a page.

Over the life of a printer, the cost of consumables can quickly exceed what you paid for the printer. More importantly, consumables costs differ with various printer models. Over the life of the typical printer, the difference in consumables cost can far overwhelm a difference in purchase price.

Some printers appear wasteful in their need for consumables. Hewlett-Packard's LaserJets, for example, are designed with one-piece cartridges that contain both the drum and toner. The whole assembly is replaced as a single unit when the toner runs out. Other laser printers are designed so that the toner, drum, and sometimes the fuser, can be replaced individually.

The makers of the latter style of printer contend that the drum lasts for many times more copies than a single shot of toner, so dumping the drum before its time is wasteful. On the other hand, the all-in-one cartridge folks contend that they design their drums to last only as long as the toner.

Surprisingly, from a cost standpoint the choice of technology does not appear to make a difference. (From an ecology standpoint, however, the individual replacement scheme still makes more sense.)

Ink and Toner

When a printer makes a mark, it generally must use ink or toner. The exceptions include the direct thermal printer that uses a special pigment embedded in its special paper and the dye-sublimation printer that uses a dye, which all but the most persnickety minds can consider an ink.

The difference between ink and toner is that one is wet and the other dry. That's one distinction that's hard to miss, but the differences go deeper. At the physical level, ink and toner differ in how they get to the paper and bind to it.

Inks

Ink relies on a binder to make it adhere to paper. The basic black of inks still used by artists, *India ink*, uses a gum (yes, akin to chewing gum) to hold its black pigment to paper. In technical terms, the gum acts as a *binder*. In order to make the ink flow, the coloring matter and binder are mixed with a *solvent*. Ordinary water works for many inks, but some use more esoteric and elaborate solvents. The solvent is a vehicle that carries the pigment and binder along with it. It makes the ink workable but after the ink has been used—that is, applied to the paper—the solvent's role ends and the solvent ignominiously evaporates, ideally without a trace.

The classic printer's ink is essentially an oil paint. It combines a coloring substance in an oil-based medium often combined with a resin. These inks use special drying oils as their medium, vegetable-based oils that polymerize through oxidation. That is, they change their chemical composition by absorbing oxygen from the air, transforming themselves from a free-flowing liquid into a tough, dry plastic. Because the vegetable oils are viscous (that is, syrupy), a solvent often is mixed with them to thin them and make them flow more freely. Once spread on paper, the solvent quickly evaporates but the ink doesn't truly dry and set until it oxidizes. Once oxidized, the ink can no longer be thinned or removed by the solvent because it has changed form into a different compound through the oxidation process. The vegetable oils used in such inks (primarily linseed oil, although others may be used as well) also acts as a binder or adhesive to hold the coloring substance to the paper. Soya inks replace the linseed oil, which is made by squeezing the seeds of the flax plant (the fibers of which make linen), with an oil pressed from soybeans.

Some modern printing processes rely on inks more like India ink, which use another binder instead of oil, and take their working properties primarily from the solvent. These inks dry primarily by evaporation. For example, the inks used in plotters are much thinner than classic printers' ink and use water as a solvent. Unlike the classic printers' ink, these work by a different process. The solvent thins the ink and provides a medium for the coloring matter. But after the ink is applied, the solvent has performed its function and evaporates. Another substance added to the ink, a binder, forms a bond between the color and the paper. This binder may be a vegetable gum or resin or some more elaborate chemical concoction. As soon as the solvent has evaporated, the ink enters its final form. But the binder may remain soluble, so a subsequent application of the solvent can cause this kind of ink to run (or remove the coloring matter entirely).

Toner

Toners are dry powers. They lack any solvent because the printing processes using them don't require them. In fact, a toner looks as if it were nothing more than the coloring matter, typically something black and noxious, finer than dust and even more difficult to rid from your household. In fact, the toner can be just as complex–or even more complex–than an ink. A toner requires a coloring material and a binder. The toner binder is heat sensitive. It is activated by heat, the fuser in the printer. The toner must also have its composition controlled so that it maintains an electrostatic attraction to the print drum. Some toners, such as those used in Kyocera's "green" printers, also incorporate abrasive ceramic compounds to help maintain the finish of the print drum.

Waxes

The wax-based inks used by the thermal transfer processes and phase change printers blur the distinction between ink and toner. Although dry and heat sensitive like toner, most printer manufacturers call them inks. The nomenclature is a result more of appearance than technology. Wax-based inks visibly resemble the classic inks used on Mylar typewriter ribbons more than they do the dry power of toner even though they act chemically more like toner than ink. Although you can think of the colored waxes of thermal transfer printers as ink like the manufacturers, they work like toners. Heat makes them bind to paper, and they undergo no curing or setting process as do oil-based inks. They adhere to paper rather than combine with it. The wax in the ink acts as a vehicle, carrying the pigment along with it, but is not a solvent because it remains a part of the ink on the paper.

Pigments and Dyes

Inks and toners use two types of coloring matter, pigments and dyes. A *pigment* has a color of its own. A *dye* affects and infuses a base substance with color.

In general, pigments fade less readily than dyes, although many modern dyes are regarded as permanent and some old pigments changed color and faded with amazing speed. For most purposes, the colors of modern inks last as long as the information they contain is useful. Most will last as long as the acid-rich paper on which they are printed. Archival acid-free paper and a good black ink may outlast civilization.

The list of pigments is long. Some, like Paris green, are deadly chemicals thankfully left in the past. Many of the more permanent bright colors of modern inks rely on heavy metals (particularly cadmium) and aren't exactly among the most earth-friendly (or human-friendly) compounds.

Solubility

Inks differ in the solvent they use and they way in which they dry. Ink makers base their choice of solvent on the characteristics that are required to make a particular printer technology work. After all, a thick, gloppy ink would quickly clog the nozzles of ink-jet printers while a thin, volatile ink would quickly dry on impact printer ribbons.

Although strictly speaking, the solvent in an ink is not supposed to play a role in binding to paper, many solvents do double duty as binders. As a result, the choice of solvents in inks (and, of course, the binders the work with) affects the permanence of the ink. Some printer inks are permanent or at least waterproof; others are not.

Oil-based inks such as those used on impact printer ribbons dry through oxidation and are resistant even to most solvents after they dry. They are as permanent as printing gets. Toners come close. They are chemically stable and don't rely on solubility to work, so most are as permanent as the paper they are printed on. Printer makers regard toner to be archival in quality, able to stand up to the ages. However, documents printed with toner remain susceptible to abrasion (rubbing) and thermal smearing (although you'll have to get them hot, indeed, to loosen the toner). Toners may also be degraded by petroleum-based solvents and plasticizers. A common culprit is the plastic folder made from PVC (polyvinyl chloride), which can leach out its plasticizer and damage toner on documents into which it comes into contact.

Wax-based inks as used by thermal-wax and phase-change printers are naturally water repellent. Waxes, however, are soluble in a variety of common chemicals, although few of their solvents are used in the typical office. They may also suffer degradation from plasticizers in vinyl folders.

Ink-jet inks are generally water resistant. Although soluble in water (many use water as their principal solvent), when they dry they will resist smudging from fingers. These inks remain vulnerable to environmental water—rain from leaky ceilings, tears, and drool all can make your words run and your graphics blur.

If you need to make ink-jet output permanent, you have several choices. The most rugged is laminating it with plastic. Spray sealants (sometimes called *fixatives*) available at art supply stores allow you to put an impervious layer of water-insoluble lacquer or varnish over your printout. Most of these have the disadvantage of yellowing with age, so they cannot be regarded as a completely permanent solution. Use these sprays frugally because a thick application—one that actually wets the page—may dissolve the ink and make it run.

If you use water-soluble ink-jet printing for package labels or envelopes and fret about the letter carrier getting soaked in a downpour (neither rain nor sleet nor snow will keep the carrier from his rounds, but beware the ordnance in the post office), you can take steps to prevent addresses from running. The tried-and-true technique is to cover the printing with transparent tape. Ordinary cellophane tape works but isn't truly waterproof. A better choice is wide Mylar packing tape that can resist both nature's best efforts and those of your recipient. You can avoid printing labels or envelopes at all and use envelopes with see-through windows that let the world read the inside addresses of your correspondence.

In truth, ink-jet output will withstand anything but immersion. You can improve its chance of survival and good legibility by giving it time to set before exposing it to the elements. After a couple of hours of drying time the ink should reach its state most resistant to water damage.

Coverage

No measure of ink or toner consumption as a cost per page can be meaningful without considering the simple concept of *coverage*. It represents how much of a blank page your printer must cover with ink or toner. The more densely you cover the page, the higher the covers.

Look at the specifications of a given printer, and you'll see that how long an ink or toner cartridge lasts is usually specified at a given coverage. The more of each page you cover, the faster you'll go through ink. Simple. Life would be even simpler if all printer manufacturers could agree on a given figure for coverage. You could then directly compare every manufacturer's figures for toner and ink cartridge life. No such luck.

The abstinence and variance among printer manufacturers has one justification. Coverage depends on what you do, so no single figure can take care of every situation. Some applications naturally use more coverage than others.

Coverage will always be between zero and 100%. At zero, not a trace of ink finds its way to the paper, and you're just giving each sheet a joy ride around your printer as it rolls through. When coverage reaches 100%, you can see no paper, anywhere, because it's totally covered with ink. Although you'll never want to print a page a solid color unless you're Tristram Shandy in mourning, thermal-transfer printers race through ink as if they were constantly applying 100% coverage in each color they use. That's an issue we'll discuss separately.

The least coverage you're likely to apply is garden variety text. Text characters themselves put ink in a small fraction of the character cell they use. Leading (the space between lines), double-spacing between paragraphs, margins, and other dramatic white spaces all pare down the coverage used by text. Depending on the printer manufacturer, most consider text-based printing to require from 3 to 5% coverage.

Reverse printing, that is, putting white characters against a background of solid ink color, reverses the relationship between ink and paper and flips the coverage to from 95% to 97%. Typically the coverage will fall on the low side because legibility requires using heavier characters in reverse printing.

Graphics vary even more widely. Lay a simple line graph on a sheet of paper, and you may cover less than one percent. Halftones come close enough to 50% coverage that the name seems a rightful fit. A four-color photo image may push cover to beyond 50% per color. Graphic art can require 100% coverage in some colors, turning backgrounds delightful hue mixtures.

The basic rule is that if you print a lot of graphics, consider the number of copies quoted per toner or ink-jet cartridge bunk. You won't even come close. If you constantly use graphics that cover a good fraction of each page, you might get one-tenth as many copies for each ink or toner refill as your printer maker promises.

Thermal-wax and dye-sublimation printers are the exception, technologies that add amazing certainty to the cost of consumables. No matter how much of a page they cover, they use the same amount of inksheet. Each page requires a full page of ink. Consequently, the number of pages quoted for each inksheet role is exactly what you should expect. A 180-sheet roll will produce 180 pages, whether laced with text or blanketed with graphics.

The difference coverage has a direct and important on the overall cost per page of ink-jet and thermal-wax technologies when you need color output. When coverage is low, ink-jets are much less expensive than thermal wax machines. The high cost of ink-jet inks makes thermal transfer machines more economical when coverage gets high. Figure 7.1 illustrates this relationship.

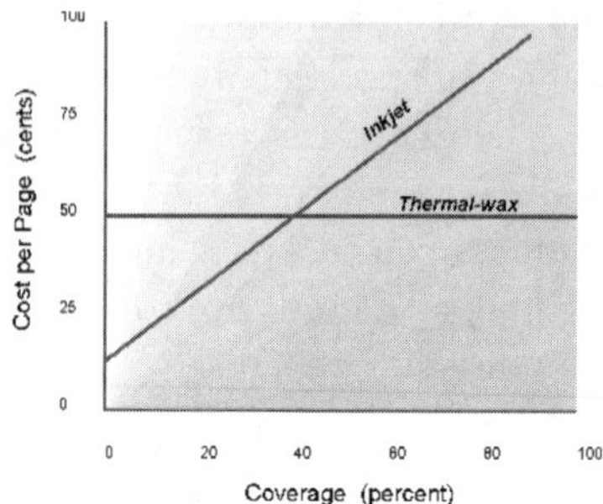

Figure 7.1 The effect of coverage on the cost per page for different technology.

Although the actual cost per page varies with the particular models of printers you compare, this overall relationship always applies to the two technologies. This relationship explains why ink-jet printers are the best choice for spot color applications while thermal transfer machines excel at presentation and prepress graphics, which usually require high coverage.

Purging

Clogs are the biggest problem faced by ink-jet printers. In fact, ink-jet printer makers report that clogging is the biggest complaint lodged by users. A bit of ink drying inside a nozzle can incapacitate it, ruining print quality forever afterward. Consequently printer makers go to great lengths to keep their printheads clean. Many ink-jet printers periodically purge their printheads to remove old ink before it can dry. This clean-up process is called *purging* and is usually part of the printer's start-up process, utterly invisible to you. In addition, most ink-jet machines let you manually activate the purge process to clean out clogged nozzles in their printheads.

The purge process has a hidden side, however. Ousting the old ink requires an injection of new ink. Inevitably, some ink that you could use for printing gets purged away. Although the quantity of ink used is minuscule (on the order of a tenth of a drop for the typical cleaning cycle), if you switch your printer on and off often, purging can amount to a measurable fraction of the ink used by your system.

Worse than the ink consumption is the time consumption involved in purging. You may have to wait a minute or more for your printer to clean up its head and start a print job.

The purge cycle often is the most aggravating aspect of operating an ink-jet printer. Some machines are programmed to purge their printheads whenever they are switched on and at periodic intervals during operation. Purge programming may also involve levels of cleaning. For example, the Epson Stylus Color series has several levels of automatic purging programmed into it. Every few lines of print, it performs a minor cleaning, which takes less than one-half second. After about every fifth startup, it runs a medium cleaning, which takes about 30 seconds. If the printer senses that its ink supply may have been compromised by leaving the printhead uncapped, when powering up, or after a lapse of several hours before use, it performs a major cleaning, which takes about one minute.

You can reduce the number of purge cycles your ink-jet runs—you can never eliminate them entirely—by operating your printer wisely.

Because most ink-jet printers purge their printheads whenever you turn them on, you can avoid many cycles by simply not turning the printer on. Of course, the only way to do that and still have an operable machine is to leave it on all the time. Most ink-jet printers consume a trivial amount of electricity—even less when they are idle, on the level of a watt or two.

If you do decide to switch off your ink-jet printer, use the power switch on the printer itself. Don't unplug it or switch it off at a terminal strip, surge protector, or UPS. The power switch on many ink-jet machines doesn't actually switch the printer entirely off. Instead, the switch shuts down most of the printer's electronics but leaves enough on to keep the printhead clean. The Tektronix phase change printers, for example, keep their ink liquid to avoid clogs and help the printer quickly leap into action when you do switch it back on. Cutting off power completely kills everything and makes the printer believe it may have been put into storage and expects the print-head nozzles to be clogged with dry ink. Your printer, being just a dumb machine, can't tell the difference between your unplugging it and the failure of the whole power grid. In other words, use the switch or pay the purge penalty.

In particular, you should never switch your printer off while it is in the middle of a job. Most ink-jet printers will automatically perform a major purge when they are switched back on. There's good reason for this. The print-head nozzles get covered when the print-head returns to its rest position at the left or right side of the printer. If the machine stops without the printhead in the rest position, there's a good chance ink will dry up in the uncovered nozzles, and the printer automatically assumes the worst. If you do have to switch off the printer in the middle of a job, press the **Pause** button and wait for the printhead to move to its rest position before throwing the off switch.

Cartridge Refilling

One way to tiptoe around the high cost of laser printer consumables is to get toner cartridges refilled. Most manufacturers do not recommend this; because they have no control over the quality of the toner, they can't guarantee that someone else's replacement works right in their machines. Besides, they miss the profits in selling toner.

Quality really can be an issue, however. The Resolution Enhancement technology of the HP's LaserJet III-series, for example, requires toner with a particle size much smaller than that of toner used by other printers. You cannot tell the difference in toner just by looking at it, but you can when blotchy grey pages pour out of the printer. When you get cartridges refilled, you must be sure to get the proper toner quality.

Another consideration: with all-in-one cartridges, just refilling the cartridge with toner will not affect the drum or charger in the cartridge. Although these are engineered with extra life, the extra might not stretch twofold. Order a refilled cartridge, and you could get fresh toner packed with a worn-out drum.

On the other hand, some people report excellent results with refilled toner cartridges. Whether you are going to be happy with refills depends on your personal standards, as well as the quality of the refill work.

Color printers that use cartridges that combine all their hues in one convenient package naturally waste ink or toner. After all, it's rather unlikely that you'll run out of all three (or four) colors at exactly the same instant. As a consequence, when you run out of one color, you have to replace the entire cartridge and toss out what might be a substantial amount of other colors.

If you're really frugal, you can squeeze more pages from those partly full cartridges. Although the lack of one hue will prevent you from making full color printouts, if you have jobs that require one or more of the remaining colors, the partly empty cartridge can fill the need.

Cartridges are not designed for convenient removal and reinstallation. Typically they have seals that get broken once you install them in your printer. Pull them out, and air will pour in or ink will pour out. To preserve both the ink and the native colors of the furnishing in your office, you'll want to seal the cartridge back up. Cellophane tape applied over the openings in the cartridge will do the trick. Be sure to cover both where the ink flows out of the cartridge and any air holes in the top.

For short periods, you can just slide the open cartridge into a sealable plastic bag. The plastic bag is also the best choice for cartridges with built-in printheads. You should never apply tape to the print-head face with the nozzles because the adhesive on the tape may permanently plug the holes.

This technique does not work for all printers. Some machines refuse to draw more ink from a cartridge when any one color runs out. Some ink-jet printers can be damaged if they are left without a cartridge installed for long periods, so be sure to always keep a cartridge (even a partly empty one) installed in your printer.

Ribbons

Printer ribbons have three essential parts: the ink itself, a carrier or substrate (the ribbon itself), and a package. The last may be spools or a complete cartridge assembly.

Printers use either of two kinds of substrate. Fabric ribbons use a long web of a woven fabric, most often nylon, which has been soaked in a heavy oil-based ink. Film ribbons use a continuous tape of thin plastic, most often polyester. Because Mylar is a well-known trade name for polyester, film ribbons are often called Mylar ribbons. Film ribbons are coated on one side with a nearly dry ink. Each class of ribbon has its advantages and disadvantages.

Fabric ribbons are the low-cost alternative. Although they may cost about the same as or even more than a film ribbon, they have a substantially longer life, one limited only by your eyesight and tolerance for a slow fade to grey. Fabric ribbons give up only a tiny fraction of their ink each time they are hit, so they can run through your printer dozens of times. You can re-ink old and fading ribbons and further extend their lives (except in the case of four-color ribbons, which usually cannot be re-inked because you cannot keep the color separate). In fact, some printer ribbon cartridges have built-in re-inkers to keep your output dark for a long time. The fabric ribbon itself rarely wears out unless your printer develops a problem such as improperly advancing the ribbon.

On the other hand, the output from a fabric ribbon is fuzzy. The weave of the fabric itself adds a fuzzy texture and grain to the characters printed out. Although the look of a fabric ribbon is definitely second rate with fully formed character printers, it doesn't detract from the already hazy look of most dot-matrix output.

Film ribbons can make text and graphics look razor sharp. With but a thin layer of plastic between hammer and paper, the ink on a film ribbon can follow each curve of a character exactly. Not only can the output of a fully formed character printer with a film ribbon look close to typeset quality, little more than a decade ago many typesetters actually used film ribbons to mash out text.

The quality of the film ribbon has its price. The ribbons have a definite, and short, life. In fact, *single-strike ribbons* can run through the printer exactly once, reserving a small space on the ribbon for each character that is typed. *Multistrike ribbons* use inks that allow the same area of ribbon to tap ink to paper several times. In most cases, multistrike ribbons only make a single journey through a printer before you must replace them. However, a multistrike ribbon lets you hammer out more characters from each ribbon with little loss in quality. Usually the printer that uses multistrike ribbons overlaps the places characters strike a ribbon, so the ribbon moves more slowly through the machine rather than making multiple journeys. Multistrike ribbons are usually more economical and require changing less frequently.

Process Embossing

Printers use a process called *intaglio* for their highest quality work (such as bank notes and $100 bills). The intaglio process uses printing plates on which a engraver has cut a recessed image. Ink fills the recesses and, when a press pushes paper against the plate, the ink sticks to the paper and is pulled from the plate. In conventional printing, the image is raised on the plate, coated with ink, and squeezed against the paper. The chief difference is that regular printing squishes the ink flat; intaglio leaves the ink rising above the surface of the paper as raised printing. Engraved wedding invitations and engraved stationery are printed with the intaglio process.

Printers reserve intaglio for quality work because it is expensive. The necessary engraved plates are difficult to make. Moreover, getting ink into those little engraved lines requires coating the entire printing plate with ink, then wiping off the ink that is *not* recessed in the engraved areas.

To give printing the look and feel of quality without the expense of intaglio, the printing industry developed *process embossing*. The process doesn't involve embossing at all. Printers use special inks and print normally, typically with offset presses. The ink is heat-sensitive. After the ink has been pressed onto the paper, the printer heats the paper, and special compounds in the ink swell up. The result is printing with a raised feel that you might imagine to be intaglio, although it neither looks nor feels the same. Letters pressed using process embossing have fuzzy edges (intaglio lines are the sharpest that can be printed) and the raised process-embossed ink has a slightly bubbly surface.

All that said, you might not care. After all, processing embossing is a matter for the professional printer, not the PC. You face one problem, however. If you have process-embossed stationery (and if yours has raised type, odd favor it being process embossed), you should never run it through your laser printer. The heat-sensitive ink will be softened by your laser printer's fuser. The ink may come off the paper and stick to the drum of your printer leaving speckles of insensitive surface. The quality of your printouts will deteriorate. In other words, you should never run process embossed stationery through your laser printer.

Two-Pass and Two-Sided Ink Issues

Printing on two sides of a sheet of paper is governed as much by the ink as by the paper that you use.

Ordinary laser printers do not excel at double-sided printing because of the characteristics of their toner. Remember, toner gets affixed to the page by thermal fusing. Heat makes the bond, but heat can also break it. When you run paper through a laser printer to put toner on the second side, the heat of the fuser will soften the already-printed toner on the first side. As a result, some of the toner may come off in the printer mechanism, not only gumming up the works but also rubbing off on sheets that you later run through the printer.

The same problem results when you try to make multiple passes on the same side of a single sheet. The toner can come off in the fuser and pollute both the mechanism and subsequent printouts.

With other printer technologies, you usually face few catastrophic problems in printing on both sides of a sheet. Your only concern with the ink is that you be sure the printing on the first side has dried before you start the second pass. Wet ink will coat the inside of the printer, smearing across not only the sheet with the wet ink but subsequent sheets as well. If you're not careful, you'll probably smear wet ink even before you run it through the printer a second time as simply rubbing sheets with wet ink together will cause smears.

The wet-ink problem is aggravated by ink-jet technology. Ink-jets use more fluid inks than other technologies, inks that readily run. (They have to or else they'd never get through the print-head nozzles.) Moreover, higher quality printing demands coated papers (see below) which naturally make the ink dry more slowly.

Using uncoated papers with ink-jets minimizes drying time (because the ink actually gets absorbed by the paper) but the ink may bleed through the sheet and the ensuing blur may make both sides unreadable.

The surface characteristics of the two sides of a sheet of paper are often quite different. One side may absorb ink more readily than the other (for reasons we'll discuss below). The individual sides of special "ink-jet" papers are more different than those of ordinary bond or "plain" paper.

The result of this difference is that ink-jet printers will look different on the two sides of a single sheet. Ordinarily this is not a problem–making direct comparisons is difficult because you can only *see* one side of a sheet at a time. But you may notice the difference and wonder what's wrong with your printer. Nothing. It's just the paper doing what paper does.

Paper

When comparing the costs of using different printer technologies, do not forget to make allowances for machines that require special paper. In most cases, approved media for such printers is available only from the machine's manufacturer. You must pay the price the manufacturer asks, which, because of the controlled distribution and special formulation, is sure to be substantially higher than buying bond paper at the office supply warehouse.

Certainly, you can load any kind of paper that fits into a printer. With some printers, particularly thermal machines, you do not get any image output at all if you use the wrong medium. With most printers, however, the penalty is a substandard image or more frequent jams. Ink-jet images, for instance, are blurrier with less saturated colors when printed on the wrong stock because of the ink absorption by the paper. When you use unsuitable stock on your laser printers, blacks might become spotty or grey. Other effects of inappropriate paper choice may be more subtle. With laser printers, for example, the passage of paper through the mechanism may be erratic, leading to sheets sticking together and more frequent jams, which are often blamed on the printer itself. The real cause is subtle differences in the paper stock itself. Many laser printers make particular requirements for the humidity content of the paper to ensure proper operation.

Paper makers classify their products into types based upon the application for which it is meant. Highest quality are bond papers, and these are the type that you are most likely to use in your computer printer. Table 7.1 lists some of the major classifications of paper and their applications.

Table 7.1 Paper Types and Their Uses

Paper Type	Primary Uses
High-rag bond	The good stuff of the best stationery
Sulfite bond	Workhorse paper for computer printers
Book	Medium-quality paper for bulk printing
Bristol	Heavier card stock
Groundwood	Newsprint for short-lived mass printing
Kraft	Paper for wrapping, packaging, and construction
Paperboard	Thick board for packaging and construction
Sanitary	Toilet tissue and the like

Within these categories, paper can differ widely. The primary differences you'll encounter in selecting paper stock include size, weight, fiber content, finish, and color.

Size

Historically, printers have used a number of quaint names to describe the size of the paper on which they print. A *folio* is a single sheet folded in once to make two leaves, each half the size of a full sheet, on which they printed four pages (two sides of each leaf). Fold each folio again, and you get *quarto*, one-quarter the size of the basic sheet with four leaves and eight pages each measuring about 9.5x12 inches. Another fold produces *octavo*, eight leaves or 16 pages, each measuring about 6x9 inches.

Another ancient term describing paper size is *foolscap*, named from its watermark which was a fool's cap and bells. For printers, the nominal size of foolscap is 13.5x17 inches, although when the term was used for writing (as opposed to printing) paper it could describe sheets that measured from 12x15 inches to 12.5x16 inches.

In the United States, we continue the tradition of giving names to paper sizes, although our choices are somewhat less interesting and more business oriented. We use terms like letter, legal, and executive. In the metric world, all the heritage has been bled out of paper designations, and the standard metric sizes bear identifications like A3, A4, and B5 (to name the more popular sizes). Table 7.2 lists the more widely use size of paper by name and dimensions.

Table 7.2 Common Paper Sizes

Designation	Height Inches	Width Inches	Height Millimeters	Width Millimeters
A9	1.5	2.1	37	52
B9	1.8	2.5	45	64
A8	2.1	2.9	52	74
B8	2.5	3.6	64	91
A7	2.9	4.1	74	105
B7	3.6	5.0	91	128
A6	4.1	5.8	105	148
B6	5.0	7.2	128	182
A5	5.8	8.3	148	210
Octavo	6	9	152	229
B5	7.2	10.1	182	256
Executive	7.25	10.5	184	267
A4	8.3	11.7	210	297
Letter	8.5	11	216	279
Legal	8.5	14	216	356
Quarto	9.5	12	241	309
B4	10.1	14.3	257	364
Tabloid	11	17	279	432
A3	11.7	16.5	297	420
Folio	12	20	309	508
Foolscap	13.5	17	343	432
B3	14.3	20.3	364	515
A2	16.5	23.4	420	594
B2	20.3	28.7	515	728
A1	23.4	33.1	594	841
B1	28.7	40.6	728	1030
A0	33.1	46.8	841	1189
B0	40.6	57.3	1030	1456

Most printers are rated as to the size of paper that they will handle. All except ancient pin-fed machines will accept paper of lesser dimensions than their maximum size, either directly or through slight adjustment. The specifications of a given printer will usually express the range of paper sizes that you can use.

Continuous-form paper may be described one of two ways: its width including the removable perforated strips at the edges of the sheet or the final size once the drive strips are removed. Because of the looseness of the interpretation of these widths, descriptions of the paper-handling of continuous-form printers are best reflected in their carriage width. Tractor-fed printers that describe themselves as having 8.5-inch or 9.5-inch paper handling (so-called *narrow-carriage printers*) have essentially identical paper handling. Wide-carriage printers, rated for paper widths of 14 or 15 inches, are similarly the same. Tractor-fed printers can, of course, use paper of width narrower than the maximum dimension.

Weight

Many people judge the quality of paper by touch. Some sheets feel more substantial than others, giving the impression that the person or organization using the paper is itself more substantial.

Thicker paper is, of course, more substantial. In general, thicker paper will be sturdier and better able to withstand the rigors of the workaday world. Presentation covers often are far thicker than standard paper to better protect the contents. Paperback book covers are made from thicker paper called cover stock. Business cards, too, use thicker paper for its ruggedness, earning the name card stock.

In the paper industry, the thickness of paper is rarely measured directly. Instead the more common measurement is weight. Thicker sheets weigh more so they are labeled with heavier weights. The weight or thickness of a given paper is also called its *basis*.

The measurement system of paper weights superficially seems to bear little relationship to reality, however. The most common weight of paper for printing is 20-pound stock, but a single sheet comes nowhere near weighing that much. The number of pounds describing the weight of paper is actually two steps removed from the single sheet.

Paper weights apply en masse, to paper in bulk rather than individual sheets. The common measuring unit is the ream, 500 sheets. Just to make things interesting, a ream used to mean 20 quires, each of which was 24 sheets, for a total of 480 sheets. Occasionally you'll run into references to these smaller reams, particularly in older publications aimed at the kind of printers who run presses.

Further complicating matters, paper weights apply to the paper in its raw state, after it has been manufactured but before it is cut down to its final size. All commercial printing papers start out as large sheets of somewhat standardized dimensions called the *basic size*. Different kinds of paper have different basic sizes. Table 7.3 lists the basic sizes of common paper types.

Table 7.3 Basic Sizes for Various Kinds of Paper

Paper Type	Basic Size (inches)
Bond	17x22
Cover	20x26
Bristol	22.5x28.5
Index	25.5x28.5
Tag	24x36
Book	25x38

Paper weights apply to a ream of paper in the basic size. These large sheets are cut down to the common sizes used in printing. For example, the basic size of a bond paper traditionally is 17x22 inches. Two cuts bring one ream of this basic size down to four reams of 8.5x11-inch letter size, so a ream of letter-size paper typically tips the scales about one-quarter its nominal weight. That is, a ream of 20-pound letter-size paper actually weighs 5 pounds. (And if you want to go further, each sheet weighs 0.16 ounce.)

Note that this relationship between the weight of a ream and the nominal paper weight–that is, 1 to 4–only applies to letter-size paper. A legal-size ream of a given basis (that is, the same weight) will tip the scales more than letter size.

Three weights of bond paper are used for general office printing: 16, 20, and 24 pounds. You might nickname these weights economy, regular, and high test.

Sixteen-pound paper is the thin, flimsy stuff used in office copiers and duplicating machines. The line paper used in schools most often is also 16-pound stock. Its chief benefit is that you get 20% more sheets from a given amount of raw material (compared to 20-pound paper), making it cheaper. Ordinarily, you'll want to use 16-pound paper for hand-outs and other short-lived distributions. Because of its thinness, it is not the best choice for double-sided printing.

Twenty-pound paper is today's norm for most computer printers. Most sheet-fed printers are optimized for this thickness and perform best with 20-pound stock. It will serve just about any purpose for which you need paper (rather than card stock).

The additional thickness of 24-pound paper makes it the choice when you want to impress the impressionable, when you want a bit more durability, or you want to optimize the legibility of two-sided printing. Twenty-four pound paper is often used for certificates and stationery because of its greater strength and prospective life as well as its more substantial subjective feel.

Most printers are rated for a given range in paper weights, which you should find listed in the machine's specifications or owner's manual. You typically will find a preferred range as well as minimums and maximums.

Laser printers and other sheet-fed machines are typically more stringent about the thicknesses of paper they will willingly handle than are friction-fed printers. Thick, heavy papers often require manual feeding in lasers and cut-sheet ink-jets. If you use paper that's too light or too heavy with a sheet-fed mechanism, you're likely to encounter extensive paper jamming. Rollers may not have enough "give" to accommodate thick sheets, causing the paper to slip and jam. Thin, lightweight sheets also jam more than moderate weight sheets because they wrinkle inside the mechanism. Table 7.4 lists the recommended paper weights for best operation with the most common Hewlett-Packard LaserJet printers.

Table 7.4 Paper Weight Recommendations for HP LaserJets

Printer Model	Feed Path	Paper Basis
Color LaserJet	All paths	20 to 24
LaserJet II	Manual feed and cassette	16 to 28
LaserJet IID	Manual feed and cassette	16 to 36
LaserJet IID	Lower bin	16 to 24
LaserJet IIP	Multipurpose tray, cassettes	16 to 28
LaserJet III	Manual feed and cassette	16 to 28
LaserJet IIID	Manual feed and cassette	16 to 36
LaserJet IIID	Lower bin	16 to 24

Table 7.4 continued

Printer Model	Feed Path	Paper Basis
LaserJet IIIP	Multipurpose tray, cassettes	16 to 28
LaserJet IIISi	Manual feed and cassette	16 to 28
LaserJet IIISi	Duplex	16 to 24
LaserJet 4	Multipurpose tray	16 to 36
LaserJet 4	250-sheet cassette	16 to 28
LaserJet 4	500-sheet lower tray	16 to 24
LaserJet 4 Plus	Multipurpose tray	16 to 36
LaserJet 4 Plus	250-sheet cassette	16 to 28
LaserJet 4 Plus	500-sheet lower tray	16 to 24
LaserJet 4Si	Upper tray (simplex)	16 to 36
LaserJet 4Si	Lower tray (simplex)	16 to 28
LaserJet 4Si	Both trays (duplex)	16 to 24
LaserJet 4L	Cassette	16 to 28
LaserJet 4L	Manual feed	16 to 36
LaserJet 4P	Cassette	16 to 28
LaserJet 4P	Manual feed	16 to 42
LaserJet 4V	Multipurpose tray	17 to 28
LaserJet 4V	250-sheet tray	17 to 28
LaserJet 4V	500-sheet lower tray	17 to 28
LaserJet 5p	Mulitpurpose tray (1)	16 to 42
LaserJet 5p	Cassette (2)	16 to 28

The metric system uses a different method for measuring paper basis. Called *grammage*, it expresses the weight of a sheet of paper one meter square in units of grams per square meter. Grammage is thus independent of basic size and the number of sheets in a package. You can convert substance or weight to grammage using the following formula:

```
(Weight * 1409) / Basic size (square inches)
```

The constant, 1409, takes into account the conversion from square inches to square meters (1550) and pounds to grams (0.0022) as well as the number of sheets in a ream (500).

Paper substance (and therefore its weight) is also measured by *caliper*, which is a fancy way of saying thickness. Standard 20-pound bond paper has a caliper of about 0.003 inches or about 76 micrometers. Friction-feed printers are most likely to specify their paper requirements in a caliper measurement.

Content

The primary ingredient in most commercially made paper is *cellulose*, a natural material produced by most plants. Chemically, cellulose is a polysaccharide, a carbohydrate, though one that is indigestible by humans. Biologically, cellulose is the primary constituent of the cell walls of plants.

By itself, cellulose wouldn't be much interest to the paper maker. Its chief novel quality is ubiquity. But when plants form cellulose into fibers, it becomes the basis for paper. Cellulose fibers are relatively inert, light in weight, and readily bind together. Like a nest of snakes, cellulose fibers can tangle together by twisting around one another and flopping one atop each other. Better still, machines can spread and mash clumps of cellulose fibers into the sheets we call paper. Certainly papermaking is a bit more complex than that, involving slurries of cellulose fibers, water, and a variety of other chemicals, but paper remains only an embellished mat of tangled fibers pressed flat.

The biggest division between types of paper depends on the origin of the cellulose fibers making up the paper. Just about any plant fiber can make paper. Egyptians pressed papyrus into the eponymous sheets from which our word "paper" derives. Japanese squeeze mulberry fibers into sheets we call rice paper. Hemp fibers, linen, even straw have been pressed into service as paper. In the modern world, however, two materials dominate paper manufacture: cotton and wood pulp.

Rag Papers

The first papers were made from rags along with a stew of other fibers by Ts'ai Lun in about 105 AD in China. Since that time, the paper-making process has changed little. Rags, in fact, remained the primary fiber in most paper until little more than a century ago. Paper makers would shred old cloth, stir it, and soak it until the weave separated into fibers. They would bleach the daylights into it, then mat the fibers back together, unwoven, as sheets of paper. Today most paper makers use raw cotton, even the lint left over from weaving cloth, instead of old rags to brew up their paper slurries. In the end, however, the result is the same–well, almost, but we'll get to that. No matter the origins of the cotton fibers, however, the result is called *rag paper*.

Pulp Papers

Rags and cotton fibers are expensive, at least more expensive than paper makers were happy to pay. Consequently printers have long sought alternatives. As commercial printing became widespread and the number of people reading for enjoyment increased, rags fell into short supply, making them even more expensive. Some publishers went so far as to admonish, "Save you rags!" in their publications. Although experiments into using wood as the basis for paper date from the end of the eighteenth century, through the middle of the nineteenth century, however, for its first millennium and a half, paper remained rag based.

Wood had long been eyed as the leading alternative to rags. Wood is fibrous and made from exactly the same cellulose as cotton. Unfortunately, along with the cellulose comes a lot of other materials that give wood its strength and rigidity–and prevents the cellulose fibers in the wood from being separated out. The challenge for paper makers was to separate the cellulose and eliminate the adulterants.

By the middle of the nineteenth century, the process for making paper from wood pulp had been perfected, although printers were slow to adopt the product made through the process. For example, the first edition of the *New York Times* to be published on wood pulp paper came out on 23 August 1873 (though the German-language paper Staats-Zeitung was first in the United States to use pulp-based paper in 7 January 1868). Consequently they sought a cheaper and more plentiful substitute.

While they didn't find anything that exactly grew on trees, they actually found even better, something that grew *inside* trees, wood. By beating the bejabbers out of logs, they reduced wood to pulp–a thick slurry of cellulose fibers, *lignin*, the natural binder that holds the wood fibers together, and water. Press it flat, squeezing the water out in the process, let it dry, and you get something resembling rag-based paper.

The similarity is superficial. Cotton and wood fibers are substantially different in their working properties. Cotton fibers are generally long and flexible. They are naturally white or close to it. Wood fibers from softwood measure about two to four millimeters long (superior for papermaking to hardwoods, which have fibers about a quarter as long), no matter their original length, are hammered down into short lengths in the pulping process. They are relatively inflexible. And they are typically far from white because of all the other tree constituents that mix with them. Put simply, wood makes second rate paper.

The pulp used in paper doesn't have to come directly from trees. It can also originate as other plant fibers or as used paper. Both are regarded as alternatives more ecologically sound than felling forests to make newsprint.

Paper makers improve the quality of pulp-based paper by mixing in cotton fibers. The amount of cotton making up the blend is called the *rag content* of the paper. The most common blends are 25% rag and 50% rag, both of which are often called high-rag papers. The addition of cotton fibers greatly strengthen the paper. Where pulp paper gets much of its strength from the lignin and other glues in the mixture, high-rag papers also have benefited from the tangle of long fibers holding the sheets together mechanically.

Pulp is prepared for papermaking either by grinding or chemical action. Groundwood pulp contains all the lignin, hemicellulous, resins, and discolorants present in the raw wood. Often it is bleached to make a usable white, but it quickly reverts back to its natural yellowish form. Moreover, the mechanical grinding shortens the cellulose fibers, so papers made from groundwood do not have high strength. Newsprint is the best common example of a groundwood pulp, although it is also used in book publishing because it has good opacity and printing qualities.

Chemical pulps rely on a process called *digesting* to separate their fibers and wash away unwanted adulterants such as the lignins. Using sulfurous acid (along with other chemicals) results in sulfite papers, which are suitable for a wide variety of print purposes. Using caustic soda to digest the raw pulp results in a weak paper. Adding sodium sulfate to caustic soda in the digester produces stronger paper, which was called exactly that by its maker, in German, *kraft*. Papers made by the kraft process originally were limited to dark brown because of difficulties bleaching it, although new processes yield bright white sheets from the kraft process. Semichemical pulps have intermediate qualities between groundwood and chemical processes and are often used for corrugated boxes and low-cost printing papers.

Recycled paper is almost never made purely from paper that has been previously used. Rather, it is a combination of wastepaper, tailings from the paper cutting before the paper is sold, and stuff rescued from the trash bin. In preparing the cellulose in the recycling brew for re-use, it is washed to remove ink and most contaminants. Nevertheless, the final recycled paper often contains dark, even-colored specks or may appear an overall dirty grey. Although the look of recycled paper is only a matter of appearance, the paper must otherwise meet the requirements of your printer. For example, if you want to use recycled paper in your laser printer, the paper must be rated for use in that kind of printer.

Paper is often bleached to make it whiter. The first bleaching processes used a single-stage of bleaching with calcium hypochlorite. Modern bleach processes use multiple stages of chlorine bleaching. The brightest papers are made by using chlorine dioxide in the later bleaching stages.

Papers are graded for whiteness by comparing them to pure magnesium oxide, which is assigned a whiteness value of 100. Table 7.5 compares the brightness of various paper types and bleaching processes.

Table 7.5 Paper Brightness from Preparation Method

Paper or Medium	Brightness
Unbleached sulfite or groundwood	50–62
Peroxide-bleached groundwood	66–72
Single-stage hypochlorite sulfite	80–85
Multiple-stage bleached pulp	85–88
Multistage bleaching with chlorine dioxide	90–94
Magnesium oxide	100

Printer manufacturers may make specific recommendations as to the brightness of paper that you should use with their machines. These are truly recommendations. The choices affect only the appearance of your print outs. If you prefer a grey paper, there is no reason why you cannot use it if you're willing to accept somewhat less contrast and legibility.

Opacity

Paper makers blend in a variety of other substances called *fillers* with the basic cellulose of paper to give the resulting paper's desired characteristics. Some of these add whiteness or brightness to the paper beyond that which can be bleached into it. Other materials help control the absorbency of the paper. Others are designed to alter the natural translucency of the cellulose fibers and make the paper more opaque. A more opaque paper allows you to print on both sides without the characters on one side becoming visible on the other.

Common fillers include *kaolin*, a white clay, that imparts both opacity and whiteness, and compounds like barium oxide (baryta), zinc oxide, or titanium dioxide that would otherwise be considered white pigments.

Paper makers use the term *opacity* to describe a given paper's ability to block text showing through from side to side. The paper industry quantifies opacity on a 100-point scale with 100 being the most opaque. A paper rated 85 or higher usually is good enough to block show through on two-sided printouts. You can use paper with lower opacities when you print on only one side of each sheet.

Acid Content

The real enemy to the life of paper is acid. As a result of the paper manufacturing process, many papers contain acids. The concentration is so low that you need to worry about injury from handling the paper, but the small amount of acid locked inside each sheet gradually eats away at the rest of the paper, fibers, and binders alike. With time the paper yellows, becomes brittle, and eventually flakes apart. Papers with high acid content came into use in the last half of the nineteenth century, and books printed on them are now in deplorable condition.

Paper makers can control and neutralize the acid content of paper by adding alkaline materials as buffers. (Conservators can neutralize the acid in modern papers long after manufacture, but the process is time-consuming and expensive.) Papers buffered against acid deterioration are called *archival papers* because their substantially lengthened lives makes them suitable for permanent archives. In fact, in suitable storage, the life of a well-made paper is indefinite.

Acid content of paper is measured by its pH. From the standpoint of longevity, the closer to neutral–a pH of 7.0–the paper is, the better. Very acidic papers may have problems with some print mechanisms and technologies. For example, Hewlett-Packard recommends a minimum pH of 5.5 for paper for its LaserJet printer.

Moisture Content

The matted cellulose fibers that make up paper readily absorb water, which alters its working characteristics. When paper becomes too dry, it becomes stiff, even brittle. Damp paper becomes flexible but also may tear more readily.

For laser printers, the moisture content of paper is important because it alters how the paper reacts to static charges. Charges drain off damp paper more quickly and linger longer when paper is very dry. Laser printers use static electricity to attract toner to the paper. If the paper does not react properly when charged, the toner will not properly bind to the paper and output quality will be substandard. In addition, the buildup in static charge in dry paper results in sheets clinging together and running through the printer mechanism that way, wasting a sheet for each one printed.

Printer makers often prescribe certain levels of moisture content for proper operation of their equipment. For example, Hewlett-Packard recommends a moisture content of within 1% of 4.7% by weight for paper used in its LaserJet machines.

Although you normally cannot buy paper based on its moisture content, you can control the moisture content of the paper that you have by how you store it. For the most part, the moisture content of paper reflects its environment. Store it in a damp basement, and the paper will become damp. Store it in a hot and dry area, and the paper will dry out. Consequently, most printer makers recommend that you store paper in a cool, controlled environment. The best strategy is to keep it sealed in its original packaging until you're ready to load it into your printer.

The only exception to this rule is that you should allow paper to acclimate to room temperature if it is stored cold. You should never use paper that you've just brought in from a cold car. Let it reach room temperature before running it through your printer.

Curl

One of the biggest bugaboos in laser printing is curl. The heat of the fusing process causes some papers to pucker or curve in one or another direction. If you've used ordinary paper in a laser printer, you might have discovered that the entire stack in the output tray has a definite cupped shape caused by this natural tendency to curl.

Although curling seems little more than a cosmetic problem, it can cause difficulties in your printer's paper-feeding mechanism. Curled sheets increase the likelihood that the paper will jam as it travels out of your printer. It can also lower the print quality of your output if the paper curls away from the fuse. And that big stack of curled sheets will likely give whoever binds them into a booklet a big headache.

Both electrostatic copies and laser printers use similar, heat-fused technologies. However, they have different requirements on paper in regard to curl. The paper path in copiers is substantially longer than that of a laser printer, and the longer path helps paper endure the heat. The short path of a laser printer results in a more intense heat treatment, which can cause papers rated only for copier use to curl or even wilt. Consequently, paper that works well in your photocopier may curl and jam in your laser printer. You'll want to use paper specifically rated for laser printing in a laser printer.

Finish

Run your hand over several different kinds of paper and you'll probably notice different textures. Some papers are smoother than others. Some are almost glassy in their finish; others could substitute for sandpaper in a pinch.

The surface texture of paper is not a matter of chance but is carefully controlled during the paper-making process. To squeeze the water out of raw paper, paper-making machines run the embryonic sheets between rollers. As the water drips out, the paper gets flattened. On its journey from pulp to finished product, the paper winds through several sets of rollers.

The final step in the process sends the paper, now through finishing rollers called *calenders*. These give the paper its final smooth finish. When paper makers want to give the finished paper a particularly smooth finish, they repeat the calendering process. This extra smooth paper is called *supercalendered.*

Four finishes are common for book papers. Antique or eggshell has the roughest surface, lightly calendered to produce a surface smoothness but preserving some of its texture. Machine-finished paper is calendared at the dry end of the paper-making process and is smooth enough to print on with a 100-line screen. English finish is smoother still. The final degree of finish is supercalendared, capable of taking a 120-line halftone screen.

Coated Paper

Supercalendered paper may be smooth, but it is not the smoothest paper. Its surface still retains the feel of individual fibers. Moreover, supercalendered paper is absorbent, wicking wet ink into its fibers and causing a slight blur. But this finish is perfect for some uses, for example ballpoint pens need the slight coarseness to spin their balls. The thick, oil-based ink of the ballpoint hardly gets absorbed at all. More fluid inks, however, take on a fuzzy edge when the ink is sucked in before it dries. The effect is usually slight and hardly bothersome with handwriting. When you're trying to make a 720 dot-per-inch ink-jet image, however, the slight absorbency destroys the finest details.

The smoothest of papers take another step in processing. They are coated with a special clay or chemicals. When calendered, the coating is squeezed into the fibers and fills the gaps between them. The paper loses its absorbency and takes on an almost glassy sheen. Sometimes paper makers add white pigments or brighteners to the coating to make the paper whiter and brighter. Photographic paper, for example, is typically coated with barium oxide (one of the whitest substances known).

Besides making the paper smooth, the coating has another effect. By preventing absorption, it forces ink printed on it to dry on the surface. All of the pigment of the ink remains on the surface and gives printed images a bright, more saturated look. Colors can be rendered more vividly. And because there's no wicking of the ink into fuzziness, edges and dots are tack sharp.

Clay-coated papers have a slight absorbency that can be carefully controlled during manufacture. The special ink-jet papers are of this type. They absorb a bit of ink, which helps the image dry faster and makes it more permanent, locked to the fiber of the paper instead of layered on its surface. Some of the most glossy papers are coated with gelatin or plastic, which gives them a perfectly smooth, nonabsorbent surface. Thermal transfer printers often use this sort of paper.

Sometimes paper manufacturers apply coatings for special purposes. For example, when you use the output of your laser or ink-jet to paste-up a printing master (it's sometimes quicker than using desktop publishing software, particularly if you're old-fashioned or haven't gotten around to buying a DTP package), the glue or rubber cement can discolor the paper and speed its decomposition. Papers specially coated on the backside prevent the absorption of glues and waxes. You'll want to print on the *uncoated* side of this paper. Fortunately most manufacturers indicate the paste-up side with faint printing (often in pale blue) so that you can identify it.

Textured Paper

The opposite of coated paper is that purposely made to have a rough finish. In handmade papers, a rough finish is the natural one. To make individual sheets of paper by hand, paper makers lift a screen through a slur of pulp and water. The pulp collects on the screen. The paper maker then presses the water out of the sheet. This process leaves an impression of the screen in the paper, marking it unmistakably as hand made–well, almost.

To add a touch of class to their higher-end products, many paper manufacturers imitate the hand-laid look, sometimes by pressing long rolls of paper through textured rollers as part of the finishing process. The result is a screen-like finish to the paper and a definite pattern that's visible when you hold an individual sheet up to the light. Every manufacturer has its own name for this kind of textured paper, for example "Classic laid" or "Linen finish."

Although the effect is mostly made to give a classic, expensive look to the paper, you can use any kind of pulp as the raw stock, even kraft paper. The texture has a definite effect on printed output, too. Textures and nonimpact printing methods don't get along well. The texture does not lay flat against a laser fuser, so character printing will be uneven. Textured paper usually is not coated, so it happily sucks in ink-jet ink giving blurry images.

Old-time paper makers learned that by putting shaped wires atop the screen used for paper making, they could make images appear in the paper when it was held up to light. The image was called a *watermark*, and printers use watermarks like brand names to label paper as their own. Some of these watermarks have made a lasting impression. For example, the cap and bells of the fool used as a watermark gave its name to the foolscap size of paper.

The visible image of the watermark arises from a change in the thickness of the paper. Where the raw paper lays upon the wire image on its screen, it is slightly thinner. Thinner paper allows more light to pass through, so the watermark appears brighter by transmitted light. Better papers today still bear watermarks to identify the origin or quality of the paper, boasting, for example, 100% cotton content.

Ink-Jet Paper

The thin inks used by ink-jet printers put special demands on the paper you use if you want to gain the full benefit of the extraordinary resolutions offered by modern machines. Plain paper absorbs too much ink to make 720 dpi printing worthwhile. The individual dots not only blend together but spread out so their precise placement is essentially irrelevant. Text printed at 720 dpi on plain paper often looks worse than printing it at lower resolutions because the spreading ink becomes too dark and edges get rough or wiggly.

Coated paper and ink-jet paper superficially appear the same with smooth, almost glossy surfaces. Ink-jet paper is not fully coated, so it's a step lower in quality. A few fibers still poke through to the surface, allowing the ink to penetrate and grab onto the paper a bit but not so much as to wick all over creation into massive blurs. Coated paper works better because it forces the ink to dry at the surface. The ink droplets keep their shape as they dry, which results in sharp, fine dots. In addition, because the ink is not absorbed under paper fibers, you can see more of its color. It consequently appears more saturated.

Paper manufacturers generally coat paper only on one side. If you print on the uncoated side, you'll waste the extra money you paid for better paper. Be careful. The coated side is not always the shinier side. Some manufacturers recommend that you use the side that appears brighter and whiter. If you look closely–particularly with a magnifying glass or loupe–you may be able to see which side is coated. The coating will cover all of the paper fibers, so if you can see the fibers clearly you are looking at the *uncoated* side.

Plain paper has definite sides, too. If you must use plain paper with ink-jets, be sure to use the roller side. During the manufacture of plain paper, it gets squeezed between a roller and a screen. Although the screen provides the water an exit path, it also makes the paper surface coarse and opens the grain. The roller smoothes the paper and packs down the paper fibers. Consequently the roller side, absorbs less and makes a sharper image. You can feel the difference between the two sides. The smoother side is the roller side, and it should be your first surface choice for printing. If you can't feel the difference, try printing on both sides of a sheet. If you can see the difference, use the side that produces the best results.

You can also get glossy coated ink-jet paper that appears to be the same material as used by photographs. You won't get photographic results, however, because the ink will sit on top of the paper while photographic dyes are actually inside the coating. This kind of paper is available from many manufacturers and is quite expensive, $1 or $2 per sheet. Epson sells its version as part number S041033. Hewlett-Packard offers a similar paper as its LX Jet-series glossy paper.

Preprinted Paper

Modern computer printers turn anyone into a chameleon: you can be anyone you want by printing your own stationery and business cards. To give a more finished, more impressive, even more established look to these business trapping (as well as just make them look better) a number of companies now sell preprinted pages and card sets. All the embellishments–color patterns, clever graphics, even logotype cuts–are already printed on the paper. You only need to add your name and address with your laser or ink-jet printer. Similar preprinted paper allows you to make decorative menus, brochures, announcements, and all the other stuff you once had to run to the print shop to buy.

Apart from concerns about fraud and forgery, you have one worry when using these preprinted papers with your computer printer. If you want top quality that approaches the old print shop, the paper *and* its printing must match the printer technology you plan to use.

As with any paper, the basic stock should match your printer technology. Most of these preprinted sheets are designed for laser printers and use laser-quality paper. This choice poses a problem should you want to use an ink-jet to add your own touch of color. The laser paper will likely be more absorbent than ink-jet paper, resulting in a slight blurring of characters. You may not be able to use the highest resolution mode of your printer (for example, 720 dpi) with these papers.

On the other hand, the ink poses no problem for ink-jet printers, but is a concern for lasers. A laser printer briefly heats both paper and ink to a high temperature (for example, 392°F or 200°C for 0.1 second for most Hewlett-Packard LaserJets, twice as long for the Color LaserJet) to fuse its toner to the paper. Some inks scorch or liquefy at this temperature. Not only will you lose some of the quality of the pre-preprinted ornamentation but some of the loosed ink may adhere to your printer's mechanism and gum up the works. In other words, be certain that any pre-preprinted papers you use are rated for laser applications if you want to run them through your laser printer.

Color

Another way to make printout distinctive is by using colored paper. You can pick your favorite hue to gain the most impact or best impression. Other than aesthetic considerations, your only concern is the same as with picking any printer paper. The paper itself must be designed to match the rigors of your printer technology. In a laser printer, colored paper must be able to withstand the heat of the fuser. Colored ink-jet papers must have the same tailored smoothness and absorbency of any ink-jet paper.

Printer manufacturers warn against using paper with color *coatings* rather than paper with color dispersed through the stock. Such coatings may be adversely affected by the heat of a laser printer. They may curl severely and jam in the machine.

Note that the color of the paper stock you use will have an effect on the hues produced by a color printer. Most color printers render intermediary tones with halftone dots that allow the color of the paper base to shine through. Most software assumes that you'll be printing on white paper, so mixed colors will not look exactly as you had intended them. The shades of transparent inks will also change with the color of the paper stock, but the background color will have only minor effect on opaque inks and the toner used by color laser printers in areas of solid color.

White is also a color, and papers come in various white tones. You have your choice not only of various off-whites (such as yellowed "antique" white or a greyish beige "dove") but also in what is regarded as pure white. As noted above, the brightness (and thus, whiteness) of paper varies with the bleaching and fillers used in making it.

Because it yields a higher contrast image, a whiter paper will make blacks appear darker. In general, photocopier papers are not as white as true laser paper. Printer makers recommend a brightness above 80 for general printing and over 90 for critical applications such as preparing reproduction masters.

Paper to Avoid

Certain kinds of paper are prone to producing problems with most printers. To avoid hassles and headaches, you're best to avoid them. Among the troublemakers are:

- **Perforated paper or sheets with cut-out areas.** Any irregularity in the surface of paper is apt to cause problems with cut-sheet-feed mechanisms. Perforations often present a raised edge that can get caught during travel through a tortuous paper path. Moreover, the perforations weaken the paper, raising the potential that it may tear as it moves through the printer. Cut-out areas–essentially holes made in individual sheets, usually for some aesthetic effect–can cause jams as well. The hole may fall where a rubber roller grabs the sheet to pull it through the printer, and the mechanism may lose its grip on one side of the sheet but not the other. The paper goes askew and jams.
- **Paper that is irregularly shaped, damaged, or wrinkled.** Printers make the assumption that paper is smooth and square, and any deviation from that will likely cause problems to the feed mechanism. If a sheet is not rectangular, it may not line up properly with the mechanism and it may prove more likely to slip, causing a jam. Wrinkled or damaged paper may likely suffer the same problem. In addition, the wrinkled paper may unevenly unwrinkle during its journey, slipping in the mechanism. It, as well as damaged paper, is also likely to be weak and liable to tear or crumple in the machine.
- **Extreme finishes, either very glossy or very rough.** Extreme finishes pose multiple problems for printers. Very smooth, glossy paper can slip through feed rollers, as can very rough paper. Problems also arise with the actual print mechanism. Glossy coatings may react unfavorably to the fuser heat in laser printers and the volatile inks of jet printers. Very rough paper surfaces will take toner unevenly and may even brush against and clog ink-jet nozzles.
- **Heavily textured or embossed papers.** To a printer, a heavily textured paper is the same as one with a rough finish. It is apt to cause feed problems and difficulties in the print process. Embossed papers–that is, those that

have text or patterns impressed into them for decorative effect—similarly present an uneven surface to the printer. Toner may not properly adhere around the embossed area. In fact, the laser process may tend to flatten out those impressive embossed impressions.

- **Paper from carbonless form or other chemically treated papers.** The odd chemical coatings used for carbonless form paper can have a number of untoward effects on the printing process. The coating adds a bit of slipperiness to the paper, which can lead to feed problems. Worse, the chemical coating may be incompatible with the print process. Toner may not adhere to it. The chemicals may repel ink-jet ink, causing it to bead up, smear, or simply not stick at all to the paper. The chemical treatment may also give off odd—and possibly hazardous—fumes when subjected to the high-temperature fusing process.

Envelopes

For the printing perspective, envelopes are something you want to stuff rather than push. The envelope carries your correspondence through the rigors of the real world and the postal system. And they challenge your printer with their quirks and idiosyncrasies.

For the most part, envelopes are simply folded paper, so all the characteristics of paper describe them well. They are different, too. Their folds and odd shapes test the mettle of your printer's feed mechanism.

For purposes of our discussion, we can divide your concerns in printing envelopes that differ from those of the base paper stock into three areas: the odd sizes of envelopes, the variation in thickness caused by folding, and the problem of feeding them through your printer.

Size

Ordinarily a container must be slightly larger inside than the thing it is suppose to contain, a fact that needs no explanation. But because it is customary to fold the individual sheets we stuff into envelopes, the typical envelope can be smaller than the size of a normal sheet of paper. This expedient of folding correspondences have saved countless rags and trees over the centuries, allowing each envelope to use less paper. It also results in a number of odd sizes for envelopes and challenges for the printer that must process them.

Most envelopes are wider than standard individual cut sheets to accommodate them folded lengthwise twice over. This poses a problem for some narrow-carriage printers that may have mechanisms too small to accommodate the full envelope width. Table 7.6 lists the sizes of the more common envelopes.

Table 7.6 Common Envelope Sizes (flap folded)

Designation	Height Inches	Width Inches	Height Millimeters	Width Millimeters
6_	3.6	6.5	91.4	165
Monarch	3.875	7.5	98.4	190.5
Com-10	4.125	9.5	195	241
DL	4.33	8.66	110	220
C5	6.5	9.01	165	229

Tractor-fed printers easily accommodate this additional width when you manually feed envelopes. Their carriages are naturally an inch wider to accommodate sprocket-fed paper, and the most common business-size envelope (Com-10) fits right into even narrow-carriage machines.

Most sheet-fed printers have greater difficulty, limited as they are to the normal paper widths. These most readily accept envelopes sideways. Of course, you must alter character orientation from portrait to landscape so that you don't further irritate your letter carrier with the need to crane his head to read the addresses you print. You also need to set your margins properly to reflect the size of the envelope. These settings must be downloaded to your printer.

Most software packages let you select standard envelope sizes as well as paper sizes for your printer and automatically make these accommodations. They will then automatically send the correct commands to your printer to handle the envelopes. You can also send the commands yourself through your own programs. Using the Hewlett-Packard PCL instruction set, the commands you want to send to your printer are given as follows.

To set the page size to:

```
COM 10              Ec&181A
Monarch             Ec&180A
DL                  Ec&190A
C5 International    Ec&191A
```

To set page orientation to:

```
Landscape     Ec&l1O
Portrait      Ec&l0O
```

To set the top margin properly for a given envelope size:

```
COM10         Ec&l12E
Monarch       Ec&l10E
DL            Ec&l12E
```

To set the left margin properly for a given envelope size:

```
COM10         Ec&a35L
Monarch       Ec&a30L
DL            Ec&a35L
```

For more exacting control of your printer in handling envelopes, you'll find a full reference to PCL and other common printer command sets in Chapter 11.

Folds

For the most part, stationery sets are matched: paper sheets and envelopes are cut from the same stock. Typically, however, even matching envelopes may use heavier paper than ordinary single sheets to help them better withstand the rigors of the postal system. You need to make allowance for the slightly thicker stock when calculating what fits through your printer.

A problem worse from the perspective of your printer than the use of heavier stock is the uneven thickness of envelopes. Because the paper in envelopes is folded over, an envelope is multiple sheets thick. Even worse, this extra thickness varies over the surface of the envelope. When open with its flap up, a conventional envelope varies from one to three thicknesses of its paper basis where the folded sheets overlap.

Further complicating the matter of variable thickness of the overlap is where it occurs. In a conventional envelope, overlaps that build the envelope to three thicknesses run in a V shape right through the middle of the envelope where you normally print the recipient's address. Figure 7.2 shows the areas of double- and triple-overlap on a conventional envelope.

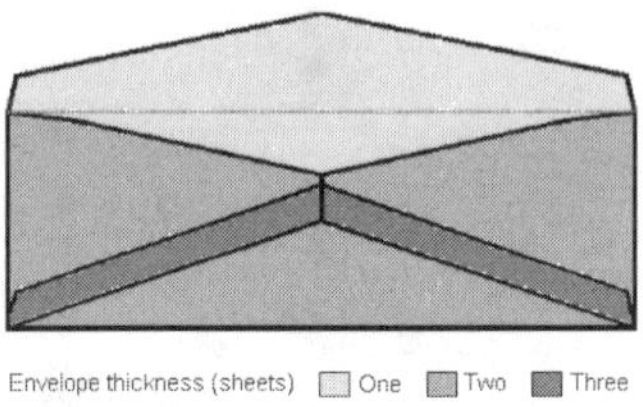

Figure 7.2 Variations in thickness in the common folded envelope.

To smooth the way for computer printers, some stationers offer redesigned envelopes that move the triple overlap and all uneven thicknesses out of the address area. To accomplish this design goal, the entire envelope must be redesigned with a different system of folds and even an altered flap. Interior and exterior dimensions are unaltered. Figure 7.3 shows an envelope that uses this new style of fold.

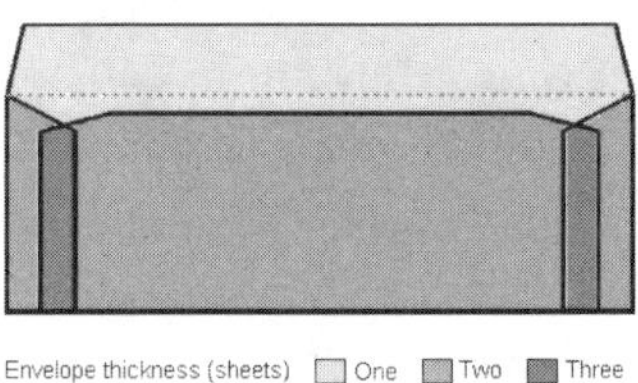

Figure 7.3 Envelope fold redesigned for computer printers.

All good ideas have their down side, and that includes the revised enveloped design. The conventional envelope minimizes the amount of paper needed to make an envelope. The revised design uses more. Not only is its unfolded shape more wasteful when cutting out the pattern, it also uses more paper in the actual envelopes. Even disregarding the tooling costs to convert a folding machine from the conventional to the newer style of envelope, the new design will naturally be more costly.

Feeding

To print an envelope, you somehow must get it through your printer. To print a lot of envelopes, you need a way of moving them automatically. Through the ages, progress has been backward—the first computer printers accommodated envelopes only by making modifications to the envelopes themselves. Later, as PCs came into widespread use, exactly when you'd think the paper industry could stand redesigning envelopes, printers changed to accept ordinary envelopes. Along the way to today's envelope-compatible printers, we've had the dubious pleasure of using continuous-form envelopes and tipped-on envelopes. Both were designed to cope with the need for tractor-feed mechanisms.

Continuous-form envelopes are an orgamist's challenge—envelopes folded to allow feed sprocket holes on their edges. As with continuous-form sheets, these envelopes load into your printer's tractors, using their edge holes for a smooth drive. Later, you tear off the edges to produce a workable, if marginally ugly, envelope with rough edges and an odd fold. Of course you had the fun of unthreading your ordinary paper and loading the envelopes every time you needed to address a few, a chore that kept typewriters in offices long past the time they were otherwise outmoded.

Tipped-on envelopes take conventional envelopes and glue them to a continuous-carrier web, essentially a long sheet of paper with perforated holes for the sprocket drive mechanism at the edges. The carrier web serves to carry each envelope into the proper position for printing. They leave a lot of waste—the entire carrier web gets left over. Moreover, the web adds another layer of thickness to the already thick (and uneven) envelope. The total thickness of the envelopes and web may be more than some modest printers can deal with.

Dedicated envelope feed mechanisms are today's answer to the envelope problem. Many printers now incorporate an envelope path in their normal feed mechanism, although often good only for manually feeding individual envelopes. Other printers make an automatic envelope feeder an easily installed but extra-cost option. Latch one on, and you can print on envelopes as easily as switching your source paper tray.

For example, many Hewlett-Packard LaserJets such as the LaserJet IID/IIID and IIISi/4Si/4Si MX make adding an envelope feeder a simple four-step process (only two of which actually involve the feeder). Installation goes like this:

1. Turn off the printer.
2. Remove the envelope feeder access cover, which you'll find just above the upper paper tray.
3. Slide the envelope feeder into the printer.
4. Turn the printer back on.

If you can cope with pulling out an ordinary paper tray to fill it with paper, you can deal with the envelope feeder.

Of course, you have another alternative to the hassle of feeding envelopes through your printer: you can always use labels and slap them on the envelopes as you need them.

Labels

Labels raise their own issues when used with computer printers. For example, dedicated label printers often require their own special label stock that matches their thermal print mechanism. Moreover, labels come in a variety of sizes and styles, most of which have little resemblance to the stuff your printer wants to work with.

Again clever designs have come up with a variety of solutions. You can slide ordinary sheets of labels through the manual paper feeding mechanism of most friction-fed printers. Continuous-form labels complete with sprocket holes on their backing let you use almost any tractor-fed printer as a label maker. And large sheets of labels matching standard stationery size (8.5x11 inches) make running labels through your laser printer a breeze.

Apart from the easily solved mechanics of feeding labels, however, you'll find that label-printing is still fraught with traps for the unwary. Use the wrong label on the wrong printer and you may be looking at a large repair bill.

The problems you're likely to encounter depend on the kind of label and printer that you have. First we'll offer some general advise that applies to most printers. Then we'll take a look at the applications used by the two primary kinds of computer printer labels, continuous-form and sheet-style labels.

General Advice

Labels are available in various sizes to match whatever your particular needs might be, from identifying file folders to routing packages across the continent. Get the size and shape that suit your application. You'll want to be sure that the labels are designed for computer printer applications. Those that come in continuous rolls and stationery-size cut sheets are usually printer compatible.

Not only must your labels be compatible with your printer, your printer must be compatible with label printing. For example, Epson warns against printing labels (as well as envelopes) unless a printer was specially designed to handle such media. In any case, the thickness of the envelope or the label should not be greater than the maximum rated for the printer. (Check the specifications in your instruction manual.)

If you use only a few labels, buy them in small quantities so your label stock is kept fresh. Avoid using old labels. As the adhesive ages, it tends to lose its stickiness, making the labels easier to peel off—or fall off—their backing. Old labels may separate as they travel through your printer. Although they don't stick to their backing, they will stick to your printer and literally gum up the works.

Continuous-Form Labels

In impact printers or any continuous-form printer, the best choice is labels with a continuous base sheet that has built-in sprocket holes to feed the tractor mechanism. The glossy backing of the labels, made slippery to allow you to remove and use the labels, has a tendency to slip in friction-feed mechanisms. The result is uneven line spacing and, potentially, paper jamming. Be sure to adjust the printer for the thickness of the labels before you start printing. A single label is the equivalent to two or three thicknesses of ordinary paper because it comprises the label itself (with a bit of extra thickness from the adhesive) and the backing, which is usually a heavier paper. Otherwise, load continuous form labels exactly as you would continuous-form paper.

Continuous-form labels have a definite front and back edge. To avoid such problems even with new labels, you should try to feed labels through your printer in the proper direction. Feeding them backwards usually increases the likelihood that they will come off the backing and jam the mechanism. If your printer has automatic paper parking, defeat this option while you use labels to avoid backfeeding of the stock. This may involve setting a DIP switch or sending a specific set-up command to the printer.

Never leave labels threaded through your printer for a long period while the printer is idle, particularly continuous-form labels in a friction-fed printer. The adhesive will be slowly squeezed from between the label and backing, causing the label to stick to the mechanism. The result is, of course, a jam. A couple of hours wait between print jobs probably isn't long enough to worry about, but leaving labels threaded up overnight is tempting fate.

Sheet Labels

As with continuous-form labels, the adhesive on label sheets has a slight but definite tendency to squeeze out as the label sheet gets fed and squeezed through a printer. Although this seepage is insignificant in most printers, the heat of the fuser in laser printers makes the adhesive less viscous and more readily able to squeeze out. If you feed many sheets of labels through your laser printer, you can eventually cause a significant adhesive buildup in the paper path inside the printer.

According to label-maker Avery, this buildup is particularly a problem in Hewlett-Packard's LaserJet 4, 4 Plus, 4L, and 4Si models. The LaserJet II, LaserJet IIP, LaserJet III, LaserJet IIIP, and LaserJet 4P are much less susceptible to this adhesive buildup. In the problematic machines, the slight buildup can cause paper jams. Consequently Avery recommends that you follow a rigorous maintenance schedule. After each 500 sheets of labels you run through your printer, you should clean your LaserJet 4 printer's fuser output guides (see Chapter 12).

Avery makes several other recommendations when using sheets of labels with a laser printer. You should ensure that the sheets are in pristine condition and that the individual label sheets are flat and do not have bent corners. Any irregularity to the edge of the label makes a jam more likely. For example, a bent edge could cause a label to momentarily catch somewhere in the paper path, slightly bucking the sheet and lifting off some of the labels. The loosened labels may later stick to the feed mechanism and–you guessed it–cause a jam.

When loading a stack of label sheets into the feed tray of your printer, riffle through them or fan them out to ensure that they separate. This will help you guard against a label that has become stuck to the backing sheet above it. You'll find the culprits before they find a nesting spot inside your printer.

If your printer allows you to choose between paper paths, always use the straightest one when printing labels. The more twists and turns the label sheet must endure, the more likely a label will separate from it. The straight and narrow path always has less temptation along the way. The best choice if you are using a Hewlett-Packard Laser-Jet 4Si printer is the multipurpose paper tray and the rear-exit paper path. With a LaserJet 4L or 4P printer, choose the straight-through paper path.

Sheet labels have a definite front and back edge just like continuous-form labels. In general, you should feed the front edge in first. However, Avery notes that if forward-feeding causes problems, you should try feeding the labels in backwards. In other words, do what works best for you and your printer.

You can buy labels preprinted with your return address, colorful patterns, or other decorations. Warnings that apply to ordinary stationery also apply to labels. The ink on the labels (as well as the labels themselves) must be designed to withstand the heat of the laser printer fuser. Although pre-decorated commercial labels that let you add your own return address usually comply with this requirement, address labels that you have printed at the corner print shop might not. Inquire about the ink before you run the label through your printer.

Transparencies

One of the chief applications for color printers is preparing transparencies for presentations. Transparencies for overhead projectors are easy to prepare. You simply substitute transparency stock for the paper you'd normally run through your printer. The only problem is that the transparency medium you use must match your printer's technology. Impact dot-matrix, ink-jet, thermal-wax, and laser printers all can make transparencies, but they all make different demands on the medium. For example, ink-jet transparency medium must be specially coated to provide what artists call *tooth*, surface roughness that helps the thin ink adhere to the otherwise slippery surface. Thermal-wax printers work best with almost glassy smooth transparencies. Hot and temperamental laser printers require a medium that's resistant to melting during its quick journey through the fuser.

Transparencies differ in the material from which they are made, their surface preparation, their thickness, and size. All of these factors must match your printer to yield optimal output—and when you're showing your work to the entire outside world during a presentation, you want optimal output.

Two plastics are commonly used for transparencies, cellulose *acetate* and *polyester*, which is often sold under the tradename Mylar. Acetate is a traditional drafting medium that is often mechanically finished with a matte surface akin to that of ground glass. Acetates are comparatively stiff but can readily be torn. Mylar sheets are smooth and flexible and usually receive a surface treatment to match their particular application. They are tougher than acetate and usually stretch rather than tear.

In the United States, the thickness of transparency media is measured in mils, one-thousandth of an inch. Metric measurements are made in fractions of a millimeter. Overall size of transparency sheets typically matches normal paper sizes so that printer mechanisms accept the sheets without adjustment.

Printer makers often recommend that you use only the transparency media that they sell. That's good for their business. It also ensures that you'll get the proper kind of medium to match your printer. You can substitute generic media as long as you ensure that the medium is compatible with your printer's technology.

Power

As with any electronic device, computer printers use electricity. Although the amount used by most printers over their lifetimes is trivial—probably less than the lightbulb that illuminates your work area—it *is* a consumable and requires some consideration.

Power Requirements

Unlike PCs and monitors that almost invariably have universal power supplies that you can plug in anywhere in the world, most PC printers are designed to match one particular power system. Printers for the United States, for example, are manufactured to run solely on the 120-volt, 60-Hertz power that is standard there. Printers made for the European Community run 240-volt, 50-Hertz power. Epson, for example, makes only one printer that can run on either kind of electrical system, the DFX-5000, which needs only a fuse change to convert from one power system to another.

Converting other printers to match different systems is a thorny issue. Inexpensive power converters sold to allow you to use a 120-volt shaver on 220 volts in Europe should never be used with anything that you value. These inexpensive devices usually comprise nothing more than a diode that reduces voltage by clipping off half of each cycle. They do not alter the frequency of the current (your shaver will sound funny when you use one). Moreover, electrical equipment that uses switching-type power supplies will attempt to compensate for the odd input, often with fatal results.

You can convert from one power system to another using a *step-down transformer* (to run U.S.-style equipment in Europe) or a *step-up transformer* (to use European-style equipment in the United States) The transformer must match both the power available, the power your printer needs, and must be able to handle the number of volt-amperes (VA) or watts used by your printer. Whether the expedient of using a transformer to match printer to power systems is recommended depends on your printer type.

For example, Epson endorses this strategy for its dot-matrix printers. The transformer takes care of the voltage difference. Epson printers can handle the frequency difference because they are built to tolerate a frequency range from 49.5 to 60.5 Hertz. Epson even recommends two step-down transformers for use in Europe. These are Stancore step-down transformers models Model GSD-150 (for printers drawing up to 150 VA) and GSD-250 (for printers drawing up to 250 VA).

Hewlett-Packard, on the other hand, warns that transformers should never be used with its laser printers. The company neither endorses nor provide information to assist with converting any of its LaserJet printers between power systems. The company specifically recommends *against* using transformers because of the sudden power demands made when the printer's fuser switches on.

HP's reluctance to advise about conversions is based on the need to convert several critical components in the printer to match the available power. The cost of making the changes may be more than buying a new printer. Moreover, if you attempt a conversion yourself, you'll void your printer's warranty.

Saving Power

Most new printers are designed with the United States government's *Energy*Star* program in mind. They minimize their power usage by shifting into an idle mode when not actively printing. Most printers will draw less than 30 watts when idle. From a power consumption standpoint, you need not worry about whether you leave your printer on all the time or switch it on only when you need to print.

Older printers often do not have such an idle mode and can consume substantial power between print jobs. Some manufacturers now offer power monitoring and switching devices that can minimize the electrical usage of these older machines. For example, Digital Products offers its NetPrint PowerMinder, a $169 device the company claims can save to $200 annually in cost of power for a network printer. The PowerMinder plugs in like a surge protector (which it resembles) and attaches to your network through Digital Products' NetPrint module. The PowerMinder then activates your printer when a job comes along, and shuts it down when it finishes.

Backup Power

Most makers of *uninterruptible power systems* (*UPSs*) recommend that you do *not* connect your printer to a protected output of your UPS. This advice makes sense for several reasons. It conserves on the size of UPS that you need to buy. You don't have to add your printer's power requirements to the total number of volt-amperes (VA) that you call upon the UPS to supply. Because you can always restart your print job after the power is restored after an outage, keeping your printer going is not much of a priority anyhow.

There's a more important reason not to connect printers to UPSs. When the fuser in a laser printer switches on, the power consumption of the printer jumps dramatically. For a brief period, a tenth of a second or so, the printer may draw a kilowatt from your wall outlet. This brief gulp is enough to overload most smaller UPSs. Typically the UPS will shut down when confronted with such an overload, subverting the purpose for which you bought the UPS. Worse, poorly designed UPSs (and there are a lot of them out there) may be damaged by such immense power drains.

Modern ink-jet printers present no problems for UPSs except their normal electrical needs. Older impact printers, however, can be problematic. Industrial-strength printers may have large induction motors to move printheads and paper. These motors create nonlinear (reactive) loads that can damage UPSs. These motors may also cause electrical surges as they switch on and off, which can also be detrimental to your UPS.

To stay on the safe side, then, the best practice is to avoid connecting *any* printer to your UPS. You'll face fewer risks.

CHAPTER EIGHT

The Interface

An interface is where you connect your printer to your PC. It can be either a parallel or serial port, a network connection, or something else entirely. While linking a printer can be as simple as plugging it in, you sometimes have to deal with the details of the interface, particular when your setup varies from the normal (and don't they all). This primer will help you through troubled times, dark and stormy nights, and other patience-testing situations

An interface is a joining of two separate things, and at that the definition falls inches short of a fasten-your-seatbelts collision. It lacks only a bit of force and bloodshed. Anyone who has tangled with a particularly pernicious printer port connection knows even that distinction disappears somewhere around the twelfth try that by all accounts is by the book and infallible. Right. You force together the recalcitrant connectors and the blood flows—either from your raw knuckles, from the plans you start hatching for the printer's design engineer, or from the sacrifice you make to the gods of digital illogic.

Even simple connections can be troublesome when what you expect and what you get are as different as diamonds and cubic zirconia. Most printer interfaces follow respected industry standards, and most printer connections are straightforward and trouble free. But push the envelope and you're sure to get paper cuts. When manufacturers try to add features by tiptoeing around the edge of the standard, you're apt to fall off. When you push the limits yourself—by stretching a cable too long or by trying to salvage a wire you once thought worked with another printer—your assumptions crash and burn like alien ships in the sites of the hero's laser.

The good news is that most simple connections work as easily as plugging in your toaster. Slide the cable connectors into the jacks on your printer and PC, and in seconds you should be wasting paper on a par with your favorite bureaucracy. In fact, you can live your entire life without knowing that even the simple parallel port comes in four distinct varieties or that serial printers can be made to work with your PC. You might never need a book that purports to tell you all the secrets of printers. But then again, you bought this one, so that something must be up. You either have a problem or want to know the inner cabal of printers and their interfaces so that you can thwart difficulties even before they arise. And you can.

You have at least four interface options that will let you connect a printer to a PC. Some printers will let you use two or more of these choices; others stodgily restrict you to one. Given the right circumstances, one of them will be best for you and your equipment. Your interface choices include:

- **Parallel ports** These are the popular means of connecting printers to PCs. In addition to covering the basics and providing a general reference (such as a pin-out of cables), recent changes in parallel ports (EPP, ECP) are also discussed.
- **Serial ports** Although serial printers are becoming rare, they are among the most troublesome to connect. This section guides the reader into establishing a serial connection and making it work.
- **Video interfaces** Some early models of laser printers allowed high-speed data transfer through video (raster) interfaces. This section describes them and points out how they are used (and products that use them).
- **Network links** Many modern printers allow direct network connections. Because a network connection allows you to share a single printer among several people, we'll discuss them in the next chapter, "Printer Sharing."

Parallel Ports

Printers and parallel ports were made for each other–literally. When engineers dreamed up the first PC, they added the parallel port as a convenient way of connecting line printers to the machine. The put signals in the connection that exactly matched the needs of printers and printing and even gave DOS a name for the port that described its function: LPT for Line PrinTer.

As printer ports, the parallel connection is one of the easiest to make. You can usually just plug in your printer and expect it to work, although you need an adapter cable to match the connectors on your PC and printer (which are explicably different). But even these are available anywhere for a few dollars.

If all you want to do is print, that's about all you need to know about parallel ports. But engineers have covetously eyed the parallel port because of its simplicity and speed. A few years ago, they took it over, redefined it, and put it to work tying in everything from CD-ROM drives to networks. Then, after 13 years of use throughout the PC industry, the parallel port finally became an official standard.

In its new guise you might not even recognize it. It may even use a brand new connector on your PC or printer or computer-controlled tachyon modulator or whatever you might connect to it. But in its heart remains a parallel port the old familiar LPT port. Even the latest, fastest versions deign to step backward and power your favorite parallel printer. Indeed, the rigors of standardization haven't so much as locked down what the parallel port can do as opened it up. The latest parallel ports do everything they always have and much more. Its new extended capabilities mean that the parallel port will be around for years more and that you'll probably plug it into other peripherals besides your printer. But even with this new versatility, the parallel port will remain the main means for your printer work.

Strategy

From what once was regarded as merely a printer port–and even retains the name of its origins–the parallel port has become an universal interface for PCs. In its latest incarnation, the parallel port now has the speed and much of the power of the SCSI interface without the hassles and extra cost. Pushed to its current-day limits, a parallel port can link dozens of peripherals to your PC and move data at speeds comparable to those of yesterday's general purposes expansion buses. From a simple circuit made from a handful of parts, the modern parallel port is a sophisticated high-speed interface rife with operating modes and transfer protocols.

The latest innovations in the parallel port are a peripheral maker's dream come true. It gives them access to virtually any PC. They can plug their network adapters, cartridge disks, tape backup, and CD-ROM drives into any PC including the tiniest of subnotebooks that have no other expansion provisions of their own. The IEEE 1284 standard gives them a rigorous model on which to base their designs and on which they can rely without worries about timing or other compatibility issues. The standard is complete, complex, and confusing.

That said, the parallel port is your friend. It is the easiest and most convenient way of linking a printer to your PC–or any PC. Slide a plug at one end of a cable into a jack on your printer and dissimilar plug at the other end into your PC, and your involvement with this most elementary of interfaces is over. In most cases (or at least with most printers and PCs), you can put the pulp mills into overtime immediately.

With nearly every combination of PC and printer, you have the option of using a parallel port. The requirements that enable you to use a parallel connection are minimal, essentially two:

- Both your printer and your PC have parallel ports available.
- Your printer and PC are no more than 10 feet apart.

The benefits of using a parallel connection for your printer are enormous. The highest recommendation of the parallel port is for its installation simplicity. In the vast majority of circumstances, the parallel port is no more difficult to manage than plugging an appliance into a wall outlet. If you can make your refrigerator work, you can get a parallel port to play. In most cases, all you need is a printer cable, an inexpensive and standardized commodity item you can buy anywhere that sells PCs or peripherals.

The Plug-and-Play standard further simplifies your installation concerns. Link your printer to your PC with a parallel port, and Windows 95 and more recent operating systems can automatically take a peek at your printer and pick the right driver software to make it work best. Your PC and your software will *know* what kind of printer you have, and you don't have to worry about telling them. And that means no tangling with driver software or installation programs with laundry lists of printer names that never seem to include the machine you've bought.

From that description, you'd expect the parallel port to be the first interface canonized and granted a festival day. But the parallel port has its limitations, and it remains a specialized interface that works well in only certain circumstances. Although its application is wide, it has its drawbacks and may not always be the one right choice for linking up a particular printer.

One drawback of the parallel port design is the profusion of connection it requires. A plain vanilla printer cable requires 25 separate connections. A serial cable gets by with three. From that perspective a parallel cable is necessarily more expensive than one used by a serial interface. Fortunately, at practical cable lengths the difference is minimal. Most of the cost of a short cable arise from the connectors at either end and the labor in assembling it. You'll find no appreciable difference between the price of serial and parallel cables at the typical two-meter (six-foot) length.

Cabling issues rise in prominence with distance. The very design of the parallel interface makes it impractical if not unworkable for connections much in excess of ten feet. That pack of data and control signals travel in a tight parallel ground down the fat printer cable. The various signals interact with each other and the wire and quickly lose their digital integrity. The longer the cable, the worse things get. The higher the signal speed, the shorter the connection must be. For example, even though the Enhanced Parallel Port specification required a special cable, it limited cable length to six feet.

Of course, a parallel connection won't work if you don't have both a parallel port on your PC and one on your printer. As ubiquitous as the parallel port may be, it's sometimes an option that's not available to you. Some old printers were equipped with only serial ports. Some machines spout only SCSI ports. Some printer sharing systems prefer a serial connection. A few printers use proprietary connections.

Odds are you will never face one of those anomalies. And the odds favor you needing a parallel connection for not only your printer but, in the future, any of a variety of peripherals. Even modems are moving to the parallel port. It is simply the most important basic connection you will make with your PC, one that will become only more valuable in the future.

Background

The parallel port reflects a hardware engineer's concept of the way in which communication should work. A signal that is in one place is connected to the distant location at which it is wanted by running a wire from point to point. For every signal, another wire is added. Eight data signals take eight wires. In addition, all the control functions–for example, the signaling back and forth between PC and printer to prevent buffer overflow–also get their own separate wires.

Such a design saves on the complex circuitry needed to bundle signals together to travel down one or two conductors. The whole connection, in fact, works like a marionette–the PC operates the printer or remote device by electrically tugging on the appropriate strings. It is difficult to imagine a simpler, more straightforward system.

No conversion circuitry impedes the flow of information. The eight conductors serve as an expressway for information, moving bytes at the same speed at which a single bit can traverse the connection.

In truth, the contribution of PC makers to the first parallel port was minimal. They added a new connector that better fit the space available on the PC. The actual port design was already being used on computer printers at the time. Originally created by printer-maker Centronics Data Computer Corporation and used by printers throughout the 1960s and 1970s, the connection was electrically simple, even elegant. It took little circuitry to add to a printer or PC even in the days when designers had to use discrete components instead of custom-designed circuits. A few old-timers still cling to history and call the parallel port a *Centronics* port.

The PC parallel port is not identical to the exact Centronics design, however. In adapting it to the PC, IBM substituted a smaller connector. The large jack used by the Centronics design had 36 pins and was too large to be put where IBM wanted it–sharing a card retaining bracket with a video connector on the PC's first Monochrome Display Adapter. In addition, IBM added two new signals to give the PC more control over the printer and adjusted the timing of the signals traveling through the interface. All that said, most Centronics-style printers worked just fine with the PC.

For the first half of its life, the PC parallel port had few higher aspirations. It did its job, and did it well. It, or subtle variations of it, became ubiquitous if not universal. Any printer worth connecting to a PC used a parallel port (or so it seemed). But when IBM broke tradition and released a new series of computers with revolutionary 3.5-inch floppy disk drives (previous machines all used 5.25-inch disk drives) in 1987, it changed the parallel port.

IBM had a particular purpose in mind. To let you transfer your files from floppy disks on your old computer to your new machine with its then-odd disk drives, IBM offered its *Data Migration Facility*. Rather than some exotic new technology, it was simply a fancy name for a cable that plugged into the parallel ports of your old and new machines. Evidently someone reasoned the more impressive the name, the higher the price could be.

The Data Migration Facility fundamentally changed the parallel. On the new computer, it had to receive data rather than just send it out to a printer. The parallel ports had bidirectional capabilities. Your old PC with an old parallel port could only send out data.

Using the parallel port for data transfer inspired the programmers struggling with moving files between notebook and desktop PCs through slow serial ports. By using the parallel port, they could double or triple their file transfer throughput. They began to tinker with parallel ports for their own purposes.

And makers of other peripherals for notebook PCs took note, too. Soon they were taking advantage of the speed of the parallel port to add networks and CD ROM drives to portable PCs.

As manufacturers began adapting higher performance peripherals to use the parallel port, what was once fast performance became agonizingly slow. Although the parallel port more than met the modest data transfer needs of printers and floppy disk drives, it lagged behind other means of connecting hard disks and networks to PCs.

Engineers at network adapter maker Xircom Incorporated decided to do something about parallel performance and banded together with notebook computer maker Zenith Data Systems to find a better way. Along the way, they added Intel Corporation, and formed a triumphirate called Enhanced Parallel Port Partnership. They explored two ways of increasing the data throughput of a parallel port. They streamlined the logical interface so that your PC would need less overhead to move each byte through the port. In addition, they tightly defined the timing of the signals passing through the port, minimizing wasted time and helping ensure against timing errors.

On August 10, 1991, the organization released its first description of what they thought the next generation of parallel port should be and do. They continued to work on a specification until March, 1992, when they submitted Release 1.7 to the Institute of Electrical and Electronic Engineers (the IEEE) for consideration as an industry standard.

Although the EPP version of the parallel port can increase its performance by nearly tenfold, that wasn't enough to please everybody. The speed potential made some engineers see the old parallel port as an alternative to more complex expansion buses like the SCSI system. With this idea in mind, Hewlett-Packard joined with Microsoft to make the parallel port into a universal expansion standard called the Extended Capabilities Port (ECP). In November, 1992, the two companies released the first version of the ECP specification aimed at computers that use the ISA expansion bus. This first implementation adds two new modes transfer modes to the EPP design–a fast two-way communication mode between a PC and its peripherals, and another two-way mode with performance further enhanced by simple integral data compression–and defines a complete software control system.

The heart of the ECP innovation is a protocol for exchanging data across a high-speed parallel connection. The devices at the two ends of each ECP transfer negotiate the speed and mode of data movement. Your PC can query any ECP device to determine its capabilities. For example, your PC can determine what language your printer speaks and can set up the proper printer driver accordingly. In addition, ECP devices tell your PC the speed at which they can accept transmissions and the format of the data they understand. To ensure the quality of all transmissions, the ECP specification includes error detection and device handshaking. It also allows the use of data compression to further speed transfers.

Knowing a good thing when they see it, the IEEE parallel port committee incorporated the ECP design into its new specification. On March 30, 1994, the IEEE Standards Board approved its parallel port standard, *IEEE-1284-1994*. It was submitted to the American National Standards Institute and approved as a standard on September 2, 1994.

The IEEE 1284 standard marks a watershed in parallel port design and nomenclature. The standard defines (or redefines) all aspect of the parallel connection, from the software interface in your PC to the control electronics in your printer. It divides the world of parallel ports in two: *IEEE 1284-compatible devices*, which are those that will work with the new interface, which in turn includes just about every parallel port and device ever made; and *IEEE 1284-compliant devices*, those which understand and use the new standard. This distinction is essentially between pre- and poststandardization ports. You can consider IEEE 1284-*compatible* ports to be "old technology" and IEEE 1284-*compliant* ports to be "new technology."

Before IEEE 1284, parallel ports could be divided into four types: Standard Parallel Ports, Bidirectional Parallel Ports (also known as PS/2 parallel ports), Enhanced Parallel Ports, and Extended Capabilities Ports. The IEEE specification redefines the differences in ports, classifying them by the transfer mode they use. Although the terms are not exactly the same, you can consider a Standard Parallel Port one that is able to use only nibble-mode transfers. A PS/2 or Bidirectional Parallel Port from the old days can also make use of byte-mode transfers. EPP and ECP ports use EPP and ECP modes, as described by the IEEE 1284 specification.

EPP and ECP remain standards separate from IEEE 1284, although they have been revised to depend on it. Both EPP and ECP rely on their respective modes in the IEEE specification for their physical connections and electrical signaling. In other words, IEEE 1284 describes the physical and electrical characteristics of a variety of parallel ports. The other standards describe how the ports operate and link to your applications.

Connectors

The place to begin any discussion of the parallel port is the connector. The *connector* is the physical manifestation of the parallel port, the one part of the interface and standard you can actually touch or hold in your hand. It is the only part of the interface that most people will ever have to deal with. Once you know the ins and outs of parallel connectors, you'll be able to plug in the vast majority of PC printers.

Unfortunately the parallel port connector is not a single thing. It comes in enough different and incompatible forms to make matters interesting and with enough subtle wiring variations to make troubleshooting frustrating. Although the long-range prognosis is good—eventually parallel ports will gravitate to a single connector—in the short-term, matters will get only more confusing.

Before the IEEE-1284 standard was introduced, equipment designers used either of two connectors for parallel ports. On the back of your PC you would find a female 25-pin D-shell connector, IBM's choice to fit a parallel port within the confines allowed on the MDA video adapter. On your printer you would find a female 36-pin ribbon connector patterned after the original Centronics design. These connector designs have now been formalized, adopted by the IEEE as the 1284-A and 1284-B connectors. The standard also introduced a new, miniaturized connector, 1284-C, similar to the old Centronics ribbon connector but about half the size.

The A Connector

The familiar parallel port on the back of your PC was IBM's pragmatic innovation. At the time of the design of the original PC, many computers used a 37-pin D-shell connector for their printer ports that mated with Centronics-style printers. This connector was simply too long (about four inches) for where IBM wanted to put it. Slicing off 12 pins made would make a D-shell connector fit, and it still could provide sufficient pins for all the essential functions required in a parallel port as long as some of the ground return signals were doubled (and tripled) up. Moreover, the 25-pin D-shell was likely in stock on the shelves wherever IBM prototyped the PC because the mating connector had long been used in serial ports. IBM chose the opposite gender (a female receptacle on the PC) to distinguish it from a serial connection.

To retain compatibility with the original IBM design, other computer makers also adopted this connector. By the time the IEEE standardized the parallel port, the 25-pin D-shell was the standard. The IEEE adopted it as its 1284-A connector. Figure 8.1 shows a conceptual view of the A-connector.

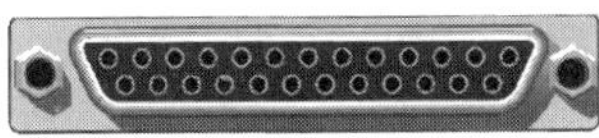

Figure 8.1 The IEEE-1284 A connector, a female 25-pin D-shell jack.

The individual contacts appear as socket holes, spaced at intervals of one-tenth inch, center-to-center. On the printer jack as it appears in the illustration, pin 1 is on the upper right, and contacts are consecutively numbered right-to-left. Pin 14 appears at the far right on the lower row, and again the contacts are sequentially numbered right to left. (Because you would wire this connector from the rear, the contact number would appear there in more familiar left to right sequence.) The socket holes are encased in plastic to hold them in place, and the plastic filler itself is completely surrounded by a metal shell that extends back to the body of the connector. The entire connector measures about two inches wide and half an inch tall when aligned as shown in the illustration.

The studs at either side of the connector are 4-40 jack screws, which are essentially extension screws. The fit into the holes in the connector and attach it to a chassis. Instead of slotted heads, they provide another screw socket to which you can securely attach screws from the mating connector.

As a receptacle or jack for mounting on a panel such as the back of your PC, this connector is available under a number of different part numbers, depending on their manufacturer. Some of these include AMP 747846-4, Molex 82009, and 3M Company 8325-60XX and 89925-X00X. Mating plugs are available as AMP 747948-1, Molex 71527, and 3M 8225-X0XX.

Of the 25 contacts on this parallel port connector, 17 are assigned individual signals for data transfer and control. The remaining eight serve as ground returns. Table 8.1 lists the functions assigned to each of these signals as implemented in the original IBM PC parallel port and most compatible computers until the IEEE 1284 standard was adopted. In its compatibility mode, the IEEE standard uses these same signal assignments.

Table 8.1 The Original IBM PC Parallel Port Pin-Out

Pin	Function
1	Strobe
2	Data bit 0
3	Data bit 1

4	Data bit 2
5	Data bit 3
6	Data bit 4
7	Data bit 5
8	Data bit 6
9	Data bit 7
10	Acknowledge
11	Busy
12	Paper end (Out of paper)
13	Select
14	Auto feed
15	Error
16	Initialize printer
17	Select input
18	Strobe ground
19	Data 1 and 2 ground
20	Data 3 and 4 ground
21	Data 5 and 6 ground
22	Data 7 and 8 ground
23	Busy and Fault ground
24	Paper out, Select, and Acknowledge ground
25	AutoFeed, Select input, and Initialize ground

Under the IEEE 1284 specification, signals are defined differently as the operating mode of changes. Note that a single physical connector on the back of your PC can operate in any of these five modes, and the signal definitions and their operation will change accordingly. Figure 8.2 lists these five modes and their signal assignments.

Table 8.2 IEEE 1284-A Connector Signal Assignments in All Modes

Pin	Compatibility Mode	Nibble Mode	Byte Mode	EPP Mode	ECP Mode
1	nStrobe	HostClk	HostClk	nWrite	HostClk
2	Data 1	Data 1	Data 1	AD1	Data 1
3	Data 2	Data 2	Data 2	AD2	Data 2
4	Data 3	Data 3	Data 3	AD3	Data 3
5	Data 4	Data 4	Data 4	AD4	Data 4
6	Data 5	Data 5	Data 5	AD5	Data 5
7	Data 6	Data 6	Data 6	AD6	Data 6
8	Data 7	Data 7	Data 7	AD7	Data 7
9	Data 8	Data 8	Data 8	AD8	Data8
10	nAck	PtrClk	PtrClk	Intr	PeriphClk
11	Busy	PtrBusy	PtrBusy	nWait	PeriphAck
12	PError	AckDataReq	AckDataReq	User defined 1	nAckReverse
13	Select	Xflag	Xflag	User defined 3	Xflag
14	nAutoFd	HostBusy	HostBusy	nDStrb	HostAck
15	nFault	nDataAvail	nDataAvail	User defined 2	nPeriphRequest
16	nInit	nInit	nInt	nInt	nReverseRequest
17	nSelectIn	1284 Active	1284 Active	nAStrb	1284 Active
18	Pin 1 (nStrobe) ground return				
19	Pins 2 and 3 (Data 1 and 2) ground return				
20	Pins 4 and 5 (Data 3 and 4) ground return				
21	Pins 6 and 7 (Data 5 and 6) ground return				
22	Pins 8 and 9 (Data 7 and 8) ground return				
23	Pins 11 and 15 ground return				
24	Pins 10, 12, and 13 ground return				
25	Pins 14, 16, and 17 ground return				

Along with standardized signal assignments, IEEE 1284 also gives us a standard nomenclature for describing the signals. In the Table 8.2 and all following that refer to the standard, signal names prefaced with a lowercase "n" indicate the signal goes negative when active–that is, the absence of a voltage means the signal is present.

Mode changes are negotiated between your PC and the printer or other peripheral connected to the parallel port. Consequently both ends of the connection switch modes together so that the signal assignments remain consistent at both ends of the connection. For example, if you connect an older printer that only understands compatibility mode, your PC cannot negotiate any other operating mode with the printer. It will not activate its EPP or ECP mode, so your printer will never get signals it cannot understand. This negotiation of the mode ensures backward compatibility among parallel devices.

The B Connector

The parallel input on the back of your printer is the direct heir of the original Centronics design. Figure 8.2 offers a conceptual view of this connector.

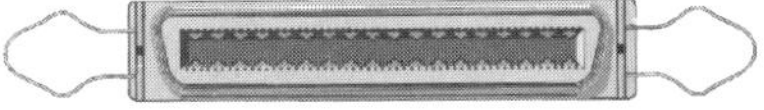

Figure 8.2 The IEEE-1284 B connector, a 36-pin ribbon jack.

At one time this connector was called an "Amphenol" connector, after the name the manufacturer of the original connector used on the first ports, an Amphenol 57-40360. Amphenol used the trade name "Blue Ribbon" for its series of connectors that included this one, hence the ribbon connector name.

Currently this style of connector is available from several makers, each of which uses its own part number. In addition to the Amphenol part, some of these include AMP 555119-1, Molex 71522, and 3M Company 3367-300X and 3448-62. The mating cable plug is available as AMP 554950-1 or Molex 71522.

The individual contacts in the 36-pin receptacle take the form of fingers or ribbons of metal. In two 18-contact rows they line the inside of a rectangular opening that accepts a matching projection on the cable connector. The overall connectors from edge to edge measure about 2.75 inches long and about 0.66 inches wide. The individual contacts are spaced at 0.085 inch center-to-center. On the printer jack as it appears in the illustration, pin one is on the upper right, and contacts are consecutively numbered right-to-left. Pin 19 appears at the far right on the bottom row, and again the contacts are sequentially numbered right to left. (In wiring this connector, you would work from the rear, and the numbering of the contacts would rise in the more familiar left to right.)

The assignment of signals to the individual pins of this connector has gone through three stages. The first standard was set by Centronics for its printers. In 1981, IBM altered this design somewhat by redefining several of the connections. Finally, in 1994, the IEEE published its standard assignments, which, like those of the A-connector, vary with operating mode.

The Centronics design serves as the foundation for all others. It, with variations, was used by printers through those made in the early years of the PC. Table 8.3 shows its signal assignments. This basic arrangement of signals has been carried through, with modification, to the IEEE 1284 standard. As far as modern printers go, however, this original Centronics design can be considered obsolete. Those printers not following the IEEE standard invariably use the IBM layout.

Table 8.3 Centronics Parallel Port Signal Assignments

Pin	Function
1	Strobe
2	Data bit 0
3	Data bit 1
4	Data bit 2
5	Data bit 3
6	Data bit 4
7	Data bit 5
8	Data bit 6
9	Data bit 7
10	Acknowledge
11	Busy
12	Paper end (Out of paper)
13	Select

14	Signal ground
15	External oscillator
16	Signal Ground
17	Chassis ground
18	+5 VDC
19	Strobe ground
20	Data 0 ground
21	Data 1 ground
22	Data 2 ground
23	Data 3 ground
24	Data 4 ground
25	Data 5 ground
26	Data 6 ground
27	Data 7 ground
28	Acknowledge ground
29	Busy ground
30	Input prime ground
31	Input prime
32	Fault
33	Light detect
34	Line count
35	Line count return (isolated from ground)
36	Reserved

The Centronics layout includes some unique signals not found on later designs. The Line count (pins 34 and 35) connections provide an isolated contact closure each time the printer advances its paper by one line. The Light detect signal (pin 33) provides an indication whether the lamp inside the printer for detecting the presence of paper is functioning. The External oscillator signal (pin 15) provides a clock signal to external devices, one generally in the range of 100 KHz to 200 KHz. The Input Prime signal (pin 31) serves the same function as the later Initialize signal. It resets the printer, flushing its internal buffer.

The IBM design eliminates the signals (but essentially only renames Input prime) and adds two new signals, Auto feed and Select input, discussed below (Operation). This layout remains current as IEEE 1284 compatibility mode on the 1284-B connector. Its signal assignments are listed in Table 8.4.

Table 8.4 IBM Parallel Printer Port Signal Assignments

Pin	Function
1	Strobe
2	Data bit 0
3	Data bit 1
4	Data bit 2
5	Data bit 3
6	Data bit 4
7	Data bit 5
8	Data bit 6
9	Data bit 7
10	Acknowledge
11	Busy
12	Paper end (Out of paper)
13	Select
14	Auto feed
15	No connection
16	Ground
17	No connection
18	No connection
19	Strobe ground
20	Data 0 ground
21	Data 1 ground
22	Data 2 ground
23	Data 3 ground

24	Data 4 ground
25	Data 5 ground
26	Data 6 ground
27	Data 7 ground
28	Paper end, Select, and Acknowledge ground
29	Busy and Fault ground
30	Auto feed, Select in, and Initialize ground
31	Initialize printer
32	Error
33	No connection
34	No connection
35	No connection
36	Select input

As with the A connector, the IEEE 1284 signal definitions on the B connector change with the operating mode of the parallel port. The signal assignments for each of the five IEEE operating modes are listed in Table 8.5.

Table 8.5 IEEE 1284-B Connector Signal Assignments in All Modes

Pin	Compatibility Mode	Nibble Mode	Byte Mode	EPP Mode	ECP Mode
1	nStrobe	HostClk	HostClk	nWrite	HostClk
2	Data 1	Data 1	Data 1	AD1	Data 1
3	Data 2	Data 2	Data 2	AD2	Data 2
4	Data 3	Data 3	Data 3	AD3	Data 3
5	Data 4	Data 4	Data 4	AD4	Data 4
6	Data 5	Data 5	Data 5	AD5	Data 5
7	Data 6	Data 6	Data 6	AD6	Data 6
8	Data 7	Data 7	Data 7	AD7	Data 7

Table 8.5 continued

Pin	Compatibility Mode	Nibble Mode	Byte Mode	EPP Mode	ECP Mode
9	Data 8	Data 8	Data 8	AD8	Data8
10	nAck	PtrClk	PtrClk	Intr	PeriphClk
11	Busy	PtrBusy	PtrBusy	nWait	PeriphAck
12	PError	AckDataReq	AckDataReq	User defined 1	nAckReverse
13	Select	Xflag	Xflag	User defined 3	Xflag
14	nAutoFd	HostBusy	HostBusy	nDStrb	HostAck
15	*Not defined*				
16	Logic ground				
17	Chassis ground				
18	Peripheral logic high				
19	Ground return for pin 1 (nStrobe)				
20	Ground return for pin 2 (Data 1)				
21	Ground return for pin 3 (Data 2)				
22	Ground return for pin 4 (Data 3)				
23	Ground return for pin 5 (Data 4)				
24	Ground return for pin 6 (Data 5)				
25	Ground return for pin 7 (Data 6)				
26	Ground return for pin 8 (Data 7)				
27	Ground return for pin 9 (Data 8)				
28	Ground return for pins 10, 12, and13 (nAck, PError, and Select)				
29	Ground return for pins 11 and 32 (Busy and nFault)				
30	Ground return for pins 14, 31, and 36 (nAutoFd, nSelectIn, and nInit))				
31	nInit	nInit	nInit	nInit	nReverseRequest
32	nFault	nDataAvail	nDataAvail	User Defined 2	nPeriphRequest
33	*Not defined*				
34	*Not defined*				
35	*Not defined*				
36	nSelectIn	1284 Active	1284 Active	nAStrb	1284 Active

Again, the port modes and the associated signal assignments are not fixed in hardware but change dynamically your PC uses the connection. Although your PC acts as host and decides which mode to use, it can only negotiate those that your printer or other parallel device understands. Your printer (or whatever) determines which of these five modes could be used while your PC and its applications picks which of the available modes to use for transferring data.

The C Connector

Given a chance to start over with a clean slate and no installed base, engineers would hardly come up with the confusion of two different connectors with an assortment of different, sometimes compatible operate modes. The IEEE saw the creation of the 1284 standard as such an opportunity, one that they were happy to exploit. To eliminate the confusion of two connectors and the intrinsic need for adapters to move between them, they took the logical step: They created a third connector, IEEE 1284-C.

All devices compliant with IEEE 1284 Level 2 must use this connector. That requirement is the IEEE's way of saying, "Let's get rid of all these old, confusing parallel ports with their strange timings and limited speed and get on with something new for the next generation." Once the entire world moves to IEEE 1284 Level 2, you'll have no need of compatibility, cable adapters, and other such nonsense. In the meantime, as manufacturers gradually adopt the C connector for their products, you'll still need adapters but in even greater variety.

All that said, the C connector still can be strongly recommended. It easily solves the original IBM problem of no space. Although it retains all the signals of the B connector, the C connector is miniaturized, about half the size of the B connector. As a PC-mounted receptacle, it measures about 1.75 inches long by 0.375 inch wide. It is shown in a conceptual view in Figure 8.3.

Figure 8.3 Conceptual view of the 1284-C parallel port connector.

The actual contact area of the C connector is much like that of the B connector with contact fingers arranged inside a rectangular opening that accepts a matching projection on the mating plug. The spacing between the individual contacts is reduced, however, to 0.05 inches, center-to-center. This measurement corresponds to those commonly used on modern printed circuit boards.

The C connector provides a positive latch using clips that are part of the shell of the plug. The clips engage latches on either side of the contact area, as shown in the figure. Squeezing the side of the plug spreads the clips and releases the latch.

The female receptacle (as shown) is available from a number of manufacturers. Some of these include AMP 2-175925-5, Harting 60-11-036-512, Molex 52311-3611, and 3M 10236-52A2VC. Part numbers of the mating plug include AMP 2-175677-5, Harting 60-13-036-5200, Molex 52316-3611, and 3M 10136-6000EC.

Every signal on the C connector gets its own pin and all pins are defined. As with the other connectors, the signal assignments depend on the mode in which the IEEE 1284 port is operating. Table 8.6 lists the signal assignments for the 1284-C connector in each of the five available modes.

Table 8.6 IEEE 1284-C Connector Signal Assignments In All Modes

Pin	Compatibility Mode	Nibble Mode	Byte Mode	EPP Mode	ECP Mode
1	Busy	PtrBusy	PtrBusy	nWait	PeriphAck
2	Select	Xflag	Xflag	User defined 3	Xflag
3	nAck	PtrClk	PtrClk	Intr	PeriphClk
4	nFault	nDataAvail	nDataAvail	User Defined 2	nPeriphRequest
5	PError	AckDataReq	AckDataReq	User defined 1	nAckReverse
6	Data 1	Data 1	Data 1	AD1	Data 1
7	Data 2	Data 2	Data 2	AD2	Data 2
8	Data 3	Data 3	Data 3	AD3	Data 3
9	Data 4	Data 4	Data 4	AD4	Data 4
10	Data 5	Data 5	Data 5	AD5	Data 5
11	Data 6	Data 6	Data 6	AD6	Data 6
12	Data 7	Data 7	Data 7	AD7	Data 7
13	Data 8	Data 8	Data 8	AD8	Data8
14	nInit	nInit	nInit	nInit	nReverseRequest
15	nStrobe	HostClk	HostClk	nWrite	HostClk
16	nSelectIn	1284 Active	1284 Active	nAStrb	1284 Active

17	nAutoFd	HostBusy	HostBusy	nDStrb	HostAck
18	Host logic high				
19	Ground return for pin 1 (Busy)				
20	Ground return for pin 2 (Select)				
21	Ground return for pin 3 (nAck)				
22	Ground return for pin 4 (nFault)				
23	Ground return for pin 5 (PError)				
24	Ground return for pin 6 (Data 1)				
25	Ground return for pin 7 (Data 2)				
26	Ground return for pin 8 (Data 3)				
27	Ground return for pin 9 (Data 4)				
28	Ground return for pin 10 (Data 5)				
29	Ground return for pin 11 (Data 6)				
30	Ground return for pin 12 (Data 7)				
31	Ground return for pin 13 (Data 8)				
32	Ground return for pin 14 (nInit)				
33	Ground return for pin 15 (nStrobe)				
34	Ground return for pin 16 (nSelectIn)				
35	Ground return for pin 17 (nAutoFd)				
36	Peripheral logic high				

Adapter Cables

The standard printer cable for PCs is an adapter cable. It rearranges the signals of the A connector to the scheme of the B connector. Ever since the introduction of the first PC, you needed this sort of cable just to make your printer work. Over the years they have become plentiful and cheap.

Unfortunately, as cables get cheaper and sources become more generic and obscure, quality is apt to slip. Printer cables provide an excellent opportunity for allowing quality to take a big slide. If you group all the grounds together as a single common line, you're left with only 18 distinct signals on a printer cable. In that some of the grounds are naturally grouped together, this approach might seem feasible, particularly since you can save the price of a 25-conductor cable. In fact, IBM took this approach with its first printer cable. Low-cost printer cables still retain this design. The wiring of this adapter cable is given in Table 8.7.

Table 8.7 Printer Cable, 18-Wire Implementation

PC END 25-pin connector	FUNCTION	PRINTER END 36-pin connector
1	Strobe	1
2	Data bit 0	2
3	Data bit 1	3
4	Data bit 2	4
5	Data bit 3	5
6	Data bit 4	6
7	Data bit 5	7
8	Data bit 6	8
9	Data bit 7	9
10	Acknowledge	10
11	Busy	11
12	Paper end (Out of paper)	12
13	Select	13
14	Auto feed	14
15	Error	32
16	Initialize printer	31
17	Select input	36
18	Ground	19-30,33
19	Ground	19-30,33
20	Ground	19-30,33
21	Ground	19-30,33
22	Ground	19-30,33

23	Ground	19-30,33
24	Ground	19-30,33
25	Ground	19-30,33

Some PC and printer manufacturers did not exploit all the control signals that were part of the basic parallel port design. In fact, many early printers would not function properly if they received these control signals. Many of these printers (and some early PCs) required proprietary adapter cables to make them work. Table 8.8 gives one example of this kind of cable, one that works with early Tandy computers but will also function with other PCs and some persnickety printers. Because of the number of omitted connections, this wiring scheme is more easily described using the printer end of the cable as reference.

Table 8.8 Early Tandy to Centronics Adapter Cable

Printer Connector	PC Connector	Function
1	1	Strobe
2	2	Data bit 0
3	3	Data bit 1
4	4	Data bit 2
5	5	Data bit 3
6	6	Data bit 4
7	7	Data bit 5
8	8	Data bit 6
9	9	Data bit 7
10	10	Acknowledge
11	11	Busy
12	12	Paper end (Out of paper)
13	No pin	No connection

Table 8.8 continued

Printer Connector	PC Connector	Function
14	No pin	No connection
15	No pin	No connection
16	No pin	No connection
17	No pin	No connection
18	13	Select
19	No pin	No connection
20	No pin	No connection
21	No pin	No connection
22	No pin	No connection
23	18	Ground
24	19	Ground
25	20	Ground
26	21	Ground
27	22	Ground
28	23	Ground
29	24	Ground
30	25	Ground
31	No pin	No connection
32	15	Error
33	16	Initialize printer
34	No pin	No connection
35	No pin	No connection
36	No pin	No connection

A modern printer cable contains a full 25 connections with the ground signals divided up among separate pins. For example, OS/2, unlike DOS, requires the use of all 25 pins in the IBM parallel printer connection. A generic printer cable that makes only 18 connections may not work with OS/2. If your printer doesn't work properly with OS/2 and does with DOS, the cable is the first place to suspect a problem.

Using all 25 wires is the preferred and correct wiring for a classic parallel printer adapter cable. If you buy or make a cable and plan to use it with classic parallel connections, it should connect all 25 leads at both ends. The IEEE recognizes this cable layout to adapt 1284-A to 1284-B connectors. Table 8.9 shows the wiring of this adapter. (The different nomenclature given for names of signal functions reflects the official IEEE usage. We've modified a few of the official IEEE signal designations for clarity, particularly those of the ground return lines.)

Table 8.9 25-Wire Parallel Printer Adapter (IEEE 1284-A to 1284-B)

Host End A connector	Function	Peripheral End C connector
1	nStrobe	1
2	Data bit 1	2
3	Data bit 2	3
4	Data bit 3	4
5	Data bit 4	5
6	Data bit 5	6
7	Data bit 6	7
8	Data bit 7	8
9	Data bit 8	9
10	nAck	10
11	Busy	11
12	PError	12
13	Select	13
14	nAutoFd	14
15	nFault	32
16	nInit	31
17	nSelectIn	36
18	Pin 1 (nStrobe) ground return	19
19	Pins 2 and 3 (Data 1 and 2) ground return	20 and 21

Table 8.9 continued

Host End A connector	Function	Peripheral End C connector
1	nStrobe	1
20	Pins 4 and 5 (Data 3 and 4) ground return	22 and 23
21	Pins 6 and 7 (Data 5 and 6) ground return	24 and 25
22	Pins 8 and 9 (Data 7 and 8) ground return	26 and 27
23	Pins 11 and 15 ground return	29
24	Pins 10, 12, and 13 ground return	28
25	Pins 14, 16, and 17 ground return	30

As new peripherals with the 1284-C connector become available, you'll need to plug them into your PC. To attach your existing PC to a printer or other device using the C-connector, you'll need an adapter cable to convert the A-connector layout to the C-connector design. Table 8.10 shows the proper wiring for such an adapter as adopted in the IEEE 1284 specification (again with a modification in signal nomenclature from the official standard for clarity).

Table 8.10 Parallel Interface Adapter, 1284-A to 1284-C Connectors

Host End A connector	Function	Peripheral End C connector
1	nStrobe	15
2	Data bit 1	6
3	Data bit 2	7
4	Data bit 3	8
5	Data bit 4	9
6	Data bit 5	10
7	Data bit 6	11
8	Data bit 7	12
9	Data bit 8	13

10	nAck	3
11	Busy	1
12	PError	5
13	Select	2
14	nAutoFd	17
15	nFault	4
16	nInit	14
17	nSelectIn	16
18	Pin 1 (nStrobe) ground return	33
19	Pins 2 and 3 (Data 1 and 2) ground return	24 and 25
20	Pins 4 and 5 (Data 3 and 4) ground return	26 and 27
21	Pins 6 and 7 (Data 5 and 6) ground return	28 and 29
22	Pins 8 and 9 (Data 7 and 8) ground return	30 and 31
23	Pins 11 and 15 ground return	19 and 22
24	Pins 10, 12, and 13 ground return	20, 21, and 23
25	Pins 14, 16, and 17 ground return	32, 34, and 35

If your next PC or parallel adapter uses the C connector and you plan to stick with your old printer, you'll need another variety of adapter, one that translates the C connector layout to that of the B connector. Table 8.11 lists the wiring required in such an adapter.

Note that although both the B and C connectors have 36 pins, they do not have the same signals. Several signals share ground connections on the B connector while several other pins are not connected.

Table 8.11 Parallel Interface Adapter, 1284-C to 1284-B

HOST END C connector	FUNCTION	PERIPHERAL END B connector
1	Busy	11
2	Select	13
3	nAck	10

Table 8.11 continued

HOST END C connector	FUNCTION	PERIPHERAL END B connector
4	nFault	32
5	PError	12
6	Data 1	2
7	Data 2	3
8	Data 3	4
9	Data 4	5
10	Data 5	6
11	Data 6	7
12	Data 7	8
13	Data 8	9
14	nInit	31
15	nStrobe	1
16	nSelectIn	36
17	nAutoFd	14
18	Host logic high	No connection
19	Ground return for pin 1 (Busy)	29
20	Ground return for pin 2 (Select)	28
21	Ground return for pin 3 (nAck)	28
22	Ground return for pin 4 (nFault)	29
23	Ground return for pin 5 (PError)	28
24	Ground return for pin 6 (Data 1)	20
25	Ground return for pin 7 (Data 2)	21
26	Ground return for pin 8 (Data 3)	22
27	Ground return for pin 9 (Data 4)	23
28	Ground return for pin 10 (Data 5)	24
29	Ground return for pin 11 (Data 6)	25
30	Ground return for pin 12 (Data 7)	26
31	Ground return for pin 13 (Data 8)	27

32	Ground return for pin 14 (nInit)	30
33	Ground return for pin 15 (nStrobe)	19
34	Ground return for pin 16 (nSelectIn)	30
35	Ground return for pin 17 (nAutoFd)	30
36	Peripheral logic high	18

Note: The following pins on the 1284-B connector are not connected: 15, 16, 17, 33, 34, and 35. Connector shields are connected at each end.

Cable

The nature of the signals in the parallel port are their own worst enemy. They interact with themselves and the other wires in the cable to the detriment of all. The sharp transitions of the digital signals blur. The farther the signal travels in the cable, the greater the degradation that overcomes it. For this reason, the maximum recommended length of a printer cable was ten feet. Not that longer cables will inevitably fail–practical experience often proves otherwise–but some cables in some circumstances become unreliable when stretched for longer distances.

The lack of a true signaling standard before IEEE 1284 made matters worse. Manufacturers had no guidelines for delays or transition times, so these values varied among PC, printer, and peripheral manufacturers. Although the signals might be close enough matches to work through a short cable, adding more wire could push them beyond the edge. A printer might then misread the signals from a PC, printing the wrong character or nothing at all.

Traditional printer cables are notoriously variable. As noted in the discussion of adapters, manufacturers scrimp where they can to produce low-cost adapter cables. After all, cables are commodities and the market is highly competitive. When you pay under $10 for a printer cable that comes without a brand name, you can never be sure of its electrical quality.

For this reason, extension cables are never recommended for locating your printer more than ten feet from your PC. Longer distances require alternate strategies–opting for another connection (serial or network) or getting a printer extension system that alters the signals and provides a controlled cable environment.

What length you can get away with depends on the cable, your printer, and your PC. Computers and printers vary in their sensitivity to parallel port anomalies like noise, cross-talk, and digital blurring. Some combinations of PCs and printers will work with lengthy parallel connections, up to fifty feet long. Other match-ups may balk when you stretch the connection more than the recommended ten feet.

The high speed modes of modern parallel ports make them even more finicky. When your parallel port operates in EPP or ECP modes, cable quality becomes critical even for short runs. Signaling speed across one of these interfaces can be in the megahertz range. The frequencies far exceed the reliable limits of even short runs of the dubious low-cost printer cables. Consequently, the IEEE 1284 specification precisely details a special cable for high speed operation. Figure 8.4 offers a conceptual view of the construction of this special parallel data cable.

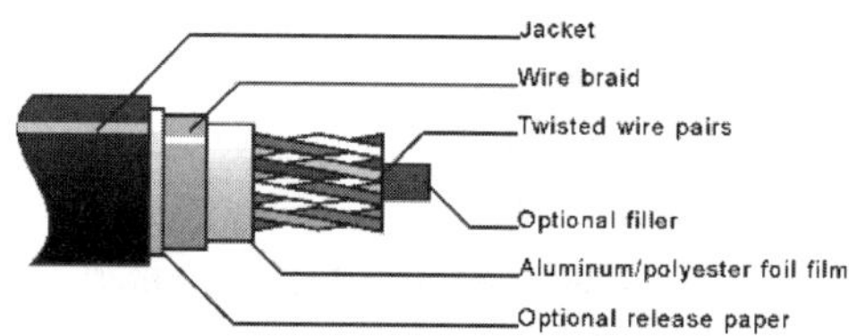

Figure 8.4 IEEE 1284 cable construction details.

Unlike standard parallel wiring, the data lines in IEEE 1284 cables must be double-shielded to prevent interference from affecting the signals. Each signal wire must be twisted with its ground return. Even though the various standard connectors do not provide separate pins for each of these grounds, the ground wires must be present and run the full length of the cable.

Electrical Operation

In each of its five modes, the IEEE 1284 parallel port operates as if it were some kind of complete different electronic creation. When in compatibility mode, the IEEE 1284 port closely parallels the operation of the plain vanilla printer port of bygone days. It allows data to travel in one direction only, from PC to printer. Nibble mode gives your printer (or more likely, another peripheral) a voice, and allows it to talk back to your PC. In nibble mode, data can move in either of two directions, although asymmetrically. Information flows faster to your printer than it does on the return trip. Byte mode makes the journey fully symmetrical.

With the shift to EPP mode, the parallel port becomes a true expansion bus. A new way of linking to your PC's bus gives it increased bidirectional speed. Many systems can run their parallel ports ten times faster in EPP mode than in compatibility, nibble, or byte modes. ECP mode takes the final step, giving control in addition to speed. ECP can do just about anything any other expansion interface (including SCSI) can do.

Because of these significant differences, the best way to get to know the parallel port is by considering each separately as if it were an interface unto itself. Our examination will follow from simple to complex, which also mirrors the history of the parallel port.

Note that IEEE 1284 deals only with the signals traveling through the connections of the parallel interface. It establishes the relationship between signals and their timing. It concerns itself neither with the data that is actually transferred, command protocols encoded in the data, nor with the control system that produces the signals. In other words, IEEE 1284 provides an environment under which other standards such as EPP and ECP operate. That is, ECP and EPP modes are not the ECP and EPP standards although those modes are meant to be used by the parallel ports operating under respective standards.

Compatibility Mode

The least common denominator among parallel ports is the classic design that IBM introduced with the first PC. It was conceived strictly as a interface for the one-way transfer of information. Your PC sends data to your printer and expects nothing in return. After all, a printer neither stores information nor creates it on its own.

In conception, this port is like a conveyor that unloads ore from a bulk freighter or rolls coal out of a mine. The raw material travels in one direction. The conveyor mindlessly pushes out stuff and more stuff, perhaps creating a dangerously precarious pile, until its operator wakes up and switches it off before the pile gets much higher than his waist.

If your printer had unlimited speed or an unlimited internal buffer, such a one-way design would work. But like the coal yard, your printer has a limited capacity and may not be able to cart off data as fast as the interface shoves it out. The printer needs some way of sending a signal to your PC to warn about a potential data overflow. In electronic terms, the interface needs feedback of some kind–it needs to get information from the printer that your PC can use to control the data flow.

To provide the necessary feedback for controlling the data flow, the original Centronics port design and IBM's adaptation of it both included several control signals. These were designed to allow your PC to monitor how things are going with your printer–whether data is piling up, whether it has sufficient paper or ribbon, whether the printer is even turned on. Your PC can use this information to moderate the outflowing gush of data or to post a message warning you that something is wrong with your printer. In addition, the original parallel port included control signals sent from your PC to the printer to tell it *when* the PC wants to transfer data and to tell the printer to reset itself. The IEEE 1284 standard carries all of these functions into compatibility mode.

Strictly speaking, then, even this basic parallel port is not truly a one-way connection, although its feedback provisions were designed strictly for monitoring rather than data flow. For the first half of its life, the parallel port kept to this design. Until the adoption of IEEE-1284, this was the design you could expect for the port on your printer and, almost as likely, those on your PC.

Each signal flowing through the parallel port in compatibility mode has its own function. These signals include:

Data Lines

The eight *data lines* of the parallel interface convey data in all operating modes. In compatibility mode, they carry data from the host to the peripheral on connector pins 2 through 9. The higher numbered pins are the more significant to the digital code. To send data to the peripheral, the host puts a pattern of digital voltages on the data lines.

Strobe Line

The presence of signals on the data lines does not, in itself, move information from host to peripheral. As your PC gets its act together, it may change the pattern of data bits. No hardware can ensure that all eight will always pop to the correct values simultaneously. Moreover, without further instruction your printer has no way knowing whether the data lines represent a single character or multiple repetitions of the same character.

To ensure reliable communications, the system requires a means of telling the peripheral that the pattern on the data lines represents valid information to be transferred. The *strobe line* does exactly that. Your PC pulses the strobe line to tell your printer that the bit pattern on the data lines is a single valid character that the printer should read and accept. The strobe line gives its pulse only after the signals on the data lines have settled down. Most parallel ports delay the strobe signal by about half a microsecond to ensure that the data signals have settled. The strobe itself lasts for at least half a microsecond so that your printer can recognize it. (The strobe signal can last up to 500 microseconds.) The signals on the data lines must maintain a constant value during this period and slightly afterward so that your printer has a chance to read them.

The strobe signal is negative-going. That is, a positive voltage (+5VDC) stays on the strobe line until your printer wants to send the actual strobe signal. Your PC then drops the positive voltage to near zero for the duration of the strobe pulse. The IEEE 1284 specification calls this signal *nStrobe*.

Busy Line

Sending data to your printer is thus a continuous cycle of setting up the data lines, sending the strobe signal, and putting new values on the data lines. The parallel port design typically requires about two microseconds for each turn of this cycle, allowing a perfect parallel port to dump out nearly half a million characters a second into your hapless printer. (As we will see, the actual maximum throughput of a parallel port is much lower than this.)

For some printers, coping with that data rate is about as daunting as trying to catch machine gun fire with your bare hands. Before your printer can accept a second character, its circuitry must do something with the one it has just received. Typically it will need to move the character into the printer's internal buffer. Although the character moves at electronic speeds, it does not travel instantaneously. Your printer needs to be able to tell your PC to wait for the processing of the current character before sending the next.

The parallel port's *busy line* gives your printer the needed breathing room. Your printer switches on the busy signal as soon as it detects the strobe signal and keeps the signal active until it is ready to accept the next character. The busy signal can last for a fraction of a second (even as short as a microsecond) or your printer could hold it on indefinitely while it waits for you to correct some error. No matter how long the busy signal is on, it keeps your PC from sending out more data through the parallel port. It functions as the basic flow-control system.

Acknowledge Line

The final part of the flow control system of the parallel port is the *acknowledge line*. It tells your PC that everything has gone well with the printing of a character or its transfer to the internal buffer. In effect, it is the opposite of the busy signal, telling your PC that the printer is ready rather than unready. Where the busy line says "Whoa!" the acknowledge line says "Giddyap!" The acknowledge signal is the opposite in another way; it is negative going where busy is positive going. The IEEE 1284 specification calls this signal *nAck*.

When your printer sends out the acknowledge signal, it completes the cycle of sending a character. Typically the acknowledge signal on a conventional parallel port lasts about eight microseconds, stretching a single-character cycle across the port to ten microseconds. (IEEE 1284 specifies the length of nAck to be between 0.5 and 10 microseconds.) If you assume the typical length of this signal for a conventional parallel port, the maximum speed of the port works out to about 100,000 characters per second.

Select

In addition to transferring data to the printer, the basic parallel port allows your printer to send signals back to your PC so that your computer can monitor the operation of the printer. The original IBM design of the parallel interface includes three such signals that tell your PC when your printer is ready, willing, and able to do its job. In effect, these signals give your PC the ability to remote sense the condition of your printer.

The most essential of these signals is *select*. The presence of this signal on the parallel interface tells your PC that your printer is on-line. That is, that your printer is switch on and is in its on-line mode, ready to receive data from your PC. In effect, it is a remote indicator for the on-line light on your printer's Control Panel. If this signal is not present, your PC assumes that nothing is connected to your parallel port and doesn't bother with the rest of its signal repertory.

Because the rest state of a parallel port line is an absence of voltage (which would be the case if nothing were connected to the port to supply the voltage), the select signal takes the form of a positive signal (nominally +5VDC) that in *compatibility mode* under the IEEE 1284 specification stays active the entire period your printer is on-line.

Paper Empty

To print anything your printer needs paper, and the most common problem that prevents your printer from doing its job is running out of paper. The *paper empty* signal warns your PC when your printer runs out. The IEEE 1284 specification calls this signal *PError* for "paper error," although it serves exactly the same function.

Paper empty is an information signal. It is not required for flow control because the busy signal more than suffices for that purpose. Most printers will assert their busy signals for the duration that they are without paper. Paper empty tells your PC about the specific reason that your printer has stopped data flow. This signal allows your operating system or application to flash a message on your monitor to warn you to load more paper.

Fault

The third printer-to-PC status signal is *fault*, a catch-all for warning of any other problems that your printer may develop—out of ink, paper jams, overheating, conflagrations, and other disasters. In operation, fault is actually a steady-state positive signal. It dips low (or off) to indicate a problem. At the same time, your printer may issue its other signals to halt the data flow including busy and select. It never hurts to be extra sure. Because this signal is negative-going, the IEEE specification calls it *nFault*.

Initialize Printer

In addition to the three signals, your printer uses to warn of its condition, the basic parallel port provides three control signals that your PC can use to command your printer without adding anything to the data stream. Each of these three provides its own hard-wired connection for a specific purpose. These include one to initialize the printer, another to switch it on-line condition if the printer allows a remote control status change, and a final signal to tell the printer to feed the paper up one line.

The *initialize printer* signal helps your computer and printer keep in sync. Your printer can send a raft of different commands to your printer to change its mode of operation, change font, alter printing pitch, and so on. Each application that shares your printer might send out its own favored set of commands. And many applications are like sloppy in-laws that come for a visit and fail to clean up after themselves. The programs may leave your printer in some strange condition, such as set to print underscored boldface characters in agate size type with a script typeface. The next program you run might assume some other condition and blithely print out a paycheck in illegible characters.

Initialize printer tells your printer to step back to ground zero. Just as your PC boots up fresh and predictably, so does your printer. When your PC sends your printer the **Initialize Printer** command, it tells the printer to boot up, that is, reset itself and load its default operating parameters with its start-up configuration of fonts, pitches, typefaces, and the like. The command has the same effect as you switching off the printer and turning back on and simply substitutes for adding a remote control arm on your PC to duplicate your actions.

During normal operation, your PC puts a constant voltage on the initialize printer line. Removing the voltage tells your printer to reset. The IEEE 1284 specification calls this negative-going signal *nInit*.

Select Input

The signal that allows your PC to switch your printer on-line and off-line is called *select input.* The IEEE 1284 specification calls it *nSelectIn.* It is active, forcing your printer on-line, when it is low or off. Switching it high deselects your printer.

No all printers obey this command. Some have no provisions for switching themselves on- and off-line. Others have set-up functions (such as a DIP switch) that allow you to defeat the action of this signal.

Auto Feed XT

At the time IBM imposed its print system design on the rest of the world, different printers interpreted the lowly carriage return in one of two ways. Some printers took it literally. Carriage return mean to move the printhead carriage back to its starting position on the left side of the platen. Other printers thought more like typewriters. Moving the printhead full left also indicated the start of a new line, so they obediently advance the paper one line when they got a **Carriage Return** command. IBM, being a premiere typewriter maker at the time, opted for this second definition.

To give printer developers flexibility, however, the IBM parallel port design included the *Auto Feed XT* signal to give your PC command of the printer's handling of carriage returns. Under the IEEE 1284 specification, this signal is called *nAutoFd.* By holding this signal low or off, your PC commands your printer to act in the IBM and typewriter manner, adding a line feed to every carriage return. Making this signal high tells your printer to interpret carriage returns literally and only move the printhead. Despite the availability of this signal, most early PC printers ignored it and did whatever their setup configuration told them to do with carriage returns.

Nibble Mode

Early parallel ports used unidirectional circuitry for their data lines. No one foresaw the need for your PC to acquire data from your printer, so there was no need to add the expense or complication of bidirectional buffers to the simple parallel port. This tradition of single-direction design and operation continues to this day in the least expensive (which, of course, also means "cheapest") parallel ports.

Every parallel port does, however, have five signals that are meant to travel from the printer to your PC. These include (as designated by the IEEE 1284 specification) nAck, Busy, PError, Select, and nFault. If you could suspend the normal operation of these signals temporarily, you could use four of them to carry data back from the printer to your PC. Of course, the information would flow at half speed, four bits at a time.

This means of moving data is the basis of *nibble mode*, so called because the PC community calls half a byte (or those four bits) a nibble. Using nibble mode, any parallel port can operate bidirectionally–full-speed forward but half-speed in reverse.

Nibble mode requires that your PC take explicit command and control the operation of your parallel port. The port itself merely monitors all of its data and monitoring signals and relays the data to your PC. Your PC determines whether to regard your printer's status signals as backward-moving data. Of course this system also requires that the device at the other end of the parallel port–your printer or whatever–know that it has switched into nibble mode and understands what signals to put where and when. The IEEE 1284 specification defines a protocol for switching into nibble mode and how PC and peripherals handle the nibble-mode signals.

The process is complex, involving several steps. First your PC must identify whether the peripheral connected to it recognized the IEEE standard. If not, all bets are off for using the standard. Products created before IEEE 1284 was adopted relied on the software driver controlling the parallel port to be matched to your parallel port peripheral. Because the two were already matched, they knew everything they needed to know about each other without negotiation. The pair could work without understanding the negotiation process or even the IEEE 1284 specification. Using the specification, however, allows your PC and peripherals to do the matching without your intervention.

Once your PC and peripheral decide they can use nibble mode, your PC signals to the peripheral to switch to the mode. Before the IEEE 1284 standard, the protocol was proprietary to the parallel port peripheral. The standard gives all devices a common means of controlling the switchover.

After both your PC and parallel port peripheral have switched to nibble mode, the signals on the interface get new definitions. In addition, nibble mode itself operates in two modes or phases, and the signals on the various parallel port lines behave differently in each mode. These modes include reverse idle phase and reverse data transfer phase.

In *reverse idle phase*, the PtrClk signal (nAck in compatibility mode) operates as an attention signal from the parallel port peripheral. Activating this signal tells the parallel port to issue an interrupt inside your PC, signaling that the peripheral has data available to be transferred. Your PC acknowledges the need for data and requests its transfer by switching the HostBusy signal (nAutoFd in compatibility mode) low or off. This switches the system to *reverse data transfer phase*. Your PC switches the HostBusy signal high again after the completion of the transfer of a full data byte. When the peripheral has mode data ready and your PC switches Host Busy back low again, another transfer begins. If it switches low without the peripheral having data available to send, the transition re-engages reverse idle phase.

During reverse data transfer phase, information is coded across two transfers as listed in Table 8.12. In effect, each transfer cycle involves to epicycles, which move one nibble. First your peripheral transfers the four bits of lesser significance, then the bits of more significance.

Table 8.12 Data Bit Definitions In Nibble Mode

Signal	First Epicycle Contents	Second Epicycle Contents
nFault	Least significant bit	Data bit 5
Xflag	Data bit 2	Data bit 6
AckDataReq	Data bit 3	Data bit 7
PtrBusy	Data bit 4	Most significant bit

Because moving a byte from peripheral to PC requires two nibble transfers each of which requires the same time as one byte transfer from PC to peripheral, reverse transfers in nibble mode operate at half-speed at best. The only advantage of nibble mode is its universal compatibility. Even before the IEEE 1284 specification, it allowed any parallel port to operate bidirectionally. Because of this speed penalty alone, if you have a peripheral and parallel port that lets you choose the operating mode for bidirectional transfers, nibble mode is your *least* attractive choice.

Byte Mode

Unlike nibble mode, byte mode requires special hardware. The basic design for byte mode circuitry was laid down when IBM developed its PS/2 line of computers and developed the Data Migration Facility. By incorporating bidirectional buffers in all eight of the data lines of the parallel port, IBM enabled them to both send and receive information on each end of the connection. Other than that change, the new design involved no other modifications to signals, connector pin assignments, or the overall operation of the port. Before the advent of the IEEE standard, these ports were known as PS/2 parallel ports or bidirectional parallel ports.

IEEE 1284 does more than put an official industry imprimatur on the IBM design, however. The standard redefines the bidirectional signals and adds a universal protocol of negotiating bidirectional transfers.

As with nibble mode, a peripheral in byte mode uses the PtrClk signal to trigger an interrupt in the host PC to advise that the peripheral has data available for transfer. When the PC services the interrupt, it checks the port nDataAvail signal, a negative-going signal that indicates a byte is available for transfer when it goes low. The PC can then pulse off the HostBusy signal to trigger the transfer using the HostClk (nStrobe) signal to read the data. The PC raises the HostBusy signal again to indicate the successful transfer of the data byte. The cycle can then repeat for as many bytes as need to be sent.

Because byte mode is fully symmetrical, transfers occur at the same speed in either direction. The speed limit is set the performance of the port hardware, the speed at which the host PC handles the port overhead, and by the length of timing cycles set in the IEEE 1284 specification. Potentially, the design could require as little as four microseconds for each byte transferred, but real-world systems peak at about the same rate as conventional parallel ports, 100,000 bytes per second.

Enhanced Parallel Port Mode

When it was introduced, the chief innovation of the Enhanced Parallel Port was its improved performance, thanks to a design that hastened the speed at which your PC could pack data into the port. The EPP design altered port hardware so that instead of using byte-wide registers to send data through the port, your PC could dump a full 32-bit word of data directly from its bus into the port. The port would then handle all the conversion necessary to repackage the data into four byte-wide transfers. The reduction in PC over head and more efficient hardware design enabled a performance improvement by a factor of ten in practical systems. This speed increase required more stringent specifications for printer cables. The IEEE 1284 specification does not get into the nitty-gritty of linking the parallel port circuitry to your PC, so it does not guarantee that a port in EPP mode will deliver all of this speed boost. Moreover, the IEEE 1284 cable specs are not as demanding as the earlier EPP specs.

EPP mode of the IEEE 1284 specification uses only six signals in addition to the eight data lines for controlling data transfers. Three more connections in the interface are reserved for use by individual manufacturers and are not defined under the standard.

A given cycle across the EPP mode interface performs one of four operations: writing an address, reading an address, writing data, or reading data. The address corresponds to a register on the peripheral. The data operations are targeted on that address. Multiple data bytes may follow a single address signal as a form of burst mode.

- **nWrite**. Data can travel both ways through an EPP connection. The *nWrite* signal tells whether the contents of the data lines is being sent from your PC to a peripheral or from a peripheral to your PC. When the nWrite signal is set low, it indicates data is bound for the peripheral. When set high, it indicates data sent from the peripheral.
- **nDStrobe**. As with other parallel port transfers, your system need a signal to indicate when the bits on the data lines are valid and accurate. EPP mode uses a negative-going signal called *nDStrobe* for this function in making data operations. Although this signal serves the same function as the strobe signal on a standard parallel port, it has been moved to a different pin, that used by the nAutoFd signal in compatibility mode.
- **nAStrobe**. To identify a valid address on the interface bus, the EPP system uses the nAStrobe signal. This signal uses the same connection as does nSelectIn during compatibility mode.
- **nWait**. To acknowledge that a peripheral has properly received a transfer, it deactivates the negative-going *nWait* signal (making it a positive voltage on the bus). By holding the signal positive, the peripheral signals the host PC to wait. Making the signal negative indicates that the peripheral is ready for another transfer.
- **Intr**. To signal the host PC that a peripheral connected to the EPP interface requires immediate service, it sends out the *Intr* signal. The transition between low and high states of this signal indicates a request for an interrupt (that is, the signal is edge-triggered). EPP mode does not allocate a signal to acknowledge that the interrupt request was received.
- **nInit**. The escape hatch for EPP mode is the *nInit* signal. When this signal is activated by making it low, it forces the system out of EPP mode and back to compatibility mode.

Extended Capabilities Port Mode

When operating in ECP mode, the IEEE 1284 port uses seven signals to control the flow of data through the standard eight data lines. ECP mode defines two data transfer signaling protocols—one for forward transfers (from PC to peripheral) and one for reverse transfers (peripheral to PC)—and the transitions between them. Transfers are moderated by closed-loop handshaking that guarantees that all bytes get where they are meant to go, even if the connection be temporarily disrupted.

Because all parallel ports start in compatibility mode, your PC and its peripherals must first negotiate with one another to arrange to shift into ECP mode. Your PC and its software initiate the negotiation (as well as managing all aspects of the data transfers). Following a successful negotiation to enter ECP mode, the connection enters its forward idle phase.

- **HostClk.** To transfer information or commands across the interface, your PC starts from the forward idle phase and puts the appropriate signals on the data line. To signal to your printer or other peripheral that the values on the data lines are valid and should be transferred, your PC activates its *HostClk* signal, setting it to a logical high.
- **PeriphAck.** The actual transfer does not take place until your printer or other peripheral acknowledges the HostClk signal by sending back the *PeriphAck* signal, setting it to a logical high. In response, your PC switches the HostClk signal low. Your printer or peripheral then knows it should read the signals on the data lines. Once it finishes reading the data signals, the peripheral switches the PeriphAck signal low. This completes the data transfers. Both HostClk and PeriphAck are back to their forward idle phase norms, ready for another transfer.

  nPeriphRequest. When a peripheral needs to transfer information back to the host PC or to another peripheral, it makes a request by driving the *nPeriphRequest* signal low. The request is a suggestion rather than a command because only the host PC can initiate or reverse the flow of data. The nPeriphRequest typically causes an interrupt in the host PC to make this request known.
- **nReverseRequest.** To allow a peripheral to send data back to the host or to another device connected to the interface, the host PC activates the *nReverseRequest* signal by driving it low, essentially switching off the voltage that otherwise appear there. This signals to the peripheral that the host PC will allow the transfer.
- **nAckReverse.** To acknowledge that it has received the nReverseRequest signal and that it is ready for a reverse-direction transfer, the peripheral asserts its *nAckReverse* signal, driving it low. The peripheral can then

send information and commands through the eight data lines and the PeriphAck signal.

- **PeriphClk.** To begin a reverse transfer from peripheral to PC, the peripheral first loads the appropriate bits onto the data lines. It then signals to the host PC that it has data ready to transfer by driving the *PeriphClk* signal low.
- **HostAck.** Your PC responds to the PeriphClk signal by switching the *HostAck* signal from its idle logical low to a logical high. The peripheral responds by driving PeriphClk high. When the host accepts the data, it responds by driving the HostAck signal low. This completes the transfer and returns the interface to the reverse idle phase.
- **Data Lines.** Although the parallel interface uses the same eight data lines to transfer information as do other IEEE 1284 port modes, it supplements them with an additional signal to indicate whether the data lines contain data or a command. The signal used to make this nine-bit information system changes with the direction of information transfer. When ECP mode transfers data from PC host to a peripheral (that is, during a forward transfer), it uses the HostAck signal to specific command or data. When a peripheral originates the data being transferred (a reverse transfer), it uses the PeriphAck signal to specify command or data.

Logical Interface

All parallel ports, regardless of speed, technology, or operating mode, must somehow interface with your PC, its operating system, and your applications. After all, you can't expect to print if you can't find your printer, so you shouldn't expect your programs to do it, either. Where you might need a map to find your printer, particularly when your office makes the aftermath of a rock concert seem organized, your programs need something more in line with their logical nature that serves the same function. You look for a particular address on a street. Software looks for function calls, interrupt routines, or specific hardware parameters.

That list represents the steps that get you closer and closer to the actual interface. A function call is a high-level software construct, part of your operating system or a driver used by the operating system or your applications. The function call may in turn ask for an interrupt, which is a program routine that either originates in the firmware of your PC or is added by driver software. Both the function call and interrupt work reach your interface by dipping down to the hardware level and looking for specific features. Most important of these are the input/output ports used by your parallel interface.

Input/Output Ports

The design of the first PC linked the circuitry of the parallel port to the PC's microprocessor through a set of *input/output ports* in your PC. These I/O ports are not ports that access the outside world but rather are special way a microprocessor has to connect to circuitry. An I/O port works like a memory address–the microprocessor signals address value to the PC's support circuitry, then it sends data to that address. The only difference between addressing memory and I/O ports is that data for the former goes to the RAM in your PC. In the latter case, the addressing is in a separate range that links to other circuitry. In general, the I/O port addresses link to registers, a special kind of memory that serves as a portal for passing logical values between circuits.

The traditional design for a parallel port used three of these I/O ports. The EPP and ECP designs use more. In any case, however, the I/O ports take the form of a sequential block. The entire range of I/O ports used in a parallel connection usually gets identified by the address of first of these I/O ports (which is to say the one with the lowest number or address). This number is termed the *base address* of the parallel port. Every parallel port in a given PC must have a unique base address. Two parallel ports inside a single PC cannot share the same base address, nor can they share any of their other I/O ports. If you accidentally assign two parallel ports the same base address when configuring your PC's hardware, neither will likely work.

The original PC design made provisions for up to three parallel ports in a single system, and this limit has been carried through to all IBM-compatible PCs. Each of these has its own base address. For the original PC, IBM chose three values for these base addresses, and these remain the values used by most hardware makers. These basic base addresses are 03BC(Hex), 0378(Hex), and 0278(Hex).

Manufacturers rarely use the first of these, 03BC(Hex). IBM originally assigned this base address to the parallel port that was part of the long-obsolete IBM Monochrome Display Adapter or MDA card. IBM kept using this name in its PS/2 line of computers, assigning it to the one built-in parallel port in those machines. There was no chance of conflict with the MDA card because the MDA cannot be installed inside PS/2s. Other computer makers sometimes use this base address for built-in parallel ports. More often, however, they use the base address of 0378(Hex) for such built-in ports. Some allow you to assign either address–(or even 0278(Hex)–using their set-up program, jumpers, or DIP switches.

Device Names

These base address values are normally hidden from your view and your concern. Most programs and operating systems refer to parallel ports with port names. These names take the familiar Line PrinTer form: LPT1, LPT2, and LPT3. In addition, the port with the name LPT1 can also use the alias PRN.

The correspondence between the base address of a parallel port and its device name varies with the number of ports in your PC. There is no direct one-to-one relationship between them. Your system assigns the device names when it boots up. One routine in your PC's BIOS code searches for parallel ports at each of the three defined base addresses in a fixed order. It always looks first for 03BC(Hex), then 0378(Hex), then 0278 (Hex). The collection of I/O ports at the first base address that's found gets assigned the name LPT1; the second, LPT2; the third, LPT3. The BIOS stores the base address values in a special memory area called the *BIOS data area* at particular absolute addresses. Because I/O port addresses are 16 bits long, each base address is allocated two bytes of storage. The base address of the parallel port assigned the LPT1 is stored at absolute memory location 0000:0408; LPT2, at 0000:040A; LPT3, 0000:040C. This somewhat arcane system assures you that you will always have a device called LPT1 (and PRN) in your PC if you have a parallel interface at all, no matter what set of I/O ports it uses.

Interrupts

The design of the original PC provided two interrupts for use by parallel ports. Hardware interrupt 07(Hex) was reserved for the first parallel port, and hardware interrupt 05(Hex) was reserved for the second.

DOS, Windows, and most applications do not normally use interrupts to hardware or control printers. When interrupts run short in your PC and you need to find one for a specific feature, you can often steal one of the interrupts used by a printer port.

The key word in the discussion of parallel port interrupts is *printer*. If you use your parallel port for some other purpose, you may not be able to steal its interrupt. Drivers for EPP and ECP ports may use interrupts, and modems that use parallel ports usually make use of interrupts. If you need an interrupt and you're not sure whether your parallel port needs it, try reassigning it where you need it. Then try to print something while you use the feature that borrowed the interrupt. If there's a problem, you'll know it before you risk your data to it.

Unlike DOS, versions of OS/2 before Warp had printer drivers that took advantage of interrupts to control access to your printer. Under these earlier versions of OS/2 you must configure your LPT1 port to use IRQ7 and your LPT2 port to use IRQ5. If another device pre-empted IRQ7—multimedia sound cards are notorious for doing so—your OS/2 system will print slowly if at all. Although OS/2 does permit the sharing of interrupts between different devices, as a practical matter you should avoid this strategy because it drastically and adversely affects parallel port performance.

As its default, OS/2 Warp does *not* use interrupts to control your printer. Instead it polls the parallel port to determine its status. This polling strategy avoids the problem of interrupt conflicts, but it can significantly slow printing. Interrupts let your printer demand that your PC send it data as soon as the printer is ready for it; polling means that printer has to wait until your PC decides to check your printer port to see if your printer has said it can accept more data.

You can force Warp to use interrupts to control your parallel printer port by altering the parallel port driver in your CONFIG.SYS file. In most PCs, the parallel port driver will be PRINT01.SYS. In Micro Channel machines, the driver is PRINT02.SYS. In either case, you only need to add the command line option **/IRQ** to the driver entry in CONFIG.SYS. For example, if you have an ISA-based PC, the line to load your parallel port driver should look like this:

```
BASEDEV=PRINT01.SYS /IRQ
```

Port Drivers

The PC printer port was designed to be controlled by a software driver. Under DOS, you might not notice these drivers because they are part of your PC's ROM BIOS. The printer interrupt handler is actually a printer driver.

In reality, only a rare program uses this BIOS-based driver. It's simply too slow. Because the hardware resources used by the parallel port are well known and readily accessed, most programmers prefer to directly control the parallel port hardware to send data to your printer. Many applications incorporate their own print routines or use printer drivers designed to take this kind of direct control.

More advanced operating systems similarly take direct hardware control of the parallel port through software drivers, which take over the functions of the BIOS routines. Windows, up through version 3.11, automatically used its own integral drivers for your printer ports, although EPP and ECP operation require that you explicitly load drivers to match. More advanced operating systems including OS/2 and Windows 95 always use external drivers to take control of your PC's ports.

You can check or change the parallel port driver your system uses when you run Windows 95 through the Printer Port Properties folder. To access this folder, run Device Manager. From the Start button, select **Settings**, then **Control Panel.** Click on the **System** icon in Control Panel. Select the **Device Manager** tab. Click on the line for Ports (**COM** and **LPT**), then highlight the **LPT** port for which you want to check the driver. Finally, click on the **Properties** button. You'll see a screen like that shown in Figure 8.5.

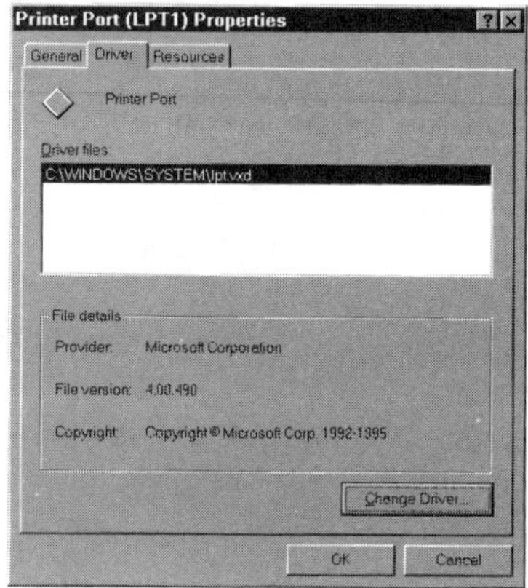

Figure 8.5 The Windows 95 Parallel Port Properties folder.

Under the heading Driver files: you'll see your parallel port drivers listed. You can change the driver used by this port by clicking on the **Change Driver** button. When you do, you'll see a window like that shown in Figure 8.6.

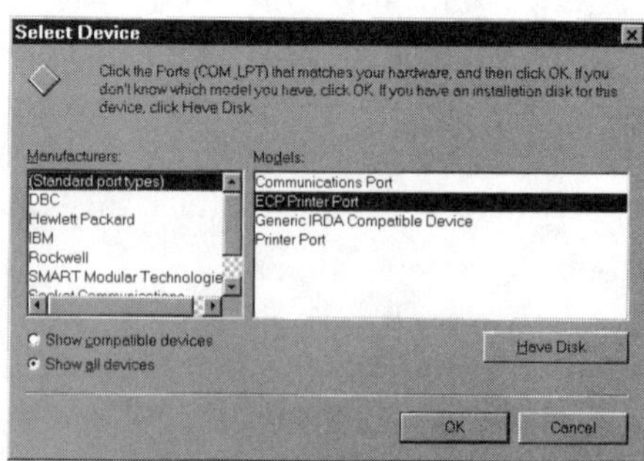

Figure 8.6 Updating your parallel port driver under Windows 95.

By default, the Models list will include only those drivers that are compatible with the port that the Windows Plug-and-Play system has detected in your PC. The list will change with the Manufacturer you highlight. You can view all the available drivers from a given manufacturer (or the standard drivers) by selecting **Show all devices.** If the driver you want is not within the current repertory of your Windows 95 system, you can install a driver from a floppy or CD ROM disk (or one that you've copied to your hard disk) by clicking on the **Have Disk** button, which prompts you for the disk and path name leading to the driver.

To install a new driver, highlight it and click on the **OK** button. Windows takes care of the rest.

Control

Even in its immense wisdom, a microprocessor can't fathom how to operate a parallel port by itself. It needs someone to tell it how to move the signals around. Moreover, the minutiae of constantly taking care of the details of controlling a port would be a waste of the microprocessor's valuable time. Consequently system designers created help systems for your PC's big brain. Driver software tells the microprocessor how to control the port. And port hardware handles all the details of port operation.

As parallel ports have evolved, so have these aspects of their control. The software that controls the traditional parallel port that's built into the firmware of your PC has given way to complex system of drivers. The port hardware, too, has changed to both simplify operation and to speed it up.

These changes don't follow the neat system of modes laid down by IEEE 1284. Instead, they have undergone a period of evolution in reaching their current condition.

Traditional Parallel Ports

In the original PC, each of its parallel ports is linked to the PC's microprocessor through three separate I/O ports, each controlling its own register. The address of the first of these registers serves as the base address of the parallel port. The other two addresses are the next higher in sequence. For example, when the first parallel port in a PC had a base address of 0378(hex), the other two I/O ports assigned it had addresses of 0379(Hex) and 037A(Hex).

The register at the base address of the parallel port serves a data latch called the *printer data register*, which temporarily holds the values passed along to it by your PC's microprocessor. Each of the eight bits of this port is tied to one of the data lines leading out of the parallel port connector. The correspondence is exact. For example, the most significant bit of the register connects to the most significant bit on the port connector. When your PC's microprocessor writes a value to the base register of the port, the register latches those values until your microprocessor sends newer values to the port.

Your PC uses the next register on the parallel port, corresponding to the next I/O port, to monitor what the printer is doing. Termed the *printer status register*, the various bits that your microprocessor can read at this I/O port carry messages from the printer back to your PC. The five most significant bits of this register directly correspond to five signals appearing in the parallel cable: bit 7 indicates the condition of the busy signal; bit 6, acknowledge; bit 5, paper empty; bit 4, select; and bit 3, error. The remaining three bits of this register (bits 2, 1, and 0–the least significant bits) served no function in the original PC parallel port.

To send commands to your printer, your PC uses the third I/O port, offset two ports from the base address of the parallel port. The register there, called the *printer control register*, relays commands through its five least significant bits. Of these, four directly control corresponding parallel port lines. Bit 0 commands the strobe line; bit 1 the Auto Feed XT line; bit 2, the initialize line; and bit 3, the select line.

To enable your printer to send interrupts to command the microprocessor's attention, your PC uses bit 4 of the printer control register. Setting this bit high causes the acknowledge signal from the printer to trigger a printer interrupt. During normal operation your printer, after it receives and processes a character, changes the acknowledge signal from a logical high to a low. Set bit 4, and your system detects the change in the acknowledge line through the printer status register and executes the hardware interrupt assigned to the port. In the normal course of things, this interrupt simply instructs the microprocessor to send another character to the printer.

All of the values sent to the printer data register and the printer control register are put in place by your PC's microprocessor, and the chip must read and react to all the values packed into the printer status register. The printer gets its instructions for what to do from firmware that is part of your system's ROM BIOS. The routines coded for interrupt vector 017(Hex) carry out most of these functions. In the normal course of things, your applications call interrupt 017(Hex) after loading appropriate values into your microprocessors registers, and the microprocessor relays the values to your printer. These operations are very microprocessor intensive.

They can occupy a substantial fraction of the power of a microprocessor (particularly that of older, slower chips) during print operations.

Enhanced Parallel Ports

Intel set the pattern for Enhanced Parallel port by integrating the design into the 386SL chip set (which comprised a microprocessor and a support chip, the 386SL itself, and the 82360SL I/O subsystem chip, which together required only memory to make a complete PC). The EPP was conceived as a superset of the standard and PS/2 parallel ports. As with those designs, compatible transfers require the use of the three parallel port registers at consecutive I/O port addresses. However, it adds five new registers to the basic three. Although designers are free to locate these registers wherever they want because they are accessed using drivers, in the typical implementation, these registers occupy the next five I/O port addresses in sequence.

EPP Address Register

The first new register (offset three from the base I/O port address) is the called the *EPP address register*. It provides a direct channel through which your PC can specify addresses of devices linked through the EPP connection. By loading an address value in this register, your PC can select among multiple devices attached to a single parallel port, at least once parallel devices using EPP addressing become available.

EPP Data Registers

The upper four ports of the EPP system interface (starting at offset four from the base port) link to the *EPP data registers*, which provide a 32-bit channel for sending data to the EPP data buffer. The EPP port circuitry takes the data from the buffer, breaks it into four separate bytes, then sends the bytes through the EPP data lines in sequence. Substituting four I/O ports for the one used by standard parallel ports moves the conversion into the port hardware, relieving your system from the responsibility of formatting the data. In addition, your PC can write to the four EPP data registers simultaneously using a single 32-bit double-word in a single clock cycle in computers that have 32-bit data buses. In lesser machines, the EPP specification also allows for byte-wide and wordwide (16-bit) write operations through to the EPP data registers.

Unlike standard parallel ports that require your PC's microprocessor to shepherd data through the port, the Enhanced Parallel Port works automatically. It requires no other signals from your microprocessor after it loads the data in order to carry out a data transfer. The EPP circuitry itself generates the data strobe signal on the bus almost as soon as your microprocessor writes to the EPP data registers. When your microprocessor reads data from the EPP data registers, the port circuitry automatically triggers the data strobe signal to tell whatever device that's sending data to the EPP connection that your PC is ready to receive more data. The EPP port can consequently push data through to the data lines with a minimum of transfer overhead. This streamlined design is one of the major factors that enables the EPP to operate so much faster than standard ports.

Fast Parallel Port Control Register

To switch from standard parallel port to bidirectional to EPP operation requires only plugging values into one of the registers. Although the manufacturers can use any design they want, needing only to alter their drivers to match, most follow the pattern set in the SL chips. Intel added a software-controllable *fast parallel port control register* as part of the chipset. This corresponds to the unused bits of the standard parallel port printer control register.

Setting the most significant bit (bit 7) of the fast parallel port control register high engages EPP operation. Setting this bit low (the default) forces the port into standard mode. Another bit controls bidirectional operation. Setting bit 6 of the fast parallel port control register high engages bidirectional operation. When low, bit 6 keeps the port unidirectional.

In most PCs, an EPP doesn't automatically spring to life. Simply plugging your printer into EPP hardware won't guarantee fast transfers. Enabling the EPP requires a software driver that provides the link between your software and the EPP hardware.

Extended Capabilities Ports

As with other variations on the basic parallel port design, your PC controls an Extended Capabilities Port through a set of registers. To maintain backward compatibility with products requiring access to a standard parallel port, the ECP design starts with the same trio of basic registers. However, it redefines the parallel port data in each of the ports different operating modes.

The ECP design supplements the basic trio of parallel port registers with an additional set of registers offset at port addresses 0400(Hex) higher than the base registers. One of these, the *extended control register* controls the operating mode of the ECP. Your microprocessor sets the operating mode by writing to this port, which is located offset by 0402(Hex) from the base register of the port. The ECP uses additional registers to monitor and control other aspects of the data transfer. Table 8.13 lists the registers used by the ECP, their mnemonics, and the modes in which they function.

Table 8.13 Extended Capabilities Port Register Definitions

Name	Address	Mode	Function
Data	Base	PC, PS/2	Data register
ecpAFifo	Base	ECP	ECP FIFO (Address) buffer
DSR	Base+1	All	Status register
DCR	Base+2	All	Control register
cFifo	Base+400	EPP	Enhanced Parallel Port FIFO (data) buffer
ecpDFifo	Base+400	ECP	ECP FIFO (data) buffer
tFifo	Base+400	Test	Test FIFO
cnfgA	Base+400	Configuration	Configuration register A
cnfgB	Base+401	Configuration	Configuration register B
ecr	Base+402	All	Extended control register

As with other improved parallel port designs, the ECP behaves exactly like a standard parallel port in its default mode. Your programs can write bytes to its data register (located at the port's base address just as with a standard parallel port) to send the bits through the data lines of the parallel connection. Switch to EPP or ECP mode, and your programs can write at high speed to a register as wide as 32-bits. The ECP design allows for transfers 8, 16, or 32 bits wide at the option of the hardware designer.

To allow multiple devices to share a single parallel connection, the ECP design incorporates its own addressing scheme that allows your PC to separately identify and send data to up to 128 devices. When your PC wants to route a packet or data stream through the parallel connection to a particular peripheral, it sends out a channel address command through the parallel port. The command includes a device address. When an ECP parallel device receives the command, it compares the address to its own assigned address. If the two do not match, the device ignores the data traveling through the parallel connection until your PC sends the next channel address command through the port. When your PC fails to indicate a channel address, the data gets broadcast to all devices linked to the parallel connection.

Performance Issues

Compatibility, Nibble, and Byte Modes

The speed of a parallel connection can be difficult to pin down. Several variables affect it. For example, the parallel cable itself sets the upper limit on the frequencies of the signals that the port can use, which in turn limits the maximum data rate. At practical cable lengths, which means those less then the recommended ten-foot maximum, cable effects on parallel port throughput are minimal. Other factors that come into play include: the switching speed of the port circuitry itself, the speed at which your PC can write to various control and data registers, the number of steps required by the BIOS or software driver to write a character, the ability of the device at the other end of the connection to accept and process the data sent to it, and the delays necessary in the timing of the various parallel port signals that are necessary to ensure the integrity of the transfer.

The timing of parallel port signals is actually artificially slow to accommodate the widest variety of parallel devices. Because the timing was never standardized before the IEEE 1284 specification, manufacturers had to rely on loose timing–meaning a wider tolerance of errors achieved through a slower signaling rate–to ensure any PC could communicate with any printer or other parallel peripheral.

When system timing of an older standard parallel port is set at the minima that produces the widest compatibility, the transmission of a single character requires about ten microseconds. That speed yields a peak transfer rate of 100,000 bytes per second. Operated at the tightest timing allowed by the IEEE 1284 specification, a conventional parallel port can complete a single character transfer cycle in four microseconds, yielding a peak throughput of 250,000 bytes per second.

Add in all the overhead at both ends of the connection, and those rates can take a bad tumble. With a fast PC and fast peripheral, you can realistically expect 80 to 90 kilobytes per second through the fastest conventional parallel port.

EPP Speed

The EPP specification allows for a cycle time of one-half microsecond in its initial implementations. That translates to a peak transfer rates of two megabytes per second. In actual operation with normal processing overhead, EPP come close to half that rate, around 800 kilobytes per second.

Such figures do not represent the top limit for the EPP design, however. In future versions of the EPP standard, timing constraints may be tightening to require data on the interface to become valid within 100 nanoseconds. Such future designs allow for a peak transfer rate approaching eight megabytes per second. Such a rate is actually exceeds the speed of practical transfers across the ISA bus. Taking full advantage of an EPP connection will require a local bus link.

Data Compression

One very effective way of increasing the speed of information through any interface is to minimize the number of bytes you have to move. By compressing the digital code–that is, reducing it to a more bit-efficient format–you can reduce the number of bytes needed to convey text, graphics, and files. Already popular in squeezing more space from disks (for example, with DriveSpace and Stacker), tapes in backup systems, and modem connections, data compression is also part of the Extended Capabilities Port standard.

As an option, the ECP system allows you to data compress the data you send through the parallel interface to further increase the speed of transfers. The port circuitry itself handles the compression and decompression, which is invisible to your PC and its software as well as to the peripheral at the other end of the connection. The effect on your transfers is the same as increasing the speed of the signals across the parallel cable but without all the electrical problems.

The ECP design uses a simple form of compression called *Run Length Encoding* or RLE. As with any code, RLE can take many different forms but the basic principle is the same. Long repetitions of the same digital pattern get reduced to a single occurrence of the pattern and a number indicating how many times the pattern is repeated. The specific RLE algorithm used by the ECP system works at the byte level. When the same byte is repeated in a sequence of data, the system translates it into two bytes: one indicating the original code and a multiplier. Of course, if bytes do not repeat, this basic form of RLE is counterproductive. Using two bytes to code one increases the number byte required for a given amount of data. To minimize the impact of this expansion, the RLE algorithm used by the ECP system splits the difference. Half the possible byte values are kept untouched and are used by the code to represent the same single byte values as in the incoming data stream. The other byte values serve as multipliers. If the same byte used by a multiplier appears in the incoming data stream, it must be represented by two bytes (the byte value followed by a multiplier of one). This system allows two bytes to encode repeated character streams up to 128 bytes long.

At its best, this system can achieve a compression ratio of 64 to 1 on long repetitions of a single byte value. At worst, the system expands data by a ratio of 1 to 2. With real-world data, the system achieves an overall compression ratio approaching 2 to 1, effectively doubling the speed of the parallel interface whatever its underlying bit-per-second transfer rate.

RLE data compression can be particularly effective when you transfer graphics images from your PC to your printer. Graphic images often contain long sequences of repeated bytes representing areas of uniform color. RLE encoding offers little benefit to textual exchanges because text rarely contains long repetitions of the same byte or character. Of course, sending ordinary text to a printer usually doesn't strain the capabilities of even a standard parallel port, so the compression speed boost is unnecessary.

Bus Mastering

System overhead is the bane of performance in any data transfer system. The more time your PC's microprocessor spends preparing and moving data through the interface, the less time there is available for other operations. The problem is most apparent during background printing in PCs using older, slower microprocessors. Most applications give you the option of printing in the background so you can go on to some other task while your PC slowly spools out data to your printer. All too often, the PC slows down so much during background printing that it's virtually useless for other work. This problem occurs in PCs as powerful as 486-based machines.

The slowdown has several sources. Your microprocessor may have to rasterize a full-page image itself (as it often does when printing from Windows) or it may spend its time micromanaging the movement of bytes from memory to the registers of the parallel interface. Although system designers can do anything to improve the speed of the former case, short of using a more powerful microprocessor, they have developed several schemes to minimize system overhead. One dramatic improvement comes with sidestepping the printer BIOS routines and taking direct control of the interface circuitry. Another is to take transfer job from the microprocessor and give it to some other circuit. This last expedient underlies the technology of *bus mastering*.

Bus mastering can improve overall system (and printing) performance two ways. The circuit managing the transfers can be more efficient that your microprocessor at the chore. It may be able to move bytes faster. And, by removing responsibility from your microprocessor, it prevents data transfers from bogging down the rest of your PC. Your microprocessor has more time for doing whatever a microprocessor does.

In systems that allow the bus mastering of parallel port, the transfers are typically managed by your system's DMA (Direct Memory Access) controller. Your microprocessor sets up the transfer–specifying where the bytes are coming from, where they are to go, and how many to move–and lets the DMA controller take over the details. The DMA controller then takes control of the bus, becoming its master, and moving the bytes across it.

Bus-mastered parallel transfers have not won wide favor. The technology does not work well on the ISA expansion bus, and IBM introduced it late in the life of the micro channel system. Moreover, the high processing speed of modern 486 and better microprocessors coupled with comparatively low throughput of the standard parallel interface makes the bus mastering an unnecessary complication. Although not currently applied to PCI or VL bus systems (both of which support bus mastering), the technology could give a boost to EPP and ECP performance because of the higher throughput and simplified means of transfer bytes to those interfaces.

Plug-and-Play

The Plug-and-Play system developed by computer manufacturers with the intention of making your life simpler–or at least dealing with the setup of your PC easier–extends to input/output ports and printers. Plug-and-Play technology allows your PC to detect and identify the various hardware devices that you connect to your computer. For example, a printer that understands and uses the Plug-and-Play system can identify itself to your PC and tell your PC which is the best software driver.

The basic mechanism required for the Plug-and-Play system to work for printers is built into the IEEE 1284 specification. The actual identification and matching of drivers get handled by your PC's operating system.

Benefits

The information that equipment made in accord with the Plug-and-Play specification tells your PC the system resources the equipment needs, and your PC can then automatically assign those resources to the equipment. Unlike when you set up hardware yourself, your PC can infallibly (or nearly so) keep track of the resource demands and usages of each device you connect. Plug-and-Play technology lets your PC not only resolve conflicts between devices that need the same or similar hardware resources, but also the system prevents conflicts from occurring in the first place.

When connecting a printer, you only need to concern yourself, if at all, with two aspects of Plug-and-Play: how it configures your ports and how it deals with your printer itself. Although you shouldn't even have to worry about these details most of the time, understanding the magic can help you better understand your PC and subvert the system when it creates instead of eliminates a problem.

Printers that conform to the requirements of the Plug-and-Play system enable several automatic features. A printer can then specify its *device class*, and the Plug-and-Play operating system will install features and drivers that work with that device class. The system allows your printer to identify itself with a familiar name instead of some obscure model number and use that name throughout the configuration process. That way you can understand what's going on instead of worrying about some weird thing in your computer with a name that looks eerily like the markings on the side of a UFO. And the Plug-and-Play printer can tell you what other peripherals it works with.

Requirements

For the Plug-and-Play system to work, you need to run an operating system that has Plug-and-Play capabilities. Windows 95 is the first operating system to fully support the technology. DOS offers no Plug-and-Play support, and OS/2 Warp includes only a trifling bit of Plug-and-Play technology, used chiefly in administering PC Card slots. It cannot automatically identify your printer.

Ideally, your PC and all the peripherals connected to it will comply with the Plug-and-Play specifications. If you buy a new PC in these enlightened times, you should expect that level of compliance. If you have an older system (or a new system into which you've installed old peripherals), however, you probably won't have full Plug-and-Play compliance. That's okay because in most cases a Plug-and-Play operating system can make do with what you have. For example, Windows 95 can identify your printer as long as it follows the Plug-and-Play standard even if you have cluttered your PC with old expansion boards that don't mesh with the standard.

To automatically identify your printer, the Plug-and-Play system needs only to be able to signal to your printer and have it send back identification data. Your parallel port is key to this operation, but the demands made from it for Plug-and-Play operation are minimal. The port may use any of the standard IEEE connector designs. It must also support, at minimum, nibble-mode bidirectional transfers. Nearly every parallel port ever made fits these requirements. Plug-and-Play prefers a port that follows the ECP design, and for the sake of maximum printer performance, so should you.

Of course, a printer must have built in support of the Plug-and-Play standard if it is to take advantage of the technology. The primary need is simple. Your printer must be able to send to your PC Plug-and-Play identification information so your PC will know what kind of printer you've connected. Your printer requires three forms of identification called *key values* so that your system can be certain of its identification. Three additional key values optimize the operation of the Plug-and-Play system.

Operation

The IEEE 1284 specification provides a mechanism through which your PC's operating system can query a device connected to a parallel port. When your PC sends out the correct command, the printer responds first by sending back two bytes indicating how much identification data it has stored. This value is the length of the identification data in bytes, including the two length-indicating bytes. The first byte of these is the more significant.

After your PC gets the length information, it can query your printer for the actual data with another command. Your Plug-and-Play printer responds by sending back the key value information stored inside its configuration memory (which may be ROM, Flash RAM, or EEPROM).

The three required identifications for Plug-and-Play to work are the manufacturer, command set, and model of your printer. Each of these is stored as a string of case-sensitive characters prefaced by the type of identification. The IEEE 1284 specification abbreviates these identifications as MFG, CMD, and MDL. For example, your printer might respond with these three required values like this:

```
MFG: Acme Printers; CMD: PCL; MDL: Roadrunner 713
```

The manufacturer and model identifications are unique to each manufacturer. These values should never change and typically will be stored in ROM inside your printer. Ideally the command set identification tells your computer what printer driver to use, Hewlett-Packard's Printer Control Language (PCL) in the example line. Although it is often a fixed value in a given printer, if your printer allows you to plug in additional emulations or fonts, the value of the command set identifier should change to match. Note that Windows 95 ignores the command set key value. Instead, when it automatically sets up your printer driver, it relies on manufacturer and model information to determine which driver to use.

Windows 95 generates its own internal Plug-and-Play identification for working with key value data. It generates its ID value by combining together the Manufacturer and Model values and appending a four-digit checksum. If the manufacturer and model designations total more than 20 characters, Windows 95 cuts them off at 20 characters but only *after* it calculates the checksum. The result is a string of 24 or fewer characters. Finally Windows 95 adds the preface LPTENUM\ (indicating the parallel port enumerator) so that it knows the path through which the printer can be found. The result is the printer's Plug-and-Play ID that Windows 95 uses internally when matching device drivers to your printer. For example, the internal Windows 95 ID for a Hewlett-Packard LaserJet 4L printer would be the following character string:

```
LPTENUM\Hewlett-PackardLaserC029
```

Printer manufacturers can add, at their option, other identification information to the Plug-and-Play key values. The IEEE 1284 specification envisions Comment and Active Command Set entries. Microsoft defines its own trio of options: Class (abbreviated CLS), Description (or DES), and Compatible ID (or CID). These values are not case-sensitive.

The Class key value describes the general type of device. Microsoft limits the choices to seven: FDC, HDC, Media, Modem, Net, Ports, or Printer.

The Description key value is a string of up to 128 characters that is meant to identify the Plug-and-Play device in a form that human beings understand. Windows 95 uses the Description when referring to the device on screen when it cannot find a data (INF) file corresponding to the device. Normally Windows would retrieve the on-screen identification for the device from the file. The Description key value keeps things understandable even if you plug in something Windows has never encountered before.

The Compatible ID key value tells Windows if your printer or other device will work exactly like some other product for which Windows might have a driver. For example, it allows the maker of a printer cloned from an Epson MX-80 to indicate it will happily use the Epson printer driver.

Once Windows 95 identifies your printer, its command set, and compatibilities, it uses these values to search through for the data it needs to find the drivers required by your printer and properly configure them. Of course, you always have the option to override the automatic choices when you think you know better than Mother Microsoft.

Serial Ports

Consider the serial port the *other* kind of connection you can make to your printer. The connectors are waiting on the back of your PC. Compared to the parallel port, they're backwards, holes where the pins should be. In operation, too, serial port is a bit backwards (as you'll soon see). But the port is there, it's available, and sometimes you'll be tempted–or cursed by fate–to use a serial connection.

The serial port goes by a number of different names. When hobbyists and engineers dominated the realm of PCs, they gave the port the descriptive name only hobbyists and engineers could love, the "asynchronous data communications port." Many of them still speak fondly of their "async" connections. Those who love to rattle off model numbers like the names of their children speak of serial ports as RS-232C ports, referring to the designation bequeathed by standardization (of sorts) under the auspices of the Electronic Industry Association (EIA).

Serial ports are more than a bit sneaky. Although they seem to be more straightforward than parallel ports and were standardized more than a dozen years before any official organization stamped its imprimatur on parallel technology, serial ports offer you more variety than a candy store. Unfortunately, the variations don't go down nearly as well as your favorite sweetmeats, and coping with them can lead to deterioration of your mental health instead of dentistry.

Physically, serial ports take only two forms, a pair of connector designs now accepted by the entire PC industry. But the signals in each of these connectors can take on two different arrangements. Different devices use different combinations of the signals. The signals themselves take a variety of forms. Failure to make a perfect match between your PC and printer on every count will keep the connection from making a proper link. Complicated? Yes. But the serial connection can serve your printer (which is not to say that's what you want to do, as you'll soon see).

We'll approach the serial system systematically. First, we'll examine why you may (or more importantly may not) want to tangle with the serial morass. Then we'll examine what makes a serial signal serial, how it gets that way, and why. We'll check out the essential hardware circuitry that makes serial ports work. Finally, we'll go through the nitty-gritty of linking a serial printer to your PC and making it work. But first, let's consider why a serial port is tempting you at all.

Strategy

For years the primary alternative to the parallel port for connecting printers to your PC has been the serial port. When the PC was first created, serial ports were a viable alternative for parallel ports. In fact, any printer you bought was as likely to be serial as it was parallel. Of course, at the same time, monitors screens were an evil green, hard disks were less common than flying saucers (and about as likely to be connected to any affordable PC), and printer quality was usually compared, unfavorably, to that of the typewriter. The world has changed in more than a decade and a half. Unfortunately the PC's serial port has not. Today the serial connection and PC printer go together about as well as Alaskan water and North Slope crude.

In today's high-speed world, you have exactly one reason to connect your printer to your PC using a serial port: because you have to. Other than need, there is very little reason for using the serial port, but when you have the need you have no alternative. The needs include:

- You have a serial printer and you want to make it work.
- You don't have a spare parallel port.
- You want to locate your printer more than ten feet from your PC.
- You are a masochist.

In each case, you can easily find a better alternative than linking your printer to your PC with a serial port. If you have a printer that only has a serial port, your better strategy is to buy a better printer. The number of new PC printers that have only serial ports totals about zero, which means any serial printer you might have is more a museum piece than modern office tool. If you can replace a clanky old contraption harboring such plagues as a serial connector you'll be much better off investing the $200 or so in a new ink-jet printer. In fact, the price of the new printer will probably be less than the value of the time you'll waste sorting through the serial connection.

If you don't have a spare parallel port in your PC, don't immediately start searching for a serial printer. Instead, buy a port board. An extra parallel port will cost less than $20. If you've exceeded the official three-port maximum for parallel connections to your PC, buy a switch box so you can connect two or more parallel printers to one port. Under most circumstances, you won't be using more than one printer at a time, so you can easily get away with splitting a single port.

Although a serial connection will let you stretch the cable between your computer and printer to nearly a mile, you face a substantial penalty for every foot of wire you add to the link: speed. The longer the wire in a serial connection, the slower you need to run the serial ports. At a quarter mile, you'll be running 1200 bits per second or less to avoid communication errors. You could wait all day to print out a full page of graphics. This sort of nonsense connection is worthwhile only if you're paid by the hour. Otherwise you'll find much better alternatives: Port extenders double-convert signals to give you a proprietary distance-compatible link that matches to both PC and printer with parallel connections. If you're willing to put up with the complication of a serial port, you'll find that adding a small network is no more difficult–and you'll have a thousand times the speed and ten times the reach (or more).

If you're really into masochism, mastering a serial connection might sound appealing, but you'll have more fun with an equivalent investment in leather, chains, and a subscription to *Readers' Digest*.

The serial connection just doesn't make sense in today's world of huge graphics based printouts. It persists because it sometimes is unavoidable. If you can't avoid it, you'll have to deal with it. Fortunately, a serial connection can be made to work. All it takes is a bit of knowledge and a lot of patience. This book will give you the knowledge, but for the patience you're on your own.

Background

In computers, a serial signal is one in which the bits of data of the digital code are arranged in a series. They travel through their medium or connection one after another as a train of pulses. Put another way, the pattern that makes up the digital code stretches across the dimension of time rather than across the width of a data bus. Instead of the bits of the digital code getting their significance from their physical position in the lines of the data bus, they get their meaning from their position in time. Instead of traveling through eight distinct connections a byte of data, for example, makes up a sequence of eight pulses in a serial communications system. Plot signal to time, and the serial connections turn things sideways from the way they would be inside your PC.

Do you detect a pattern here? Time, time, time. Serial ports make data communications a matter of timing. Defining and keeping time become critical issues in serial data exchanges.

Engineers split the universe of serial communications into two distinct forms, *synchronous* and *asynchronous*. The difference between them relates to how they deal with time.

Synchronous communications require the sending and receiving system—for our purposes, the PC and printer—to synchronize their actions. They share a common time base, a serial *clock*. This clock signal is passed between the two systems either as a separate signal or by using the pulses of data in the data stream to define it. The serial transmitter and receiver can unambiguously identify each bit in the data stream by its relationship to the shared clock. Because each uses exactly the same clock, they can make the match based on timing alone.

In asynchronous communications the transmitter and receiver use separate clocks. Although the two clocks are supposed to be running at the same speed, they don't necessarily tell the same time. They are like your wristwatch and the clock on the town square. One or the other may be a few minutes faster even though both operate at essentially the same speed: A day has 24 hours for both.

An asynchronous communications system also relies on the timing of pulses to define the digital code. But they cannot look to their clocks as infallible guidance. A small error in timing can shift a bit a few positions, say from the least significant place to the most significant, which can drastically affect the meaning of the digital message.

If you've ever had a clock that kept bad time—for example, the CMOS clock inside your PC—you probably noticed that time errors are cumulative; they add up. If your clock is a minute off today, it will be two minutes off tomorrow. The longer time elapses, the bigger the difference in two clocks will be apparent. The corollary is also true: If you make a comparison over a short enough period, you won't notice a shift between two clocks even if they are running at quite different speeds.

Asynchronous communications banks on this fine slicing of time. By keeping intervals short, they make two unsynchronized clocks act as if they were synchronized. The otherwise unsynchronized signals can identify the time relationships in the bits of a serial code.

The basic element of digital information in a serial communication system is the data *frame*. Think of the word as a time frame, the frame bracketing the information like a frame surrounds a window. The bits of the digital code are assigned their value in accord with their position in the frame. In a synchronous serial communications system, the frame contains the bits of a digital code word. In asynchronous serial communications, the frame also contains a word of data, but it has a greater significance. It is also the time interval in which the clocks of the sending and receiving systems are assumed to be synchronized.

When an asynchronous receiver detects the start of a frame, it resets its clock and then uses its clock to define the significance of each bit in the digital code within the frame. At the start of the next frame, it resets its clock and starts timing the bits again. The only problem with this system is that an asynchronous receiver needs to know when a frame begins and ends. Synchronous receivers can always look to the clock to know, but the asynchronous system has no such luxury. The trick to making asynchronous communications work is unambiguously defining the frame. Today's asynchronous systems use *start bits* to mark the beginning of a frame and *stop bits* to mark its end. In the middle are a group of *data bits.*

The start bit helps the asynchronous receiver find data in a sea of noise. In some systems, the start bit is given a special identity. In most asynchronous systems, it is twice the length of the other bits inside the frame. In others, the appearance of the bit itself is sufficient. After all, without data, you would expect no pulses. When any pulse pops up, you might expect it to be a start bit.

Each frame ends with one or more stop bits. They assure the receiver that the data in the frame is complete. Most asynchronous communication systems allow for one, one and a half, or two stop bits. Most systems use one because that length makes each frame shorter (which, in turn, means that it takes a shorter time to transmit).

The number of data bits in a frame varies widely. In most asynchronous systems, there will be from five to eight bits of data in each frame. If you plan to use a serial port to connect a printer to your PC, your printer will use either seven or eight bits, the latter being the most popular.

In addition, the data bits in the frame may be augmented by error correction information called a parity bit which fits between the last bit of data and the stop bit. In modern serial systems, any of five varieties of parity bits are sometimes used: odd, even, space, mark, and none.

The value of the parity bit is keyed to the data bits. The serial transmitter counts the number of digital ones in the data bits and determines whether this total is odd or even. In the odd parity scheme, the transmitter will turn on the parity bit (making it a digital one) only if the total number of digital ones in the data bits is odd. In even priority systems, the parity bit is set as one only if the data bits contain an even number of digital ones. In mark parity, the parity bit is always a mark, a digital one. In space parity, the parity bit is always a space, a digital zero. With no parity, no parity bit is included in the digital frames, and the stop bits immediately follow the data bits.

By convention, the bits of serial data in each frame are sent least significant bit first. Subsequent fits follow in order of increasing significance. Figure 8.7 illustrates the contents of a single data frame that uses eight data bits and a single stop bit.

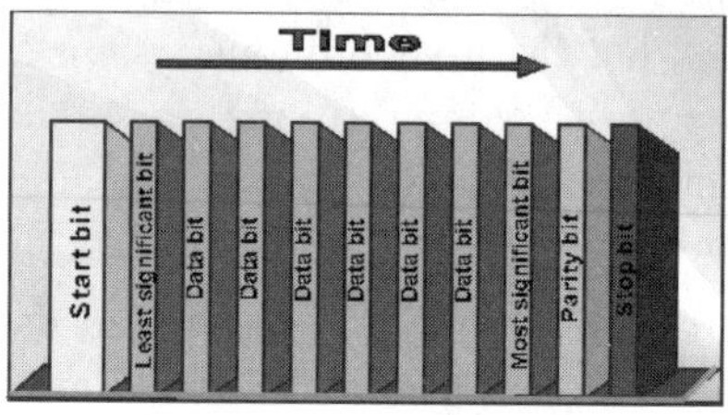

Figure 8.7 A serial data frame with eight data bits and one stop bit.

So far we've discussed time in the abstract. But serial communications must occur at very real data rates, and those rates must be the same at both ends of the serial connection, if just within a frame when transmissions are asynchronous. The speed at which devices exchange serial data is called the *bit rate,* and it is measured in the number of data bits that would be exchanged in a second if bits were sent continually. You've probably encountered these bit rates when using a modem. The PC industry uses bit rates in the following sequence: 150; 300; 600; 1200; 2400; 4800; 9600; 19,200; 38,400; 57,600; and 115,200.

This sequence results from both industry standards and the design of the original IBM PC. The PC developed its serial port bit rate by using an oscillator that operates at 1.8432 MHz and associated circuitry that reduces that frequency by a factor of 1600 to a basic operating speed of 115,200 bits per second. For this base bit rate, a device called a *programmable divider* mathematically creates the lower bit rates used by serial ports. It develops the lower frequencies by dividing the starting rate by an integer. By using a divisor of three, for example, the PC develops a bit rate of 38,400 (that is, 115200/3). Not all available divisors are used. For example, designers never set their circuits to divide by five.

You may have noticed that some modems use speeds not included in this sequence. For example, today's popular V.34 modems operate at a base speed of 28,800 bits per second. The modem generates this data rate internally. In general, you will connect your PC to the modem so that it communicates at a higher bit rate, and the modem repackages the data to fit the data rate is uses by compressing the data or telling your PC to halt the flow of information until it is ready to send more bits.

When you connect a serial printer, you'll usually use a data rate slower than that of most modern modems. That should be a good hint why not to use a serial port for printers. Older printers often accepted data at a maximum speed of 9600 bits per second. In fact, older PCs were so encumbered by software overhead that they could not exceed this rate when using their built-in serial port control firmware, which is part of your PC's ROM. Even today, when Pentium and more powerful computers could blast serial data rates skyward, 9600 bps is the most common data rate at which to run PC-to-printer links.

As you can see, even the accepted standard in asynchronous communications allows for a number of variables in the digital code used within each data frame. When you configure your printer and your serial port, you'll encounter all of these variables: speed, number of data bits, parity choices, and number of stop bits. The most important rule about choosing which values to use is that the transmitter and receiver–your PC and your printer–must use exactly the same settings. Think of a serial communications as being an exchange of coded messages by two spies. If the recipient doesn't use the same code key as the sender, he can't hope to make sense out of the message. If your printer isn't configured to understand the same settings as your PC sends out in its serial signals, you can't possibly hope to print anything sensible.

Normally you'll configure your printer's serial port bit rate using DIP switches or the printer's menu system. How to make the settings will vary with the printer, so you should check your printer's instruction manual to be sure. You set your PC's serial port speed at the DOS prompt using the **MODE** command (see Chapter 6). This setting only affects what you print from DOS. Most programs and other operating systems take direct control of the PC's serial ports when they need them, and these program override the values set using the **MODE** command. You adjust the bit rates (and other serial parameters) used by your programs as part of the setup procedures of your applications or operating system.

In general, you should set the fastest data that both ends of your connection will allow. The place to start with modern PCs and serial printers is 9600 bits per second. If all you print is text from DOS, this rate will be adequate for any printer. Graphic applications (including printing TrueType text from Windows) require the highest possible speed you can muster.

Electrical Operation

Serial signals have a definite disadvantage compared to parallel: bits move one at a time. At a given clock rate, fewer bits will travel through a serial link than a parallel one. The disadvantage is on the order of 12 to 1. When a parallel port moves a byte in a single cycle, a serial port take around a dozen–eight for the data bits, one for parity, one for stop, and two for start. That 9600 bit per second serial printer connection actually moves text at about 800 character per second.

Compensating for this definite handicap, serial connections claim versatility. Their signals can go the distance. Not just the mile or so that you can shoot out the signal from your standard serial port, but the thousands of miles you can make by modem–tied, of course, to that old serial port.

The trade-off is signal integrity for speed. As they travel down wires, digital pulses tend to blur. The electrical characteristics of wires tend to round off the sharp edges of pulses and extend their length. The farther a signal travels, the less defined it becomes until digital equipment has difficulty telling where the one pulse ends and the next begins. The more closely spaced the pulses are (and, hence, the higher the bit rate), the worse the problem becomes. By lowering the bit rate and extending the pulses and the time between them, the farther the signal can go before the pulses blend together. (Modems avoid part of this problem by converting digital signals to analog signals for the long haul. PC networks achieve length and speed by using special cables and signaling technologies.)

The question of how far can a serial signal reach depends on both the equipment and wire that you use. You can probably extend a 9600-bps printer connection to a 100 feet or more. At a quarter mile, you'll probably be down to 1200 or 300 bps (slower than even cheap printers can type).

Longer wires are cheaper with serial connections, too, a point not lost on system designers. Where a parallel cable requires 18 to 25 separate wires to carry its signals, a serial link does with three: one to carry signals from your PC to printer, one to carry signals from printer to PC, and a common or ground signal that provides a return path for both.

The electrical signal on a serial cable is a rapidly switching voltage. Digital in nature, it has one of two states. In the communications industry, these states are termed space and mark like the polarity signals. *Space* is the absence of a bit, and *mark* is the presence of a bit. On the serial line, a space is a positive voltage and a mark is a negative voltage. In other words, when you're not sending data down a serial line, it has an overall positive voltage on it. Data will appear as a serial of negative-going pulses. The original design of the serial port specification called for the voltage to shift from a positive 12 volts to negative 12 volts. Because 12 volts is an uncommon potential in many PCs, the serial voltage often varies from positive five to negative five volts.

Connectors

The physical manifestation of a serial port is the connector that glowers on the rear panel of your PC. It is where you plug your printer into your computer. And it can be the root of all evil–or so it will seem after a number of long evenings during which you valiantly try to make your serial printer work with your PC only to have text disappear like phantoms at sunrise. Again the principle problem with serial ports is the number of options that it allows designers. Serial ports can use either of two styles of connectors each of which has two options in signal assignment. Worse, some manufacturers venture bravely in their own directions with the all-important flow control signals. Sorting out all of these options is the most frustrating part of serial port configuration.

25-Pin

The basic serial port connector is called a 25-pin D-shell. It earns its name from having 25 connections arranged in two rows that are surrounded by a metal guide that takes the form of a rough letter D. The male variety of this connector–the one that actually has pins inside it–is normally used on PCs. Most, but hardly all, printers use the female connector (the one with holes instead of pins) for their serial ports. Although both serial and parallel ports use the same style 25-pin D-shell connectors, you can distinguish serial ports from parallel ports because on most PCs the latter use female connectors. Figure 8.8 shows the typical male serial port DB-25 connector that you'll find on the back of your PC.

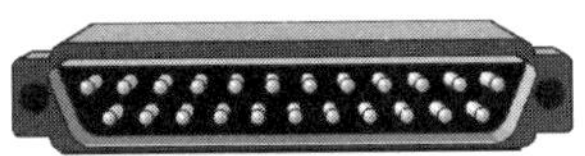

Figure 8.8 The male DB-25 connector used by serial ports on PCs.

Although the serial connector allows for 25 discrete signals, only a few of them are ever actually used. Serial systems may involve as few as three connections. At most, PC serial ports use ten different signals. Table 8.14 lists the names of these signals, their mnemonics, and the pins to which they are assigned in the standard 25-pin serial connector.

Table 8.14 25-Pin Serial Port Connector

Pin	Function	Mnemonic
1	Chassis ground	None
2	Transmit data	TXD
3	Receive data	RXD
4	Request to send	RTS
5	Clear to send	CTS
6	Data set ready	RTS
7	Signal ground	GND
8	Carrier detect	CD
20	Data terminal ready	DTR
22	Ring indicator	RI

Note that in the standard serial cable, signal ground (which is the return line for the data signals on pins 2 and 3) is separated from the chassis ground on pin 1. The chassis ground pin is connected directly to the metal chassis or case of the equipment much like the extra prong of a three-wire AC power cable and provide the same protective function. It ensures that the case of the two devices linked by the serial cable are at the same potential, which means you won't get a shock if you touch both at the same time. As wonderful as this connection sounds, it is often omitted from serial cables. On the other hand, the signal ground is a necessary signal that the serial link cannot work without. You should never connect the chassis ground to the signal ground.

9-Pin

If nothing else, using a 25-pin D-shell connector for a serial port is a waste of at least 15 pins. Most serial connections use fewer than the complete ten; some as few as four with hardware handshaking, three with software flow control. For the sake of standardization, the PC industry sacrificed the cost of the other unused pins for years until a larger—or smaller, depending on your point of view—problem arose: space. A serial port connector was too big to fit on the retaining brackets of expansion boards along with a parallel connector. Because each pin in the parallel connector had an assigned function, the serial connector met its destiny and got miniaturized.

The problem arose when IBM attempted to put both sorts of ports on one board inside its Personal Computer AT when it was introduced in 1984. To cope with the small space available on the card retaining bracket, IBM eliminated all the unnecessary pins but kept the essential design of the connector the same. The result was an implementation of the standard serial port that uses a nine-pin D-shell connector. To trim the ten connections to nine, IBM omitted the little-used chassis ground connection.

As with the 25-pin variety of serial connector, the nine-pin serial jack on the back of PCs uses a male connector. This choice distinguishes it from the female nine-pin D-shell jacks used by early video adapters (the MDA, CGA, and EGA systems all used this style of connector). Figure 8.9 shows the nine-pin male connector that's used on some PCs for serial ports.

Figure 8.9 The male DB-9 plug used by AT-class serial devices.

Besides eliminating some pins, IBM also rearranged the signal assignments used in the miniaturized connector. Table 8.15 lists the signal assignments for the nine-pin serial connector introduced with the IBM PC-AT.

Table 8.15 IBM Nine-Pin Serial Connector

Pin	Function	Mnemonic
1	Carrier detect	CD
2	Receive data	RXD
3	Transmit data	TXD
4	Data terminal ready	DTR
5	Signal Ground	GND
6	Data set ready	DSR
7	Request to send	RTS
8	Clear to send	CTS
9	Ring indicator	RI

Other than the rearrangement of signals, the nine-pin and 25-pin serial connectors are essentially the same. All the signals behave identically regardless of the size of the connector on which it appears.

Signals

Serial communications is an exchange of signals across the serial interface. First we'll look at the signals and their flow in the kind of communication system for which the serial port was designed, linking a PC to a modem. Then we'll examine how attaching a printer to a serial port complicates matters and what you can do to make the connection work.

Definitions

The names of the signals on the various lines of the serial connector sound odd in today's PC-oriented lingo because the terminology originated in the communications industry. The names are more relevant to the realm of modems and vintage teletype equipment.

Serial terminology assumes that each end of a connection has a different type of equipment attached to it. One end has a *data terminal* connected to it. In the old days when the serial port was developed, a terminal was exactly that–a keyboard and a screen that translated typing into serial signals. Today a terminal is usually a PC. For reasons known only to those who revel in rolling their tongues across excess syllables, the term *data terminal equipment* is often substituted. To make matters even more complex, many discussions mention *DTE* devices, which are exactly the same as "data terminals."

The other end of the connection had a *data set*, which corresponds to a modem. Often engineers substitute the more formal term *data communication equipment* or talk about *DCE* devices.

The distinction between data terminals and data sets (or DTE and DCE devices) is important. Serial communications were originally designed to take place between one DTE and one DCE, and the signals used by the system are defined in those terms.

> **Transmit data.** The serial data leaving the RS-232 port travels is called the *transmit data* line, which is usually abbreviated TXD. The signal on it comprises the long sequence of pulses generated by the UART in the serial port. The data terminal sends out this signal, and the data set listens to it.

Receive data. The stream of bits going the other direction–that is, coming in from a distant serial port–goes through the *receive data* line (usually abbreviated RXD) to reach the input of the serial port's UART. The data terminal listens on this line for the data signal coming from the data set.

Data terminal ready. When the data terminal is able to participate in communications, that is, it is turned on and in the proper operating mode, it signals its readiness to the data set by applying a positive voltage to the *data terminal* ready line (DTR).

Data set ready. When the data set is able to receive data, that is, it is turned on and in the proper operating mode, it signals its readiness by applying a positive voltage to the *data set ready* line (*DSR*). Because serial communications must be two-way, the data terminal will not send out a data signal unless it sees the DSR signal coming from the data set.

Request to send. When the data terminal is on and capable of receiving transmissions, it puts a positive voltage on its *request to send* line (RTS). This signal tells the data set that it can send data to the data terminal. The absence of a RTS signal across the serial connection will prevent the data set from sending out serial data. This allows the data terminal to control the flow of the data set to it.

Clear to send. The data set, too, needs to control the signal flow from the data terminal. The signal it uses is called *clear to send*, which is abbreviated CTS. The presence of the CTS in effect tells the data terminal that the coast is clear and the data terminal can blast data down the line. The absence of a CTS signal across the serial connection will prevent the data terminal from sending out serial data.

Carrier detect. The serial interface standard shows its roots in the communication industry with the *carrier detect* signal, which is usually abbreviated CD. This signal gives a modem, the typical data set, a means of signaling to the data terminal that it has made a connection with a distant modem. The signal says that the modem or data set has detected the carrier wave of another modem on the telephone line. In effect, the carrier detect signal gets sent to the data terminal to tell it that communications are possible. In some systems, the data terminal must see the carrier detect signal before it will engage in data exchange. Other systems simply ignore this signal.

Ring indicator. Sometimes a data terminal has to get ready to communicate even before the flow of information begins. For example, you might want to switch your communications program into answer mode so that it can deal with an incoming call. The designers of the serial port provided such an early warning in the form of send the ring indicator signal, which is usually abbreviated RI. When a modem serving as a data set detects ringing voltage–the low-frequency, high-voltage signal that makes telephone bells ring–on the telephone line to which it is connected, it activates the RI signal, which alerts the data terminal to what's going on. Although useful in setting up modem communications, you can regard the *ring indicator* signal as optional because its absence usually will not prevent the flow of serial data.

Signal ground. All of the signals used in a serial port need a return path. The signal ground provides this return path. The single ground signal is the common return for all other signals on the serial interface. Its absence will prevent serial communications entirely.

Flow Control

This hierarchy of signals hints that serial communications can be a complex process. The primary complicating factor is handshaking or flow control. The designers of the serial interface recognized that some devices might not be able to accommodate information as fast as others could deliver it, so they built handshaking into the serial communications hardware using several special control signals to compensate.

This flow control signals become extremely important when you want to use a serial connection to a printer. Simply put, printers aren't as quick as PCs. As you sit around playing Freecell for the fourteenth hand while waiting for a ten-page report to roll out, that news comes as little surprise. Printers are mechanical devices that work at mechanical speed. PCs are electronic roadrunners. A modern PC can produce a printout much quicker than your printer can get it on paper.

The temptation for your PC is to force-feed your printer, shooting data out like rice puffs from a cannon. After the first few gulps, however, your printer will choke. With a serial connection, the printer might let the next salvo whiz right by, missing it and your paper and leaving large gaps in your text. Flow control helps throttle down the onslaught of data.

The concept underlying flow control is the same as that for parallel ports: your printer signals when it cannot accept more characters to stop the flow from your PC. When it is ready for more, it signals its availability back to your PC. Where the parallel port uses a simple hardware scheme, flow control for the serial port is more complex. As with every other aspect of serial technology, flow control is a theme overwhelmed by variations.

The chief division in serial flow control is between hardware and software. *Hardware flow control* involves the use of special control lines that can be (but don't have to be) part of a serial connection. Your PC signals whether it is ready to accept more data by sending a signal down the appropriate wire. *Software flow control* involves the exchange of characters between PC and printer. One character tells the PC your printer is ready and another warns that it can't deal with more data. Both hardware and software flow control take more than one form. As a default, PC serial ports use hardware flow control (or hardware handshaking). Most printers do, too.

Hardware Flow Control

Several of the signals in the serial interface are specifically designed to help handle flow control. Rather than a simple on-and-off operation, however, they work together in an elaborate ritual.

The profusion of signal seems overkill for keeping printouts under control, and it is. The basic handshaking protocol for a serial interface is built around the needs of modem communications. Establishing a modem connection and maintaining the flow of data through it is substantially more complex then simply pouring data into a printer. Even a relatively simple modem exchange involves about a dozen steps with a complex interplay of signals. The basic steps of the dance would go something like this:

1. The telephone rings when a remote modem wants to make a connector. The data set sends the ring indicator signal to the data terminal to warn of the incoming call.
2. The data terminal switches on or flips into the proper mode to engage in communications. It indicates its readiness by sending the data terminal ready signal to the data set.
3. Simultaneously, it activates its request to send line.
4. When the data set knows the data terminal is ready, it answers the phone and listens for the carrier of the other modem. If it hears the carrier, it sends out the carrier detect signal.
5. The data set negotiates a connection. When it is capable of sending data down the phone line, it activates the data set ready signal.
6. Simultaneously, it activates its clear to send line.

7. The data set relays bytes from the phone line to the data terminal through the receive data line.
8. The data terminal sends bytes to the data set (and thence the distant modem) through the transmit data line.
9. Because the phone line is typically slower than the data terminal-to-data set link, the data set quickly fills its internal buffer. It tells the data terminal to stop sending bytes by deactivating the clear to send line. When its buffer empties, it reactivates clear to send.
10. If the data terminal cannot handle incoming data, it deactivates its request to send line. When it can again accept data, it reactivates the request to send line.
11. The call ends. The carrier disappears, and the data set discontinues the carrier detect signal, clear to send signal, and data set ready signal.
12. Upon losing the carrier detect signal, the data terminal returns to its quiescent state, dropping its request to send and data terminal ready signals.

Underlying the serial dance are a two rules: 1) the data terminal must see the data set ready signal as well as the clear to send signal before it will disgorge data; and 2) the data set must see the data terminal ready and request to send signals before it will send out serial data. Interrupting either of the first pair of signal will usually stop the data terminal from pumping out data. Interrupting either of the second pair of signals will stop the data set from replying with its own data.

The carrier detect signal may or may not enter the relationship. Some data terminals require seeing the carrier detect signal before they will transmit data. Others just don't give a byte one way or the other.

Software Flow Control

The alternative means of handshaking, software flow control, requires your printer and PC to exchange characters or tokens to indicate whether they should transfer data. The printer normally sends out one character to indicate it can accept data and a different character to indicate that it is busy and cannot accommodate more. Two pairs of characters are often used, XON/XOFF and ETX/ACK.

In the XON/XOFF scheme, the XOFF character sent from your printer tells your PC that its buffer is full and to hold off sending data. This character is also sometimes called DC1 and has an ASCII value of 19 or 013(Hex). It is sometimes called Control-S. (With some communications programs, you can hold down the

Control key and type **S** to tell the remote system to stop sending characters to your PC). Once your printer is ready to receive data again, it sends out XON, also known as DC3, to your PC. This character has an ASCII value of 17 or 011(Hex). It is sometimes called Control-Q. When you hold down **Control** and type **Q** into your communications program, it cancels the effect of a Control-S.

ETX/ACK works similarly. ETX, which is an abbreviation for End TeXt, tells your PC to hold off on sending more text. This character has an ASCII value of 3 (decimal or hexadecimal) and is sometimes called Control-C. ACK, short for Acknowledge, tells your PC to resume sending data. It has an ASCII value of 6 (decimal or hexadecimal), and is sometimes called Control-F.

There's no issue as to whether hardware or software flow control is better. Both work, and that's all that's necessary. The important issue is what kind of flow control your printer and software use. You must ensure that your PC, your software, and your printer use the same flow control.

Your software will either tell you what it prefers or give you the option of choosing when you load a printer driver. On your printer, you select serial port flow control when you set it up. Typically this will involve making a menu selection or adjusting a DIP switch.

Hardware flow control is normally used by graphic printers because the characters used by software flow control may be interpreted by a printer as bit-image data when printing graphics. Because they are out of the normal text range, however, they can be embedded in purely text printouts without difficulty. On the other hand, hardware flow control often poses problems with cabling, which we will discuss as follows.

Cables

The design of the standard RS-232 serial interface anticipates that you will connect a data terminal to a data set. When you do, all the connections at one end of the cable that links them are carried through to the other end, pin for pin, connection for connection. The definitions of the signals at each end of the cable are the same, and the function and direction of travel (whether from data terminal to data set or the other way around) of each is well defined. Each signal goes straight-through from one end to the other. Even the connectors are the same at either end. Consequently, a serial cable should be relatively easy to fabricate.

In the real world, nothing is so easy. Serial cables are usually much less complicated or much more complicated than this simple design. Unfortunately, if you plan to use a serial connection for a printer, you have to suffer through the more complex design.

Straight-Through Cables

Serial cables are often simpler than pin-for-pin connections from one end to the other because no serial link uses all 25 connector pins. Even with the complex handshaking schemes used by modems, only nine signals need to travel from the data terminal to the data set, PC to modem. (For signaling purposes, the two grounds are redundant–most serial cables do not connect the chassis ground.) Consequently, you need only make these nine connections to make virtually any data terminal to data set link work. Assuming you have a 25-pin D-shell connector at either end of your serial cable, the essential pins that must be connected are 2 through 8, 20, and 22 on a 25-pin D-shell connector. With nine-pin connectors at either end of your serial cable, all nine connections are essential.

Not all systems use all the handshaking signals, so you can often get away with fewer connections in a serial cable. The minimal case is a system that uses software handshaking only. In that case, you need only three connections: transmit data, receive data, and the signal ground. In other words, you need only connect pins 2, 3, and 7 on a 25-pin connector or pins 2, 3, and 5 on a nine-pin serial connector–providing, of course, you have the same size connector at each end of the cable.

Although cables with an intermediary number of connections are often available, they are not sufficiently less expensive than the nine-wire cable to justify the risk and lack of versatility. So you should limit your choices to a nine-wire cable for systems that use hardware handshaking or three-wire cables for those that you're certain use only software flow control.

Manufacturers use a wide range of cable types for serial connections. For the relatively low data rates and reasonable lengths of serial connections, you can get away with just about everything, including twisted-pair telephone wire. To ensure against interference, you should use shielded cable, which wraps a wire braid or aluminum-coated plastic film about inner conductors to prevent signals leaking out or in. The shield of the cable should be connected to the signal ground. (Ideally the signal ground should have its own wire, and the shield should be connected to chassis ground, but most folks just don't bother.)

Adapter Cables

If you need a cable with a 25-pin connector at one end and a nine-pin connector at the other, you cannot use a straight-through design even when you want to link a data terminal to a data set. The different signal layouts of the two styles of connector are incompatible. After all, you can't possibly link pin 22 on a 25-pin connector to a nonexistent pin 22 on a nine-pin connector.

This problem is not uncommon. Even though the nine-pin connector has become a de facto standard on PCs, most other equipment including serial printers and modems has stuck with the 25-pin standard. To get from one connector type to other, you need an adapter. The adapter can take the form of a small assembly with a connector on each end or of an adapter cable, typically from six inches to six feet long.

Although commercial adapters are readily available, you can readily make your own. Table 8.16 shows the proper wiring for an adapter to link a 25-pin serial device to a nine-pin jack on a PC, assuming a data terminal-to-data set connection.

Table 8.16 Wiring for 9-to-25 Pin Serial Port Adapter

25-Pin Connector	9-Pin Connector	Mnemonic	Function
2	3	TXD	Transmit data
3	2	RXD	Receive data
4	7	RTS	Request to send
5	8	CTS	Clear to send
6	6	RTS	Data set ready
7	5	GND	Signal ground
8	1	CD	Carrier detect
20	4	DTR	Data terminal ready
22	9	RI	Ring indicator

Again, nine wires in a cable will suffice. For systems using only software flow control, you need link only the three essential pins. Note, however, the three pins do not get connected one-for-one. Pin 2 on the 25-pin connector goes to pin 3 on the nine-pin connector; pin 3 on the 25-pin goes to pin 2 on the nine-pin. The ground on pin 7 of the 25-pin connector goes to pin 5 of the nine-pin connector.

Apple sometimes uses its own variation on the serial port with an entirely different connector than the D-shells used in the PC environment. The Apple connector is about three-eighths of an inch round and is called a mini-DIN connector. At that it resembles those used by some PC bus mice, PS/2 mice, and miniature keyboard connectors. The Apple scheme of things supports hardware handshaking using the CTS or DTR signals. Figure 8.17 shows how to wire an adapter to match an Apple Imagewriter II printer to a PC serial port.

Table 8.17 IBM to Apple (Imagewriter II) Serial Cable Adapter

Signal	Function	DB-25	DB-9	Mini-DIN
TXD	Transmit data	2	3	5
RXD	Receive data	3	2	3
CTS	Clear to send	5	8	1
GND	Ground	7	5	4 & 8
DTR	Data terminal ready	20	4	2

Cross-Over Cables

As long as you want to connect a computer serial port that functions to a modem, you should have no problem with serial communications. You will be connecting a data terminal to a data set, exactly what engineers designed the serial systems for. Simply sling a cable with enough conductors to handle all the vital signals between the computer and modem and, voila! Serial communications without a hitch. Try it, and you're likely to wonder why so many people complain about the capricious nature of serial connections.

When you want to connect a printer to a PC through a serial port, however, you will immediately encounter a problem. The architects of the RS-232 serial system decided that both PCs and printers are data terminals or DTE devices. The designations actually made sense, at least at that time. You were just as likely to connect a serial printer (such as a teletype) to a modem as you were a computer terminal. There was no concern about connecting a printer to a PC because PCs didn't even exist at that time.

When you connect a printer and PC—or any two DTE devices—with an ordinary serial cable, you will not have a communication system at all. Neither machine will know that the other one is even there. Each one will listen on the serial port signal line that the other is listening on, and each one will talk on the line that the other talks on. One device won't hear anything the other is saying.

The obvious solution to the problem is to switch around some wires. Move the transmit data wire from the PC to where the receive data wire goes on the printer. Route the PC's receive data wire to the printer's transmit data wire. A simple *cross-over cable* does exactly that, switching the transmit and receive signals at one end of the connection.

Many of the devices that you plug into a PC are classified as DTE or data terminals just like the PC. All of these will require a cross-over cable. Table 8.18 lists many of the devices you might connect to your PC and whether they function as data terminals (DTE) or data sets (DCE).

Table 8.18 Common Serial Device Types

Peripheral	Device Type	Cable Needed To Connect To PC
PC	DTE	Cross-over
Modem	DCE	Straight-through
Mouse	DCE	Straight-through
Trackball	DCE	Straight-through
Digitizer	DCE	Straight-through
Scanner	DCE	Straight-through
Serial printer	DTE	Cross-over
Serial plotter	DTE	Cross-over

Some serial ports on PCs (and some serial devices, too) offer a neat solution to this problem. They allow you to select whether they function as DTE or DCE with jumpers or DIP switches. To connect one of these to a printer using an ordinary straight-through cable, configure the PC's serial port as DCE.

This simple three-wire cross-over cable works if you plan on using only software flow control. Most printers, as noted earlier, use hardware handshaking so the three-wire connection won't work. You need to carry the hardware handshaking signals through the cable. And then the fun begins.

Your problems begin with carrier detect. The carrier detect signal originates on a data set, and many data terminals need to receive it before they will send out data. When you connect two data terminals together, neither generates a signal anything like carrier detect, so there's nothing to connect to make the data terminals start talking. You have to fabricate the carrier detect signal somehow.

Because data terminals send out their data terminal ready signals whenever they are ready to receive data, you can steal the voltage from that connection. Most cross-over cables link their carrier-detect signals to the data terminal ready signal from the other end of the cable.

Both data terminals will send out their data terminal ready signals when they are ready. They expect to see a ready signal from a data set on the data set ready connection. Consequently most cross-over cables also link data terminal ready on one end to data set ready (as well as carrier detect) at the other end. Making up this link allows the two data terminals at either end of the cable to judge when the other is ready.

The actual flow control signals are request to send and clear to send. The typical cross-over cable thus links the request to send signal from one end to the clear to send connection at the other end. This link will enable flow control, providing that the two data terminal devices follow the signaling standard we outlined previously. Table 8.19 summarizes these connections.

Table 8.19 Basic Cross-Over Cable for Hardware Handshaking (25-pin connectors)

PC End	Function	Printer End
2	Transmit data	3
3	Receive data	2
4	Request to send	5
5	Clear to send	4
6	Data set ready	20
7	Signal ground	7
8	Carrier detect	20
20	Data terminal ready	6
20	Data terminal ready	8

Unfortunately, this cable may not work when you link many printers to the typical PC. A different design that combines the request to send and clear to send signals and links them to carrier detect at the opposite end of the cable often works better than the above by-the-book design. The wiring connections for this variety of cross-over cable are listed in Table 8.20.

Table 8.20 Wiring for a Generic Cross-Over Serial Cable (25-pin connectors)

PC End	Function	Printer End
2	Transmit data	3
3	Receive data	2
4	Request to send	8
5	Clear to send	8
6	Data set ready	20
7	Signal ground	7
8	Carrier detect	5
8	Carrier detect	4
20	Data terminal ready	22
20	Data terminal ready	6
22	Ring indicator	20

A number of printers vary from the signal layout ascribed to RS-232 connections and use different connections for flow control. DEC serial printers, among others, use pin 19 instead of pin 20 for hardware flow control. These require another variation on the generic cross-over cable to make them work properly with PCs. The proper wiring is shown in Table 8.21.

Table 8.21 Wiring for Cross-Over Serial Cable (25-pin to 25-pin) for DEC Printers Using Pin 19 Handshake

PC End	Function	Printer End
2	Transmit data	3
3	Receive data	2
4	Request to send	8
5	Clear to send	8

Table 8.21 continued

PC End	Function	Printer End
6	Data set ready	19
7	Signal ground	7
8	Carrier detect	5
8	Carrier detect	4
20	Data terminal ready	22
20	Data terminal ready	6

Some of the newer and more popular serial printers are in the LaserJet series made by Hewlett-Packard. These use a simplified hardware flow control system that involves only the DTR signal on the printer end of the cable. Earlier printer models use 25-pin connectors, and Hewlett-Packard sells an crossover cable for these as its part number 17255D. Its wiring is shown in Figure 8.22.

Table 8.22 Serial Adapter Cable, PC 25-Pin to Hewlett-Packard 25-Pin LaserJet, As Used By HP Cable #17255D

PC End		LaserJet End	
Pin	Signal	Pin	Signal
1	Chassis ground	1	Chassis ground
2	Transmit data	3	Receive data
3	Receive data	2	Transmit data
5	Clear to send	20	Data terminal ready
6	Data set ready	20	Data terminal ready
7	Signal ground	7	Signal ground

You can directly connect a PC-style nine-pin serial port to a LaserJet with a 25-pin serial connector using Hewlett-Packard's adapter cable model 2424G. Its wiring is shown in Table 8.23.

Table 8.23 Serial Adapter Cable, PC Nine-pin to Hewlett-Packard 25-Pin, As Used By HP Cable #24542G

PC End Pin	Signal	LaserJet End Pin	Signal
2	Receive data	2	Transmit data
3	Transmit data	3	Receive data
5	Signal ground	7	Signal ground
6	Clear to send	20	Data terminal ready
8	Data set ready	20	Data terminal ready

More recent LaserJets use nine-pin serial connectors instead of the 25-pin variety. The machines do not follow the IBM nine-pin standard used by the nine-pin jacks on PCs but instead use its complement. If you consider the IBM-style connector DTE, then the Hewlett-Packard LaserJet nine-pin connector is DCE. It requires its own adapter cable to plug into standard 25-pin PC-style serial ports. The necessary adapter cable is available from Hewlett-Packard as model number C2933A. Figure 8.24 shows its wiring.

Table 8.24 Serial Adapter Cable, PC 25-Pin to Hewlett-Packard Nine-Pin LaserJet, As Used By HP Cable #C2933A

PC End Pin	Signal	LaserJet End Pin	Signal
2	Transmit data	3	Receive data
3	Receive data	2	Transmit data
4	Request to send	7	Not used
5	Clear to send	8	Data terminal ready
6	Data set ready	6	Data terminal ready
7	Signal ground	5	Signal ground
8	Carrier detect	1	Request to send

Table 8.24 continued

PC End Pin	Signal	LaserJet End Pin	Signal
20	Data terminal ready	4	Data set ready
22	Ring indicator	9	Not used

The Hewlett-Packard redefinition of the nine-pin serial connector for its printers has one big benefit. You can connect a nine-pin PC serial port directly to a nine-pin HP printer port using a straight-through cable. Moreover, only HP's printers use only seven of the nine connections. Table 8.25 shows the wiring of this cable, which is available from Hewlett-Packard as its model C2932A.

Table 8.25 Serial Adapter Cable, PC Nine-Pin to Hewlett-Packard 9-Pin LaserJet, As Used By HP Cable #C2932A

PC End Pin	Signal	LaserJet End Pin	Signal
1	Carrier detect	1	Carrier detect
2	Receive data	2	Transmit data
3	Transmit data	3	Receive data
4	Data terminal ready	4	Data set ready
5	Signal ground	5	Signal ground
6	Clear to send	6	Data terminal ready
7	Request to send	7	Not used
8	Data set ready	8	Data terminal ready
9	Ring indicator	9	Not used

One way to avoid the hassle of finding the right combination of hardware handshaking connections would appear to be letting software do it–avoiding hardware handshaking and instead using the XON-XOFF software flow control available with most serial devices. Although a good idea, even this expedient can also cause hours of head-scratching when nothing works as it should–or nothing works at all.

When trying to use software handshaking, nothing happening is a common occurrence. Without the proper software driver, your PC or PS/2 has no idea that you want to use software handshaking. It just sits around waiting for a DSR and a CTS to come rolling in toward it from the connected serial device.

Sometimes you can circumvent this problem by connecting the data terminal ready to data set ready and request to send to clear to send within the connectors at each end of the cable. This wiring scheme satisfies the handshaking needs of a device with its own signals. But beware. This kind of subterfuge will make systems that use hardware handshaking print, too, but you'll probably lose large blocks of text when the lack of real handshaking lets your PC continue to churn out data even after your printer shouts "Stop!"

Finally, note that some people call cross-over cables *null modem cables*. This is not correct. A null modem is a single connector used in testing serial ports. It connects the transmit data line to the receive data line of a serial port as well as crossing the handshaking connections within the connector ad described above. Correctly speaking, a null-modem cable is equipped with this kind of wiring at both ends. It will force both serial ports constantly on and prevent any hardware flow control from functioning at all. Although such a cable can be useful, it is not the same as a cross-over cable. Substituting one for the other will lead to some unpleasant surprises–text dropping from sight from within documents as mysteriously and irrecoverably as D. B. Cooper.

UARTs

A serial port has two jobs to perform. It must repackage parallel data into serial form and it must send power down a long wire with another circuit at the end, which is called driving the line.

Turning parallel data into serial is such a common electrical function that engineers created special integrated circuits that do exactly that. Called *Universal Asynchronous Receiver/Transmitter* chips (UARTs), these chips gulp down a byte or more of data and stream it out a bit at a time. In addition, they add all the other accouterments of the serial signal–the start, parity, and stop bits. Because every serial practical connection is bidirectional, the UART works both ways, sending and receiving, as its name implies.

Because the UART does all the work of serializing your PC's data signals, its operation is one of the limits on the performance of serial data exchanges. PCs have used three different generations of UARTs.

The choice of chip is particularly critical when you connect your serial port to modem to it. When you communicate on-line with a modem, you're apt to receive long strings of characters through the connection. Your PC must take each character from a register in the UART and move it into memory. When your PC runs a multitasking system, it may be diverted for several milliseconds before it turns its attention to the UART and gathers up the character. Older UARTs must wait for the PC to take away one character before they can accept another from the communications line. If the PC is not fast enough, the characters pile up. The UART doesn't know what to do with them, and some of the characters simply get lost. The latest UARTs incorporate small buffers or memory areas that allow the UART to temporarily store characters until the PC has time to take them away. These newer UARTs are more immune to character loss and are preferred by modem users for high-speed communications.

When you connect a printer to a serial port, you don't have such worries. The printer connection is more a monologue than a dialogue–your PC chatters out characters and gets very little backtalk from your printer. Typically it will get only a single XOFF or XON character to tell the PC to stop or start the data flow. Because there's no risk of a pile up of in-bound characters, there's no need for a buffer in the UART.

If you have both a modem and a serial printer attached to your PC, your strategy should be obvious: The modem gets the port with the faster UART. Your printer can work with whatever UART is left over.

The three UART chips that PC and peripheral makers install in their products are the 8250, 16450, and 16550A.

8250

The first UART used in PCs was installed in the original IBM PC's Asynchronous Communications Adapter card in 1981. Even after a decade and a half, it is still popular on inexpensive port adapter expansion boards because it is cheap. It has a one-byte internal buffer that's exactly what you need for printer applications: it can hold the XOFF character until your PC gets around to reading it. It is inadequate for reliable two-way communications at high modem speeds.

16450

In 1984, designers first put an improved version of the 8250, the 16450 UART, in PCs. Although the 16450 has a higher speed internal design, it still retains the one-byte buffer incorporated into its predecessor. Serial ports built using it may still drop characters under some circumstances at high data rates. Although functionally identical, the 16450 and 8250 are physically different (they have different pin-outs), and you cannot substitute one in a socket meant for the other.

16550A

The real UART breakthrough came with the introduction of the 16550 to PCs in 1987. The first versions of this chip proved buggy, so it was quickly revised to produce the 16550A. It is commonly listed as 16550AF and 16550AFN, with the last initials indicating the package and temperature rating of the chip. The chief innovation incorporated into the 166550 was a 16-byte *first-in, first out buffer* (*FIFO*). The buffer is essential to high-speed modem operating in multitasking systems, making this the chip of choice for communications.

To maintain backward compatibility with the 16450, the 16550 ignores its internal buffer until it is specifically switched on. Most communications programs activate the buffer automatically. Physically, the 16550 and 16450 will fit and operate in the same sockets, so you can easily upgrade the older chip to the newer one.

Buffer Control

Operating system support for the buffer in the 16550 appeared only with Windows 3.1. Even then it was limited in support to Windows applications only. DOS applications require internal FIFO support even when they run inside Windows 3.1. Windows for Workgroups (version 3.11) extended buffer support to DOS applications running within the operating environment. The standard communications drivers for OS/2 Warp and Windows 95 operating systems will automatically take advantage of the 16550 buffer when the chip is present.

Windows 3.1 uses its COMM.DRV for controlling the buffer of the 16650. You control whether the buffer is activated by altering the COMxFIFO entries for each of your serial ports in the [386Enh] section of your SYSTEM.INI file of any member of the Window 3.1 family. To activate the buffer for a specific port, set COM*x*FIFO to one where the *x* is the port designation. To deactivate the buffer, make the entry zero. For example, the following entries in SYSTEM.INI will switch on the buffer for COM3 only:

```
[386Enh]

COM1FIFO=0
COM2FIFO=1
COM3FIFO=0
```

```
COM4FIFO=0
```

By default, Windows will activate the buffers in any 16550 chip that it finds.

Under Windows 95, you can control the FIFO buffer through the Device Manager section of the System folder found in Control Panel. Once you open on Control Panel, click on the **System** icon. Click on the **Device Manager** tab, then the entry for Ports, which will then expand to list the ports available in your system. Click on the **COM** port you want to control, then click on the **Properties** button below the listing, as shown in Figure 8.10.

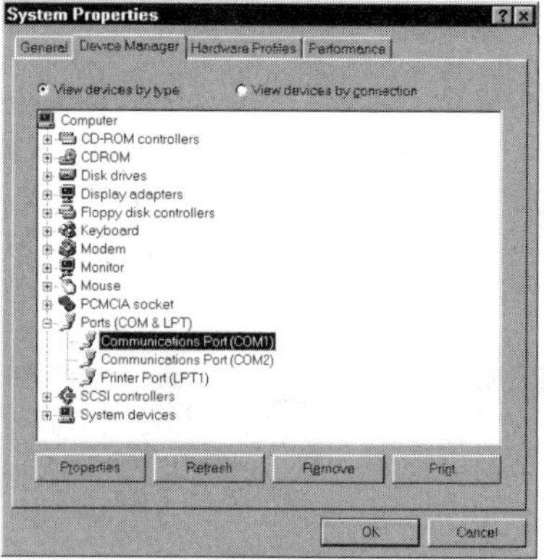

Figure 8.10 Windows 95 Device Manager folder.

From the Communications properties screen, click on the **Port Settings** tab. In addition to the default parameters set up for your chosen port, you'll see a button labeled **Advanced**. Clicking on it will give you control of the FIFO buffer, as shown in Figure 8.11.

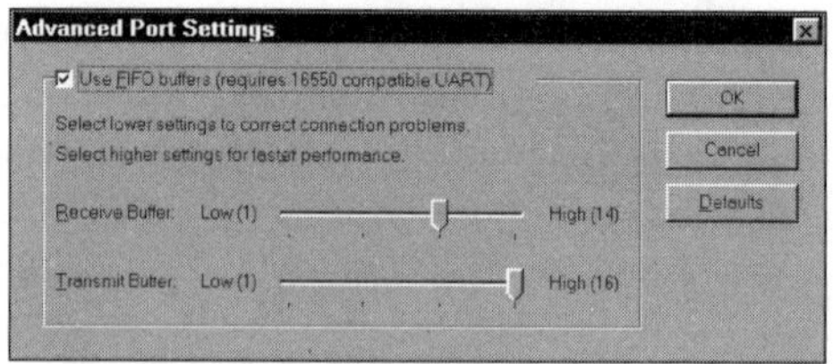

Figure 8.11 Disabling or enabling your UART FIFO buffer under Windows 95.

Windows 95 defaults to setting the FIFO buffer on if you have a 16550 UART or the equivalent in your PC. To switch the buffer off, click on the checked box labeled User FIFO buffers. The settings shown in Figure 8.3 are the defaults.

Identifying UARTs

One way to identify the type of UART installed in your PC is to look at the designation stenciled on the chip itself. Amid a sea of prefixes, suffixes, data codes, batch numbers, and other arcana important only to the chip makers, you'll find the model number of the chip.

First, of course, you must find the chip. Fortunately, UART are relatively easy to find. All three basic types of UART use exactly the same package, a 40-pin DIP (Dual In-line Package) black plastic shell that's a bit more than 2 inches long and 0.8 inch wide. Figure 8.12 shows this chip package. These large chips tend to dominate multifunction or port adapter boards on which you'll typically find them. Some older PCs have their chips on their motherboards.

Figure 8.12 The 40-pin DIP package used by UARTs.

Unfortunately, the classic embodiment of the UART chip is disappearing from modern PCs. Large ASICs (Application-Specific Integrated Circuits) often incorporate the circuitry and functions of the UART (or, more typically, two of them). Most PCs consequently have no UARTs for you to find, even though they have two built-in serial ports.

The better way to identify your UARTs is by checking their function. That way you don't have to open your PC to find out what you've got. Better still, you can be sure that the chip will act the way it's supposed to. Snooper programs will check out your UART quickly and painlessly. Better still, you can determine the kind of UARTs in your PC (as well as a wealth of other information) using Microsoft Diagnostics, the program MSD.EXE, which is included with the latest versions of Windows. After you run MSD, you'll see a screen like the one shown in Figure 8.13.

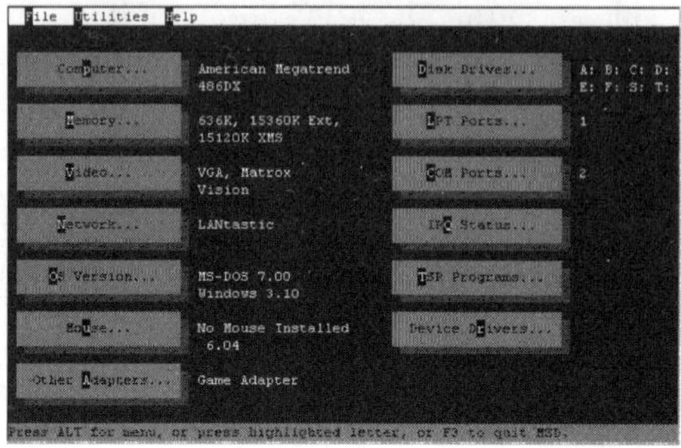

Figure 8.13 The opening screen of the Microsoft Diagnostics program.

From the main menu, choose the COM ports option by pressing **C** on your keyboard. The program will respond by showing you the details of the serial ports that you have installed in your system with a screen like the one shown in Figure 8.14.

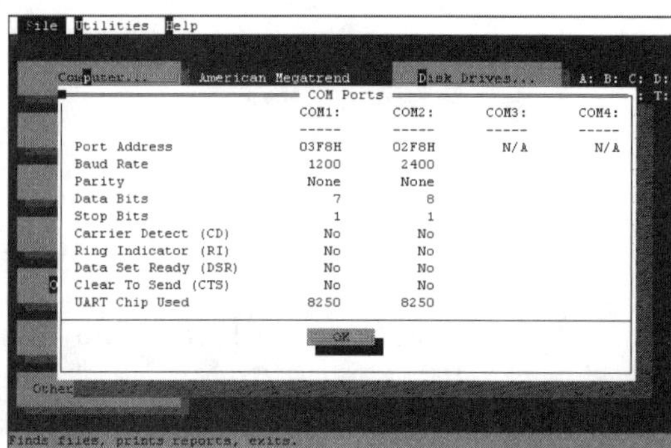

Figure 8.14 The Microsoft Diagnostics display of communications port parameters.

The last line of the display lists the UART chip used by each of your PC's serial ports. Use the more recent chip for your external modem if you have the choice; the 8250 chips (as shown in the example screen) are suitable for printers, mice, and other slow-moving critters.

Enhanced Serial Ports

Serious modem users may install an Enhanced Serial Port in their PCs, which act like a 16550 but incorporate higher speed circuitry and a much larger buffer.

Because you have to install such an option yourself, you should know if you have one. Most enhanced serial ports are identified as 16550 UARTs by snooping programs. They are unnecessary for serial printers.

Logical Interface

Your PC controls the serial port UART through a set of seven registers built into the chip. Although your programs could send data and commands to the UART (and, through it, to your serial printer) by using the hardware address of the registers on the chip, this strategy has disadvantages. It requires the designers of systems to allocate once and forever the system resources used by the serial port. The designers of the original IBM PC were loathe to make such a permanent commitment. Instead they devised a more flexible system that allows your software to access ports by name. In addition, they worked out a way whenever port names would be assigned properly and automatically even if you didn't install ports in some predetermined order.

Port Names

The names they assigned were COM1 and COM2. In 1987, they expanded the possible port repertory to include COM3 and COM4. The names that get assigned to a serial port depend on the input/output port addresses used by the registers on the UART. PCs reserve a block of eight I/O ports for the seven UART registers. These eight addresses are sequential, so they can be fully identified by the first, the *base address* of the serial port.

Because of their long use, the first two base addresses used by the serial ports are invariant, 3F8(Hex) and 2F8(Hex). Although the next two sometimes vary, the most widely used values for the next two base addresses are 3E8(Hex) and 2E8(Hex). Windows automatically assumes you will use these base addresses.

IBM devised an elaborate scheme for assigning port names to base addresses. When a PC boots up, DOS reads all base address values for serial ports, then assigns port names to them in order. Serial port names are consequently always sequential. In theory, you could skip a number from the ordered listing of base addresses and still get a sequence of serial port names starting with COM1. In practice, however, this can create setup difficulties. You're better off assuming that the defaults listed in Table 8.26 for DOS and Windows default serial port parameters are a hard and fast rule.

Table 8.26 Default Settings for DOS and Windows Serial Ports

Port Name	Base Address	Interrupt
COM1	03F8(Hex)	4
COM2	02F8(Hex)	3
COM3	03E8(Hex)	4
COM4	02E8(Hex)	3

Assigning alternate base addresses for higher port names when using the Windows 3.1 family requires adjusting settings in your PC's SYSTEM.INI file, which is normally located in your WINDOWS directory. If you look under the [386Enh] section of SYSTEM.INI, you'll find entries for the variables COM3Base and COM4Base. You can change the base address assignments by altering these values.

OS/2 does not abide the serial port scheme used by DOS and Windows, however. It makes provision for eight rather than four serial ports, and it uses different values for the all but the first two addresses. Instead of naming its ports COMx, it calls them SERIAL x. Table 8.27 lists the OS/2 serial port base address values.

Table 8.27 OS/2 Serial Port Base Addresses

Port Name	Base Address
SERIAL 1	03F8(Hex)
SERIAL 2	02F8(Hex)
SERIAL 3	3220(Hex)
SERIAL 4	3228(Hex)
SERIAL 5	4220(Hex)
SERIAL 6	4228(Hex)
SERIAL 7	5220(Hex)
SERIAL 8	5228(Hex)

Interrupts

Serial ports normally operate as interrupt-driven devices. That is, when they must perform an action immediately, they send a special signal called an interrupt to your PC's microprocessor. When the microprocessor receives an interrupt signal, it stops the work it is doing, saves its place, and executes special software routines called the *interrupt handler.*

A serial port generates a hardware interrupt by sending a signal down an *interrupt request line* (IRQ). PC expansion buses typically have six to twelve separate interrupt request lines. The ISA expansion bus is designed to allow one interrupt and one device to use each IRQ line. More advanced expansion buses like EISA and PCI allow more than one device to share each IRQ line.

Unless interrupts are shared, each serial port needs its own interrupt. Unfortunately, the number of available interrupts is typically too small for four serial ports to get their own IRQs. In most ISA computers, only interrupts 3 and 4 are typically used by serial ports. When you have more than two serial ports installed in such a system, some ports must share interrupts. Because ISA makes no provision for sharing these interrupts, conflicts can arise when two devices ask the microprocessor to use the same interrupt at the same time. The result can be characters lost in serial port communications, mice that refuse to move, and even system crashes.

The usual culprits in such problems are modems and mice sharing a port. Printers rarely cause problems because their interrupt demands are small–they usually need interrupt service only for flow control. If you have to share interrupts between devices, making the serial port used by your printer share usually is the best choice. It will happily share an interrupt with your modem's serial port and will rarely cause problems, particularly if you refrain from printing and using your modem at the same time.

Windows helps resolve serial port interrupt conflict problems. It lets you designate your own choice of interrupt for serial ports 3 and 4. As with the base addresses used by these ports, you tell Windows the values you want to use in your PC's SYSTEM.INI file. You'll find entries for COM3Int and COM4Int under the heading [386Enh] in SYSTEM.INI. Windows 95 normally will automatically identify your serial ports. However, you can change the settings using the **Resources** tab in the Communications Port Properties folder, as shown in Figure 8.15. You access this folder exactly as you would change FIFO buffers settings as described previously.

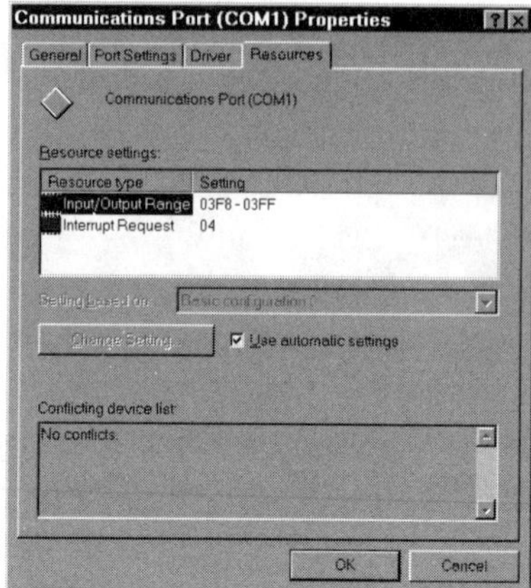

Figure 8.15 The **Resources** tab in the Communications Port Properties folder.

In any case, you cannot haphazardly assign any value to serial port interrupts and expect the serial port to automatically work. You also have to configure the port hardware to use the same address you've indicated to Windows. Most serial ports allow you to choose the interrupt from a short list using jumpers or DIP switches. You'll have to consult the manual accompanying your PC or serial port adapter to determine the proper settings.

Video Interfaces

Once a powerful interface that enabled you to push the limits of laser printing technology, the video interface now rates as little more than a historic footnote to laser printing. With current technologies and printers, it is completely unnecessary. Modern laser printers do not include video interfaces. They simply have no need to, and you have no need to use one.

Nevertheless, you may still encounter products that use a video interface, particularly if you go scrounging through the discards of graphic arts departments before other circuit scavengers get there. The video interface allowed you to push the limits of computer-generated output.

The video interface was a direct channel to the laser inside your laser printer. Through the video interface, you could control the exact instants the laser switched on and off which, eventually, would make marks on paper. Other signals in the video interface controlled the laser's scan so you could specify the position of each mark the laser would make. Because the interface allowed you to control the laser beam and its scan much like video signals control the electron beam and its scan in a video monitor, it was called a video interface.

In effect, the video interface allowed you to sidestep the raster image processor in your printer and substitute another of your own. Although few people have spare RIPs lying around, a number of third-party manufacturers offered their own for the LaserJet II series. Using an alternate RIP allowed you to advance beyond some of the limitations inherent in the Hewlett-Packard design. You could gain speed, resolution, and extra language abilities.

The typical third-party RIP was one or more expansion boards that fit inside your PC. You would then run a thick cable to a small interface board that slid into the video interface slot of your LaserJet.

You could increase the effective speed of your printer because most third-party RIPs used processors more powerful than those inside the LaserJets. Because the RIPs could race through image rasterization, they cut the most time-consuming part of the print job and push throughput closer to engine speed.

By the precise control of the laser signals, the external RIPs could improve the resolution of a given printer. After all, the size of the dots made by a laser printer depends on how long the laser stays lit as it scans across a line. Shorten the burn, and the dot size shrinks. The most precise third-party RIPs pushed up laser resolution from the then-standard 300 dots per inch to 600 or 1200 dpi. Usually the resolution increase was in the horizontal direction only. The vertical resolution of the laser was fixed by mechanical and scanning considerations.

Third-party RIPs could also add fluency in additional languages to your LaserJet. Most importantly, you could add PostScript. The necessary language interpreter was built into the RIP's ROM.

Note that modern laser printers boast all of these capabilities. Standard resolution in lasers is as high as 1200 dpi even in low-cost models. Most use power RISC processors in their RIPs for the fastest possible rasterization. And most laser printers now include PostScript (or a compatible language) as an option or even an add-in cartridge. Considering that the add-on RIP cost about the same as a PC, you can understand why the technology and the need for video interfacing has disappeared.

CHAPTER NINE

Printer Sharing

A modern computer printer can churn out more paperwork than you can produce on your PC, so sharing a printer among several people and PCs makes economic sense. One printer can serve many masters (and users). A printer sharing system can be as simple as a box with a switch inside or as complex as a complete local area network. Which you need depends on the printer you have (or will buy), how many people want to share, and the cost, effort, and frustration you're willing to endure to gain the benefits of printer sharing.

Two printers are not necessarily better than one—they are just more expensive. Like unwanted in-laws, printers usually spend most of their time simply sitting around and not doing very much, seemingly gloating that you can't get rid of them without a divorce. Although they might be ready to work, you may be pressed to come up with enough for them to do to keep them busy and justify the expense of having them around.

Yet the printer, unlike the in-law, has its redeeming value. Adding a second printer can even be tempting, if just for convenience sake. Better, however, would be finding a way to get more out of what you already have, to locate a full-time job for in-law and printer alike. You're in luck, at least if you want to get more from your printer. (The in-law problem is never solved but might be accommodated with family counseling.) Several technologies under the umbrella called *printer sharing* allow you to share a printer and its costs among several PCs and their users. In effect, by sharing you can turn your printer's idle time into productive time and eliminate the need for attaching a separate printer to every PC.

This strategy works because people don't print all the time—if we did, we would have no time left to create anything worth printing. Because normal office work leaves your printer with spare time, you can put it to work for someone else.

So goes the classic line of reasoning, the primary justification for printer sharing. But times have changed, and so have strategies. The biggest change, however, is that printer prices have plummeted. Today you can buy a new printer for less than the cost of classic printer sharing devices. Moreover, the cost-effectiveness of your options has changed. You can buy a pair of network adapters and configure Windows 95 to share a printer for a fraction the cost of yesterday's dedicated printer sharing device.

Then again, the cost of sharing has gone down, too. Today you can find a simple sharing device for under $20. Although elaborate sharing systems with management capabilities still are costly, you can stretch the usefulness of any printer to two to four PCs with little more than your lunch money.

Specialized printers, too, keep the need for printer sharing alive almost regardless of the cost. Top-quality color printers remain expensive, much more costly than even the most elaborate the sharing devices. For example, an art department might want to share a $5000 thermal-wax machine or a group of editors a tabloid-size laser printer for full-page previews. Spending a few hundred or even a thousand dollars on a sharing device to get access without the irritations of administering a network however modest can still make sense. In other words, printer sharing is alive and well. New technologies, rather than bringing its death, have brought you new options. And with every new option, comes new confusion.

In today's market many technologies hold the potential for allowing multiple PCs to share one or more printers. The range runs from the full-blown network to the simplest toggle switch. Which is best–and the best way to use each one–depends on what you want to share and how you work. One technique won't work in every situation. You need to know your options, their potentials, and their weaknesses before you can star sharing.

Overview

Printer sharing can be simple and physical. For example, you could just pull out a chainsaw, then dole the out small pieces of printer to each PC. But a printer sharing device makes more sense and lets you print more sensibly. With a printer sharing device, you can connect two, three, or a dozen PCs to a single printer, spreading the cost of an expensive, feature-laden printer among several people and PCs. If you're not prepared, however, connecting up the printer sharing device itself can cause enough of a headache to make the chainsaw a tempting alternative.

Background

In the early days of mainframe computers, printer sharing among multiple users was natural. After all, the power of the entire computer system got shared, and the printer was simply part of that power. Everything was centralized including the printer—or printers—a company's entire quota.

The PC changed that. Everyone got his or her own computer, separate and isolated from the rest of the organization, maybe even in a separate location (like your home). Printers migrated and multiplied along with the computers. Continuing a design tradition begun with mainframes, every printer had a single input designed for plugging into a single computer. No one noticed the limitations of this carry-over from days gone by. No one cared. They had just broken free from the bonds of the centrally managed computer and were reveling in their freedom. A personal printer for every PC was the price to pay for the autonomy gained.

When the PC moved from being a novelty to a business necessity and found its way onto every desk, the business bean-counters got involved and started mumbling mysterious mantras like "cost-benefit analysis." Suddenly printer sharing looked like a good thing, and the industry was born.

Sharing grew in two directions. Small businesses that had installed their first few computers sought low-cost ways of linking printers together. They had no established computer management system and didn't want to add an expensive layer of support to save a much smaller amount by sharing a printer. The sharing solution had to be simple, both in setup and operation.

At the other end of the spectrum, the folks who once had mainframes already had an established system of computer management. As they moved from big computers to PCs, the management people kept components together by linking them in networks. The complicated interconnections were already there, so it was only natural to add printers to the network to serve multiple users just as the mainframe printers had served everyone. In this situation, the sharing solution was complex but printers were only a small part of the overall plan.

The usefulness of connectivity and the computer network is not limited only to businesses that once had mainframes. Anywhere PCs are plentiful you can benefit by linking them together. Consequently, networks quickly moved down the business spectrum. To adapt the technology to organizations lacking skilled system management, a wave of new, software companies developed less complex networks such as Artisoft's Lantastic and Novell's Netware Lite. Finally Microsoft incorporated simplified networking into Windows for Workgroups (3.11) and Windows 95.

As a result, anyone with a few PCs and a printer to share among them faces the question of direction: whether to opt for a simple hardware sharing device or to go for the entire parcel of connectivity benefits, of which printer sharing is but one. The choice depends on how deeply you want to become involved in managing multiple PCs.

The dedicated printer sharing device lets you continue with what's essentially a hands-off approach. Your commitment ends as soon as you plug in everything. Nothing changes except what you plug into what. Every PC works exactly as it used to without changes to applications, drivers, or the operating system.

The network approach takes more involvement but pays greater benefits. Every PC must be equipped for sharing, both in hardware and software. Setup becomes more complex. The simple job of installing an operating system can stretch several times as long and may lead to interminable headscratching. Nor does the work stop with installation.

Strategy

In concept, setting up a printer sharing system is simple. You just run a wire from each PC that's to share the printer to the sharing device and then run another wire to the printer. You'd hardly think you'd need a degree in astronautics to figure everything out. But as soon as you try connecting up the cables, the complexities will be as obvious as the plugs that won't fit the jacks–and often won't work even if they do.

The confusion in cabling a printer sharing system results from all the available port choices. While simple sharing devices may all have the use of only parallel ports, more sophisticated equipment will offer you the choice (either when you order or when you hook everything up) of either parallel or serial ports. These port choices must be made at two places–going to and from the sharing device.

From the sharing device to the printer is often the easiest port choice to make. In most cases, standard PC printers offer only a parallel connection, so there's no port choice to make. Use parallel.

You have your choice of several printer sharing strategies, including those that use nothing but software and those that are hardware based.

The least expensive–in terms of out-of-pocket cost–is a simple A/B switch box. As the name implies, this device consists of a box of some kind that protects a multiple switch. The switch allows you to reroute all 25 connections of a printer cable from one PC to another. For example, in position A, your computer might be connected to the printer; in position B, a coworkers PC would be connected. It is the equivalent of moving the printer cable with the convenience of a switch.

True sharing systems give you the greater convenience of automatic operation. Of the various techniques, software printer sharing is generally the least costly. Most zero-slot local area networks have provisions for sharing printers. A zero-slot LAN allows you to connect several PCs together as a network using their serial ports. The only expenses involved in sharing printers this way are the software itself and some (relatively cheap) cable to connect the systems.

But a nonmonetary cost exists, too—the performance hit the printer server suffers. The PC connected to the printer is forced to spend some of its time spooling the print job and controlling the printer, which can steal a good deal of performance. No worker in your office is likely to want to use that PC for his daily work, unless his work mostly involves checking the output quality of the office coffee maker.

Arbitration systems determine which PC has priority when two or more try to print at once. The best sharing systems allow you to assign a priority to every PC based upon its need and the corporate pecking order. You should expect to get control software to let you manage the entire printing system to accompany the more versatile sharing devices.

Sharing devices also differ as to the number and kind of ports that they make available. You need a port for every PC you want to connect. You want parallel ports for easy connections, but serial ports if PCs are located some distance (generally over 10–25 feet) from the sharing device.

Some printer sharing devices plug into the I/O slots of printers. Although these devices limit the number of available ports because of size constraints, they also minimize costs because no additional case or power supply is required. A few printers are designed to be shared, having multiple or network inputs built-in.

When printers are expensive—as are better-quality machines like lasers and thermal-wax printers—sharing the asset is much more economical than buying a separate printer for everyone and smarter than making someone suffer with a cheap printer while the quality machine lies idle most of the day.

The fundamental difference between true networks and a peripheral sharing system is that the goal of the network is an increase in versatility and functionality. The peripheral sharing device uses the same topology but different technology to make more cost-effective use of equipment.

Peripheral sharing devices are often compared to networks, and in fact the two connectivity schemes often share the same topology. Nearly all peripheral sharing devices are arranged in a star configuration.

They differ from true star-LANs in that most are designed for one-way data flow, most often from several PCs to a shared printer. They do not allow file interchange or communication between their inputs. In effect, they function as a degraded form of network.

A peripheral sharing device is the best choice when the power of the network is unnecessary. For instance, electronic messaging is unnecessary in a work group in which individuals can communicate freely just by looking up from their monitor screens.

Peripheral sharing devices help make better use of a hardware investment without the headaches and overhead of a true network. They are generally easier to set up and much simpler to maintain.

Dedicated Sharing Hardware

The easiest way to share a printer is to use specialized hardware designed for that specific purpose. The chief advantage of this approach is that it adds the least complication to the operation and management of your computer systems. The other technique, the network (or subnetwork), makes printer sharing just one of many features from which your group of PC benefits. Along with the extra benefits come big headaches in setup, configuration, and day-to-day management. Given a choice, most people with only a couple of PCs want to avoid the hassles and costs of a full-fledged network, hence the market for dedicated printer sharing hardware is flourishing.

Most printer sharing hardware fits into one of two classes. The *switch box* is conceptually the easier to understand and certainly the most rudimentary inside. The true printer sharing device adds a wealth of features at surprisingly little extra cost. And, despite its added complexity, the printer sharing device is operationally easier to use and definitely much less susceptible to human error.

Choosing between the two should be a no-brainer. The printer sharing device should win every time. Often you'll find printer sharing devices with two or three inputs priced for less than comparable hardware switch boxes. Even when the sharing device costs more, the price difference (and often the overall price itself) is so small that it is inconsequential to all but the tiniest budgets. You can find some printer sharing devices for $20 to $30 from distributors of off-shore products.

When you need to connect four or more PCs to a single printer, you should always opt for the true printer sharing device. Trying to arbitrate between four people and their conflicting needs is more than a simple switch (and anyone less than a professional mediator) can handle.

Switch Boxes

The most basic of printer sharing systems is the humble switch box. Electrically, the switch box functions exactly the same as physically removing the printer plug from the back of one PC and moving it to the other. The only feature the switch box adds is convenience. You don't have to reach behind each system, fiddle with a screw driver (you *do* screw in your cable plugs into the back of your PC for proper grounding, don't you?), and fumble the plug back into place every time you want to link a different PC to your printer. A twist of a knob, and you've connected a different printer.

At heart, the switch box is exactly what it says it is: one big switch in a metal (usually) box that has a place to plug in cables. For such a simple device, however, you'll find an amazing range of variations. Switch boxes differ in the number of connections they switch, the number of devices you can connect, and the connectors and cables they use. Getting your printer sharing system to work requires matching a switch box to your particular needs.

Passive and Active Switches

Most switch boxes are *passive* devices. That is, they lack any electronic circuits inside except for a old-fashioned switch. Electrically, it is a wire that can be disconnected from one source and reconnected to another. In fact, the switch box is simply a convenient way of changing connections, letting you do with a knob what would otherwise require a journey to the back of your PC with a screwdriver.

The passive nature of the switch box has some substantial benefits. There's little to go wrong inside one. While lightning and other power line problems plague electronic devices, the passive switch box is immune. Moreover, the switch box is versatile. Just as you can connect a wire any way you want, you have the freedom to plug in the switch box any way that you like. The same box that lets two PCs share one printer will let one PC share two printers. The signal can find its way through the switch box no matter which direction it flows in. Moreover, switch boxes handle parallel and serial printer signals equally well (providing they carry through a sufficient number of connections for a parallel printer).

The passive nature of the switch box also has its downside. Because there's no active circuitry inside, you cannot change the port type or protocol. All devices connected to a switch box must therefore use the same interface–all must be parallel or serial (or whatever) devices. By itself, a switch box will not convert serial signals to parallel or vice versa. For that, you need a *protocol converter.*

An *active* switching device has electronics built in that may limit the travel of signals to one direction alone. With such a box, you cannot turn the connections around to tie two printers to one PC. Some active switches are designed for bi-directional operation and impose no such limit. To avoid surprises, you have to check the specifications of active printer switches carefully.

On the other hand, the circuitry inside an active switch often handles protocol conversion so you can link together any assortment of parallel and serial connections. Once an engineer goes to the trouble of designing an active switch with protocol conversion, he can easily make the switch automatic and add internal buffering to make a true printer sharing device. Consequently true active printer switch boxes are rare.

Poles and Throws

Switch boxes differ in the internal wiring they use. As with the rest of electronics and most of the universe, something more complex is more costly. Switch box makers economize wherever they can, simplifying the wiring and sometimes shortchanging you along the way.

Switches are classed by the number of poles and throws. A switch *pole* is an isolated wire connection. For a switch box, that means a single signal. A switch *throw* is a separate pathway these signals can take. A switch with two throws can route its signals down either of two paths, for example to one of two different printers. A normal light switch is classed as an SPST switch–a single pole, single throw switch. It has one circuit, the electrical power, and one signal pathway. Either it lets power down the path or it stops it, switching off the power.

Each pole and each throw add to the number of contacts required in a switch. The number of contacts is the product of the poles and throws. The more pole and the more throws, the more complicated and the more expensive the switch.

One way that switch box makers economize is by trimming the number of poles on their switches. They only need to include a number of poles equal to the number of active signals that you want to switch. With a serial connection that uses software flow control, three wires and three poles are sufficient. If you want hardware handshaking to switch through a box, the handshaking signals must be switched as well. A parallel port switch box requires at least 18 poles.

Advertisements and specification typically list the signals handled by a switch box. Serial switch boxes are often listed no only by the number of poles but also by the connector pin number that they switch. For example, an eight-wire box might switch pins 2, 3, 5, 6, 7, 8, 9, and 20.

Parallel port switch boxes typically have 18 or 25 poles. The former is sufficient to handle all of the separate signals used by a parallel port (pins 19 through 25 are the same as pin 18, ground, so they need not be duplicated). The latter insures that all wires in any cable will be switched through the box. An 18-pole switch box may not work with all parallel printers nor all software. OS/2 explicitly requires all 25 connections. Advanced parallel port designs like EPP and ECP also require a full complement of signals.

In fact, only the last kind of switch box, one with 25 poles, can be considered universal, able to handle both parallel and serial connections (but not, of course, at the same time). A box advertised as parallel may not work properly with serial printers that use hardware handshaking because pin 20 might not be connected. In other words, if you want a universal switch box, you'll want one with 25 poles.

Cables and Connectors

Switch boxes use a variety of connectors, and the connector choice directly influences the type of cable that you need if you want to have any hope of plugging everything together. You'll need to order cables to match the connectors your switch box uses.

Most current switch boxes designed for parallel port switching come equipped with either Centronics-style connectors (IEEE 1284 Type B connectors) as used on printer inputs or D-shell connectors as used on PC parallel port outputs (IEEE 1284 Type A connectors). Ideally, you might want a pair of female Centronics inputs and a female 25-pin D-shell so that you can link your printer sharing system together using nothing but standard IBM-style printer cables. Unfortunately most switch boxes use only one connector style. As a result, you'll need two or more different cable types to wire in your switch box.

In general, most switch boxes with 25 or fewer poles use 25-pin D-shell connectors. These allow you to use straight-through cables similar to those you'd use to link up a modem, only you must ensure that the cables provide a full complement of 25 connections. (Standard modem cables usually only use the basic nine signals.) Ideally you'll want this kind of 25-pole switch box to have *male* D-shell connectors so ordinary extension cables will work. If a switch box has *female* D-shells for its inputs, you'll need cables with male connectors on box ends or a gender changer (with male connectors on either side) for each cable, which will add substantially to your cost of wiring.

Switch boxes with 36 poles typically use IEEE 1284 Type B connectors. You link each of your PCs to the box with a standard printer cable. Then you need a cable with Centronics-style connectors at each end (and of the proper gender) to link the box to your printer. In general, a *printer extension cable* will work with these switch boxes, but be sure to double-check the connector gender on the switch box before ordering a cable. (The connector on the printer is a *female* Centronics.)

You have one additional concern with parallel switch box wiring: cable length. The total circuit path from either PC to your printer should never exceed the ten-foot limit for standard printer ports. (If you use a high-speed connection, the maximum recommended cable length is six feet, but the bus-like nature and individual device addressing of the advanced parallel signaling system like EPP and ECP make switch boxes unnecessary.)

A-B Switches

The basic switch box is usually called the *A-B switch*. The name is not an acronym. Rather the A and B are simple labels for the two PCs that share the switch. The typical A-B switch has two positions labeled A and B, hence the name. The inputs are correspondingly labeled. When the switch is in the A position, the A input gets connected to the output. When in the B position, the switch connects the B input to its output.

With an A-B switch, you plug the printer port of each of two PCs into the input of the switch box. Then you run a cable from the single output of the switch box to your printer. Figure 9.1 shows the layout of an A-B switch connection.

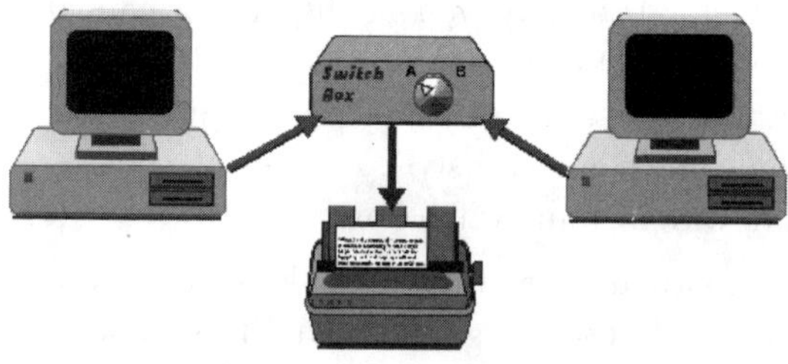

Figure 9.1 Printer sharing with an A-B switch.

Because most A-B switches are passive, you can turn the switch around and use the inputs as outputs to let a single PC link to two printers. This isn't nearly as clever as it sounds. You can get the same result more conveniently (and usually cheaper) simply by adding a second parallel port to your PC. You can then handle your printer switching through software by using LPT1 as the name for one printer and LPT2 for the other.

A-B-C Switches

There's nothing magical about two inputs on a printer switch box. Increasing the number of throws of the switch allows more inputs and lets us journey farther down the alphabet, from A-B switch to A-B-C switch to A-B-C-D switch and so on until you pass the limits of practicality. One big constraint is the availability to switches with so many throws and poles.

Another limit is management. Two people and PCs can usually share a single printer without hassle, but the more you add the more likely trouble will occur. When deadlines approach, you can expect open warfare when several people need to print reports in a hurry. Inevitably someone will have to stand guard on the switch box to ensure that each job gets through without some sniper sneaking in and killing a job by flicking the switch so he or she can get his or her own work done.

X Switches

Slightly more sophisticated than the A-B switch is the *X switch*, sometimes called a *crossover* switch. The basic X switch has four connectors that let you connect two printers to two PCs. In one position, the switch links Computer A to Printer A and Computer B to Printer B. In the other position, the switch links Computer A to Printer B and Computer B to Printer A. In other words, the connections cross over. If you connect only one printer, the X switch functions as an A-B switch.

The X switch doesn't accomplish the basic goal of printer sharing, cutting down on the number of printers that you need. Rather, it is for more specialized situations. For example, it allows you to share a laser and ink-jet printer between two PCs so you can select the technology you want to use for a particular application. In addition, an X switch can be effective when you want to share a printer and some other device between two PCs, for example, a parallel-port-based backup system.

Operation

The biggest recommendation for a switch box is the simplicity of its operation. Most people can readily grasp the basic concept involved. But the switch is not so simple in actual operation. You need to be very careful *when* you throw the switch.

You should change positions of the switch only when your printer is idle. Flick the switch in the middle of a print job and you'll jumble one job together with the other. Realize your mistake and switch back, and you'll mess things up further.

To share a printer effectively, the software on both PCs must be configured to initialize the printer before each print job. Otherwise, you can get some unexpected results. For example, consider what would happen if someone printed out a banner with six-inch-tall characters, and the next person wanted to send a 50,000 word report–and the printer obediently rattles out each word a full six inches high.

Other than those concerns, a printer switch box should work without trouble for a long time. There's little inside to go wrong. With the plummeting cost of other kinds of printer sharing, however, there's little to recommend the switch box. You can share for less with a more complicated technology and never have to worry about throwing the switch at the wrong time.

Printer Sharing Devices

The difference between a printer switch box and a printer sharing device is the knob on the front panel. A switch box requires that you give the switch a turn when you need to route a different PC to your printer. A printer sharing device does away with the switch by automatically sensing when one or another PC needs to use the printer. A switch box requires constant attention and good twist now and again. The printer sharing device is a set-in-one-and-forget-it peripheral.

When you shop for a printer sharing device, the magic behind its automatic abilities will be hidden deep below the surface. The sharing device is a mysterious black box (or more often, beige) that has several connectors marked "input" and one or two more marked "output." Somehow signals travel from one to the other, never crashing into each other along the way.

Printer sharing devices, particularly the lowest cost models, are more than anything else defined by the connections that they provide. As with the switch box, the inputs of the printer sharing device are connected to the outputs of several computers, and one or more outputs from the sharing device are connected to the shared printer (or printers). The inputs can differ in number and interface. Most people look no farther. They buy the box based on the number and kind of inputs it offers.

The differences between models of printer sharing device go deeper, and these under-the-skin subtleties can dramatically affect the apparent performance of your printer and even how well the members of the work group sharing the printer get along. A poorly designed sharing device can keep everyone waiting while some idle soul prints out ever more detailed bit maps of the Mandelbrot set. A good sharing device lets everyone print at the same time, then go on to the rest of their work. The printer sharing box sorts everything out and tells the printer how to pile up the jobs at the end.

The most important internal aspect of a printer sharing device is how it decides which of its inputs to send to the printer. It needs to exercise judgment, which in computer terms means it needs *intelligence* which invariably takes the form of a microprocessor of some sort. After all, any electronic device that has its own, native intelligence almost by definition today contains its own microprocessor. Only the most rudimentary (and increasingly rare) scan-based sharing devices get away with operating without the benefit of a microprocessor.

Then again, selecting an input isn't that arduous a chore, at least compared to the challenge of running 16 multimegabyte applications simultaneously faced by the microprocessor in your PC. The microprocessor need concern itself with something on the level of an electronic eeny-meeny-mieny-moe, and chips left over from the days before the first true PCs actually work commendably well. Many printer sharing devices are based on Zilog Z80 microprocessors, eight-bit chips dating back to the 1970s.

Most of the intelligence we credit to the printer sharing device actually results from the wisdom exercised by its designer. The combination of the hardware intelligence and wisdom in the design determines how well a given printer sharing device serves its users, how effectively it can divide up the time of the printer or printers it links to, and the cost of buying and using the shared printing system. The designer can take advantage of the microprocessor power of the sharing device to provide auxiliary functions such as protocol conversion.

In addition to intelligence, most printer sharing devices hold a substantial supply of *memory*. Acting as a hardware print buffer, the memory smoothes out the operation of the sharing device and helps minimize the waiting time at individual PCs. Most sharing devices will accept from all of their inputs even though they can only route one stream to the printer at a time. Print jobs not currently online build up in the buffer. Consequently most modern printer sharing devices not only help you get more out of your printer investment, but also speed up the printing process (at least from the perspective of a user connected to the device. The speed of your printer is, of course, unaltered.)

Scanning and Arbitration

Two different selection processes are used by various printer sharing devices, scanning, and arbitration.

Scanning is simplest, both in design and operation. The sharing device that uses scanning checks each of its inputs in sequence at a predefined interval (usually in the range of milliseconds) to see if a PC is sending it a job to print. Like a police-band radio scanner, it listens in briefly to check for activity–a PC sending a data signal out of its printer port–and, finding none, checks the next channel in a predefined sequence, typically something inventive like 1-2-3-4-5. The first active signal the scanning system finds gets routed to the printer. When the job is done, the scanning device continues its quest for print job requests.

The scanning system doesn't have to think much at all, and it only looks at a single input at a time. It can achieve a degree of fairness by resuming its scan after a print job at the next input instead of starting back at the beginning. That way if two or three jobs pile up while one is printing, the scanning device will service each one in order before going back to the beginning and giving the first input to print another whack at the printer.

In actual operation, a simple scanning-type printer sharing device constantly fishes for something to print. The sharing device holds all of its inputs continuously "not ready" except the one that it is monitoring at any given instant. Each PC that's connected to the sharing device sees a "not ready" printer at its output port and holds back its output. When the sharing device scans a given input, it switches the port to "ready," in effect dropping its bait in front of the selected PC. Then the sharing device waits to see if there's a nibble at the bait.

If the computer connected to the scanned input has nothing to print, it won't take the bait. But if the "not ready" signal has dammed up the PC, the change to "ready" will unleash the flood waters, and the print job data will come pouring out. The sharing device routes this data to the printer.

PCs may not respond instantly to the change from "not ready" to "ready," so most sharing devices wiggle their bait for a present period, typically in the range of a few milliseconds to a few seconds. You're often given the choice of the waiting period when you set up the sharing device.

If a PC doesn't take the bait during the scanning interval, the sharing device changes the status of that input port from "ready" back to "not ready," then switches to monitoring the next port. It keeps up its switching between ports, in sequence, after the waiting interval elapses for each one.

During the print job, the sharing device monitors the data flow, listening for a pause. When it detects a pause, the sharing device starts timing. If the pause exceeds a preset period (often one that you may choose when you set up the sharing device), the sharing device assumes the print job has ended and resumes its scan.

Some older sharing systems require an explicit "end of job" or "end of transmission" character in the stream of printer-bound data to indicate the conclusion of a job so the scanning process can resume.

You can readily see the primary drawback of this scan-and-latch mode of operation in a simple sharing device. The outputs of all but one computer are put on hold while that single machine monopolizes your printer. All the other PCs wanting to print may turn into vegetables or, more likely, complain with error messages like "Time out error on LPT1." Although the spooling systems built into modern application software will prevent your PC from locking up entirely, it can complicate the operation of this kind of sharing device. For example, the printer time-out error may abort the print job, requiring you to send it again (and hope that you get access to the printer soon enough). Or you may have to manually restart the spooler to try again. Although you save the effort of printing again, you're still stuck hoping for access.

Adding buffer memory to the sharing device helps ameliorate this problem but doesn't eliminate it entirely. Someday you'll run out of buffer memory—sooner than you'd think, of course—and face the problem.

You can also minimize the problem by adjusting the time-out settings for your printer. For example, in Windows 95 you select the Properties folder for your printer. Under the Details tab you'll find the time-out settings, which you can adjust to avoid errors. Figure 9.2 shows where you make this adjustment.

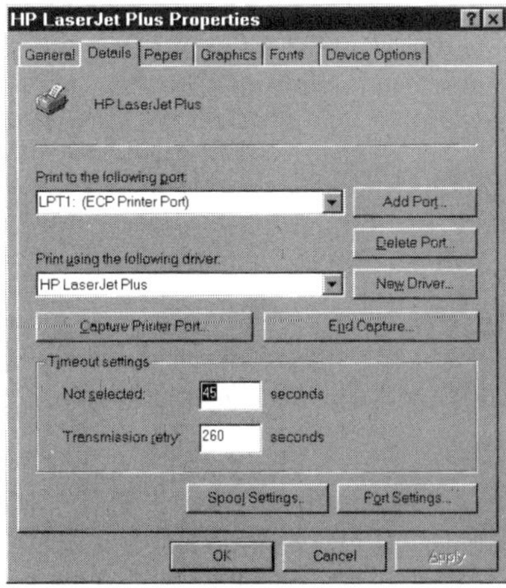

Figure 9.2 Setting the printer time-out period under Windows 95.

Although setting the time out to infinity (which is what you get when you set the displayed value to zero) would seem to be a sure-fire way to eliminate pesky error messages and needing to restart stalled print jobs, it will leave you with no way of detecting real printer and sharing device problems. In other words, exercise caution; it isn't nice to try to fool Windows. You're better off using the built-in Windows 95 printer sharing abilities, discussed as follows.

Simple scanned hardware printer sharing is mostly a convenience, the switch box without the switch, a way of permanently wiring together several PCs and a printer. It works well enough in the home or small business where printing traffic is light. The least expensive printer sharing devices use this technology.

Arbitration takes a more holistic approach. The printer sharing device constantly monitors *all* of its inputs. As with the scanning device, during a period of inactivity, the first PC to send out a print job gets its signals routed directly to the printer. If other PCs send out tasks while another job is printing, however, the arbitration process takes over. Because it monitors all inputs, the sharing device knows which want time on the printer. When the printer finishes one job, the sharing device does not simply look at the next port but instead considers the order in which request to print came in. It can then award printer access to the job and input that has been waiting the longest. Or it may have a list of priorities. The work of one PC may be deemed more important than the rest (it could be the boss's PC, for example) so it automatically gets raised to the top of the priority list for printing. Arbitration is the process used by the sharing device to select the next job.

Any arbitration system requires management of some kind. Someone has to assign priorities to each PC so that the sharing device knows which is the more important and requires access most often. The means of supplying this information to the sharing device varies with the device itself. More advanced sharing systems come complete with software that lets you manage the most intimate details of the system. In general, you'll get a menu-controlled interface that sends encoded commands from one of your PCs to the sharing device, which then holds its configuration in memory. Other systems have their arbitration setting fixed in their hardware and require that you prioritize by plugging into the proper ports. For example, port 1 may have the highest priority in printing, port 2 the next most, and so on.

Because of this need for management (which implies a need for a manager who will grapple with user needs and set priorities for them), the most powerful printer sharing devices are also more complex to set up than many people wish to deal with, particularly for smaller installation of just a few PCs.

Buffering

Prioritizing systems by itself will not eliminate the problem of PCs waiting for a time slot to use your printer, however. At best, prioritizing merely makes the delays more tolerable–at least if you're one of the users who has been assigned a high priority. Otherwise your frustration will mount with every moment you wait for control of your PC to return to you.

The wait can be eliminated almost entirely by adding buffering, either in your PC or in the sharing system. Most printer sharing devices include some amount of RAM that's devoted to buffering, using it to give the user of each attached computer the impression that he has direct access to–and the exclusive use of–the shared printer. With an arbitrated printer sharing device, the buffer can be split so that more than one of the attached PCs can simultaneously send print jobs to the sharing device and have the data stored until the printer becomes available to take care of it. The sharing device constantly monitors each input and routes whatever data it finds to the buffer.

When multiple print jobs get buffered at the same time, the sharing device cannot simply dump all the data into memory. The result would be a jumble of words and bits mixed into an incomprehensible mess. Instead the sharing device splits its memory into *partitions*, one for each job that it stores.

Of course, the data from only one computer at a time is truly linked to the shared peripheral. The sharing device merely collects the information that's sent from the rest of the attached computers and stores it in solid-state memory.

Although inputs are still scanned to find activity, the scanning process is handled differently by buffered systems. The microprocessor in control of the sharing device peeks at each port as quickly as possible–perhaps every few milliseconds–and looks for any kind of activity. If it finds a character ready for transmission, the microprocessor collects it and sends it off the buffer. In between the moments the microprocessor is examining its inputs and shuffling data into the buffer, it also sends data to its output port as quickly as the shared device can absorb it.

The earliest intelligent peripheral sharing systems enforced partitions of a fixed size, typically assigning one to each input port. These inflexible partition functioned as if they were dedicated print spoolers connected between the computer and sharing device. Each could hold multiple jobs, but each one faced its own, unalterable capacity limit. Once that limit was reached, the sharing device could accept no more data from the computer associated with that partition, even if other partitions are not full and the sharing device have available memory overall.

When such sharing devices have a large number of input ports, they may actually dole out relatively small amounts of buffer to each partition (and hence input) even when they have seemingly large memory endowments.

More modern and more sophisticated peripheral sharing devices allocate memory partitions dynamically. Each input then has potential access to all of the available buffer space. In that way large jobs won't necessarily run into partition limits. This scheme uses memory much more effectively and efficiently. A dynamically partitioned sharing device with a relatively small buffer can often actually perform better than a fixed-partition system with a massive amount of memory.

Dynamically partitioned systems usually allocate one partition to each job rather than each input. They are limited to the number of jobs they can handle simultaneously by a mixture of hardware and firmware considerations that determine the maximum number of partitions. Usually, this maximum is so large–for instance, 99 or 255–that it imposes no functional limit on the use of the system. In fact, the biggest constraint on the performance of such a peripheral sharing system is the microprocessor and its operating speed.

The housekeeping involved in maintaining a smoothly functioning sharing system can be formidable. The task is made even more complex when the microprocessor is charged with protocol conversion (for instance, converting serial input data to parallel output) or controlling several serial ports simultaneously.

As with any data processing device, an intelligent printer sharing device can suffer from overload. It receives more data than it can handle in real time. The usual symptom of overloading is a slowdown in the rate that data is accepted at each input. For instance, while a typical peripheral sharing device based on a Z80 microprocessor may be able to handle two or three serial input ports at a data rate of 9600 bits per second, adding a fourth input may slow throughput to a 7200 or 4800 bps rate. Data are still transferred at the peak rate, but handshaking intermittently stops data flow and constrains total system throughput.

Although bothersome, such degradation is a transient phenomenon. Throughput increases as soon as the input load decreases. Further, a simple slowdown is often more acceptable than denying one or more computers access to the shared peripheral.

Management

Managing the partitions in a hardware printer sharing device is exactly the same as managing print queues in a local print spooler. By issuing commands, you can alter the order in which jobs print, halt them, restart them, even duplicate jobs to make multiple copies. Not all hardware printer sharing devices give you the ability to manage these features, but higher quality ones (meaning more expensive) do.

The difference between managing a sharing device and a local print queue is only a matter of getting the commands to the sharing device. The only route available without further complication is through the same cable that carries data to the printer (and thus, the sharing device). Consequently the management systems for sharing devices often embed control codes in the data stream. The microprocessor in the sharing device detects these commands and carries them out.

The only problem is distinguishing commands from data bound for the printer. Text-only systems can take advantage of nonprinting characters like control codes and escape sequences for encoding commands. Modern graphics-based printing doesn't take kindly to such tinkering. The control characters would be indistinguishable from graphic data, so some images might inadvertently trigger the control system of the sharing device. To guard against such potentialities, most sharing devices use long sequences of characters to actuate their control functions. Adding a character to the sequence reduces the likelihood of a false trigger. Instead the sharing device might use drivers in each individual PC that would capture the printer output and suppress interfering data sequences, restoring them at the output of the sharing device.

The sharing device responds by sending data back through the printer port of the host PC. The form of control and user interface of the control system are the prerogative of the designer of the sharing device. Typically you can expect a menu system that translates your commands and the device's responses into an understandable format.

Wireless Sharing Systems

One of the most troubling aspects of a hardware printer sharing system is the task of snaking all the cables around your office. Ultimately they all converge in a snarl at the sharing device. After a few weeks, you might lose all track of which device is plugged into what port, and when you want to make changes or disconnect a PC, you face a selection process almost as random as playing scissors-paper-stone. One way to eliminate the confusion is to carefully document all the connections you make. Of course that's exactly contrary to human nature. This brings us to choice two: eliminating the wires entirely. You can buy a sharing system that works without wires, using instead infrared or radio waves.

One commercially available system is sold as the Printer Sharing Kit by Merritt Computer Products, Dallas, Texas. Retailing for about $240, the basic kit includes one small transmitter that plug into the printer port of each PC and a receiver that plugs into your printer. You can expand the system to as many as 16 PCs per printer by adding a transmitter to each PC (at a retail cost of about $120 each).

Each transmitter and receiver is switch-selectable to operate on any of four frequencies, allowing for a large degree of creative installation. For example, you can put four different and isolated systems in a single office or use the switch to allow a PC to access any of four printers. Both the transmitter and receivers are compact, measuring about 5.75 by 3.75 by 2.2 inches (HWD).

Besides the expense, the drawbacks of the system twofold. Its range is limited. The manufacturer quotes a maximum range of 100 feet, but practical installations may not reach half that far. Moreover, the system is slow because of the transmitter's low data rate. Switching from a hard-wire connection to wireless can slow a print job so that it may take six times longer.

Networked Printer Sharing

Sharing resources ultimately means adding a network. Although a network in itself does not automatically let you to share the various peripherals and files on multiple PCs, the network is necessary to enable you to share. The network provides the physical and logical connection between your PCs through which you can send any kind of data you want. All you need is the software to package and move what you want.

Printer sharing is one of the basic capabilities built into most networks. After all, the net results of printer sharing are exactly what networks are designed for–getting more from your investment in having multiple PCs.

Computer networks have a knack for knocking even knowledgeable PC gnostics down to size. They bring together the worst of all possible worlds: impenetrable software, inhospitable hardware, and cabling as confused as a pit of epileptic snakes. Installing a network operating system can take system managers days; deciphering its idiosyncrasies can keep users and operators puzzled for weeks. Network host adapters often prove incompatible with other PC hardware–their required interrupts and I/O addresses locking horns with SCSI boards, port controllers, and other peripherals. As to cabling–weaving the wiring for a network is like threading a needle while wearing boxing gloves during a cyclone that has blown out the electricity, the candles, and the last rays of hope.

In fact, no one in his right mind would tangle with a network if the benefits were not so great. File sharing across the network alone will eliminate a major source of data loss, duplication of records, out-of-sync file updates. Better still, a network lets you get organized. You can put all your important files in one central location where they are easier to protect, both from disaster and theft. Instead of worrying about backing up half a dozen PCs individually, you can easily handle the chore with one command.

Electronic mail can bring order to the chaos of tracking messages and appointments, even in a small office. With network-based E-mail, you can communicate with your coworkers without scattering memo slips like grass seed or felling a forest for paper.

Sharing a costly laser printer or large hard disk (with some networks, even modems) can cut your capital cost of a computer's equipment by thousands or tens of thousands of dollars. For example, instead of buying a flotilla of personal laser printers, you can serve everyone's hardcopy need with just one machine.

Fortunately, you can get all the benefits of network connectivity without its biggest headaches if you keep your needs modest and pick the right technologies. Although you still won't be able to plug PCs together with the same impunity as with Christmas lights, modern cabling will make the chore hardly more difficult than connecting a few telephones. Using such a modern smaller network won't require any more PC savvy than copying a file from a different disk drive. And installing the hardware–well, it will still take a bit of forethought and knowledge, but you can master those needs relatively easily.

Most computer networks are structured in several layers, piled on top of one another and linked together. Although this wedding-cake approach is great when you're designing network software, when all you want to do is get down to work, a birthday-cake approach that considers only two layers is much more tractable. Consequently, when setting up a small network with the principal intention of sharing resources, your primary concerns are two: hardware and software.

Network hardware involves three parts: a *network adapter*, the device installed inside your PC that sends and receives network-compatible signals; *network cabling* that provides a pathway for moving the signals between various PCs; and, optionally, a network *hub* or network concentrator that serves as a central exchange, linking together all the signals from PCs. Some networks do without hubs. More elaborate networks may involve other hardware devices such as gateways, but such complex arrangements are well beyond the realm of our discussion.

The cabling used by the network determines the kind of network adapter you need to use. In turn, the cabling is, at least in part, determined by the networking system that you want to use.

Over the years a true menagerie of networks types has been developed and unleashed on an unsuspecting market. Among the more familiar names you'll find ArcNet, StarLAN, and Token Ring. The most popular is the oldest of all, *Ethernet*, was originally developed in the 1970s at the Xerox Corporation's Palo Alto Research Center and usually credited to Robert Metcalf, who later went on to found 3Com Corporation. In September 1980, however, Ethernet became an open system when Xerox joined with minicomputer maker Digital Equipment Corporation and semiconductor manufacturer Intel Corporation to publish the first Ethernet specification. That original was superseded in January 1985, when the Institute of Electrical and Electronic Engineers published the industry-standard system now known as Ethernet as its IEEE 802.3 specification. Although derived from the original Xerox Ethernet, IEEE 802.3 is not identical and uses a different system for packaging the data that are transmitted over the network wires.

Network software takes many forms. It can involve a dedicated *network operating system*, which is software that in complex networks runs on a special PC called the *network server*. The network operating system (occasionally rendered as NOS) is like any other PC operating system in that it tells the computer how to run and use its disk drives. The NOS, however, is designed to read requests sent to it through the network, find the request files on its own hard disk drives, and dispatch the file back down the network. The NOS also handles requests and data sent to the printers shared by the network.

Individual PCs use *network drivers* that make the network resources (for example, the shared disk drives and printers) appear as if they were directly connected to the PC. The network printer driver intercepts commands and data that your system sends to its printer port and redirects it across the network.

Most smaller networks that you might use chiefly for printer sharing don't use network operating systems. Instead they use more elaborate drivers that allow individual PCs to perform some of the functions of servers. Because all of the PCs in such a network are theoretically equal and able to perform the server functions, they are considered peers and such network link-ups are called *peer-to-peer networking*.

Peer-to-peer means no dedicated file server as you will find in big, complex networks. Instead all PCs exist as equals. In general, one PC is simply granted access to the disk drives and printers connected to another. The same DOS commands apply to both the drives local to an individual computer and those accessed remotely through the network. Because most people already know enough about DOS to change drive letters, they can almost instantly put the network to work.

The most successful small networks today are built using two concepts–this peer-to-peer architecture combined with a simplified wiring scheme called *10Base-T*, which uses twisted-pair cables that are much like telephone wires (you can even substitute one for the other in a pinch). The combination of peers and pairs means simple installation, understandable operation, and low costs.

The twisted-pair wiring of 10Base-T means that you use exactly the same kind of cable as you would when putting in an extension telephone. You can even plug everything together with simple modular connectors. In fact, the biggest 10Base-T cabling trick may be keeping the wires from wrapping around your feet. A complete 10Base-T network can be easier to plug together than a printer switch.

In the past, you have also had the choice of subnetworks, sometimes called *zero-slot LANs* (Local Area Networks), which take use of one of the serial ports that's probably built into your PC to link up with other PCs. It's like a printer sharing device using serial ports but without the box. As with a true 10Base-T network, a zero-slot LAN needs nothing more than unshielded twisted-pair wiring. Because they use the serial port circuitry, however, their signals are single-ended rather than differential, and speeds are modest. At most, zero-slot LANs run at about one-hundredth the rate of Ethernet, 115,200 bits per second versus 10,000,000. Most take advantage of the handshaking signals available in the serial port to control the transfer of data. Most also require special cables or adapters to allow you to link together multiple ports. Worse, the software needed to run a zero-slot LAN is no less complex than that of a simple network, and it is just as complex to set up and operate. Once you consider the low cost of 10Base-T network adapters, their easy wiring, and the intrinsic connectivity of Windows 95, you can easily see why this technology has fallen from favor.

Network Hardware

Hardware doesn't make a network, it enables it. You need network hardware to provide the links between PCs you need for sharing resources such as printers. Although by itself the hardware won't let you share anything but your wealth with your computer dealer, you can't have a network without it. Moreover, the hardware you choose will determine how easily you can install the network as well as its maximum capabilities. Although the hardware won't be the actual network, it will be its physical embodiment.

Choosing network hardware involves two considerations: the hardware itself and how it is connected. The hardware comprises those network adapters, the wire between them, and the connectors that let you plug in the wires. The way you connect the PCs and printers together is called the *topology* of the network.

Wiring

You have your choice of two basic kinds of cables to wire a simple network for printer sharing, twisted-pair wire or coaxial cable.

Twisted-pair wiring is much the same stuff used for wiring in telephone systems. In fact, network twisted-pair cables look very similar to the telephone type, down to the modular connectors, but under their plastic jackets the two kinds of cable are quite different. Network people often use the acronym *UTP* to mean Unshielded Twisted-Pair wiring. In the Ethernet scheme of things, twisted-pair wiring is called *10Base-T*. The "10" indicates the clock speed of the network signals, 10 megahertz, and the "T" stands for twisted-pair. Figure 9.3 shows one of the more common forms of twisted-pair cabling, one with four pairs of wires in a single jacket used in wiring telephone (and many network) systems.

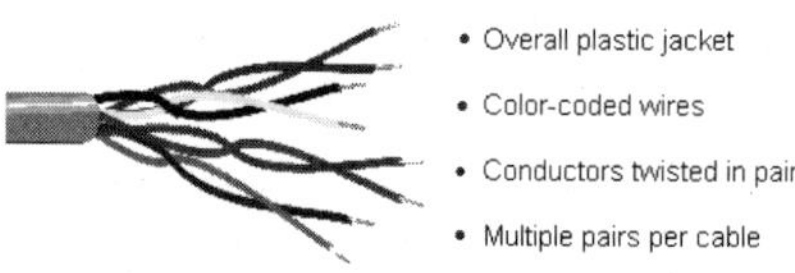

Figure 9.3 Unshielded twisted-pair cable.

Coaxial cable is similar to the wires you use to connect up your VCR or cable television box. Again, appearances are deceiving. Network and television cables are both round, black, and about a quarter inch around. The two cable types differ in their electrical characteristics, however. Ethernet wiring systems use two types of coaxial cables, 10Base-2 and 10Base-5, which differ in their diameters (and thus their signal loss over a given distance). Figure 9.4 gives a generalized view of a coaxial cable.

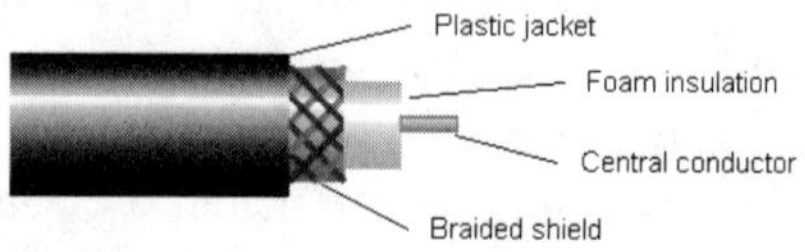

Figure 9.4 Generalized view of coaxial cable.

Modern networking systems favor twisted-pair wiring. One reason is that it's less expensive to manufacture and sell than coaxial cable. Moreover, the twisted-pairs themselves are easier to work with. And its familiar stuff, too, because zillions of miles of it have been installed in offices around the world in the last century to handle telephone communications. On the other hand, coaxial cable is better able to preserve high-speed signals when they are shipped across great distances. Using coaxial cables, a computer network can stretch for miles, probably farther than you'd ever need for simple printer sharing.

NOTE

Although you can use twisted-pair and coaxial cable for the same purposes in creating a network, they embody different philosophies and rely on distinct technologies.

Twisted-pair wiring earns its name from its construction. One connection comprises two separate conductors–a pair of wires–that are twisted together and wrapped around one another in a loose double-helix, sort of a enlarged, relaxed DNA strand. Because the electrical signals used by networks are quite faint (they're only about five volts), the actual wires in the twisted-pair are quite small, as thin as 28 gauge. The magic of the twisted pair results from the signaling system used across the wires.

Designers of network systems face many problems, but with the FCC breathing down their backs, one of the biggest is keeping radiation and interference under control. Like all wires, the cables used to wire together a network act as antennae, sending and receiving signals to the delight of spies and the dismay of nearby television viewers. As frequencies of signals increase and wire lengths grow longer, the radiation potential increases. The pressure is on network designers to increase both the speed (with higher frequencies) and reach of networks (with longer cables) to keep up with the increasing demands of industry.

To combat interference, most high-speed twisted-pair wiring systems in computer networks use *differential signals*. That is, the each conductor carries the same information at different polarities (plus and minus), and the equipment signal subtracts the signal on one conductor from the other before it is amplified (thus finding the difference between the two conductors and the name of the signal type). Because of the polarity difference of the desired signals on the conductors, subtracting them from one another actually doubles the strength of the signal. Noise that is picked up by the wire, however, appears at about equal strength in both wires. The subtraction thus cancels out the noise. Twisting together the pair of wires helps ensure that each conductor picks up the same noise so that it will cancel perfectly.

In addition, any radiation from the wire tends to cancel itself out because the signals radiated from the two conductors at any reasonable distance blend together. Because they are exact opposites, the blend results in nothing, no apparent radiation. Again, the twist helps ensure that the two signals are equally radiated so that they properly cancel.

The other physical properties of twisted-pair have won great favor from the networking industry. The thin wires are reasonably flexible and are relatively easy to hide. Telephone installers have been working with (and stapling down) millions of miles of the wire for decades. Moreover, multiple twisted-pairs are easy to bundle together, and major cables with 50, 100, or more pairs are readily available for wiring in businesses.

Making connections in twisted-pair networks is easy, too. Although some specialized tools are required to add connectors to cables, basic wiring takes little more than a screwdriver. When you need to do a lot of wiring, a *punchdown tool* ties a wire to a terminal block in less than a second.

Coaxial cable is a special two-conductor wire in which a central signal-carrying conductor is surrounded by a shield (a continuous braid or metalized plastic film) at ground potential which prevents stray signals from leaking out of the central conductor or noise seeping in. The shield makes coaxial cable naturally resistant to interference. It's called coaxial because the shield is centered at the same point as the inner conductor. The center of the inner conductor forms a long axis around which the shield wraps. Hence, both conductors share the same axis and the coaxial name.

The shield makes coaxial cable more difficult to work with than twisted-pair. Somehow you've got to wad all the braid or foil together to make a connection. In fact, coaxial cables require special (and costly) coaxial connectors which require special (and even more costly) tools to install.

The construction of coaxial cables makes them difficult to work with. They are relatively inflexible. Moreover a sharp bend can damage the cable, breaking the wires within. A kink in the cable can be similarly fatal. Compared to twisted-pair, it's fat and difficult to tuck under carpets or otherwise hide. Moreover, cables with multiple coaxial sets are rare and expensive. Every coaxial connection consequently require a separate cable and separate installation job.

Connectors

In computer networks, twisted-pair wiring uses connectors similar to telephone modular plugs and jacks. Where most telephone connectors use four or six contacts, the network systems use wider connectors with eight contacts. The standard plug used in 10Base-T wiring is called *RJ-45*.

Only four of the eight contacts on the RJ-45 connector are active. The rest are unconnected. The signal layout is such that inadvertently plugging a telephone won't affect the network.

The 10Base-T system uses pins 1 and 2 (corresponding to the blue and orange wires in the standard color code used by modular jacks) for one signal and pins 3 and 6 (corresponding to the black and yellow wires) for the other signal. Telephone circuits normally use pins 4 and 5 (the red and green wires). The wires in a 10Base-T cable are connected pin-for-pin, straight-through, from one end of the cable to the other. As long as you connect network adapters to hubs the way you're supposed to, you'll never need a cross-over adapter or other such nonsense used in other wiring systems. Figure 9.5 illustrates the correct wiring for a 10Base-T cable.

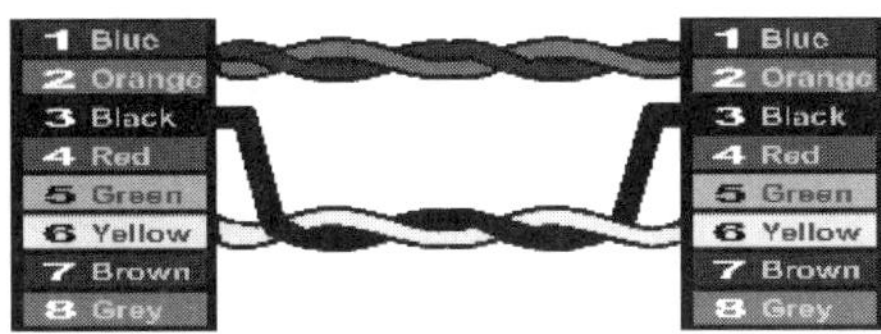

Figure 9.5 Correct wiring of a 10Base-T cable.

Despite their similarities, cables for 10Base-T are not the same as standard modular telephone wires. The 10Base-T system requires the pairs be twisted for their entire length. Modular telephone cables, where lying flat is more of a virtue than is controlling interference, typically don't twist their pairs.

Coaxial cables are less complicated to wire and connect, consisting as they do of but a single central conductor and a shield. With one conductor to worry about, it's difficult to screw up the wiring.

In the small networks you're likely to connect for printer sharing, you'll likely use only the 10Base-2 wiring system, which is sometimes called *thin-wire* Ethernet. This cabling system uses 100-ohm wire and BNC connectors. The latter provide positive locking so you cannot inadvertently pull a plug from a jack. Plugging in a BNC connector requires pushing it firmly into its jack and giving a clockwise twists until it turns no further. Releasing pressure locks the plug in place. To remove the plug, push it in again, twist it counterclockwise until it stops, and pull it out of the jack.

If all your PCs are in one room or reasonably close proximity, your best wiring choice for putting together a small network aimed chiefly at printer sharing is to use the 10Base-T system and buy prefabricated RJ-45 cables, which are available direct from several sources, in standard lengths (for example, 10, 25, 50, and 100 feet). You can loosely coil up several feet of extra cable without a problem. The only restriction imposed by 10Base-T is that the length of cable between PC and hub cannot exceed 100 meters (328 feet).

If you're planning a more permanent installation, however, you'll want to think about other alternatives. Few people enjoy tripping over cables or the look of a round, black line of a coaxial cable streaking across the living room carpet from one room (and PC) to another. While you could roll out the duct tape to keep the cabling under control, the easy way out may lead directly to the doghouse. If you plan on making your printer sharing connections more than a temporary measure, you'll want to find a more attractive course for your cables to follow.

Because of the similarity between 10Base-T cable and standard telephone wiring, you can permanently install printer sharing connections almost exactly the way you'd add a telephone. For example, you can hide wires within walls or staple them to baseboards, just as phone company installers are wont to do. Better still, for most of the cabling you can use ordinary telephone wiring and other supplies.

Telephone wiring has at least three big advantages: it costs very little, is widely available, and requires few tools and even less skill to connect up. You should be able to locate what you want in discount, appliance, and electronics stores–nearly anywhere telephones are sold. The only tools you'll need are an ordinary screw-driver and wire-stripper. No soldering is usually necessary. You need to avoid only those flat modular cables used by telephones because they lack wiring twists.

Perhaps the biggest advantage of telephone wiring is that you don't have to know how it works or what the signals are to connect wires together properly. It's all a matter of consistently matching colors. Standard telephone cables have four wires, one each green, red, yellow, and black. You'll find that many of the terminal blocks to which you connect the wires are similarly coded with the initials G, R, Y, and B molded into their plastic. The eight-wire jacks used by 10Base-T simply expand the color range with four new colors, blue, orange, brown, and grey. If you just match colors with those shown in Figure 9.5, you're sure to get everything right.

Modular jacks come in several styles based on the connector type and mounting style. Modular connectors vary in the number of gold-plated wires they use as contacts. The most common–the type you're most likely to find in the drugstore hardware department–is the RJ-11, which has four contacts. RJ-13 and RJ-14 modular jacks have more contacts, which are used by some low-cost networks, but 10Base-T wiring requires RJ-45 jacks. These look like overweight RJ11 jacks with their eight connections.

Both flush and surface-mount styles of jacks of every connector style are available. The flush mount allows you to hide all the wiring inside the wall. Double flush-mount jacks are available; these are great because you can use one jack for your existing telephone connection (to plug in your modem) and the other for your printer sharing connection, hiding all the wires in the wall. Surface-mount jacks are for the less fastidious. They allow you to run wires along baseboards, within walls, or wherever you want.

The easy part of a permanent installation is connecting the jacks to the wires at the ends of the cable. You need only strip the each conductor of the cable by removing about one-half inch of its plastic insulation, bend a half-loop in the stripped end of the wire, put the bare wire half-loop around the screw terminal so that twisting the screw in place cause the loop to close, and tighten the screw. Getting the wire between PC locations is the big challenge, one that you'll have to suffer through yourself.

Network Adapters

The signals across most network wires consist of packets of serial data, essentially blocks of bytes sent out one bit at a time. As strange as that sounds to you, it's even stranger to your PC which prefers to deal with synchronous parallel data. About the only things the two kinds of signals have in common is their electrical nature and the data they contain.

The network *host adapter* converts your data from one form to the other (and back again). In addition, the host adapter incorporates a control system that monitors the network wire, listening for data that is meant for your PC as well as pauses into which it can interject its own conversations. It also holds driver circuitry to boost the level of its signals so that they are strong enough to travel the length of the network cable unscathed. It's an amazingly complex electronic device that clever engineers have compressed into a single, low-cost chip.

Because the most common cabling and signaling systems for networks are widely recognized standards, the network side of these chips is also standardized, ready to plug in to your wiring. Unfortunately, the other side of the chip, where it makes its connection with your PC, follows no standard. Makers of network adapters have gone in their own directions in choosing ports, registers, and signals to operate their host adapters. They make up for their differences with driver software. Like a new paint job on an old car, the driver can cover up a lot of sins. On the positive side, however, driver software makes all host adapters work much the same (though with different speeds and capabilities) with most networks–as long as you have the right driver to match your network. Without the proper driver, a host adapter is scrap circuitry awaiting a scavenger. The network adapter circuitry built into some PCs and system boards uses the same chips and circuitry as dedicated (in-slot) host adapters, so they have the same need for driver software.

Some host adapters are widely enough used that other manufacturers have looked upon them as de facto standards and crafted their own products to match. The most popular of these are Novell's NE1000 and NE2000 host adapters. The principal difference between them is that the former matches eight-bit expansion buses, the latter matches 16-bit buses. Host adapters that emulate either of these products will likely work with most networks. Both are directly supported by Windows 95 (as are a raft of other host adapters). In addition, NetBIOS compatibility will ensure that the host adapter will work with most network software.

In the peer-to-peer network scheme you're most apt to use for printer sharing, you will be less likely to need to load programs through the network line. Consequently you need not worry about squeezing out the utmost in speed. Almost any network connection will far exceed the speed capabilities of the parallel port that you data takes on the final leg of its journey. A minimal host adapter, one using an eight-bit interface and only a single modular jack for plugging in the cable, with usually suffice for simple networked printer sharing. A 16-bit network adapter does give you more installation versatility, however, including a wider range of interrupts (15 for a 16-bit board versus eight for the eight-bit board) that you can assign to the board to avoid conflicts. If you've already got a number of peripherals inside a PC, you may need this wider interrupt selection.

For all intents and purposes, a network host adapter is just another expansion board for your PC. You slide it into a slot like any other board and have the same worries about resource usage. You will, of course, need one host adapter for every PC from which you'd like to share your printer.

Topologies

Linking together network nodes is more than a matter of cables and connectors. It also requires that you put the network in the proper arrangement, that is, how you run the wires from one network node to another. This configuration of the network is called its *topology*. You can imagine the topology of a network to be a geometric shape, which is where the name came from. In mathematics, it is the study of geometric forms and their distortions.

Three topologies dominate in networking: the bus (which is a line), the star, and the ring. Ethernet uses the first two; IBM's Token Ring networking system uses the last. For a simple network that aims primarily at printer sharing, the two Ethernet configurations are most important.

The original Ethernet design was based on a bus. Each PC (or other device in the network) was connected to the next with a coaxial cable, and so on down the line. In early Ethernet systems, each network adapter actually had two connectors to accommodate the connections to the PCs on either side. The first and last machines on the bus, which would connect to only one PC, required a terminator on the other network adapter jack. Figure 9.6 shows this prototypical Ethernet bus.

Figure 9.6 The basic bus configuration of a computer network.

In most modern Ethernet systems, this configuration is altered somewhat in the quest of wiring convenience. Each network adapter has only one connector. The network bus is a single cable. A short, separate tap from the main cable (or backbone) runs to each individual PC. A terminator caps each end of the network bus. Because only a single coaxial cable runs to each PC, you don't have to wrestle as much with wiring. The backbone cable can be tucked out of the way, for example running overhead in the ceiling with a tap line dropping down to each individual PC. Moreover, unplugging a cable from the back of a PC (for example, to repair or replace it) no longer breaks the network connection. Figure 9.7 shows the typical modern bus configuration of a modern Ethernet installation.

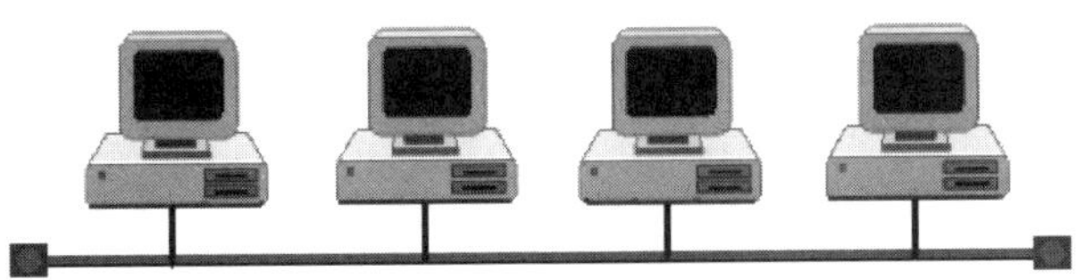

Figure 9.7 Typical modern Ethernet bus implementation.

The bus configuration is often inconvenient. It requires that an installer snake a coaxial cable throughout the area of the installation. Tapping in to the backbone cable to add a new PC inevitably interrupts the network (which means installers have to do their work when no one else is). And most other wiring in buildings doesn't fit well with the bus configuration. In most cases, all wiring from desks and workstations converges on a single place, the wiring closet. The bus is like a snake that sneaked out and won't go back in.

The most common application of twisted-pair wiring is the telephone system which puts a big box of switch gear in the wiring closet and runs a single cable out to each telephone set. You can easily transform the bus topology into such an arrangement by squashing the background cable into an interconnection box. All the tap lines plug into the bus but instead of being spread out throughout the installation, the bus gets confined to the wiring closet along with the telephone switch gear and dust bunnies that time forgot. In effect the bus becomes the network hub, as shown in Figure 9.8.

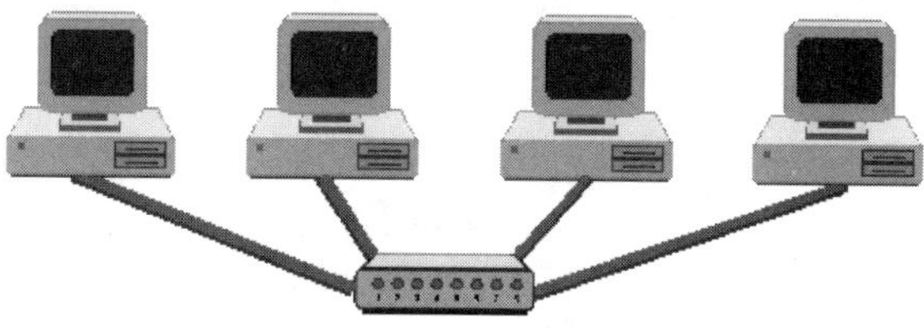

Figure 9.8 The hub or star configuration of a computer network.

The hub is more than a wire. The distance between the wiring closet and individual desks can be dozens or hundreds of feet, far longer than Ethernet allows for a cable tap. Consequently each connection to the hub is electrically isolated and amplified. Moreover, the wire connecting the hub and each workstation is actually two twisted-pairs. As with other species of Ethernet, a separate pair of wires runs to and from each PC even in this hub configuration, but the four wires used by the connected fit inside a single jacket.

In the basic hub configuration meant mostly for printer sharing, you need know little more about wiring or hubs. All you need is a hub with sufficient jacks to connect all the PCs and printers you want to use. As networks become more elaborate, however, differences become more important. Hubs, for example, differ in their management abilities (better, more expensive hubs respond to management commands from the system administrator to reorganize the network). In addition, you can like hubs together. Most hubs designed for 10Base-T Ethernet have extra jacks for coaxial cable for such interconnections. The 10Base-T specifications allow for up to four hubs in a network segment. (You can add even more using special network hardware, but that's beyond the scope of our discussion of simple printer sharing.)

Perhaps the most important aspect of the 10Base-T system is that it uses common modular connectors at both the hub and network adapter so that you can plug a complete network together even easier than hooking up a dedicated printer sharing device. The biggest practical difference in hardware installation is that you've got to add in a network host adapter in each PC instead of using a parallel port. (A number of new PCs have built-in host adapters for 10Base-T networking.) After you pass that hurdle, however, you've nothing to fear in installing hardware for a simple network.

Printer Connections

If you opt for the 10Base-T hub configuration, you're still left with two chief alternatives in connecting a printer to be shared. You can plug the printer into any of the workstation nodes and designate it as a network printer. All other PCs in the network can then access the printer through the designated PC. This arrangement is shown in Figure 9.9.

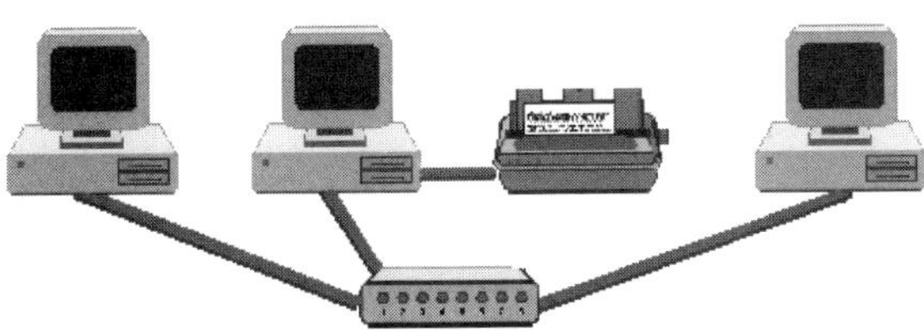

Figure 9.9 Connecting a network printer through a PC node.

Linking the printer through a PC eliminates the need for a network adapter for the printer, and it also saves a port on the network hub, allowing you to plug in an additional PC. On the other hand, the printer uses some of the resources of the PC to which it is connected. The microprocessor in the PC must manage the print job whether it is local or from another PC in the network. If the PC to which the printer is connected acts only as a server, this is not a handicap. But if the host PC also must function as a workstation, the need for printer management can hold back its performance. The PC will also have to give up some of disk space to spool print jobs. On the other hand, the rest of the PCs in the network will see the combination of printer and its PC host as a print spooler. Several PCs can print at once, probably at full speed, leaving the host PC to sort things out.

The alternative is to link the printer directly through the hub. All PCs can then communicate directly with the printer. This configuration requires either that the printer itself has a compatible network input or that you add a standalone network adapter to connect the printer to the hub. Figure 9.10 shows this arrangement.

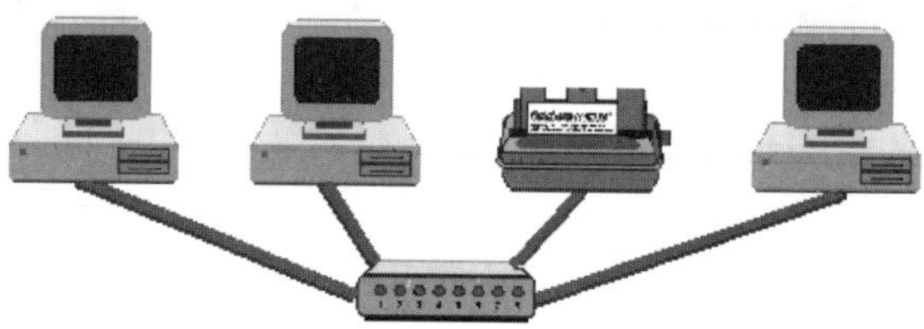

Figure 9.10 Network printer connected as standalone node.

Printers designed for networking have their own built-in network adapter connections. They plug right into the network wire. Of course, the connector used by the printer must match your network wiring system. More importantly, the printer must understand your network protocol, which means it must be compatible with your network operating system. More advanced printers have a feature called *automatic protocol switching* that allows them to identify the protocol used by the data they receive, decipher the data, and print it out. Such printers can accept data from different networking systems and make sense from it. You can connect such a printer to networks with nodes that run different operating systems yet still print from each node.

Sometimes direct network inputs are an option. One of the more popular alternatives is Hewlett-Packard's *JetDirect* system. Depending on the kind of printer you have, JetDirect takes one of two forms: a card that slides into the MIO slot of many LaserJet printers or as a standalone unit that plugs into your printer's parallel port. The system is available to mate with various network topologies and cabling systems including standard coaxial cables and 10Base-T twisted pair. The JetDirect hardware comes complete with software that allows you to directly address the attached printer using all of the most common network software systems including the networking features built into Microsoft Windows (such as Windows for Workgroups 3.11 and Windows 95).

When a printer has a direct network input, this is the easiest to install wiring system. Everything can plug together with modular jacks. The only penalty is the loss of a single port on the hub. Printers that have their own network jacks typically have sufficient internal memory to buffer several print jobs from different PCs so that the printer itself acts as a spooler. When you substitute an ordinary printer and associated network adapter, however, this system relies on the individual workstations to handle their own print spooling–fine for Windows 95 or OS/2 but problematic for systems that still run DOS. In any case, your network software must be able to directly address the printer for this topology to work. (Most do.)

Software

All networks need software to work. Nearly all use drivers (or, in the case of Windows, dynamic link libraries) to enable their necessary networking features: giving access to shared resources, passing data through the network adapter, and accessing data from remote PCs. All three of these functions involve matching of some kind: the sending and receiving ends must match their respective PCs and their software. The data that's passed must, of course, match the needs of the systems at either end. The bottom line is that your network software must match the operating system you run on your PC, and the two ends of the network must speak the same language to understand one another. That is, they must use the same networking *protocol*. The protocol dictates the form of the data such as the size of the *packets* (or blocks of bytes) that get transferred between systems, the addresses added to each packet so that it can find its destination, and the means of arbitrating network access and routing the data.

The software for building a network ranges from the trivial to sorts more complex than can be comprehended by the mortal mind. After all, the Internet that connects nearly every computer in the world together one way or another (through modem or direct connection) is just one computer network. No one understands the full complexity of the system or all of its software. Fortunately, to simply share a printer you don't have to understand all of computer networking or even the intimate details of how networking works. The software used by a printer sharing network need not be quite that complex or incomprehensible. For printer sharing, the lowest of the low end of computer networks will serve you well. Certainly networking is complex even that this level, but it is at least manageable. Although even the smallest networks involve a complicated software setup, many have automatic installation programs that let your PC do most of the work.

The networking software to use can be a religious issue. Some people still believe that there is only one true network. For the purpose of printer sharing, however, you can make a few simplifying assumptions that should guide your choice. First is that you'll want to go the peer-to-peer route so you don't have to waste an entire PC to act as your server or worry about the complexities of administering a major network. Second, you'll want something simple, proven, and inexpensive.

Your choice depends on what operating system you plan to use. If you're sticking with DOS, you need to buy a third-party networking software package. For small peer-to-peer networks, one of the more popular choices is Artisoft Corporation's Lantastic. If you're using Windows (either 3.11 or 95), the connectivity features you need to link a printer to multiple PCs are built into the basic operating system. You won't need any additional software.

Both Lantastic and Windows supposedly make printer sharing easy to install, almost automatic. Unfortunately, they don't make it entirely obvious. What follows is a discussion of what you need to know to start sharing a printer using either of these networking systems.

DOS Networking

To help unskilled people to set up a small network, Artisoft includes an automatic installation program with Lantastic. Run the program INSTALL.EXE from the distribution disks, and you need only answer a series of questions to install the network on an individual PC.

Before you start the installation, you need to assign a name to each of the PCs in your network so that both you and Lantastic have a way of identifying individual machines. You have other decisions, too. You need decide which machines you want to act as servers and which as workstations. The difference is that a server can share the printers connected to it (as well as its disk drives) with other PCs in the network. A workstation can use shared printers but cannot provide access to its local printers or disk drives to other PCs. A server can do anything a workstation can do and more, so you might as well make all your PCs servers–except that server software takes up more memory (about 30K) than does that used by a workstation node. In addition, a print server needs several megabytes of disk space to devote to spooling print jobs. If you're going to share disk drives, you also have to decide what drive letter to assign the shared drive on the workstations that will have access to it (you can use the same letter on each PC or a different letter on different workstations).

Once you've made all the decisions, you can quickly step through the installation process and let Lantastic tinker with all the vital files on your PC. You also won't know a thing about what's going on if you have to troubleshoot things.

Lantastic operates as a series of software drivers that interact with one another. One driver takes control of your network adapter. One provides a NetBIOS interface. One redirects file commands to the network operating system so that it can intercept your data requests. And a final driver links you and your PC to the network software.

Lantastic or any network operating system requires a bit of support in your PC's configuration files. So that DOS will recognize any shared disk drives, you'll usually have to add a **LASTDRIVE** command to your CONFIG.SYS file. As a default, Lantastic will add **LASTDRIVE=Z** so you can use any letter of the alphabet that's not the name of another disk drive for your network drives. Lantastic will also increase the FCBS, FILES, and STACKS statements in your CONFIG.SYS file (if their values are inadequate) so that the resources needed by the network operating system are available. The following values work for the majority of Lantastic installations (and are the defaults of the installation program):

```
FCBS=32,8
FILES=50
LASTDRIVE=Z
STACKS=9,256
```

In order to Lantastic to find the files and settings that it needs, it also makes changes or additions to your AUTOEXEC.BAT file. It adds the name of its own directory, nominally \LANTASTI, to your path statement so that the Lantastic programs will run without your explicitly typing the full path for accessing them. In addition, Lantastic adds two new settings to your environment in the form of **SET** commands. These are as follows:

```
SET LAN_DIR=C:\LANTASTI.NET
SET LAN_CFG=C:\LANTASTI
```

To set up the basic network, Lantastic loads four drivers from the DOS command line or through a batch file. As a default, Lantastic sets up the file STARTNET.BAT to load these drivers.

Four drivers are required, and they must be loaded in the proper order. The first must configure your network adapter hardware. Lantastic comes with a separate driver for a variety of different network adapters. The installation program automatically picks the correct one based on the board that you tell it you have installed. For example, the driver for a NE2000 network adapter is called

NEX000.EXE. This driver require several switches, IRQ= to indicate the interrupt used by the adapter, IOBASE= to indicate the base address of the I/O ports used by the adapter, a switch to indicate eight- or 16-bit mode, and a VERBOSE switch which turns on diagnostic messages. The NetBIOS takes the form of the next driver, AILANBIO.EXE; the network redirector REDIR.EXE, and the server program, SERVER.EXE. Workstations will substitute the NODERUN.EXE driver for SERVER.EXE.

A typical STARTNET.BAT file for a server would have these entries:

```
NEX000 IRQ=5 IOBASE=300 VERBOSE
AILANBIO
REDIR OFFICE LOGINS=5
SERVER
```

Once you have loaded these drivers, your network is enabled but is not functional. It is capable of passing data back and forth but has not established the names to use for the various PCs to which it is connected. The Lantastic NET.EXE program provides these details and enables network file and printer sharing. In a normal configuration, you must call NET.EXE several times. First, you must log in to establish a network connection. All PCs must log in before they are accessible by the network. Logging in uses NET.EXE to give the network the name you've assigned your workstations and servers.

After you've logged in, you can then make connections between one PC and another through the network. NET.EXE allows you to assign a printer attached to a server to one of the ports on a workstation. It also allows you to assign drive letters to networked disk drives.

The Lantastic installation process normally incorporates all of the required logging in and resource assignments into your STARTNET.BAT file. The entries of a typical setup using arbitrary names might look like this:

```
NET LOGIN/WAIT \\PRT_SRV OFFICE
NET USE E: \\PRT_SRV\C-DRIVE
NET USE LPT1: \\PRT_SRV\LPT1
```

The first line adds the PC called OFFICE to the network, linking it to a server called PRT_SRV. If the server is not available, the /WAIT option tells NET.EXE to keep control of the PC (and prevent further processing) until the server becomes available. The next line assigns the C: drive on the server to drive letter E: on the local PC using the option **USE** to the NET.EXE program. The last line enables the actual printer sharing, telling the local PC to reroute program output nominally sent to the LPT1 printer port to the printer connected to the LPT1 port on the server PRT_SRV.

The NET.EXE program also provides queue management for your print jobs. Running NET.EXE without command line switches loads the program in its menu-driven mode. Using cursor keys, you can select its various functions, among them being queue management. Using this facility, you can pause, cancel, or reorder print jobs as you would with a local print spooler.

Lantastic provides a wide range of other features that go far beyond basic printer sharing. You can control access to various devices as well as full network administration. Fortunately you don't have to deal with such details to make your printer sharing system work.

Windows 95

The connectivity features of Windows 95 are more than sufficient to share a printer (as well as disk drives and other resources) among a dozen PCs. Similar size groups of PCs running under DOS can use any of a number of small network programs, the most popular of which is Artisoft's Lantastic. More complex installations work best with full-fledged networks, which are beyond the scope of this book–or any single volume.

The set-up process involves two types of PCs, servers that will provide access to the printer or printers you want to share and workstations that will use the network to send print jobs to those printers. Each of these two classes of PCs requires its own distinct setup.

Server Setup

Before you can begin thinking about setting up your network software for printer sharing, you must have a working network. Installing the network hardware is only the first step. You must then configure your network workstations and servers to use the hardware you've installed. Windows 95 won't even consider letting you set up printer sharing until your network is operational.

The plug-and-play capabilities of Windows 95 helps expedite network setup. When you install Windows, it should be able to automatically identify your network adapter and set it up for proper operation.

Once your network hardware is properly set up, you must enable the PC that you want to act as a print server to share its printer. The control for this function is sufficiently buried so that you need a treasure map to find it. Start your quest by opening Control Panel by selecting it from the Settings menu from the **Start** button. From Control Panel, double-click on the **Network** icon to open the Network folder. You'll see a screen that tells you about all the network components that Windows has installed for you, which will look something like Figure 9.11.

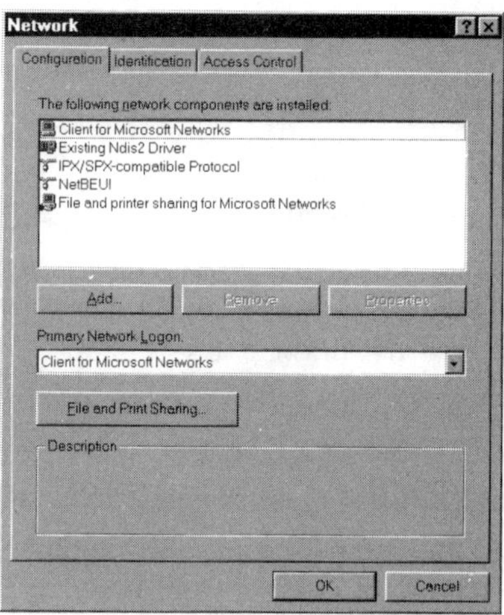

Figure 9.11 The Windows 95 Network folder.

If your network is operating, you don't have to worry about all the obscure entries on this screen. For your purposes, its only important aspect is the File and Printer Sharing button about two-thirds the way down the screen. Clicking on it will open a small window giving you the choice of whether or not to share system resources, as shown in Figure 9.12.

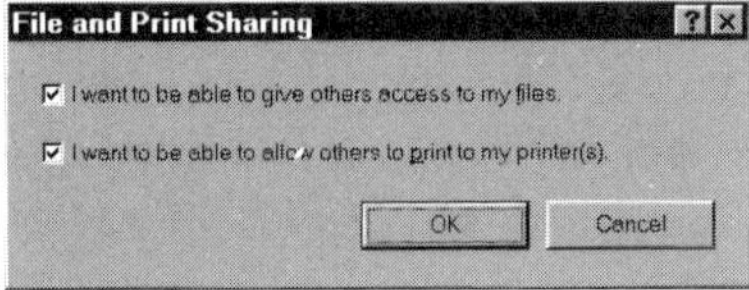

Figure 9.12 The File and Printer Sharing menu of Windows 95.

Your choices are twofold, sharing files and sharing printers. To share a printer, you only need to select that option. In most cases, however, you'll want to share files as well as put the machine to work as a server.

Once you've made your choices, clicking on **OK** will take you back to the previous screen, the Network folder. Click on **OK** again to exist back to Control Panel. At this point you've enabled the overall sharing abilities of your PC, but you haven't made any of the system's resources available to other PCs. To do that, you must alter the properties of each resource you want to share.

You have two ways of altering the properties of your printer. First, double-click on the **Printer** icon inside Control Panel. Windows 95 will display icons for each of the printers installed in your PC (as well as give you the option to install another). You can right-click on a **Printer's** icon and select **Properties** from the pop-up menu. Alternately, double-click on the **Printer** icon, opening the associated folder. From the Printer menu, select properties. In either case, you'll have a variety of tabs to choose from. Among them you should see a Sharing tab. If you do not, you've not properly enabled the printer sharing abilities of your PC, and you'll have to go back to the Network folder to enable sharing.

Once you select the **Sharing** tab, you'll see a screen like the one shown in Figure 9.13.

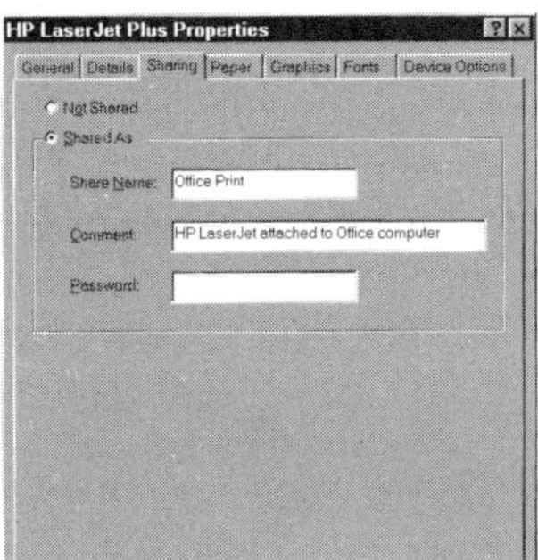

Figure 9.13 The **Sharing** tab of the Printer Properties folder.

When this tab initially pops up, it will default to Not Shared, and the lower part of the screen will be greyed out. Selecting **Sharing** will activate your other choices. You must give the printer a name by which PCs in the network will refer to it. You can optionally supply a comment so you can remember what you've done. This tab also provides for password protection for printer access. If you want to restrict printer access, you can enter a password here; otherwise printer access won't be limited.

When you're finished with your entries, click on **OK**, and you're done. Your printer can now be shared with other workstations attached to your network.

Workstation Setup

After you've enabled printer sharing from the system that is to act as your print server, you must individually connect each PC to it through Windows 95. In effect, you must install the network printer exactly as you would install a local printer.

Start by double-clicking on the **Printer** icon from the Control Panel in the workstation in which you want to install the networked printer. Windows 95 will respond by letting you choose to add a printer and, should you have already installed another printer, the choice of controlling the already-installed printers. If you've not previously installed a printer in the workstation, you'll see a screen like that shown in Figure 9.14.

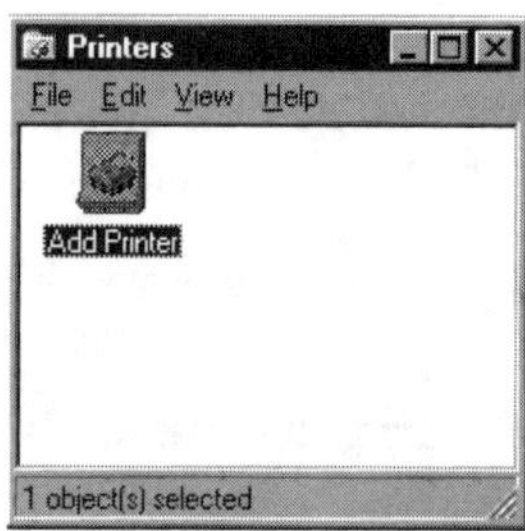

Figure 9.14 The Windows 95 Printer folder.

Choose **Add Printer** from the Printers folder. This will activate the Add Printer Wizard, which will manage the installation process for you.

When the Add Printer Wizard starts, your first choice will be whether to install a local or networked printer, as shown in Figure 9.15. The wizard defaults to installing a local printer, so you'll want to select **Network** printer. Then click on the **Next** button.

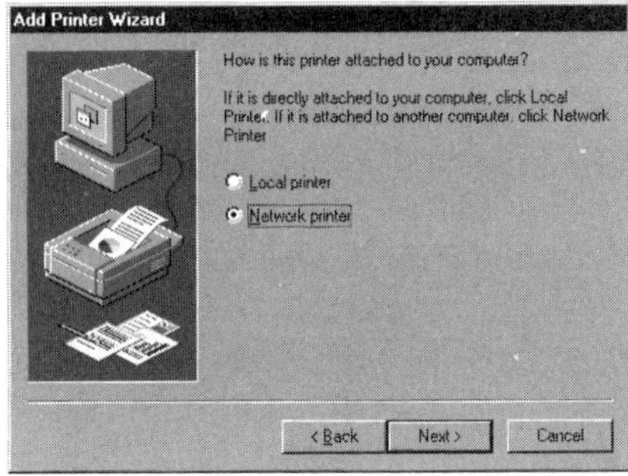

Figure 9.15 The first screen of the Add Printer Wizard.

In order to install a printer, the Wizard needs to know which printer you want. The Wizard identifies printers by name, and it prompts you to type in the name of the printer to install, as shown in Figure 9.16. This screen also gives you the choice of routing the print commands from your DOS programs to the networked printer. Odds are you'll want to use one printer for all your output needs, so you'll want to select the **Yes** button, too.

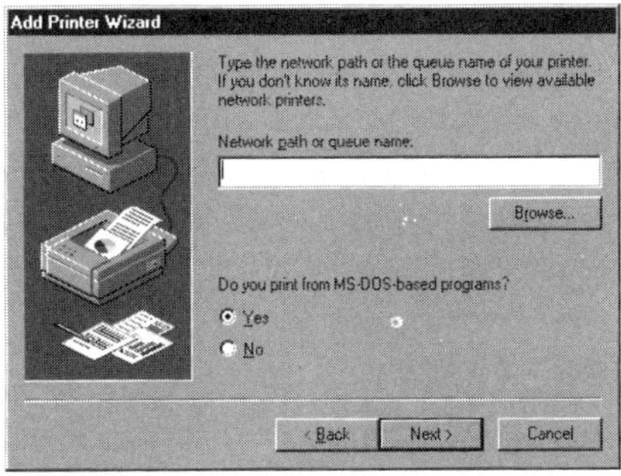

Figure 9.16 The Add Printer Wizard prompting for a network printer name.

Of course, you may not remember the complete name and path of all the printers in your network–or you may have given your printer a name so obscure that even you cannot remember it. You can ask the Wizard to find the available printers for you by clicking on the **Browse** button and looking in the likely places on the network. The **Browse** button is a good choice even if you know your printer's name because by selecting a printer from the names it presents you can avoid typing errors.

When you select **Browse**, the Wizard will let you examine your network using a tree-structured display. Click on the PC that acts as your server. The Wizard will then list the shared printers attached to that server, as shown in Figure 9.17. Click on the printer that you want to connect through the network to the workstation.

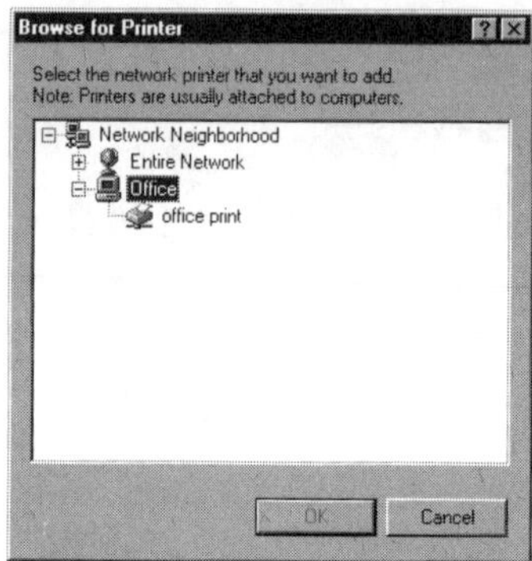

Figure 9.17 Browsing for a networked printer using the Add Printer Wizard.

If you've told the Add Printer Wizard to route your DOS print jobs to your networked printer, it will prompt you as to whether you want to capture a printer port to use as a channel for the printer-bound data. You'll see a screen like that shown in Figure 9.18.

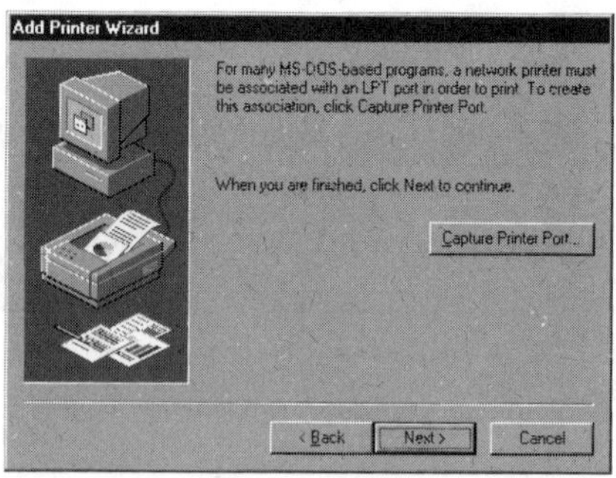

Figure 9.18 The Add Printer Wizard prompting for port capture.

Most DOS applications want to send their output directly to a printer port, so you're well advised to capture the port and route the data pumped into it by your DOS programs to your networked printer.

Click on the **Capture Printer Port** button and the Add Printer Wizard will respond by asking you *which* printer port to capture. You'll see a screen like that shown in Figure 9.19. The normal default choice, LPT1, is a good one. If you opt for that selection, install all your DOS applications to use LPT1 as their printer port. Of course, you can specify other ports to capture. If you do, you'll want to install your DOS applications to match.

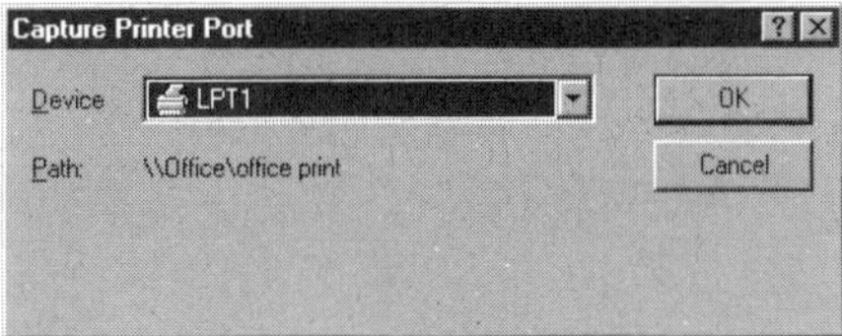

Figure 9.19 Selecting a port to capture for DOS printing.

Once you've chosen a port to capture, click on **OK** to finish the networked printer installation. The Add Printer Wizard will ask one more question, the name to use for your newly installed printer, as shown in Figure 9.20. This is the name that will appear on the icon in the Printers folder for the printer you select. It does not need to be the same as the network printer name.

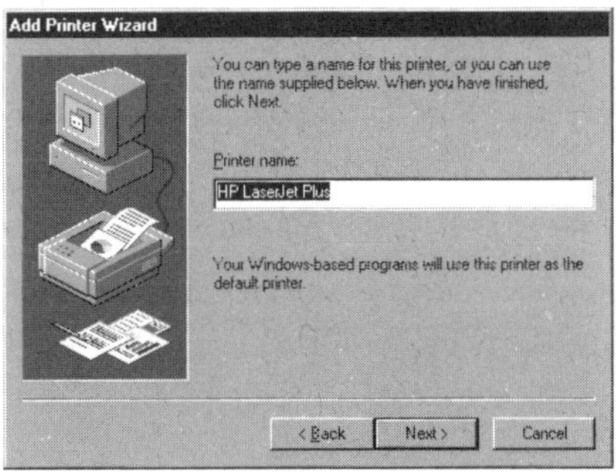

Figure 9.20 Giving a name to your networked printer.

To finish up, click on Next. The Add Printer Wizard will then copy the driver files necessary for your applications and printer to your local PC automatically. You can then take control of the network printer as if it were locally connected to your workstation–only you'll have to walk farther to fill the paper tray.

CHAPTER TEN

Fonts

Although you might consider the look of your text a simple matter of aesthetics, it is a major influence on the impact and feeling of what you print–in other words, how well you communicate. Today's bit-image printers are adept at forming your text into characters of virtually any size, alignment, and look. The shapes of the various characters of an alphabet define a font, and printer fonts are available in wide variety–and various compatibilities. This chapter helps you understand fonts and how to manage them effectively.

When you print text, every letter is important, and if you care about what you print, the look of each character is an important part of the overall expression and impression of your work. The appropriate choice of the visual look of your documents can add weight or airiness, authority or frivolity, readability or confusion. At this point, you're dealing with the aesthetics of printing at its most intimate level, the shapes and characteristics of each letter and figure you print, that is, typefaces.

Modern printer technology makes working with different typefaces more than a matter of aesthetics. The character designs have to come from somewhere. Ultimately, of course, typeface designs originate in the minds of artists. But once the typeface designs are created and perfected, they must somehow get to your printer and, through it, to your printed output. In order that you can save, manipulate, and move around fonts, you must reduce their aesthetics to some form your PC and printer can store and move around. They require a storage format. As with anything else where a PC requires a standard, developers have come up with several that embrace various technologies.

Background

Before we can discuss how you work with and what you can do with text characters, you need to know what distinguishes them. The characters you print have both aesthetic and technical characteristics. The aesthetics define how each character looks. The technical qualities define how you get the character to begin with, what your PC can do with it, and finally how it prints.

The aesthetic characteristics at least can trace their heritage back to the primeval days of printing, when newspapers, books, and broadsides were made by but one method, the *letterpress*. The technology was essentially the durable rubber stamp. The printer smeared ink on a raised letters, then pressed them against a sheet of paper. The high points on the characters contacted the paper and pushed off the ink onto it. Each character was an individual piece of type made from lead, molded into the desired shape when the lead was hot and molten. Modern day typographers call this technology *hot type* because of the high temperature process used to form the individual pieces of type. Each character or piece of lead in a hot type font is called a *slug*.

Modern commercial printing has cast aside the letterpress in favor of *offset printing*. Instead of molded characters, offset uses printing plates made photographically. Text characters are made by phototypesetting machines that set pages of type by exposing film to character shapes, and character sizes could be adjusted optically much like zooming a camera lens. The typesetting technique is commonly called *cold type* to contrast it with the hot type process. This technology dates from the middle of the twentieth century, with the first photocomposition machines debuting in France (the Photon and Fotosetter) in 1944.

Although computer printers don't use ordinary offset technology, they do compose documents using optical technology that's based on principle similar to cold type composition. The supply of characters is limitless, each one dutifully copied from a master, used as often as needed.

Typefaces

The aesthetics of textual printing begins with the *typeface*, a set of characters that includes the standard alphabet, the various numerals, punctuation marks, and often addition symbols used for expressing written ideas. Each typeface has a unique design that is defined by the shapes of all of the characters it contains as well as the thickness of the lines that make up the shapes. The shapes of individual characters varies widely and includes such elements as height (including whether a character towers over the others or hangs its tail down below the rest), width, and slant. The line weight can be uniform throughout all characters or it can vary within shapes much as the width of lines of written text vary in old-fashioned formal handwriting (like Spencerian script).

Families

A *typeface family* is a collection of several typefaces that shares the same underlying aesthetics but vary in some essential aspects of their design such as line weight or slant. Several of these variations are common among popular typefaces and have names that have become essentially generic. Among these are the following:

- **Roman** describes characters that stand in normal, straight-backed fashion. They are the normal characters used for printing and, in PC applications, are simply called *normal* characters.
- **Italic** describes the alternative characters that, instead of printing bolt upright, lean to the right. Italic characters often have a bit more flair, a more calligraphic touch with broader curves and wiggly tails. Because they stand out when contrasted with normal Roman characters, italics are often used for emphasis. Note that some typeface families use the word "Roman" in their names (such as Times Roman), and the italic faces of these families bear names that are somewhat self-contradictory (such as Times Roman italic).
- **Boldface** or simply bold characters have a heavier or thicker line width, putting more ink on paper and more emphasis in the text. A typeface family sometimes offers several variations in boldface design. For example, a demibold face is in between Roman and boldface in weight.

Some typefaces use the term *heavyweight* to describe boldface. Typefaces in which the boldface characteristics are particularly exaggerated are often called *extra heavy*. Alternately, bold characters may be termed *dark*. The choice of term depends on little more than the whim of the typeface designer.

- **Light** characters are the opposite of boldface. The individual lines or strokes of each character are finer than those of the normal or Roman face, giving a lighter, more airy feel to the typeface.

- **Condensed** characters get horizontally squeezed. Although they maintain the same height as the normal face, they end up narrower, so more will fit on a line of type. When characters are squeezed very tightly, they may be described as *extra condensed*. Some typefaces simply call their condensed variations *narrow*.
- **Expanded** characters stretch out horizontally. They, too, are the same height as the normal characters of a given face but are wider. They take up more room and provide an additional means for emphasizing words or lines of text. Expanded characters are sometimes called *wide*.

Many of these characteristics can be combined in a single typeface, for example, condensed boldface. Boldface and light characters are mutually exclusive, as are the condensed and expanded characteristics, although some computer printers allow you to combine condensed and expanded characters to get additional effects for extra emphasis. Most PC and printer typefaces include four basic variations: Roman, italic, boldface, and bold italic.

Designers typically give each typeface an individual name. These typically are based on the name of the designer (for example, Baskerville, Caslon, or Goudy), a particular purpose (Times Roman was specifically designed for the print of the *London Times*), an aesthetics objective (think Avant Garde or Futura), or simply the whim of the designer (like Ransom Note). Individual members of a typeface family are descriptively distinguished by how they vary from the normal or Roman face, for example Caslon bold.

Some designers have opted to designate typeface variations with numbers instead of increasingly abstruse names. In general, the designer uses these *typeface numbers* to distinguish variations in weight and width for large typeface families. Most numbering schemes use two digits. The first indicates the character weight with low numbers indicating light faces and higher numbers being increasingly bold. The second digit indicates character width. Low numbers indicate wide face, and higher values indicate narrower or more condensed characters.

- **Effects** is the name Microsoft gives to some alterations made to typefaces that really do not define a new typeface or family but simply emphasize or enhance an existing typeface. Under Microsoft's definition these effects include underlining, strike-through, and color. In effect, these typeface effects are character attributes applied to a typeface.

Design

The design of typefaces is an art, one that's little appreciated except by other typeface designers. Most people take typefaces for granted. Good faces are often ignored like clean water and pure air until the moment you encounter an illegible one. In years past, designers have devoted years of their lives to creating their version of the perfect typeface. Some of these designs have won their own preeminent places in typography, highly regarded and well used even unto today. Today the PC and font creation and manipulation programs (like Typographer) have made font design almost easy, and fonts have proliferated, some designers churning out a new one every few weeks. Yet some old fonts still persevere, a testament to all the work and artistry that went into their design.

Every line of type has a single unifying characteristic, the one that makes it a line. All characters on the line have a single base or foundation upon which they sit called the *baseline*. Rather than real, the baseline is imaginary, simply a horizontal position that defines the bottom of most characters.

All characters rise above the baseline. A few, however, have extensions that dip below it. The low-reaching portions of these characters are *descenders*. (The characters with descenders are themselves often termed descenders, too.) In most typefaces, the lowercase letters g, j, p, q, and y have descenders. In some typefaces (most often italic) a few capital letters also descend, most commonly J and Y.

In most typefaces, characters rise to one of two distinct heights above the baseline, the tallest characters being the capital letters. The height of the top of most capital letters above the baseline is called *cap height*. Most lowercase characters extend only about halfway up to cap height. The height of these lowercase characters is termed *x-height*, which is nominally the height of the lowercase letter x. Figure 10.1 illustrates these concepts.

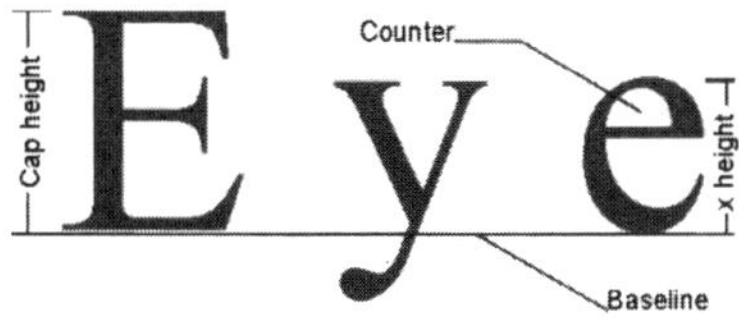

Figure 10.1 Typeface measurement nomenclature.

The portion of the few lowercase characters that rises above x-height is called an *ascender*. In most typefaces, the ascending lowercase characters include b, d, f, h, k, l, and t. The lowercase i and j typically have an ascending dot. Figure 10.2 illustrates these definitions.

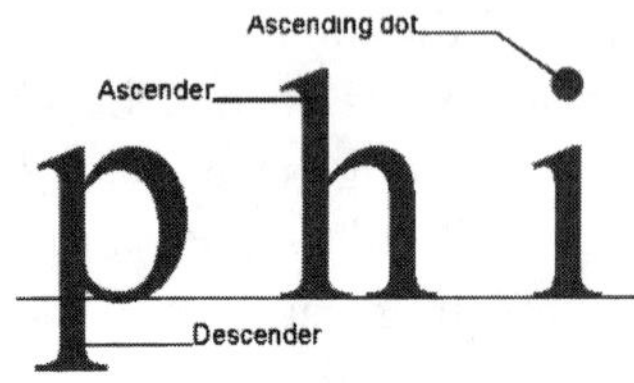

Figure 10.2 Ascenders and descenders.

The height of ascenders and descenders varies within a font at the typographer's discretion. Making all the same often is not aesthetically pleasing because the human eye perceives rounded characters as taller than those that are straight. Rounded characters must ascend higher or descend lower than the flat characters in a font in order to appear to have the same height.

Most characters are initially defined by a single vertical stroke. In typeface terminology, that vertical stroke is called the *stem* of the character. Several characters in our alphabet have round or circular portions that totally enclose a white space. This white space is called the *counter.*

By convention a single design element called the *serif* separates all typefaces into two classes. A serif is a short finishing stroke or fillip that crosses the main stroke of a character most often at the baseline and top of the character, although some serifs may be vertical (as on the letter s). Serifs, at least in theory, help define the baseline and make lines of type easier to follow. Serif (or serifed) typefaces have serifs. *Sans serif* (sometimes called nonserif or Gothic) typefaces lack serifs.

The serifs of most typefaces vary in weight. They start wide at the main stroke of the character and thin out to points. In effect, they make the character flow almost organically into the baseline. Serifs with a rounded join to the main stroke of the character are called *bracketed* serifs. A few modern faces use serifs of a single, unvarying weight that meet the main character strokes square-on. These are called *slab serif* or *square serif* typefaces. The three basic serif designs are illustrated in Figure 10.3 using the Arial, Times New Roman, and Courier New typefaces, all TrueType faces that come with Windows 95.

Figure 10.3 Serif types.

Two other terms define specific characteristics of some typefaces. *Script* emulates cursive handwriting made with a flexible steel nib pen with flowing lines, loops, flourishes, and, usually, an italic slant. *Blackletter* follows the pattern originated with Gutenberg and emulates the hand lettering of monastic manuscripts, what we commonly think of as Old English lettering with ornate capital letters, thick black strokes, and diamond- or triangle-shape serifs.

A normal character of type fits separately into an invisible rectangle or box on the paper defined by its width and height with nothing intruding into its sacred territory. This characteristic harks back to the days when type was cast in lead, and each letter was a rectangle that lined up next to the rest. Characters of different shapes occupied different areas of their boxes, leaving white space at various positions around the character. In general, designers try to make the space between individual characters within their boxes appear uniform. Sometimes, however, combinations of certain characters results in a white space between them that appears abnormally wide. For example, when a capital T and capital A are adjacent, a river of white seems to run between them.

To improve the appearance of these combinations, the typeface designer sometimes trims the white space between particular characters like T and A to improve the appearance of these combinations. The process of spacing characters closer together to make letter spacing appear more uniform is termed *kerning*. Often kerning is manual. When a document is composed, the typesetter (not the type designer) adjusts the character spacing using any tools that are available in the publishing program being used. Figure 10.4 shows an example of character kerning. Note that if the cells of the individual kerned characters were kept square, the cells would overlap.

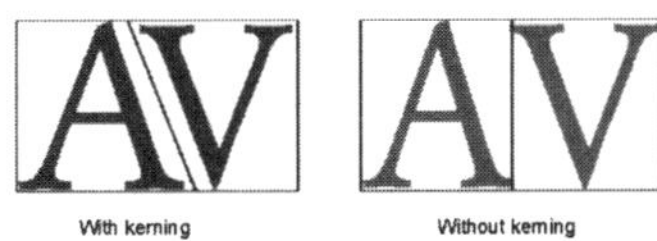

Figure 10.4 An example of kerning.

Some typefaces include *kerning pairs*, sets of two-letter combinations that have had their spacing optimally adjusted by the typeface designer. When font control software detects the letter sequence of a kerning pair, it automatically substitutes the pair for the individual characters.

Ligatures are related to kerning pairs. Ligatures are combinations of characters that have been merged by the typeface designer to make them more elegant or readable. Ligatures originated in the old scriptoria where monks hand-copied manuscripts with quill pens. The ligatures, combining characters, saved space and effort. Ligatures were later carried into moveable-type printing to help it look more like the lettering of old manuscripts. Even centuries ago, the world loathed too-quick changes of technology. As people became more familiar with mass-produced printing, ligatures fell out of favor. Most disappeared in the fifteenth and sixteenth centuries. Only a few survived into the eighteenth and nineteenth centuries, and many modern typefaces lack them entirely.

The most common ligature is the combination of lowercase f followed by i in which the dot of the i becomes part of the f character. Other common ligature sequences include f l, ft, and ffi. In PCs, font control programs automatically substitute ligatures when they detect the key character combinations.

Aesthetics

Typefaces are also classed aesthetically. Typeface styles evolved with changes in taste and the emergence of typography as an art form independent of *calligraphy*, the art of ornate writing. Each of these styles has a characteristic look that can add (or detract) from the force and feeling of what you try to communicate.

Old face style, that used by the first printers, was greatly influenced by Renaissance handwriting, the kind produced with a flat, broad quill pen. In typefaces influenced by this design philosophy, you'll find only a slight difference between the hairlines and stems. In rounded characters, the widest part of the opening is offset in some direction from the center of the character. In other words, the hole in the "o" may lean. The capital letters, which generally follow the style set by Roman majuscule characters, are slightly shorter than the ascending lowercase characters. Some of the best known old faces styles include Bembo, Caslon, and Garamond.

- **Transitional typefaces** thinned the hairlines and serifs of individual characters, thereby making the stems more pronounced. The weight of rounder letters appears to be centered. In part, this style emerged as typographers and printers became able to create fine detail in their lead-work and print with greater delicacy. One of the most beautiful faces of the transitional style was created in about 1750 by John Baskerville and now bears his name. Today's Times New Roman, originally developed for the *London Times*, carries on the transitional typeface tradition.

- **Modern typefaces** take the transitional style further, increasing and emphasizing the difference in weights between the hairlines and stems. Letters are still narrower, more rigid, and austere. Serifs are straight and fine. The modern style in typeface design reflects a quest for the return to classicism that arose at the end of the eighteenth and beginning of the nineteenth centuries. Bodoni (designed by Giambattista Bodoni) and Didot (designed by Francois Ambroise Didot) are two of the best known examples.
- **Egyptian typefaces** represent the reverse swing of the pendulum. Dating from the nineteenth century, Egyptian typefaces are characterized by pronounced serifs that have a weight nearing that of the stem. Clarendon is the classic example. Close to the same time, sans serif typefaces arose as an aesthetic development that pushed the limits in the opposite direction.

Measurement

Printing and typography were (and are) arts of their own. As they developed, they incorporated their own measurement systems as arbitrarily as any other system and based on their own demands. The same measurement system used in the days of landset lead type survives today in the common designations of typefaces.

The basic unit of measurement for type is the *point*, which in digital typography today is set to measure exactly 1/72 (or 0.01383) of an inch. This is actually a bit smaller than the point measurement of traditional typesetting, where 72.27 points made an inch. Twelve points make one *pica*, and six picas make an inch. Although a point system of measurement was first proposed by Pierre Simon Fournier in 1737, the current scheme was developed by Francois Ambroise Didot.

Typefaces are invariably described by their height in points. This measurement typically (but not always) extends from the bottom of the lowest descender to the top of the highest ascender. These positions are sometimes given the names *maximum descender* and *maximum ascender*. Because most capital letters do not have descenders (the exception being J in some fonts), point size does not designate the height of capitals. That is, a 24-point capital letter does not measure 24 points tall.

Nevertheless, the larger the number, the larger the type. The width of characters varies proportionally with height within a given typeface, so all character widths are dependent on type size.

Just as characters do not fill the entire space within the vertical reaches of a line, they do not fill the entire width assigned to them. In the days of hot type, the lines of the character were inset from the edges of the slug so that one letter did not appear to touch the next one on the line. The space between the edge of the character and the edge of the slug (or the edge of the matrix of the character cell in digital topography) is called a *sidebearing*. The left sidebearing precedes the character, and the right sidebearing follows it.

Sidebearings can be positive or negative. The white space around a character is a positive sidebearing. Italic characters often have negative sidebearings. The characters lean over the edges of the cells and overlap adjacent cells. Despite the overlap, italic characters maintain a uniformly spaced appearance because the slants of every character match, and one character leans into the space vacated by those adjacent.

Most typefaces are *proportionally spaced*, that is, the width of individual characters varies. An M is wider than an I. The variation in character width helps you identify letters more easily and makes text more legible. *Monospaced typefaces* contrive to make every character exactly the same width by extending serifs of narrow characters and condensing wide characters. Although a nightmare for the typeface designer, monospacing offers advantages in some special circumstances. In general they make character management easier for primitive equipment like typewriters, dot-matrix printers, and text-based video systems.

Two units of width are often used in typography. An *em* is a horizontal unit of space that traditionally corresponded to the width of a capital M in the given typeface. Characteristically in early hot-type typefaces, the letter M was exactly as wide as it was tall, so an em is a square that's as wide as the typeface size is high. Traditionally one em was the amount of indentation provided individual paragraphs. An *en* is half as wide as an em, corresponding to the width of the character N. Traditionally words were spaced an en apart when spacing was not modified for justification.

In digital font technology, the em unit is the basis of a measurement system used in scaling fonts to specific point sizes. The amount of detail in a character can be measured independently of the resolution of the display or printing system in units of *pixels per em* (ppem). The em, representing a square equal to character height and width, forms the basis of the character matrix and can be equated to the point size in whatever units are used by the device. The higher the ppem value, the more detail in each character.

Alternately, you can determine the size characters displayed or printed in a given system from a given font if you know the font's ppem value and the pixel size (which is equivalent to the resolution) of the system. The formula used in these calculations is as follows:

```
Point Size = 72 / (ppem / Resolution)
```

where resolution is given in dots or pixels per inch. You can also determine the ppem value for a font used by a particular device from its point size and the system resolution using the following formula:

```
ppem = (Point Size/72) * Resolution
```

For example, a 12 point font that's rendered on a 300 dpi laser printer has a ppem value of 50. A 12 point font rendered on a 1200 dpi laser printer would have a ppem value of 200. On a 72 dpi monitor, a 12 point font is rendered at 12 ppem.

When PC printing does not aspire to the level of typesetting, it often uses measurements based on the terminology of the typewriter. Instead of height, typewriter text was measured by width. Because of the constraint in the design of mechanical typewriters, every character had exactly the same width. The distance between the corresponding edges of adjacent character boxes (that is, the left edge of each box) is termed the *pitch* of the typewriter and is measured by the number of characters that fit in one inch.

The most common typewriter pitches are individually named, and these names are often used in reference to the output of impact dot-matrix and some ink-jet printers. *Pica* describes a 10 character per inch pitch or 10-pitch. (Note that one-tenth inch pica typewriter character pitch does not correspond to the one-sixth inch width of a typesetters pica.) *Elite* describes a 12 character per inch pitch or 12-pitch. *Micro-elite* describes a pitch of 15 characters per inch or 15-pitch. Note that if you consider a single monospaced typewritten character to be an em (as some folks do), the sizes of typewriter characters are more than a little confusing–10-pitch equates to 12-point type, and 12-pitch is 10-point type. Micro-elite 15-pitch equates approximately to seven point type.

Leading

When lines of type are squashed together so that the descenders from one line touch the ascenders from the line below it, your eye has difficulty discerning and smoothly following the individual lines. To make text more legible, most typesetters add extra spacing between lines. This extra space is called *leading* (which rhymes with "bedding"), a carryover from the days of setting individual characters of metal type when typesetters inserted thin strips of lead between lines.

Leading is traditionally measured in points. In the days of hot type, the measurement specified the width of the actual lead that was used. With today's cold type, however, the measurement system has become more refined. Leading now refers to the total height of a line of type, measured from baseline to baseline. Typically the line width is specified with two numbers, one (the numerator) indicating the character height without leading and the other (the denominator) the baseline-to-baseline height with leading. For example, a book that is printed with 10-point characters with 12-point spacing between lines would be described as 10/12 or 10.12. This same leading might also be described as 10 over 12 or 10 on 12. Double-spaced typing is actually an extreme case of leading.

In digital typography, leading can be negative as well as positive, squeezing lines of text closer together. Negative leading was not possible with hot type because with zero leading one line of type actually touched the next line with nothing that could be removed between them. In some particular circumstances, negative leading is preferred. For example, lines of solid capital letters may appear too widely spaced because of the lack of descenders. Negative leading would compensate and make all-caps text look properly spaced.

Fonts

From the aesthetic viewpoint, a *font* collects together all the characters—all the letters, numerals, symbols, and punctuation marks—of a given size and style of typeface. In the days of hot type, a font comprised all the characters that fit in a job case, multiple copies of each letter because each could only be used once in a given setup. Phototypesetting made the issue of copies of characters immaterial. The typesetting machine could produce as many of any character as were needed at any instant. Consequently, in the modern definition, a font includes one pattern for each character of the desired size and style of typeface.

Types

In PCs and printers, however, there's more to fonts than mere aesthetics. Fonts differ in how the information for coding these light and dark patterns is stored. Generally, fonts are stored using one of two technologies, termed bit mapped and outline. In addition, fonts are often named for some specialized purpose for which they are designed. Screen fonts and OCR fonts are special bit-mapped fonts. Vector fonts printer fonts are much like outline fonts but designed for devices that draw characters rather than print them. Printer fonts is a catch-all used by Microsoft to refer to fonts of any kind used by a printer.

Bit-mapped fonts encode each character as the pattern of dots that form the matrix, recording the position and color of each individual dot. They are also called *raster* fonts because they are drawn with raster techniques much like television images. Because larger character sizes require more dots, they require different pattern codes than smaller characters. In fact, every size of character, weight of character (bold, condensed, light, and so on), even each character slant (Roman versus Italic), requires its own code and collection of individually defined characters. A given face cannot be readily scaled from one size to another, and when they are the results are rarely pleasing–scaling upward magnifies the jaggedness of each character; scaling downward makes detail disappear faster than beer on a hot summer's day. As a result, a single type family may require dozens of different, bit-mapped fonts. Worse, bit-mapped fonts hog memory, and every size and character weight requires more.

Screen fonts are specialized bit-mapped fonts used for rendering text on your video display. Because they are bit mapped, they display with the same number of dots regardless of your display resolution. At higher resolutions, a given font takes up a smaller fraction of the screen and consequently looks smaller.

Microsoft Windows treats screen fonts as a special case of bit-mapped fonts and uses them to make menus, messages, window captions, and miscellaneous text. The Windows 3.1 family packages include a number of screen fonts keyed to match the resolutions of leading display standards (CGA, EGA, VGA, and SVGA/8514). As a default, the Windows 3.1 uses a specially designed proportionally space bit-mapped font called System. When you install Windows or a new video driver, Windows selects the appropriate screen font (or gives you a choice) for the resolution of the system. It stores this selection in the [fonts] section of the WIN.INI file.

The Windows 3.1 family also includes a number of monospaced screen fonts for the display of DOS applications that run under Windows in Enhanced Mode. Window 95 also allows the use of monospaced TrueType fonts in DOS windows.

Printer fonts are special Windows constructs. The Microsoft definition of a printer font is simple: any font that your printer can print out. Windows recognizes three different types of printer fonts. *Device* fonts are fonts that are integral to your printer, either recorded inside its ROM memory, on a hard disk associated with the printer, or stored in a font cartridge or font card. *Printable screen* fonts are screen fonts that Windows can translate into a form that can be printed by your printer. *Downloadable soft* fonts are fonts designed to be used by your printer that are stored inside your PC and are sent to your printer as they are called for in your print jobs. Whether a given printer can use a type of printer font depends on its design. For example, nearly all printers have at least one device font, but printers using Hewlett-Packard's Printer Control Language (PCL) cannot print Windows screen fonts. Most plotters do not accept downloadable soft fonts. Table 10.1 lists the types of fonts supported by different types of printers when you use the Windows 3.1 family. Because Windows 95 uses basically the same font technology as Windows 3.1 (TrueType), its font handling is much the same.

Table 10.1 Windows 3.1 Printer Font Support

Printer	TrueType	Raster	Vector	Outline
Dot matrix	Yes	Yes	No	Yes
HPPCL	Yes	No	Yes	Yes
PostScript	Yes	No	Yes	Yes
Plotter	Yes	No	Yes	No

Vector fonts define each character by the strokes needed to draw it, essentially the directions needed for you or your equipment to wield a pen to write text. In simplest form, vector font characters look like what you'd write with a felt-tip marker, a single stroke for each essential element of each character. However, more elaborate characters are not necessarily off-limits to vector fonts. Serifed typefaces and variable stroke widths of the more readable fonts can be drawn with sufficiently precise and detailed instructions. The instructions needed for making big, bold characters can be complex, however. For example, the font would contain instructions for drawing the outline of the character as well as fill instructions comprising a multitude of short, overlapping strokes within the character outline.

As with vector-based drawing images, simple vector fonts readily lend themselves to scaling, rotation, and other manipulations. Simple vector fonts don't look the same at every scale, however, as the stroke weight does not change as size is altered. Small characters run together, and large characters look spindly. The success of scaling more complex, filled characters varies with the font definition. In any case, however, increasing the size of filled characters can dramatically increase the drawing time.

Vector fonts are designed primarily for one specialized application, plotters. Their stroke-by-stroke approach corresponds exactly to the method by which plotters must work. Consequently vector fonts are used by plotters to annotate their drawings. Moreover, most programs that produce vector-based output, which means CADD and similar drawing applications, use vector fonts for text production. In fact, plotters can only use vector fonts. They cannot print any kind of bit-map or raster screen fonts.

Most plotters have at least one built-in vector font (Hewlett-Packard plotters include one called Plotter. Microsoft's Windows include three additional fonts, which it can print through plotters as vector commands. The three Windows vector fonts are Modern, Roman, and Script.

Sometimes applications shift to using vector fonts when very large characters are required. (The other scalable technology, outline fonts, typically lays out characters in a large size matrix, which scales downward well but not upward.) Because of their drawing-based nature, vector fonts easily scale to large sizes although rendering large sizes may be time consuming. Some Windows applications allow you to specify at what font size to switch from outline to vector fonts. In PageMaker, for example, the **Vector Above** setting specifies this switch.

Outline fonts encode individual characters as mathematical descriptions, essentially the stroke you would have to make to draw the character. These strokes define the outline of the character, hence the name for the technology. Your computer or printer then serves as a *raster image processor* (often termed a RIP) that executes the mathematical instructions to draw each character in memory to make the necessary bit pattern for printing. With most typefaces, one mathematical description makes any size of character–the size of each individual stroke in the character is merely scaled to reflect the size of the final character (consequently outline fonts are often termed *scalable* fonts). One code, then, serves any character size, although different weights and slants require somewhat different codes. A single type family can be coded with relatively few font descriptions–normal, bold, Roman, and Italic combinations.

The equations required for storing an outline font typically require more storage (more bytes on disk or in memory) than a single bit-mapped font, but storing an entire family of outline fonts requires substantially less space than a family of bit-mapped fonts (because one outline font serves all sizes). For normal business printing, which generally involves fewer than a dozen fonts (including size variations), this difference is not significant. For graphic artists, publishers, and anyone who likes to experiment with type and printing, however, outline fonts bring greater versatility with less cost in resources.

On the other hand, bit-mapped fonts print faster. Outline fonts have to go through an additional step—all of that raster image processing—computations, which add to the time it takes to print out anything. Bit-mapped fonts get directly retrieved from memory and set to your printer without any additional footwork.

OCR fonts are another special case in font technology and design. Unlike most typefaces that are designed to be aesthetically appealing and readily readable by us human beings, these *Optical Character Recognition* fonts pay little heed to beauty or elegance, sacrificing all to the ability to be quickly and unambiguously recognized by machine. Three OCR typefaces are common in everyday commerce. *OCR-A* appears on book covers for encoding ISBN numbers and is used increasingly by libraries for their circulation systems. *OCR-B* digits augment the many bar codes (see below) that appear on products to key them to inventory systems. *Magnetic Ink Character Recognition* or MICR is the typeface that the international banking system uses to identify institutions and record account and check numbers on each document. Although readable optically, MICR earns its name from the use of inks containing magnetic particles, which allows the code to be read by magnetic scanners in the banking system's processing equipment. Several decorative fonts simulate the look of OCR characters without their machine-readable functionality, just in case you want to pollute what you publish with arcane characters.

Scaling

One way or another, all fonts can be scaled from one size to another, although not necessarily by your printer or application software. The quality of the results of scaling vary wildly, however, depending on whether the font was *meant* to be scaled. For example, when bit-mapped or screen fonts are scaled to larger sizes (for example, using a painting program), quality suffers because the individual pixels that make up each character get magnified. Enlarge a bit-mapped font sufficiently, and it will look like it was built by stacking a child's building blocks and will seem just as likely to fall apart. Moreover, scaling a bit-mapped font requires substantial computing power, as values need to be determined for each pixel position of each character.

Vector fonts scale more easily. The drawing vectors of the characters are formulae of which the scaling factor is one element. Substituting one scale for another does not alter the complexity of the calculation, so vector fonts can be computed with equal speed and facility regardless of their size. As noted before, however, the quality of the characters that are actually rendered suffers as scaling factors increase.

Outline fonts are designed for scaling. Again, the formulae used for rendering the fonts have built-in scaling factors, so making characters of various sizes is quick and natural. When scaling becomes extreme, however, quality can still suffer even with outline fonts, however. Simply scaling outline fonts generally produces acceptable, though not outstanding results. To make the clearest, most readable text, small characters must typically be shaped somewhat differently than large characters. For example, the serifs on each letter may need to be proportionally larger for smaller characters, or else they would disappear. The process of adjusting character design to suit different type sizes is called *optical scaling*. In general, to properly scale a typeface optically, the relative weight of the thick strokes of each character are maintained while the thinner strokes are adjusted–made thicker at small point sizes and thinner at large sizes.

Bit-mapped fonts of different sizes are typically optically scaled when they are designed so each size has optimal readability and reproduction potential. In outline fonts, the equations describing each stroke can include *hints* on what needs to be changed for best legibility at particular sizes. Outline fonts that include this supplementary information are termed *hinted*, and produce clearer characters, particularly in large headlines and tiny, eye-straining contract fine-print sizes.

In addition to hinting, TrueType uses another process to achieve optimum rendering of small type sizes called *nonlinear scaling*. This technique avoids many scaling problems including round-off errors. These occur when the calculation of the size of a character results in noninteger values. Screen pixels and printer dots all occur only in integral values, so the match between the calculated character and that which can possibly be displayed can be substantially off. The errors are larger in relation to character size at smaller point values. If they are simply rounded off, character spacing, and even character shape suffer. Worse, characters will appear differently at different resolutions. Nonlinear scaling adjusts the character width so that the visual results at different resolutions make the best match.

Character Sets

Every font includes a full alphabet, numerals, and the most common punctuation marks. Computer fonts usually include more, often much more. Because most computer systems reserve a full byte to encode character values, designers can define 256 character possibilities. Because these possibilities encode all the possible characters that can be coded in a given system, they are collectively called the *character set* of a given system. The Roman alphabet takes 52 characters for upper- and lowercase, the numerals take ten more, and punctuation marks may need another dozen. That leaves 182 free values for encoding different characters. Moreover, the encoding of even the basic 74 values alphanumeric values is entirely arbitrary, anything the designer of the system might want. A value of the letter "A" could be 1, 15, 53, or anything else the designer chooses.

The computer industry has come together to develop several standards for making these assignments. The greatest degree of standardization comes with the infamous ASCII code (the American Standard Code for Information Interchange), which gives a byte value to each of the basic 74 characters as well as 54 additional definitions to use up all 128 possible values of a seven-bit code. But ASCII isn't the only system. IBM created the *Extended Binary Coded Decimal Interchange Code* (EBCDIC) for encoding data in its 360-series and later mainframe computers, and other languages require their own character definitions for alphabets that involve accents, diacritical marks, and characters beyond the most common 26 of the Roman alphabet. Moreover, the extra available bit leaves room for 128 characters beyond the basic ASCII codes.

In the fonts used by PCs, two character set standards are dominant. The native character set used by most PCs is that which IBM developed in 1981 for its first Personal Computer. The lower 128 bit values follow the ASCII standard, and the upper 128 bit values code a collection of foreign character and symbols, block graphic characters, and special characters for drawing frames and boxes. Most printer manufacturers call this assignment of values the *IBM character set.* Microsoft classifies it as an OEM (Original Equipment Manufacturer) character set. Microsoft Windows does not follow this standard but instead recognizes the ANSI (American National Standards Institute) character set definition. Most fonts, including those used by TrueType, use the ANSI definition.

To cope with the requirement of different languages, PCs use a system of *code pages*. Each page stores a list that assigns byte values to characters. Many fonts are design to correspond to a particular code page. For example, the bit-mapped screen fonts used by Windows are separately defined for each code page available, identified by a number appended to their filenames. For example, the number 437 identifies the United States code page, the default used by Windows for its screen fonts.

Note that some printers may use their own proprietary character sets and may default to different code pages than those used by your PC and its software. If your software and printer do not use the same character definitions, what you see on your monitor and what your printer slides out may be unexpectedly different.

Sometimes you want to use a character that's not directly accessible to you, for example to insert a special character such as a trademark sign in a document. One way of adding such special characters to documents is by taking advantage of the Windows Character Map facility. Although when you map a character, the on-screen representation may not be accurate, the character will print properly according to its definition in the font that you're using.

Printer manufacturers follow their own stars when it comes to choice of character set, for their products. For example, early Epson printers used the standard ASCII character set while the mechanically identical machines from IBM used the IBM character set. In that most early PC software was written to expect the IBM character set, printouts on Epson machines sometimes could get strange. To eliminate such difficulties, Epson recapitulated and added an understanding of the IBM character set to is newer machines. However, the Epson design makes the IBM characters inaccessible through WordPerfect using Epson's standard printer drivers. To get the IBM characters, you have to install the Epson printer in IBM mode and use a driver designed for the related IBM printers, for example using the IBM Graphics Printer driver for the EX-800, EX-1000, FX-85, or FX-185. The Epson LQ-800 and LQ-1000 use *identity modules* that define the language and character set used by the printer. The module with Epson part number 7695 lets the printer understand IBM commands and codes. The ESC/P (#7696) module includes Epson commands as well as the IBM character set.

Hewlett-Packard printers demonstrate the mismatch character set problem, too, but requires a different solution. HP LaserJet printers use their Roman-8 font for their default symbol set, and this font contains only alphanumeric and foreign characters. The line and box characters necessary for emulating the IBM character set are part of the PC-8 symbol set. If you need to print the IBM character set (for example, to execute a **Print Screen** command when running DOS) you must change the default symbol set to PC-8. To make this change, you can use the printer's front-panel menu controls.

Storage and Retrieval

The information describing font characters has to be stored somewhere. Considering that many megabytes may be involved, the location of font storage can have important implications on how you use your PC and printer.

Internal Fonts

Nearly every printer has at least one built-in font. Without an internal font, the printer could not create characters from the ASCII or other codes sent from your PC. The most basic impact dot-matrix printers include just one font design–and a primitive one at that–which the printer modifies mechanically or electrically to yield various widths and weights, for example, slowing the printhead to make a more compressed typeface.

Like every dot-matrix printer, nearly every laser and ink-jet printer has a few fonts built in. Ubiquitous among printers is the familiar, old 10-pitch Courier or one of its kin, the default typeface held over from typewriter days. Probably the most endearing and desirable characteristic of Courier (at least to software and printer designers) is that it is monospaced–every character from "i" to "m" is exactly the same width, making page layout easy to control. The bit patterns for this typeface, consequently, are forever encoded into the ROMs of nearly every machine. It can, and usually is, pulled up at an instant's notice simply by giving a command to print a character.

For example, the Hewlett-Packard LaserJet printers running PCL use Courier as the default typeface and will use it for everything you print if you don't tell the machine otherwise.

More recent machines give you a wider choice, adding in scalable or outline fonts. These and other faces may be resident in the ROM of the printers. Exactly how many fonts are included and which ones depends on many factors–mostly the whim of the manufacturer. Generally if the manufacturer is large, as few faces as possible are packed in ROM; smaller manufacturers include more to give their products a competitive edge.

In addition to the basic Courier, you can expect certain fonts in some varieties of printer, particularly PostScript machines. Table 10.2 lists the 17 fonts included with the most basic of PostScript interpreters and the additional 18 fonts that make the basic 35 included with most modern PostScript printers.

Table 10.2 Fonts Included with PostScript Interpreters

Basic 17 Fonts
Courier
Courier Bold

Courier Bold Oblique

Courier Oblique

Helvetica

Helvetica Bold

Helvetica Bold Oblique

Helvetica Narrow

Helvetica Narrow Bold

Helvetica Narrow Bold Oblique

Helvetica Narrow Oblique

Helvetica Oblique

Symbol

Times Bold

TimesBold Italic

Times Italic

Times Roman

Additional Fonts to Make 35

Zapf Chancery Medium Italic

Zapf Dingbats

Avant Garde Book

Avant Garde Book Oblique

Avant Garde Demi

Avant Garde Demi Oblique

Bookman Demi

Bookman Demi Italic

Bookman Light

Bookman Light Italic

New Century Schoolbook Bold

New Century Schoolbook Bold Italic

New Century Schoolbook Italic

Table 10.2 continued

New Century Schoolbook Roman
Palatino Bold
Palatino Bold Italic
Palatino Italic
Palatino Roman

Many applications programs packages and operating systems also include one or more fonts to allow you to take advantage of the power or features of the software. The most important of these are the fonts included with Windows. Since version 3.1, the design of Windows allows the operating system to print its software fonts through nearly any bit-image printer. These built-in fonts are always available to your Windows applications. Table 10.3 lists the fonts that came with the Windows 3.1 family and are also included with Windows 95.

Table 10.3 Fonts Shipped with Windows 3.1

Name	Type	Spacing	Sizes	CharacterSet
Arial Bold Italic	TrueType	Proportional	Scalable	ANSI
Arial Bold	TrueType	Proportional	Scalable	ANSI
Arial Italic	TrueType	Proportional	Scalable	ANSI
Arial	TrueType	Proportional	Scalable	ANSI
Courier New Bold Italic	TrueType	Monospaced	Scalable	ANSI
Courier New Bold	TrueType	Monospaced	Scalable	ANSI
Courier New Italic	TrueType	Monospaced	Scalable	ANSI
Courier New	TrueType	Monospaced	Scalable	ANSI
Courier	Raster	Monospaced	10, 12, 15	ANSI
Modern	Vector	Proportional	Scalable	ANSI
MS Sans Serif	Raster	Proportional	8, 10, 12, 14, 18, 24	ANSI
MS Serif	Raster	Proportional	8, 10, 12, 14, 18, 24	ANSI

Roman	Vector	Proportional	Scalable	ANSI
Script	Vector	Proportional	2, 4, 6	ANSI
Symbol	Raster	Proportional	8, 10, 12, 14, 18, 24	Symbol
Symbol	TrueType	Proportional	Scalable	Symbol
System	Raster	Proportional	Varies with display	ANSI
Terminal	Raster	Monospaced	Varies with display	OEM
Times New Roman Bold Italic	TrueType	Proportional	Scalable	ANSI
Times New Roman Bold	TrueType	Proportional	Scalable	ANSI
Times New Roman Italic	TrueType	Proportional	Scalable	ANSI
Times New Roman	TrueType	Proportional	Scalable	ANSI

Once you install the proper version of Windows, all of these fonts will be available for display and printing by your Windows applications. Although with Windows 95 you can substitute monospaced TrueType fonts (essentially Courier New) to display your DOS applications, you still cannot use the TrueType fonts for printing documents made by DOS applications.

Font Cartridges

You can add more fonts to your system in any of several ways. The easiest of these to manage is the font cartridge. The dot patterns for the character designs of the fonts are stored in ROM chips soldered inside each cartridge. The cartridge functions mostly as a shell and handle, itself providing little more than a housing for the chip and a connector that plugs into a mate in your printer. When you slide in a cartridge, you simply add the bit patterns or character definitions in the ROM inside the cartridge to those already in your printer. Impact, ink-jet, and laser-image printers have all been designed to use font cartridges.

On the downside, many font cartridges don't give you much. They hold only a few fonts to keep the amount of memory and the licensing requirements low. The small contents of these cartridges couple with the limited number of cartridge slots in most printers (rarely more than two) means that cartridges really don't put many fonts at your disposal. The typical printer-maker's cartridge holds six to 12 fonts. Aftermarket cartridge suppliers may pack 25 or more fonts in a single cartridge. Although that sounds like a generous endowment, tens of thousands of fonts are available in digital form (and sometimes documents look like they've been printed with them all, but that's another story).

The HP design is flexible enough to accommodate more than mere ROM in cartridges. For example, you can often add a PostScript language interpreter to your PCL-only LaserJet by sliding in a PostScript-compatible cartridge. The cartridge includes not only code for drawing outline fonts but a language interpreter that changes the entire personality of the printer, and it reacts not to PCL but as a true PostScript.

Font cartridges are not necessarily interchangeable between printer manufacturers. Often each manufacturer's cartridges follows its own design specifications. Sometimes the cartridges used by two models of printers made by the same manufacturer are incompatible.

The closest thing to a standard is the design developed by Hewlett-Packard for its laser printer cartridges because of HP's dominance in the market. Most font cartridges are designed to be compatible with HP printers. In general, other laser printers emulate the HP machines and usually support most font cartridges designed for HP machines. Such compatibility is not always complete, however. Some cartridges may not work with particular printer models. Compatibility information is usually available from cartridge or printer manufacturers. For example, Table 10.4 lists the published font cartridge compatibilities of three leading Epson laser printer models. Note that these machines must be in their HP compatibility modes to use these font cartridges.

Table 10.4 Epson Laser Printer Cartridge Compatibility

Cartridge maker	Cartridge model	Printer		
		Action Laser II	EPL-8000	EPL-7000
Anacom	Alfajet MX-1 Maxi-One Cartridge	Yes	Yes	Yes
Anacom	Alfajet PC Maxi-Pro Cartridge	Yes	Yes	Yes
Computer Peripherals	JetFont SuperSet	Yes	Yes	Yes
Computer Peripherals	JetFont 12/30	Yes	Yes	Yes

Computer Peripherals	JetFont 4-in-1	Yes	Yes	Yes
Computer Peripherals	JetFont SuperSet International	Yes	Yes	Yes
Computer Peripherals	JetFont 425-in-one SuperSet Plus	No	Yes	No
Everex	HardFont Cartridge B	Yes	Yes	Yes
Everex	HardFont Cartridge F	Yes	Yes	Yes
Everex	HardFont Cartridge T	Yes	Yes	Yes
Everex	HardFont Cartridge Z	Yes	Yes	Yes
Everex	HardFont Cartridge LGL	Yes	Yes	Yes
Everex	HardFont Cartridge SST	Yes	Yes	Yes
Everex	HardFont Cartridge BST	Yes	Yes	Yes
Everex	HardFont Cartridge All-in-1	Yes	Yes	Yes
Everex	HardFont Cartridge A-TO Z	Yes	Yes	Yes
Hewlett-Packard	92286A Courier 1	Yes	Yes	Yes
Hewlett-Packard	92286B Tms Proportional	Yes	Yes	Yes
Hewlett-Packard	92286C International	Yes	Yes	Yes
Hewlett-Packard	92286D Prestige Elite	Yes	Yes	Yes
Hewlett-Packard	92286E Letter Gothic	Yes	Yes	Yes
Hewlett-Packard	92286F Tms Proportional 2	Yes	Yes	Yes
Hewlett-Packard	92286G Legal Elite	Yes	Yes	Yes
Hewlett-Packard	92286H Legal Courier	Yes	Yes	Yes
Hewlett-Packard	92286J Math Elite	Yes	Yes	Yes
Hewlett-Packard	92286K Math TmsRmn	Yes	Yes	Yes
Hewlett-Packard	92286L Courier P&L	Yes	Yes	Yes
Hewlett-Packard	92286M Prestige Elite P&L	Yes	Yes	Yes
Hewlett-Packard	92286N Letter Gothic P&L	Yes	Yes	Yes
Hewlett-Packard	92286P TmsRmn P&L	Yes	Yes	Yes
Hewlett-Packard	92286Q Memo 1	Yes	Yes	Yes
Hewlett-Packard	92286R Presentations 1	Yes	Yes	Yes
Hewlett-Packard	92286T Tax 1	Yes	Yes	Yes
Hewlett-Packard	92286U Forms Portrait	Yes	Yes	Yes

Table 10.4 continued

CARTRIDGE MAKER	CARTRIDGE MODEL	PRINTER		
		Action Laser II	EPL-8000	EPL-7000
Hewlett-Packard	92286V Forms Landscape	Yes	Yes	Yes
Hewlett-Packard	92286W Bar Code 3-of-9/0CR-A	Yes	Yes	Yes
Hewlett-Packard	92286X EAN/UPC/OCR-B	Yes	Yes	Yes
Hewlett-Packard	92286Y PC Courier 1	Yes	Yes	Yes
Hewlett-Packard	92286Z Microsoft 1A	Yes	Yes	Yes
Hewlett-Packard	92290S1 Courier Document 1	Yes	Yes	Yes
Hewlett-Packard	92290S2 TmsRmn/Helv Report 1	Yes	Yes	Yes
Hewlett-Packard	92286PC ProCollection	Yes	Yes	Yes
Hewlett-Packard	C2055A #C01 Great Start	Yes	Yes	Yes
Hewlett-Packard	C2053A #C01 WordPerfect	Yes	Yes	Yes
Hewlett-Packard	C2053A #C02 Microsoft	Yes	Yes	Yes
Hewlett-Packard	C2053A #C03 Polished Worksheets	Yes	Yes	Yes
Hewlett-Packard	C2053A #C04 Persuasv Presentations	Yes	Yes	Yes
Hewlett-Packard	C2053A #C05 Forms Etc.	Yes	Yes	Yes
Hewlett-Packard	C2053A #C06 Bar Codes & More	Yes	Yes	Yes
Hewlett-Packard	C2053A #C07 Text Equations	Yes	Yes	Yes
Hewlett-Packard	C2053A #C08 Global Text	Yes	Yes	Yes
Hewlett-Packard	C2053A #C09 Pretty Faces	No	Yes	No
Intercon	PHONT+	Yes	Yes	Yes
Intercon	PROIIP	Yes	Yes	Yes
IQ	Super Cartridge 1	Yes	Yes	Yes
IQ	Super Cartridge 2	Yes	Yes	Yes
IQ	Super Cartridge 2L	Yes	Yes	Yes
IQ	Super Cartridge LC	Yes	Yes	Yes
IQ	Super Cartridge 2WP	Yes	Yes	Yes
IQ	Super Cartridge 2LS	No	Yes	No
IQ	Series 11 Packages	No	Yes	No

Pacific Data	25 Cartridges in One 172 Headlines	Yes	Yes	Yes
Pacific Data	25 Cartridges in One Original Version	Yes	Yes	Yes
Pacific Data	25 in One! III	No	Yes	No
UDP	DT1-TMS RMN	Yes	Yes	Yes
UDP	DT2-HELV	Yes	Yes	Yes
UDP	H-65 65-in-One	Yes	Yes	Yes
UDP	I-65 International 65-in-One	No	Yes	No
UDP	PRO 65	No	Yes	No
UDP	86-1C	No	Yes	No
UDP	25 Plus	No	Yes	No
UDP	Turbo 25	No	Yes	Yes
UDP	Super Times	No	Yes	No
UDP	T&F Tax and Finance	No	Yes	No
UDP	WP Plus C1	No	Yes	No
UDP	MS Plus C2	No	Yes	No
UDP	Spreadsheets C3	No	Yes	No
UDP	Presentation Plus C4	No	Yes	No
UDP	Forms C5	No	Yes	No
UDP	Bar Codes C6	No	Yes	No
UDP	Equations C7	No	Yes	No
UDP	Global C8	No	Yes	No

Downloadable Fonts

Cartridge fonts have fallen from favor because, despite all their conveniences, they still have one big inconvenience: the cartridge itself. ROM chips, connectors, and plastic shells add bulk to fonts they don't need. After all, a font is just a collection of ideas without mass or matter. Strip a font cartridge down to its essentials, and that's what you have–the descriptions that make up the font itself. Although directly dealing with something so intangible as font metrics might have been inconceivable a few decades ago, today we buy, install, modify, and otherwise work with ideas all the time. We just call them software. Stripped to the essence, a font is nothing more than software and can be stored and manipulated exactly like program or data files.

Most bit-image printers are designed to work directly with these font definitions, loading the code directly into their memory for use when making printouts. The immaterial fonts used for this purpose are sometimes called soft fonts because of their software nature. They are more familiarly called downloadable fonts because your PC must download them into your printer before you can use them to print out your documents. You can buy soft fonts just like software, on floppy disk or CD, that you can copy to your PC's hard disk. You can store as many soft fonts as your hard disk can hold for use in your laser printer.

Today, this software-only approach to fonts is the principle form of distribution and use. If a reference uses no other qualifier to describe a font, it almost invariably refers to a soft font.

In the old days of printing, you had to download each font into your printer before you could use it. Modern technology relieves you of this responsibility. Your application or operating system handles the copying for you, checking the fonts you've used in a document and sending only them to the printer before they are needed.

Soft fonts have other disadvantages, however. For example, every soft font you load into your printer lodges in a chunk of your printer's RAM, removing it from the memory available for buffering or rasterizing pages. The memory limit of a given printer may constrain how many soft fonts you can load at any given time, although the bounty of megabytes installed in newer printers ameliorates the problem somewhat (but not, of course, the cost of additional printer memory).

A different approach uses software-based fonts but doesn't bother loading them into your printer. Instead, your software rasterizes the font definitions and sends the bit patterns rather than characters and font definitions to your printer. In effect, it is the equivalent of having soft fonts built into the program. Windows versions since 3.1 sometimes take advantage of this font generation method, depending on the fonts and printer you choose. This feature is part of the TrueType system and helps you get what-you-see-is-what-you-get text for anything you can display on your screen. While this technique eliminates most of the need to download fonts to your printer, it does impose a hefty penalty–bit patterns take more memory than characters, requiring more memory inside your laser printer, more than a megabyte to print a full page at highest resolution. Worse, the greater amount of data requires a longer period to transmit to the printer, increasing print time. Windows sidesteps the former problem with banded printing. You sidestep the latter problem by buying a faster PC (which you need in order to run the latest versions of Windows, anyhow).

Most PostScript printers also accept downloadable fonts. PostScript soft fonts usually come with their own installation utilities. With most PostScript fonts, you have a choice of three programs to aid you in downloading the font data to your printer: PCSEND, PSDOWN, and WINDOWN. You use PCSEND to download fonts to your printer through a parallel connection. Command-driven, PCSEND runs under DOS and can be controlled through a batch file so you can load the appropriate fonts before you start a DOS application that needs them. If you have connected your printer through a serial port, you'll want to use PSDOWN, which also runs under DOS and features an interactive menu for choosing the functions to carry out. To download PostScript fonts to either parallel or serial printers from Windows, use WINDOWN. Besides the Windows interface, this more advanced program has additional capabilities, including the ability to format and download fonts to a SCSI hard disk connected to your printer. WINDOWN also updates your WIN.INI file after downloading a font to keep your system apprised of what's available for printing. It also allows you to preview fonts by printing out samples of all the fonts accessible by your printer including downloaded, cartridge, and resident fonts.

Note that the Windows PostScript driver makes no provisions of its own for the installation of soft fonts. If you don't have a font manager, you'll also need to install screen fonts to match the downloadable PostScript fonts. Because Windows cannot scale screen fonts, you need to install screen fonts of the size with which you plan to print. A font manager like Adobe Type Manager lets your system render fonts for the display as they are needed by interpreting your printer fonts. ATM rasterizes and scales your printer fonts so that the image on your display matches (within the limits of current technology) what your printer generates.

Font Formats

Two eyewitnesses rarely describe an event identically. In fact, from their descriptions you might doubt that they are talking about the same event. A similar descriptive diversity befalls fonts. You can describe the same font in an infinity of ways. For example, the letter "O" is little more than a circle, and a simple mathematical expression (X^2-Y^2=0) suffices for a circle–providing the circle is centered on the origin. But you can describe the circle mathematically from any point, so you have an infinity of options right there–not to mention details like measuring units (inches, millimeters, points, cubits, links, chains, furlongs, etc.) and even the number system (binary, decimal, hexadecimal, Roman numeral, Klingon) you want to use. The need for a standard font format should be obvious.

Bit-Mapped Fonts

By their very nature, bit-mapped fonts tend to be device specific. They are designed for optimum quality at a given size and resolution, and they suffer whenever you try to manipulate their designs to suit other systems. As a consequence of this specificity, bit-mapped fonts get stored in a format that best suits the device they serve.

Most bit-mapped font files take the same general form, a header that describes the font and the format of its data followed by the data itself. When the font is meant for a specific device or purpose with a set resolution or format, the header data may be omitted. The bit map itself comprises a table with one entry for each character, the data for each entry defining the associated bit pattern. This data may be compressed to reduce the size of the file.

The size of an uncompressed bit-mapped font file increases with resolution because there are more bits in the matrix of every character. At moderate resolutions, the storage requirements of a single font can be quite small. The minimum storage size of a bit-mapped font is easy to calculate: It's just the number of characters in the font times the size of the matrix in dots divided by eight to reduce bits to bytes. If you want to use the full ANSI character set, you need 256 different characters, although most fonts get along with many fewer. You can compute the storage needs of a bit-mapped font with the following formula:

```
Minimum size = (Number of characters * Size of matrix)/8
```

For example, the standard VGA character font uses a 126-bit matrix (the character cell measures 9 by 14 dots), so a full font of 256 characters fits in 1 kilobyte (that is, 1024 bytes) of storage with 16 bytes to spare.

Note that the size of the matrix is a two-dimensional (area) measurement. As a result, the storage requirements for a bit-mapped font increase with the square of the character size. Make the font twice as big, and it requires four times as much storage. At large sizes or high resolutions, the bit-mapped font data can get large, indeed.

Outline Fonts

All outline fonts are not the same. Several standards have arisen, and you must match the fonts you add to the standard used by your hardware and software. Your principal choices are Adobe (subdivided into Types 1, 3, 4, and 5), Intellifont, Speedo, and TrueType.

For PCs, the two big guns are Adobe and TrueType. Adobe got a headstart, entering the scene in 1984, but TrueType has new momentum thanks to direct support in both Windows and Macintosh systems. The big difference between the two (besides origin) is how characters are described. Adobe uses Bezier curves to record the geometry of each character. TrueType uses B-spline curves. There are other differences. The principle Adobe format, Type 1 (see the following section) allows encoding the font data to prevent people (chiefly competitors) from peeking at the underlying descriptions. In other words, Adobe Type 1 fonts can and often are copy protected. Although TrueType has built-in hooks to support encryption, no TrueType fonts are encrypted.

Adobe Type 1

At one time the most common outline font format used with PCs, the Type 1 format developed by Adobe remains a major standard in the industry for desktop publishing and by service bureaus. Introduced in 1984, Type 1 fonts are essentially synonomous with the principal form of fonts used in the PostScript language and the character shapes themselves are defined as mathematical equations using PostScript language code. Type 1 fonts allow the full flexibility of the outline design, including full scaling to almost any point size, rotation, twisting, bending, and other manipulations. To provide for the highest quality at all sizes, most Type 1 fonts are hinted. Although designed for use in printers, the same fonts can be rendered for video displays using Adobe Type Manager. Although support for Type 1 fonts is built into OS/2 versions 1.3 and later, you must specifically add ATM to Windows to enable your Windows programs to give an exact preview of what your PostScript printer will output.

The fonts that are built into all PostScript printers are based on the Type 1 design. Early PostScript printers had 17 built-in Type 1 fonts. Most recent models have 35. You can download additional Type 1 fonts into PostScript printers. Some printers store large numbers of Type 1 fonts using hard disk memory. When Windows prints a file to a PostScript printer, even one displayed on the screen in TrueType, it sends the data as Type 1 fonts except when the text is to be rendered in small type sizes.

The complete definition of the Adobe Type 1 font format is given in the appropriately named book, *The Adobe Type 1 Font Format*, published by Adobe. This book is also called the "black book" because of the color of its cover.

Type 1 fonts are commonly distributed in downloadable form for use with PCs in files with the PFB extension, which are called PFB files. The initials stand for *Printer Font Binary*. Downloadable Type 1 fonts for Macintosh systems use a different format. PFB files cannot be directly downloaded to PostScript printers because they are encrypted and their font definitions are preceded by a header that's unintelligible to PostScript interpreters.

Type 1 font files that can be directly downloaded to PostScript printers wear the PFA extension, which stands for *Printer Font ASCII*. These files are essentially unencrypted versions of the PFB distribution files with font descriptions stored as ASCII hex, which means two ASCII characters represent each byte of the data. You can download fonts by copying PFA files directly to your PostScript printer before any data to be printed using the fonts within the file. Several utility programs are able to decrypt and convert PFB files into PFA format. In addition, Adobe supplies a font downloader that makes the conversion on the fly as it send the font data to a PostScript printer.

The 17 or 35 fonts built into most PostScript Level 1 printers use Type 1 but are hidden in memory, inaccessible to PostScript code that would allow you to copy them. This restriction was removed for most fonts with PostScript Level 2 interpreters, although some particularly valuable fonts remain protected.

Adobe Type 3

To accommodate more complex designs, Adobe developed its Type 3 font format, which is sometimes called *user-defined font format*. Although the Type 3 format supports scalable outline fonts, it does not allow for hinting. Most often, the Type 3 format is used for storing bit maps such as logos and small, detailed (but nonscalable) typefaces.

As with Type 1 fonts, Type 3 definitions are PostScript programs. However, the Type 3 format allows the use of functions not permitted in the Type 1 design. They require a full PostScript interpreter to be properly rendered, so they are incompatible with Adobe Type Manager and cannot be previewed by ATM systems. Type 3 fonts are normally stored as uncompressed text files (PFA).

A major application for Type 3 fonts is printing characters in small point sizes where font scaling—even when enhanced with hinting—fails. Typographers can individually hand-tool Type 3 character bit maps for best readability. In fact, Windows 3.1 relies on Type 3 fonts for small point sizes when sending TrueType data to PostScript printers. You can control the switchover between use of Type 1 and Type 3 fonts in such Windows applications using the *minoutlineppem=xxx* setting in your WIN.INI file. For example, the entry

```
minoutlineppem=25
```

would switch over from Type 1 outline fonts to Type 3 bit-mapped fonts at type sizes below 6 points when printed to 300-dpi laser printers. (See the preceding formula for converting ppem values to point sizes at various resolutions.)

Adobe Type 4

In some very particular cases, the storage needs of Type 4 fonts exceeds the resources that you want or can devote to them, for example extremely large character sets such as Japanese Kanji (which contains about 8000 characters). Adobe developed its Type 4 fonts to take care of such situations. A Type 4 font is little more than a Type 1 font embedded in a Type 3 font and stored in a compressed format once downloaded into PostScript printers. To handle Type 4 fonts, printers require special versions of PostScript (specifically one that has the special operator CCrun).

Adobe Type 5

Storage space become particularly critical when data must be crammed into the confines of ROM. To make font storage more compact, Adobe developed its Type 5 font format. Based on Type 1 font definition, Type 5 fonts are specially compressed for efficient ROM storage. Consequently they are sometimes called *Compressed ROM* (or CROM) fonts. Although Type 5 fonts are typically rendered identically to their Type 1 equivalents, their coding may be subtly different. For example, CharStrings entries may differ.

Adobe MMF

The latest update to the Adobe font design is its *Multiple Master Font* format. This enhancement to the Type 1 definition allows for greater flexibility in fonts rendering, allowing fonts not only to be scaled but also altered along one or more additional design axes. In the context of a Multiple Master Font, a design axis can be any font characteristic such as weight or serif size. For example, using Multiple Master Font technology, a PostScript interpreter can use a single font definition to create light, normal, and bold typefaces.

The first font to use the Multiple Master Font design was Adobe's Myriad, which allows control of two design axes in addition to size: character weight and character width. The weight axis allows the single Myriad font definition to produces faces that vary in boldness. Width allows the font to render faces that vary from condensed to expanded. The Myriad font definition thus can create an infinite variety of typefaces varying in three dimensions (size, weight, and width).

MMF does more than give you the densest available storage for a variety of fonts—on the order of one definition for all your font needs. It also gives you more control than ever possible in the precise rendering of fonts. For example, with the three-axis design of Myriad, you can adjust character weight to something between demibold and bold and width in between condensed and extra condensed to suit your exact needs in any size. Moreover, you can create a variety of absolutely unique typefaces from a single font definition.

Multiple Master Font technology is compatible with all PostScript printers in that the code will be understood but not necessarily acted upon. To allow you to vary the parameters available on the various design axes, your printer's PostScript interpreter needs to understand a new PostScript operator called *makeblendedfont*. Although this operator can be built into a specific PostScript interpreter, all current Multiple Master Fonts include an emulation of this operator so ordinary PostScript printers can take advantage of the technology.

Intellifont

The native font format of the Hewlett-Packard LaserJet printers since the LaserJet III series and part of the PCL5 printer control language is called *Intellifont*. Developed jointly by Agfa Compugraphic and Hewlett-Packard, Intellifont supports both bit-mapped and outline fonts. It is likely the system in the most widespread use, considering the popularity of LaserJet printers. Its chief benefit is speed. Intellifont technology can scale and rasterize a font on the fly in real time during the printing process. Although you do not have to worry about font formats with cartridge fonts—if the cartridge fits, it should work—the cartridges you plug into your LaserJet or compatible printer use Intellifont characters. Downloadable outline fonts for LaserJet III and compatible printers use Intellifont format.

Speedo

Many programs use Bitstream fonts, which have their own format called Speedo. In general, this software works by generating the characters in your PC and transferring them in bit-image form to your printer. Speedo fonts are used by Lotus 1-2-3 and Freelance (in their DOS versions). You also can use Bitstream's Speedo fonts with Windows using Bitstream's FaceLift for Windows.

TrueType

Most font systems were conceived for printers. Microsoft, in developing a font system for its own Windows 3.1 operating environment and working with Apple to develop a font technology for Macintosh System 7, developed a universal format that would work effectively with any kind of output device. The end product, called TrueType, has quickly grown to become the most popular font format, if just because of the wide acceptance of Windows.

The universal scope of the TrueType design results in the first true WYSIWYG (What You See Is What You Get) font system for PCs. TrueType uses exactly the same fonts for video displays and printers, relying on drivers to render them to produce optimum quality at the resolution of the display device. TrueType actually adjusts the size and dot placement of characters to suit device resolution to compensate for scaling and rasterization effects. Moreover, because TrueType fonts are the same no matter what the output device is–which means they are also the same no matter which printer model you use–TrueType output from different devices will match within the resolution limits of each system. Output will even look the same should you move a document across computer platforms, for example shifting from PC to Macintosh.

At heart, TrueType is an outline font system, but it also takes advantage of bit-map technology when appropriate. In addition, the TrueType system matches and translates fonts, rendering them itself (then transferring bit maps to printers) or passing through the rasterizing to the printer.

Matching fonts can be surprisingly challenging. Whenever one of your program attempts to put a character on the screen as a preview or send it out to your printer, a graphic operating system like Windows must locate the right font to use. Difficulties arise when a document uses fonts that are not available to your printer or multiple fonts with the same name are installed in your system.

The Windows environment has a set of strict rules for font matching. TrueType is the first priority. When TrueType fonts are used in a document, TrueType renders the characters into bit mapped and sends the bit maps to your display system or printer. When an application uses a font that is not TrueType, Windows relies on a *font mapping table* to determine the most appropriate font for the device that your application wants to access. TrueType fonts are always the first choice in the font mapping table. Matches are made based on several characteristics in the following order of importance: the character set, character spacing (monospaced versus proportionally spaces), typeface family, typeface name, point size, width, weight, slant, underline, and strike-through.

Because they are designed as outlines, TrueType fonts can be scaled to any size. They are designed in a 2048 x 2048 matrix but stored mathematically. TrueType supports optical scaling through the use of hints. As with other outline fonts, TrueType fonts also can be easily rotated.

In addition, TrueType incorporates speed enhancement features to accelerate rendering in the time-demanding video display application. For example, properly displaying justified lines of text requires that an application knows the widths of each displayed character. To eliminate the time required to compute individual character widths, which is dramatically increased by the need to calculate hints at lower point sizes, each TrueType font includes a *Horizontal Device Metrics* (HMDX) table storing precomputed widths for characters at the most often used sizes–the fonts for Windows 3.1 distributed by Microsoft cover integer character sizes from 9 to 24 ppem and 15 larger sizes. At the largest character sizes hinting no longer comes into play, and character widths can be computed quickly. Another table, called the *Linear Threshold* (LTSH) table in each font file indicates the point at which hinting no longer needs to be considered (hence the font scales linearly).

To give the best possible video performance, TrueType uses a *font caching* system. The first time an application asks for a TrueType character for display or printing in a Windows session, TrueType renders the entire font from the outline definition and hints. The rendered characters are then stored in the font cache and mapped into place as they are needed. Although this system imposes a slight delay when the font is initially rendered (which can be as long as one second on 386-based PCs), all subsequent uses of the font are essentially instantaneous, the same speed as retrieving bit-mapped characters.

The more fonts you use in a Windows session, the larger the font cache must be. If your PC's memory sources are limited and you go wild on the number of fonts you use, including multiple different typefaces, sizes, and styles, the font cache may force Windows to use virtual memory, swapping font data to disk. Although this slows performance in displaying text, in general the penalty is less than the alternative–discarding fonts and regenerating them on the next occasion they are required.

Each TrueType font requires two files for complete definition, one with the extension FOT holding the font tables and one with the extension TTF that stores the actual outline data. From these two files, the TrueType system can create fonts in any size at any resolution to suit display and output needs. You'll note that a TTF file is about the same size as a FON file used by a normal-size bit-map font, but where the bit-map file only hold a single size, the data in a TrueType font file can create any point size.

Identifying Font Files

Although you can tell a font by looking at it–after all, appearance is what defines the font–you can't tell one font from another when it is squeezed down into the form of digital data. They all look the same: a bunch of byte codes representing bit patterns, numbers, and formulae. To use a font effectively, the first step is to identify it, determining exactly what it is, the format in which its data has been organized.

As with all the other data your PC uses, your system stores fonts in the form of files. The files contain various details about the font, be they bit patterns, mathematical formulae, or other such nonsense comprehensible only to bit heads and microprocessors.

Most manufacturers and applications characteristically use their own filename extensions to identify fonts or their components. Table 10.5 lists some of the most common filename extensions used for storing fonts.

Table 10.5 Common Font File Extensions

Extension	File Type
AFM	Adobe Type 1 metric information (in ASCII)
BCO	Bitstream compressed outline
BDF	Adobe Bitmap Distribution Format
BEZ	Bezier outline information
CHR	Borland stroked font file
F3B	Sun Microsystems format
FB	Sun Microsystems format

Table 10.5 continued

Extension	File Type
FF	Sun Microsystems format
FF	Sun Microsystems format
FON	Generic font file (could be almost anything)
FOT	Windows TrueType font format
GF	Generic font (for example, TeX MetaFont)
FLI	Font libraries used by emTeX
INF	PC Font information file used by ATM
MF	TeX MetaFont font file
PFA	Adobe Type 1 Postscript font in ASCII
PFB	Adobe Type 1 PostScript font in binary
PFM	Adobe Printer font metrics for Windows (binary)
PK	TeX packed bitmap font
PL	TeX property list
PS	PostScript file
PXL	TeX pixel bitmap font
SFL	HP bit-mapped downloadable landscape font
SFP	HP bit-mapped downloadable portrait font
SFS	HP scalable downloadable font
TFM	TeX font metrics
TTF	TrueType font
VF	TeX virtual font
VPL	TeX property list in ASCII

Note that a single file suffices for some font formats, but multiple files are often required for some fonts and applications. For example, primitive systems require both screen and printer fonts. Adobe Type Manager requires both .PFB and .PFM font files to give you WYSIWYG text. Deleting or losing one required file of the several used by a given font can be sufficient to make that font unusable. You want to be careful as you manipulate font files. Better still, you want a program that will take care of the font management details for you.

Font Managers

A font in your hand isn't worth two in the bush; it's hardly worth anything. After all, you can't do anything with a font unless your software and printer have access to it. Your hardware and software must be aware of the font and know how to use it.

A program that controls the storage and use of fonts is called a *font manager.* Ideally, a font manager takes care of all the details of using a font. You use your application software without worrying about downloading or matching fonts. Everything you see on your screen dutifully appears in your printouts.

Most font managers do more than merely download fonts as your documents call for them. Most include three basic font management functions: installation, downloading, and substitution.

Installation

Publishers deliver most fonts in a form other than that in which they are meant to be used. To save space, both in distribution and storage on your hard disk, most fonts are distributed compressed and must be decompressed before your applications will even know that the data represents a font. In fact, you must tell your applications that you have new fonts before the application can use them. A font manager typically handles both functions. It converts a given font from its distribution format into a form accessible to your software. In addition, the font manager moves the font to a disk directory in which your applications can find it. The font manager also will register the font with your application or operating system so that your software knows that the font is available.

Downloading

For your printer to be able to rasterize text into printable form, it needs access to the character definitions represented by a given font. Ordinarily your printer cannot reach into the files stored on your hard disk. You must send the font data to your printer, downloading it from your PC to your printer. Font managers normally take care of this chore.

Early font managers required that you specify which fonts you wanted to download, and it was up to you to ensure that the fonts your printer required got downloaded before your documents called for that font. State-of-the-art font managers operate interactively with your applications, checking which fonts are needed and downloading them into your printer as necessary.

Substitution

When someone sends you a document file that calls for a font that you don't have, you have a problem. Your system can't invent new font definitions (at least not easily), but it cannot rasterize the characters in the document either on the screen or in your printer without a font definition. Rather than leave big blank spaces, the font manager will substitute a font it knows for one it doesn't. In primitive systems, the result of this font substitution is that everything invariably turns up in Courier. Smarter font managers are able to make better substitutions, usually finding a close match for the fonts you need.

Several dedicated font managers are in wide use with today's software, operating systems, and printers. These include Adobe Type Manager, Hewlett-Packard's FontSmart, and Windows TrueType.

Adobe Type Manager

The best known font manager is Adobe Systems's Adobe Type Manager. The primary purpose of ATM is to allow you to see on screen exactly what you're printouts will look like. To accomplish that, ATM acts as a font rasterizer, taking the character shape definitions of the outline fonts used by your programs and converting them into bit maps that can be displayed on your screen. IBM's OS/2 Warp includes ATM as standard equipment, and you can add ATM to both Mac systems and Windows. The latest version, called Super ATM or SATM, adds on-the-fly font substitution to the functions of the program.

ATM's font substitution lets you see an approximation of fonts you don't have. For example, if you are editing a document that calls for a Baskerville font and you've not installed Baskerville, ATM displays a close match for it. ATM derives the substitute font from one of two standard-equipment fonts (Adobe Serif and Adobe Sans) using Adobe's Multiple Master Font technology. ATM only uses these fonts for making substitutes (they don't appear in any menu, so you can't use them in your documents). To make substitutions, ATM relies on a database that lists about 1300 fonts from the Adobe type library that provides the descriptive data necessary for making its approximations. Consequently, ATM cannot substitute for fonts not in the Adobe library, such as Bitstream fonts, and makes no attempt to do so. In the Mac environment, ATM operates from two components, a Control Panel Device (CDEV) and a driver that differs according to your Mac model (specifically, the microprocessor in your Mac determines which driver you need. Different versions are available for PCs that use the 68000 microprocessor and those that use the 68020 and later chips. Machines in the former class include the original Mac, the Mac Plus, the Mac Classic, the original Portable, the PowerBook 100, and Mac SE with the 68000 microprocessor. These all use the ~ATM68000 driver. Other Macs use the ~ATM68020/030 driver.

The Mac version of ATM has gone through many revisions, each adding new features. Table 10.6 lists the most recent of these.

Table 10.6 Adobe Type Manager for Macintosh Summary History

Version	Feature
ATM 2.0	Faster performance (two times faster than version 1.2)
ATM 2.0.2	Bugs removed, better searching abilities
ATM 2.0.3	As above for 68040 Macs such as Centris and Quadra
ATM 3.0	Multiple Master font support
ATM 3.5 (SuperATM™)	Font substitution

The PC version of ATM has gone through a similar evolution. The primary innovation brought by ATM 2.0 was a move to 32-bit technology. This increases ATM's rasterization speed to give you faster on-screen response. To match 16-bit systems (286 processor and earlier) ATM 2.0 included a special link library called ATM16.DLL. Modern 32-bit PCs use ATM32.DLL.

Version 2.5 endowed ATM with the ability to add and remove fonts without having to restart Windows, although some applications such as AmiPro 3.0 and PageMaker 4.0 require that you reselect your current printer to update the font menu. Others, such as Adobe Illustrator 4.0 and QuattroPro for Windows 1.0, require that you restart the individual application because they generate their font menus only when they start.

Although a single package, the current version of ATM for Windows comprises several files including the main program, ATMCNTRL.EXE, two link libraries, a driver file, and an .INI file. It also requires access to your PostScript font files. Table 10.7 lists these essential files and the disk locations that ATM prefers to find them in.

Table 10.7 Adobe Type Manager for Windows File Locations

File	Location	Notes
ATMCNTRL.EXE	\WINDOWS	All version
ATM16.DLL	\WINDOWS\SYSTEM	ATM 2.0 or newer
ATM32.DLL	\WINDOWS\SYSTEM	ATM 2.0 or newer
ATM.DLL	\WINDOWS\SYSTEM	ATM 1.15 or newer
ATM.INI	\WINDOWS	all versions
ATMSYS.DRV	\WINDOWS\SYSTEM	all versions
PFM files	\PSFONTS\PFM	(recommended)
PFB files	\PSFONTS	(recommended)
PCL files	\PCLFONTS	(recommended)
FON files	\WINDOWS\SYSTEM	(recommended)

These locations are not mandatory, however. You can, for example, move your fonts to other locations. ATM finds font files by looking in the [Fonts] section of your ATM.INI file, which lists the locations of the .PFM and .PFB files for your fonts. The .INI file also contains lists of font substitutions and other ATM configuration details.

Under Windows, ATM uses the .PFB and .PFM files to rasterize fonts on your screen. Files with the extension .PFB store the outline data that describe each character in the font as well as printer information concerning the font, both in binary form; .PFM files store the font metric and pair kerning information used in creating a screen replica of the individual characters, also in binary form. In addition, most fonts come with an .INF file that holds information about the font. In order to properly rasterize and display a given font on your screen, ATM needs both the .PFB and .PFM files associated with the font.

NOTE

Note that OS/2 also uses .PFM files but an OS/2 .PFM file holds different descriptions than a Windows .PFM file so the two are not compatible.

The .PFM file contains a subset of font metrics data stored in ASCII form in an Adobe .AFM file. When you install a font using ATM under Windows, ATM generates the .PFM file from the .ATM and .INF files.

Although included as standard equipment with OS/2, ATM is also sold as a standalone application. So you can use Adobe font packages without ATM, most include their own installation programs and instructions for using it. The preferred method of installing and managing a font is with ATM, however.

To install a font using ATM, you only need to click on the **Add** button once you've opened the ATM Control Panel. ATM will respond by asking you for a drive letter from which to install your font. Slide the distribution disk into your floppy or CD drive, and select the proper drive letter by highlighting it and double-clicking on it.

ATM will respond by searching the disk for installable fonts. It will list all of those that it finds in the Available Font box. Select the font you want to install by highlighting it, then click on the **Add** button again. ATM will then install the font and create a .PFM file for the font if it found none on the distribution disk.

FontSmart

Having the largest share of the printer market essentially guaranteed Hewlett-Packard the lion's share of support headaches fostered by people who bought expensive hardware but couldn't get their fonts to work. To help get more quality from their printers with less confusion, HP developed its own font control software to accompany the fonts it sold for its machines. From simple installation software, the HP product has grown to a true font management system called FontSmart, which was introduced in conjunction with the company's LaserJet 5P and 5MP printers operating in conjunction with Windows 3.1 and later versions.

FontSmart is a bridge between the worlds of PostScript and TrueType, integrating management of both TrueType and Abode Type 1 fonts with bit-mapped fonts. All fonts install using the same simple Windows-based user interface so that all become accessible to your applications on essentially equal terms. The FontSmart system not only includes a wide variety of fonts (110 TrueType fonts, 45 TrueType fonts resident in the LaserJet 5P printer or 35 in the LaserJet 5MP, the balance on disk) but it handles any other font in its three compatible formats.

In addition to installing fonts, FontSmart also provides a mechanism for archiving them or keeping them in near-line storage. It helps you pare down the number of fonts you keep loaded to the essentials to keep Windows up to speed while providing quick access to the fonts you occasionally use. In addition, it will compress little-used fonts so they take a minimum of disk space so you don't have to risk losing them in off-line storage. The compression algorithm used by FontSmart can squeeze a font so that it takes up as little as 10% of the space it would require in native form. FontSmart also lets you view fonts and will magnify them for a detailed look.

Older Hewlett-Packard printers used a more primitive Hewlett-Packard font management system called the HP Font Installer. Both FontSmart and Font Installer use the same metaphor for installing fonts. The process requires only that you move the name of the font from one side of the screen to the other to install or remove a font.

For example, to install downloadable fonts to your Hewlett-Packard LaserJet using Windows, you select the FontSmart using its icon or the HP Font Installer program (which is buried inside Print Manager). To launch Font Installer, choose **Printer Setup** under the Options menu at the main Print Manager screen, then choose the **Setup** option from the Printer dialog box, then the **Fonts** button from the dialog box associated with your printer. You'll then see a screen like the one shown in Figure 10.5:

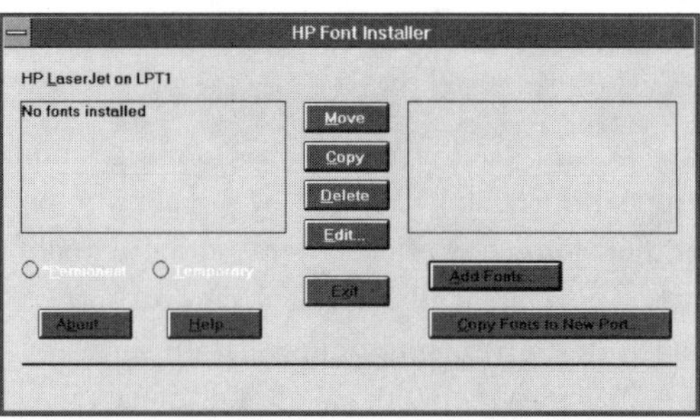

Figure 10.5 The user interface of the Hewlett-Packard Font Installer.

To install a font, select Add Fonts, then slide your font disk into a disk drive (A: is the default). The Font Installer will make entries to load your soft fonts in your PC's WIN.INI file. These entries are specific to a single printer, keyed by port number and driver. The Font Installer allows you to add the same downloadable font entries to another printer using its **Copy Fonts to New Port** button in the main Font Installer dialog box. Most third-party fonts for LaserJet printers that are not recognized by the Font Installer come with their own downloading utilities.

The process for FontSmart's three essential functions (installing, uninstalling, and deleting fonts) is the same. When you run FontSmart, fonts available for installing are listed on the left side of the screen. To install a font, FontSmart decompresses the font from its distribution to usable form, adding an entry for the font to your WIN.INI file. The listing of the font name in FontSmart then moves from the left to the right side of the screen. Uninstalling a font compresses the font file and deletes the reference to the font in your WIN.INI file so that your programs can no longer use it, at least until you install the font once again. The uninstalled font is again listed on the left side of the FontSmart screen, making it available for re-installation. Deleting a font first uninstalls it, removes any reference to it in FontSmart, and physically erases the font from your hard disk. (A few special FontSmart fonts don't actually get deleted but are kept in a highly compressed format on your disk.) As a default, FontSmart keeps its font files in your \WINDOWS\SYSTEM subdirectory.

FontSmart is relatively resource intensive and can steal a substantial share of your system's processing power when it its activated. When you start FontSmart, by default it searches your entire system disk for installable fonts to build the list it shows on your screen. With a large drive with many fonts, this process can be quite time consuming. Installing fonts, too, takes time; and more complex fonts require commensurately more time to install. It's best to run as few other applications as possible when you run FontSmart. That way more of your system's power will be available to FontSmart. Moreover, FontSmart must call each running application to advise it that the list of available fonts has changed. (Even so, some applications might not register newly installed fonts until the next time you launch them.)

Fonts downloaded to HP LaserJet and compatible printers using Font Installer or FontSmart are treated either as temporary or permanent. Temporary fonts are downloaded only when they are needed–when the printer driver encounters one while printing through a file. The temporary font remains in memory only until the end of the print job, at which point it is discarded. Permanent fonts are loaded into the printer upon initialization of any print job and remain in the printer's memory until specifically discarded or the printer's power is switched off.

NOTE

Note that you cannot assume that all so-called HP compatible printers will accept downloaded fonts identically with HP's own machines. For example, some printers that emulate the LaserJet allow you to load soft fonts only at the beginning of a print job, not during it. These machine, which include the Apricot Laser and Kyocera F-1010, cannot use temporary soft fonts with the standard Windows PCL driver.

Windows

Microsoft improved font management in Microsoft Windows with the addition of TrueType technology to version 3.1, making font management almost invisible in the everyday operation of your PC. Once you've installed a font, you can use it with impunity in all your Windows applications, get very good what-you-see-is-what-you-get performance, and never have to worry about downloading files to your printer.

With Windows 95, Microsoft improved TrueType handling to tie it more tightly to the user interface and give it 32-bit speed thanks to a new image rasterizer. The new power allows the rasterizer to generate more complex characters with more accuracy, for example smoothing the rough edges of characters.

About the only time you need to worry about fonts with Windows 95 is during installation. To install, remove, or simply check out fonts, you only need to click on the **Fonts** icon in Control Panel. (You load Control Panel from the **Settings** selection at the **Start** button.)

The default display in the Windows 95 font manager assigns each font file an icon. In that the icons are nearly identical, differing only in the characters identifying the type of font file, such as TT for TrueType, the icon display is generally a waste of screen space, as is apparent in Figure 10.6. The **List** option available under **View** in the menu (as shown in the figure) displays all of your installed fonts in a much more compact form.

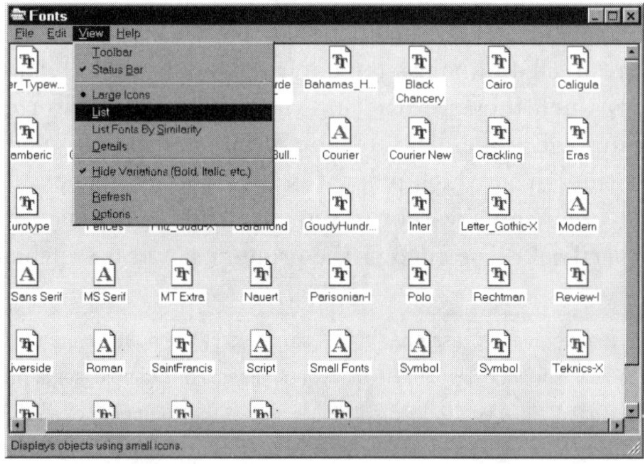

Figure 10.6 The Windows 95 font manager showing the icon view.

Clicking on any font icon or font name in the list will display font identifying data (such as the complete typeface name, its version, its developer, and the size of the font file) as well as a sample of the font itself in various sizes. The Windows 95 font manager also allows you to print a sample of the font so that you can better judge its on-paper look. For example, Figure 10.7 shows the Windows 95 display of the TrueType font Times New Roman.

Figure 10.7 The Windows font manager display of a TrueType font.

Installing a new font using the Windows 95 font manager requires nothing more than selecting Install New Font from the font manager's File menu, as shown in Figure 10.8.

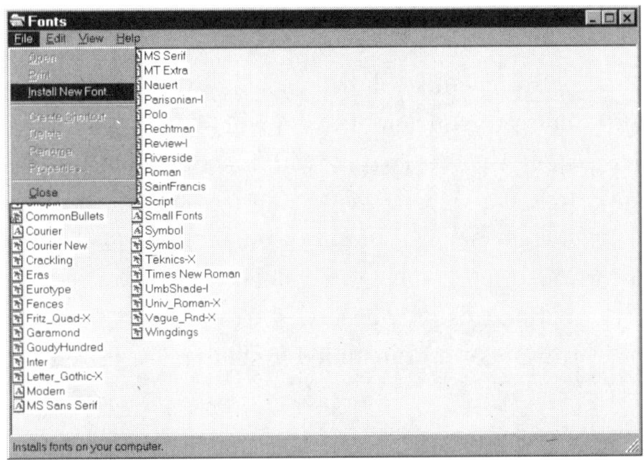

Figure 10.8 Selecting to install a new font through Windows 95.

When you select **Install New Font**, the font manager will open its Add Fonts window, which lists the fonts available for installation in the path that you specify. Once you've opened this window, select the drive and directory that holds your new font, typically your floppy disk or CD drive. The font manager will search it and display the fonts, as shown in Figure 10.9.

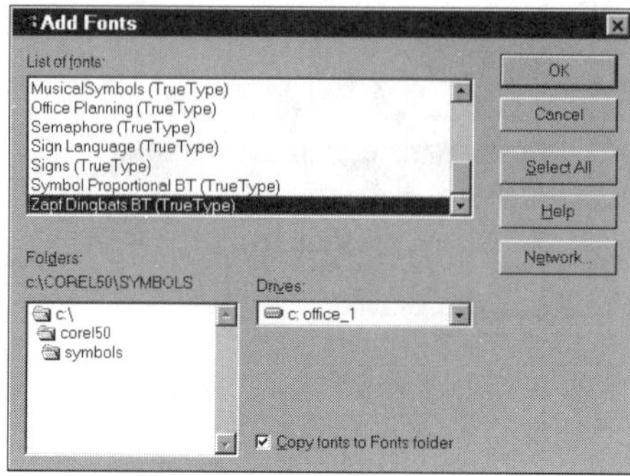

Figure 10.9 Selecting a font to install through the Add Fonts window.

Installing a font through Windows 95 merely makes your applications aware that the font exists. The font installer makes no fundamental change in the font. Indeed, unless you tell it to do so, it won't even move your fonts from your distribution disk. To ensure that your new fonts are loaded into your system for future use, be sure that the **Copy Fonts to Fonts Folder** option box is checked, as shown in the figure, when you install new fonts. By default, Windows 95 locates the Fonts Folder inside your \WINDOWS directory.

After installation, all your fonts will be available to all your Windows applications. Selecting the font function in your application will allow you to choose which of the installed fonts to use. Note that every time you select the font function in your application, the Windows font manager scans the entire list of installed fonts to display the menu selections. If you install a large number of fonts–hundreds rather than dozens–you're apt to encounter substantial delays when you select a font feature. Unless your supply of patience is only exceeded by your love of variety in typesetting, you'll want to limit your selection of installed fonts to a few dozen favorites.

Creating Bit-Mapped Fonts

When you can't find the one font your really want among the 10,000 or more that are available commercially, you're not out of luck, although you may run short of patience questing the alternative. You can design your own bit-mapped font, download it to your printer, and rattle out text the way you want it to look, paying no royalties and no heed to such trivial considerations as aesthetics. You might even create a font that's so beautiful that it will forever commemorate your name like that of Frederic Goudy or Charles Courier.

Designing a bit-mapped font can be as easy as playing checkers. In fact, you can even use a checkerboard and playing pieces to help you visualize what you're creating. The whole process is little more than stacking the dots. Instead of skill, you need patience and the single-mindedness to work your way through an entire alphabet.

The character design process involves four basic steps: designing the character grid, laying out each character in the grid, calculating the code values that describe the character layouts, and sending the resulting codes to your printer. You can design characters for any bit-addressable printer. The higher the resolution of the printer and of each character, however, the more data you need to create and the more complex and tedious the design process.

The most basic but still useful case is the nine-pin dot-matrix printer. What follows is such an example, one that uses the industry-standard Epson ESC /P command system.

Design the Character Cell

Before you can begin to lay out a character, you need to design the cell into which it will fit. In other words, you need to calculate the size of each character in dots.

The character size will vary with the printer and the mode in which you choose to print. Characters printed with nine-pin printers will obviously need smaller cells than those for 24-pin printers.

For most line printers, the height of the character cell in Draft mode corresponds to the number of pins or nozzles in a line. Therefore, a nine-pin printer will use a character cell nine dots high in draft mode. The width of the cell varies with the printer and its operating mode. For Epson nine-pin printers in monospaced Draft mode, the character cell is eleven dots wide. Therefore, each character cell for an Epson nine-pin printer in Draft mode will be a grid measuring nine dots high by eleven dots wide. In near letter quality mode (in printers that have one), Epson nine-wire printers use a character cell measuring 18 dots high by 12 dots wide.

When you want to design proportionally spaced characters, you can vary with width of the character cell. In the Epson system, you can begin a proportionally spaced character with any column in the character cell from one to seven and end the character with any column (but, obviously, it must be a later column than the starting column). You will later specify the width of the character when sending the downloadable code to the printer using the values of the starting and ending columns.

To make the design process easier, you'll want to mark off on graph paper a number of character cells of the appropriate dimension that matches the number of characters you want to design—52 for a full alphabet, for example. Alternately, you can use that old checkerboard, marking off an area of the appropriate size. You can then use the checkerboard and its pieces to preview your characters without a lot of penciling in and erasing on paper.

Lay Out Each Character

The next step is to actually fill in the character cell to indicate which dots you want to print on paper to form each character. If you're unerringly sure of yourself, you can simply ink in each square in the character cell that should get printed. If you suspect that you may need a bit of experimentation and adjustment to get each character perfectly, you can lightly sketch the character shape over the cell and then ink in the appropriate squares, or you can use the checkerboard as a sketch pad, arranging the pieces to see which alignment is most pleasing.

Epson imposes a few odd rules on downloadable character design. Although the character cell has nine vertical positions, you can only use eight in a given character. You must leave blank either the top row or the bottom row in a given character. In general, you'll want to leave the bottom row blank if the character to appear in the cell does not have descenders. If the character does have descenders, you'll want to leave the top row blank. You will specify whether to leave the top or bottom row blank when you send the character code to your printer.

The speed at which the printhead travels and the firing rate of individual print wires results in a second rule: You cannot print two adjacent dots in any row (at least with older Epson printers). In other words, you must make your solid horizontal lines out of alternating dots and blanks.

For text characters, you should leave the last two dot columns blank to provide space between characters and improve legibility. If you want to make graphic characters, however, you can fill any column with dots.

Calculate the Codes

Your printer can see or understand the patterns that you've crafted. In other words, to download the patterns into your printer, you have to translate them into codes that the printer understands. At this point, you enter in the territory of your printer's language, which may be specific to the make and model that you own.

Machines that follow the Esc /P standard require that you reduce your bit patterns into numbers following a very specific formula. You assign a numeric value to each column of dots individually by summing up the weighted value of each printed dot. In the Esc /P system, the column positions of dots are assigned in ascending powers of two (1, 2, 4, 8, 16, 32, 64, 128) from the bottom row up. For example, if you want a printed dot in the third from the bottom, fifth, and eight rows of a given column, you'd sum up 4, 16, and 128 to get 148. This number indicates to the printer which print wires to fire in that column position.

Because each character comprises 11 columns, you must calculate 11 of these numerical codes for each character in the font that you design. The string of 11 values is the code the printer will use to generate the character.

For example, to print a diamond shape, you would derive the numerical codes, as shown in Figure 10.10. If no prints are to fire in a given column, you must assign a value of zero to that column to maintain 11 separate values to code each character.

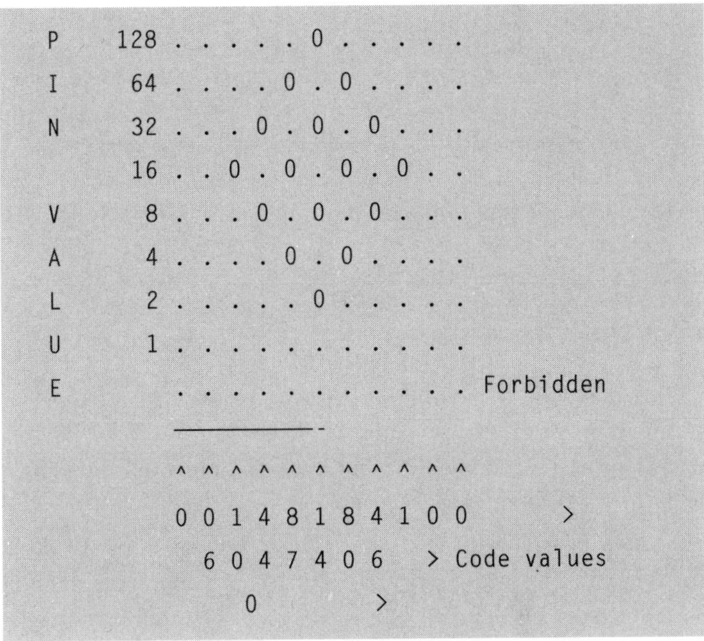

Figure 10.10 Determining code values for firing print wires.

In the example in Figure 10.11, the numerical values for the diamond shape would be the following:

Column	Code	Calculation
1	0	0+0+0+0+0+0+0+0
2	0	0+0+0+0+0+0+0+0
3	16	0+0+0+0+16+0+0+0
4	40	0+0+0+8+0+32+0+0
5	84	0+0+4+0+16+0+64+0
6	170	0+2+0+8+0+32+0+128
7	84	0+0+4+0+16+0+64+0
8	40	0+0+0+8+0+32+0+0
9	16	0+0+0+0+16+0+0+0
10	0	0+0+0+0+0+0+0+0
11	0	0+0+0+0+0+0+0+0

Figure 10.11 Calculating byte values to be sent to the printer.

The numerical values to be sent to the printer would thus be 0, 0, 16, 40, 84, 170, 84, 40, 16, 0, and 0.

Download the Characters

If you simply tried to send these numbers to your printer, all you'd get would be a series of numbers printed out on paper. In other words, to make your printer accept these values as a downloadable character, you must tell the printer what to do with the data by sending the appropriate escape codes.

Your first step is to determine *which* character you want to download. In other words, you need to assign an ASCII value to each character you download so your printer can trigger on that ASCII value to print the appropriate character. In general, you can assign a given character any value between 32 and 127 (decimal). Of course the value you assign must be unique to that download session. Not all printers allow you to define this full range, and some allow even a larger range. To be certain of the allowable range, you'll need to consult your printer's manual.

If you do not want to define an entire set of characters, you need to load a basic character set into your printer's RAM to fill in the characters you do not define. The easiest way to do this is to copy the character definitions from your printer's ROM into RAM before you define new characters. (If you copy from ROM to RAM after you define new characters, the ROM codes will erase and overwrite the definitions you download.)

The command to download ROM character codes into RAM is as follows:

```
ESC : NUL n NUL
```

This command corresponds to the string of ASCII values 27, 58, 0, *n*, 0, where the *n* encodes whether to use Roman or sans serif characters. An *n* value of zero corresponds to Roman; one, sans serif.

Next you must create an escape code to define and download each character. In the Esc /P system, the escape sequence to create a user-defined character takes the following form:

```
ESC & NUL n1 n2 a1 d1...dn
```

The first three characters, ESC & NUL, are distinct ASCII values that specify the beginning of the printer's character definition mode. (See Chapter 11, "Languages," for a full listing of Esc /P codes.) These characters are represented in ASCII by the sequence (in decimal) of 27, 38, and 0.

The next two variables, represented as *n1* and *n2* in the above command line, indicate the character range that you wish to define. The first variable is the first character of the range; the second variable, the last character. To define a single character, make n1 and n2 equal the same value. For example, to define an entire new alphabet of capital letters, make n1 = A and n2 = Z. To redefine only the % sign, make n1 = % and n2 = %. In most cases, you'll define a limited range or even one character at a time, particularly when you want to use proportionally spaced characters or those that vary between using the upper eight print wires and the lower eight.

The third variable, *a1*, encodes those print wires the printer should use for the characters you define and the width of proportionally spaced characters. The encoding is somewhat elaborate. To calculate it, you must know the starting and ending columns of each proportionally spaced character and which rows of print wires to use. You determine the value of a1 by summing up three numeric values, one representing each variable (starting column, ending column, and print wires).

When you use proportionally spaced characters, the Esc /P system assigns each starting column 1 through 7 a distinct (and nonobvious) value as multiples of 16, as listed in Table 10.8. Ending columns take a value that corresponds to their position. For monospaced characters, both values are zero.

Table 10.8 Values for Calculating Variable a1 in the Esc /P Define Character Command

Beginning Column	Value	Ending Column	Value	Pin group	Value
0	0	1	1	Upper 8	128
1	16	2	2	Lower 8	0
2	32	3	3		
3	48	4	4		
4	64	5	5		
5	80	6	6		
6	96	7	7		
7	112	8	8		
		9	9		
		10	10		
		11	11		

Leaving the bottom row blank and only using the upper eight print wires takes a numeric value of 128. Leaving the top row blank and only using the lower eight print wires takes a numeric value of zero. When you use monospaced characters, the value for a1 will thus always be 0 or 128.

The *dn* variables are a series of numbers corresponding to the character cell definitions you created. The n1, n2, and a1 values define how many numbers must be in the command. You must provide a numerical value for each column in each character you define.

Once you've downloaded all the characters you want to use, you must explicitly tell your printer to use them. The Esc /P system includes a command that switches the printer between using the built-in ROM-based character codes and the downloaded codes you put into RAM. The command takes the following form:

```
ESC % n
```

This command corresponds to the ASCII code 27, 36, *n*, where *n* indicates whether to use ROM- or RAM-based characters. When *n* equals zero, the printer is instructed to use the built-in ROM-based character codes. When *n* equals 1, the printer is instructed to use downloaded RAM-based character codes.

CHAPTER ELEVEN

Languages

When you want to tell your printer what to do, you have to learn its language; it won't learn yours. Printer languages range from single character controls to elaborate and labyrinthine descriptions of every point on a page. The names are all familiar and include Epson Esc/P2, Hewlett-Packard PCL-5e, and PostScript Level 2. Each control system has its own syntax and idiosyncrasies. Understanding them will give you direct and intimate control over all the details of your printer's the operation.

The primary difference between a wild mustang and a computer printer is that you can get the mustang under control with a lariat. A couple spare cowhands, a lot of rope, a tranquilizer gun, and a lot of patience come in handy, too. Getting a printer to do what you want isn't as easy. For that you have to learn a new language and develop a tolerance for frustration that makes bronco busting seem as soothing as a sip of brandy by a warm hearthside.

Certainly you've gotten your printer running by now. You've probably put a pulp mill or two on overtime to make the paper for all your printouts. But odds are your printer is not obeying your commands. Instead, it's listening only to your programs and the operating system on your PC. The control is indirect. When you have a specific intent, it can be as imprecise as relying on the rumor mill for your news, with the vital information filtered through other ears on its way to you.

Because a microprocessor governs the entire operation of any modern printer, you can tell your printer to do anything within its repertory by sending commands to the chip. The only limits are what the printer's programming allows it to do and what the printer's language lets you say.

Using printer languages is simply a matter of learning what to say and how to say it. As a consequence, any guide to printer languages must offer long listings of commands. This chapter includes a reference to the most important commands in the most-used printer languages so that you can become the master of your machinery.

PRINTER CONTROL

Your application software and operating system take advantage of your printer's language to help make what you see on paper resemble what you preview on your monitor screen. Using the printer's language to communicate, your PC's software gives the printer guidance on exactly how to make each printout look exactly as you'd like.

The most elementary command to your printer is sending a printable character. The printer's microprocessor reads the character from its input port, looks up the pattern the character encodes, and sends the proper timing instructions to the print engine. Printer language commands work similarly, but instead of making the microprocessor look up a pattern, they instruct the chip to check and carry out a series of instructions. For example, one command might tell the chip to move the printhead, another could tell it to substitute a new location for the map of character patterns (and thus change the font), or to use a different paper tray.

The instructions from the computer must be embedded in the character stream because that is the only data connection between the printer and its host. These embedded instructions can take on any of several forms.

Command Types

Printers consider themselves big-shot bureaucrats. They are so self-important that they won't even listen to you if you don't use the proper form of address. You can't just tell one what to do. It will so obstinately refuse that you'd think you were asking a favor without first making a contribution to a campaign fund.

Unlike mere human beings, most PC printers are immovable by money. They extract their toll in precision. They require the commands you make to precisely match those they deign to obey. Form is as important as function. If you don't put your instructions in the proper form, the printer will neither distinguish them from the sea of noise called data nor act in the way you want.

Printer commands use two means to stand out from other data. In one, they gain attention by oddity. They don't look like other data to the printer because they use special, reserved code values. The other form uses a waving flag to draw attention to the command. One special code serves as the attention getter, making a sequence of ordinary data stand out as a printer instruction. The first form, the special codes, are called *control characters*; the second, *escape sequences*.

Control Characters

Some of the most necessary instructions for your PC printer are ones that you naturally type at the keyboard, for example, the space, backspace, and tab. Keyboards use special, noncharacter codes to transmit these instructions to your PC. The same codes (or similar ones with the same purposes) can be sent to your printer to elicit the required responses. These commands in addition to a number of the most commonplace typing functions proved so important that they were granted privileged status when the ASCII code was developed.

These special ASCII values are the set of control characters. Your printer recognizes them by their special values and carries out the appropriate action. For example, when the ASCII value 08 appears in the data stream, your printer recognizes it as a control character telling it to backspace. The printer then moves its carriage back one space or positions the cursor in its raster buffer one position backward.

Note that these control characters can only work when a printer deals with text data. When printing graphics, most PC printers recognize any byte value as a bit pattern representing printable data. Control characters would not stand out from data representing printable dot patterns. Consequently control characters are often not recognized or acted upon when they are included in an instruction to a printer to generate graphic output.

Nearly all documents and printing jobs call upon the same range of text printing functions, so most printers need to carry out the same control functions. To give a standard the means to elicit the most basic of those functions, the American National Standards Institute defined a standard set of control characters in developing the ASCII code. Table 11.1 lists these standardized control characters.

Table 11.1 ANSI Control Characters

Decimal	Hex	Code	Name	Function
0	00	^@	NUL	Used as a fill character
1	01	^A	SOH	Start of heading (indicator)
2	02	^B	STX	Start of text (indicator)
3	03	^C	ETX	End of text (indicator)
4	04	^D	EOT	End of transmission; disconnect character
5	05	^E	ENQ	Enquiry; request for an answerback message

Table 11.1 continued

Decimal	Hex	Code	Name	Function
6	06	^F	ACK	Acknowledge
7	07	^G	BEL	Sounds audible bell tone
8	08	^H	BS	Backspace
9	09	^I	HT	Horizontal tab
10	0A	^J	LF	Line feed
11	0B	^K	VT	Vertical tab
12	0C	^L	FF	Form feed
13	0D	^M	CR	Carriage return
14	0E	^N	SO	Shift out; changes character set
15	0F	^O	SI	Shift in; changes character set
16	10	^P	DLE	Data link escape
17	11	^Q	DC1	Data control 1, also known as XON
18	12	^R	DC2	Data control 2
19	13	^S	DC3	Data control 3, also known as XOFF
20	14	^T	DC4	Data control 4
21	15	^U	NAK	Negative acknowledge
22	16	^V	SYN	Synchronous idle
23	17	^W	ETB	End of transmission block (indicator)
24	18	^X	CAN	Cancel; immediately ends any escape sequence
25	19	^Y	EM	End of medium (indicator)
26	1A	^Z	SUB	Substitute (also, end-of-file marker)
27	1B	^[	ESC	Escape; introduces escape sequence
28	1C	^\	FS	File separator (indicator)
29	1D	^]	GS	Group separator (indicator)
30	1E	^^	RS	Record separator (indicator)
31	1F	^_	US	Unit separator (indicator)
32	20		SP	Space character
127	7F		NUL	No operation
128	80		Reserved	Reset parser with no action (Esc)
129	81		Reserved	Reset parser with no action (Esc A)

130	82	Reserved	Reset parser with no action (Esc B)
131	83	Reserved	Reset parser with no action (Esc C)
132	84	IND	Index; increment active line (move paper up)
133	85	NEL	Next line; advance to first character of next line
134	86	SSA	Start of selected area (indicator)
135	87	ESA	End of selected area (indicator)
136	88	HTS	Set horizontal tab (at active column)
137	89	HTJ	Horizontal tab with justification
138	8A	VTS	Set vertical tab stop (at current line)
139	8B	PLD	Partial line down
140	8C	PLU	Partial line up
141	8D	RI	Reverse index (move paper down one line)
142	8E	SS2	Single shift 2
143	8F	SS3	Single shift 3
144	90	DCS	Device control string
145	91	PU1	Private use 1
146	92	PU2	Private use 2
147	93	STS	Set terminal state
148	94	CCH	Cancel character
149	95	MW	Message writing
150	96	SPA	Start of protected area (indicator)
151	97	EPA	End of protected area (indicator)
152	98	Reserved	Function same as Esc X
153	99	Reserved	Function same as Esc Y
154	9A	Reserved	Function same as Esc Z
155	9B	CSI	Control sequence introducer
156	9C	ST	String terminator
157	9D	OSC	Operating system command (indicator)
158	9E	PM	Privacy message
159	9F	APC	Application program command

Wonderful as it is to have a standard, this one is usually ignored. For example, the IBM character set (see Chapter 10) provides its own definitions to ASCII code values higher than 127 to accommodate a wider range of printable characters, such as things like block graphics, foreign language accents, and smiley faces. (One rationale for this choice is that these high-value characters—often called *high-bit characters*—could not be accessed through a seven-bit digital code and consequently were not universal even before IBM sidestepped the standard.) Because of the appropriation of these high-bit characters for higher purposes, only the lower 32 ASCII values are actually used as universal control characters.

Escape Sequences

To augment the handful of control characters available to printers operating with a seven-bit connection, ANSI added a second means of sending instructions to printers, using the ASCII code 27 (decimal) as an attention-getting character. Because the ASCII code calls this character Escape and it serves to mark the beginning of a string or sequence of several characters making up a printer instruction, this form of command is often called an escape sequence.

As your printer processes the data stream it receives through its interface, it watches for the appearance of the Esc character. When the printer sees the character, it reads it as well as the next few characters, comparing them to the table of commands that it understands. When it makes a match, it carries out the associated function, suppressing the print of the characters in the instruction. After the printer identifies the command and all the characters associated with it (which can be a string of several hundred additional bytes), it resumes its monitoring of the data stream and begins again to print the textual part of the data stream.

ANSI defined several escape sequences designed for use by printers working with seven-bit characters. Table 11.2 lists some of the most common of these escape sequences. Some people use the term *escape code* to mean the same thing.

Table 11.2 Escape Sequences for Seven-Bit Environments

Escape sequence	Decimal Value	Hex Value	Function
Esc D	27 68	1B 44	Index
Esc E	27 69	1B 45	Vertical line
Esc H	27 72	1B 48	Set horizontal tab

Esc Z	27 90	1B 5A	Set vertical tab
Esc K	27 75	1B 4B	Partial line down
Esc L	27 76	1B 4C	Partial line up
Esc M	27 77	1B 4D	Reverse index
Esc N	27 78	1B 4E	Single shift 2
Esc O	27 79	1B 4F	Single shift 3
Esc P	27 80	1B 50	Device control string
Esc [	27 91	1B 5B	Control sequence introducer
Esc \	27 92	1B 5C	String terminator
Esc]	27 93	1B 5D	Operating system command
Esc ^	27 94	1B 5E	Private message
Esc _	27 95	1B 5F	Application program command

The list of ANSI standard escape sequences hardly covers the range of possibilities of even a modest modern printer. After all, the ANSI list was composed in the days when the only thing anyone ever wanted to print was text, pecked out one character at a time as if it were the work of a typewriter. In the modern world, printers handle graphics as adroitly as text, sometimes treating text *as* graphics, rendering it from bit images generated by your PC's software.

To take care of the needs of modern graphic printing, most manufacturers have created their own systems of commands based on an expansion of the escape sequence concept. Of the three most important languages for controlling printers in use today, two (Epson Esc/P and Hewlett-Packard PCL) are based on the use of escape sequences. Only PostScript goes in its own directions, and that is because it is meant to describe the appearance of printed material rather than control the operation of printers.

You can consider both Esc/P and PCL to be escape sequence dialects. The concepts behind the two and the means by which they issue commands are the same. Different are the functions assigned the characters in the sequence themselves. Just as someone speaking with a strong dialect might be incomprehensible to you, a printer meant for one family of escape sequences can understand the codes used by another unless it is explicitly able to emulate the other printer (in effect, speak a second language).

Sending Printer Commands

During the normal execution of an application's print routine, your software generates the language commands necessary for all the details of printing a line or a page. The command are automatically embedded in the data your PC sends to the printer. You don't have to worry about them or even know about the details.

Your software may not know or understand some of the features of your printer, or it may simply not deign to give you control over them. The reluctance of your software shortchanges the capabilities of your printer–and it may add immeasurably to your frustration and blood pressure. In some cases you can take direct command by pressing the appropriate button combinations on your printer's control panel.

The solution is to send software commands to your printer yourself. While that sounds good in the abstract, carrying out the transmission is another matter entirely. You can't just stand there and chant commands at your printer to get them carried out, at least not today. Nor are the other, more human means of communicating available to you, not smoke signals, semaphore flags, or even blackboard scribblings.

Without a channel for sending commands, knowing a printer language doesn't seem especially useful. In fact, you don't have a single way of working with a printer language directly. You have at least four: creating your own programs, embedding commands in the documents you print, sending setup strings to your printer, or embedding control codes. Which of these four are useable depends on what you want to do, your dedication, and what your software allows you.

Custom Programs

The most direct and powerful way of controlling your printer is to write a program that sends the commands you want out through your printer port.

In the olden days when DOS was king, writing your own programs that issued printer commands was easy. You could put your commands in a file and simply copy them to your printer or, more efficiently, create a simple program that sent out the commands. Although crafting custom programs to run under Windows 95 can take more effort than most folks are willing to use just to send a control code to a printer, you can still use the old DOS techniques with the newer operating system.

The Copy Technique

The DOS **COPY** command can be your friend when you want to send commands to your printer. It will diligently send almost anything you want to any printer you can name under the DOS naming conventions (PRN or LPTx). All you have to do is supply **COPY** with the data to send. You have two ways of giving the information to **COPY**, interactively or through a file.

To supply data to the **COPY** command interactively, you specify the keyboard (which DOS calls the console or CON) as the origin of the data. Once you give the proper command, you only need to type the printer commands at your keyboard and **COPY** will relay them to your printer.

To start copy in interactive operation, type the following command at the DOS prompt:

```
COPY CON LPT1
```

If you've connected your printer to some port other than the first parallel port, substitute the port designation in the command.

The **COPY** command will continue to relay everything you type to the printer until you tell it to stop. You can type in any ASCII code by pressing and holding down the **Alt** key and typing the ASCII code in decimal on the numeric keypad, releasing **Alt** after the last number. The brakes take the form of the end-of-file character, **Ctrl-Z**, which you can send by holding down **Ctrl** and pressing **Z** or by simply pressing **F6** (if you haven't redefined your PC's function keys, of course).

Although working interactively can be satisfying, it has its shortcomings. Make an error, and you suffer the punishment, without recourse the moment your mistake permanent by pressing the **Enter** key. Typing the Byzantine commands themselves can be a gymnastic challenge to type, often made from keystroke combinations only a contortionist could master. Even when the commands involve only plain text characters, some printer languages make even simple operations long strings that challenge both your fingers and memory.

Substituting the mind and memory of the PC for your own simplifies sending commands to your printer. You can encapsulate all of your commands in a file and use **COPY** to forward the details out your parallel port. The process involves only one extra step compared to the interactive technique, and the extra step will save immeasurable effort in the future.

All you have to do is substitute a file name for the LPT1 in the interactive command, which tells DOS to take the keystrokes that you type and save them as a file under t he name you specify. Later, you can use the **COPY** command again to send the file to your printer, reusing the same file as often as you want.

Although you can use any file name you want to store your keystroke commands, you'll want to use something memorable. If you stick with the old DOS eight-plus-three file name convention, you'll probably want to assign an identifiable extension to your command file names, for example, .BIN to indicate the contents are binary data. Avoid the likely choices that you might later confuse with other file types, such as .COM or .CMD for "command" (which you might mistake for executable files).

Using Windows 95's long file names lets you be more explicit. Moreover, you can avoid file name extensions and make the file names read like real commands. For example, "Change to landscape with banner type" would be perfectly acceptable as a Windows 95 file name. (Avoid manipulating the file with older applications that might cause the name to be truncated to obscurity, like CHANGE~1.)

Once you have a file of printer commands, you can build a batch file around it so that you can type a command or click on an icon to send the instructions to your printer. All you have to do is put the **COPY** command in a batch file. Again, use a readily comprehensible name. Under the DOS 8+3 file name convention, you could use the same name as the command file, substituting the extension .BAT to make it a batch file. Under Windows 95, things are even better. You can give your batch file a name like "Send Form Feed to Printer.BAT." The batch file will appear as an icon labeled exactly that (but, by default without the extension appearing) that you can click on to send your command.

The .COM File Technique

The COPY technique has only a few limitations, but they can be fatal. For example, you won't be able to puts an end-of-file character in your command because DOS will think you've finished typing in command characters as soon as you press the **Ctrl-Z** combination. Moreover, some purists think that the batch file technique is messy because it requires two files for each command set. To avoid these shortcomings, you can make your own short programs that issue printer commands.

The trick is to take advantage of the function calls that have been part of every version of DOS since 2.0. By making a function call, you let DOS do the work of transferring individual bytes to your printer using a file that's only a few bytes longer than the command itself. You can quickly type in everything you need and produce your own machine language program.

In machine language a program takes the form of a set of instructions, each of which is only a byte or two long. The program you will want to build requires only these steps:

1. Tell your PC where to find the command to send your printer;
2. Tell your PC what part of the interrupt routine to use;

3. Tell your PC to execute the interrupt routine;
4. List the data to send to your printer; and
5. Tell your PC the program is finished.

In the realm of PCs, sometimes you have to do things backward. In a working version of this program, for example, you tell your PC the program is over *before* you give it the data to use. This expedient allows this general form of program to issue a command string of any reasonable length. In addition, note that the two bytes specifying the string location are in reverse order because of the *little endian* numbering system used by Intel microprocessors.

The general form of the printer command program is as follows:

```
Byte          Assembler           Function
values        instructions

BA 09 01      MOV DX,0109H        ;Loads string location
B4 09         MOV AH,09H          ;Loads function call number
CD 21         INT 21H             ;Calls interrupt
CD 20         INT 20H             ;Ends program
??                                ;Command string data bytes
24                                ;Ends data string
```

To make this printer command program work, create a file using the byte values shown in the first column. You can use a disk editor to enter the byte values. If you have the DOS program DEBUG available on your PC, you can enter the assembler instructions into it after giving the A (for assemble) instruction. Substitute the string of byte comprising the printer command for the ?? in the example above, appending the hexadecimal value 24 (a dollar sign) at the end to tell DOS the command is over. Write the complete file to disk, naming it with the file name extension .COM.

Creating and writing a file using Debug requires three steps, as follows:

1. Give the file a name. To be an executable program, you must give the file the extension **.COM**. The name can be anything that's valid under the DOS naming convention, but should be memorable and short so that you don't mind typing it. For example, you could name a file **FORMFEED.COM** or if your fingers tire readily, **FF.COM**. You tell Debug what name to use with the **N**

command. At the Debug-prompt, type **N**, a space, and the name you want to give your new program.

2. Next, you must tell Debug how long your program is. Specify the length of the program by loading it into the CX register. You don't have to know what that means; just type the command **RCX** at the Debug-prompt. Debug will reply with the value zero and a new prompt, a colon. After the colon, type in the length of your program in hexadecimal characters. If you use the **Assemble** command, you'll find the length in hex as the last four digits of the last number Debug shows on the left of your screen minus 100 (hex). In other words, if Debug ends with 09F8:013F, your program is 3F (Hex) bytes long. Type this value in response to the colon prompt after the **RCX** command.
3. Finally, you must instruct Debug to write your new program to disk using the write command, **W**. Simply type **W** at the Debug- prompt and press **Enter**. Debug will tell you how many bytes it wrote to disk. Your new program is now complete.

Once your program has been successfully written to disk, typing the name you gave the program will send the commands you've written into it to your PC's PRN device.

Embedded Commands

Because most printer commands are little more than strings of text, you can sometimes include–or in computer terminology, embed–them inside the files that you want to print. The program then obediently sends the commands to your printer as if they were ordinary text, and your printer interprets the command and then carries it out.

The only difficulty you'll encounter is getting characters beyond the normal text range to your printer. Many programs won't accept characters other than those that you could normally read on the screen; others might let you type these unreadable characters but they will strip them from the data stream that they send to your printer. Since most printer commands start with the special Esc character, this small difficulty is sometimes an insurmountable obstacle.

A few programs make specific provisions for embedding printer commands, for example, MultiMate Advantage II and Professional Write. Most of the time, however, the software may restrict the use of embedded characters, for example, to the top of the document only. Moreover, most more recent programs omit this feature. If your software offers this ability, you'll find instructions for using it (if at all) in your application program's manual typically in the section called something like "Printer Commands." Each program with this feature uses its own technique and syntax, which you should find in the same place.

Other program packages, mostly the disappearing breed written to exploit the capabilities of old dot-matrix printers, allow you to embed control codes into your files so that you can send commands to your printer. For example, the Edit program that accompanies DOS 5.0 or later lets you embed printer commands by holding down the **Ctrl** key and pressing the letter P, releasing the **Ctrl** key, then pressing **Esc** followed by the value you want to send to your printer. Table 11.3 lists some other programs that allow this form of embedding as well as the keystrokes needed to carry out the process.

Table 11.3 Sending Escape Sequences Through Popular Programs

Program	Escape Key	Example (Reset)
Borland Quattro	\027	\027E
dBase III+	?? CHR(27)+	?? CHR(27)+"E"
dBase IV	??? CHR(27)+	??? CHR(27)+"E"
Edlin (DOS 3.0 to 4.1)	(Control key +V) [	^V[E
Enable	%^27,	%^27,69
Framework	CHR(27)+	?? CHR(27)+"E"
GWBASIC	LPRINT CHR$(27);	LPRINT CHR$(27);"E";
Lotus 1-2-3	\027	\027E
Lotus Symphony	\027	\027E
MS Word (DOS)	[Alt]027	[Alt]027 069
MultiMate	(ALT Key + A) 027	027 E
Professional Write	*P 27, *	*P 27,69*
Q&A	*P 27, *	*P 27,69*
Quicken	\027	\027E
WordPerfect	<27>	<27>E
WordStar	^[	^[E

The extra keystrokes that you type serve as "introducers," telling the program to expect the next character as a printer command. Because this form of command makes no provision for indicating the end of a command, it serves only for sending single characters to your printer. To send longer sequences, you have to retype the introductory keystrokes for each character of the printer command. After awhile, all that typing gets pretty tedious, so you'll probably want to assign a macro to the most embedded common printer commands that you issue.

Setup Strings

Some application programs (such as versions of Lotus 1-2-3, Paradox, Quattro, and WordStar) allow you to specify a setup string, a list of commands that get sent to your printer every time the program starts sending out a print job. The setup string is meant to initialize your printer and ensure that some other program has not left the printer in some strange, obscure mode such as printing vector curves in blue. You can alter the setup string to put your printer in the state you want, specifying a font, paper bin, orientation, and so on.

The opportunities for using this technique are limited. Not all programs make provisions for your customizing setup strings. Moreover, the setup string technique allows control only at the beginning of a print job. You can't change fonts in the middle of the data stream.

Again, the technique and syntax of adding custom setup strings to software that supports them is application specific. You will want to check your program's manual to find out how to use this technology and even whether your software has the required capability.

STANDARDS

The reigning printer language standards are all classed as *de facto* standards. That is, rather than wearing the imprimatur of a disconsolate industry committee, they are like celebrities who are famous chiefly for being famous. The printer language standards are popular primarily because they are popular. A lot of people and printers use them, so the people designing new printers go with the flow and use whatever everyone else is using.

This lack of imagination is immaterial. What really matters is that the decision to follow the leader means that you can have some degree of assurance. When a printer emulates a leader (or is the leader itself), you can be sure that you'll be able to use the widest range of applications successfully.

Many printer makers have developed what they have believed to be superior printer control languages. In face of dominance of PCL and PostScript, however, all have fallen by the wayside. Neither size of the promoter nor innovation has been able to derail the dominance of these two systems. For example, both the Canon and Lexmark languages, the latter originally developed by IBM's printer division before it was spun off to make Lexmark, failed to gain any acceptance beyond their original promoters. Both are now languages dead as Latin, fixed forever in time and destined to be spoken less and less.

Antecedents

The first important group of printers to be used with PCs were the fully formed character machines that help word processors push the typewriter out of the secretarial pool. Although most of those old daisy wheels have been retired, their memory lingers. Escape sequences designed for them are still in use, incorporated into the command sets of some of the most recent printers.

As you should expect, the escape sequences used by these text-only printers were centered around the needs of typing and mostly concern the exact and speedy movement of the printhead. Because these printers were slow, both in comparison to modern machines and the ability of even early PCs to grind out documents, their commands were mostly meant for shaving the time needed for printing each page by letting your PC determine the most efficient way to move the printhead, a job these early machines weren't smart enough to handle themselves. Other commands concerned the minutiae of running a balky impact printer.

Diablo and Qume

Two manufacturers led the early fully formed character printer industry, the Diablo division of Xerox Corporation and Qume, a company that has passed through many hands since establishing its place in the industry as part of the ITT conglomerate. Working from the same foundation of ANSI escape codes, each manufacturer developed its own elaboration on the standard for its printer products. In fact, the command sets developed by each are quite similar, differing by but a few instructions, reflecting their shared origin and the common needs of daisy-wheel printing. Table 11.4 summarizes the escape sequences used by some of the last models of daisy-wheel printers made by these two manufacturers, the Diablo 630 and Sprint 11.

Table 11.4 Fully Formed Character Printer Escape Sequences

Escape Sequence	Function
Esc BS	*Backspace 1/120 inch
Esc LF	*Negative (backwards) line feed
Esc SO	Shift to primary mode
Esc SI	Return to normal mode
Esc RS n	*Define vertical spacing increment as n-1
Esc US n	*Set horizontal space increment to n-1
Esc VT n	*Absolute vertical tab to line n-1
Esc HT	*Absolute horizontal tab to column n-1
Esc SP	Print special character position 004
Esc SUB I	Initialize printer
Esc SUB SO	Terminal self-test
Esc CR P	Initialize printer
Esc 0	*Set right margin
Esc 1	*Set horizontal tab stop
Esc 2	*Clear all horizontal tab stops
Esc 3	*Graphic on with 1/60 inch resolution
Esc 4	*Graphics off
Esc 5	*Forward print
Esc 6	*Backward print
Esc 8	*Clear horizontal tab stop
Esc 9	*Set left margin
Esc .	Auto line feed on
Esc ,	Auto line feed off
Esc <	Auto bidirectional printing on
Esc >	Auto bidirectional printing off
Esc +	Set top margin
Esc -	Set bottom margin

Esc @ T	Enter user test mode
Esc #	Enter secondary mode
Esc $	*WPS (proportional spaced printwheel) on
Esc %	*WPS (proportional spaced printwheel) off
Esc (n	Set tabs at n (n can be a list)
Esc) n	Clear tabs at n (n can be a list)
Esc /	Print special character position 002
Esc C n m	Absolute horizontal tab to column n
Esc D	*Negative half-line feed
Esc E n m	Define horizontal space increments
Esc F n m	Set form length
Esc G	*Graphics on 1/120 inch
Esc H n m l	Relative horizontal motion
Esc I	Underlining on
Esc J	Underlining off
Esc K n	Bold overprint mode on
Esc L n m	Define vertical spacing increment
Esc M n	Bold overprint off
Esc N	No carriage movement on next character
Esc O	Right margin control on
Esc P n	Absolute vertical tab to line n
Esc Q	Shadow print on
Esc R	Shadow print off
Esc S	No print on
Esc T	No print off
Esc U	*Half-line feed
Esc W	Auto carriage return/line feed on
Esc V n m l	Relative vertical paper motion
Esc X	Force execution
Esc Y	Right margin control off

Table 11.4 continued

Escape Sequence	Function
Esc Z	Auto carriage return/line feed off
Esc e	Sheet feeder page eject
Esc I	Sheet feeder insert page from tray one
Esc x	Force execution of command

Note: Qume Sprint 11 commands shown; asterisk indicates commands shared by Diablo 630.

Most of these commands are irrelevant to a modern printer. Lasers don't have printheads to move; ink-jets know the most efficient means of putting an image on paper better than your PC does. Their character control abilities are trifling compared to today's simple manipulation of fonts. But these command sets remain relevant because they established the basic escape code control system used by the overwhelming majority of printers today.

Canon CaPSL

The advent of laser printer technology spelled the end for daisy-wheel printing but not for the use of their escape codes. When Canon developed its first laser machines, the company used daisy-wheel commands as part of the foundation for its own printer programming language, CaPSL. The initials stand for *Ca*non *P*rinting *S*ystem *L*anguage.

Since its introduction in 1985, CaPSL has undergone two major revisions. In 1987, Canon introduced the first update, CaPSL II; and the current and final version, CaPSL III, came in 1989. Bowing to the dominance of PCL in the controlling laser printers, however, Canon ceased development of CaPSL and moved to making PCL chosen the language for its laser printer products.

Two important Canon printers use CaPSL as their native tongue, the LBP-4 (in several versions) and LBP-8 Mark III machines, although they also highlight one of the weaknesses of the system. Even Canon found the language so extensive and overwhelming that even the programming language used by the top-of-the-line LBP-8 (which Canon calls LBP-8A1/A2/II) is not the same as CaPSL III but rather a subset of it. The LBP-4 and LBP-8 consequently do not recognize all CaPSL III codes.

The CaPSL III itself represents the cross-breeding of the other control systems, each of which is a recognized standard in its own right. The Diablo set of escape sequences serves as the foundation of the emulation mode of CaPSL III. It is augmented by the ISO control codes, escape sequences, and their extensions as well as the VDM (Vector Drawing Mode) language standards defined by ANSI X3H33. Despite adherence to these official international standards, however, Canon carried on the daisy-wheel tradition by making the factory default emulation of the LBP machines Diablo.

The major portion of CaPSL derived from the several ISO standards including ISO 646 for the basic character set and control codes; the ISO 2022 character set extension; and ISO 6429 for extension codes and expansion methods. The majority of the ISO commands takes the form of CSI sequences. CSI sequences are like escape sequences but use a different introducer, the ASCII code 9B(Hex), which is termed the *C*haracter *S*equence *I*ntroducer, hence the name. In seven-bit environments, the CSI is rendered as a two-character introducer, Esc followed by a left square bracket, Esc[. In ASCII characters, these two characters appear as the sequence 27 91 using decimal notation or 1B 5B in hexadecimal.

The CSI printer commands usually take a three- or four-part form. The first part must be the CSI introducer (otherwise it wouldn't be a CSI command). The next character defines the function of the command and is optionally followed by one or more characters that specify the parameters of the command to be carried out. Some commands end with an explicit terminator to mark the end of the data contained in the command.

The mixed heritage of CaPSL is readily evident from a look at its most often used commands, as listed in Table 11.5. These include shifting into Diablo mode to emulate a daisy-wheel printer (and use the escape sequences shown in Table 11.5) as well as instructions more suited to dot-matrix printers than laser machines.

Table 11.5 Common CaPSL III Printer Commands

Function	Escape Code	Decimal Code	Hexadecimal Code
Initialization (ISO)	ESC;	27 59	1B 3B
Diablo emulation	ESC:	27 58	1B 3A
Hard reset	ESCc	27 99	1B 63

Table 11.5 continued

Function	Escape Code	Decimal Code	Hexadecimal Code
Soft reset	ESC<	27 60	1B 3C
Underscore on	ESC[4m	27 91 52 109	1B 5B 34 6D
Double underline	ESC[21m	27 91 50 49 109	1B 5B 32 31 6D
Bold on	ESC[1m	27 91 49 109	1B 5B 31 6D
Italic on	ESC[3m	27 91 51 109	1B 5B 33 6D
Inverse	ESC[7m	27 91 55 109	1B 5B 37 6D
Shaded	ESC[5m	27 91 53 109	1B 5B 35 6D
End underline/ bold/ italics/ inverse/shaded	ESC[0m	27 91 48 109	1B 5B 30 6D
Outline on	ESC[?7m	27 91 63 55 109	1B 5B 3F 37 6D
Outline off	ESC[?27m	27 91 63 50 55 109	1B 5B 3F 32 37 6D
Shadow on	ESC[?6m	27 91 63 54 109	1B 5B 3F 36 6D
Shadow off	ESC[?26m	27 91 63 50 54 109	1B 5B 3F 32 36 6D
Subscript on	ESC[2 K	27 91 50 32 75 139	1B 5B 32 20 4B 8B
Subscript off	ESC[0 K	27 91 48 32 75 140	1B 5B 30 20 4B 8C
Superscript on	ESC[2 K	27 91 50 32 75 140	1B 5B 32 20 4B 8C
Superscript off	ESC[0 K	27 91 48 32 75 139	1B 5B 30 20 4B 8B
Wide characters	ESC[100;200 B	27 91 49 48 48 59 50 48 48 32 66	1B 5B 31 30 30 3B 32 30 30 20 42
Tall characters	ESC[200;100 B	27 91 50 48 48 59 49 48 48 32 66	1B 5B 32 30 30 3B 31 30 30 20 42
Wide and tall characters	ESC[200;200 B	27 91 50 48 48 59 50 48 48 32 66	1B 5B 32 30 30 3B 32 30 30 20 42
End wide and tall characters	ESC[100;100 B	27 91 49 48 48 59 49 48 48 32 66	1B 5B 31 30 30 3B 31 30 30 20 42
Upright character	ESC[22m	27 91 50 50 109	1B 5B 32 32 6D

Medium character	ESC[23m	27 91 50 51 109	1B 5B 32 33 6D
10 CPI	ESC(%$2 ESC[0 K ESC[3y	27 40 37 36 50 27 91 48 32 75 27 91 51 121	1B 28 25 24 32 1B 5B 30 20 4B
12 CPI (requires BM3 card)	ESC[1 K ESC[2y	27 91 49 32 75 27 91 50 121	1B 5B 31 20 4B 1B 5B 32 4B
15 CPI	ESC(%$2 ESC [2 K ESC[3y	27 40 37 36 50 27 91 50 32 75 27 91 51 121	1B 28 25 24 32 1B 5B 32 20 4B
17 CPI	ESC('$2 ESC [1666 K	27 40 39 36 50 27 91 63 49 54 54 54 32 75	1B 28 27 24 32 1B 5B 3F 31 36 36 36 20 4B
6 LPI	ESC[0 L	27 91 48 32 76	1B 5B 30 20 4C
4 LPI	ESC[1 L	27 91 49 32 76	1B 5B 31 20 4C
3 LPI	ESC[2 L	27 91 50 32 76	1B 5B 32 20 4C
12 LPI	ESC[3 L	27 91 51 32 76	1B 5B 33 20 4C
8 LPI	ESC[4 L	27 91 52 32 76	1B 5B 34 20 4C
10 cpi "HMI"	ESC[;60 G	27 91 59 54 48 32 71	1B 5B 3B 36 30 20 47
12 cpi "HMI"	ESC[;72 G	27 91 59 55 50 32 71	1B 5B 3B 37 32 20 47
Page eject	FF	12	0C
Line drawing font	ESC('$2 ESC)' 2	27 40 39 36 50 27 41 39 32 50	1B 28 27 24 32 1B 29 27 20 32
Portrait mode	ESC[0%r	27 91 48 37 114	1B 5B 30 25 72
Landscape mode	ESC[1%r	27 91 49 37 114	1B 5B 31 25 72
Legal-size paper	ESC[32p	27 91 51 50 112	1B 5B 33 30 70
Letter-size paper	ESC[30p	27 91 51 48 112	1B 5B 33 32 70
Envelope tray	ESC[7 I ESC[81;2400; 1200;p "Line 11 Pos 31"	27 91 55 32 73 27 91 56 49 59 50 52 48 48 59 49 50 48 48 59 112 "Line 11 Pos 31"	1B 5B 37 20 49 1B 5B 38 31 3B 32 37 30 30 3B 31 32 30 30 3B 70 "Line 11 Pos 31"

Table 11.5 continued

Function	Escape Code	Decimal Code	Hexadecimal Code
Manual feed on (LBP-4 multipurpose tray)	ESC[1q	27 91 49 113	1B 5B 31 71
Cassette (LBP-4 optional cassette) on	ESC[0q	27 91 48 113	1B 5B 30 71
Top bin (LBP 8IIIT/R)	ESC[3q	27 91 51 113	1B 5B 33 71
Bottom bin (LBP 8III T/R)	ESC[2q	27 91 50 113	1B 5B 32 71
Optional feeder (LBP 8III T/R)	ESC[4q	27 91 52 113	1B 5B 34 71
Duplex printing (LBP 8III R)	ESC[1#x	27 91 49 35 120	1B 5B 31 23 78
Single-sided printing (LBP 8III R)	ESC[0#x	27 91 48 35 120	1B 5B 30 23 78

CaPSL III represents an extreme form of headstrong accommodation, incorporating a the widest possible range of backward compatibilities without seeing the real future, the dominance of PCL. Unless you have a printer that uses it, CaPSL is but a footnote in printer control.

Epson Esc/P2

Being first by itself doesn't guarantee the wide acceptance that fosters becoming a de facto industry standard, but being first with the right product does. Fully-formed character printing proved to be as much of a deadend as dedicated word processors. The versatile bit-image printer, as programmable as the PC that powered it, would lead the way into the future, from impact machines to lasers to whatever's next.

Epson made the first significant bit-image printers, both under its own name and the IBM label. The command system designed for them evolved into one of the most successful and widely used instruction sets for printers, the Esc/P2 system.

The Esc/P2 command set has its roots in the same ground as other early systems, arising from a combination of control characters and escape codes. Over time, the system grew into an elaborate control system for dot-matrix printers, adding to its repertory as Epson added new features such as color and higher resolution to its printer products. When Epson added state-of-the-art high-resolution ink-jet printers to the line-up, instead of shifting to another control system, it expanded Esc/P to include support for scalable fonts, raster graphics, and page-printer oriented advanced paper handling to create the Esc/P2 system in 1992. Most Epson laser printers also understand Esc/P codes in their emulation modes. For example, the EPL8000 has three modes–HP LaserJet Series III emulation (PCL-5), ESC/P 24-pin printer emulation, and ESC/P 9-pin emulation–so you can use one set of commands across the entire Epson line.

Command Sets

Functionally, Esc/P2 printers can be divided into four sets, each with its own set of compatibilties and commands. The original Esc/P printers were nine-wire impact dot-matrix printers, which now understand only a limited subset of all Esc/P commands. What Epson considers the true Esc/P standard applies to higher resolution, 24-wire and 48-wire dot-matrix printers, including ink-jet machines. The latest Epson machines understand the full Esc/P2 system. The fourth class under Esc/P includes those printers that follow IBM's proprietary Graphic Printer nine-wire command set, which differs in several functions from the Epson repertory. We'll consider separately the commands available under each of these four classes.

All Esc/P printers up to–but not including–the most recent implementation of Esc/P2 understand only a small subset of the full listing ANSI control codes. Table 11.6 shows the one-byte control codes these printer recognize. The latest revision of Esc/P2 and the printers using it eliminate several more control characters from this limited repertoire, including BEL, BS, DC1, DC3, CAN, and DEL.

Table 11.6 Control Codes Recognized by Esc/P Printers

Decimal	Hex	Control Code	Mnemonic	Function
7	07	^G	BEL	*Sounds audible bell tone
8	08	^H	BS	*Backspace
9	09	^I	HT	Horizontal tab

Table 11.6 continued

Decimal	Hex	Control Code	Mnemonic	Function
10	0A	^J	LF	Line feed
11	0B	^K	VT	Vertical tab
12	0C	^L	FF	Form feed
13	0D	^M	CR	Carriage return
14	0E	^N	SO	Turns enlarged print mode on
15	0F	^O	SI	Turns condensed print mode on
17	11	^P	DC1	*Select printer
18	12	^R	DC2	Turns condensed print mode off
19	13	^S	DC3	*Deselect printer
20	14	^T	DC4	Turns enlarged print mode off
24	18	^X	CAN	*Cancel line
127	7F	None	DEL	*No operation

Note: Control codes designated with an asterisk in the ***Function*** *column are no longer supported under the most recent revision of Esc/P2.*

The early series of Epson printers based their measurements on the system reigning in typography at the time, the point, 1/72 inch. The basic increment of printhead movement was one point, and the machines rendered normal density graphics at a resolution of 72 dots per inch.

These early machines included one basic resident typeface. Printer commands allowed the adjustment of the printhead speed to render condensed, extended characters, emphasized or double-struck characters. Printing graphics relied on the complex **Esc** * command, which not only set mode but served as an introducer for the bit-image data, which followed after the mode indication as a sequence of byte values. Table 11.7 lists the escape sequences used by these early Epson dot-matrix machines.

Table 11.7 Epson Escape Codes for Nine-Wire Printers

CODE	BYTE VALUES Decimal	Hex	FUNCTION
Esc SO	27 14	1B 0E	Turns on enlarged print mode
Esc SI	27 15	1B 0F	Turns on condensed print mode
Esc EM	27 25	1B 19	Cuts sheet feeder control
Esc SP	27 32	1B 20	Selects character space
Esc !	27 33	1B 21	Selects mode combinations
Esc #	27 35	1B 23	MSB mode cancel
Esc $	27 36	1B 24	Sets absolute horizontal tab
Esc %	27 37	1B 25	Selects active character set
Esc :	27 58	1B 3A	Copies ROM to user RAM
Esc &	27 38	1B 26	Defines user characters
Esc (t	27 40 116	1B 28 74	Assigns character table
Esc /	27 47	1B 2F	Sets vertical tab
Esc \	27 92	1B 5C	Moves printhead
Esc <	27 60	1B 3C	Turns on unidirectional (left-to-right only) printing
Esc >	27 62	1B 3E	MSB set (MSB=0)
Esc =	27 61	1B 3D	MSB reset (MSB=1)
Esc @	27 64	1B 40	Initializes printer
Esc - n	27 45 n	1B 2D n	Underlines mode
			n=1 or 49, turns on underline mode
			n=0 or 48, turns off underline mode
Esc * n	27 42 n	1B 2A n	Selects bit-image mode (data follows n)
			n=0, normal density
			n=1, dual density
			n=2, double-speed dual density

Table 11.7 continued

Code	Byte Values Decimal	Hex	Function
			n=3, quadruple density
			n=4, CRT graphics
			n=6, CRT graphics II
Esc ^	27 94	1B 5E	Nine-pin graphics mode
Esc 0	27 48	1B 30	Sets line spacing at 1/8 inch
Esc 1	27 49	1B 31	Sets line spacing at 7/72 inch
Esc 2	27 50	1B 32	Sets line spacing at 1/6 inch
Esc 3 n	27 51 n	1B 33 n	Sets line spacing at n/216 inch (n between 0 and 255)
Esc 4	27 52	1B 34	Turns on alternate character (italics) set
Esc 5	27 53	1B 35	Turns off alternate character (italics) set
Esc 6	27 54	1B 36	Deactivates high-order control codes
Esc 7	27 55	1B 37	Restores high-order control codes
Esc 8	27 56	1B 38	Turns off paper-end detector
Esc 9	27 57	1B 39	Turns on paper-end detector
Esc A n	27 65 n	1B 41 n	Sets line spacing at n/72 inch (n between 0 and 85
Esc B	27 66	1B 42	Sets vertical tab stop
Esc C n	27 67 n	1B 43 n	Sets form length to n inches (n between 1 and 22)
Esc D	27 68	1B 44	Sets horizontal tab stop
Esc E	27 69	1B 45	Turns on emphasized mode
Esc F	27 70	1B 46	Turns on emphasized mode
Esc G	27 71	1B 47	Turns on double-strike mode
Esc H	27 72	1B 48	Turns off double-strike mode
Esc I	27 73	1B 49	Controls code select
Esc J n	27 74 n	1B 4A n	Tentative n/216-inch line spacing

Esc K	27 75	1B 4B	Normal-density bit-image data follows
Esc L	27 76	1B 4C	Dual-density bit-image data follows
Esc M	27 77	1B 4D	Elite-sized characters on
Esc N n	27 78 n	1B 4E n	Sets number of lines to skip-over perforation
			n=number of lines to skip between 1 and 127
Esc O	27 79	1B 4F	Turns off skip-over perforation
Esc P	27 80	1B 50	Elite mode off/Pica-sized characters on
Esc Q n	27 81 n	1B 51 n	Sets the right margin at column n
Esc R n	27 82 n	1B 52 n	Selects international character set
			n=0, USA
			n=1, France
			n=2, Germany
			n=3, England
			n=4, Denmark I
			n=5, Sweden
			n=6, Italy
			n=7, Spain
			n=8, Japan
			n=9, Norway
			n=10, Denmark II
Esc S n	27 83 n	1B 53 n	Superscript/subscript on mode
			n=0 or 48, superscript mode on
			n=1 or 49, subscript mode on
Esc T	27 84	1B 54	Turns off superscript/subscript
Esc U n	27 85 n	1B 55 n	Unidirectional/bi-directional printing
			n=0 or 48, turn bi-directional printing on
			n=1 or 49, turn unidirectional printing on
Esc W n	27 87 n	1B 57 n	Enlarged (double-width) print mode
			n=1 or 49, enlarged print mode on
			n=0 or 48, enlarged print mode off

Table 11.7 continued

Code	Byte Values Decimal	Hex	Function
Esc Y	27 89	1B 59	Double-speed, dual-density bit image data follows
Esc Z	27 90	1B 5A	Quadruple-density bit-image data follows
Esc a	27 97	1B 61	Justification
Esc b	27 98	1B 62	Sets vertical tab
Esc g	27 103	1B 67	Selects 15 width
Esc R n	27 82 n	1B 52 n	Selects international character set
Esc i	27 105	1B 69	Immediate print (typewriter mode)
Esc j	27 106	1B 6A	Immediate temporary reverse paper feed
Esc k	27 107	1B 6B	Select family of type styles
Esc l n	27 108	1B 6C n	Sets the left margin at column n
Esc m n	27 109 n	1B 6D n	Special character generator selection
			n=0, control codes accepted
			n=4, graphics characters accepted
Esc p n	27 112 n	1B 70 n	Proportional printing
			n=0 or 48, turn proportional printing off
			n=1 or 49, turn proportional printing on
Esc s	27 115 n	1B 73 N	Half-speed printing
			n=0 or 48, turn half-speed printing off
			n=1 or 49, turn half-speed printing on
Esc z	27 122	1B 7A	Selects letter quality or draft

Note: The character n in the above chart may represent one or more parameters that are included in a complete command.

When dot-matrix technology advanced from nine-wire printers to 24-wire designs, Epson had to augment its graphics commands to take additional print modes into account. In addition, Epson changed the smallest unit of measure under Esc/P to units of 1/360th of an inch in text mode, as represented by the Esc + command. In graphics mode, Esc/P extended resolution as high as 1/240th of an inch with the **Esc Z** command or 1/360th of an inch using **Esc** *. Of course, your printer must support these higher resolutions you choose.

What Epson called the Esc/P standard accommodates both 24-wire and 48-wire dot-matrix printers and has become as close to a standard as that which exists among dot-matrix and other line printers throughout the personal computer industry. Table 11.8 summarizes the escape sequences used by the Esc/P standard.

Table 11.8 Esc/P Escape Codes (24- and 48-Wire Printers)

CODE	BYTE VALUES Decimal	Hex	FUNCTION
Esc SO	27 14	1B 0E	Turns on enlarged print mode
Esc SI	27 15	1B 0F	Turns on condensed print mode
Esc EM	27 25	1B 19	Cuts sheet feeder control
Esc SP	27 32	1B 20	Selects character space
Esc !	27 33	1B 21	Selects mode combinations
Esc #	27 35	1B 23	MSB mode cancel
Esc $	27 36	1B 24	Sets absolute horizontal tab
Esc %	27 37	1B 25	Selects active character set
Esc (-	27 40 116	1B 28 74	Selects line/score
Esc :	27 58	1B 3A	Copies ROM to user RAM
Esc &	27 38	1B 26	Defines user characters
Esc /	27 47	1B 2F	Sets vertical tab
Esc \	27 92	1B 5C	Moves printhead
Esc <	27 60	1B 3C	Turns on unidirectional (left-to-right only) printing
Esc >	27 62	1B 3E	MSB set (MSB=0)
Esc =	27 61	1B 3D	MSB reset (MSB=1)
Esc @	27 64	1B 40	Initializes printer

Table 11.8 continued

Code	Byte Values Decimal	Hex	Function
Esc - n	27 45 n	1B 2D n	Underline mode n=1 or 49, turns on underline mode n=0 or 48, turns off underline mode
Esc * n	27 42 n	1B 2A n	Bit-image mode (See Table 11.10)
Esc 0	27 48	1B 30	Sets line spacing at 1/8 inch
Esc 2	27 50	1B 32	Sets line spacing at 1/6 inch
Esc 3 n	27 51 n	1B 33 n	Sets line spacing at n/180 inch
Esc 4	27 52	1B 34	Turns on alternate character (italics) set
Esc 5	27 53	1B 35	Turns off alternate character (italics) set
Esc 6	27 54	1B 36	Deactivates high-order control codes
Esc 7	27 55	1B 37	Restores high-order control codes
Esc 8	27 56	1B 38	Turns off paper-end detector
Esc 9	27 57	1B 39	Turns on paper-end detector
Esc A n	27 65 n	1B 41 n	Sets line spacing at n/60 inch
Esc B	27 66	1B 42	Sets vertical tab stop
Esc C n	27 67 n	1B 43 n	Sets form length to n inches (n between 1 and 22)
Esc D	27 68	1B 44	Sets horizontal tab stop
Esc E	27 69	1B 45	Turns on emphasized mode
Esc F	27 70	1B 46	Turns off emphasized mode
Esc G	27 71	1B 47	Turns on double-strike mode
Esc H	27 72	1B 48	Turns off double-strike mode
Esc J n	27 74 n	1B 4A n	Tentative n/216-inch line spacing
Esc K	27 75	1B 4B	Normal-density bit-image data follows
Esc L	27 76	1B 4C	Dual-density bit-image data follows
Esc M	27 77	1B 4D	Elite-sized characters on

Esc N n	27 78 n	1B 4E n	Sets number of lines to skip-over perforation
			n=number of lines to skip between 1 and 127
Esc O	27 79	1B 4F	Turns off skip-over perforation
Esc P	27 80	1B 50	Elite mode off/Pica-sized characters on
Esc Q n	27 81 n	1B 51 n	Sets the right margin at column n
Esc R n	27 82 n	1B 52 n	Selects international character set
			n=0, USA
			n=1, France
			n=2, Germany
			n=3, England
			n=4, Denmark I
			n=5, Sweden
			n=6, Italy
			n=7, Spain
			n=8, Japan
			n=9, Norway
			n=10, Denmark II
Esc S n	27 83 n	1B 53 n	Superscript/subscript on mode
			n=0 or 48, superscript mode on
			n=1 or 49, subscript mode on
Esc T	27 84	1B 54	Turns off superscript/subscript
Esc U n	27 85 n	1B 55 n	Unidirectional/bidirectional printing
			n=0 or 48, turns on bidirectional printing
			n=1 or 49, turns on unidirectional printing
Esc W n	27 87 n	1B 57 n	Enlarged (double-width) print mode
			n=1 or 49, enlarged print mode on
			n=0 or 48, enlarged print mode off
Esc Y	27 89	1B 59	Double-speed, dual-density bit image data follows
Esc Z	27 90	1B 5A	Quadruple-density bit-image data follows

Table 11.8 continued

Code	Byte Values Decimal	Hex	Function
Esc a	27 97	1B 61	Justification
Esc b	27 98	1B 62	Sets vertical tab
Esc e n	27 101 n	1B 65 n	Sets tab unit
			n=0 or 48, sets horizontal tab unit
			n=1 or 49, sets vertical tab unit
Esc f n	27 102 n	1B 66 n	Set skip position setting
			n=0 or 48, sets horizontal skip position
			n=0 or 49, sets vertical skip position
Esc g	27 103	1B 67	Selects 15 width
Esc k	27 107	1B 6B	Selects family of type styles
Esc l n	27 108	1B 6C n	Sets the left margin at column n
Esc p n	27 112 n	1B 70 n	Proportional printing
			n=0 or 48, turns off proportional printing
			n=1 or 49, turns on proportional printing
Esc s	27 115 n	1B 73 n	Half-speed printing
			n=0 or 48, turns off half-speed printing
			n=1 or 49, turns on half-speed printing
Esc z	27 122	1B 7A	Selects letter quality or draft

Note: The character n in the above chart may represents one or more parameters that are included in a complete command.

By 1992 manufacturers endowed even inexpensive printers with the ability to use scalable fonts, and Epson revised the Esc/P system to accommodate them. In addition, Epson added higher resolution abilities to take advantage of the trend toward ever-sharper bit-image graphics. The result was the Esc/P2 command system.

The actual changes between Esc/P and Esc/P2 appear modest, a mere handful of commands, but they add tremendous power to the system and making the system sufficient even for modest desktop publishing applications.

Key among the additions was the **Esc X** command that allows you to specify the pitch and point size of scalable fonts. The command takes three parameters. The first sets the character pitch: set at 0, it does not alter the current pitch setting; 1 switches on proportional spacing; and values greater than 5 set the character pitch to the designated pitch, expressed in units of 1/360th of an inch. The next two parameters are actually a single 16-bit value expressing the character height in points. In Intel little endian fashion, the first byte holds the least significant bits. Because Epson defined point sizes of 8, 10, 12, 14, 16, 18, 20, 22, 24, 26, 28, 30, and 32, the second byte indicating the character height (that is, the third parameter) will always be zero–at least until Epson allows for characters larger than 3.5 inches high.

Esc/P2 also adds a new raster graphics mode accessible through the command **Esc.** (that is, Escape-period). The raster graphics command allows you to describe images as does a line printer or television, a single row of dots at a time, each line sent sequentially to the printer. Previously graphic images had to be sent in multiple rows to match the number of printhead wires. In addition, raster graphics allows for run-length encoded data compression, which can trim the amount of data your PC must send to your printer to print graphics (and, of course, the time spent sending that data).

Before you can use the raster graphics command, you must set your printer to **Esc/P2** graphics mode with the new command **Esc** (G followed by the parameters 01(Hex) 00(Hex) 01(Hex). The raster graphics command itself takes six parameters. The first indicates whether the data bytes are compressed (0 means not compressed, 1 means compressed). The next two set vertical and horizontal resolution in units of 1/3600th of an inch, with only the values 10 and 20 allowed (for 180- or 360-dpi resolution). The next byte indicates the number of rows in the data stream that follows the command. The final two parameter bytes form a data word expressing the number of dots per row (0 to 65,535) in Intel little endian format. The data bytes representing the raster image follow the parameter bytes. Switching from this graphics mode to text mode requires re-initializing the printer with an **Esc @** command.

To accommodate higher resolution printers, the Esc/P2 system includes a series of commands based on 1/3600th of an inch measuring units including those to set the default measuring unit–Esc (U–and others in the Esc (form for setting page length and vertical print position.

The Esc/P2 system also adds several more esoteric commands in the Esc (form including those to print data values as characters to allow enlarged fonts with printable characters assigned to nonprintable control code values. The command **Esc ^** must be followed by a two-byte little endian word specifying the number of characters to print and the character values themselves. **Esc (c** allows you to set the page format for cut-sheet printers. And **Esc (t** allows you to set a character table to suit several foreign languages. Table 11.9 summarizes the escape codes used in the original implementation of the Esc/P2 standard.

Table 11.9 Esc/P2 Escape Codes, Original Implementation (1992)

CODE	BYTE VALUES Decimal	Hex	FUNCTION
Esc SO	27 14	1B 0E	Turns on enlarged print mode
Esc SI	27 15	1B 0F	Turns on condensed print mode
Esc EM	27 25	1B 19	Cuts sheet feeder control
Esc SP	27 32	1B 20	Selects character space
Esc !	27 33	1B 21	Selects mode combinations
Esc #	27 35	1B 23	MSB mode cancel
Esc $	27 36	1B 24	Sets absolute horizontal tab
Esc %	27 37	1B 25	Selects active character set
Esc (-	27 40 116	1B 28 74	Selects line/score
Esc (^	27 40 94	1B 28 5E	Prints data as characters
Esc (C	27 40 67	1B 28 43	Sets page length (defined unit)
Esc (G	27 40 71	1B 28 47	Selects graphics mode
Esc (U	27 40 85	1B 28 55	Sets unit
Esc (V	27 40 86	1B 28 56	Sets absolute vertical position
Esc (c	27 40 99	1B 28 63	Sets page format
Esc (i	27 40 105 n	1b 28 69 n	Microweave mode; on=1, off=0
Esc (t	27 40 116	1B 28 74	Assigns character table
Esc (v	27 40 118	1B 28 76	Sets relative vertical position
Esc :	27 58	1B 3A	Copies ROM to user RAM
Esc &	27 38	1B 26	Defines user characters
Esc .	27 46 *	1B 2E *	Prints raster graphics; for *, see below
Esc /	27 47	1B 2F	Sets vertical tab
Esc \	27 92	1B 5C	Moves printhead

Esc <	27 60	1B 3C	Turns on unidirectional (left-to-right only) printing
Esc >	27 62	1B 3E	MSB set (MSB=0)
Esc =	27 61	1B 3D	MSB reset (MSB=1)
Esc @	27 64	1B 40	Initializes printer
Esc - n	27 45 n	1B 2D n	Underline mode
			n=1 or 49, turns on underline mode
			n=0 or 48, turns off underline mode
Esc * n	27 42 n	1B 2A n	Bit-image mode (See Table 11.10)
Esc 0	27 48	1B 30	Sets line spacing at 1/8 inch
Esc 2	27 50	1B 32	Sets line spacing at 1/6 inch
Esc 3 n	27 51 n	1B 33 n	Sets line spacing at n/216 inch (n between 0 and 255)
Esc 4	27 52	1B 34	Turns on alternate character (italics) set
Esc 5	27 53	1B 35	Turns off alternate character (italics) set
Esc 6	27 54	1B 36	Deactivates high-order control codes
Esc 7	27 55	1B 37	Restores high-order control codes
Esc A n	27 65 n	1B 41 n	Sets line spacing at n/60 inch
Esc B	27 66	1B 42	Sets vertical tab stop
Esc C n	27 67 n	1B 43 n	Sets form length to n inches (n between 1 and 22)
Esc D	27 68	1B 44	Sets horizontal tab stop
Esc E	27 69	1B 45	Turns on emphasized mode
Esc F	27 70	1B 46	Turns off emphasized mode
Esc G	27 71	1B 47	Turns on double-strike mode
Esc H	27 72	1B 48	Turns off double-strike mode
Esc I	27 73	1B 49	Controls code select
Esc J n	27 74 n	1B 4A n	Tentative n/216-inch line spacing
Esc K	27 75	1B 4B	Normal-density bit-image data follows
Esc L	27 76	1B 4C	Dual-density bit-image data follows
Esc M	27 77	1B 4D	Elite-sized characters on

Table 11.9 continued

CODE	BYTE VALUES Decimal	Hex	FUNCTION
Esc N n	27 78 n	1B 4E n	Sets number of lines to skip-over perforation
			n=number of lines to skip between 1 and 127
Esc O	27 79	1B 4F	Turns off skip-over perforation
Esc P	27 80	1B 50	Elite mode off/Pica-sized characters on
Esc Q n	27 81 n	1B 51 n	Sets the right margin at column n
Esc R n	27 82 n	1B 52 n	Selects international character set
			n=0, USA
			n=1, France
			n=2, Germany
			n=3, England
			n=4, Denmark I
			n=5, Sweden
			n=6, Italy
			n=7, Spain
			n=8, Japan
			n=9, Norway
			n=10, Denmark II
Esc S n	27 83 n	1B 53 n	Superscript/subscript on mode
			n=0 or 48, superscript mode on
			n=1 or 49, subscript mode on
Esc T	27 84	1B 54	Turns off superscript/subscript
Esc U n	27 85 n	1B 55 n	Unidirectional/bidirectional printing
			n=0 or 48, turns on bidirectional printing
			n=1 or 49, turns on unidirectional printing
Esc W n	27 87 n	1B 57 n	Enlarged (double-width) print mode
			n=1 or 49, enlarged print mode on
			n=0 or 48, enlarged print mode off

Esc X	27 88 n	1B 58 n	Selects font by pitch and point
Esc Y	27 89	1B 59	Double-speed, dual-density bit image data follows
Esc Z	27 90	1B 5A	Quadruple-density bit-image data follows
Esc g	27 103	1B 67	Selects 15 width
Esc k	27 107	1B 6B	Selects family of type styles
Esc l n	27 108	1B 6C n	Sets the left margin at column n
Esc p n	27 112 n	1B 70 n	Proportional printing
			n=0 or 48, turns off proportional printing
			n=1 or 49, turns on proportional printing
Esc z	27 122	1B 7A	Selects letter quality or draft

Note: The character n in the above chart may represent one or more parameters that are included in a complete command.

Despite Epson's calling Esc/P2 a standard, the company did not cast the command set in bronze. In recent years, the company has update the list of escape sequences used by its printers, eliminating the control codes in the previous table as well as some little used escape sequences. Table 11.10 lists the escape codes used in the most recent implementations of Esc/P2 used by such printers as the Color Stylus.

Table 11.10 Esc/P2 Escape Codes as Currently Implemented (1995)

CODE	BYTE VALUES Decimal	Hex	FUNCTION
Esc EM	27 25	1B 19	Cuts sheet feeder control
Esc SP	27 32	1B 20	Selects character space
Esc !	27 33	1B 21	Selects mode combinations
Esc $	27 36	1B 24	Sets absolute horizontal tab
Esc %	27 37	1B 25	Selects active character set
Esc (-	27 40 116	1B 28 74	Selects line/score
Esc (^	27 40 94	1B 28 5E	Prints data as characters

Table 11.10 continued

CODE	BYTE VALUES Decimal	Hex	FUNCTION
Esc (C	27 40 67	1B 28 43	Sets page length (defined unit)
Esc (G	27 40 71	1B 28 47	Selects graphics mode
Esc (U	27 40 85	1B 28 55	Sets unit
Esc (V	27 40 86	1B 28 56	Sets absolute vertical position
Esc (c	27 40 99	1B 28 63	Sets page format
Esc (i	27 40 105 n	1b 28 69 n	Microweave mode; on=1, off=0
Esc (t	27 40 116	1B 28 74	Assigns character table
Esc (v	27 40 118	1B 28 76	Sets relative vertical position
Esc :	27 58	1B 3A	Copies ROM to user RAM
Esc &	27 38	1B 26	Defines user characters
Esc .	27 46	1B 2E	Prints raster graphics
Esc \	27 92	1B 5C	Moves printhead
Esc @	27 64	1B 40	Initializes printer
Esc - n	27 45 n	1B 2D n	Underline mode
			n=1 or 49, turns on underline mode
			n=0 or 48, turns off underline mode
Esc * n	27 42 n	1B 2A n	Select bit-image mode (See Table 11.10)
Esc 0	27 48	1B 30	Sets line spacing at 1/8 inch
Esc 2	27 50	1B 32	Sets line spacing at 1/6 inch
Esc 3 n	27 51 n	1B 33 n	Sets line spacing at n/216 inch (n between 0 and 255)
Esc 4	27 52	1B 34	Turns on alternate character (italics) set
Esc 5	27 53	1B 35	Turns off alternate character (italics) set
Esc 6	27 54	1B 36	Deactivates high-order control codes
Esc 7	27 55	1B 37	Restores high-order control codes
Esc A n	27 65 n	1B 41 n	Sets line spacing at n/60 inch

Esc B	27 66	1B 42	Sets vertical tab stop
Esc C n	27 67 n	1B 43 n	Sets form length to n inches (n between 1 and 22)
Esc D	27 68	1B 44	Sets horizontal tab stop
Esc E	27 69	1B 45	Turns on emphasized mode
Esc F	27 70	1B 46	Turns off emphasized mode
Esc G	27 71	1B 47	Turns on double-strike mode
Esc H	27 72	1B 48	Turns off double-strike mode
Esc I	27 73	1B 49	Controls code select
Esc J n	27 74 n	1B 4A n	Tentative n/216-inch line spacing
Esc K	27 75	1B 4B	Normal-density bit-image data follows
Esc L	27 76	1B 4C	Dual-density bit-image data follows
Esc M	27 77	1B 4D	Elite-sized characters on
Esc N n	27 78 n	1B 4E n	Sets number of lines to skip-over perforation
			n=number of lines to skip between 1 and 127
Esc O	27 79	1B 4F	Turns off skip-over perforation
Esc P	27 80	1B 50	Elite mode off/Pica-sized characters on
Esc Q n	27 81 n	1B 51 n	Sets the right margin at column n
Esc R n	27 82 n	1B 52 n	Selects international character set
			n=0, USA
			n=1, France
			n=2, Germany
			n=3, England
			n=4, Denmark I
			n=5, Sweden
			n=6, Italy
			n=7, Spain
			n=8, Japan
			n=9, Norway
			n=10, Denmark II

Table 11.10 continued

CODE	BYTE VALUES Decimal	Hex	FUNCTION
Esc S n	27 83 n	1B 53 n	Superscript/subscript on mode
			n=0 or 48, superscript mode on
			n=1 or 49, subscript mode on
Esc T	27 84	1B 54	Turns off superscript/subscript
Esc U n	27 85 n	1B 55 n	Unidirectional/bidirectional printing
			n=0 or 48, turn bidirectional printing on
			n=1 or 49, turn unidirectional printing on
Esc W n	27 87 n	1B 57 n	Enlarged (double-width) print mode
			n=1 or 49, enlarged print mode on
			n=0 or 48, enlarged print mode off
Esc X	27 88 n	1B 58 n	Selects font by pitch and point
Esc Y	27 89	1B 59	Double-speed, dual-density bit-image data follows
Esc Z	27 90	1B 5A	Quadruple-density bit-image data follows
Esc g	27 103	1B 67	Selects 15 width
Esc k	27 107	1B 6B	Selects family of type styles
Esc l n	27 108	1B 6C n	Sets the left margin at column n
Esc p n	27 112 n	1B 70 n	Proportional printing
			n=0 or 48, turns off proportional printing
			n=1 or 49, turns on proportional printing
Esc z	27 122	1B 7A	Selects letter quality or draft

Graphics Printing

The Esc/P system incorporates several commands to print bit-image graphics. Epson now recommends use of the **Esc** * command for this purpose. Epson has designed **Esc** * to handle the resolution capabilities of all of its printers and replace the earlier single resolution commands **Esc ^**, **Esc K**, **Esc L**, **Esc Y**, or **Esc Z**.

As a catch-all, the **Esc** * command is consequently one of the most complex Esc/P instructions. It takes three parameters and a series of data bytes. The first of the parameters sets the printer resolution. Table 11.11 lists the value of this parameter for various printing resolutions.

Table 11.11 Esc/P2 Graphics Printing Resolution Parameters

Esc * Parameter (dpi)	Horizontal Resolution (dpi)	Vertical Resolution (dpi)		Print Adjacent Dots?	Dots per Column
		24-Wire	**48-Wire**		
0	60	60	60	Yes	8
1	120	60	60	Yes	8
2	120	60	60	No	8
3	240	60	60	No	8
4	80	60	60	Yes	8
6	90	60	60	Yes	8
32	60	180	180	Yes	24
33	120	180	180	Yes	24
38	90	180	180	Yes	24
39	180	180	180	Yes	24
40	360	180	180	No	24
64	60	N/A	60	Yes	48
65	120	N/A	120	Yes	48
70	90	N/A	180	Yes	48
71	180	N/A	360	Yes	48
72	360	N/A	360	No	48
73	360	N/A	360	Yes	48

Table 11.11 continued

Generalized command form:

Esc * m c1 c2 [graphics data]

where m is the code number from the table above, and c1 and c2 specify the number of columns to use for graphics.

Note 1 Computing c1 and c2: The values of c1 and c2 specify the number of columns of dots to use for the graphics display. Because one byte can code only 256 values, a second byte must be used to encompass the total number of possible dot-columns. The c1 value is least significant. To determine the proper values, divide the desired number of graphics columns by 256. The quotient is the value of c2; the remainder is c1.

Note 2 Graphics data: Each column of data is a line encoded multiple bytes using the formula x/8 where x is the number of printhead wires. For example a 24-wire printer will use with three separate bytes for each column; the first byte codes the top eight wires, the second byte codes the middle eight, and the last byte codes the bottom eight. The least significant bit in each byte codes the bottom dot of the octet associated with that byte; the most significant bit codes the top dot of the octet. A value of one indicates a dot will appear on paper.

Two bytes specifying the number of columns to be printed follow the mode byte. The values of these bytes, c1 and c2, are determined mathematically. Because one byte can code only 256 values, two bytes are required for a reasonable line length. The value of the first byte, c1, is of lesser significance. To determine the proper values, you divide the desired number of graphic columns by 256. The whole number value of the quotient represents the value of c2; the remainder is c1.

The total number of data bytes depends both on the resolution and the number of columns to be printed. In nine-wire printing (in which only eight wires are used), one byte defines a column; 24-pin printing requires three bytes per column; 48-wiring printing, six bytes. When multiple bytes are used for each column, the first byte codes the top eight wires; the second codes the next eight; and so on. The least significant bit in each byte codes the bottom dot of the eight that are associated with that byte; the most significant bit codes the top dot of the octet of bits. In each bit position, a value of 1 indicates that a dot will appear on paper; a zero indicates the paper will be left unprinted in that bit position.

Under Esc/P2, you can print at higher resolution than available under the earlier command set by using the **Esc .** instruction for printing raster graphics. This command takes several parameters. The first indicates whether the data following the command is compressed using the code 0 for uncompressed and 1 for compressed data. The next two parameters express the vertical and horizontal dot density in measuring units of 1/3600th of an inch. The highest density available with current Epson printers is 720 dpi represented by a value of 5 for each of these parameters. The next parameter tells the number of row of dots the data within the command represents. The next two bytes indicate the width of the printed rows of data. The command ends with a string of bytes representing the data to be printed.

For example, to select 720-dpi graphics mode using uncompressed data, you would issue the command:

```
Esc . 0 5 5 1 nL nH d1 ... dn
```

The variables nL and nH represent the lesser and more significant bytes enumerating the number of horizontal dots, respectively. To determine these values, divide the number of dots on a horizontal row by 256. The nonfractional part of the quotient is nH; the remainder is nL.

High-density graphics can create thermal stress because the printhead cannot cool itself fast enough. When printing in 720-dpi mode with impact printers, Epson recommends restricting data to a maximum duty cycle of 65% to prevent damage from overheating.

Offshoots

During the period in which Epson Esc/P system was becoming an accepted industry standard, many printer makers took their own liberties with it to match special features of their own products or simply to express their own corporate individuality. Among the first of these was IBM, which modified the Epson list of escape sequences to suit its own purposes when it relabeled Epson's machines under its own name. Table 11.12 lists the set of commands (not including control characters) used by the IBM Graphics Printer. IBM no longer manufacturers or offers printers under its own name.

Table 11.12 IBM Graphics Printer Escape Codes

CODE	BYTE VALUES Decimal	Hex	FUNCTION
Esc <	27 60	1B 3C	Turns on unidirectional (left-to-right) printing
Esc - n	27 45 n	1B	Underline mode
			n=1 or 49, turns on underline mode
			n=0 or 48, turns off underline mode

Table 11.12 continued

Code	Byte Values Decimal	Hex	Function
Esc ^	27 94	1B 5E	Nine-pin graphics mode
Esc 0	27 48	1B 30	Sets line spacing at 1/8 inch
Esc 1	27 49	1B 31	Sets line spacing at 7/72 inch
Esc 2	27 50	1B 32	Sets line spacing at 1/6 inch
Esc 3 n	27 51 n	1B 3C n	Sets line spacing at n/216 inch (n=0 to 255)
Esc 6	27 54 n	1B 36	Selects character set 1
Esc 7	27 55	1B 37	Selects character set 2
Esc 8	27 56	1B 38	Turns off paper-end detector
Esc 9	27 57	1B 39	Turns on paper-end detector
Esc A n	27 65 n	1B 41 n	Sets line spacing at n/72 inch (n between 0 and 85
Esc C n	27 67 n	1B 43 n	Sets form length to n inches (n between 1 and 22)
Esc D	27 68	1B 44	Sets horizontal tab stop
Esc E	27 69	1B 45	Turns on emphasized mode
Esc F	27 70	1B 46	Turns off emphasized mode
Esc G	27 71	1B 47	Turns on double-strike mode
Esc H	27 72	1B 48	Turns off double-strike mode
Esc J n	27 74 n	1B 4A n	Tentative n/216-inch line spacing
Esc K	27 75	1B 4B	Normal-density bit-image data follows
Esc L	27 76	1B 4C	Dual-density bit-image data follows
Esc M	27 77	1B 4D	Elite-sized characters on
Esc N n	27 78 n	1B 4E n	Sets number of lines to skip-over perforation, 1 TO 127
Esc O	27 79	1B 4F	Turns off skip-over perforation

Esc R	27 82	1B 52	Returns to default tabs
Esc S n	27 83	1B 53 n	Superscript/subscript on mode
			n=0 or 48, superscript mode on
			n=1 or 49, subscript mode on
Esc T	27 84	1B 54	Turns off superscript/subscript
Esc U n	27 85 n	1B 55 n	Unidirectional/bidirectional printing
			n=0 or 48, turns on bidirectional printing
			n=1 or 49, turns on unidirectional printing
Esc W n	27 87 n	1B 57 n	Enlarged (double-width) print mode
			n=1 or 49, enlarged print mode on
			n=0 or 48, enlarged print mode off
Esc X	27 88	1B 58	Sets margins
Esc Y	27 89	1B 59	Double-speed, dual-density bit image data follows
Esc Z	27 90	1B 5A	Quadruple-density bit-image data follows
Esc b	27 98	1B 62	Sets vertical tab
Esc e n	27 101 n	1B 65 n	Sets tab unit
			n=0 or 48, sets horizontal tab unit
			n=1 or 49, sets vertical tab unit
Esc f n	27 102 n	1B 66 N	Set skip position setting
			n=0 or 48, sets horizontal skip position
			n=0 or 49, sets vertical skip position
Esc l n	27 108 n	1B 6C n	Sets the left margin at column n
Esc m n	27 109 n	1B 6D n	Special character generator selection
			n=0, control codes accepted
			n=4, graphics characters accepted
Esc p n	27 112 n	1B 70 n	Proportional printing
			n=0 or 48, turns off proportional printing
			n=1 or 49, turns on proportional printing

Table 11.12 continued

Esc s n	27 115 n	1B 73 n	Half-speed printing
			n=0 or 48, turn half-speed printing off
			n=1 or 49, turn half-speed printing on
Esc z	27 122	1B 7A	Selects letter quality or draft

Other printer manufacturers have adopted their own variations of the Esc/P system for their products. In most cases, they have extended the Epson system to include exclusive features of their products by latching onto codes unused in the Epson system. As an example, we offer the command set understood by early Star Micronics printers in Table 11.13.

Table 11.13 Star Micronics Gemini-10 Command Set

Mnemonic	Hex Codes	Function
SO	0E	Turns on double width; canceled with DC4 or CR
SI	0F	Turns on compressed mode
DC1	11	Selects printer
DC2	12	Cancels SI mode
DC3	13	Deselects printer
DC4	14	Cancels SO mode
ESC #	1B 23	Accepts eighth bit "as is" from host CPU
ESC-1	1B 2D 01	Starts underlining
ESC-0	1B 2D 00	Cancels the ESC-1 underlining
ESC 0	1B 30	Changes line feed to 1/8"
ESC 1	1B 31	Changes line feed to 7/72"
ESC 2	1B 32	Changes line feed to 1/6"
ESC 3n	1B 33 n	Changes to n/144" line spacing; n=1 to 127
ESC 4	1B 34	Changes to italics

ESC 5	1B 35	Cancels ESC 4
ESC 8	38	Disable "Paper Out" switch
ESC 9	39	Cancels ESC 8 mode
ESC =	3D	Sets 8th bit to 0
ESC >	3E	Sets 8th bit to 1
ESC @	40	Printer reset
ESC An	41 n	Sets line spacing to n/72"; n=1 to 127
ESC B1	42 01	Sets 10 cpi
ESC B2	42 02	Sets 12 cpi
ESC B3	42 03	Sets 17 cpi
ESC Cn	43 n	Sets form length to n lines; n=1 to 127
ESC C0n	43 30 n	Sets form length to n inches; n=1 to 32
ESC DnnNUL	44 n n 0	Sets tabs; n=1 to 255; clears old tab settings
ESC E	45	Selects emphasized printing
ESC F	46	Cancels emphasized printing
ESC G	47	Selects double strike mode
ESC H	48	Cancels double strike mode
Esc Jn	4A n	One-time line feed of n/144"
ESC Kn1n2	4B n1 n2	480 dots pitch of bit-image n1 + n2*255
ESC Ln1n2	4C n1 n2	960 dots pitch of bit-image n1 + n2*255
ESC Mn	4D n	Sets LH margin n columns
ESC Nn	4E n	Sets skip-over perforation to n lines
ESC O	4F	Resets skip-over perforation to 0 lines
ESC PnnNUL	50 n n 00	Sets vertical tab positions - default 6 lines
ESC Qn	51 n	Sets RH margin to n columns
ESC Rn	51 n	Sets header line position - valid values 1 to 16
ESC S0	53 00	Superscript mode selected
ESC S1	52 01	Subscript mode selected
ESC T	54	Cancels super- or sub-script mode
ESC U1	55 01	Selects uni-directional print mode

Table 11.13 continued

Mnemonic	Hex Codes	Function
ESC U0	55 00	Cancels uni-directional print mode
ESC V1	56 01	Selects slashed-zero option
ESC V0	56 00	Cancels slashed-zero option
ESC W1	57 01	Selects double-wide print
ESC W0	57 00	Cancels double-wide print
ESC X1	58 00	Selects 9x9 matrix optional ROM
ESC X0	58 00	Cancels 9x9 matrix optional ROM
ESC Y1	59 01	Enables buzzer
ESC Y0	59 00	Disables buzzer
EEC Zn	5A n	Selects proportional characters; n dot spacing
Additional commands recognized by Gemini 10X-15X		
ESC yn1n2m1m2	79 n1 n2 m1 m2	Prints dual-density graphics double speed
ESC zn1n2m1m2	7A n1 n2 m1 m2	Prints quadruple-density graphics
ESC + ... RS	2B ... 1E	Defines the macro-instruction
ESC *0	2A 30	Copies fonts from ROM to RAM
ESC *1n1n2m1m2	2A 31 n1 n2 m1 m2	Defines download character into RAM

Mnemonic	Hex Codes	Function
ESC $0	24 30	Cancels the download character set
ESC $1	24 31	Selects the download character set
ESC 7n	37 n	Selects the international character set
ESC !	21	Selects the macro instruction
ESC a n	61 n	Sends one-time n line feeds
ESC b n	62 n	Sends one-time horiz tab of n columns

For the most part, you'll find these commands nearly identical to those used by Epson. The chief variations appear in the bit-image graphics modes. Star Micronics defines the Esc K and Esc L commands differently from Epson. If you don't take these differences into account and set up a Star Micronics printer with the expectation of exact Epson emulation, strange images may appear in your output.

PCL 5e

Most modern laser printer and many ink-jet machines use what has become the common tongue of today's high-end printers, Hewlett-Packard's Printer Control Language. Most often abbreviated with its initials, PCL starts with the same basic capabilities as Esc/P but carries them even further. Its power follows that of HP's printers themselves, starting as a control system for a humble ink-jet and evolving into the command system for some of the most sophisticated page printers. But despite the evolution, PCL remains rooted in the same escape-sequence technology that underlies most other printer languages.

The success of PCL stems from HP's forethought, which allowed the language to expand without compromising backward compatibility. Now offered in an enhanced form of its fifth major revision and called PCL 5e, it still accommodates the earliest PCL machines. Each revision builds upon the previous ones to provide backward and forward compatibility. For example, an application that only understands PCL 1 and output printer commands at that level can still control today's latest PCL 5e machines–sacrificing, of course, the features added to the language since the application was written.

According the HP, PCL is designed to function independently from its computer host, its device drivers, the interconnection interface, and networking system. It gives software writers a consistent control structure that can command any PCL printer, which means that you don't have compatibility worries when you upgrade your software or drivers.

Although designed to control the function of page printers such as HP's line of LaserJets, PCL is not a true page description language. Its functions are machine dependent, and it controls the look of the printout by making specific commands to the hardware rather than describing the final look of the image. Rather than saying "draw a line across the middle of the page," it tells the printer to move its cursor to the middle of the page, start drawing a line, and move the cursor to the opposite side of the page. The important difference is that the commands under PCL are dependent on the resolution of the printer. The line-drawing command specifies the number of dots in the line, not its final length in inches on the sheet.

PCL 5 can yield on-paper images that are effectively identical to those made on printers using the PostScript language (below), but there are substantial differences between PCL 5 and PostScript. PostScript is essentially device independent. It describes the image rather than telling the printer what to do. PostScript depends on the printer being able to figure out what to do to make the image on its own. More importantly, the PostScript code sent out from your PC will be the same no matter whether it is meant to control a relatively inexpensive desktop laser or an expensive typesetting machine. PCL 5, on the other hand, is a device dependent. It currently works only with printers that operate at the resolution levels that it supports, which in the latest version (PCL 5e) is limited to 600 dpi. In the form that its instructions come from your PC, the PCL 5 language cannot drive typesetters.

This characteristic makes PCL little more than an elaborate printer command set, one with length strings of characters to initiate and control the various LaserJet functions. Just as with Exc/P printers, PCL machines accept their commands as escape sequence codes that are embedded in the data stream making up the print job.

According to Hewlett-Packard, the design of this method of sending instructions minimizes both the time and code required for data transmission and reduces the power required in the printer for decoding and carrying out printing instructions. HP notes that the fonts and formats used by PCL were designed to allow the quick translation of the printer instructions generated by your applications into high-quality, raster print images.

PCL 5 would be a curiosity if it were only to be used in Hewlett-Packard printers, but it has proven to be a cost-effective printer control system. It's less expensive than the other desktop publishing-capable language, PostScript, because it does not require printer makers to get a license in order to use it. Several manufacturers offer chips and controllers that smaller printer makers can use to build PCL-compatible products.

History

The history of PCL tracks the development of Hewlett-Packard's various printer products. HP had added enhancements to the language to match the new features and capabilities the company put into its printers to increase their power, performance, and suitability to various applications–not just desktop publishing but also presentation graphics, networked printer sharing, and other business-related needs.

Although PCL is normally associated with laser printers and particularly the HP LaserJet line, the two earliest versions of PCL were designed for simple line printers.

PCL 1 was developed to give the basic control to simple line printers, what HP calls "print and space functionality." Its commands allow for printing characters and moving the printhead and paper.

The first printer to use the original version of PCL was the HP ThinkJet, an ink-jet engine. Although the ThinkJet was introduced in 1984, its development began in 1979. The languages was designed around the capabilities of that printer, which had 96-dpi resolution.

PCL 2 added electronic data and transaction processing abilities to PCL 1, features aimed at making the printer more of a general purpose, multi-user system printing tool.

PCL 3 was introduced along with the printer the language was designed to control, HP's first laser printer, the original LaserJet, which was also introduced in May 1984. The more recent language stems from the shorter development of the LaserJet, which HP notes began in 1983.

In HP's technospeak, PCL 3 adds "office word processing" functionality to high-quality office document production. In other words, PCL 3 lets you choose among fonts (although printers compatible with the PCL 3 standard can use only cartridge fonts in their text modes) and draw simple lines and borders. Because PCL 3 includes few other drawing commands, full pages of graphics must be generated by your PC and transferred bit-by-bit to your PCL 3 printer.

PCL 4 was the next major revision to PCL, developed in response to the needs of early desktop publishing and similar applications that demanded more than just a few cartridge-based fonts. In addition, PCL 4 enhanced the page formatting functions of PCL 3 to give you more control over the look of your documents. PCL 4 also added the ability to have multiple fonts on the same page as well as to download fonts. However, PCL 4 allows only for downloading bit-mapped fonts, and you could only print one orientation on a given page no matter the type or number of fonts you selected. PCL 4 also improved PCL 3's line drawing abilities and added some rudimentary box drawing and filling to its command repertory. The first printer to use PCL 4 was HP's LaserJet Series II, which was introduced in March 1987.

PCL 5 pushed the LaserJet family into the world of scaleable fonts, making it a workable language to handle desktop publishing. In addition, PCL 5 added other features needed for serious publishing, including sophisticated page formatting capability, the ability to handle portrait and landscape orientations on the same page, to print white-on-black, and to turn fonts into some pattern or shade. PCL5 also added vector graphics drawing abilities based on HP's own plotter language, HP-GL, which has become an industry standard in its own right as a means of commanding plotters (see p. 526).

PCL 5 was formally introduced with the announcement of the LaserJet III on February 26, 1990.

PCL 5e enhanced the language to increase the maximum resolution to 600 dpi to support the LaserJet 4 series of printers introduced in October 1992.

Architecture

PCL brings together three control systems under a single banner, control characters, PCL commands, and HP-GL commands. Each has a specific role in controlling your printer and creating on-paper images.

Control Characters

As with Esc/P, it starts with a basic set of control codes, special nonprinting characters that elicit a specific response from the printer. These include the most basic printer functions such as carriage-return, line-feed, and form feed.

PCL Commands

The heart of PCL are the native commands of the language, which provide access to the printer's control structure. These commands operate all of the features of the printer beyond the range of control characters with the exception of drawing vector graphics.

Every PCL printer command is an escape sequence that comprises two or more characters. The first is the introducer, the ubiquitous Esc character, which tells the printer that the next characters represent a command rather than text.

Among other functions, PCL commands can elicit an immediate action from the printer or set a parameter that controls subsequent functions, for example, shifting from portrait to landscaping printing mode or specifying a font. Once a PCL command sets a parameter, that setting remains in effect until another PCL command sends a new setting for that parameter, another command alters the parameter, or the printer is reset (either by command or by switching it off). For this reason most commercial applications reset PCL printers at the beginning of each print job so that they can be sure the machine will operate with known parameter settings.

HP-GL Commands

To draw images on paper, PCL printers using version 5 or later of the language, use the HP plotter language, HP-GL. It creates images by drawing vector graphics. That is, images are built from drawing straight or curved lines, which can later be filled in. HP-GL commands take the form of mnemonic two-letter codes, which may be followed by one or more parameters, which tell the printer the specifics of carrying out the command.

Command Structure

PCL commands can take two forms, two character escape sequences and parameters escape sequences.

In the two-character form of PCL command escape sequences comprise only the introducer and a second character that defines the operation for the printer to carry out. The second character may be any ASCII value between 48 and 126 (decimal). PCL uses its two-character commands for only a few functions including the three that follow:

Esc E	Printer reset
Esc 9	Resets left and right margins
Esc =	Half-line feed

PCL's parameterized escape sequences add one or more parameters after the introducer and command-identifying characters. In general, these commands take the following form:

```
<Esc> X Y # z1 # z2 # Zn
```

Hewlett-Packard gives a specific name to each character in a parameterized command. These are as follows:

X is the *parameterized character*, which identifies the command and additionally lets the printer know to expect additional parameters. Its value must be within the range of byte values between 33 and 47 (decimal) inclusive.

Y is the *group character*, which informs your printer the type of function to carry out. It may range in byte value from 96 to126 (decimal) inclusive.

is a *value field*, which specifies a numerical value using one or more binary-code decimal (BCD) characters. That is, the individual bytes will have values within the range 48 to 57 (decimal) inclusive, corresponding to the ASCII characters 0 to 9. This numerical value may optionally be preceded by a plus or minus sign or may also include a decimal point, these additional characters not being counted in the five total. The numeric value expressed in this field can range from -32,767 to

+3,767. If a value field contains no number in a PCL command requiring one, your printer will assume a value of zero.

Z1 and **Z2** are *parameter characters*, which specify the parameter associated with the preceding numerical value field. PCL uses characters within the range 96 to 126 (decimal) inclusive to specify parameter characters. Although two are shown, a given PCL command may contain one or several parameter characters. They are used to combine or concatenate escape sequences.

Zn is the *termination character*, which specifies a parameter for the preceding value field exactly as does a parameter field but also notifies your printer that the escape sequence has ended. A termination character must be within the range 64 to 94 (decimal) inclusive.

PCL allows the combining of two related escape sequences into one. In order to concatenate escape sequences, you must follow two rules:

1. The parameterized and group characters–the first two characters after the Esc–in the commands to be combined must be the same. In other words, the function of the commands must be drawn from the same PCL group.
2. The termination character in the string is the only one to be uppercase. All the other alphabetic characters in the command must being lowercase.

You combine multiple escape sequences by dropping the introducer (Esc), the parameterized character, and the group character from subsequent issuances of the command and changing the case of the termination characters from uppercase to lowercase. For example, you would combine the sequences Esc & l 1 O with Esc & l 2 A to make the sequence Esc & l 1 o 2 A. When escape sequences are combined, your printer executes them in left to right order as they appear on the line.

Commands

Escape sequences must be sent to PCL printers in the proper order to control the production of documents. Hewlett-Packard calls this ordering the command hierarchy and arranges the commands into eight groups: job control commands, page control commands, cursor positioning commands, font selection commands, font management commands, graphics commands, print model features, and macro commands. (You can also find the command groups listed in order of significance in the printer command section your printer's users manual.)

Job control commands tell your printer how to handle the mechanics of the print job–where the image appears on the page, which sides of the sheet or paper bin to use, and what measurement units to use. All job control commands are usually sent at the beginning of a print job as a group. They remain in effect throughout the print job and ordinarily are not sent again until the beginning of the next print job. Table 11.14 lists and describes the PCL 5 job control commands.

Table 11.14 PCL 5 Job Control Commands

DOUBLE-SIDED PRINTING

Sets printer to print on both sides of paper (if printer supports double-sided printing)

Text Form	Hexadecimal Form	Definition
Esc&l1S	1B 26 6C 31 53	Sets duplex printing with long-edge binding
Esc&l2S	1B 26 6C 32 53	Sets duplex printing with short-edge binding

DOWNWARD IMAGE OFFSET

Sets the top edge of image area in relation to top edge of sheet

Text Form	Hexadecimal Form	Definition
Esc&l<#>Z	1B 26 6C <#> 5A	<#> indicates offset in 1/720th of an inch increments

HORIZONTAL IMAGE MOVE

Moves image area left or right in relation to physical page

Text Form	Hexadecimal Form	Definition
Esc&l+<#>U	1B 26 6C 2B <#> 55	<#> indicates distance to move left in 1/720th-inch increments
Esc&l-<#>U	1B 26 6C 2D <#> 55	<#> indicates distance to move right in 1/720th-inch increments

Table 11.14 continued

Job Separation

Toggles printer's job separation mechanism

Text Form	Hexadecimal Form	Definition
Esc&l1T	1B 26 6C 31 54	Separates print jobs

Left Image Offset

Sets the left edge of image area in relation to left edge of sheet

Text Form	Hexadecimal Form	Definition
Esc&l<#>U	1B 26 6C <#> 55	<#> indicates offset in 1/720th-inch increments

Number of Copies

Specifies number of copies of each page to be printed

Text Form	Hexadecimal Form	Definition
Esc&l<#>X	1B 26 6C <#> 58	<#> indicates number of copies (up to 99 for LJIII series; 32,767 for LJIIISi and LJ4)

Output Bin

Selects which tray to use for finished printing

Text Form	Hexadecimal Form	Definition
Esc&l0G	1B 26 6C 30 47	Selects upper output tray
Esc&l1G	1B 26 6C 31 47	Selects lower or rear output tray

RESET

Restores printer to default environment settings, deletes temporary fonts and macros

Text Form	Hexadecimal Form	Definition
EscE	1B 45	Resets, printing any remaining data

SIDE SELECTION

Chooses which side of page to print upon

Text Form	Hexadecimal Form	Definition
Esc&a0G	1B 26 61 30 47	Selects next side
Esc&a1G	1B 26 61 31 47	Selects front side
Esc&a2G	1B 26 61 32 47	Selects rear side

SINGLE-SIDED PRINTING

Sets printer to print only on one side of sheets

Text Form	Hexadecimal Form	Definition
Esc&l0S	1B 26 6C 30 53	Sets simplex printing mode

UNITS OF MEASURE

Establishes units of measure for subsequent PCL commands

Text Form	Hexadecimal Form	Definition
Esc&u96D	1B 26 75 39 36 44	Sets units of measure at increments of 96 to the inch
Esc&u100D	1B 26 75 31 30 30 44	Sets units of measure at increments of 100 to the inch

Table 11.14 continued

Esc&u120D	1B 26 75 31 32 30 44	Sets units of measure at increments of 120 to the inch
Esc&u144D	1B 26 75 31 34 34 44	Sets units of measure at increments of 144 to the inch
Esc&u150D	1B 26 75 31 35 30 44	Sets units of measure at increments of 150 to the inch
Esc&u160D	1B 26 75 31 36 30 44	Sets units of measure at increments of 160 to the inch
Esc&u180D	1B 26 75 31 38 30 44	Sets units of measure at increments of 180 to the inch
Esc&u200D	1B 26 75 32 30 30 44	Sets units of measure at increments of 200 to the inch
Esc&u225D	1B 26 75 32 32 35 44	Sets units of measure at increments of 225 to the inch
Esc&u240D	1B 26 75 32 34 30 44	Sets units of measure at increments of 240 to the inch
Esc&u288D	1B 26 75 32 38 38 44	Sets units of measure at increments of 288 to the inch
Esc&u300D	1B 26 75 33 30 30 44	Sets units of measure at increments of 300 to the inch
Esc&u360D	1B 26 75 33 36 30 44	Sets units of measure at increments of 360 to the inch
Esc&u400D	1B 26 75 34 30 30 44	Sets units of measure at increments of 400 to the inch
Esc&u450D	1B 26 75 34 35 30 44	Sets units of measure at increments of 450 to the inch
Esc&u480D	1B 26 75 34 38 30 44	Sets units of measure at increments of 480 to the inch
Esc&u600D	1B 26 75 36 30 30 44	Sets units of measure at increments of 600 to the inch
Esc&u720D	1B 26 75 37 32 30 44	Sets units of measure at increments of 720 to the inch

Esc&u800D	1B 26 75 38 30 30 44	Sets units of measure at increments of 800 to the inch
Esc&u900D	1B 26 75 39 30 30 44	Sets units of measure at increments of 900 to the inch
Esc&u1200D	1B 26 75 31 32 30 30 44	Sets units of measure at increments of 1200 to the inch
Esc&u1440D	1B 26 75 31 34 34 30 44	Sets units of measure at increments of 1440 to the inch
Esc&u1800D	1B 26 75 31 38 30 30 44	Sets units of measure at increments of 1800 to the inch
Esc&u2400D	1B 26 75 32 34 30 30 44	Sets units of measure at increments of 2400 to the inch
Esc&u3600D	1B 26 75 33 36 30 30 44	Sets units of measure at increments of 3600 to the inch
Esc&u7200D	1B 26 75 37 32 30 30 44	Sets units of measure at increments of 7200 to the inch

Universal Exit Code

Forces printer to leave current language

Text Form	Hexadecimal Form	Definition
Esc-12345X	1B 2D 31 32 33 34 35 58	Return control to PCL

Vertical Image Move

Moves image area up or down in relation to physical page

Text Form	Hexadecimal Form	Definition
Esc&l+<#>Z	1B 26 6C 2B <#> 5A	<#> indicates distance to move down in 1/720th-inch increments
Esc&l-<#>Z	1B 26 6C 2D <#> 5A	<#> indicates distance to move up in 1/720th-inch increments

Page control commands give you the power to select the page source, size, orientation, margins, and text spacing used in the documents that you print. PCL commands let you specify both vertical and horizontal motion indices, which set the distance between rows and columns, set left and right margins, change the orientation of the page and text, and alter the line spacing and page size. Table 11.15 lists the page control commands used by PCL 5.

Table 11.15 PCL 5 Page Control Commands

Eject Page

Ejects current page from printer

Text Form	Hexadecimal Form	Definition
Esc&l0H	1B 26 6C 30 48	Prints current page from current source

Horizontal Motion Index

Sets distance between columns

Text Form	Hexadecimal Form	Definition
Esc&k<#>H	1B 26 6B <#> 48	<#> specifies distance in 1/120 inch increments, up to 9999

Left Margin

Sets left margin to column specified

Text Form	Hexadecimal Form	Definition
Esc&a<#>L	1B 26 61 <#> 4C	<#> specifies column
Esc9	1B 39	Clears left and right margins

Line Spacing

Sets number of lines printed per inch

Text Form	Hexadecimal Form	Definition
Esc&l1D	1B 26 6C 31 44	Prints 1 line per inch
Esc&l2D	1B 26 6C 32 44	Prints 2 lines per inch
Esc&l3D	1B 26 6C 33 44	Prints 3 lines per inch

Esc&l4D	1B 26 6C 34 44	Prints 4 lines per inch
Esc&l6D	1B 26 6C 36 44	Prints 6 lines per inch
Esc&l8D	1B 26 6C 38 44	Prints 8 lines per inch
Esc&l12D	1B 26 6C 31 32 44	Prints 12 lines per inch
Esc&l16D	1B 26 6C 31 36 44	Prints 16 lines per inch
Esc&l24D	1B 26 6C 32 34 44	Prints 24 lines per inch
Esc&l48D	1B 26 6C 34 38 44	Prints 48 lines per inch

Page Orientation

Indicates logical orientation of image on page

Text Form	Hexadecimal Form	Definition
Esc&l0O	1B 26 6C 30 4F	Portrait
Esc&l1O	1B 26 6C 31 4F	Landscape
Esc&l2O	1B 26 6C 32 4F	Reverses portrait
Esc&l3O	1B 26 6C 33 4F	Reverses landscape

Page Size

Specifies paper size

Text Form	Hexadecimal Form	Definition
Esc&l1A	1B 26 6C 31 41	Executive (7.25 by 10.5 inches)
Esc&l2A	1B 26 6C 32 41	Letter (8.5 by 11 inches)
Esc&l3A	1B 26 6C 33 41	Legal (8.5 by 14 inches)
Esc&l80A	1B 26 6C 38 30 41	Number 7 3/4 envelope
Esc&l81A	1B 26 6C 38 31 41	Number 10 envelope
Esc&l90A	1B 26 6C 39 30 41	International DL (110 by 220 mm)
Esc &91A	1B 26 6C 39 31 41	International C5 (162 by 229 mm)
Esc&l100A	1B 26 6C 31 30 30 41	International B5 (176 by 250 mm)

Table 11.15 continued

Paper Source

Indicates where paper is fed from

Text Form	Hexadecimal Form	Definition
Esc&l1H	1B 26 6C 31 48	Feeds sheets from main source
Esc&l2H	1B 26 6C 32 48	Feeds sheets from manual tray
Esc&l3H	1B 26 6C 33 48	Feeds envelopes from manual tray
Esc&l4H	1B 26 6C 34 48	Feeds sheets from alternate source
Esc&l5H	1B 26 6C 35 48	Feeds sheets from optional large paper source
Esc&l6H	1B 26 6C 36 48	Feeds envelopes from automatic feeder

Perforation Skip

When enabled, printer skips from end of text to top of text on next page

Text Form	Hexadecimal Form	Definition
Esc&l0L	1B 26 6C 30 4C	Disables perforation skip
Esc&l1L	1B 26 6C 31 4C	Enables perforation skip

Print Direction

Rotates image on page the specific angle

Text Form	Hexadecimal Form	Definition
Esc&a0P	1B 26 61 30 50	No rotation
Esc&a90P	1B 26 61 39 30 50	Rotates image 90∞
Esc&a180P	1B 26 61 31 38 30 50	Rotates image 180∞
Esc&a270P	1B 26 61 32 37 30 50	Rotates image 270∞

Right Margin

Sets right margin to column specified

Text Form	Hexadecimal Form	Definition
Esc&a<#>R	1B 26 61 <#> 4D	<#> specifies column
Esc9	1B 39	Clears left and right margins

Text Length

Sets number of lines of text per page

Text Form	Hexadecimal Form	Definition
Esc&l<#>F	1B 26 6C <#> 46	<#> specifies number of lines

Top Margin

Sets number of blanks lines between top of page and top of text

Text Form	Hexadecimal Form	Definition
Esc&l<#>E	1B 26 6C <#> 45	<#> specifies number of lines

Vertical Motion Index

Sets distance between rows

Text Form	Hexadecimal Form	Definition
Esc&l<#>C	1B 26 6C <#> 43	<#> specifies distance in 1/48th-inch increments, up to 9999

Cursor positioning commands tell your printer where to place the cursor that marks the active printing position. The commands give you several ways to indicate the cursor position–moving it to an absolute position to a fixed position on the page; making a relative move, one in which the new cursor position is measured in relation to the old position. In addition, the commands provide a form of memory, a stack, that allows you to move the cursor back to a previous position. Table 11.16 lists the PCL 5 cursor positioning commands.

Table 11.16 PCL 5 Cursor Positioning Commands

HORIZONTAL CURSOR MOVE

Moves cursor to designated horizontal location

Text Form	Hexadecimal Form	Definition
Esc&a<#>C	1B 26 61 <#> 43	Moves to indicated column
Esc&a<#>H	1B 26 61 <#> 48	Moves to position located indicated number of 1/720 inch increments right of edge
Esc*p<#>X	1B 2A 70 <#> 58	Moves to position located indicated number times current units of measure right of edge

Moves cursor by designated distance

Text Form	Hexadecimal Form	Definition
Esc&a+<#>C	1B 26 61 2B <#> 43	Moves right indicated number of columns
Esc&a-<#>C	1B 26 61 2D<#> 43	Moves left indicated number of columns
Esc&a+<#>H	1B 26 61 2B<#> 48	Moves right indicated number of 1/720 inch increments
Esc&a-<#>H	1B 26 61 2D<#> 48	Moves left indicated number of 1/720 inch increments
Esc*p+<#>X	1B 2A 70 2B<#> 58	Moves right indicated number times current units of measure
Esc*p-<#>X	1B 2A 70 2D<#> 58	Moves left indicated number times current units of measure

Moves cursor to left edge of text area

Text Form	Hexadecimal Form	Definition
CR	0D	Carriage return

Moves cursor left one column

Text Form	Hexadecimal Form	Definition
BS	8	Backspace

Moves cursor right one column

Text Form	Hexadecimal Form	Definition
SP	20	Space

Moves cursor left one tab width

Text Form	Hexadecimal Form	Definition
HT	9	Horizontal tab

Line Termination Select

Chooses end-of-line codes

Text Form	Hexadecimal Form	Definition
Esc&k0G	1B 26 6B 30 47	CR, LF, and FF interpreted literally
Esc&k1G	1B 26 6B 31 47	LF added to each CR; LF and FF interpreted literally
Esc&k2G	1B 26 6B 32 47	CR added before each LF and FF; CR itself interpreted literally
Esc&k3G	1B 26 6B 33 47	LF added to CR; CR added before each LF and FF

Pop Cursor Position

Moves cursor to position saved on top of stack, decrements stack

Text Form	Hexadecimal Form	Definition
Esc&f1S	1B 26 66 31 53	Returns cursor to position saved with previous push

Push Cursor Position

Saves current cursor position to top of stack

Text Form	Hexadecimal Form	Definition
Esc&f0S	1B 26 66 30 53	Saves cursor position for subsequent pop

Table 11.16 continued

Vertical Cursor Move

Moves cursor to designated vertical location

Text Form	Hexadecimal Form	Definition
Esc&a<#>R	1B 26 61 <#> 52	Move to indicated row
Esc&a<#>V	1B 26 61 <#> 56	Move to position located indicated number of 1/720 inch increments below top edge
Esc*p<#>Y	1B 2A 70 <#> 59	Move to position located indicated number times current units of measure below top edge

Moves cursor by designated distance

Text Form	Hexadecimal Form	Definition
Esc&a+<#>R	1B 26 61 2B <#> 52	Move down indicated number of rows
Esc&a-<#>R	1B 26 61 2D<#> 52	Move up indicated number of rows
Esc&a+<#>V	1B 26 61 2B<#> 56	Move down indicated number of 1/720 inch increments
Esc&a-<#>V	1B 26 61 2D<#> 56	Move up indicated number of 1/720 inch increments
Esc*p+<#>Y	1B 2A 70 2B<#> 59	Move down indicated number times current units of measure
Esc*p-<#>Y	1B 2A 70 2D<#> 59	Move up indicated number times current units of measure

Moves cursor down one-half row

Text Form	Hexadecimal Form	Definition
Esc=	1B 3D	Half-line feed

Moves cursor down one line

Text Form	Hexadecimal Form	Definition
LF	0A	Line feed

Moves cursor to next page

Text Form	Hexadecimal Form	Definition
FF	0C	Form feed

Font selection commands are used to access internal, cartridge, and soft fonts. Font attributes should be addressed in the order of their significance (i.e., primary spacing before stroke weight).

A PCL 5 printer identifies a font by several of its characteristics including its symbol set, spacing, pitch, height, style, stroke weight, and typeface family. The printer understands a range of seven commands (one corresponding to each typeface characteristic) with various parameters to specify the fonts with which you want to print. Table 11.17 lists these font selection commands.

Table 11.17 PCL 5 Font Selection Commands

Symbol Set

Identifies symbol set in a font

Text Form	Hexadecimal Form	Definition
Esc(<ID>	1B 28 <ID>	Defines primary symbol set
Esc)<ID>	1B 29 <ID>	Defines secondary symbol set

Spacing Command

Selects proportional or fixed spacing

Text Form	Hexadecimal Form	Definition
Esc(s0P	1B 28 73 30 50	Fixed spacing on primary font
Esc(s1P	1B 28 73 31 50	Proportional spacing on primary font
Esc)s0P	1B 29 73 30 50	Fixed spacing on secondary font
Esc)s1P	1B 29 73 31 50	Proportional spacing on secondary font

Table 11.17 continued

PITCH COMMAND

Sets letter spacing of fixed-spaced fonts

Text Form	Hexadecimal Form	Definition
Esc(s<#>H	1B 28 73 <#> 48	Sets pitch of primary font at <#> characters per inch
Esc)s<#>H	1B 29 73 <#> 48	Sets pitch of secondary font at <#> characters per inch

HEIGHT COMMAND

Sets height of proportionally spaced scalable fonts

Text Form	Hexadecimal Form	Definition
Esc(s<#>V	1B 28 73 <#> 56	Sets height of primary font at <#> points
Esc)s<#>V	1B 29 73 <#> 56	Sets height of secondary font at <#> points

FONT STYLE COMMAND

Identifies the posture, width, and structure of font symbols

Text Form	Hexadecimal Form	Definition
Esc(s<#>S	1B 28 73 <#> 53	Sets style of primary font to <#>
Esc)s<#>S	1B 29 73 <#> 53	Sets style of secondary font to <#>

STROKE WEIGHT COMMAND

Sets the thickness of the strokes making up font characters

Text Form	Hexadecimal Form	Definition
Esc(s<#>B	1B 28 73 <#> 42	Sets stroke weight of primary font to <#>
Esc)s<#>B	1B 29 73 <#> 42	Sets stroke weight of secondary font to <#>

Typeface Family Command

Selects the design of the font being used

Text Form	Hexadecimal Form	Definition
Esc(s<#>T	1B 28 73 <#> 54	Sets typeface family of primary font to <#>
Esc)s<#>T	1B 29 73 <#> 54	Sets typeface family of secondary font to <#>

A PCL printer tracks the fonts that it has available to it using two font select tables that store the characteristics of two fonts. The font that the printer is actively using is termed the primary font. The other is the secondary font. A single control character allows you to shift between the two fonts, changing to printing with the secondary instead of the primary font.

To change the characteristics listed in the font select table, you (or your printer driver) send a font select command to the printer. The printer then searches out a matching typeface to use, or, if it can't find an exact match, the typeface closest to matching that which it has access to.

The font style command uses numerical values to designate ten basic styles of character, which are listed in Table 11.18. Special fonts may use additional style designations within the range 0 to 32767.

Table 11.18 PCL Font Styles

Value	Font Style
0	Upright or solid
1	Italic
4	Condensed
5	Condensed italic
8	Compressed or extra condensed
24	Expanded

Table 11.18 continued

Value	Font Style
32	Outline
64	Inline
128	Shadowed
160	Outline shadowed

PCL 5 recognizes 15 different stroke weights, designated with values from -7 to 7. Table 11.19 lists the corresponding stroke weights for the values given in the stroke weight command. Out-of-range values are interpreted as the closet in-range value. If you specify a stroke weight less than -7, a PCL 5 printer will use ultra-thin weight. If you specify a stroke weight greater than 7, a PCL printer will use ultra black.

Table 11.19 PCL Stroke Weights

Value	Weight
-7	Ultra thin
-6	Extra thin
-5	Thin
-4	Extra light
-3	Light
-2	Demi light
-1	Semi light
0	Medium, book, or text
1	Semi bold
2	Demi bold
3	Bold
4	Extra bold
5	Black
6	Extra black
7	Ultra black

When attempting to match a font in its repertory, a PCL 5 printer looks for fonts in four places in the order listed: in its random access memory, in cartridge memory, in the ROM installed in the printer in the form of SIMMs (single in-line memory modules), and those stored in its main board read-only memory (ROM).

Font management commands provide mechanisms for downloading and manipulating soft fonts. These commands allow you to select a font for printing text at the cursor position, remove fonts from memory, or carry out other housekeeping functions. Table 11.20 lists the PCL 5e font management commands.

Table 11.20 PCL 5e Font Management Commands

FONT ID COMMAND

Selects the font used in subsequent font management commands

Text Form	Hexadecimal Form	Definition
Esc*c<#>D	1B 2A 63 <#> 44	Selects font <#>

FONT CONTROL COMMAND

Manipulates soft fonts

Text Form	Hexadecimal Form	Definition
Esc*c0F	1B 2A 63 30 46	Deletes all soft fonts
Esc*c1F	1B 2A 63 31 46	Deletes all temporary soft fonts
Esc*c2F	1B 2A 63 32 46	Deletes last soft font ID specified
Esc*c3F	1B 2A 63 33 46	Deletes last character code specified in last soft font specified
Esc*c4F	1B 2A 63 34 46	Makes last font specified temporary
Esc*c5F	1B 2A 63 35 46	Makes last font specified permanent
Esc*c6F	1B 2A 63 36 46	Copies/assigns current font as temporary

Graphics commands provide the ability to build dot-per-bit raster images and to fill or shade rectangular areas with a predefined pattern. For its graphics commands, PCL 5e has a few of its own built-in commands (see Table 11.21). In addition, it uses the Hewlett-Packard Graphics Language/2 command set, developed for HP's line of plotters. We'll take a closer look at this language and its command set in the next section.

Table 11.21 PCL 5e Rectangular Area Fill Commands

HORIZONTAL RECTANGLE SIZE COMMAND

Specifies width of rectangle in units of 1/720th of an inch

Text Form	Hexadecimal Form	Definition
Esc*c<#>H	1B 2A 63 <#> 48	Sets width to <#>1/720th of an inch

HORIZONTAL RECTANGLE SIZE COMMAND

Specifies width of rectangle in PCL units

Text Form	Hexadecimal Form	Definition
Escc<#>A	1B 2A 63 <#> 41	Sets width to <#> times the currently set unit of measure

VERTICAL RECTANGLE SIZE COMMAND

Specifies height of rectangle in units of 1/720th of an inch

Text Form	Hexadecimal Form	Definition
Esc*c<#>V	1B 2A 63 <#> 56	Sets height to <#>1/720th of an inch

VERTICAL RECTANGLE SIZE COMMAND

Specifies height of rectangle in PCL units

Text Form	Hexadecimal Form	Definition
Esc*c<#>B	1B 2A 63 <#> 42	Sets height to <#> times the currently set unit of measure

Pattern ID Command

Specifies a shading, pattern, or fill

Text Form	Hexadecimal Form	Definition
Esc*c<#>G	1B 2A 63 <#> 47	Sets pattern ID to <#>

Fill Rectangular Area Command

Fill rectangle of specified height and width with specified color or pattern

Text Form	Hexadecimal Form	Definition
Esc*c0P	1B 2A 63 30 50	Solid black (default)
Esc*c1P	1B 2A 63 31 50	Solid white
Esc*c2P	1B 2A 63 32 50	Shading pattern
Esc*c3P	1B 2A 63 33 50	Cross-hatch pattern
Esc*c4P	1B 2A 63 34 50	User-defined pattern

Print model features allow you to fill images and characters with a predefined color (which, for monochrome PCL printers means black, white, or grey) or a pattern. You can even design the pattern yourself and tile it across a full page. Table 11.22 lists the printer model commands available under PCL 5e.

Table 11.22 PCL 5e Print Model Features Commands

Source Transparency Mode Command

Sets source image mode to transparent or opaque

Text Form	Hexadecimal Form	Definition
Esc*v0N	1B 2A 76 30 4E	Sets source image transparent
Esc*v1N	1B 2A 76 31 4E	Sets source image opaque

Table 11.22 continued

Text Form	Hexadecimal Form	Definition
Esc*v0O	1B 2A 76 30 4F	Sets pattern transparent
Esc*v1O	1B 2A 76 31 4F	Sets pattern opaque

PATTERN ID COMMAND

Specifies a shading, pattern, or fill

Text Form	Hexadecimal Form	Definition
Esc*c<#>G	1B 2A 63 <#> 47	Sets pattern ID to <#>

SELECTS CURRENT PATTERN COMMAND

Identifies pattern sent to destination

Text Form	Hexadecimal Form	Definition
Esc*v0T	1B 2A 76 30 54	Solid black (default)
Esc*v1T	1B 2A 76 31 54	Solid white
Esc*v2T	1B 2A 76 32 54	Shading pattern
Esc*v3T	1B 2A 76 33 54	Cross-hatch pattern
Esc*v4T	1B 2A 76 34 54	User-defined pattern

USER-DEFINED PATTERN COMMAND

Sends user-defined pattern data to the printer

Text Form	Hexadecimal Form	Definition
Esc*c<#>W	1B 2A 63 <#> 57 <data>	Sends <#> bytes of data to the printer as a pattern

Sets Pattern Reference Point Command

Sets height of proportionally spaced scalable fonts

Text Form	Hexadecimal Form	Definition
Esc*p0R	1B 2A 70 30 52	Rotates pattern with print direction
Esc*p1R	1B 2A 70 31 52	Keeps pattern fixed

Pattern Control Command

Manipulates user-defined patterns

Text Form	Hexadecimal Form	Definition
Esc*p0Q	1B 2A 70 30 51	Deletes all patterns
Esc*p1Q	1B 2A 70 31 51	Deletes temporary patterns only
Esc*p2Q	1B 2A 70 32 51	Deletes last pattern specified
Esc*p3Q	1B 2A 70 33 51	Reserved
Esc*p4Q	1B 2A 70 34 51	Makes last pattern specified temporary
Esc*p5Q	1B 2A 70 35 51	Makes last pattern specified permanent

Macro commands can be used when tasks need to be performed repeatedly. By using macros, you can reduce the number of commands that you have to send to your printer to carry out everyday tasks. A single macro instruction can describe a complete page format and even add a graphic design to a letterhead. PCL 5 also allows you to nest macros, so one macro may call another.

In PCL 5, you can make a out of any escape sequences, control codes, and data that you can download to your printer with but a few exceptions. Although one macro can call or execute another, macros cannot manage other macros (that is, define or delete them). Macros cannot reset a printer. Not all PCL printers allow the use of HP-GL/2 commands within a macro.

Once you've defined a macro, your printer will then carry out the entire sequence of commands each and every time that you send the appropriate single macro command to it.

Defining a macro command takes four steps.

1. You tell your printer you want to define a macro command by assigning an unique identification number to the macro.
2. You must next signal to the printer to make it start recording the commands and data that will make up your macro.
3. You send the data and command sequences that will make your macro.
4. You signal to your PCL 5 printer that you've finished sending commands and data to stop the recording process.

This process requires only three explicit commands. These and all other macro commands are listed in Table 11.23.

Table 11.23 PCL 5 macro commands

MACRO ID NUMBER

Specifies the ID number by which the macro can be created, called, or executed

Text Form	Hexadecimal Form	Definition
Esc&f<#>Y	1B 26 66 <#> 59	Assigns <#> as ID

MACRO CONTROL COMMAND

Defines, invokes, or deletes macros

Text Form	Hexadecimal Form	Definition
Esc&f0X	1B 26 66 30 58	Starts macro recording
Esc&f1X	1B 26 66 31 58	Stops macro recording
Esc&f2X	1B 26 66 32 58	Execute last macro ID specified
Esc&f3X	1B 26 66 33 58	Calls last macro ID specified
Esc&f4X	1B 26 66 34 58	Enables last macro ID specified for automatic overlay
Esc&f5X	1B 26 66 35 58	Disables automatic overlay
Esc&f6X	1B 26 66 36 58	Deletes all macros

Esc&f7X	1B 26 66 37 58	Deletes all temporary macros
Esc&f8X	1B 26 66 38 58	Delete last macro ID specified
Esc&f9X	1B 26 66 39 58	Makes last macro ID specified temporary
Esc&f10X	1B 26 66 31 30 58	Makes last macro ID specified permanent

Once you've defined a macro, you can start it in three ways–by executing it, by calling it, and by using it in an automatic overlay. The difference between these three invocation methods is how the macro treats the current environment settings of your printer. When your printer *executes* a macro, the macro causes changes in the printer environment, and those changes remain in effect after the macro completes. When your printer *calls* a macro, whatever changes the macro makes to your printer environment are effective only during the execution of the macro. When the macro completes, the environment reverts back to what it was before the macro began. The cursor position is not considered part of the printer environment, so the cursor may be at a new position at the end of a called macro. A macro that runs as an *automatic overlay* is called at the completion of printing of each page. The changes it makes to the printer environment are effective only during its execution. Printing starts on the next page using the environment that was in effect before the automatic overlay was called.

Macros can be permanent or temporary. The difference affects what happens to the macro when the printer receives a reset command. A reset erases *temporary* macros but leaves *permanent* macros in memory. Switching off your printer will erase all RAM-based macros.

The two basic macro commands work together. First you specify a macro, be it to record the macro or to apply some other macro management function to it. Then you issue a macro control command, which acts on the last macro that you specified. Most of the time you will combine the macro ID and macro control commands into a single escape sequence that both identifies the macro and the action to carry out on it.

HP-GL/2 Commands

When HP updated PCL 4 to PCL 5, the company needed a means of giving the language graphic abilities in keeping with the needs of desktop publishing. Fortunately the company had a fully developed graphic language already at hand–the Hewlett-Packard Graphic Language that was the native tongue of the company's line of desktop plotters. Giving PCL printers drawing abilities was simply a matter of adding the HP-GL commands to the PCL language.

The union is not complete, however. PCL 5e printers handle HP-GL2 commands by changing modes. That is, when you want to draw an image, you must explicitly tell your printer to shift into HP-GL2 mode. Once you do, your printer will not recognize ordinary PCL 5e instructions until you shift back to PCL 5e mode.

Designed for plotters, HP-GL is a vector drawing language. That is, its controls are the equivalent to drawing vector strokes across paper with a pen. Drawing commands tell the printer to move its imaginary pen equivalent in its rasterizer from point to point. In general, the pen starts drawing at the current cursor position and draws the length or shape specified in the command.

Nearly all commands in HP-GL take the form of two-letter *mnemonics*, and nearly all accept one or more parameters to specify positions, sizes, and other variables. In HP/GL, the individual parameters used in a command are separated by a special character, which in HP/GL terminology is called a *separator*. Although you can use four characters as separators including a comma, space, plus sign (which also indicates positive numerical values), or minus sign (which also indicates a negative value), HP recommends using commas. You do not need to separate the mnemonic from the first parameter. Each command ends with another special character called a *terminator*. Most use semicolons as terminators, although in some cases you can use a space or tab. The polyline encoded command requires a semicolon as a terminator; the label command requires the ASCII character 03(Hex) as its terminator; and the comment command uses a double quote as its terminator. In cases where you can use a semicolon as a terminator, the mnemonic of the next command also acts as a terminator. Figure 11.1 shows the form of a typical HP-GL2 command.

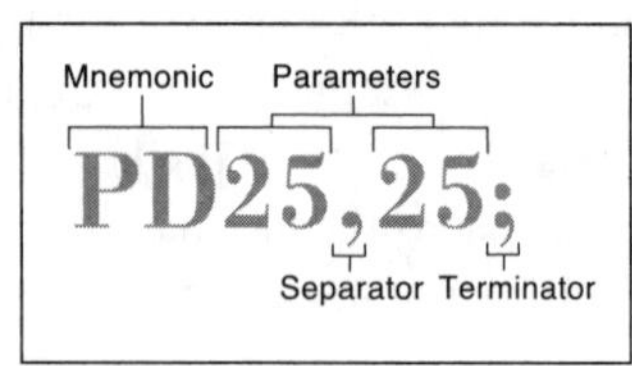

Figure 11.1 The elements of an HP-GL/2 command.

You specify a cursor locations for drawing in HP-GL using a Cartesian coordinate system. PCL also uses a coordinate system for specifying text locations. But, showing that

PCL and HP-GL were united by the equivalent of a shotgun marriage, the coordinate systems used in the two languages are different. PCL locates the origin of its coordinate system at the upper-left corner of the sheet, and coordinate values increase downward and to the right. HP-GL puts the origin at the *lower*-left corner, and coordinate values increase upward and to the right. When you shift between giving PCL command and HP-GL commands, the coordinate system changes even though you may be working on the same sheet.

HP-GL locates the points in its coordinate system in terms of its prevailing measuring units. The default measuring units for HP-GL are called *plotter units* and each measures 0.025 millimeter. You can change the measuring units using the HP-GL scale (**SC**) command. There are about 1016 plotter units in one inch.

Hewlett-Packard divides HP-GL2 commands into seven functional groups. These include dual-context commands, configuration and status commands, vector commands, polygon commands, line and fill attribute commands, palette extensions, and character commands.

Dual-context commands are those that interact with the PCL language. They allow you to switch from HP-GL to PCL, use the fonts you've installed in your printer, and send a reset to your printer. Table 11.24 describes the dual-context commands of HP-GL2.

Table 11.24 HP-GL/2 Dual-Context Commands

Function	Command	Parameters	Comments
Enter PCL mode	Esc%#A	0	Retains previous PCL cursor position
	Esc%#A	1	Uses current HP-GL/2 pen position
Resets	EscE	None	
Selects primary font	FI	Font ID	
Selects secondary font	FN	Font ID	
Scalable fonts only	SB	0	Scalable fonts only
Enables bit-mapped fonts	SB	1	Bit-mapped fonts allowed

Configuration and status commands allow you to set up the measuring units and other drawing defaults (such as rotating the coordinate system) used by HP-GL2. Two of these commands, advance full page (**PC**) and replot (**RP**), are relevant only to HP-GL2 plotters and are ignored by laser printers using the language. Table 11.25 lists the HP-GL2 configuration and status commands.

Table 11.25 HP-GL/2 Configuration and Status Commands

Function	Command	Parameters	Comments
Scale	SC	[x1,x2,y1,y2[,type[,left, bottom]]]	
	SC	[x1,xfactor,y1,yfactor,2]	Alternate form
Input window	IW	[xLL,yLL,xUR,yUR]	
Input P1 & P2, absolute	IP	[p1x,p1y[,p2x,p2y]]	
Input P1 & P2, relative	IR	[p1x,p1y[,p2x,p2y]]	
Default values	DF		
Initialize	IN	[n]	
Rotate coordinate syst.	RO	[angle]	
Advance full page	PC	[n]	Ignored by printers
Replot	RP	[n]	Ignored by printers

Vector commands are the basic HP-GL2 drawing instructions. The two most important are pen down (**PD**) and pen up (**PU**). After you give a pen up instruction, pen movement instructions move the cursor but do not produce a drawn line. The effect is the same as lifting your pen from the paper. After giving a pen down command, the movement made by the pen register as lines in your drawing.

Other vector commands allow you to draw lines and arcs. The commands may call for relative movement in which the specified coordinates refer back to the current pen position or absolute movements in which the specified coordinates are made in reference to the origin. For example, the plot absolute and plot relative instructions draw one or more straight lines from the current pen position to the coordinates given as parameters.

Table 11.26 lists the vector commands included in HP-GL2.

Table 11.26 HP-GL/2 Vector Commands

Function	Command	Parameters
Arc absolute	AA	x_center,y_center,sweep_angle [,chord_angle]
Arc relative	AR	x_increment,y_increment,sweep_angle [,chord_angle]
Arc absolute three-point	AT	x_inter,y_inter,x_end,y_end [,chord_angle]
Plot absolute	PA	[x,y ... [,x,y]]
Plot relative	PR	[x,y ... [,x,y]]
Pen down	PD	[x,y ... [,x,y]]
Pen up	PU	[x,y ... [,x,y]]
Arc relative three-point	RT	x_incr_inter,y_incr_inter,x_incr_end,y_incr_end [,chord_angle]
Polyline encoded	PE	[flag[val] | coord_pair ... [flag[val] coord_pair]]

Polygon commands allow you to draw circles and rectangles and fill them without listing tedious strings of basic plot and arc commands. You indicate rectangle size by giving the coordinates of the corner of the finished rectangle that will be diagonally opposite the current pen position. In HP-GL terminology, an edge figure is an outline; a fill figure is a solid drawing.

Table 11.27 lists the HP-GL2 polygon commands.

Table 11.27 HP-GL/2 Polygon Commands

Function	Command	Parameters
Circle	CI	radius [,chord_angle]
Fill rectangle absolute	RA	x_coordinate,y_coordinate

Table 11.27 continued

Function	Command	Parameters
Fill rectangle relative	RR	x_increment,y_increment
Edge rectangle absolute	EA	x_coordinate,y_coordinate
Edge rectangle relative	ER	x_increment,y_increment
Fill wedge	WG	radius,start_angle,sweep_angle[, chord_angle]
Edge wedge	EW	radius,start_angle,sweep_angle[, chord_angle]
Polygon mode	PM	polygon_definition
Polygon fill	FP	
Polygon edge	EP	

Line and fill attributes commands are closely allied with the polygon commands. They enable you to change the characteristics of the lines that you draw, both its width and pattern. Similarly, these commands specify the pattern to be used for filling shapes. Because HP-GL works in the same order that you would ordinarily, you specify the line or fill type before you draw a shape.

Table 11.28 lists the line and fill attributes commands.

Table 11.28 HP-GL/2 Line and Fill Attributes Commands

Function	Command	Parameters	Comments
Line type	LT	[line_type[,pattern_length [,mode]]]	
Line attributes	LA	[kind,value ... [,kind,value]]	
Pen width	PW	[width[,pen]]	
Pen width units	WU	[type]	
Select pen	SP	1	Black
	SP	0	White

Symbol mode	SM	[char]
Fill type	FT	[fill_type[,option1[,option2]]]
Anchor corner	AC	[x_coordinate,y_coordinate]
Raster fill definition	RF	[index[,width,height,pen_nbr ... pen_nbr]]
User-defined line type	UL	[index[,gap1 ... gapn]]

Palette extension commands extend a bit of extra versatility to your drawings. The transparency mode command affects how HP-GL/2 treats areas of white fill. When transparent, other line, shapes, and text show through as if the white fill were clear. When opaque, white fill covers up anything drawn underneath it. The screened vectors command allows you to specify dot screen, cross-hatch patterns, or custom patterns to use as fill inside shapes.

Table 11.29 lists the HP-GL/2 palette extension commands.

Table 11.29 HP-GL/2 Palette Extension Commands

Function	Command	Parameters	Comments
Transparency mode	TR	0	Off (opaque)
	TR	1	On (transparent)
Screened vectors	SV	[screen type [,shading [,index]]]	

Character commands add text handling to HP-GL2's drawing mode because PCL text commands are not available while you are drawing. These allow you to select a font, its size, slant, and the character orientation (portrait, landscape, or anything in between). As with PCL mode, HP-GL/2 allows for a primary and secondary font but calls them standard and alternate.

Table 11.30 lists the HP-GL/2 character commands.

Table 11.30 HP-GL/2 Character Commands

Function	Command	Parameters
Selects standard font	SS	
Selects alternate font	SA	
Standard font definition	SD	[kind,value ... [,kind,value]]
Alternate font definition	AD	[kind,value ... [,kind,value]]
Character size, absolute	SI	[width,height]
Character size, relative	SR	[width,height]
Character slant	SL	[tangent_of_angle]
Extra space	ES	[width[,height]]
Character fill mode	CF	[fill_mode[,edge_pen]]
Direction, absolute	DI	[run,rise]
Direction, relative	DR	[run,rise]
Label origin	LO	[position]
Label	LB	[char ... [char]]1bterm
Defines label terminator	DT	[1bterm[,mode]]
Character plot	CP	[spaces,lines]
Transparent data	TD	[mode]
Defines variable text path	DV	[path[,line]]

PostScript

Laser printers are more than mere printers; most have the brains of a complete computer. Many are smarter than the computers that they are plugged into. Their understanding of certain instructions reflects this intelligence. Rather than mere commands, the software controls for laser printers are more like programming languages.

The advantage of PostScript is its versatility. It uses outline fonts, which can be scaled to any practical size. PostScript is device and resolution independent, which means that the same code that controls your 300-dpi printer runs a 2500-dpi typesetter–and produces the highest possible quality image at the available resolution level. You can print a rough draft on your LaserJet from a PostScript file and, after you have checked it over, send the same file to a typesetter to have a photo-ready page made.

Among people working extensively with graphics, the most popular printer control method is Adobe System's PostScript page description language. Originally developed in 1985, PostScript comprises a group of commands and codes that describe graphic elements and indicate where they are to appear on the printed page. Your computer sends high-level PostScript commands to your laser printer, and the printer executes the commands to draw the image itself. In effect, the data processing load is shifted to the printer which, in theory, has been optimized for implementing such graphics commands. Nevertheless, it can take several minutes for the printer to compute a full-page image after all the PostScript commands have been transferred to it. (Older PostScript printers might take half an hour or more to work out a full page of graphics.)

In June, 1990, Adobe Systems announced a new version of PostScript, Level 2, which incorporated several enhancements. The most obvious are speed and color. PostScript Level 2 can dash through documents four to five times quicker thanks to getting the font-rendering technology used in Adobe Type Manager. In addition, PostScript incorporates a new generalized class of objects called "resources" that can be precompiled, named, and cached and downloaded to the memory (or disk) inside a PostScript device. Nearly anything that is printed can be classed as a resource–artwork, patterns, forms and handled in this streamlined manner. PostScript Level 2 also manages its memory uses much better, no longer requiring that programs preallocate memory for downloaded fonts and bit-mapped graphics. It also incorporates new file-management abilities to handle disk-based storage inside PostScript devices. In addition, PostScript Level 2 has built-in compression/decompression abilities so that bit-mapped images (and other massive objects) can be transmitted more quickly in compressed form, then expanded inside the printer or other device.

The PostScript color extensions were first grafted onto the language in 1988, but PostScript Level 2 takes color to heart. Where each PostScript device had its own proprietary color-handling methods, with PostScript Level 2, color is device independent. To improve color quality, the new version also allows color halftone screening at any angle, which helps to eliminate more patterns and to make sharper renderings.

Under the original PostScript language, you could specify color using either of two display-oriented systems, red-green-blue (RGB) and hue-saturation-brightness

(HSB). The color extensions added a print-oriented color model, cyan-magenta-yellow-black (CMYK). It also added black generation and undercolor removal functions, screen and transfer functions for four separate color components, and a new operator (command) called *colorimage* for rendering color sampled images.

Level 2 also enhances the handling of font by increasing the number of characters per font and by adding composite font technology. PostScript Level 1 limited fonts to 256 characters each. Level 2 allows for composite fonts, which allow an essentially unlimited number of characters. Larger fonts are particularly useful for languages that do not use the Roman alphabet. For example, a typical Japanese language font includes more than 7000 kanji, katakana, and hiragana characters. The larger character sets also allow for fonts with a wealth of diacritical marks so that PostScript fonts can accommodate virtually any language.

Composite font technology helps typographers use the same font for portrait and landscape orientations by allowing a font to include two sets of character spacing details (called metrics) in a single font. One set of metrics can describe the characters when used horizontally; the other, for vertical orientation. Composite font technology also allows two fonts to be merged into one, for example, combining symbols with text characters so that both are immediately accessible without changing fonts. A composite font could make both the IBM extended character set and ANSI character set available within a single font. Because combining fonts can minimize the need to switch between multiple fonts, it can streamline image processing.

Level 2 also incorporates Display PostScript, an extension that is designed to translate PostScript code into screen images. Display PostScript gives the language the ability to deal with monitor images and windowing systems. It also includes device-independent support for many of the more generalized printer features also available so that paper trays, paper sizes, paper feeding, even stapling, can be controlled through PostScript.

Of course, ordinary PostScript printers cannot take advantage of these new features, while Level 2 machines are generally (though not completely) backwardly compatible with older code. In most cases, a PostScript Level 2 printer handles ordinary PostScript commands without a problem, but realizing the full features of Level 2 requires new PostScript 2 software drivers.

Operation

The PostScript language instructions created by your application or printer driver actually generate a computer program that's written in the PostScript language. As a program, it is a set of step-by-step instructions. Rather than telling your printer what to do, however, the PostScript program tells your printer what the page you want to print is supposed to look like.

The controller in a PostScript printer is essentially a computer, one that is programmed to run a program called the PostScript language interpreter. You don't have to load this program because it is coded into the read-only memory (ROM) of the printer, much like your PC's BIOS is part of its ROM. The PostScript interpreter functions as the operating system of the printer.

When the PostScript interpreter receives a program or PostScript file from your PC, it steps through it one instruction at a time, carrying them out to draw an image. In PostScript terminology, each instruction is an operator. The operators in the program tell the printer two essentials for making the page image: where on the page to locate specific image features and what character to place or kind of image to draw at the given point.

PostScript describes page images in terms of a coordinate system with the bottom edge of the paper representing the horizontal axis and the left edge the vertical axis. The origin, with coordinates (0,0) is consequently at the lower-left corner of the page. The numbers assigned to coordinates increase as you go up the page or move to the right across it. All coordinate values are positive–a negative value would be off the sheet where it could not print.

Measurements under PostScript are figured in units of points, 1/72nd of an inch. A standard sheet of paper measures 792 points high and 612 points wide. Table 11.31 lists the PostScript coordinates at various points around a standard sheet of letter-size paper.

Table 11.31 PostScript Page Coordinates for an 8.5x11 Inch Sheet

Coordinate	Location
0,0	Bottom-left corner
0,792	Top-left corner
612,0	Bottom-right corner
612,792	Top-right corner
306,396	Center of page

To draw a graphic image, PostScript traces the path of an imaginary pen across the coordinate system. Note that the coordinate measurements are referenced to the size of the image on the page rather than the number of dots required to make up a line. This design makes PostScript device independent. No matter the resolution of the printer drawing the line, the line will always appear at the same place or coordinate position on the paper.

Although PostScript is supposed to be device independent, PostScript programs can call upon specific features of a given printer. To generate the proper code, PostScript uses PostScript Printer Description (PPD) files to tell it how to use the special features of a given printer. The PPD file is supposed to be in plain language that you can read, but the commands (like all PostScript) are meaningful only to those conversant in the language.

Text printing works in the same manner as graphic printing. The PostScript instructions from your PC tell the printer where to place the cursor and what kind of characters to type. PostScript accepts a string of characters, from one to an entire line, then with an explicit command, prints them. You can change fonts, cursor position, color, or any other parameter with every character you print.

One consequence of this design is that a PostScript printer won't work like an ordinary line printer. Blast a plain string of text at it, and your PostScript printer will probably just sit there, blinking an error message at you because it attempted to read PostScript commands in your text. Because plain text doesn't include a command to PostScript to print the text, it won't know what to do with the data that you sent. To print a plain text file, you need a utility that sends the text to your PostScript printer along with the commands to print it out. Dozens of such utilities are available.

Another consequence of the PostScript design is that while you can read a PostScript file with any text editor, you're as likely to make as much sense from it as you would a treatise in Romulan runes. Even the plain text part of a document isn't in very plain text–you'll find each line surrounded by positioning and printing instructions. In fact, when text is kerned, each character may have its own positioning operators.

One of the most distinctive parts of the PostScript language is its memory system. PostScript uses a stack to store the numbers that it works on. As a number appears in a PostScript program or file, the language interpreter puts the number on the top of the stack memory. All the other numbers in the stack notch down one position. The interpreter can access only the top number on the stack, so it must peel off layers of numbers to get one that is buried deeply down and move it to the top of the stack. PostScript uses several stacks for its various functions.

PostScript uses only seven-bit characters (those with ASCII values less than 128). Data and operators for PostScript programs are written with printable plain-text characters. The language uses only a handful of control codes, listed in Table 11.32.

Table 11.32 Serial Commands to PostScript Printers

Character	Code	Hex	To Printer	From Printer	Definition
Carriage return	CR	13	X	X	End of line
Control-C	ETX	03	X	-	Stops execution
Control-D	EOT	04	X	X	End of file
Control-H	BS	08	X	X	Deletes previous character
Control-Q	DC1	17	X	X	Resumes output
Control-R	DC2	18	X	-	Redisplays line
Control-S	DC3	19	X	X	Suspends output
Control-T	DC4	20	X	-	Status query
Control-U	NAK	21	X	-	Erases current line
Delete	DEL	7F	X	-	Deletes previous character
Line-Feed	LF	12	X	X	End of line

Documenting the syntax and operators of the PostScript language is complex enough to require a book in its own right, and Adobe has prepared one called *The PostScript Language Reference Manual* [ISBN 0-201-10174-2], published by Addison-Wesley.

PostScript Drivers

From the standpoint of using your printer, PostScript is no different than any other printer language. Your application software sends commands to your PostScript printer using a PostScript driver. Nearly every DOS program that's likely to benefit from PostScript–in particular, desktop publishing programs–has its own PostScript driver.

Windows applications rely on the printer drivers that you install in the operating system. Under the Windows 3.1 family, the default PostScript driver is called

PSCRIPT.DRV. This program is meant to be a universal driver, so it will run nearly any PostScript printer but will not be able to control manufacturer-specific features.

Windows 3.1 originally shipped with PostScript driver version 3.5, which proved so full of problems that Microsoft quickly released an update, version 3.51. (In particular, it had problems converting TrueType to PostScript fonts and dealing with custom page sizes.) Within the period of several months (in 1992) Microsoft quickly released several more updates, from version 3.52 to 3.55. Version 3.56, which was relatively bug free, shipped with PageMaker 5.0 and was also distributed free through various Microsoft distribution channels (including CompuServe and Internet FTP). If your Windows PostScript driver is older than this, you should get an update to avoid the known problems with earlier drivers.

In addition, Windows has many manufacturer-specific drivers built in for PostScript printers. If your printer appears in the **List Of Printers** box in the Printers dialog box, then Windows has the driver and will install it for you. However, printer manufacturers often update their drivers to fix bugs (such as those in the universal driver) or enhance features. The manufacturer-specific driver version built into Windows won't be as current as the drivers available from your printer's manufacturer. For this reason the PostScript driver (if any) that came with your printer probably will be more up to date than the one built into Windows. The better choice is the driver that accompanied your printer. Better still is to download the latest driver available from your printer's manufacturer.

To install a new version of the universal PostScript driver or a manufacturer-specific driver, start by choosing the **Printers** icon in the Control Panel window, then select **Install Unlisted Or Updated Printer** from the List of Printers box that appears in the Printer Setup dialog box. When Windows requests which driver to use, click on the **Have disk** option and slide your driver disk into the appropriate slot. Windows will then install a Windows PostScript Definition (.WPD) file for your printer.

The Windows PostScript driver is better at detecting errors than Print Manager and can document the errors it encounters to aid in troubleshooting. If you want to print out the errors encountered in printing a document, select the **Print PostScript Error Information** check box in the Advanced Options dialog box of the **Printer Setup** command after the document prints.

PostScript drivers install into Windows 95 exactly like other printer drivers, as described in Chapter 6. The same caveat about aging drivers applies, although because Windows 95 is newer (both to you and the programmers writing drivers) the PostScript drivers included with it are more likely to be current.

PostScript Files

The PostScript language is designed to be more than immediate commands sent through a parallel interface to your printer. Because a page description under PostScript is nothing more than text commands, you can create a text file from them just as you can make a document with a word processor. Most programs that offer PostScript output allow you to send that output to a file rather than directly to your printer. You can then copy the file to floppy disk, a disk cartridge, or a tape and send it to a service bureau. The service bureau can copy the file to a high-resolution typesetter to produce an offset master with 2500-dpi resolution. Alternately, you can create a PostScript file on disk and later copy it to your own printer and print out the document as if your program were generating the code afresh.

By convention, PostScript files use the file name extension .PS, although some manufacturers use similar but different codes for PostScript files that have device-specific features. For example, Hewlett-Packard uses .HPS for files that are code-specific to its PostScript printers.

You can read a PostScript file with your word processor or other text editor as if it were an ordinary document, although you have to be intimately familiar with the PostScript language in order to sort out what all the operators and data mean. You can even edit a PostScript file to add commands that are outside the repertory of your printer driver (or just be malicious).

Encapsulated PostScript files are special-purpose files containing PostScript code that are often used in exchanging images. As with ordinary PostScript files, encapsulated PostScript files contain a list of commands written in the PostScript page description language. Unlike regular PostScript files that may hold multipage documents, an encapsulated PostScript file usually stores a single-page image, although it may hold text, drawing commands, and bit-images without restriction. Optionally, the encapsulated PostScript file may contain a bit-mapped preview image.

Many PC graphics programs are able to import Encapsulated PostScript images and use them as bit maps. Programs that cannot interpret the PostScript instructions in the file often can display the bit map to give you a crude view of what the file contains. Exchanging files in the encapsulated PostScript format is useful because PostScript is a fully documented standard, so the encapsulated form offers a convenient means of storing a simple image or other page.

The primary difference between an encapsulated PostScript and ordinary PostScript file is that the former contains one extra line to describe a *bounding box* that gives the limits of the image's edges on the page. This bounding box allows the graphics applications that manipulate bit images to determine how to import the image, position it on the page, and resize it when necessary. The encapsulated PostScript file also includes a header that identifies its format.

The bounding box in an encapsulated PostScript file is described by the command **%%BoundingBox:** Four parameters describe the coordinates of the upper-left and lower-right corners of the image in the standard PostScript measuring units, points (1/72 of an inch). For example, the first two lines of an encapsulated PostScript file that contains a full page image in portrait format would have a header and %%BoundingBox command like this:

```
%!PS-Adobe-3.0 EPSF-3.0
%%BoundingBox: 0 0 612 792
```

You can ordinarily identify encapsulated PostScript files by their file name extension, .EPS. As with other standards, however, even encapsulated PostScript has its variations (mostly in regard to the preview image), and these may wear different extensions.

CHAPTER TWELVE

Maintenance and Troubleshooting

Getting the most from your printer means keeping it running as long as you can with as few as possible migraines and other disasters. Preventive maintenance will help minimize your problems, no matter the technology your printer uses. This chapter will tell you what to do and how. However, if things eventually do go wrong, the tips in these pages will help you troubleshoot your way through the most common problems encountered in printing with your PC.

Bytes don't break. Although your data may get stale, the bits won't wear out. Your PC keeps everything fresh with minimal up-keep; no care, no feeding, no maintenance. Printers are different. They use things up and wear themselves out. The require periodic maintenance of one kind or another just to keep going. Although you can avoid the work for a while, eventually the needs of the real world will catch up with you. Your printer and your printouts will come grinding to a halt, sometimes literally.

Thankfully, routine printer maintenance isn't tough. You don't have to stoke the boiler, swab the decks, or change the oil. A damp rag and some well-placed fingers will take care of the routine chores. And a little forethought will keep all the chores routine.

Sometimes, however, things do go wrong. Your masterpiece that once and for all explains the meaning of life might print out as only little black squares. Or your best efforts might come out a garble suitable for the puzzle page of the *New York Times* or the lead story on the network news. Your printer might quit working entirely, or simply never start.

Most of your printer problems are not unique. The odds favor someone encountering exactly the same kind of difficulties that plague you. Although someone, somewhere may be quietly cackling to himself in a full-fledged hebephrenic daze pushing his ink-jet's printhead slowly back and forth between his finger, facing the problem still unsolved with a mind proven quite solvable, your particular problem has likely been fixed a dozen times over. You could do the work of solving it yourself or better still, find guidance in these pages that will help you through most of the more common difficulties in printerdom.

If you're lucky, you'll find this book's diagnostic advice entirely optional, the pages a waste of good ink and pulp that might have been better used on some celebrity's memoirs. If you're realistic, you'll read through the maintenance section and try preventive medicine. Although taking good care of your printer won't guarantee its long, trouble-free life, you can be sure mistreating your machine will only shortchange you on your printer investment.

MAINTENANCE

With any mechanical device, the basic maintenance issues are two: dirt and wear. Dirt is Nature's way of bringing entropy home, piling particles of contamination, dust, and grime atop precision parts, making them stick, bind, and grind. Wear is part of the universal aging process but, unlike human aging, in printers it broadens tolerances. As the machine ages, parts rubbing against one another wear themselves down. Some materials simply degrade with time as plasticizers evaporate away, ozone nibbles away at rubber drive belts and rollers (and your lungs), and ultraviolet light breaks molecular bonds and embrittles some plastics. As precise tolerances become loose tolerances, print quality degrades. As aging parts break, print quality (and any output at all) stops.

Dirt and wear are related. Dirt accelerates wear, adding grit to the grind. Although you cannot slow the passage of time or its ravages, you can cut the contribution from dirt. That's the key to maintenance. By keeping your machine clean, you prevent the added problems that dirt and contamination add to the aging process.

Ink-Jet Issues

The quiet of ink-jet operation is reassuring, particularly to mechanical engineers. They know that every noise a printer makes means some part is getting a workout, and that means an increased opportunity for wear and failure. Ink-jet printers have fewer moving parts than the impact technology they have essentially replaced, and that means fewer things to go wrong and a longer, trouble-free life.

But even paradise has its plagues. Although ink-jets reduce the need for maintenance, they don't entirely eliminate it. After all, that printhead still runs back and forth. Moreover, all the pollutants that infest the world can still find their way inside. The printer, too, brews its own.

Left to itself, an ink-jet printer will have a long, trouble-free life. Give it periodic maintenance, and it will have a longer, even more trouble-free life. You simply exchange the few moments it takes for cleaning for unplanned work stoppages, ensuring frustration, and possible repair bills. All in all, periodic maintenance of an ink-jet is a pretty good deal.

Preventing Clogs

The key concern with ink-jet printers is preventing clogs; ink *wants* to dry. That's its whole purpose and design in life. Given a chance, it will dry wherever it can. You're delighted when it dries quickly enough on paper that one sheet sliding onto the last on printed doesn't smear. But the same fast-drying is an anathema to your printhead. Given a chance, the ink will happily dry on your ink-jet's nozzles, clogging them and preventing the spray of one or more dots into the on-paper character matrix.

The constant spray of ink keeps enough solvent flowing so that clogs ordinarily won't form during your printouts. Stop the spray, and clogging potential skyrockets. Printer makers know this and have designed their printers so that they cover their nozzles when you're not printing. You can, however, subvert this protection by careless operation of your printer.

Most ink-jet printers cap their printheads after they complete each print job, but you have to give the printer a chance to take care of itself. Most ink-jets cap their nozzles by sliding their printhead to the rest position at one side of the carriage. The capping operating is simple, quick, and part of the process of completing a print job. If you're eager to switch off the printer to get on with the rest of your life, for example, to finish a job and then move the printer to a different office, you can subvert the capping process. Although most printers allow for you sneakily switching them off before they cap their nozzles (the off switch only starts the shutdown process, which the printer completes itself), unplugging the printer instantly cuts off its supply of electricity. The cover-up process can't complete, the nozzles are left uncovered, the ink dries, and you face formidable clogs when you get around to printing again. The morale is that your printer knows what's best. Let it finish its shutdown process before you unplug it. After the last print job, switch the machine off and wait the few seconds until everything inside quiets down.

Ink can dry even when not in the printer, so it's important to take proper care of cartridges when they are not installed in your printer. When you buy a new cartridge for your ink-jet printer, leave it in its factory-sealed package until you're ready to install it. Don't be tempted to peek at your purchase to marvel at how little money buys these days or you'll get an even worse deal when the cartridge clogs even before you install it.

When you do install a new cartridge, be sure to let it acclimate to your office. Sliding in a cartridge fresh from a ride home from the computer store *al fresco* will result in lower quality until the cartridge fully warms up. Cartridges too hot from sitting in your sedan in the hot sun will also print poorly until they cool off to printer temperature.

If you remove a cartridge from your printer while it still contains ink with the though of reusing it, be sure to cover it well to prevent clogs. For example, you may want to switch from straight black ink to a color cartridge and later switch back again. Some ink-jet makers like Hewlett-Packard supply a cradle in which to store your cartridge when it is outside your printer. The cradle caps the nozzles and keeps the ink free flowing. Don't just leave the cartridge lying around but put it into the cradle when not in the printer. If, by some lack of prescience, you happen to have thrown out the cradle after you installed a cartridge, seal your cartridge in a plastic bag while it's out of your machine.

Cleaning Your Ink-jet

Regular maintenance involves cleaning your ink-jet printer. The cleaning process has three aspects: outside the printer, inside the printer, and the ink-jet cartridge or printhead.

Exterior Clean Up

Cleaning the outside of any printer is mostly a matter of cosmetics. If you keep your printer looking good, you'll mostly satisfy your own soul. As long as it looks new, you'll be happier with the machine and less likely to think about replacing it. But a good exterior cleaning has its positive preventive aspects, too. Removing dirt from the outside of the machine improves the chance that it won't migrate to the inside of the machine. Let a lot of dust and other crud build up on your printer, and mysterious cosmic forces will ensure some of it will work its way inside your machine to gum things up.

Most printer makers recommend the mildest of cleaning methods for the outside of their products. Typically you're told to use a soft cloth moistened with nothing but water to wipe away stains, smudges, and dust. The moisture in the cleaning cloth will help it collect the dust and help prevent it getting brushed inside the printer. It will also loosen and dissolve most light smudges and stains.

Often, however, plain water isn't enough. At most, printer manufacturers recommend a *mild* detergent. A good choice is a few drops of liquid dish detergent in a cup of warm water. If you need something with more smudge-removing power, you have to carefully select more powerful solvents to do the job. Two that work well are glass cleaner (such as Windex) and isopropyl alcohol (rubbing alcohol).

Glass cleaner is the milder of the two and the one better to start with. If you want to play it safe, moisten the soft cloth with the glass cleaner and wipe the smudges away. Of course that spray bottle will tempt you to spray glass cleaner all over your printer. Try to resist the temptation. And when you don't, be careful not to spray so much that the glass cleaning drips inside the machine. Better still, avoid spraying near any opening in the machine, including the cracks in the case. If you let the glass cleaner stand for a few dozen seconds before wiping it away, you can often dissolve more stubborn stains.

Rubbing alcohol is the most powerful solvent you should ever use on the plastic case of a printer. Stronger solvents (like acetone) can melt many plastics and destroy paint finishes. Again, moisten your soft cloth with the alcohol and gently wipe away the smudges and stains from your printer's case.

Don't use other household cleaners. Most bathroom cleaners contain bleach as an antibacterial. Bleach can be harmful to the plastic and rubber parts of your printer. Kitchen cleaners often leave an oily residue that can bind dust to your printer. The result of using a kitchen cleaner can be worse in the long run than not cleaning your printer at all.

The Inside Job

The dirt that builds up inside an ink-jet printer comes from both the paper and ink that you use. Almost all types of paper shed tiny pieces of dust as they twist through a printer. And all ink-jet printers build up a small amount of residue from ink that misses the mark and the paper. After a while you may see this residue build up inside the case of your printer.

Cleaning the inside of an ink-jet printer is little different than the outside. In general you should use exactly the same materials and techniques: the same soft cloth (or better still, a clean one) moistened but not wet with water. If stains prove stubborn, you can venture as far as using alcohol as a cleaning solvent but never use anything stronger. Hewlett-Packard recommends using rubbing alcohol *only* on the printhead contacts. According to the company, alcohol may damage other parts of the printer mechanism.

If you want to be thorough in your cleaning, clear out any dust and debris. You can brush away the loose pieces with a soft brush, an unused paintbrush will work as well as anything else. Of course, the debris has to go somewhere, and brushing it is as likely to push it deeper into your printer as it is to get it out. Better to get the dirt to go somewhere you can control, like into a vacuum cleaner.

A hand vacuum cleaning with an extended nozzle works best. Some manufacturers even offer special vacuums for cleaning computers and delicate electronics gear. Get as deeply inside your printer as you can *without* touching the vacuum nozzle to any part of the printer mechanism. If you can obtain one, use a soft rubber nozzles designed to prevent damage to delicate mechanisms.

Deciding where to wipe your printer clean is easy. Clean everywhere you can reach. Wipe the inside of the case and the outside of the internal mechanism. Get into all the nooks and even the crannies.

You can use cotton swabs such as Q-Tips to get into tight spots, but be careful. A bit of cotton fiber unravels from the tip of the cotton swab can be worse for your printer's health than the dirt you're cleaning out. A better choice are the special rubber foam cleaning tips that you'll find in electronics stores for cleaning VCRs.

Note that Hewlett-Packard recommends against cleaning the guide rod in some of its ink-jet printers (particularly the 600, 660, and 850 series). The company notes that any ink build-up on the rod should not hinder the printer's normal operation. Cleaning the rod, the company cautions, can shorten its life and thereby the useful life of your printer.

On the other hand, HP recommends you look in one surprising place for your cleaning that they don't mention in your printer manual–under the cartridge. To give your machine a thorough cleaning, switch it off, slide the cartridge mechanism left and away from its resting spot, and wipe up underneath. Heavy use of the printer can lead to a lot of build-up here, and according to HP wiping up here can help clean up your printing. Be sure to put the cartridge back in its resting position when you're done to cap the printhead and prevent clogs.

Besides removing ink stains from the case, you should also clean the paper path and mechanism. Although every printer model is different in the twists and turns it gives your every sheet, the cleaning procedure for most is about the same.

Start by switching off your printer. You don't want to fight with the mechanism, and in particular, you don't want the printer to win and run your necktie around the platen.

Next, unload the paper. You don't want it in the way, and since you'll be using solvents, you won't want it to get wet.

Remove the removable parts in the paper path. For example, remove the paper trays from printers that use them.

Open your printer. In some cases that means folding open a cover. In others, you'll need to open an access door. You'll want to access everything as you would to clear a jam from the paper path. Remove whatever debris you find. Vacuum as necessary.

Clean the rollers in the printer path. Special solvents are available for cleaning rubber parts. Use it sparingly and avoid getting it on any other part of your printer. Rotate the rollers against a cloth lightly wetted with the solvent. Allow it to evaporate.

Close your printer and replace whatever you earlier removed (tray and paper). Switch it on and verify that everything works and you haven't left the cleaning cloth inside the machine.

Some manufacturers make special cleaning provisions that vary from these guidelines. With some Hewlett-Packard ink-jet machines, for example, you should leave the printer switched *on* and plugged in when clean the paper path. Once you have access to the drive rollers, pressing the **Resume** button will make the printer spin them so that you can more easily clean the rollers. Other HP models require you switch off the printer before you start the clean-up disassembly then switch it on to spin the drive rollers. (The access door is interlocked and must be open to spin the rollers with the Resume button.) Your printer's manual should tell you the proper procedure. In any case, be sure to clean all of the driver rollers (most HP machines have three sets) before closing up the printer.

Another often neglected place to clean is the paper tray sled in printer models that have one. According to Hewlett-Packard, contamination there can sometimes cause printing problems. The most common of these is scratching transparencies as they run through the printer. Often the scratches are invisible until you project the transparencies, then they appear as long, distracting lines running from top to bottom the length of the page (or across the page, if you print them in landscape mode). If you notice such scratches on your transparencies, HP recommends that you clean the sled attached to the Out tray of your printer with tissue paper.

Cartridge and Nozzle Cleaning

Printers tell you when its time to clean their print cartridges—or, rather, they tell you when you should have cleaned the cartridge a few days earlier. Just look at the print-outs. If you see line or dots missing from text or graphics, it's time to do the job.

Although you should clean printer cartridges at the first sign of clogging, you should never clean too often or unnecessarily. Every time you clean the cartridge, you waste some ink, which shortens the life of the cartridge (and when you consider what you pay for them, their life is already too short).

Depending on the model of your printer, you may have several methods of cleaning available to you. For example, many of the newer Hewlett-Packard DeskJets have three different cartridge cleaning modes: light cleaning, intensive cleaning, and prime pens. When each finishes, it shows you a sample of the work so you can verify the cleaning was effective.

Light Cleaning

Every time you switch your printer on, it gives itself a quick going over to ensure that it will print cleanly and with its best quality. It purges its printhead to help ensure that all of its nozzles are clear. You can force your printer to go through a more thorough but still light cleaning cycle when you suspect or suffer small problems, such as the missing row of dots that marks a single clogged nozzle.

The procedure to activate the light cleaning cycle varies with printers and manufacturers. A few might force you to switch your printer off and back on. Other machines understand explicit commands.

With the HP machine, the activation process is a bit obscure. You press the **Power** button down and hold it on. At the same time press and release the **Resume** button seven times. Then release the **Power** button. The printer should start in its light cleaning mode.

Alternately, you can activate the printer's light cleaning mode with commands from your PC. For example, if you're running Windows 3.1, double-click on the **HP DeskJet Status Monitor** icon that's located by default in the HP DeskJet Utilities program group. In Windows 95, click on **Start**, then **Programs**, and look for the HP DeskJet Utilities Group. Click on it, then on **HP DeskJet Status Monitor**. Select the **Maintenance** menu, and from there choose **Clean Print Cartridge**. Click on **Clean**. The program will tell you what to do to complete the process.

Intensive Cleaning Mode

When a light cleaning doesn't clear the clogs, you need to try the next step up in clean-up power, intensive cleaning mode. The intensive cleaning takes longer and consumes more of your printer's ink, so you resort to it only as necessary.

In the case of the HP 850, the only way to start intensive cleaning is from the printer's Control Panel. Its starts much like the light cleaning but requires an additional press of the **Resume** button. In other words, press and hold down the **Power** button, then press and release the **Select** button eight times. Release the **Power** button and the process will begin and automatically run to completion.

Prime Pens Mode

The most thorough purge in the HP repertory is prime pens mode, designed for getting new cartridges ready for operation. You can also use it for stubborn cartridges that might have been idle for long periods. Because it can consume a great deal of ink and time, you should use this mode only when necessary. On the HP 850, you activate it from the front Control Panel much like the other cleaning modes only using nine presses of the **Resume** button while holding the **Power** button on.

As part of the cleaning process, each of the cleaning modes prints a test on paper (the also serves to serves to suck up the ink the cleaning mode uses to clean the printhead). Consequently, in order to carry out any of the cleaning cycles, you must have paper loaded into your printer. You should use your normal paper stock, although you can the backsides of old printouts if you have a New England-style frugal streak or want to save at least a small branch of a tree from the papermakers.

This printout also serves to let you judge the effectiveness of the cleaning process. You should see that all the nozzle of your printer are firing as the printout comes near its end. Other printers may not have such an elaborate hierarchy of cleaning modes. The Epson Color Stylus, for example, gets by with one that serves to clean the nozzles and purge new cartridges. To get a more thorough cleaning, you simply repeat the cycle.

With the Stylus, you start a cleaning cycle of the black jets by pressing the **Pause** button followed by **Alt** and **Load/Eject**. To start a color jet cleaning cycle, press the **Pause** button followed by **Alt** and **Economy/Condensed**. A clogged printhead may require three to five cycles to clear all of its nozzles.

Laser Issues

Laser technology has come a long way since the days of ruby rods and pulsed xenon tubes, the only purpose for which seemed to slice James Bond in half—and never successfully at that. Today the laser is tiny silicon junction in a diode, taken for granted in millions of CD drives and printers (not to mention fiber optics, surveying equipment, and weapons systems). In printers, we take the coherent, collimated beam for granted, expecting to pour data and paper in one side of the machine and have them come out combined on the other.

Regular maintenance ensures the steady flow of paper through your laser printer. Not that improperly maintaining your printer will prevent the paper from getting out. It inevitably does, even if you have to crossbar the case open to yank out the shards. An improperly maintained laser results in output not up to your expectations: spotty, pale, or never making it to the out tray at all.

Although you can regard a modern laser printer as a beige box that only requires you dump in paper and toner as it clamors for more, such cavalier treatment is akin to limiting your car maintenance to pumping in gas. You can expect trouble-free travels for thousands of miles, till the sludge throttles your engine or reams of print-out until the grime starts grabbing every other sheet on its way through.

Normal Maintenance

Laser printer makers have thought hard about the maintenance of their machines, mostly with the goal of minimizing and simplifying it. In fact, improved maintenance put laser printer and its associated copier technology into individual hands. The first generation of photocopiers required so much attention that many seemed to come with a service technician as standard equipment. Toner came like an unruly genie in a bottle and burst out in a cloud of dust that would never return to its home. Machines were so large they threatened to swallow technicians without leaving a trace. The breakthrough of Canon photocopiers that was carried through the first Hewlett-Packard laser printers combined all the maintenance items into a single cartridge: toner, drum, and fuser. Regular maintenance only meant replacing the cartridge, and the most common repairs involved little more.

Moving a Laser Printer

For most people moving or shipping, a printer is merely a matter of yanking the power cord from the wall, throwing the machine in a box, pulling it out at the end of its travels, and plugging it back in. You can't be so cavalier about moving a laser printer. Certainly the mechanisms are strong enough to withstand even the hired gorillas at the freight company. But every laser printer comes complete with its own bomb called toner. Shake, rattle, or roll the printer and the toner will come seething out, coating everything it comes near with a fine black (usually) power is that is as difficult to remove as bloodstains from the hands of Scottish royalty.

The toner inside a laser printer ordinarily is not sealed in place. Moving a laser printer without preparation can cause toner to sift out of its reservoir and let it drift throughout the printer. If you're particularly evil about moving the printer, you can shake out the entire supply of toner and cover not only the inside of the printer but the outside and much of the rest of the world as well. The stuff inside is trouble for your printouts, added grey speckles to every sheet. On the outside it can make you look like a coal miner whenever you touch the machine. Worst of all, it's almost impossible to clean up a laser printer after a bad toner spill. You have to disassemble the entire machine to get out all the toner.

In this case, an ounce of prevention can be worth the cost of a new printer. Before shipping or moving a laser printer, remove the toner from inside it. Take out the entire cartridge. If your machine has a separate container for used toner (as do some Data Products, Sharp, and Texas Instruments machines), remove that, too. Cover the openings as best you can and move the toner and printer separately. If you plan to ship the printer to a distant locale, you're probably best off tossing the old toner and getting a new supply for the printer's new home. The cost is insignificant compared to the damage that toner can do.

Emergency Toner Replenishment

The nightmare is more common than you might think–you have a 1000-page report due at 9 a.m. and you've been printing it out since you got home. On page 998 your printer beeps and stops, flashing an ugly green light at you with the message "Out of Toner" on the LCD display. Of course you don't have a replacement toner cartridge, and the only computer supply stores open are 12,000 miles away on the daytime side of the planet. If you're lucky (although, at this point there's no reason to expect any luck other than bad), you can find enough toner inside your printer to finish the job, grab ten minutes of sleep, and get off to the office.

While some printers count the number of copies made by a toner cartridge to tell you when you need a new one, most actually judge the level of toner. The cartridge is wide, however, and the sensor is narrow. Often, there's enough toner piled up at one or the other end of a cartridge to finish your print job. The trick is to pull the cartridge out of the printer, hold it horizontally with either end in each of your hands, then gently rock it back and forth to distribute the toner. Replace the cartridge, press the **Reset** button, and if you said your prayers properly you should be able to finish the job.

Some printers have used toner reservoirs. In an emergency, you can puff some of this old toner into the main cartridge to get a few more pages. Be careful. The process can be messy and is recommended by no one. In an emergency, however, you'll want to try anything.

Cleaning a Laser Printer

Ordinary maintenance cleaning of a laser printer need not involve disassembly or any more trouble than cleaning an ink-jet printer. In fact, because the toner is kept under better control than spraying ink, cleaning can be quicker and easier despite the greater size and complexity of most laser printers.

A dirty or gummy fuser is the likely culprit when labels jam and fold up like an accordion in your printer. The heat of the fuser causes the adhesive in some labels to ooze out, and it may stick to the fuser mechanism. The fuser sticks, in turn, to the label sheet or the next sheet that rolls through, preventing the sheet from sliding through while the paper feed unknowingly keeps stuffing it in until it jams. Clearing the jam alone does not solve the problem. If the adhesive residue remains in the fuser, jams will repeat until you run out of patience or labels.

Unlike impact and ink-jet print technologies, lasers involve intense heat to complete the image-making process. The fuser rollers in a laser printer reach nearly 400°F and remains hot long after the last page has rolled through your printer. Touching the fuser or parts adjacent to it can cause severe burns. You should wait about 20 minutes after switching off a laser printer before you attempt a clean-up around the fuser. For safety's sake, unplug your laser printer from the wall outlet, and wait for the fuser to cool down.

After the printer has cooled, start by opening the printer to gain access to the paper path. Different models of laser printer use different paper paths, so the access method and the exact cleaning procedure will vary. The general technique is the same for all, however. We'll use the HP LaserJet 4 as an example.

Open the LaserJet by pulling away the long latch in the center of the rear cover that extends almost to the top of the printer. Inside the back cover near the bottom of the printer you will find the lower fuser door. Open it to gain access to the fuser. The fuser rollers are colored silver and black. If your printer has not cooled sufficiently, touching these rollers can cause severe burns, so be careful.

The usual cause of jams is adhesive residue on the exit guides from the fuser. Use a mild solvent to clean them, nothing stronger than rubbing alcohol. Solvents containing acetone will attack the plastic of the guides and damage them, which will likely *increase* the frequency of jamming. Use a coarse rag, such as terry cloth to wipe away any residue. Use Q-Tips or, better still, foam covered swaps to clean into the corners of the guides.

The LaserJet 4 has upper and lower guides in the fuser assembly and additional guides on the fuser door. You should clean all guides, the paper sensor lever, and all areas against which paper slides in its course through the printer. Close the fuser cover when you're finished.

A thorough cleaning of the fuser guides will solve most jamming problems. Other parts of the printer are less likely culprits in paper jams. Cleaning the rest of your printer will, however, help avert other problems.

While you have your printer open, examine the interior for paper scraps left behind from clearing jams. Carefully pick out the individual pieces of paper from wherever you find them, then vacuum inside. To avoid surprises, remove the toner cartridge or reservoir before you vacuum.

Examine the guides and rollers throughout the paper path. Clean those you find to be dirty, particularly any that have a black residue on them. Again, use no solvent stronger than alcohol. You can also use alcohol to clean the rubber drive rollers or, better still, use a solvent formulated for cleaning *rubber* rollers, being careful not to get any of this solvent on the plastic parts of the printer including plastic guide rollers.

If the output quality of your printer has been uneven, pay particular attention to the imaging system when you are cleaning. Contaminants such as errant toner and paper dust can interfere with the distribution of the static charge used in forming the toner image during the printing process. Areas of particular concern include the primary corona wire, the transfer corona, and the antistatic teeth. The latter two parts are outside the HP toner cartridge while the primary corona wire is inside the cartridge. You should carefully clean them all. If you are in doubt, check the Cleaning and Maintenance section of your printer's manual for model-specific guidance.

One particular area to clean in the LaserJet 4 is the output guide, which you will find at the top of the back of the printer. The guide comprises a set of rollers that are hard to see under the top of the printer. According to HP, most of the residue buildup occurs on the hard plastic rollers under the rubber rollers that are connected by a shaft. You'll also see guide ribs at the rear of the printer. Clean these as well.

When you're done cleaning, replace the toner cartridge and anything else you've removed from inside the printer. Remove your cleaning rag and other cleaning supplies from inside the printer. Then close the printer cover.

Impact Issues

Periodic cleaning of impact printers is needed more often than with nonimpact technologies. All those tiny little hammers pound paper to pieces, tiny little pieces at that, a light dust of paper fibers that collects inside the printer. Most perniciously, the dust can coat the platen roller, giving it a slick, hard surface. Without the firm grip of fresh rubber, cut sheets can slip as they roll through, giving your printed pages a definite skew. Special solvents are available for cleaning rubber platen rollers. As a rule, you should use these solvents only on the roller for which they are designed. The solvent may attack other parts of the printer with which it comes in contact.

Continuous-form printers often collect the edges from pages using a process akin to spontaneous generation. Although you might never see a piece disappear as you run a ream of paper through your printer, those edges miraculously appear inside the printer. When you least expect or want it, the paper edge pops up and lodges itself on the printhead. Prevent problems by occasionally brushing or vacuuming out the inside of your impact printer.

With the exception of the particular needs of the impact printhead, cleaning an impact printer is much the same as any other machine, both in the material you need and the technique. There is, however, one additional caveat. Impact printheads often get extremely hot during operation. Before you attempt maintenance of an impact printer, allow its printhead to cool down.

Although impact printheads don't clog, they do wear out and sometimes jam. Replacing them is standard maintenance on hard-working machines.

Cleaning a Printhead

Most impact printer manufacturers have one rule for the cleaning of the printheads in their products: Don't! You're apt to do more damage than good. You can push contaminants into the printhead and jam its wires. You may bend wires or damage the face of the printhead and impede the smooth operation of the wires. You may press the printhead out of alignment.

In general, the only maintenance required by modern impact printheads is replacement when they wear out. Should you decide your printer's printhead needs cleaning, you'll find the process even more complicated than replacing it. After all, to do a thorough job, you should remove the printhead from the machine so that you can access its front face, its business end.

Do not use cotton-tipped swabs, terry cloth, or abrasives when cleaning an impact printhead. You don't want to snag a wires or deform its face. If you use a solvent, exercise extreme care and be very frugal with it. You don't want the delicate wires to rust or corrode in place, or to wick the solvent along with a gummy residue into their inner works.

Changing a Printhead

Impact printheads are long-lived, able each wire able to smash against paper and ribbon tens of millions of times. But after prolonged use, the head may need replacement. The symptoms requiring this radical cure include your printouts having gradually grown too faint and neither sliding in a new ribbon nor adjusting the spacing between printhead and paper is effective in getting the blacks back. A printhead can also fail catastrophically, with one or more wires failing to fire, leaving white rows across lines of text and graphics.

Although impact printers vary in how you remove and install their printheads, the process is similar in most machines. The printhead is typically designed as a field service part, one meant to be replaced with a minimum of fuss and tools. Most printer makers provide detailed instructions in the owners manuals accompanying their products. In any case, the first step is to switch off your printer and unplug it from electrical power. Then, for safety's sake, take a break. Have a cup of coffee or play a game of racquet ball, letting the machine's printhead cool down.

The next step is to gain access to the printhead. Open the cover of your printer. Remove the ribbon. Finally remove the printhead. In most printers, the printhead either snaps in place or is screwed down. A quick inspection will reveal the method used by your printer. Release the printhead and pull it up. You'll note that it is still tethered by a ribbon-like *head cable*. Trace the cable from the printhead to its other end, which should be in an edge connector. Note the path of the cable and the direction it approaches the connector.

Next, unplug the cable. In most printers, you can simply pull the cable out of the connector. The printhead assembly should now be free. Put it aside. While you have the printhead out, give the printer a good overall cleaning.

Take the new printhead assembly and hold it in the same general position in which the old one was installed. In particular, route the head cable through the same path as the old one. Align the far end of the cable with the connector from which you removed the old cable, and press the new cable in its place. Ensure you make firm contact without damaging the cable.

Snug the printhead into its place in the carriage. It should either snap into place or fit so snugly you cannot rock it around. Secure the new printhead using the screws from the old one (if the old one used screws). Replace the ribbon, close the cover, and run the printer's self-test.

TROUBLESHOOTING

If you have more cash than pride, you'll take your printer in for repair at the slightest hint of trouble. If you have more pride than cash, you'll struggle with your screwdriver and duct tape to fix problems only a replacement can solve. In between is the vast middle ground, simple tricks to try so you don't waste your money needlessly on service calls or suffer the embarrassment of seeing "No Trouble Found" on the repair slip when you pick up your printer and the technician explains how to connect a parallel cable as he would to a not too generously endowed kindergartner.

To put it simply, the most common problem with printers is stupidity, and not necessarily your own. Many printer conventions and standards are just plain stupid, and printer designers who don't deign to follow the standards that are generally accepted are even worse.

Locating the Problem

The first step in solving a problem is finding out exactly what the problem is. Dyspepsia and heart attack have similar symptoms, but the treatments differ markedly. A doctor determines which or what is ailing you before he prescribes medication. With most illnesses, a proper diagnosis is the first and biggest step to a cure.

So it is with your printer. Before you can fix the problem, you should know what's wrong. Although many common PC problems appear to originate in the printer, many do not. Your printout is only as good as the data delivered to your printer.

Depending on how you slice up your system, there are six layers of processing that processor pass along the data bound for your printer. These include your application, the software driver, operating system, print spooler, the hardware printer interface, and the connecting cable. Any one of them can dedicate itself to making your life miserable.

Application

Your application generates the text or image that you expect your printer to make. If you screw up here and generate garbage, your printer won't be able to deliver anything but garbage to you. Certainly application software can cause printer problems itself through poor design or implementation, but usually you're the culprit because you fail to use the software in a manner consistent with the printer's abilities. For example, you could use the wrong color model for your printer or your might exceed the range of tonal values your printer expects in generating your image. When you're working with text, you might choose fonts to which your printer doesn't have access.

Most application problems are part of the learning experience. You learn the capabilities of your software and how to use them to best match what your printer can do. Along the way you may make some interesting if unusable printouts. In the vast scheme of things, a couple of sheets of paper is a small price to pay for an education.

Software Driver

The software driver must match the ideas and images from your application with the command used by your printer. Problems usually arise in two ways: (1) using the wrong driver or (2) using a defective driver. The wrong driver is a matter of improper matching, selecting a driver that sends out commands meant for a different model of printer than the one you plan to use. The defects in drivers are usually bugs, mistakes in programming not discovered until the driver is released into the real world.

Wrong drivers are usually a matter of making bad guesses. You think you're installing the proper driver for your printer but you make the wrong choice. Typically, your software will give you a choice of printers by which to select the software driver. You don't find your driver on the list, so you choose something that sounds close, hoping that it recognizes the same codes as your printer. Solving the problem is as easy as guessing again–and as hard as making the right guess.

Buggy drivers seem unavoidable in today's world of rushed deadlines and complex printers and software. Testing all the possible combinations of data and commands is impossible, and the ones that get missed during the manufacturer's debugging usually are the ones you want to use. The best way to avoid driver bugs is to be sure to get the most recent version of the driver from your printer manufacturer or the publisher of your application or operating system. Although having the latest version doesn't guarantee against bugs, it does decrease the likelihood of one biting you.

Operating System

The effect of your operating system on your printer is subtle. Its job is mostly as a messenger, routing the printer data on its way through your system. A good messenger ensures that deliveries get made quickly and that nothing gets lost along the way. A poor messenger drops a letter occasionally and may lose his way entirely.

Printing problems generated by operating systems are usually moot. You don't have that many alternatives, and you've usually made a commitment to your operating system that printing problems won't cause to waver.

Fortunately printing problems originating in operating systems are rare. The messengers are good indeed. But sometimes you bump into an idiosyncrasy. You might not be able to do anything about it, but at least you can understand the cause and why you must endure it.

Print Spooler

As a warehouse for your computer data, the print spooler is charged with keeping everything intact as well as keeping its wares organized. Problems with a spooler can lead to a mix-up among your print jobs, possibly mashing them together into confusion.

Most modern spooler carry out their task without a problem. But they give you the power to manage the jobs they spool, and with that power comes the potential for problem. You can route the jobs to the wrong place or lose a job entirely. The most common problem, however, is a failure to pay attention. The spooler may stall and fail to send your data on to the printer, leaving you to wonder what's wrong. All you have to do is tell the spooler to start spooling again, but you have to think to look at the spooler for the problem before you can work the solution. The moral is to know where to look for a problem. And when your printer stops for no apparent reason, one for the first places to look is your print spooler.

Printer Hardware Interface

The interface is the portal through which all the data going to your printer must pass. As computer hardware devices go, it's not very complex, but its failure can bring your print system to a stop. Or it can turn the text of your well-thought-out ideas into the ravings of a mad typesetter.

All things considered, the hardware interface may be the most reliable link in the chain of hardware and software between your application and the printed page. Problems that appear to be the fault of the interface are usually rooted in the cabling or connection. But your interface can fail, too, and you have to consider that possibility when troubleshooting.

Connecting Cable

What seems the simplest part of the application to output connection, the cable, can be one of the most troublesome. Use the wrong cable, and nothing can get from your

PC to your printer–and you'll likely suspect everything from the programming of the printer to the circuits in the interface before you consider the cable itself may fail. Wires do break. More commonly, however, connections come loose and suffer from undue influence–interference and even physical damage from kinking and other trauma.

When you have a printing problem, either when first setting up a new machine or suddenly, in the middle of a print job, you should check out these areas of potential failure one-by-one. By performing simple troubleshooting tests, you can quickly narrow down the suspects. In the next section, we'll take a look at how to locate typical printer problems.

Problem Finder

To help sort through the troubleshooting process, we'll divide printer problems into three groups: Dead on Arrival, Not Completely Operational, and Failures in Working Systems.

Dead On Arrival printers have never worked. Despite your best efforts, not a character from your PC, not a bit of image graphics, ever has made it to paper. Your printer sits there as if to challenge you, seemingly ready and able to print but decidedly unwilling.

Not Completely Operational printers differ in that they work but not the way you want. These, too, have never completed a perfect printout but at least hint that they might be capable of one if you could only discover the magic word to make them work properly. They may print odd characters, refuse to make graphics, or cut off parts of pages.

Failures in Working Systems are sudden turns for the worse. Your printer once was working well but suddenly your bliss evaporates. The rich blacks of your printouts fade to a sickly green, black blotches splatter across pages like the microcomputer equivalent of measles, paper slides into your printer, and confetti comes out, unwillingly at that.

Dead On Arrival

The first thing to try is your printer's self-test. Nearly all printers have a built-in routine that generates a page or more of text and graphics so you can verify that your new printer itself works, no matter the condition of the rest of your computer and connection system. Because the self-test is internally generated, it should operate regardless of whether your PC-to-printer link works, regardless of whether you have the right driver installed, regardless of whether you know what you're doing.

Every manufacturer has its own idea of what it should take to run a printer self-test. Typically you must press one of the Control Panel buttons such as **On-line** at the same time you switch the printer on. For example, the Epson Stylus Color switches on its self-test when you hold down the **Economy/Condensed** button when you turn on the printer by pressing the **Operate** button. Other manufacturers make the self-test a menu option, which you can select using the printer's LCD Control Panel. The necessary buttons to press to start the self-test will be documented in your printer's manual. Check the index under Self-test. In any case, after you set-up your printer but before you try your first print job, you should execute a self-test if just to reassure yourself that your printer is working.

Just as the key presses you use to start the self-test vary, the results you get will vary with each printer model and manufacturer. Some self-tests merely run through the alphabet one or more times. Others attempt to paint pages worthy for hanging in the Museum of Modern Art, demonstrating graphics capabilities and listing every printer parameter known to man and machine. Some self-tests print out just a few lines, others will rattle on continuously until you shut off the printer.

The details don't matter. If your printer can roll out a self-test page, you know that its electronics, mechanism, and material are all working together and properly doing their job. You can then connect your printer, install its drivers, and ensure that it works with your system.

If you connect through Windows 95, the software setup for adding a new printer will let you send out a test page so you can verify that the machine will work with all of your Windows software.

If you don't have Windows, you can try your own kind of test page. Use the DOS command **COPY** to send a text file directly from the operating system to your printer, skipping any driver software that's in the way. Just issue a command like the following:

```
COPY anyfile.txt PRN
```

substituting the name of a file that you know contains nothing but ASCII text for the *anyfile.txt* in the example. If you have a page printer like a laser-based machine, your test file may not constitute the full page required to trigger the printing of a page. You can sidestep this problem by taking your printer off line and pressing its **Form Feed** button after your PC has copied the text file to the printer.

Your two tests–the printer self-test and the test page–can conclude in any of four ways: a failed self-test, passing the self-test but failing to print the test page, getting both tests right but still not printing with your application, and perfect operation. If you get the last, then you have no need to bother reading about troubleshooting. We'll consider the other three alternatives, the causes and possible solutions, separately as follows.

Failed Self-Test

If your printer cannot complete a self-test, your first thought often is to pack it back into its box and return it to your dealer. Before you act rashly, however, consider the alternative: the printer isn't ready to carry out the self-test. This situation can arise if you have not properly loaded the printer with the consumables that it needs. To run a self-test, your printer need electricity, ink, and paper.

First, ensure that your printer is properly plugged into the correct voltage and that the outlet itself is working. ((Nothing is quite as embarrassing as discovering that your printer is plugged into a switched outlet, and the switch is turned off.) If the indicators on your printer glow normally or you can read a message on the LCDs on the Control Panel, you can be pretty sure the printer is getting electricity. If indicators don't light, either the electrical supply or the printer is defective. Check the electrical supply to be sure.

Once you're sure of the electrical supply, ensure that you've properly installed the toner cartridge, ink cartridges, or ribbon that your printer uses. If a toner or ink-jet cartridge is not properly seated, your printer might not be able to reach and use it. Double-check to be sure.

You can't expect your printer to print a page if you don't give it any paper. Check the input tray if your printer uses one. Ensure that it is properly seated in the printer and that the stack of paper is at the proper height. Some continuous-form printers sense paper in their tractors and refuse to work if nothing is there. Other printer detect paper wrapped around their platen rollers. Make sure you follow the printers exact instructions for loading paper and double-check just to be sure.

If after these efforts you still cannot get your printer to run a self-test *and you're sure you've been pressing the proper keys,* call your printer maker's technical support line. They will guide you through the proper return and replacement procedure. Or give a call to your dealer to be sure that lugging the machine back is the appropriate action.

Failed Test Page

When your printer works and your PC works but the two don't work together, the first thing to check is the communications between them. No matter the interface you use, the first place to check is the cable. In the rush to get your new printer working, it's easy to forget such an essential. Ensure that you've not only securely plugged in both ends of your printer cable but also be sure you've plugged into the right port. This check is particularly important if your PC has multiple parallel or serial ports.

Next ensure that both your PC and printer are using the same ports that you've plugged into. For example, during printer setup, Windows 95 offers you the option of using any port. You might mean to operate your printer from LPT2 and tell Windows to use LPT1. Similarly, many printers give you the option of using parallel or serial inputs during their configuration. If you don't tell the printer the right port, data may be at its doorstep and your printer will never hear it knock.

Chapter 8 covers most of the ins and outs of the popular printer interfaces. Parallel ports are essentially problem-free from the beginning, but even when they are working serial communications are troublesome. When they don't work, they are a nightmare. Getting them to work is even worse. There are so many variables that finding a working combination is more a matter of persistence and luck than genius.

Having to set up several serial ports may make you wonder whether you've inadvertently insulted a sorcerer or robbed a mummy's tomb while sleepwalking. If you ever get stuck with such a challenge, you should equip yourself with the right tools. High on the list is the serial port expert's best friend–the *break-out box*. Although it looks like little more than a glorified double serial connector, the breakout box is your secret collaborator, tattling all the secrets of the serial signals. The lights on the break-out box indicate which serial port signals are active so you can figure out whether your printer and serial port are attempting hardware handshaking. With a little educated guesswork, you can even figure out which serial signals they are using (or trying to use) for their handshake. That knowledge puts you well on your way to getting the port to work.

If you don't have a break-out box, you can still solve the mysteries of serial communications. The work will just take longer and turn more of your hair white.

The first step is to verify that your serial port is actually working properly. If you don't have a break-out box, try connecting using the port with known-to-be-good hardware and software. For example, temporarily move your mouse or modem to the serial port in question. If everything works fine from the port, you can assume the hardware doesn't have an intrinsic problem of its own.

Typical problems that will prevent a serial port from working are resource conflicts (your port wants to use the interrupt or input/output address used by another device), but with modern PCs these difficulties are rare. Windows 95 will automatically identify such conflicts, and you can check for them under the Device Manager tab of Control Panel. Windows 95 will even tell you if it thinks the port is working properly. With earlier versions of Windows and DOS, you can use Microsoft Diagnostics (the program MSD.EXE) to determine the resource assignments of your serial ports. In general you have a hardware problem if Windows 95 or Microsoft Diagnostics cannot identify a serial port.

When you're sure your serial port operates properly, the next challenge is getting the right cable. Larger printer manufacturers (e.g., DEC and HP) often offer special cables for their serial printers. Although they demand a premium over what you would pay to a discount vendor, these manufacturer-supplied cables guarantee you have the right wiring—an assurance that can be worth several hours of your time.

Application Printing Failure

The classic big buildup to the final letdown is successfully running through all the installation and setup procedures for your printer, rolling out sheets of self-test and even a Windows test page or two only to have the machine sit around listlessly after you give a print command from your software application. Everything should work yet nothing does.

The good news is that all those tests and verifications tell you that there is absolutely nothing wrong with your printer hardware. As long as the test page duly pours out of Windows, you can be sure that the entire print system from operating system and driver through the port and connecting cable all the way to your printhead is functioning fine. The failure lurks in your software. That means you need no tools, only perseverance, to fix it. The likely problems are the failure to install your applications properly, an invisible incompatibility, or lock-up inside your print-spooler.

The last of these is the first place to look. The Spooler will tell you if a print job got at least that far. Check to be sure that your print job is not stalled or that you haven't sent it to a file instead of your printer. Stalls occur for any of a number of reasons, most commonly switching on your printer after the Windows spooler tries to access the printer.

Under Windows 95, applications first go through the Windows spooler before they go to the printer driver. If the print job gets to the spooler but not through the driver, you've pretty well nailed down the problem. You've probably elicited an incompatibility between your applications expectations of the printer and between the driver and the printer. You may have installed a printer driver that's close to matching your printer but far enough off to cause problems. Check your printer's folder in Control Panel and verify that you've selected the right driver.

Versions of Windows before Windows 95 ran program instructions through the printer driver before sending them to the spooler. In this case, the spooler will reflect the successful operation of the driver.

Application-based printing problems are much more prevalent in DOS programs than those running under Windows. Each DOS program require its own configuration for the printer you want to use, even if your run the DOS application under Windows. Sometimes people forget this basic need. They install their driver for Windows but never properly configure their DOS applications to print with their hardware. As a result, the software never sends Windows the data to pass on to your printer. Any non-Windows application, that is any application that runs in an DOS box under Windows must be individually configured for your printer. Although Windows 95 does a good job of hiding the nature of DOS programs from you, you can check by looking in the program's Properties tab. Even if you assign a shortcut to your DOS applications, Windows 95 will tell you so under its properties.

In general, Windows applications require no printer setup when run under Windows. After the basic installation of the program, the **Print** option in the file menu will link through with Windows application interface to the Windows printer driver. If a test page rolls out, the program should work.

As wonderful as Windows is, things can go wrong. Some subtle interaction between the Windows program and the operating system can cause printer problems. These generally occur when you use an old application with a newer version of Windows. The best solution is, of course, upgrade to a newer version of the application.

Not Completely Operational

Once you have your system working well enough to spit a few characters into your printer, you can still encounter a number problems in successfully creating printouts with it. The most common of these are printing out only part of a page, characters disappearing from printouts, garbled characters, and the printer stopping before it finishes the job. Most of these problems arise from the hardware interface yet are so subtle that you're likely to think you have a software problem.

Although the problems related here usually occur when initially setting up your printer, they may also appear later on if you change any part of your computer system. In particular, switching printer drivers or adding a new application may cause one of these problems to pop up. The next section examines the cause of and cure for each:

Printing Only a Partial Page

One of the most common problems people encounter when first setting up a serial printer with their PCs is only being able to coax part of a page from the printer no matter how long the job to be printed. The culprit is usually a failure to set up the proper serial port handshaking. When your serial cable is wired almost correctly, your PC and printer may be able to start a job printing and squeeze out sufficient characters to fill the printer's buffer. Then the handshaking fails and the printer can't get your PC to stop. It sends out a command to stop sending characters, and it doesn't listen further to the port. Your PC, meanwhile, misses the signal and keeps sending out text until the job is done. The rest of the text falls on the printer's deaf ear and is never heard or printed. This problem is most evident when the printer is substantially slower than the serial port speed so it can miss long strings of text while it is unloading its buffer. The solution is simply to get the right cable to match your printer to your PC.

You can also experience partial pages with parallel page printers when printing graphics. Instead of just stopping dead in its tracks, however, the printer will likely put the rest of the image on the next sheet (or next several sheets) that roll out. This problem may occur at any time, not just when you're initially setting up the machine. The common cause is too little memory for the resolution level at which you want to render your image. Most page printers require at least enough internal memory to hold a page-size bit map to print a whole graphic page. At 300 dpi, you need at least 2MB; at 600 dpi, 8MB. Averting this problem means upgrading the RAM inside your printer or rendering your image at lower resolution.

Disappearing Characters

A variation of the same underlying problem manifests itself when your serial printer seems to work okay but loses characters from whatever is sent to it. Again the culprit is the failure of handshaking. The symptom appears different only because the printer reacts differently to the lack of handshaking. In this case, the printer uses its handshaking signals to tell your PC to stop sending characters when the printer's buffers gets filled. Instead of turning its deaf ear to your PC, however, the printer starts listening as soon as it has space in its buffer. Alas, it misses hearing all the text that your PC sent while it was emptying its internal buffer. If your printer is only a bit slower than the serial interface, it may miss only a few characters. As the speed difference increases, so does the amount of text that disappears.

Again, the solution is simple in principle but more difficult to carry out: fix the handshaking. Usually this means little more than getting the right cable. In more obscure configurations (odd applications, operating systems, or printers) you might have to match the form of handshaking (ETX/ACK, XON/XOFF, or hardware) between your PC system and the printer.

Truncated Print Jobs

When running a printer with DOS applications through a serial connection, you may print jobs quitting before they should, for example, before the final page is completely finished. Sometimes this problem will be encountered by an on-screen error message like "Device Timeout Error" when you print directly from the DOS prompt. When printing through DOS applications, however, you might not receive any error message at all.

This problem usually results from improperly configuring the **MODE** command when assigning a serial port to a printer. If you forget to append the final "P" to the parameters you set with the **MODE** command, DOS may expect your printer to respond faster than the printer's hardware will allow. Not getting a timely response back from the printer, DOS assumes something is wrong, pastes the error message on the screen, and kills the otherwise happy print job. The solution is simply to re-issue the **MODE** command with the proper parameter line.

Perpetual Double-Spacing

Once a common problem with some brands of printers, the double-spacing of every line of text when you really want single spacing–or quadruple spacing when you want double-spacing–results from a mismatch between the way your printer handles the ends of lines and the way that PCs do. Many printers once expected that a carriage return meant only one thing, the end of a line of text. Consequently, whenever the printer received a carriage return character from your PC, the printer automatically pushed the printhead back to the beginning of a line (which is what carriage-return actually calls for) and also rolled the paper up one line so that it did not overprint the text that it previously laid down. Although this operation sounds natural, it's not the way PCs see the end of lines. The PC is designed to explicitly generate a separate carriage return and line feed. It takes absolute control and gives its commands explicitly, accurate to the individual character.

You should see the problem. As soon as your printer gets a carriage return, it returns the character and advanced one line. Then the PC sends out a line feed character, and your printer advanced another line. As result, it advances two lines at the end of each individual line.

To correct this problem, most printer makers allow you to specify the way to treat the end of each line, whether to add an extra carriage return or not. Make the wrong choice, and you get extraneous double-spacing. You only need to consult your printer's instruction manual to see how to change the printer's end-of-line treatment. Most machines have a DIP switch to select between functions. Typically the switch will be labeled CR or CR/LF. Which position of the switch indicates which action is immaterial. If your printer is misbehaving, you automatically know the switch is set wrong. Simply move the switch to the other position. Don't forget to turn the printer off and back on so that it knows what to do–most printers only check the positions of their setup switches when they power up.

Sliding Page Breaks

After you set up your printer and run a test page through it, all might look well. The text from your sample page lines up perfectly with the margins of the page, and you assume all is well. Then, when you try your first multipage print job, you notice a problem: the last few lines at the bottom of the first page appear at the top of the second, then a wide gap, then the text of the second page begins. At the bottom of the second sheet, even more lines of text are missing, and the wide white band move farther down sheet three. The big gap slides on and on down the page. Or you might suffer the opposite problem. Text from the later pages creeps up the earlier ones, again preceded by a wide white gap.

This problem looks like the printer equivalent of loss of vertical hold on an old television set, and the cause is exactly the same: a loss of synchronization between source and set. In the case of your printer, your software is assuming one page length (as expressed in a number of lines to print per page) while your printer is working on a completely different assumption. For example, your software may be sending out a standard 66 lines per page but your printer wants only 60 to enforce top and bottom margins. As a result six lines from each page—along with the bottom and top margins—get displaced to the next page.

Solving this problem means getting your software and printer back into sync. The first step is the driver check: ensure you've installed the right driver for your printer. Some application software allows you to adjust the number of lines to print per page. With many laser printers, the correct number of 10-pitch lines is 60 rather than the 66 you'd expect would fit on an 11-inch page. Most lasers enforce a half-inch unprintable margin at the top and bottom of each sheet. Many printers, including some laser models, also have setup adjustments to set the page length they assume your PC is using. Make sure the length set on the printer is the same as the length assumed by your software.

Often, the only page length adjustment a printer will give you is for paper size, with choices of letter and legal. With these machines, you'll have to make your adjustments at the software level, either by adjusting your applications for the appropriate page length or by sending software setup commands from your PC to the printer to set its page length to the proper number of lines.

Garbled or Strange Text

If your serial system gives every indication of working except all that it produces is gibberish, text array with little smiling faces and other characters from no known human alphabet or graphics that look like your eyes have lost horizontal sync, you probably have a communications problem.

Serial Killers

Communications problems can really be killers with serial printers. Most commonly, problems will arise when you've not properly matched serial port parameters at the two ends of the connection. Your computer is sending characters at one bit rate, and the serial device is expecting to receive them at another. Similarly, you may have your computer set for odd parity when the other end of the connection is expecting even. The two devices are not speaking the same language, so it's natural that they would get confused. The solution to the problem is simply to match the communications parameters at both ends of the connection.

Driver Confusion

Windows in its various guises allow you to install multiple printers and select among them. This versatility has its own penalty if you're not careful when switching things around. If you inadvertently mix up your multiple printers, you can use the wrong settings and drivers for each machine. Close but imperfect matches between printer models are most likely to cause garble. A complete mismatch will result in obvious problems like dozens of blank pages or text instead of graphics. A close mismatch will cause subtler problems.

The solution is simple. Make sure your using the right driver for the right printer. If you're using Windows, check the printer dialog box that pops on the screen when you start to print to see which machine it plans to run.

Parallel Thoughts

Garble can sneak into parallel connections, too, although the problem is usually mechanical or electrical than logical. Losing one wire of a parallel connection, or worse, having a single intermittent connection, can produce strange results. One bit drops out of the data stream, changing all the ASCII values your printer receives and acts upon.

One common cause of such parallel communications problems is a loose cable. Ensure that the connectors at both ends of your printer cable firmly fit into their jacks. Screw or clip in the connectors in place to ensure against future problems.

Sometimes a printer cable itself can go bad. A wire can invisibly break inside the cable or the connection to a pin inside a plug can come loose, uncrimped, or unsoldered. If your cable connections appear solid at both ends yet a parallel problem persists, try a different printer cable to see if you can work a cure.

Avoid using extension cables. The high speed of parallel connections makes communications riskier with every extra foot. Moreover an extension cable adds two more connections that can go bad.

One Bad Sheet

If the garbled printing occurs only on one sheet of a print job–and invariably the first sheet–the cause is unlikely to be a bad connection or communication problem. The more likely cause is in your software or printer driver.

Start Up Problems

Sometimes the garble only appears on the first sheet of your first print out. On the second and subsequent pages, the problem clears up by itself. Later print outs are perfect from start to finish.

Such problems appear most often with Macintosh computers, although it can sometimes happen with other PCs. When powering up, the computer may send out strange signals on its communication lines that your printer interprets as commands, possibly setting itself into some weird mode. Start printing immediately, and the results can be strange. You can prevent this problem by waiting until your computer boots before switching on your printer.

Because better printer drivers start by sending out a reset or printer initialization command at the beginning of each print job, you're more likely to see this problem with programs that you write yourself rather than commercial applications.

Extended Characters Print Improperly

When you see boxes around text on the screen but your printouts are bordered with strings of capital W's or some strange combination of characters instead, you're most likely looking at a mismatch between character sets. Under DOS (or in a DOS box), your PC displays the IBM character set. Most Windows drivers use the ANSI character set. Although the basic range of text and control characters match in the two sets, the top 128 characters diverge. When your PC sends out a code for a horizontal line, your printer sees it as a code for a text character. (The opposite can happen, too–lines appearing on paper instead of the extended character set–but this mismatch is unusual with modern printers.)

Failures in Working Systems

The other major class of printer problems are those that occur in systems that were once working, the kind of thing you're tempted to call the repairman to fix. Many of them can be quickly and easily solved–or even prevented–once you know the symptom and remedy.

In general, there are two classes of these printer problems, the mechanical and the aesthetic. Mechanical problems usually involve the finer points of paper-handling or the failure to do same. Your printer may mangle your printouts, shredding them so completely and successfully you might entertain the idea of leasing the machine to the CIA. It may choke on the paper you feed it, jamming up with every sheet it sucks through. Aesthetic problems involve anything that prevents your printouts from reaching perfection. They may involve weird colors, fading text, and graphics sliding off the page.

The next section looks at the most common of these printer problems:

Paper Pick Problems

When a printer fails even to pull a sheet of paper from the feed stack, the printer is said to have a *paper pick problem*–it cannot properly pick up a sheet of paper. The obvious symptom is your printer making a lot of noise like it's trying to grab a page to print but nothing happens, no paper comes out because no paper goes in. Your printer will generally show its displeasure in another way, by flashing its Error indicator or, in the case of some HP LaserJets, flashing its Resume light.

The most common cause for a paper pick problem is no paper to pick. Printers with LCD Control Panels will usually tell you Paper Out; many machines have dedicated indicators for this condition. Resolving the problem of course involves loading more paper. But sometimes you'll pull out the paper try and find that it still has paper. In fact, you may be a paper-out message right after you load a tray full of paper into your machine.

If your printer has a multiple feed tray, the first step is to ensure yourself that the printer is trying to feed from the proper tray. The printer must not only have paper but also must be able to find it.

Once you have the paper tray out, check to be sure that it's properly loaded. If the paper stack is not square or if the width-adjuster at the side of the stack is not adjusted properly, your printer may not be able to slip sheets off the stack. You can fix both problems by removing the paper from the tray. Resquare the stack by holding its edges lightly and dropping it against a flat, horizontal surface. Carefully put the stack back in the tray ensuring that the top of the stack doesn't splay out from the bottom. Slide the width-adjuster firmly against the side of the stack but not so hard that it causes the stack to buckle. Move the length-adjuster up against the paper stack similarly. If you are attempting to feed cards through some models of HP LaserJet, be sure you flip up the card guide rather than aligning cards against the right wall of the input tray.

Make sure you don't have too much paper in the tray, too. If the stack is too tall, the drive rollers may not be able to grab the top sheet properly. The drive roller might also be dirty, coated with slippery paper dust, which can prevent them from getting a proper grip. If the rollers appear grey instead of black or covered white specks or a whitish powder, clean them using a rag dampened with water and a mild detergent.

The paper you're using can also be the root of the difficulties. If the paper pick problem started at the same time you began using a particular kind of paper, try another variety of paper. Some characteristics of your media (too smooth, too rough, too thick, too thin) may be incompatible with your printer. Even the paper recommended for your printer can cause pick problems if it is damaged, wrinkled, damp, or too dry.

Paper Jams

Hewlett-Packard 600-series printers indicate paper jams by alternately flashing their Power and Resume lights; however, these printer use the same indication for other errors (such as carriage stall or communications problems). These printers assume they have a paper jam when they continue to detect paper at the bottom of the platen after they have tried to eject the paper.

Clearing a paper jam requires several steps. The correct procedure is as follows:

1. ***Switch off the printer.*** This will remove power to the entire mechanism and ensure that you won't be working against the motors and possibly damaging the mechanism. It also ensures that the printer won't miraculously spring to life with your hands or necktie inside.
2. ***Open the printer to gain access to the paper path.*** In many printers, this will involve removing one or more paper trays. In impact printers, you may have to slide the printhead to one side of the platen.
3. ***Remove the offending paper from the mechanism.*** You should first try to remove the entire jammed sheet intact. Tearing the paper risks leaving pieces behind–and, in any case, will add dust and lint inside the mechanism. If the paper will not pull out in its normal direction of travel, try pulling it out backwards. If you must tear the paper to get it out, be sure to remove all the shreds from inside the printer and particularly the paper path.
4. ***Check the feed paper.*** Ensure that the jam has not wrinkled the top sheets in the feed tray or, with a continuous form printer, creases the paper longitudinally. If you detect so much as a curled edge in the feed tray, remove the bent sheets to prevent the jam from recurring.
5. ***Reload the in tray***, the media stack, or the tractor system, checking again to ensure the paper is flat and unwrinkled.
6. ***Close up the printer again*** after you ensure you've left nothing inside the printer (that's not supposed to be there!). If you have to remove paper trays or parts of the cover, replace them.
7. ***Switch the printer back on.*** Wait until it warms up and check to be sure the error has cleared. You may have to press the **Reset** button.

8. ***Put the printer on-line*** and resume printing.

The best way to deal with paper jams is to avoid them. Jams arise from several conditions, most of which are under your control. By taking proper care, you can avoid the problem.

Some printers, such as the HP 600-series, require that you install the out paper tray in order for their feed mechanism to operate properly. Without the out tray, the printer may not properly eject paper.

Jams often result from buckling of the paper in the in tray. Most such problems are cause by improperly loading the tray. For example, you may slide the media-length adjuster up or the width adjuster sideways too forcefully, forcing the entire stack of paper to curve upward or downward. The grippers that pull the paper through will grab the bent sheet and force the platen or rollers in the paper path to flatten it with a crease or jam the mechanism. Always be sure the paper lies flat when you move the length and width adjusters.

On the other hand, if you don't push the width adjuster against the edge of the stack of paper, the stack may shift so that it is not drawn squarely into the paper path. As the feed mechanism pulls the crooked sheet through the printer, it will force it further askew until it jams. Always make sure the paper stack in the input tray is squared off and aligned with the edge of the tray.

Adding paper to an input tray that is not completely empty can also cause jams. The width adjuster often does not properly rest on the edge of the old and new stacks, causing the misalignment that can lead to paper jams. You can avoid the problem by removing any paper in the input tray, making a single stack from it and the new paper you want to load, squaring the edges of the stack, and loading it as a unit into the input tray.

Putting too much paper in the in tray can cause jams because the feed rollers will have to pull the paper down from the top of the stack, rasping at its edges at the same time. The too-tall stack may also cause excess pressure against the paper, which can lead to multiple sheets feeding at the same time. The two sheets may be too thick for the mechanism to handle reliably or may slip against one another during their travels. One sheet might jam in the mechanism while the other sails smoothly through.

Failure to unload the out tray when it reaches its capacity can also cause jams. Paper on its way out of the printer may butt into the output stack, curl up, and jam.

Using the wrong size paper will almost inevitably cause jams. Sheets that are too short might fall between rollers. Sheets that are too long may bump against the end of the output tray while the mechanism is still attempting to roll it through the printer. Sheets that are too narrow may slip between the grippers as it courses through the printer. Sheets that are even slightly too wide will curl at the edges on their way through.

The paper must also be of the proper weight for the printer. Sheets that are too thin may tear or buckle on their way through the machine. Sheets that are too thick may bind when trying to pass through.

Paper can also be too coarse or too smooth to properly feed through the machine. Mixing different kinds of media in the input tray can also cause some printers to jam. Paper that is too dry may develop an excess static charge that can stick multiple sheets together and cause jams.

Perhaps the most common cause of jams is another jam. If you don't completely clean out all the shreds of paper when clearing a jam, an errant corner of paper could obstruct the paper path and cause a subsequent jam. If you encounter repeated jams, odds favor something obstructing the paper path. Make doubly sure when clearing the jam that the paper path is clear for its entire length.

Carriage Stall

When the printhead in a line printer suddenly stops its back and forth slide, the condition is called a *carriage stall.* Depending on its design, the printer may stop entirely or continue to print a thin line down the paper. In either case, however, you're not going to be happy with what you get.

Carriage stall usually results from a mechanical defect. The most common of these is something interfering with the free travel of the printhead carriage. A foreign object in the printer can bring the carriage to a full halt or impede its travel across the page, compressing characters or narrowing each page. In most circumstances, removing the offending foreign object will eliminate the problem.

The proper procedure for clearing a stalled carriage varies with the model and technology used by your printer. The safest procedure with most impact printers is to switch off the power and unplug the printer before delving in to the mechanism. Once the power is off, you can freely slide the carriage without the servos in the printer counteracting your every move. You'll only have to deal with the obstruction.

Many ink-jet printers lock down their printhead carriages with the printhead in its home position when you switch off the power so that the ink doesn't dry or dribble out. You'll need to keep these printers switched on to move the carriage and manually and find any impediment in its path. Once you move the printhead from its home position, switch off the printer's power and unplug it.

At this point, it will be safe with most line printers to move their printheads manually across the full path of their travel. As you slide the carriage, feel for anything that binds or a sudden increase in resistance. In many cases, simply moving the printhead with your hands will be enough to knock the obstruction out of the way. If you do, be sure to remove whatever it was from inside the printer.

If you don't find a foreign object, check the carriage guide rod for contamination. A foreign substance on it (say dried coffee particularly rich with cream and sugar) can cause the carriage to bind. Clean the guide rod carefully. Some printer models warn that careless cleaning of the guide rod can damage the mechanism.

Finding no obstruction is not good news because it usually indicates a mechanical problem with your printer that has no easy solution, one that will likely require a visit to the repair shop. These include the following problems:

Broken drive belt. If your printer uses a belt or cable to shift its carriage, inspect it for damage. If the belt or cable is broken, frayed, or worn, it may need to be replaced. Check cogged belts for missing or clogged teeth.

Damaged printhead carriage. The printhead carriage itself may be damaged, preventing its smooth travel. Suspect this problem if you clear an obstruction from inside your printer without fixing the stall.

Service station damage. Many ink-jet printers have *service stations* for performing maintenance functions at the right side of the carriage. The service station can get damaged, usually by a foreign object, and cause the printhead to stall.

Guide rod damage. The rod that guides the carriage across the printer may also become damaged by a foreign object–dinged, gouged, or bent.

These and other mechanical printer problems may require the replacement of defective parts by a skilled service technician.

Paper Not Emerging

Sometimes your printer will greedily gobble up a sheet of paper or transparency medium from the input tray and not let it go. You wait and wait and wait and nothing comes out of the printer, but it neither displays an error message nor complains of a difficulty. The likely problem is a lack of patience. Printing sometimes takes longer than you want.

With some ink-jet printers, a long wait for a transparency may be nothing more than your printer trying to outsmart you. When you shift some ink-jet printers into transparency mode, they add an additional step to their printing cycle called the automatic dry timers. The printer paints the transparency and then holds it back until the printer is sure that the ink has dried. Having no finger to poke in the ink, the only thing the printer can do is wait long enough—what often feels like too long—for the ink to dry before releasing the transparency.

If you switch off your PC before it has completed a print job, you might miss something important, such as a final form-feed character that clears the last page out of the printer. You can clear out the reluctant page by switching the printer off-line and pressing form feed. And you'll probably discover the printing on the final sheet is not complete. All you can do is switch your PC back on and print the page all over again.

Some printers will refuse to eject paper if they do not detect the output paper tray in the proper position. This probably usually occurs after you have removed the tray for some purpose such as maintenance. Although the tray may look like it is properly installed, it may not be activating the printer's sensors. Try removing the tray and reinstalling it.

Pay particular attention to the drive rollers in sheet-feed mechanisms. If you don't clean them often enough (or at all), they can build up a hard, slick layer of paper dust. Because of the coating, they may not be able to properly drive pages through your printer, resulting in the jam. The solution is, of course, to clean the drive rollers—and the rest of the printer while you're at it.

Envelope Feeding Problems

Envelopes, because of the unusual shape and uneven thickness, are more apt to cause paper feed problems than other media. The paper-handling systems of most printers are particularly sensitive to variations among envelopes. Any deviation from pristine such as torn, bent, or curled envelopes may cause feeding problems.

Printer mechanisms are also sensitive to the proper loading of envelopes. Ensure that you slide the media width and length adjusters to the proper positions when using feed trays. Also ensure that you do not place too many envelopes in the feed tray. Because of the greater thickness of envelopes (compared to sheets of paper), the maximum number the tray can properly accept is substantially less, sometimes as few as 20.

If your printer has a dedicated envelope feed slot, never attempt to slide more than one envelope through at a time. Stuffing in multiple envelopes is one of the ways most certainly guaranteed to jam your printer. On the other hand, if your printer fails to suck an envelope into the feed slot, the usual cause is simply not pushing the envelope in far enough. You should slide each envelope in until it stops. Do not push so hard that the envelope buckles.

Most manufacturers are stringent in the specifications they give for the envelopes their machines can handle. Envelopes that don't meet these specifications are likely not to advance properly through the mechanism. Sometimes substituting envelopes with rectangular flaps instead of the more common triangular flaps will solve feeding problems.

Paper Skew

When the edges of the text or printed image do not run parallel with the edges of the paper, the problem is called *paper skew*. It can result from a problem with your printer or with the paper you use.

The paper industry specification requires that paper be square within 0.3%. That is, a sheet vary no more than 0.003 inch for every inch of its length or width. Most people cannot detect an error that small–it's about one laser printer dot (at 300 dpi) in an inch, about half a point in the length of a page. Poorly cut paper may not meet this specification and may produce images that appear to skew across the sheet.

One way to judge the squareness of a sheet of paper is to print on both sides by turning the sheet over and running it through your ink-jet or impact printer a second time with the same image. (Flipping pages over to do a second side is not recommended with laser printers.) When you hold the printed page up to a bright light, you should see the edges on each side align or run parallel to one another. A graphic with horizontal and vertical lines makes paper skew most readily apparent.

An out-of-adjustment printer mechanism may also cause a skew problem. If you don't properly line up the paper when loading it into your printer (for example, not putting it squarely into a paper tray), the sheets may skew as they feed through. Skewing from no apparent outside cause (paper or loading) may be caused by an out-of-adjustment printer. Because of the tight tolerances involved, this alignment is best left to the service shop.

Overprinted Characters

If the text from your line printer appears jumbled together, check inside the printhead chamber. Something interfering with the free travel of the printhead can prevent proper spacing. The drive system may also be slipping or a belt may have become dislodged from its proper position. Inspect the mechanism and verify that all is well.

If you see one character printed on top of another in the text that rolls out of your laser printer or if the text looks wavy, stretched, or compressed, there can be several possible problems.

With all nonimpact printers, the place to start is with your paper. The paper may not feed properly through your printer if it is either too rough *or* too smooth. In addition, toner may not adhere properly to coarse paper so characters can look disjointed or otherwise malformed that may resemble overprinting. Consequently, the first thing to try with poor character printing is a change of media. If using a different paper (try one recommended for your printer) yields better results, don't use the offending medium. As the doctor says, if it hurts when you do that, don't do that.

If you hear a popping noise at the same time your printer demonstrates this problem, the cause could be your toner cartridge if it has an integrated OPC drum. Try substituting another toner cartridge to see if that clears up the problem. If it does, recycle the ailing cartridge.

In some HP LaserJet printers, this problem may be caused by high-speed operation or other advanced features with some media. If you need to use the particular medium that causes problems, you can switch off the offending features. Select the **Parallel Menu** from the Front Menu Panel and turn off the **Advanced Functions** and **High Speed** selections.

If the problem arises only when printing from Windows 3.1, another tactic is to switch off direct-to-port printing. To do this, select **Control Panel**, then **Printers**. Choose the connect option and select LPT1.DOS for the port setting. Deselect the **Fast Printing Direct to Port** option by removing the check from its option box.

According to Hewlett-Packard, sometimes you can trace the overprinting character problem to an improperly seated or defecting parallel cable. The company specifically recommends that you check for tight bends or heavy pressure from objects sitting on the cable. Running the printer's self-test will reveal whether the problem originates in the printer or from beyond (your PC or cable). To zero in more tightly on the real culprit, HP recommends removing all printer accessories if the self-test still shows the problem, then running the test again to see if you can find interference from a particular accessory.

Repeating Image Defects on a Laser Printer

Every printer technology has its characteristic failures. Those of the laser printer involve vertically repeating image defects. Every inch or two down the page appears a blotch or blank spot across page after page. Sometimes the problem fades in for fades away. More often it appears suddenly–and permanently.

The origin of the problem is a bad spot in part of the imaging system or in the paper path. For example, part of the optical photoconductor might get scraped off the imaging drum of the printer resulting in a dead spot that won't lay toner on paper. The defect repeats because the circumference of the imaging drum is smaller than the length of a sheet of paper, so the same bad spot passes over the sheet again and again.

The imaging or optical photoconductor (OPC) drum isn't the only part of the print system that can cause a repeating defect. The fusing rollers, transfer rollers, registration rollers, and other parts of the print system can also cause repeating defects.

The good news is that you can fix most of these repeating defects yourself, quickly and easily. Sometimes, however, it can be expensive, requiring you to replace the toner cartridge or drum. Other forms of the problem can be corrected with cleaning the printer or changing the printing environment.

The spacing of the defects can be an important diagnostic. The various rotating parts of printers almost all have different circumferences. Each will cause defects with different spacing. In addition, some cause defects on the front of sheets, other cause them on the back. By measuring the spacing between defect and check in the side of the sheet on which they occur, you can quickly determine the offending part and the repair action to take. Tables 12.1 through 12.5 list the spacings characteristic of problems with various Hewlett-Packard printers and the action needed to rectify the underlying problem. The charts give the vertical spacing between defects in inches.

Table 12.1 covers the first series of LaserJets, including the original LaserJet, the LaserJet 500, and the LaserJet Plus.

Table 12.1 Repeating Errors in Original HP LaserJet Printer Series

Printer	Defect Spacing	Paper Side	Cause	Repair
LaserJet	2.66	Front	Developing cylinder	Replace cartridge
LaserJet	2.88	Back	Lower fuser	Clean
LaserJet	5.12	Front	Upper fuser	Clean
LaserJet	7.38	Front	OPC drum	Replace cartridge
LaserJet 500	2.66	Front	Developing cylinder	Replace cartridge

Table 12.1 continued

Printer	Defect Spacing	Paper Side	Cause	Repair
LaserJet 500	2.88	Back	Lower fuser	Clean
LaserJet 500	5.12	Front	Upper fuser	Clean
LaserJet 500	7.38	Front	OPC drum	Replace cartridge
LaserJet Plus	2.66	Front	Developing cylinder	Replace cartridge
LaserJet Plus	2.88	Back	Lower fuser	Clean
LaserJet Plus	5.12	Front	Upper fuser	Clean
LaserJet Plus	7.38	Front	OPC drum	Replace cartridge

Table 12.2 covers the second series of LaserJets, including the LaserJet II, LaserJet D, LaserJet P, and LaserJet P Plus.

Table 12.2 Repeating Errors in HP LaserJet II Printer Series

Printer	Defect Spacing	Side	Paper Cause	Repair
LaserJet II	0.5	Back	Registration transfer roller	Clean
LaserJet II	1.5	Front	Upper registration roller	Clean
LaserJet II	1.75	Back	Lower registration roller	Clean
LaserJet II	2.00	Front	Developing cylinder	Replace cartridge
LaserJet II	2.38	Front	OPC drum	Replace cartridge
LaserJet II	2.50	Back	Lower fuser	Clean
LaserJet II	3.12	Front	Upper fuser	Clean
LaserJet IID	0.5	Back	Registration transfer roller	Clean
LaserJet IID	1.5	Front	Upper registration roller	Clean
LaserJet IID	1.75	Back	Lower registration roller	Clean

LaserJet IID	2.00	Front	Developing cylinder	Replace cartridge
LaserJet IID	2.38	Front	OPC drum	Replace cartridge
LaserJet IID	2.50	Back	Lower fuser	Clean
LaserJet IID	3.12	Front	Upper fuser	Clean
LaserJet IIP	1.5	Front	Charging roller	Replace cartridge
LaserJet IIP	1.75	Back	Lower fusing roller	Clean
LaserJet IIP	1.88	Front	Input feed roller	Clean
LaserJet IIP	2.0	Back	Transfer roller	Clean
LaserJet IIP	2.0	Front	Developing cylinder	Replace cartridge
LaserJet IIP	2.12	Back	Lower fusing roller	Clean
LaserJet IIP	2.5	Front	Upper fusing roller	Clean
LaserJet IIP	3.38	Front	OPC drum	Replace cartridge
LaserJet IIP Plus	1.5	Front	Charging roller	Replace cartridge
LaserJet IIP Plus	1.75	Back	Lower fusing roller	Clean
LaserJet IIP Plus	1.88	Front	Input feed roller	Clean
LaserJet IIP Plus	2.0	Back	Transfer roller	Clean
LaserJet IIP Plus	2.0	Front	Developing cylinder	Replace cartridge
LaserJet IIP Plus	2.12	Back	Lower fusing roller	Clean
LaserJet IIP Plus	2.5	Front	Upper fusing roller	Clean
LaserJet IIP Plus	3.38	Front	OPC drum	Replace cartridge

Table 12.3 lists the entire LaserJet III series, including the original LaserJet III, the IIID, IIIP, and IIISi.

Table 12.3 Repeating Errors in HP LaserJet II Printer Series

Printer	Defect Spacing	Paper Side	Cause	Repair
LaserJet III	0.5	Back	Registration transfer roller	Clean

Table 12.3 continued

Printer	Defect Spacing	Paper Side	Cause	Repair
LaserJet III	1.5	Front	Upper registration roller	Clean
LaserJet III	1.75	Back	Lower registration roller	Clean
LaserJet III	2.00	Front	Developing cylinder	Replace cartridge
LaserJet III	2.38	Front	OPC drum	Replace cartridge
LaserJet III	2.50	Back	Lower fuser	Clean
LaserJet III	3.12	Front	Upper fuser	Clean
LaserJet IIID	0.5	Back	Registration transfer roller	Clean
LaserJet IIID	1.5	Front	Upper registration roller	Clean
LaserJet IIID	1.75	Back	Lower registration roller	Clean
LaserJet IIID	2.00	Front	Developing cylinder	Replace cartridge
LaserJet IIID	2.38	Front	OPC drum	Replace cartridge
LaserJet IIID	2.50	Back	Lower fuser	Clean
LaserJet IIID	3.12	Front	Upper fuser	Clean
LaserJet IIIP	1.5	Front	Charging roller	Replace cartridge
LaserJet IIIP	2.0	Front	Developing cylinder	Replace cartridge
LaserJet IIIP	3.38	Front	OPC drum	Replace cartridge
LaserJet IIIP	1.75	Back	Lower fusing roller	Clean
LaserJet IIIP	1.88	Front	Input feed roller	Clean
LaserJet IIIP	2.0	Back	Transfer roller	Clean
LaserJet IIIP	2.12	Back	Lower fusing roller	Clean
LaserJet IIIP	2.5	Front	Upper fusing roller	Clean
LaserJet IIISi	1.5	Front	Primary charging roller	Replace cartridge
LaserJet IIISi	1.75	Front	Upper registration roller	Clean

LaserJet IIISi	2.0	Front	Developing cylinder	Replace cartridge
LaserJet IIISi	2.5	Back	Transfer roller	Clean
LaserJet IIISi	3.75	Either	Fuser rollers	Clean
LaserJet IIISi	3.75	Front	OPC drum	Replace cartridge

Table 12.4 lists the printers in LaserJet 4 series, including the basic LaserJet 4, the 4L, 4P, 4Si, and 4V. Note that the "M" series of models are mechanically identical to those without the "M" designation. The "M" machines differ in having built-in PostScript interpreters.

Table 12.4 Repeating Errors in HP LaserJet 4 Printer Series

Printer	Defect Spacing	Paper Side	Cause	Repair
LaserJet 4	1.5	Front	Primary charging roller	Replace cartridge
LaserJet 4	2.0	Front	Developing cylinder	Replace cartridge
LaserJet 4	2.12	Back	Transfer roller	Clean
LaserJet 4	2.5	Either	Fuser rollers	Clean
LaserJet 4	3.75	Front	OPC drum	Replace cartridge
LaserJet 4L	1.5	Back	Face down delivery roller	Clean
LaserJet 4L	1.5	Front	Developing roller	Replace cartridge
LaserJet 4L	1.5	Front	Primary charging roller	Replace cartridge
LaserJet 4L	1.75	Back	Transfer roller	Clean
LaserJet 4L	1.88	Front	Lower fuser roller	Clean
LaserJet 4L	3.0	Front	Upper fuser roller	Clean
LaserJet 4L	3.0	Front	OPC drum	Replace cartridge
LaserJet 4L	4.75	Back	Feed roller	Clean
LaserJet 4P	1.5	Back	Face down delivery roller	Clean
LaserJet 4P	1.5	Front	Developing roller	Replace cartridge
LaserJet 4P	1.5	Front	Primary charging roller	Replace cartridge

Table 12.4 continued

Printer	Defect Spacing	Paper Side	Cause	Repair
LaserJet 4P	1.75	Back	Transfer roller	Clean
LaserJet 4P	1.88	Front	Lower fuser roller	Clean
LaserJet 4P	3.0	Front	Upper fuser roller	Clean
LaserJet 4P	3.0	Front	OPC drum	Replace cartridge
LaserJet 4P	4.75	Back	Feed roller	Clean
LaserJet 4Si	1.5	Front	Primary charging roller	Replace cartridge
LaserJet 4Si	1.75	Front	Upper registration roller	Clean
LaserJet 4Si	2.0	Front	Developing cylinder	Replace cartridge
LaserJet 4Si	2.5	Back	Transfer roller	Clean
LaserJet 4Si	3.75	Either	Fuser rollers	Clean
LaserJet 4Si	3.75	Front	OPC drum	Replace cartridge
LaserJet 4V	1.5	Front	Primary charging roller	Replace cartridge
LaserJet 4V	2.0	Front	Developing cylinder	Replace cartridge
LaserJet 4V	2.38	Back	Transfer roller	Clean
LaserJet 4V	3.75	Front	OPC drum	Replace cartridge

Table 12.5 lists some printers of the LaserJet 5 series.

Table 12.5 Repeating Errors in HP LaserJet 5 Printer Series

Printer	Defect Spacing	Paper Side	Cause	Repair
LaserJet 5P	3.0	Front	OPC drum	Replace cartridge

Recurrent blotches in your printouts are not always caused by printer defects, however. Sometimes bad media can cause print problems resembling repeated defects. Moisture, weight differences, and variations in chemical composition in the paper can cause image defects that appear to repeat down the page.

You can determine whether the media or the printer is at fault with either of two quick tests. Try rotating the paper in the input tray by 180° so what was the top of a page becomes the bottom. If the repeated defect does not change, the problem is in the printer, not the paper. Alternately, you can substitute a different print medium and observe whether the problem goes away or changes. If changing the medium does not alter the problem, it's in your printer.

Blank Pages

As you collate a printout, you'll sometimes encounter blank pages among those properly printed. Two different and unrelated problems can cause these blank pages.

When two pages pass through the printer at the same time, one gets printed and the other just tags along for the ride. Typically the two sheets are stuck together lightly and your printer cannot separate them. Anything that makes paper stick together can cause this problem. The likely culprits are static charges in the paper caused by the relative humidity being too low, coarsely cut sheets clinging to one another at their edges, and using the wrong medium in your printer.

Most of the time you can eliminate the sticking sheets by fanning or riffling through the stack of paper as if you were shuffling a deck of cards before loading the paper into your printer. The shuffle separates the edges and individual sheets. Be sure to square off the stack of paper by lightly tapping its edge against a tabletop before loading it into your printer.

When the blank sheets take their own ride through your printer, separate from any printed sheet, the problem usually is one of printing too close to the bottom margin of the paper. Your printer may count lines and determine that it must go on to the next page while at the same time your application or driver sends the printer a form-feed command, telling it to advance to the next page. The printer doesn't care where the commands come from; it just knows it has two form feeds to carry out. The first ejects the sheet it has just finished printing, and the second ejects the next page, unprinted. The cure is to slightly increase the bottom margin setting in your software application.

No Landscape Mode

Many printers lack the facility in both hardware and their native drivers for printing in landscape mode, while others allow you to shift your sheets to your heart's content. One way of printing on such machine is downloading a landscape font and using it for your printout. If you have a graphic, you need to print in landscape mode and an unwilling printer, a number of utilities can help you out. Among these are the shareware program PrintGF and the commercial program Sideways.

No Graphics Printing

When your printer works but you get odd results–in appropriate spacing or good text but absurd graphics (such as nothing but a single character on every page)–the first suspect is the printer driver used by your application.

The youth of a printer driver is typically more troubled than the typical gang member. Drivers go through generations as one or another user discovers a new bug, none of which showed up in extensive beta testing. To be sure the driver you use is the best available, ensure that it is the latest available driver. Contact your printer manufacturer and check your version number. You can call technical support (and have the version number ready–you can usually find it when the driver loads or through the installation program. It may even be listed on your disk, should you have received the driver on disk with your printer and have never upgraded it.) Or you can simply contact the manufacturer's own bulletin board or support forum in an on-line service like CompuServe.

In a pinch you can work around the problem if the erratic driver is confined to a single application and you have others that do, in fact, work with your printer. Save your graphic image in a standard format (such as a .PCX or BMP file), then open the application with the known-to-be-good driver, and print it there.

If things get really desperate and cannot transfer your image to a known format, use a screen capture program and grab a snapshot of the image you want to print. This will get you a usable format that you can print with another application.

Low Resolution

Sometimes your printer may seem to shift to low resolution printing or print a small image when you expect a full page. One circumstance under which this occurs is when you try to print an encapsulated PostScript file to a non-PostScript printer. Normally you would expect no output at all because you're using the wrong language. And no output would be the tip-off that you're doing something seriously wrong. But substandard output may sidetrack you and lead you to believe that the printer rather than your expectation is wrong.

The reason you can sometimes get output when printing an encapsulated PostScript image to a non-PostScript printer is that many software programs that generate encapsulated PostScript output include a screen preview image in the file so that they can quickly display the image preview on your monitor. Because these images are meant for video display, they generally take the form of a 72-dpi bit map. The problem is that your printer may be able to read this bit map and print it out. Of course, the printer puts it on paper bit-by-bit. Because the printer typically uses a much higher resolution (perhaps as high as 720 dpi) the bit image may be as small as one-tenth the size of a normal printer image. Seeing such a postage-stamp size image may make you think your printer is operating in some obscure and indecipherable mode, even though it's doing its best.

To correctly print encapsulated PostScript images, you need a PostScript-compatible printer or cartridge. Alternately, you can convert the EPS file into a form compatible with your printer. For example, you can use the application that generated the EPS file to save the image in a different format or directly print the image using its regular printer driver. If you don't have the application that generated the EPS file, you can rasterize the EPS image using a PostScript conversion utility.

Off-Color Text

If your ink-jet printer fabricates documents that appear off-color and you're not printing out jokes of dubious taste, blacks overtoned with odd hues may be a result of an inherent part of the color printing process.

Sometimes all of your printouts have the same–and objectionable–color cast to them. Although you see a range of different colors, overall the image might look too red, too yellow, too purple, or too green. Such off-color printouts are the result of poor color balance.

The place to begin getting colors right is your color management system. You must calibrate your PC's monitor and printer so that both show the same colors.

One problem with monitors is that many manufacturers have standardized on a higher color temperature, one of about 9600 kelvins. The higher color temperature helps the monitor produce a brighter image by exploiting the power of the blue phosphors. However, the result is that the on-screen image looks too cold or too blue when you compare your printed output. Some monitors allow you to adjust their color temperature directly using their built-in menuing systems. Without this feature, direct adjustment of a monitor is difficult because it requires that you separately adjust the levels of the red, blue, and green signals inside the monitors, and few computer monitors provide you with the needed controls.

The alternative is to adjust the signals your PC produces for your monitor. A color management system, when properly used, will do exactly that. Alternately, you can use a software monitor calibration program like MONCAL.ZIP sin Library 5 of the MICROGRAFX forum.

Grey Printing (Foreground)

If your printouts look too light, there are several things to check depending on the technology your printer uses.

The most obvious problem with an impact dot-matrix printer is an old ribbon. You should suspect this problem if your printouts have gradually lost their depth. As a ribbon gets used, the ink gets squeezed off it. Even if not used, it will dry out just from sitting around in your printer. A well-used or otherwise dried ribbon can't print the same dark black as a new one. Replacing the ribbon will usually cure the problem. And don't assume that just because a ribbon came with your new printer that the ribbon is in perfect condition. They can dry out even in their little plastic bags should the bag leak only slightly.

If your printouts have never had dark blacks and the light grey tone has been consistent (and not fading with use), you might also have a driver problem. Drivers for older printer models often assume that they are being used with printers with large print wires. These make big, black dots that need not be closely spaced on the paper. If you printer is newer and has finer wires to allow it to print with higher resolution, the old driver may use the same big-dot wide spacing. The smaller dots will be far apart and put less ink on the paper, making everything look grey. The solution is to get a new driver that's matched for the printhead wire size of your printer.

Ink-jet printers are at a handicap from the start in producing rich blacks, at least when compared to laser machines. Ink-jet ink just isn't capable of producing the same intense blacks as laser toner. Some ink-jet printers aggravate the situation further by offering an "economy" mode. They achieve their economy by skimping on the ink, their most expensive consumable. As with much of the rest of life, economy and quality are at odds. If you want deep blacks, switch out of economy mode.

If you use paper that's too absorbent with an ink-jet printer, black can appear grey. The paper sucks in so much of the ink that the resulting image looks faded and flat. The solution is, of course, to use paper that's coated for use with ink-jet printers (and incidentally, more expensive). You can also try using a different color paper–an off-white or a strong hue–to alter image contrast. Some people find that a colored background helps emphasize printing and makes it appear more intense.

Epson notes that you can get blacker, more intense printing with its Stylus Color by switching to the otherwise not recommended use of 720-dpi mode with plain paper. Although you sacrifice the crisp sharpness you'd get with coated paper, the greater quantity of ink will make text appear blacker.

Background Grey

One of the more common problems is that the printer lays a pale grey cast over the whole of the printable area on your media. The problem is most prevalent with envelopes. After all, mixing envelopes and laser printers are only a bit less tricky than alchemy. The greater thickness of envelopes and the way it varies across the various overlaps challenges the laser printer to make its output appear uniform and tempts the printer to print grey. A grey background can occur on plain paper as well. The mechanism underlying the problem and its solution are the same in any case.

The basic problem relates to the distribution of electrostatic charges between the envelope and the imaging drum. You can use the **Density** setting of the printer to adjust the charge voltage. Surprisingly, adjusting the density for dark*er* printing usually reduces the background grey. (On the adjustment dial of the HP LaserJet II, IID, III, and IIID printers, move the dial toward 1 to increase density.) Be judicious in making this adjustment. Turning the density too high will cause other printer defects such as spotchy printing.

Hewlett-Packard has discovered that the relative humidity of your printer operating environment can also cause the backgrounds of envelopes to print grey. The humidity also affects the static charge distribution in laser printers. Because of the lower relative humidities in heated homes in the winter, the background grey problem appears oddly seasonal–about Thanksgiving your printing starts to turn grey and match the sky.

According to HP, you should get optimum quality when the relative humidity is 50%. Consider a humidifier in the winter months and a dehumidifier or air conditioning for the summer to eliminate the problem once and for all–and to make you more comfortable in your own work. HP also recommends that you acclimate envelopes to the printer environment for at least 24 hours before you print on them.

HP also acknowledges that background grey may appear on envelopes just after you install a new toner cartridge. According to HP's testing, the tendency to add a grey background is most visible during the first 1000 or so pages (about one-quarter the life of the average LaserJet cartridge). If you are severely bothered by background greys, you might want to consider keeping an older cartridge around just for printing envelopes.

Photo Backgrounds Muddy

The tonal range available with most printers is substantially less than that most graphics programs and monitors can handle, and most monitors have less tonal range than original photographs (as opposed to printed reproductions). One result of this is that the tonal range gets compressed. As a result, background with subtle tonal variations often print solid or flattened out.

This is a problem without a good solution in that the best solution requires technology that is not available (or would have been used already). The only way to eliminate the effect is to compensate in your artwork so that it accommodates the range of your printer. Some applications will warn you if you're trying to dish out more than your printer can handle. For example, Adobe *Photoshop* alerts you to circumstances that may cause the problem with a Gamut Warning.

The compensation in your image amounts to limiting the saturation, contrast, or brightness of your image with the tools available in your graphic application. Although such alterations may make the on-screen image look worse, the printed output often will appear better. Getting the best quality in this manner is a matter of aesthetic judgment that takes experience to develop.

Horizontal Stripes or Bands

Line printers are particularly prone to producing horizontal lines–either white, black, or colored–on the pages they print. Any defect in a single dot, be it formed by an impact printwire or ink-jet nozzle, gets magnified into a long, straight line by the movement of the printhead.

The most common of these striping problems is a thin, white horizontal line running across the entire page through your text and graphic printouts. These lines are usually produced by a single print element: a jammed print wire in an impact printer or a clogged nozzle in an ink-jet. You can usually work an effective cure by cleaning the printhead in accordance with the instructions in the Maintenance section of this chapter. If a good cleaning doesn't solve the problem, you may have to take the next, more radical step, replacing the printhead or cartridge.

When the banding problem appears inherent in your printer setup, that is, it infects your printer from the first time your start using it rather than arising *during* operation, the cause usually is a mismatch between the driver and the printer. For example, when not properly matched with your printer some impact printer drivers may advance a nine-dot-high text line during eight-dot-high graphic printing leaving a blank row of dots between every line. The cure is to shift to the proper driver for your printer.

Under Windows 3.1, some video drivers were known to interfere with printing, particularly in high resolution modes. If you suspect such an interaction, try temporarily shifting your video system to the standard Windows VGA driver using the Setup program. Then try printing the same image that gave your the banding problem when you use the high-resolution video driver. If the banding problem disappears, your system is suffering from an interaction. Report the problem to the maker of your video board and see if the board-maker has an updated driver that solves the problem.

Sometimes sequential lines overlap causing a thin, dark band where ink has been laid down in two thicknesses. This problem was inherent early in the development of some technologies (the first phase change printers were plagued by this kind of banding, though newer machines are much improved). You might see similar symptoms when friction feeding single sheets through a continuous form printer. The banding is apt to be irregular, caused by the paper slipping as it feeds through. You should verify that the bail arm is properly engaged and the friction mechanism has a firm grip on the paper. If the platen and drive rollers are particularly dirty, covered with paper dust, paper will be more apt to slip. Clean your printer.

All Colors Are Wrong

Problems with color matching are consistent throughout the life of your printer unless you do something to correct them. Other shifts in hues can arise suddenly or gradually as you use your printer. For example, red may shift to magenta, green may gradually turn blue. With ink-jet printers, the problem is often little more than a dirty printhead. Running the printer through a cleaning cycle or two can quickly clean up the colors.

If a deep cleaning (or several cleanings in printers with only one cleaning level) don't change the color cast, you may have inadvertently run out of one ink color in your cartridge. Usually the printer's self-test will exercise all colors and show you any that are missing. The problem is easily solved, of course, by replacing the depleted ink cartridge.

Blue Is Purplish

Epson notes that the blues of its Stylus Color ink-jet printer are frequently reported as being too purple. Far from being a problem, however, Epson points out the purple color cast is a feature of the printer. The purplish blue is actually a true blue. The bright blue you're familiar with on your monitor screen is actually accented with a good deal of cyan to make it appear brighter, more appealing, and more familiar.

According to Epson, the dark blue of the Stylus Color allows the printer to faithfully reproduce scanned images. Unless you calibrate your monitor, however, the printer's output will not match what you see on the screen. Epson suggests you use the Stylus Color's output as your blue reference standard and readjust your perceptions accordingly.

Black Is Greenish

With some color printers, blacks come in various off-shades and never seem black enough. Usually the problem is a result of using composite black rather than pure black. Composite black is what you get by combining ink in the three primary colors. Pure black starts out as black ink and stays that way.

The problem is that making a perfect black requires a perfect match of three perfect hues. If the mix or one of the underlying colors is a bit off, the defect will be reflected in the undertones of the black.

If you demand perfect blacks, you can follow any of several strategies. The most radical is to get a four-color printer, one that puts black as well as red, yellow, and blue ink on line at the same time.

If you're stuck with a three-color printer and still want the best blacks, put in a black cartridge. Of course, then you will not be able to mix color and black on one page.

Sometimes you can adjust the printer driver to alter the color mix and make composite black approach a neutral black. For example, if using a Windows driver, you can often experiment by switching color dithering or halftone rendering from automatic to manual control.

If you're really desperate to combine pure blacks with color, consider two-pass printing. Run each page through the printer once for black ink and a second time for color. Be forewarned that this technique is fraught with difficulties. You have to prepare your image properly, duplicating the same form in black-only and color-only, a process only slightly less complex than making color separations. Your printer driver must allow you to switch between black and color modes. And you must get the two passes through the printer to stay in register. Do this more than a couple times, and a new printer with four colors of ink will take on new value.

Out of Register Color

When images printed in multiple passes of a printer don't exactly line up, the result is that one impression looks like a drop-shadow or halo of the others. The problem is common in high-speed commercial color printing, adding a touch of blur to color photos in newspapers and a even more disheveled look to the Sunday comics. A similar problem can also occur with some PC printer technologies.

Some four-color ink-jet printers sometimes show misalignment between the black and color images they print. The black image may be out of register with the color image, there may be a white gap between the black and color, or the two may overlap where they are not supposed to, resulting in the black bleeding to the color image. The problem occurs because some machines use separate printheads for their color and black images. If the spacing between the two printheads and the timing of the signals driving them are not precisely matched, the images they form will not align with each other. This problem commonly arises when you replace one of the cartridges or printheads, particularly if you damage the alignment tabs on one of the printheads when repeatedly removing and reinstalling it.

To cure the problem, you need to align your printer. The alignment process varies among printer manufacturers and models. For example, Epson calls the alignment process a "calibration" and provides a calibration utility on the driver disk accompanying the printers that require it.

You can align most HP DeskJets requiring it through Windows. The printer must be on for the alignment process. Start by double-clicking on the **HP DeskJet Status Monitor** icon that installs by default in the HP DeskJet utilities program group. Pull down the Maintenance menu and select **Align Print Cartridges**. The screen will give you the correct instructions for aligning your particular printer.

Plotters

Plotters reach toward the same goal as do printers–putting your thoughts on paper–but they do in their own style. Although modern printer technologies can file the roles traditionally played by plotters, plotter technology retains distinct advantages in some niche applications.

Printers aren't the only means of making an image on paper or transparency. Just as there are various ways of creating an image in your PC–for example, you can either draw or paint a picture–you can do the same on paper. Today's printer is a painting machine, jetting ink to paper as dots that would be the envy of any Impressionist. Drawing on paper requires a different mind-set, technology, and device–the plotter.

In today's world, however, the plotter is a throwback, a carryover from days when microprocessors ran at a thousandth the speed of today's chips, when a curve or two would take the length of a coffee break, when software could fit on a single floppy disk and still leave room for a year's worth of data files. Despite the dramatic changes in PCs and peripherals over the last decade and a half, plotters have kept technology at bay. You probably couldn't tell the difference between a ten year old plotter and a contemporary machine. The drawings they make would appear identical.

If you switch on the most positive light, that's great because it means that plotter technology matured long ago. The bugs were squashed years ago, too. But more realistically, it means that plotters have stood still despite the race of innovation. No matter how long a head start you give any technology, the fast pace of change today will certainly leave it behind sooner or later.

Today's high-resolution inkjet printers present plotter technology with its greatest challenge yet. Although plotters still boast higher resolutions than even today's best inkjets, down to 1/1000th inch compared to 1/720th, the different is hardly visible because plotters draw with thicker lines. Moreover, the inkjet has a number of strengths. It offers a greater range of colors in a single drawing, generates complex drawing quicker, and excels at area fills that would have plotters scratching away forever.

Despite the new economies of modern printer technology, plotters still retain a number of strengths that make them particularly suited to some applications.

Most plotters are not constrained by the paper size demands of today's sheet-fed printers. Choose a plotter wisely and your choice of paper is almost unlimited. Some plotters can draw on stock as small as business cards. Others can scratch across vast pages that would dwarf wallpaper. If you have to sketch out vast diagrams, be they building plans for pyramids or a schematic diagram of the entire Internet, you can probably find a plotter that will put everything on a single sheet.

Plotters approach the spectrum differently from printers. Although plotters can't approach the range of colors available through the dithering of primary colors as can color laser, inkjet, and thermal wax machines, they do let you choose bright, pure inks of whatever color you choose. A plotter can draw in pure purple or vivid viridian green while most printers have to mix these hues from dots of different colors.

On simple drawings, making a plot can be quicker than printing a page. When you only need to draw a few lines, plotters can chase across the page in a few seconds. Making a drawing on a plotter requires little overhead in your PC or in the plotter because there's no need to rasterize. Your system never needs to imagine what your drawing will look like. Its final form is set only when the plotter's pen lifts from the sheet for the final time. On complex images, however, the balance shifts. A few minutes of rasterization in your PC and a quick run through your inkjet printer can take the place of hours of intricate plotting.

Finally, plotters have inertia on their side. Some applications–and some people as well–stay with plotting technology because, well, that's what they've always used. When they want a plot of a drawing, they want to see the pen chase across the paper in their plotter.

Background

The plotter represents a different approach to image making. Modern printers take the bit-mapped approach to graphics. Every page, every shape, every line comprises an array of dots. Put the dots close enough together or look at them far enough away, and they blend into what appears to be a continuous reality. Bit-mapping is the classic digital approach: subdivide and quantify.

Plotters approach images as vectors. Rather than a series of dots, to a plotter a line is a definition or an equation. Rather than discrete units, the line is a continuous function. The approach is the same as that of the medieval scribe: writing and drawing means making strokes with a pen. And that's exactly what the plotter does.

In today's digital world, those pen strokes seem about as out of date as the monastic scriptorium. Hardly ten years ago, however, plotter technology proved not only viable but desirable. The plotter way of looking at the world exactly matches that of drawing and drafting software. CADD (Computer-Aided Design and Development) software draws its images using equation derived from cursor movements. Converting the screen equations to plotter commands is a quick, easy translation, often little more than a matter of substitution and scaling. There's no need for rasterizing the image, which a decade ago would have strained the wimpy microprocessors that were in general use.

The stroke/vector approach holds another advantage. It allows the easy scaling of images. Just as with outline typefaces, which are described by vectors, the drawings most suited for plotting can quickly be scaled to any size without a loss of quality. The same file (and nearly the same drawing commands) can plot the same image in business card or billboard size.

The command languages used by plotters can be economical. Drawing a line takes a single command. Even a full-page drawing may involve a few hundred commands, which can be stored or transmitted in a few thousand bytes. Plotter language files can be very compact and the time to transmit a drawing between PC and plotter may be almost insignificant. Plotting time, however, is dependent on mechanical factors such as how quickly the plotter can move its pens, and is often quite substantial. Unlike printing, the time require to plot a page depends on the content of the image. Once images have been rasterized, a bit-image printer renders them all at the same rate. This difference is inherent in the technology.

Plotter Designs

Plotter technology is based on moving a pen across a sheet of paper, a concept familiar to literal people since the first quill was plucked from an unsuspecting goose. The movement is relative. What matters is the change in relationship between pen and paper, not the movement of the pen itself. Unlike the scribe, a plotter has the luxury of moving either pen or paper to draw a line.

These two line-drawing alternatives underlie the primary distinction between plotter technologies. *Flatbed plotters* are pen-movers. They operate as mechanical hands, grasping a pen and sweeping it across each sheet. The paper or other plotting medium remains stationary, held down against a flat plotting surface (the "bed" of the "flatbed" name). The flatbed plotter moves its pen across the paper in two dimensions, along the X and Y coordinates of the sheet exactly as you would draw a picture by hand. In fact, flatbed plotters are sometimes called *X-Y plotters*.

The alternate approach, moving the paper, is implemented by modern printers only in hybrid designs. That is, they move both the pen and paper. Instead of holding the paper still against a drawing board, these machines move the paper in one direction across a rotating drum while they move the pen in the perpendicular direction. These machines are commonly called *drum plottes* because of the drum that moves the paper. By precisely coordinating the spin of the drum and the race of the pen, a drum plotter can draw lines in any direction.

Nothing inherent in either technology limits what it can do. Either can make excellent plots. Implementing actual designs that work in the real world is another matter. Manufacturing and mechanical matters impose their own limits, endowing each technology with its own talents and making it suitable to its own range of purposes.

When accuracy counts, flatbed technology often proves the better choice. Because a flatbed plotter requires only one moving mechanism–the pen systems–it often yields the lowest cost designs. It hold a potential accuracy advantage, too, in that all the tolerances are confined to the single plotter mechanism itself.

Drum plotters require two distinct and fundamentally different mechanical systems, one for pen movement and one for paper control. The two must be precisely coordinated to yield drawings with acceptable accuracy However, by sacrificing the last bit of accuracy, manufacturers can often build drum plotters for less than flatbed designs.

On the other hand, roller-bed technology has an inherent performance edge. It's all a matter of inertia. It's simply easier to move lighter objects and make them change direction. Paper weighs less than a pen–and substantially less than a pen attached to an overreaching mechanical arm–letting the drum plotter start, stop, and alter its movement more adroitly than can flatbed plotters.

MEDIA HANDLING

Media handling abilities also distinguish the two schools of design. Flatbed plotters have more versatility within their limits but drum plotter technology typically has a wider limit. The flatbed design accommodates virtually any size and weight of paper that will lie flat on the bed. You can use sheets as small as you want as long as your software knows not to send the plotter's pens on excursions to Neverland.

Drum plotters constrain your choice of paper to certain widths. In order to hold the paper firmly so that it doesn't slip during quick strokes, these machines tightly grab the paper at its edges. For design reasons (most of which have to do with economy), most drum plotters put their paper grippers at fixed or preset widths. If the width of the paper doesn't match the distance between the grippers, your plots will bear little resemblance to your expectations. Some plotter makers have, however, developed drum plotters able to accommodate a variety of sheet widths. For example, Hitachi has offered a roller-bed plotter that could grasp any width paper from letter down to postcard size.

On the other hand, while the width of the paper used by drum plotters is fixed by the mechanism, the length is not. Given the proper command, many drum printers will happily roll down the full length of a wallpaper roll. Moreover, as paper widths become larger, the flatbed mechanism becomes progressively more ungainly. The drum design scales upward much more readily. Consequently, the largest plotters typically use the drum design.

All plotters must grasp the paper or plotting medium they use securely. If the paper moves from its expected position, all subsequent strokes will be inaccurate. This grasping function is inherent in the design of the drum plotter. Flatbed machines require some supplementary means of holding the paper in place. The most rudimentary means is the one long familiar to manual drafting–taping the paper in place with drafting tape. Although effective, drafting tape hardly makes an elegant solution. Consequently most plotter makers incorporate other paper-grasping technologies into their products. For example, some manufacturers have adapted static electricity to paper holding, giving the paper a charge and holding it against a contrary charge. Although this strategy works for most media, it's not foolproof and can fail in humid conditions. Another alternative to tape is magnetism. Some plotter makers include small, flat magnets that you lay atop your paper. The magnets clamp down on the steel drawing surface–securely holding the paper between the magnets and the surface.

Most plotter are characterized by the size of paper or plotting medium that they use. The most popular flatbed machines handle sheets up to ANSI B size, approximately tabloid size, 11 by 17 inches. Some of the lowest cost drum plotters may be constrained to paper 8.5 inches wide, although most inexpensive machines are capable of handling 11-inch wide sheets of any length. Some drum plotter will handle sheets six feet wide.

Output Quality

The principal quality difference between plotter is precision. A better plotter can more accurately render drawings. For plotters as with printers, the figure of merit in describing precision is resolution, but resolution has different significance for the two types of machines because of the difference in the underlying technologies.

Plotters universally use stepper motors to move their pens, and stepper motors are characterized by their rotating in discrete steps, fractions of a revolution. They quickly cog between steps, never pausing in between. When moving a pen, these steps show up as increments of movement, and because of them diagonal lines are never truly straight. Instead, a diagonal consists of a discrete vertical and horizontal steps. These steps show up in the final output as a jaggedness in diagonal lines akin to the jaggies you see on close inspection of a monitor image.

The smaller the step size, the less noticeable the jaggedness will be. In other words, higher resolution means smaller steps which, in turn, mean smoother curves.

In plotters, the size of these steps is the effective measure of the resolution of a plotter. The plotter cannot produce detail smaller than a single step. A better plotter has higher resolution, which means a smaller step size. All but the least expensive plotters claim a step size of one-thousandth inch. (This size is also the basic measuring unit of the widely used HP-GL plotter language.)

Note that this resolution is higher than that claimed by any printer except photocomposing machines. Unlike with printers, however, resolution does not translate to the fineness of detail that a plotter can render. The pens used by plotters all have discrete widths, the finest of which is about 0.3 millimeters, a bit wider than $1/100^{th}$ inch. A plotter cannot produce a dot smaller than the width of its pen. Consequently, plotter resolution translates into smoothness rather than detail.

The text generated by plotters is inferior to that made by inkjet printers. The mainstay fonts for plotters are vector fonts. Although vector fonts are scalable, the aesthetics of their design is limited by the unvarying width of the plotter's pen. Fine serifs and wide stems are difficult, even impossible, to produce. Most vector characters use the single, uniform width of a single pass of the plotter's pen for every stroke in their design. In other words, although you might do some interesting digital calligraphy with your plotter, you'll probably restrict your use of plotter text for annotations. You wouldn't want to read a page full of vector-drawn characters, nor would you want to wait while your plotter painstakingly draws them out.

Color

Drawing in color is no challenge even for the least expensive of plotters. You can make your drawings any color for which you can find a suitable pen. The plotter neither knows nor cares the color of ink you use.

In fact, for plotters color is mostly an issue of convenience. Most plotters accommodate multiple pens so you can load up several colors at once. Most software allows for *pen changes*. That is, when the software detects the need for a new color, it stops plotting and prompts you to change the pen in the plotter. In this way, a plotter with a single pen can cover the entire rainbow. You don't need a four-pen plotter to draw in four colors. An eight-pen plotter is a matter of convenience only–the extra pens mean that you don't have to baby-sit the plotter waiting to change pens.

The versatility of printing with any pen also brings the need for an extra degree of care. If you load pens of colors different from those your software expects, you're plots won't look like what you see on the screen. Although this design allows for a great deal of creativity–intentional or not–it can complicate matters when you want spectral accuracy.

The closest as there is to a standard for assigning color to pen positions is the default color palette assumed by the Hewlett-Packard Graphics Language. Table A.1 lists this default palette.

Table A.1 HP-GL/2 default pen palette

Pen	Code	Color
Pen0	SP0	white (no color)
Pen1	SP1	black
Pen2	SP2	red

Table A.1 continued

Pen3	SP3	green
Pen4	SP4	yellow
Pen5	SP5	blue
Pen6	SP6	magenta
Pen7	SP7	cyan

Besides sheer numbers and color, most plotter manufacturers let you choose the type of pens that you can load into a given plotter. One difference is the kind of ink inside the pen. Some manufacturers specially formulate the ink in their plotter pens for paper or for transparency media. To get the best results, you should choose a pen that matches your media type. Often you get your choice of pen widths as well.

Plotter pens may be refillable or disposable. The refillable pens are adaptations of the classic drafting pen. They typically allow you to use thinner, higher quality ink. Refillable pens also allow you to pick any color ink you want, even blending inks to suit your own sense of aesthetics (or lack of same). Disposable pens are convenient and remove the worry of clogs and maintenance. Most disposable pens are based on the same writing technology as fiber-tipped markers. The draw smoothly but with heavy use or abuse may grow blunt and draw wide, coarse lines.

INTERFACES

Traditionally plotters have used serial interfaces. The relatively slow rate at which the typical plotter processes and carries out drawing instructions doesn't require anything faster. Most plotter serial ports default to 9600 bit per second transmission, which should be adequate for most installation. Moreover, in the days before PC parallel ports became an accepted industry standard, serial ports guaranteed compatibility with the widest possible variety of computer equipment.

Of course, no serial interface is trouble-free. Plotters often make their own demands. Some plotter manufacturers have required their own, special interface cable to accommodate the proper handshaking signals to make their plotters work. Most of these cables are simply variations of the crossover cable design, but you will avoid setup headaches by buying the manufacturer's own cable.

Today most plotter manufacturers have shifted to using parallel ports. Plotters using the parallel connection plug in as quickly and as easily as any printer—providing you have a spare port. In general, they use the standard IBM-style PC-to-printer cable (an IEEE 1284 A connector at one end, a B connector at the other).

A few manufacturers offer plotters that use an IEEE 488 (also known as GPIB, the General Purpose Interface Bus, or HP-IB, the Hewlett-Packard Interface Bus) connection. Although this port is widely used with test instruments and laboratory equipment, you'll probably want to avoid it for simply connecting a plotter.

Control languages

Among most available plotters, there is one accepted language standard. Most modern machines used in the United States are designed to recognize the commands of Hewlett-Packard's HP-GL plotter language, the commands for which are listed in Chapter 11. Nearly all applications with provisions for controlling plotters are able to send out HP-GL commands.

The current version, HP-GL/2, represents an important advance over the original incarnation of the language. Among other features, the update has better font handling and fill algorithms. HP-GL/2 plotters will recognize and carry out all HP-GL commands, but older plotter understanding only HP-GL may find instructions set out by HP-GL/2 drivers beyond their ken.

You may encounter two other plotter languages. The General Purpose Graphic Language or GP-GL is used in a number of foreign markets and many plotters are also able to understand it. Digital Microprocessor Plotter Language or DMPL was developed by Houston Instrument for its line of plotters. Its use has been mostly supplanted by HP-GL/2.

Some plotters use their own, proprietary (generally manufacturer-specific) languages. Although these can be entirely satisfactory for general plotting needs, none has the wide support of HP-GL. If you choose a printer that only speaks a proprietary language, your software options will be limited to the programs with explicit support for that language and software for which the plotter maker has developed its own drivers.

Performance

The faster you move your pen when making a drawing, the sooner you'll finish—and the rougher your sketches will likely be. The issue with plotters is exactly the same, speed versus quality. Most plotter makers set a minimum quality standard for their products (that one-thousandth of an inch resolution) and limit their drawing speed to maintain that level.

By careful design of the plotter mechanism, some manufacturers eke out slightly higher speeds than their competitors. The gains that can be won aren't great, however, because designers have to work against the unyielding laws of physics. A different strategy often brings better improvements, intelligence. Smarter plotters can finish their drawings faster by optimizing pen movements and avoiding the waste of their drawing time in scribbling out lines that won't show in the final output.

Although the traditional plotter processes the commands it receives in true hand-to-mouth fashion, swallowing them up as soon as they come in and carrying out the instructions immediately, better plotters incorporate built-in buffer RAM. As with printer buffers, this memory helps free up your computer while you plot, absorbing commands as fast as the plotter's interface can deliver it. With a large enough buffer, a plotter can hold a complete drawing in memory and make multiple copies of it at the press of a button.

The real power of the buffer is that it allows smarter plotters to look ahead in the stream of instructions. With this little bit of prescience, it can determine the best way to finish a drawing quickest, eliminating wasted pen movement and other actions. For example, the plotter might detect several changes of pen from blue to red and back again. Based on its look into the future, the plotter could reorganize the drawing command so that it sketches out all the blue lines before changing–once only–to the red pen. The proper application of this intelligence in the design of a plotter can reap big gains. Some plotters may complete the same drawing in half the time as others.

INDEX

ABOUT THE CD

The CD-ROM packaged with this book contains the complete text of the book in a Windows Help format. There's also an Esc/P reference in the same format. For Windows 95 users, just double click on the icon of the Help file you wish to open and you'll be able to page through the book without actually having the book with you.

Windows 3.1 users will also be able to use these files by opening them from any Windows Help area. Just select File and then Open from any Help file and then select the Help document you wish.

Also included on the CD are a number of fonts and printer utilities that you can try out. Each utility has been compressed and some of them have their own installation programs. To use them, copy them to your hard drive, decompress them (you'll need a program that can handle the ZIP format), and–where necessary–run the setup or installation program.

The fonts have been separated into two folders, a PCFONTS directory and a MACFONTS directory. These files are also compressed. You'll need a program that can handle ZIP files to use the TrueType fonts in the PCFONTS directory.

Macintosh users who wish to use the fonts in the MACFONTS directory will need a utility capable of handling Stuffit! files. To use them, open them from within your Stuffit! program. You cannot simply double-click them to open them.

Many of these programs are shareware and/or freeware. If you find them useful, you should pay the shareware fee that each program's author requests. This helps make sure that programs and utilities of this caliber are available for your use in the future.